ARMS OF THE VAN METERENS OF HOLLAND

A Genealogy of the

DUKE
SHEPHERD
VAN METRE
FAMILY

FROM
CIVIL, MILITARY, CHURCH
AND FAMILY RECORDS
AND DOCUMENTS

Compiled and Edited by
Samuel Gordon Smyth

HERITAGE BOOKS
2007

HERITAGE BOOKS

AN IMPRINT OF HERITAGE BOOKS, INC.

Books, CDs, and more—Worldwide

For our listing of thousands of titles see our website
at
www.HeritageBooks.com

A Facsimile Reprint
Published 2007 by
HERITAGE BOOKS, INC.
Publishing Division
65 East Main Street
Westminster, Maryland 21157-5026

Originally published
Lancaster, Pennsylvania
1909

International Standard Book Number: 978-0-7884-2201-0

DEDICATION

With sentiments of affectionate esteem, this volume is respect-
fully dedicated to my dear friend and kinsman, MAJOR S. A.
DUKE, of Baxter, Arkansas, whose counsel and support, wisely
and practically rendered, has sustained the compiler of these pages
through many years of patient, but persistent, endeavor; and in
grateful recognition of the knowledge and the pleasure the writer
has absorbed from his genial personality, his cheering optimism
and his common-sense philosophy during the happy days of our
companionship at home and abroad.

SAMUEL GORDON SMYTH.

" RYLMONT,"
   WEST CONSHOHOCKEN, PA.,
    July 24, 1909.

"Pride in descent from men of the type of our early colonists, is held to be entirely consistent with our democratic institutions. They were the pioneer Americans, men who under great discouragements and with vast labor, planted strong and deep the foundations of our commonwealths. It is worth while to make this fact plain. . . . hence, the spirit of preserving the memory of the great though humbly worked-out deeds of our ancestors in the gloomy obscurities of the colonies in their forest days."

Boston *Transcript.*

"The very base of family feeling is respect for the past, for the best possessions of a family are its common memories. . . . We must learn again to value our domestic traditions. A precious care has preserved certain monuments of the past. So antique dress, provincial dialects, old folk-songs, have found appreciative hands to gather them up before they should disappear from the face of the earth. What a good deed to guard these crumbs of a great past—these vestiges of the souls of our ancestors! Let us do the same for *our* family traditions, save and guard as much as possible of the patriarchal—whatever its form."

From Rev. Chas. Wagner's *Simple Life.*

FOREWORD

This work now before you is a genealogy and history of the related families of John Van Meter, Thomas Shepherd and John Duke: settlers between 1730 and 1750 of the Northern Neck in the Valley of Virginia; conspicuous figures in the formative period, as their descendants have been in later developments,— of Frederick and Berkeley counties in what is now western Virginia. The annals of those earlier days are of the hardships and adventures of border-life in the pioneer-period and concerns, too, the welding of diverse racial elements into an American body-politic.

In the adventures and the work, as the annals graphically evidence, these fathers were conspicuous and foremost, and the story of their respective descendants who were related in so remarkable and unusual degree, is the story of the establishment of a community upon which the character of the fathers is indelibly stamped and which has exercised an appreciable and progressive influence in every part of the Union. It is the outgrowth of conditions in a period that has no parallel in the history of any other country at any time, and out of which, and from such as these, has been evolved this wonderful American nation.

It is not without a sense of his own personal limitations and the responsibilities of such an undertaking, that the compiler has essayed the rôle of a family biographer and genealogist. It is the fruit of many years of patient investigation and study; and of a determination to preserve, in some tangible form, the results attained. It grew out of circumstances where, in at least two instances, the work of others along the same lines was left unfinished and became subsequently lost.

The compiler has made extensive and painstaking research in state and county civil records, military rosters, church and Bible registers and in private documents and correspondence. He has industriously consulted and collated all reputable authorities, and with patience and thoroughness, has traced and compared family histories and local traditions, verifying or correcting these essentials of trustworthy genealogy.

The work is a tentative genealogy, meaning that the factor of error and omission, if not altogether eliminated, has been minimized and reduced to a negligible quantity. It is given to the reader without further apology, as the compiler's best effort to approximate the truth in the family's history.

This opportunity is taken to express the compiler's grateful appreciation of the valuable assistance and counsel given him in the preparation of this work by Mrs. C. C. Foster of Indianapolis,

Ind.; Mrs. Wm. P. Mercer of Elm City, N. C.; Miss Sally Lee Powell of Shepherdstown, W. Va.; Major S. A. Duke of Baxter, Ark.; Col. J. T. Holmes of Columbus, Ohio; Clinton Gage, Esq., of Oak Lane, and Dr. John W. Jordan, Librarian of the Historical Society of Pennsylvania, of Philadelphia; Prof. W. A. Obenchain, Pres. of Ogden College of Bowling Green, Ky.; Prof. J. C. Hubbard of Clarke College, Worcester, Mass.; Prof. Charles Magee of Conshohocken, Pa.; W. W. Van Meter, Esq., of New Orleans, La.; Hon. R. T. W. Duke of Charlottesville, Va.; Rev. F. T. McFaden, D.D., of Richmond, Va.; Mrs. W. Sam¹ Goodwyn of Emporia, Va.; and by many others whose interest in this work has been practically demonstrated either by contributions of data and information; by sensible advice or in other channels—lent a helping hand in its development: to each of whom my sincere thanks are now extended.

S. GORDON SMYTH.

WEST CONSHOHOCKEN, PA.,
July 24, 1909.

CONTENTS

PART I

PART II

CONTENTS

LIST OF ILLUSTRATIONS (AND INSCRIPTIONS)

PART I

JOHN VAN METRE

IN THE NEW WORLD

Long years before the English people had obtained a foothold in the present State of New York, the Dutch, one of the then world-powers, had carefully explored, took possession of and was rapidly planting her sons upon a vast province which extended from the Connecticut River on the east and passed over the Delaware to the eastern shore of Chesapeake Bay ere the other maritime nations were aware of the significance and extent of the Dutch dominion in the New World. Upon this magnificent territory was bestowed the name of New Netherlands. From the day, in 1609, when Henry Hudson rode the waters of the North River in the famous " Half Moon " till the present—the impress of the Dutch is ineradicably stamped upon the land and its inhabitants. The exploring expedition of Captain Hudson which ascended the river that bears his name had for its object one more attempt to find the fabled and long-sought passage to the western sea and though it failed to achieve that purpose, yet it marked one of the earliest epochs in the romance of western colonization and in this historic event one of its most interesting features is the realization that it was brought about through the influence of one of the family of Van Meteren. We are told by the late John Fiske—who was one of our most learned historians—that it was due to Emmanuel Van Meteren, himself a famous historian in his day, and at the time Dutch Consul, resident in London, that Captain Henry Hudson was persuaded to enlist in the service of the Dutch East India Company and was given command of the expedition which opened the era of Dutch influence in America. Whether or not the advice of Consul Van Meteren was extended to his own family and acted upon by some of them in later generations, it is impossible to say; they came, however, whether his counsel was responsible or not. From Hudson's period, through all the succeeding years, to Governor Leisler's time, the Dutch rule over New Netherlands was supreme. As the years passed on there came from the cities and provinces of Holland an ever-increasing stream of immigrants made up, for the greater part, by farmers, traders, burghers and mariners; men of respectability, thrift and enterprise. They found among the waterways in and about New Amsterdam snug harbors and havens so like those beyond the sea, but more promising in freedom and prosperity than those they had ever before known. They were a numerous and flourishing people; the tide of their progress met the flow of Puritan colonists who came down the coast from the bleak and

3

rock-bound shores of Massachusetts Bay; they spread over the southern end of Long Island, and here were founded the Dutch towns of New Utrecht, Flatbush, Gowanus, Gravesend, Breucklyn, until the multiplying communities interlaced each other, while over the Hudson were the villages of Bergen, Communipaw and the fishing hamlets of Staten Island. Their inhabitants were mostly rivermen, but the prosperous burgher of the busy marts of Manhattan came to abide among them and lived in the tidy boweries that stretched along the Sound shores, or up the "lordly Hudson" or down to Staten and Coney's Islands. Crossing the Kill-von-Kull, they mixed with the incoming Scotch and English settlers about Perth and when mere village limitations no longer marked their bounds they passed on, with the trader and the peltry hunter, to more distant conquests.

Grants of land—many of them of princely size—were made on the upper reaches of the Hudson; their proportions extended far into the forests until the realms claimed from the wilderness by the invading Dutchman extended to the northern lakes. It was then that the patroonships were introduced and witnessed the translation of Old World feudalism—patterned from the baronies of the fatherland—to the primitive wilds of the forest-girt Hudson. The Indians receded toward the interior, but in his passing, as in parting with his ancient possessions, he occasionally exacted revengeful recompense as he fell back before the advance of a relentless and resistless force. The love of barter was strong in the Dutch character; it was infectious and dominant, and its insidious influence drew largess from the tribesmen inhabiting the uttermost parts of these Dutch dominions; here and then was laid the foundation of that spirit of commercialism which, long since, made New York dominant in the trade of the western world.

In the second decade of the latter half of the seventeenth century a settlement was founded on the west shore of the Hudson among the foothills of the Catskill Mountains, some sixty odd miles above the bay, by the Dutch and some French Huguenot immigrants who had obtained patents there. These pioneers were joined by others from Manhattan and its surrounding communities and in a short while the fertile valleys of the Wallkill and the Esopus sheltered a group of thrifty villages. Thus in the decades between 1660 and 1680 the settlements known as New Village (Hurley), Wyltwick, Esopus, Marbletown (Mormel) and New Paltz were founded in close proximity to each other. Behind them rose the bulwark of the Catskills and beyond these mountains, and out of their western slopes, the head springs of the Delaware rose and so provided a trail for the tribes of the mountains by which they found intercourse with their southern contemporaries. Over the three thousand and more acres of fertile lands peopled by these different social refugees, a new Pala-

4

tinate arose and the pilgrims from the Rhine sought here that peace and tolerance which was denied them in their old homes beyond the sea. But, while escaping the religious and political persecutions and the devastation of their property abroad, they were destined to meet here new terrors and stranger experiences in the very sanctuary which Providence seems to have raised up for them. Suffering and disaster in terrible form awaited them from the Indians and many were thus actually martyrs for conscience sake. In 1663 the savages fell upon the inhabitants of Esopus with barbaric fury; the village of Hurley was burned, several of the settlers were killed and wounded, and, retreating toward the Minnisink Mountains, the Indians carried away many captives, among whom were the wives and children of the Du Bois and Van Metre families. This attack, styled in the narratives of colonial history the Second Esopus War, dispersed many of the settlers; some of them, going far to find security, passed down the Delaware Valley to the Dutch settlements in the vicinity of New Amstel (New Castle, Del.), where a few permanently remained. Months later, the Indians who had caused this trouble were found and punished by Captain Martin Kreiger and a band of Dutch soldiers, and the captives, on the very eve of diabolic torture, were rescued and restored to their families. It was not long after this event that peace and prosperity once again reigned over the Hudson Valley region.

One benignant feature which grew out of intercommunal relations and interests of the villagers who were of differing racial temperament, was the harmony which prevailed throughout the settlements. The Dutch and the French Huguenots forget their political antagonisms, their social and religious lines of cleavage, and fraternized in a common bond of sympathy and self-protection. These conditions were constantly strengthened and at length unified by intermarriage and its resultant kinship, so that before the first native generation had reached maturity the social, civil and economic environment had become so radically changed that the Dutch tongue was used principally in the domestic circle and the French langue in civil and ecclesiastical affairs.

There was one church in the earlier days: the Reformed Dutch. It was located at Wyltwyck (Kingston), where all might worship, where most of the children were baptized. Here was kept by successive pastors or dominies, with rare fidelity and thoroughness, the records of marriages and baptisms. These records were carefully preserved and were recently edited and published, and for the period from 1662 to a comparatively recent date now form a valuable index of the inhabitants of that part of Ulster County, N. Y. In scanning the pages of this register one finds the names of foreparents of families now scattered world-wide. From this place many of the descendants of those early settlers migrated to the newly settled parts of Pennsylvania, or were of those who pressed on into Maryland and Virginia, and later were in the forefront of that conquering host of heroic pioneers who carried civilization into the south and west, and so redeemed the wilderness and banished forever the scourge of the redmen.

Coincident with the settlement of New York by the Dutch a Swedish colony was planted on the west side of the Delaware during the reign of Gustavus Adolphus. Peter Minuit was sent over from Sweden by his sovereign to govern the little colony. In the space of the dozen or more years that New Sweden flourished, several small settlements were made on either side of the Delaware by these people, principally along the creeks and about the coves of the river. The aggressive trading propensities of these hardy men and the rapid expansion of their communities excited the jealousy and invoked the wrath of the Dutch, and very soon precipitated a dispute with the government at New Amsterdam. It was claimed that the Swedes had encroached upon the territorial rights and were colonizing the Dutch possessions. The controversy was suddenly brought to an end in 1655 by the appearance among the Swedes of the formidable and irrepressible Governor Stuyvesant, who, with an armed force behind him, compelled the surrender of the subjects of Charles X., who was then the Swedish king in the place of Queen Christina, the renunciation of the Swedish pretensions and the acknowledgement by them of the overlordship of New Netherlands to all the lands by them inhabited on both sides of the Delaware (Fiske's Dutch and Quaker Colonies, Vol. I., pp. 208–210). Stuyvesant lost no time in persuading some of his people, then living in New Amsterdam and its adjacencies and colonists freshly arriving, to emigrate to this new and subjugated country. He was successful. After this time many ships coming direct from Holland with their loads of settlers were directed to the Delaware settlements, and here, too, in time, the same process of assimilation between the Swedes and the Dutch took place as was then being enacted between the Dutch and the French Huguenots on the shores of the upper Hudson.

On the east shore of the Delaware, or South River, as it was called by the Dutch, the Swedes had been seated for some years, their possessions extending southward from Fort Nassau, nearly opposite the present city of Philadelphia, to Fort Elsinborg near Penn's Neck. There were several little settlements along the small streams intervening between these points; here the same commingling between the racial types was occurring. The river formed no barrier, but rather a convenience, for their intercourse; both races being of a maritime tendency, the river afforded them a natural highway for their trading and easier access to their villages than by the roads which had to be cut through the forests and swamps. Thus we find them on the banks of Raccoon, Cohansey, Maurice, Salem, Timber and other creeks on the eastern

6

shore, and along the Christiana, Brandywine, Misspillion, White and Red Clay and other creeks on the west side of the Delaware. These settlers often crossed the river to attend the churches on the opposite shore, the mills and the trading stations.

There was an overland path between the Dutch settlements at New Amsterdam and at New Amstel; it crossed the Passaic, the Rahway and the Raritan rivers and touched the Delaware at the Falls, now Trenton, N. J., and thence, by fording, to the Pennsylvania side and keeping along its western bank to the sites of the old Swedish plantations on the Pennepack and on the Schuylkill they passed down to the present town of New Castle, Del. At Christiana Creek they could follow its northerly direction until at a point where the Delaware peninsula was the narrowest they could cross overland to the Head of Elk and by that tributary reach the Chesapeake and farther on to the more distant points in the provinces of Pennsylvania and Maryland and the colony of Virginia. The overland path of 1675 was called the Kings Highway; later it became the main artery of communication between New York and Philadelphia. It remains to-day a well preserved and popular thoroughfare between those two important eastern cities.

Another path much traveled in colonial days was the one used by the settlers of Monmouth and Middlesex Counties, in the Province of East Jersey, to reach the settlements along the Delaware. This one crossed Burlington County from the first named points and intersected the Delaware at Matinicunk Island (between Bristol and Burlington) and joined the "King's Path" on the Pennsylvania side of the river.

It was by these primitive routes that the various and widely separated settlements in the middle colonies were connected and by which they continually acquired growth from the ever-increasing flow of pioneers, who, setting their faces southward from the earlier and more thickly settled parts eastward, formed the stream of emigration which pierced the Blue Ridge at the Potomac and rapidly absorbed the virgin valleys beyond. Thus it is set forth in order that we may more readily trace and follow the trend of our progenitors in their earlier movements and final settlement in Maryland and Virginia.

AMERICAN ORIGINS

Our first introduction to the search for the Van Metre ancestry comes to us, strangely enough, through the work of the American historian, John Fiske, in his "Dutch and Quaker Colonies" (Vol. I., p. 70 et seq.), in which he refers to Captain Hendrick Hudson and states that: ". . . the moment that history first actually knows him is the first day of May, 1607, when he sailed from Greenwich in command of an Arctic expedition; but we also know that he was a citizen of London; and the Dutch historian *Van Meteren,* who was Consul at London, tells us that there was a warm friendship existing between Henry Hudson the navigator, and Captain John Smith." Farther along, in a reference to the Dutch East India Company, he says: "Their offers were probably made through his [Henry Hudson's] friend, the Dutch consul *Van Meteren,*" and again: "it was Hudson's friend *Van Meteren* who declared that English was only 'broken Dutch';" and farther along that, "Hudson, in 1608, knew scarcely a word of Dutch."

From some notes in reference to the pedigree of Emmanuel Van Meteren, Dutch Consul, historian and chief of the College of Dutch Merchants of London, 1583, we learn that he was born in Antwerp 9th June, 1535; died in London 8th April, 1612, at the age of 77 years. He was the son of Jacob Van Meteren of Breda, who printed at Antwerp the Coverdale Bible, the first in English, and one of the rarest of printed books, a copy of which was sold in 1903 by the Appletons in New York for $3,000. Jacob Van Meteren married Ottilia Ortels, daughter of William Ortels of Augsburg, and the grandfather of Abraham Ortels, or Orteleius, the world-famed geographer. Jacob's father was Cornelius Van Meteren.

Emmanuel Van Meteren married first, in 1562, a Miss Van Loobeck, who died in 1563; he then married second, in 1564, Ester van der Corput, daughter of Nicholas van der Corput, Secretary of Breda, and son of Johan van der Corput, a former mayor of the same city. By this wife Emmanuel Van Meteren had thirteen children, of whom nine were living in 1612, three sons and six daughters, and the widow surviving. It is said that Emmanuel was buried in St. Denis' Church, London, where a monument was placed over his remains by his "wedouwe en negen kinderen."

A recent writer describes the Van Meteren coat of arms, as given in French by Riestap in his "Armorial General," as follows: "Meteren (van), Hollande, ecartellé aux 1 et 4 d'argent, à une fleur de lis de queules; Aux 2 et 3 d'or, à deux fasces de queules, accompagnies de huit merlettes du meme rangèe en orie. Comier la fleur de lis."

The coat of arms of the Van Metere family of Holland was quartered: first and fourth of silver, with a fleur de lis, red (gules); with second and third of gold (yellow), with two fesses, red; accompanied with eight martlets of the same color arranged in orle, that is, around the outer rim of the shield. The crest, a fleur de lis. [The fleur de lis was the royal emblem of France.]

The armorial bearings of the Cuicks, Van Meteren were: "Gules, with two fesses argent, accompanied by three martlets of the same, arranged two and one." In plain English: the shield had a red ground with two horizontal bands, silver or white; and

EMMANUEL VAN METEREN
DUTCH CONSUL AND HISTORIAN

THE VAN METEREN HOUSE IN HOLLAND

three martlets (in heraldry: a sort of swallow without feet, denoting cadency—a younger son) arranged two and one, either ∵ or ∴.

The "Huize Meteren," situate in the Heerlykheid Metere, in Geldermalsen, Holland, as shown in the picture, was a stately building, the residence for many generations of prominent members of the Meteren family, and subsequently by others probably stranger to the blood.

This mansion stood in a beautiful park of magnificent trees, some of which were of great height and dimensions. Rebuilt in 1768–69, it has at last served its day and was sold in December, 1906; within a short time thereafter it was torn down. The grand old trees also went under the hammer and were cut down, too; some of them sold for more than 100 florins; one, in particular, brought the sum of 154 florins; the prices ranged in American equivalent from $40 to $60 each. My correspondent writes: "All is gone! all except the money obligations which rest upon or are inherent to the Heerlykheid, of which, one of the heaviest is the annual payment of 200 florins towards the salary of the preacher at Meteren. 'Tis a pity! Sic transit gloria mundi!" [W. A. O.]

The Van Meteres who came to America from Holland derive their name, it is said, from *van,* "of," and *meteren,* a town in the province of Guelderland, Holland.

If one examines the map of Holland it will be found that the Rhine, flowing down from Germany into the Netherlands, as it approaches the sea divides itself into several branches. Upon one of these is Arnheim, the chief town in Guelderland; it is located about fifteen miles distant from Amsterdam. Utrecht is on another estuary which flows into the Zuyder Zee. The Waal is the principal branch of the Rhine and takes its course westerly until it unites with the Meuse and its waters from that point to the sea is called the river Merwe. On the right bank of the Waal, as it nears the Meuse, is situated the pretty little town of Theil, twenty-two miles W. S. W. of Arnheim, and further down on the left, where the waters of the two rivers meet, is the island of Bommel, on the west side of which stands the castle of Loevenstein, made famous in 1619 as the prison of Grotius. Thus within the radius of a few miles lies the fatherland of the Van Meteren, the Eltings and others whose names appear in documents relating to the earlier history of colonization in this country.

The first evidence found in the records of the actual presence of any of the Van Metre family in America is contained in the list of passengers arriving in the "Fox" at New Amsterdam, 12th September, 1662 [Passenger Lists: 1657–1664, Doc. Hist. N. Y., Vol. III., pp. 52–63; Year Book Hist. Soc. N. Y., 1896].

Among them were Jan Joosten, as he signs his name, from Tieder-welt, with wife and five children, aged 15, 12, 9, 6 and 2½ years. "He removed to Wyltwik [Kingston] in the summer (?) of 1662." [Doc. Hist. of N. Y.] On March 30, 1671 he had from Governor Lovelace a deed for a lot in Marbletown [N. Y. Land Papers, I., p. 37] and a confirmation, 11th October, 1671, of a thirty acre lot of ground in Marbletown [ibid., p. 42]. His wife was Macyken Hendricksen; the names of their children and the probable order of their birth were: Lysbeth, Catharine, Geertje, Joost Janse and Gysbert Janse, the two sons born probably *circa* 1656 and 1660, respectively. From the Probate Records of Ulster County, N. Y., which sets forth the testamentary disposition of Jan Joosten Van Meteren, dated 16th December, 1681, it develops that Joost Janse was the elder son, and, according to the pro-visions therein, received the heir-at-law's usual double portion. Following the custom of the time it would seem that the daughters were older than the sons, as they are named in priority to the sons. Jan Joosten's wife Macyken, is supposed to have been the sister of Femmetjen Hendricksen, who married Joost Adriensen of Pynaker, Holland, on 20th March, 1663-4. She was of Mep-pelen, Province of Dreuth, Holland. Upon the decease of Joost Ariencesen of "Boswick upon Long Island," *circa* 1685, Jan Joosten was appointed administrator and tutor to the decedent's children and arbitrator in proceedings regarding the sale of some land in Hurley which had been sold to Derick Schepmoes by Joost Adriensen in his lifetime.

Jan Joosten settled, with his wife and family, in Wyltwick [Kingston] late in the summer of 1662 and nothing more is learned of them until the Minnisink Indians came down upon the settle-ments on the Hudson, raiding and burning the villages of Hurley and Kingston on June 7, 1663, and carried away captives the wife and two of the children of Joosten. Unfortunately Captain Martin Kreiger's journal, which gives a lengthy account of his successful pursuit of the Indians and the rescue of their pris-oners, fails to name the children, but we presume that one of them was Jan's son, Joost Jans, because of his subsequent asso-ciation with the Indians and his knowledge of their ways.

In a list of the inhabitants of Ulster County, N. Y., who sub-scribed to the oath of allegiance between the 21st and 26th of October, 1664, the name of Jan Joosten appears. After this time mention of his name and his growing prominence in the civil and religious affairs occurs with more or less frequency in the records of Kingston and its vicinity, and are noted here in chronological order. In 1665 he was appointed refereee in a law-suit and sometime later the appointment of "schepen," a minor judiciary position, which, under the laws of New Nether-lands, gave him jurisdiction in all civil actions under the sum of 100 guilders [$60], but in cases above that sum they must be referred to the Director-General and his Council; he could also pronounce sentences in criminal cases, subject to appeal [Hazard's Annals, p. 223]. From about this time Jan Joosten was in active demand to witness or serve as sponsor at the baptisms of many children at the homes of his friends and relatives; in some cases the baptisms were celebrated "at Jan Joosten's, in the presence of the whole consistory." This distinction was probably due to the fact that he had been elected a deacon in the Reformed Dutch Church at Kingston in 1667. He was still "schepen" in 1668. On 6th October, 1673, he was selected as one of the four magistrates of Hurley and Marbletown, where he appears to have possessed property in 1671. The other magistrates who served with him were Louis du Bois, Roelof Hendricksen and Jan Broersen. On the overthrow of the Dutch government and its possessions coming under English rule, the inhabitants of New Netherland were required to swear allegiance to the new sovereign, and thus again we find his name among those who performed this act of fealty in Ulster County, on 1st September, 1689.

We now approach a very interesting part of Jan Joosten's career, that which relates to the land grants he obtained in the Province of East New Jersey, a period which extends from 1689 to 1706.

In partnership with Jan Hamel, who m. Gertrude Krom or Crom [alias Girty Jans] ante 1683, supposed to be the daughter of Jan Joosten; they appear in the Province of East Jersey about 1695 with other Dutch adventurers, and on the 18th October of that year they purchased jointly from Edward Hunloke, of Wingerworth, Burlington County, who was Deputy Governor under Dr. Daniel Coxe, a plantation of 500 acres, located at Lassa, or "Lazy," Point on the Delaware River, in Burlington County. The property was on the path frequented by the Dutch traders in passing between the settlements on the Delaware and the lower Hudson, and is now marked by the site of the city of Burlington, N. J. It is situated about twenty miles northeast of Philadelphia and was originally settled by three or four Dutch families, "who were there," says Governor Philip Carteret, "in 1666," and to whom he confirmed patents in 1678. It was subsequently the home of Peter Jegou, a noted colonial character, and included the island of Mattiniconch in the river opposite.

The record of purchase shows that title was acquired by "John Joosten and John Hamel both now, or late of Sopus [Esopus] New York, yeomen." On the same date Hunloke gave the purchasers a bond guaranteeing them undisputed possession of the premises. The day following Joosten and Hamel, there was executed and delivered to Edward Hunloke, a mortgage on the 500 acres [see N. J. Col. Arch., 1st Ser., Vol. XXI., p. 464].

On the 5th June, 1696, "Jan Joosten, late of Burlington Township," executes a power of attorney to William Wood, of Chesterfield Township, Burlington County, authorizing the latter to collect his debts. The inference here is that Jan had returned to Ulster County, N. Y. Joint ownership in Lassa Point, however, was held by Joosten and Hamel until the 1st May, 1699, when, by deed of conveyance, "John Joosten of Marbletown, Ulster Co., N. Y., transfers to John Hamel of Lassa Point, Burlington, his share of the plantation bought of Edward Hunloke." Jan Joosten again appears in the Province of East Jersey as an individual purchaser of lands in Somerset County. By deed from Governor Andrew Hamilton and Agnes, his wife, dated 13th September, 1700, several parcels of land were conveyed to "*Jane* [Jan] Joosten of Marbletown, Ulster County, N. Y., yeoman." The lands were designated as unappropriated and unsurveyed tracts, lying contiguous and located on the South Branch of the Raritan River, which was in the vicinity of the present town of Somerville. The plantation, aggregating 1,835 acres, was made up of four parcels: No. 1, 835 acres, adjoining lands of John Campbell and John Drummond; No. 2, 250 acres, adjoining lands of Hendrick Coursen and the waters of the South Branch; No. 3, 250 acres, adjoining the preceding, and No. 4, 500 acres, adjoining William Medford and waters of the South Branch. This section, the broad fertile meadows on the Raritan bottoms, was being rapidly settled by the Dutch, and some Scotch people from Long Island and the Lower Bay shore, who made their advent about fifteen years before this time. Jan Joosten Van Meteren is also on record as being in Piscataway [now South Amboy] Township on September 13, 1700 [see N. J. Col. Arch., 1st Ser., Vol. XXI., pp. 318, 497, 517].

The actual place of residence of Jan Joosten at this period is not learned, but in the N. J. Cal. of Wills [p. 480] is found the date of the filing of the inventory of the personal estate of "Jan Joosten of ————," dated 13th June, 1706, marked *Dutch*. This instrument gives the value of his estate at £245.14.0 and includes six negro slaves (a man, a woman and four children at £145). Appraisers were: Joris [George] Van Neste and Hendrick Reinersen; sworn to by *John Van Mator*, in Burlington. The appraisers were neighbors to each other and were residents on the South Branch of the Raritan. In the same neighborhood were other Dutch residents, emigrants from Kingston, among whom were: Thomas and George Haal, Abraham de la Meter, Cornelius du Bois, Adrian Molenaur and Hendrick Traphagen; they were scattered along the main stem of the Raritan, at Three Mile [Franklin Park] and Six Mile [New Brunswick], and at a later period there came into this vicinity the families of Bodine, Powelson, Eoff and Brown, each of whom are represented in this genealogy through the intermarriages of their descendants [see Hist. Somerset County, N. J., pp. 561 et seq.; also Dr. Messlar's Hist.]. At Raritan (now Somerville) was the Reformed Church;

it was the oldest congregation and in it the settlers, who were mostly Dutch, worshiped. About 1715 a Reformed Dutch church was organized at the head of the Raritan. Rev. Theodorus Jacobus Frelinghausen was its first pastor; among its elders in 1719 were Abraham de la Meter, Cornelius Bogart, Jans Hendrickson and Andreas Ten Eyck, all formerly of Kingston. This became subsequently the Readington church on the North Branch.

In Liber D of Deeds, p. 111, at Somerville, N. J., is found a deed dated 30th November, 1803, from Gilbert Bodine and Catharine, his wife, conveying to Gabriel Caskhuff, of Amwell Township, an undivided one-third part of a plantation, late the property of Isaac Bodine, which was purchased by the said Isaac Bodine (grandfather of the said Gilbert), one part from Volkert Doue, by indenture dated 6th September, 1746; and another part from Isaac Van Maitre by indenture dated 1714; both tracts or parts together, contained 100 acres and was situate in Bridgewater Township, Somerset County, N. J. The Isaac Van Maitre mentioned in this deed was probably the same who was "received, 7 Nov., 1731, on confession of faith" in the North Branch Church [see Readington Church Records].

When the will of Hendrix Mullinar, one of the pioneer settlers of the South Branch, was probated, 4th March, 1718–19, it was learned that Arience Mullinar (a son of the testator) and Isaac Bodine were named as executors; they both renounced, however, whereupon the court appointed *Isaac Van Metere,* of Salem County, N. J., as executor in their stead; *John* and *Henry Van Metere,* also of Salem, and probably brothers of Isaac, were his "fellow-bondsmen." The will was administered in June, 1719.

A search among the archives of the State Department at Trenton, N. J., brought out the record of another transaction which further evidences the presence of the Van Meteres in Somerset County at an early date. It is the record of a conveyance of a tract of land (area and consideration not mentioned) situate on the west side of the South Branch of the Raritan River and is identified as a part of tract No. 1 of the 835 acres granted to Jan Joosten by Governor Hamilton in 1700. The grantors are John Van Meter, of Somerset County, Province of East Jersey, yeoman, and Margerat, his wife, to Hendry Millar [Hendrix Mullinar?] of said county. The deed is dated 16th November, 1719, and the description reads as follows:

"All that tract of land situate lying and being upon the west side of the South Branch of Raraton River in the said County of Somerset aforesaid now in the peaceable possession and enjoyment of him the said Hendry Millar. Beginning at a Red Oak tree on the bank of the South Branch marked on the east side and running North West by West 120 chains, thence Southwest by South 44 chains, thence Southeast by East 147 chains to a Walnut tree at the said bank and point of the meadow marked on three sides thence along the South Branch to where it begins."

THE VAN METRE GENEALOGY

The deed is signed: John *Vanmetere* and Margret *Van Metere,* who makes her mark. The tract is bounded by lands of John Campbell, John Drummond, of "Londine," other lands of John Van Metre and the South Branch, and is estimated to contain 37 acres. John Drummond was formerly a burgess and merchant of Edinburgh and afterward Deputy Treasurer of Scotland [see Liber C, p. 2, East Jersey Deeds, at Trenton, N. J.].

It will be necessary at this point to return to the subject of Jan Joosten Van Meteren at Marbletown, from which the compiler digressed for the purpose of following the development of the emigrant ancestor into a New Jersey land-owner, and in order that the subsequent career of some of his children may be traced before entering upon the genealogy of the family beginning with John Van Metre, of Virginia.

Among the five children of Jan Joosten and Macyken Hendricksen Van Meteren was his son, Joost Jans, who was probably born in France, Holland, or in the German Palatinate, *circa* 1656. In the testamentary disposition written by Jan Joosten Van Meteren under date of 16th December, 1681, appears the following:

"Wife Macyke shall retain full possession (of the estate). She consents that the survivor shall possess everything: lands, houses, personal property, money, gold, silver—coined or uncoined. After their decease, the property to be inherited by their children. Jooste to have one-half of the entire estate first. Jooste and Gysbert to have the land at Marbletown, Jooste one half and then the other half to be divided between them. Geertje Crom to have the land at Wassemaker's land. Children of Lysbeth, deceased, to have their portion, in money, from the other children

Benjamin Bovoost } (signed) { Jan Joosten
Levereyn Ten Hout } { Macyken Hendrix (her mark).
[See Ulster Co., N. Y., Probate Records.]

It would thus appear than Jooste Jans was the eldest son, and it is believed that the daughters were older than the sons. From the records of the Reformed Dutch church at Kingston the following is abstracted:

"Jooste, Jan, J. M. of Meteren b. in Gelderland, residing in Mormur (Marbletown), and Sara Du Bois, J. D. of Kingston, residing in the Nieuwe Pals (New Paltz), married in the Pals 12 Dec., 1682. First publication of the Banns, 18 Nov.

Sara was a daughter of Louis du Bois, was baptized 14th September, 1664. The children of Jooste Jans and Sara (du Bois) Van Meteren were: Jan, b. 14 Oct., 1683; Jan Joosten, Maken Hendrikse and Jacob du Bois, sponsors; Rebekka, b. 26 April, 1686; Gysbert Crom and Catryn du Bois, sponsors. Lysbeth, b. 3 Mar., 1689; David du Bois and Janneken Meulenaer, sponsors. Isaac, b. *circa* 1692 (record missing); Hendrix, b. 1 Sept., 1695; Abram du Boys and Jan Hamel, sponsors. All further reference to Joosten Janse seems to have ceased with the record of his

14

youngest son Hendrix's birth in 1695 and the impression prevails that he either died about this time or disappeared in some hunting adventure, or Indian fatality. When Louis du Bois' will was probated at Kingston, 23d June, 1696, it was found that of the eight devisees, one share was allotted " to the heirs of Sara's deceased." This appears to be an irresistible argument that his daughter, the wife of Jooste Jans, was dead. This, however, is not proven so by subsequent records. What may have happened is probably this : Jooste Jans and his wife Sara may possibly have been absent from Kingston during the hiatus between the birth of their daughter Lysbeth, 1689 and the date of her father's will, which was in 1694. In this period Lysbeth, the child, disappears and Isaac is born. The writer is without knowledge of what ever became of the child Lysbeth, or the place and date of birth of Isaac. The parents may have gone back to Holland, or circumstances may have arisen which would have caused Louis Du Bois to consider his daughter dead, and this possibly accounts for the statement in his will. In a codicil of Louis du Bois' will, to me of unknown date, my authority says: " But in the codicil there were specified bequests altering this (the former) method, though probably possessing an equality." This language and alteration may have been due to the return of Jooste Jans and his wife Sara to Kingston, where Hendrix, their son, was born in 1695. Certain it is that Sara du Bois was alive and active for many years after the date of her father's will.

"Rebekka van Meteren, j. d. born in Mormeltown [Marbletown] and residing in Kingston, m.—Sept., 1704,—Cornelis Elten, j. m. born in Horle [Harley] and residing in Kingston. Banns first published 3 Sept., 1704 " [Kingston Marriage Register].

It is evident that the parents, or the mother, at least of Rebekka Elting, was absent from Kingston for another period during which time three or four children were born to the Eltings; but when their child "Zara" was baptized at the Kingston church, 6th February, 1715, Sara du Bois and her son, Jan Van Meteren, appeared as two of the four sponsors on that occasion. (This child Sara afterward m. Colonel John Hite, son of Jost Heydt, of Virginia.) And this was the only time among the baptisms of ten of the Elting children that Sara du Bois was present. She was busy elsewhere. The scene of the Van Meteren's activity is now shifted from the Hudson to the Raritan in New Jersey, where Jan Joosten probably died in 1706. His son, Jooste Jans, being probably deceased and the latter's son Jan being the eldest and the heir at law, according to the customs of the law of descent at that time prevailing, naturally became the successor of his father's rights and the largest beneficiary of the estate of his grandfather. He it was, undoubtedly, who administered the latter's estate and filed the inventory of Jan Joosten's personalty at

Burlington in 1706. He had, prior to this time, became identified with his grandfather's interest in the Province of East Jersey and had settled somewhere on the Raritan in Somerset County, where he is supposed to have married *circa* 1705, 1st, Sarah Bodine (or Berdine, according to traditions), probably the daughter of Peter or Isaac Bodine, who came to that locality in the trend of settlement up the Raritan Valley from Staten Island, N. Y., where a number of French Huguenots had settled many years before. Their children were: I., Sara, bap. Somerville, 30 Oct., 1706; II., Johannes, bap. 28 April, 1708; and III., Maria, bap. 26 April, 1709 [records of Ref. Dutch Church at Somerville, N. J.]. The wife of Jan Van Metre is supposed to have died about this time and he *m.*, 2d, Margerat ————, whom we know was his wife in 1719. They had issue: IV., Rebecca, b. *circa* 1711; V., Isaac, b. *circa* 1713; VI., Elizabeth, b. *circa* 1715; VII., Henry, b. *circa* 1717; VIII., Rachael, b. *circa* 1719; IX., Abraham, b. *circa* 1721; X., Jacob, b. 1723, and XI., Maudlina, b. *circa* 1725.

Isaac Van Metre, son of Jooste Janse and Sarah du Bois Van Metren, b. *circa* 1692-3, also emigrated to New Jersey, where he *m.* 1st (*sup.*), Catalina, the widow of Molenaer Hendrickse, who died *circa* 1719, in Somerset County, N. J., and whose will Isaac administered as executor [see N. J. Col. Arch., Cal. of Wills, Vol. XXIII., p. 332; Records First Presby. Church of Phila.]. He *m.*, 2d, *circa* 1725 Annetje [Hannah], daughter Gerritt Wyncoop, of Moreland Manor, near Philadelphia, Pa., who was b. 1698. They afterward removed to Salem County, N. J. Isaac had a family of eight children, some of whom emigrated with their parents to the Valley of the South Branch of the Potomac *ante* 1745.

Henry Van Metere, son of Jooste Janse and Sara du Bois Van Metere, b. Marbletown, N. Y., 1st September, 1695, also migrated to New Jersey and was of Salem County, N. J., when he became fellow-bondsman with his brother John as securities of the second brother Isaac for his faithful administration of the estate of Hendrix Mullinaer, deceased, of Somerset County, *vice* Isaac Bodine, renouncing. His name appears later in the Van Metre land transactions in Salem County, N. J.

The further movements of the Van Metres in the lower province of New Jersey may now be traced through the abstracts of deeds recorded at Salem, here chronologically arranged.

"19 June, 1714. Col. Daniel Cox [Agent of the Proprietors of West Jersey, at Burlington] grants to Jacob du Bois, of the County of Ulster, N. Y., Sarah du Bois of Salem; John and Isaac van Metre, also of Salem, —3,000 acres of land in Salem Co. [Liber D. D., p. 316, Salem Deeds, at Trenton, N. J.]." "These parties divided their lands by the compass; the du Bois taking theirs on the north side of a line; the Van Meters on the south side. The Van Metres continued to purchase until they owned a very large portion of the land reaching from the overshot mill in Upper Alloway's Creek, near Daretown, southeasterly to Fork Bridge: about

6,000 acres in all" [see Shourd's History of Fenwichs Colony, pp. 302–304].

The persons mentioned, the grantees, were Sara du Bois, wife or widow of Jooste Jans Van Metre; her brother Jacob, and her two sons, John and Isaac Van Metre, who were now moving southward from Somerset County. Here at least Isaac was to be established upon a plantation of his own near his uncle Jacob and under his advice and oversight, as Isaac then could have been but 22 years of age.

22d May, 1716, John Powell conveys to John Van Metre 600 acres of land on Alloway Creek, in Salem County [Liber DD, p. 41, Salem Deeds]. 20th day of 1st mo. [March], 1720: John Dickinson, Jr., son of John Dickinson, the elder, conveys to Isaac Van Metre certain lands, containing 50 acres which John Champney, grandson and heir of Major Fenwick, conveyed to said Dickinson and adjoining lands of the elder Dickinson, on 26th August, 1719 [Liber D, p. 206, Salem Deeds].

10th July, 1721, William Trent, of Trent town, in Province of West Jersey, conveys to Isaac Van Metre, a certain tract or piece of land, containing 320 acres, situate in Salem County, and is called "Piles Grove Mannor Plantation," which land had formerly been in possession of Thomas Hall and upon his death had reverted to his widow, Sarah Hall [Liber D, p. 209, Salem Deeds].

May 27, 1726, Sarah de Bois, of Salem, Province of West Jersey, "for and in consideration of the love, good will and affection which I have & do bear toward my loving and dutiful Son Isaac Van Meter of the above Province and County aforesaid, yeoman"—grants all that parcel and neck of land lying between Nickomus Run and the main branch of Salem Creek; bounded by Benjamin Acton's land on upper side and on Pile's Grove land on the lower side, containing 302 acres. All this said land, except 100 acres without any allowance for roads, which said 100 acres is to lay adjoining to Benjamin Acton's land, etc., etc. Witnesses: Samuel Elwell, Barent du Bois [son of Jacob du Bois], Chas. Crossthayt. Possession whereof was taken 28th May, 1726, by the said Isaac Van Metre in his own proper person in the presence of Jno. Whitall, Cornelis Eltinge and James Inskeep [Liber D, p. 203, Salem Deeds].

25th March, 1730, John Van Metre, of Prince George's County, Maryland, yeoman, conveys to Cornelius Newkirk, of Salem, N. J., 200 acres of land. The recitation in the deed shows that the land conveyed was part of the original purchase of 3,000 acres from Colonel Daniel Coxe, 19th June, 1714; that subsequently 400 acres were set apart by Jacob du Bois, Sarah du Bois and Isaac Van Metre to John Van Metre as his dividend; it consisted of fast land, marsh and swamp and 20 acres for roads, as set forth in a certificate by Benjamin Acton, surveyor. On the above date John Van Metre conveys the one-half of the said 400 acres to Cornelius Newkirk, adjoining the 200 acres that Elisha Bassett purchased of the said Van Metre. Witnesses were: Catharine Van Metre ("H" her mark), John Millar and William Burkett. [See Liber DD, p. 41, Salem Deeds.]

23d March, 1734, John Van Metre, in consideration of the sum of £200 paid by Isaac Van Metre, and for divers other good reasons, conveys all that certain land, marsh and meadow (except 110 acres sold out of the said tract to John Tyler) next adjoining to said Tyler's land (locality and quantity not mentioned). [Liber E, p. 32, Salem Deeds.]

22d March, 1739, Thomas Hill, of town and county of Salem, N. J., merchant, conveys to Henry Van Metre, of Pile's Grove, in said county, yeoman, 200 acres of land. The recitation in the deed shows that whereas William Hall, of Salem, merchant, deceased, was seized of 400 acres of land, he, by deed of sale, dated 10th March, 1701–2, conveyed the above mentioned 400 acres to John Hoffman, and he, by his will, dated 4th February, 1714, bequeathed 100 acres to his eldest son John Hoffman; and to his son Nicholas 100 acres and they became lawfully seized thereof of 200 acres which they jointly conveyed to Peter Steelman. Peter Steelman, by his deed dated 16th May, 1721, granted the said 200 acres to Thomas Hill, of the town and county of Salem, father of the said Thomas Hill, the first party to these presents, who thereafter died so seized intestate, whereupon the said 200 acres devolved upon the said Thomas Hill, the younger, as his only son and heir at law. The same was conveyed for the sum of £85 proclamation money [Liber K, p. 213, Salem Deeds].

20th March, 1750, Isaac Van Metre, of Salem, and Ann, his wife, yeoman, conveys a certain tract of land in Salem County to Aaron Burr, of Newark, E. J., clerk. Herein is recited the descent of title from Daniel Coxe and in which "Sarah du Bois als Van Metre" is specifically mentioned, and that the above Isaac had received 430 acres in a division dated 1st September, 1716 [Liber Jk, p. 391, Salem Deeds].

In further reference to Isaac Van Metre, whom, as we have seen, had his first children baptized in the First Presbyterian Church at Philadelphia, it is recorded that he and his friends residing in Pile's Grove were anxious to have a place of worship established among them and they made persevering efforts to obtain it. On the 22d of May, 1739, Isaac Van Metre, "on behalf of himself and many inhabitants of Pilesgrove," made application to the Philadelphia Presbytery to this effect, but the project met with considerable opposition from the congregation at Deerfield, in Cumberland County, a few miles away. The matter dragged along for the two succeeding years, the people meanwhile worshiping in a school house and at private residences; the movement, however, being finally successful, a covenant was signed organizing the Presbyterian Church of Pittsgrove [Pile's Grove], and among the first to sign the covenant were: Isaac Van Metre, Hannah, his wife, their son Henry and daughter Sarah; and among the thirty or more signatures following appear the names of Cornelius Newkirk, his wife Rachael and their son Abraham; Barent du Bois and his wife Jacomyntje. The first marriage there was that of Isaac's daughter Sarah to John Richman, 27th January, 1741/2. Under the influences of this church Isaac's children were reared and a number of them have been among its leading officers; Isaac was one of the first elders [see Original Records of Pittsgrove Church].

The date of John Van Metre's settlement in Maryland can only be approximated. He was perhaps long familiar with this part of the country, and may have traversed it with his father while following the trails with the Delaware Indians southward from the headwaters of the Delaware, which rose in the mountainous country adjacent to the Dutch settlements in Ulster County, N. Y. In 1730 Prince George's County, Maryland, extended from the Patuxent River to the western limits of Lord Baltimore's palatinate. This county was indebted for much of its earlier population to the emigrants from Pennsylvania and eastward. The border troubles between the two Provinces of Maryland and Pennsylvania had much to do with its settlement, and the disputes between these proprietary governments led many settlers of the adjacent counties of Pennsylvania to remove to the valley of Frederick, to the Monocacy and its neighboring streams. The Dutch element, perhaps, were the first to establish themselves in these localities; coming down from New York by way of Pennsylvania, they were found in western Maryland as early as 1725 [see Thomas Chalkley's journal]. One of the most traveled paths from the German settlements of Lancaster and York counties, Pa., which led into Maryland was the Monocacy-Conococheague road, which was evolved from an Indian trail. The Conococheague road led southward from a point five miles west of Codorus Creek in York County, Pa., where the Monocacy road makes a bend toward the southwest, and led to Fort Conococheague in the Cumberland Valley, Pa., thence to Fort Frederick on the Potomac [see Spangler Genealogy]. For those living on the east side of the Delaware, in the counties of Salem and Cumberland, N. J., they were only obliged to cross the Delaware River to reach Christiana [Wilmington] or New Amstel [New Castle] and from these points proceed, by much frequented paths, to the head of Elk and from thence by the waters of the Chesapeake and its tributaries reach their destination via the Potomac Falls [Harper's Ferry] in the Valley of Virginia. It was perhaps by one or the other of these routes that John Van Metre and his friends reached the Monocacy. It is probably due to him that his friends and relatives began to colonize along that stream, for here were found the Eltings, Vernoys, Croms, Van Metre and other families from the Hudson River communities. Cornelius Elting was a brother-in-law of John Van Metre. In the public records at Upper Marlborough, Prince George's County, Maryland, is found the record of purchase of two tracts of land by Cornelis Elting "formerly of Ulster County, N. Y., now being at Annapolis, Anne Arundel Co., Md.," from Sarah [B]radford, 17th October, 1729, one tract called "Melburn," containing 270 acres, and another tract called "Darby Island," contained 146 acres. The latter tract was conveyed by Cornelius Elting to his nephew, John Thompson, by deed dated 3d May, 1746, to which conveyance Isaac Hite, John Hite and Isaac Eltinge were witnesses.

The first record of John Van Metre is found in an entry in the Frederick County, Md., records, 8th November, 1726, being the date of a grant of land to John Van Metre, named "Metre," containing 300 acres and located at the mouth of a run called "Metre's Run," falling into the Monocacy. It is said that it was upon this property that the battle of Monocacy Junction was fought during the Civil War. At the above date the granted land lay in Prince George's County. In the sale of some of his land in Salem County, N. J., to Cornelius Newkirk, 25th March, 1730, the grantor describes himself as "of Prince George's Co." He also acquired other lands in Maryland, some of which lay upon the Antietam Creek in what is now Washington County, and it was while he was a resident in this province that he cast wistful eyes beyond the Potomac, upon the rich virgin land of the great valley leading southward and dreamed of larger conquests.

At a point in the foregoing pages it was stated that Jooste Janse Van Metre was supposed to have died about 1706. The last record concerning him is found in the baptismal register of the Reformed Dutch Church at Raritan [now Somerville], N. J., where his name appears with that of Kathleyn [wife of Isaac] Bodyn as sponsors at the baptism of his granddaughter Sarah, the eldest child of Jan [John] Van Metere, 30th October, 1706. Whether or not he died in that year, or later, and where his death occurred, are still unsolved problems. It is, however, the conviction of the writer that Jooste Janse was none other than "John Van Meter, the Indian trader," and if it be true, that fact would help to explain the periods of absence from his Ulster County home and assist in identifying him as the "John Van Meter of New York," referred to in the following sketches which, while differing in dates, generally agree in the main facts.

In an article relating to the last of the Southern Indians, which appeared in the *Virginia Historical Magazine* [Vol. III., p. 191, footnote], it states that "Mr. John Van Meter of New York gives an account of his accompanying the New York Delaware Indians in 1732 (?) on their raid against the Catawbas. They passed up the South Branch of the Potomac *and he afterward settled his boys there.*" The Catawbas and Cherokees were ancient foes of the Delawares and the latter drove them from their home in the Carolinas westward through Virginia and Pennsylvania and some of them finally settled in Kansas.

A writer in the *West Virginia Historical Magazine* [Vol. II., p. 17] states that John Van Meter was with the Delaware and Cayugas in 1725 (?), and this statement seems to have been repeated from Kercheval's "History of the Valley." Kercheval derived his information from the immediate descendants of the participants in the border wars and Indian troubles in Virginia. The "History of the Valley" [p. 51] gives a traditional account of the coming of the Van Meters to Virginia and the circumstances connected therewith :

"Tradition relates that a man by the name of John Van Meter, from New York, some years previous to the first settlement of the valley, discovered the fine country on the Wappatomaka [South Branch of the Potomac]. This man was a kind of Indian trader, being well acquainted with the Delawares, and once accompanied a war party who marched to the South for the purpose of invading the Catawbas. The Catawbas however anticipated them—met them very near the spot where Pendleton Court-House now stands, encountered, and defeated them with great slaughter. Van Meter was engaged on the side of the Delawares in this battle. When Van Meter returned to New York, he advised his sons, that if ever they migrated to Virginia, by all means to secure a part of the South Branch bottom, and described the land immediately above ' The Trough ' as the finest body of land which he had ever discovered in all his travels. One of his sons: Isaac Van Meter, in conformity with his father's advise came to Virginia about the year 1736-37, and made what is called a tomahawk improvement. Mr. Van Meter returned to New Jersey and came out again in 1740 . . . and in the year 1744 removed with his family and settled on the land."

This narrative by Kercheval has been freely accepted and copied by most writers who have had occasion to refer to the Van Metre pioneers in Virginia.

Scharf's "History of Western Maryland" [Vol. II., p. 1204] gives the following account :

"At the mouth of the Antietam [then in Prince George's Co., Md.], between 1730–1736, occurred the famous battle between the Catawbas and the Delawares, by which the Catawba secured the victory. This occurred at what is now the coke-yard of the Antietam Iron Works, three miles from Sharpsburg, where numerous skeletons and war implements have been found from time to time."

The beautiful "Valley of Virginia" lies beyond the western slopes of the Blue Ridge. The Shenandoah enfolds it on the south and the Potomac and its branches on the north and west. Lord Fairfax called it "The Northern Neck," and its settlement may fairly be said to have begun with the actual granting of an immense area of land in what then was Spottsylvania County, Virginia, by Governor Gooch and his Council, at Williamsburg, Virginia, to John and Isaac Van Metre, 17th June, 1730.

LOUIS DU BOIS

Out of much that has been written and from what has been more recently discovered by investigation concerning this interesting and influential ancestor of the Van Metre family of America the following record has been compiled for this work.

Louis du Bois, a French Huguenot, was born 28th October, 1626, in La Bassee, near Lille, in the Province of Artois, France. He died at Kingston, Ulster County, N. Y., ———— 1696 [will proved 27th March, 1696]; was *m.* at Mannheim in the Lower Palatinate of Germany, 10th October, 1655, to Catharine, daughter of Mathese Blanchan [a co-refugee with the du Bois from French Flanders] of Wicres, Artois [or Marseilles], France.

Mrs. Anna Louise Thompson, of Clinton, Iowa, a lineal descendant of the above Louis du Bois, in connection with M. Le Turcq, of the Genealogical Institute of Paris, has developed the du Bois line of ancestors running back to the days of the Scyrii, and includes descent from Charlemagne, Emperor of the West; Alfred the Great; Hugh Capet, King of France, and Henry I., Emperor of Germany. A chart has been worked out showing the most important of these lines, the correctness of which, Mrs. Thompson avers, has been verified by comparison with different sources of information; and where the line is broken, the cause is attributed to the summary action of Louis XIV.'s minister, Cardinal Mazarin, and Marshall Turenne, who decreed that the names of many of the noble families of the realm who espoused and held to the faith of Protestantism should be erased from the rolls and the documentary history of France and their property be confiscated. Such, then, was the law in respect to all "heretics." Mrs. Thompson further adds that Louis du Bois was a second son; that the titles and arms of de Fiennes were revived and that he assumed them, and that the line de Fiennes became extinct with the death of the Marchioness de Poyanne in 1761.

The first line in the chart begins with Guelph, Prince of the Scyrii (A. D. 476); a descendant of his in the fourteenth generation, Azo, Marquis of Liguria (A. D. 1030), married Marie, a descendant of the powerful house of Este in Italy. The Estes were of the Actii of Rome, who settled in Italy and Lombardy about 500 B. C.

Guelph, grandson of Azo and Marie, and Count of Bavaria and Saxe (A. D. 1107), *m.* Judith, a descendant of Charlemagne.

A great grandson of Guelph and Judith, Henry V., Duc de Bavaria and Saxe (A. D. 1195), *m.* Matilda, a descendant of

22

William the Conqueror, through Henry I. and Henry II. of England.

Henry VI., the son of the above and Duc de Bavaria and Saxe, *m*. A. D. 1200 Agnes, Countess of Palatine, a descendant of Alfred the Great.

A descendant of Henry VI. and Agnes (Mademoiselle) Claude de Lannoy, was *m*. to Charles du Bois, Seignieur des Querder, who was a descendant of Macquaire du Bois, Count de Roussey, A. D. 1110.

The line of descent from Charles du Bois and Claude de Lannoy was:

1st generation: Eustache, Seigneur des Querder and de Fiennes, *m*. 1st Gille de Renel; *m*. 2d Jeanne St. Ol.

2d generation: Guislain des Fiennes, Count de Clarmont, who *m*. Jeanne de Longueville.

3d generation: Marc de Fiennes, Seigneur des Querder, *m*. Madelaine d'Ognies.

4th generation: Maximillian de Fiennes, Seigneur des Querder, *m*. Catharine Cecil Germand.

5th generation: Maximillian des Fiennes, *m*. Louise Charlotte d' E'tamps.

6th generation: Chas. Maximillian des Fiennes, *m*. Henrietta de Reignier de Boisleau.

7th generation: Chrétien Maximillian des Fiennes, *m*. ——————
—————— (not on record, but a Huguenot, as supposed by M. Le Turcq—record erased).

8th generation: Louis du Bois de Fiennes, b. Oct., 1626, who evidently took refuge from religious persecution in Mannheim, Germany, where he *m*. Catharine Blanchan in 1655. Their two eldest children were born in Mannheim, and in 1660 the family came to America.

The du Bois des Fiennes appear to have been a military family and to have furnished to France some able soldiers. The first Maximillian beside being a Count was "Marischall des camps et des armées du roi." His son Maximillian was lieutenant-general "du armées du roi." Chrétian Maximillian, Marquis des Fiennes, was captain of cavalry in his father's regiment.

The erasure of the record of Chrétien's marriage and family, the Chrétien known to have been the father of Louis du Bois, makes a break in Louis' line of descent and it was done, obviously, to destroy official record of his ancestry because of his being a "heretic"; to prevent him or any of his descendants from ever afterward establishing a claim to the title and estates. But in this connection, continues Mrs. Thompson, "certainly there were not two branches after the resumption of the title of Marquis des Fiennes. It does not seem that Louis *could* belong to the line des Fiennes, as the writer of 'The Du Bois Family' says he does, and be other than the son of Chrétien Maximillian, Marquis de Fiennes."

Louis du Bois emigrated from Manheim to America with his family *circa* 1660 and eventually settled at New Village (now Hurley], near Kingston, Ulster County, N. Y., where he rapidly rose to prominence in the civil and religious affairs of the settlement. He was one of the twelve original patentees of New Paltz, a village next to Hurley; he later became one of the magistrates of the jurisdiction comprising the villages of New Paltz and Hurley. Before this period, however, the settlement had been attacked by Indians who burned Hurley; they killed and injured many of the inhabitants and carried into captivity all the family of Louis du Bois, the wife and three children of Jan Joosten Van Metern and others, all of whom were carried off to the fastnesses of the Catskill Mountains. This event, which occurred 7th June, 1663, was known in history as the Second Esopus War. Captain Martin Krieger, an old Dutch soldier and a familiar figure in the earlier Dutch settlements on the Delaware, organized, and, with Louis du Bois, headed an expedition to rescue the captives and chastise the Indians. After three months of ineffectual warfare they finally rounded up the savages on September 3, 1663, defeated the Indians and restored the captive women and children to their homes. In connection with these tragic experiences, Professor Obenchain, of Ogden College, Bowling Green, Ky., sends me the following relation:

"About ten weeks after the capture the Indians decided to celebrate their escape from pursuit by burning one of their captives. For their victim they selected Catharine du Bois and her baby, Sara, who afterward married Joost Janse Van Veteren. A cubical pile of logs was arranged and the mother and child were placed upon it; when the Indians were about to apply the torch, Catharine began to sing a Huguenot hymn she had learned in earlier days in France. The Indians withheld the fire and listened. When she finished they demanded another song and then another. Before the last hymn was finished Dutch Soldiers arrived, the, captives were all rescued and the Indians terribly punished."

Again, in 1670, when the Indians were on the warpath, Louis du Bois served in the colonial forces against them. He is credited with being the founder and first elder of the French Reformed Church at New Paltz. He left a family, a widow, who afterward *m.* Jean Cotton, and ten children, and their descendants are numerous, prominent and influential throughout the country, one of whom was Garrett A. Hobart, Vice-President of the United States during the first term of President McKinley's administration.

JAN GYSBERTSEN VAN METEREN

It is deemed desirable to add here the record of another of the Van Meteren family because of the popular belief that he was a near kinsman of Jan Joosten Van Meteren, *i. e.,* a first cousin of the Hudson River pioneer. This record is compiled from various historical and genealogical sources.

Jan Gysbertsen Van Metre [John Gilbert Van Metre] is said to have emigrated from Bommell, Province of Gelderland, Holland, to New Amsterdam in 1663, bringing with him a son, Kryn Jansen Van Meteren *sup.* b. in Bommell, 10th March, 1650. The compilers of the various records of Long Island state that Jan Gysbertsen settled at New Utrecht, L. I., in 1663. There is no statement referring to his wife. He was assessed on the rolls as an inhabitant of New Utrecht for the years 1675, '76, '83 and '98; that he was a magistrate in 1673; deacon of the Dutch Church in 1683. After 1698 his name disappears from that locality, but reappears at Middletown, Monmouth County, Province of East Jersey, whence he is supposed to have come in that year. In the latter locality he is supposed to have *m.* his second wife, Hester, daughter of James Grover, Jr., of Middletown, in whose will, dated 18th March, 1714/15, mention of his son-in-law, John Gysbertsen, is made. Further evidence of this fact is found in a mortgage dated 19th November, 1700, given by Jan Gysbertsen and his wife Esther, of Monmouth County, to Gerardus Beekman, of King's County, N. Y., on 149 acres of land located in the former county. The land of Jan Gysbertsen adjoined those of Captain John Bowne on Hope River in the year 1700. In the inventory of the estate of Captain John Bowne, of Mattewan, Middletown Township, filed 9th April, 1716, the name of John Ghisberson not only occurs, but also those of Cryne Jansen, John Van Metre and Thomas Shepherd, all of whom are noted as mortgagors in an exceedingly long list of debtors to Bowne's estate.

The son of Jan Gysbertsen, and the only one of whom there is any present knowledge, was Kreign, or, as it is variously given, Quryn, Kryn, Chrine, Chrynyonce, etc. Jansen Van Meteren [John Van Metre] settled at New Utrecht with his father and married there, 9th September, 1683, Neeltje Van Cleef. On the 25th March, 1675, Krein purchased " Thomas Jans new farm, in New Utrecht, for 2,000 guilders." He appears on the assessment rolls there from 1675 to 1709; a member of the Dutch Church, 1677; mentioned in Dungan's Patent, 1686; deacon, 1699; assessed for 49 acres in New Utrecht, 1701, and removed to Middletown, 1709; died there 10th March, 1720, and his wife, 1st January, 1747. Issue: 1 Jan, b. 26 April, 1687; d. y.; 2 John, b 17 April, 1688, *m.* Ida Hendrickse; 3 Ida, b. 24 Aug., 1691, *m.* John, son

25

of Adrian Bennett; 4 Gysbert, b. 24 Feb., 1694, *m.* Macyke Hendrickse; 5 Engleteje, b. 30 Sept., 1696, *m.* John Andersen; 6 Benjamin, b. 22 Jan., 1702, *m.* Elizabeth Laen; 7 Cornelia, b. 24 May, 1704, *m.* Hans Van Cleef; 8 Cyrenius, b. 28 Aug., 1706, *m.* Abigail Lefferts, and 9 Joseph, b. 5 Feb., 1710, *m.* Sarah Schenk.

1 John Van Metre, son of Chryne Jans, *m.* 17th October, 1717, Ida, daughter of Ruyk Hendricksen van Suydam (lieutenant of troop in Flatbush, L. I., 1715) on June 6, 1727, his father-in-law, residing at Flatbush conveys to John Van Metre, of Middletown Township,, Monmouth County, N. J., a tract of land adjoining lands of the heirs of Quryn Van Metre, containing 152 acres and located in Middletown. John was a communicant of the Dutch Church at Freehold 1713; deacon, 1739. He died 10 Jan., 1761. His children as noted by Beekman, were 1 Cryn Jan, b. 28 Sept., 1718. 2 Ryck, b. 16 April, 1720, *m.* Micah Osborne. 3 Gilbert, b. 14 Jan., 1722. 4 Janetje, bap. 29 Oct., 1724. 5 Nealtje, bap. 14 Aug., 1728. 6 Marija, b. 7 Jan., 1731, *m.* Daniel Polehemous. 7 Eyda, b. 12 Feb., 1733, *m.* Benj. Sutphen. 8 John, b. 1 Feb., 1735; d. y. 9 Cornelia, b. 4 July, 1737. 10 Cornelius, b. 14 Aug., 1739. 11 Geertje, b. 27 Nov., 1744, *m.* Aert Van der Bilt, 1763.

The will of this John Van Metre dated 7 March, 1758, and proved 1st April, 1761, gives the names of the testator's wife and children in the following form and order: Widow Eitie; sons: Chrineyonce; Richard; Guisbert; John; daus. Youmachie Sutphen Vally van Lery; Eitie Sutphen; Mary; Caty; Hune and Charity. The will also contains the request that his son John shall be maintained by Guisbert van Metre as long as he shall live.

The descendants of Jan Gysbertsen have been recorded here, because it has been claimed by some of the family historians that this Jan Gysbertsen van Meteren was the ancestor of the Virginia Van Metres—the father of John Van Metre, the Indian trader. As the former line has been traced in detail and all the Johns accounted for, so that now the honor claimed for Jan Gysbertsen may be eliminated from any further consideration in connection with the Virginia branch of the family.

THE VIRGINIA GRANT, AND SETTLEMENT.

At a Council held at the Capital the 17th day of June, 1730. Present: the Governor.

Robert Carter	John Carter
James Blair	Rd. Fitzwilliam
Wm. Byrd	John Grymes
John Robinson	Wm. Dandridge
	John Curtis, Esqrs.

Several petitions being this day offered to the Board for leave to take up land on the River Sherando on the North-west side of the Great

THE VIRGINIA GRANT, AND SETTLEMENT

Mountains, Robert Carter, Esqr., Agent for the Proprietors of the Northern Neck moved that it might be entered that he on behalf of the s^d. Proprietors claimed the land on the s^d. River Sherando as belonging to the sd. Proprietors & within the limits of their Grants it belonged sole to the Proprietors to grant the sd. lands wch moven at his request is entered and then the Board proceeded to the hearing of the s^d Petetions.

On reading at this Board the Petition of John Van Metre setting forth that he is desirous to take up a Tract of land in this Colony on the West side of the Great Mountains for the settlement of himself & Eleven children & also that divers of his Relations & friends living in the Government of New York are also desirous to move with their families & Effects to Settle in the same place if a Sufficient Quantity of Land may be assigned them for that purpose & praying that ten thousand acres of land lying in the forks of Sherando River including the places called by the names of Cedar Litch & Stony Lick and running up between the branches of the s^d. River to complete that Quantity & twenty thousand acres not already taken up by Robert Carter & Mann Page, Esq^{rs}., or any other,—lying in the fork between the sd. River Sherando and the River Cohongaroola [Potomac] & extending thence to Opeckon & up the South Branch thereof may be assigned for the Habitation of himself his family & friends. The Governor with the advise of the Council is pleased to give leave to the sd. John Vanmeter to take up the sd. first mentioned tract of ten thousand acres for the Set'lem't of himself and his family. And that as soon as the Petitioner shall bring on the last mentioned tract twenty families to inhabit on that this Board is satisfied so many are to remove thither Leave be & it is hereby granted him for surveying the last mentioned Tract of twenty thousand acres within the limits above described in so many Several Dividens as the pet^r. & his sd. partners shall think fit. And it is further ordered that no person be permitted to enter for or take up any part of the afsd. Lands in the meantime provided the sd. Vanmeter & his family & the twenty other families of his Relations and friends do settle thereon within the space of two years according to his proposal.

Isaac Vanmeter of the Province of West Jersey having by his petition to this Board set forth that he & Divers other Germans Families are desirous to settle themselves on the West side of the Great Mountains in this Colony he the Petitioner has been to view the lands in those parts & has discovered a place where further such Settlement may Conveniently be made & not yet taken up or possesed by any of the english Inhabitants & praying that ten thousand acres of Land lying between the Land surveyed for Robert Carter, Esqr. the fork of Sherundo River & the River Opeckon in as many several Tracts or Dividends as shall be necessary ffor the Acomodation and settlement of ten ffamilies (including his own), which he proposes to bring to the sd. Land. The Governor with the advise of the Council is pleas'd to order as it is hereby Ordered that the sd. Isaac Vanmeter for himself and his Partners have leave to take up the sd. Quantity of ten thousand acres of Land within the limits above described & that if he bring the above Number of Families to dwell there within two yeares Patents be granted him & them for the same in such several Tracts & Dividends as they shall think ffit & in the Mean time that the same shall be reserv'd free from the entry of any other p'son. [MSS. Journal of the Governor and Council (1721–1734), p. 364, Richmond, Va].

Within the two years allowed in the grant the Van Metres who were expected to carry out the conditions regarding the colonizing of the grant had negotiated a transfer of their rights to Joist Hite a native of Holland, but more recently of the Perkiomen

27

region in Philadelphia County, Pa., whence he had came via Germantown,—from Kingston. He is presumed to have been a relative of John Van Metre through his wife who was Anna Maria DuBois. At the time the grant was made to the Van Metres, Hite had a large plantation and some mill property on Perkiomen Creek in what is now Montgomery Co., Pa.,—a property now owned by Hon. Samuel W. Pennypacker, ex-Governor of Penna. After Hite had acquired the Van Metre grants it appears that he entered into a partnership with Robert McKoy, also of Penna. The transfer by the Van Metres to Hite was made on 5th Aug., 1731, and on the following 25th of October Messrs. Hite and McKoy obtained orders from Council for 100,000 acres of land on the west side of the Blue Ridge under the same conditions, as to its colonization—were exacted of them as those by which the Van Metres were bound. It was in that year, 1731, that Jost Hite and Robert McKoy made permanent settlement upon their possessions in Western Virginia (see *W. Va. Hist. Mag.*, Vol. I., pp. 53, 54; also W. S. Laidley's letters). Hite having disposed of his lands and mill in Pennsylvania in 1730—proceeded with his family of adult children, some friends and relatives—16 families in all,—to York, Pa., and thence by the way of the Indian trail along the Conococheague through the Cumberland Valley to the Potomac and by passing through the gap in the Blue Ridge at Harper's Ferry, entered the Valley of Virginia and made his first settlement, it is claimed,— at New Muhlenburg (see *Times-Despatch*, Richmond, Va., 18 Nov., 1904).

Orange Co., Va., was taken from Spottsylvania Co., in 1734 and it was within the limits of the new county of Orange that the 40,000 acres granted to the Van Metres was located, and one of the first patents issued was for 1,020 acres of land being a part of the original Van Metre grant made by Virginia to Jost Hite under date of 5 Aug., 1734 (Grant Book, 15, p. 276, Richmond).

On the third day of October, 1734, thirty four grants, for lands in varying quantities, were made to as many colonists in Orange Co., the aggregate number of acres being 19,033. Among the various grantees are the names of John Van Metre, 885 acres; Thomas Shepherd, 220 acres; Richard Morgan, 500 acres; Richard Paulson, 834 acres, and Benjamin Burden, 1,142 acres. Some of these pioneers were from the Provinces of East and West Jersey, and were in all probability, more or less intimately associated with the Van Metres and Hite in earlier days and localities.

Between 1734 and 1744—the year following the establishment of Frederick Co., out of Orange Co.—82 other grants were made to as many different persons; these grants probably absorbed the whole of the Van Metre-Hite-McKoy original interests and the passing of title by these grantors to the many grantees occasioned long years of contention and litigation between Hite and McKoy of the one part and Thomas, Lord Fairfax, of the other part, upon the latter's claim that he had prior ownership of the Northern Neck; the dispute lasted until 1786 and was finally settled by decree of Court in Hite & McKoy's favor, and after the two principals had laid long in their graves.

THE COLONY IN SPOTTSYLVANIA CO., VA.

XXVI April, 1734.

Present: The Governor

Cole Digges
John Robinson
John Grymes
Thomas Lee

Will Randolph
John Taylor
Philip Lightfoot, Esq^rs.

Present also, Com^ry. Blair, William Byrd, John Curtis, Esq^rs. On read-reading a petition from the inhabitants on the North West side the Blue Ridge of Mountains, praying that: some persons may be appointed as Magistrates to determine Differences and punish Offenders in regard; the Petitioners live far remote from any of the established Counties within the Colony. It is the Opinion of the Council that *Joost* Hyte, Morgan Morgan, John Smith, Benjamin Bourden and George Hobson be appointed Justices within the limits aforesaid and that they be added to the Com^mrs. of the Peace for the County of Spottsylvania, until there be sufficient number of inhabitants on the North West side of s^d. Mountains to make a County of itself. But that the persons above named be not obliged to give their attendance as Justices of the Court of Spottsylvania. [Journal of Councils, 1721-1734, p. 485; State Library, Richmond, Va.]

Jost Hite and McKay were in 1735, granted extension to settle "till Christmas, 1735," to comply with the terms of their grants and in the meantime they may proceed to survey [vide. p. 494].

Petition of St. Marks in Orange County, praying the descretion of the Council with regard to the poor of the new intended Parish of St. Thomas already separated from St. Marks, but not yet erected into a parish of themselves—is postponed until after the Oyer and Terminer Court;—as also, the petition of the inhabitants of the newly intended Parish of St. Thomas, praying to be erected into a distinct County from Orange by name of the County of Frederick, as by law directed, they answering the —to those now of sufficient number of inhabitants for that purpose, who are greatly distressed by reason of their distance from Orange Court—is postponed at the same time. Council held at the Capital 29 April, 1741 [Vide Vol. 1722-73, p. 35]. 1743. Justices named for County of Frederick when erected in October next—if no opposition takes place: Morgan Morgan, Richard Borden and others [Vide Vol. 1722-1773, p. 80, State Library, Richmond, Va.]

THE HITE GRANTS AND ASSIGNMENTS

On the 30th June, 1730, an Order of Council was made granting leave to John Van Metre of New York to take up 10,000 acres of land lying in the fork of Sherando River, including the places called Cedar Lick and Stoney Lick, and running up between the branches of the river for quantity, for the settlement of himself and family of eleven children; and (as soon as he should bring thirty families to settle the same) 20,000 acres more of lands not before located by Robert Carter and Mann Page, or any other persons, lying in the fork of the Sherundo and Cohongoruta, and extending thence to the Opequon. Two years were allowed to locate this entry and all others were forbidden to locate the lands in the meantime.

John Van Metre and Isaac Van Metre also obtained leave by another order of Council, to take up 40,000 acres including the other 30,000 acres. In 1731 the Van Metres assigned their rights under these orders of Council, to Joist Hite and Robert McKay of Pennsylvania; and on 1st October, in same year, on petition of Hite and McKay, setting forth that they and their families, and an hundred other families were desirous of removing to Virginia, and praying a grant of 100,000 acres of land to seat themselves upon, another Order of Council was made granting them leave to locate that quantity of land, between the lands of John Van Metre, Jacob Stoever and John Fishbach and others, and the residue upon and including the branches of the Sherundo above Stoevers, Fishbach and his partners; and that upon 100 families migrating and settling on the lands granted, patents should issue to them for such proportions as they should agree among themselves. Hite and company were thus entitled to locate 140,000 acres of land. In June, 1734, an order of Council was made declaring that Hite & Co. had complied with the terms of the grant, in respect to the first 40,000 acres, and directing that patents should be issued accordingly to the respective surveys thereof. The surveys were deposited in the Land Office, but the patents were not issued. Hite and Co., proceeded in the location of 54 families on them. But the whole 140,000 acres being within the bounds of the Northern Neck, as claimed by the Proprietor, he, in 1736, entered a caveat against the issuing of patents for them; and as we have seen, the order of the King in Council, of 1733, had restrained the Colonial government from perfecting the grants. After the determination of the dispute between the Crown and the Proprietary, covering the bounds of the Northern Neck, Hite and his company claimed their patents insisting that the order of Council under which they claimed, were grants within the intendment of the Act of 1748, and were therefore confirmed by that Act, when Lord Fairfax insisted that only the titles of lands granted by patent were confirmed by the Act. In 1749 Hite brought suit in Chancery. In 1771, Oct., the Plaintiff obtained a decree, Lord Fairfax appealed to King and Council. After the Revolution, Hite appealed to Court of Appeals. The General Court reversed . . . and case removed to High Court of Chancery. The papers and decrees in the case afford most complete information as to the origin and circumstances, etc. [See: Revised Code of Virginia, Vol. II., 1818-19, pp. 346-7.]

JOHN VAN METRE'S DEED OF GIFT

1744, Sept. 17. Deed of gift from John Van Metre of Frederick Co. Va. for love and affection to Isaac my eldest son, Henry second son, Abraham third son, Jacob fourth and youngest son; Maudlena, wife to Robert Pewsey my youngest daughter, Solomon Hedges Esqr., Thomas Shepherd, James Davis, and Robert Jones, sons in law—gives, grants, etc., all stalyons, geldings, mares and colts, running in the woods, branded on the left shoulder with letter " M," to be divided equally, the part to my said daughter shall be appropriated to her use, and under the care of my executors named in my will. 4 young mares and their increase to each of my grandsons Johannes Van Metre, son of Johannes deceased; and the same to John Lessige, son of my daughter Rachael deceased when they shall arrive at age of 21 years. If the within mentioned Robert Jones do not quit-claim to a pretended right to 100 acres of land and other pretended demands on me, the said John Van Metre, for which he hath no right, then the proportion of said creatures shall be given to my daughter, Mary wife to said Jones and to her children at the discression of my executors.

JOHN VAN METER.

Witnesses: Jonas Hedges, Joseph Carroll [Fredrick Co. Va., Records].

WILL OF JOHN VAN METRE

In the name of God Amen, the Thirteenth day of August one thousand seven hundred and forty five, I. John Van Metre in Frederick County in the Colony of Virginia being sick in body but of sound mind and Memory praise be given to God for the same and calling to mind the uncertainty of this Transitory Life, am willing through Divine Assistance to settle and Dispose of those Temporal blessings which it hath Pleased God beyond my Deserts to bestow upon me and therefore making this my Last Will and Testament Disannulling all other wills and Testaments heretofore made by me, &c. Imprimis, I commend my soul into the hands of God that gave it, hoping thro the merits of the Lord Jesus Christ it will be accepted and my body to be Interred with Deacency at the Discretion of my executors hereafter named. I also will that all my Just Debts and Demands whatsoever in Right of Conscience is Due to any to be Discharged and paid (as also funeral expenses) By my executors and as to my Real and Personal Estate, I Will, Dispose Devise Give and Bequeath it in the manner following, that is to say. First my will is that my well beloved wife Margerat Van Metre Have the third part of my moveable estate, also one room which she likes best, to Dwell in, in my dwelling House, and one third part of the Orchard next the Run with the keeping of one Riding Horse and two Milch cows, Linnin and Wolling Yarn to be wove her Bed and Bedding the said Room and Liberties to be by her possessed during Her Dureing Life, without controle hinderance or molestation of any person whatever.

Second, Item, I give Will Devise and bequeath unto my son Abraham Van Meter and his Heirs Lawfully Begotten, a Certain Parcel Tract of Land Bought by me of Francis Prichard on Opekan Run against the Land formally Bequeathed to him, said Tract Begins at an Elm Tree being the East corner of the said Tract between a Line Tree Hickory Saplin and aforesaid Elm Saplin By Opekan Run side thence down the same to the Beginning Tree of afsd. Pricherds Tract. thence South Fifty five Degrees West, one Hundred and Ten Poles, to the afsd. Beginning Elm Tree, containing by Estimation one hundred acres of land be it more or less. Provided there should be no Heirs Male or Female of my said Son or Sons (Hereafter named) Live to arise to the age of Twenty one Years, that then after the Decease of my s'd son or sons afsd. or their Heirs, that then their part of Land to be equally Divided amongst the rest of my Surviving Devisees 3d hereafter mentioned, Furthermore I also give Unto my s'd son Abraham Van Meter on Certain Tract of Land being and Situate on Opequon Run in the County afrs'd and to his Heirs Lawfully Begotton being part of Four hundred and Seventy five acres of Land Bought of Jost Hite, Beginning at or about two yards below a Pine Tree on a high Bank on Opeckon Run called the Allan Hill, and running thence by a Division Line North Sixty five Degrees East sixty Polls, to a small Hickory thence North Twenty Degrees West Twenty Eight Poles

31

to a Black Oak then North Twenty Degrees West Sixteen Poles then North Fifteen Degrees East two hundred and nine Poles to a Spannish Oak another corner of the Original survey Thence North twenty Degrees West sixteen Poles to the First Beginning head of the survey of the original Tract by Opeckon Run side near a White Oak marked thus IVM, then up Opeckon Run to the Beginning Pine, containing by estimation Two hundred and thirty seven acres of Land be it more or less &c. the same I also Give Devise and Bequeath to him my son Abraham and his Heir Lawfully Begotten, Under the same Restrictions and Limitations as I have Bequeathed unto him the above mentioned Land Bought of Francis Pricher, also I Give Devise unto my said son Abraham (a son of my wife aforesaid thirds of my Movable Estate and Legacies are paid) an equal proportioned. Childs' part therefrom as well as Lands to be Disposed of if any there be as of all things else &c.

Fourth I also Will, Give Devise and Bequeath unto my son Abraham Van Metre and to his lawful Heirs the Southernmost part and half moiety of four hundred acres of land for me and in my name to survey for him his Heirs afrs'd which land I have Jos Hite's Bond for procuring a Pattent, which if he shall not obtain the said Pattent he is to have the said Bond for Recovering so much as will amount to his share or Proportion according to his dividend of s'd Tract and the same Land to be held and enjoyed by him under the same Restrictions and Limitations as the above mentioned Land Namely the Land Bought of Francis Pricher &c.

Fifth, I Devise Will and Bequeath unto my son Isaac Van Meter and his Heirs Lawfully Begotten one Part or Tract of Land being part of the Tract of Land whereon I now Dwell, Beginning at a Bounded stake at the end of Sixteen Poles in the first Line of the Original Tract Running thence with the said Line South Thirty Degrees West Sixty full perches, then South Eighty one Degrees East One hundred and Eighty Eight Perches, the North Five Degrees East Ten Poles then South Eighty one Degrees East One hundred and Eighty Poles until it intersects the line of the Intire Tract then North one hundred Poles to two white oaks at corner of the Intire Tract then North Fifty two Degrees West Fifty Poles to a Black Oak another Corner of the Intire Tract then North Eighteen Poles then South Seventy-six Degrees West to the Beginning Stake, containing by computation Two hundred and Fifty acres of Land be it more or less. Provided the said Isaac Van Meter make sale of the Land he has at Monocacy and deliver one fourth part of the price thereof to his Brother Jacob and the other three fourths to be either applied toward improving the Land herein Bequeathed otherwise laid out in other Lands and the s'd. to be held under the same Restrictions and Limitations, as those lands Will and Bequeathed to my son Abraham as aforementioned, Also I Give and Devise unto my said son Isaac Van Meter after my afs'd wife's thirds of my Movable Estate and Legacies are paid an Equal proportional Child's part arising therefrom as well of my Lands which are to be Disposed of if any there be as of all also my Movables &c.

Sixth Item, I Give Devise and Bequeath unto my son Henry Van Meter his Heirs Lawfully Begotten one certain Parcel Tract of Land situate and being in Frederich County on Opeckon Run whereon the said Henry now dwells, Beginning at the Spannish oak standing by Opeckon at a Lick in the Branch of s'd Run and running thence into the woods East Twenty Poles to a Black Oak thence South Eighty three Degrees East Ninty two Poles to a White Oak then East one hundred and fifty one Poles to a Hickory in a Line of the original survey thence down the same to a Run that falls into Opeckon Run thence down the same into Opeckon Run where a Spring is at the mouth thereof then up Opeckan Run to the Beginning Spannish Oak containing by estimation about four Hundred acres of Land be it more or less, with Liberty to such as possessed the

32

land below the mouth of the said Run to get the water and have and possess part of the said Spring at the mouth of said Run, and hold and enjoy the said land under the same Restrictions and Limitations as my son Abraham and his Heirs &c. and if my said son should decease before his wife Eve. . . . Also I give and Devise unto my said son Henry after my aforesaid wives third of my Movable Estate and Legacies are paid an equal proportional Child's part arising therefrom as well as my lands which are to be disposed of if any there be as of all else &c.

Seventh—Item I will Devise Give and Bequeath unto my son Jacob Van Metre and his Heirs Lawfully Begotten, one piece or tract of land, being part of Tract whereon I now dwell, Beginning at a Bound Hickory standing at the end of the Eighty Poles in the first Line of the Original and running thence with the said Line North Thirty degrees West Fifty six Poles then South seventy one Degrees East two hundred and twenty four Poles then North sixty six Degrees East Twenty four Poles then North Eighty two Degrees East Eighty Poles then North Eighty five Degrees East one hundred and Forty Poles then North fifteen Degrees west twelve Poles to a Black Oak being one of the corner trees of the original Tract then North Forty two Degrees West Eighty two Poles to a Hickory then North sixty eight Poles until it intersects Isaac Van Meter's Line thence traversing the several Courses of the said Isaac's Line to the Beginning Containing by estimation two hundred and thirty three acres of Land with that part of the Plantation whereon I now dwell together with all the Houses, Orchards on the said part Parcel, Tract of Land excepting as before excepted unto my wife to hold and enjoy the same under the same Restrictions and Limitations as is aforementioned unto my son Abraham and his Heirs &c. Also I give Devise and bequeath unto my said son Jacob after my wifes Third part of my Movable Estate and Legacies are paid an equal proportional Child's part arising therefrom as well as my lands which are to be disposed of if any there be as of all else &c.

Eighth, Item, I will Devise give and Bequeath unto the Heirs Begotten [on] the body of my daughter *Sarah* wife to James Davis, one Piece or Tract of Land, part of the Tract of land whereon I now dwell Beginning for the same at the first Beginning Tree of the Intire tract and Running thence South Thirty degrees West Sixteen Poles to a stake then North Seventy-five Degrees East two hundred and ninty two Poles to a cross the Intire Tract then around the several courses Joining *Rebeccas* land to the Beginning Containing by computation two hundred and Twenty acres of Land, more or less to be held under the same Restrictions, Titles, Limitations as aforesaid. Also, I give and Bequeath unto my said Daughter after my said wife's Thirds of my Moveable Estate and Legacies are paid an equal proportional Child's part arising therefrom as well of my Lands wh are to be Disposed of if there be of all else. Provided, and it is my Soul Intent and Meaning that *James Davis* together with his wife Sarah give Good and sufficient security unto my Executors, for the sum of her Proportional part of my Moveable Estate arising to be paid unto their Heirs, equally divided amongst them when they shall arrive at the age of twenty one years, and on Refusal of such security the Proportional part so arising to remain in the hands of my Executors until the Heirs aforesaid arrive at the age aforesaid &c.

Ninth, Item, I will Devise Give and Bequeath unto my daughter *Mary* wife of *Robert Jones* and to the Heirs of her body Lawfully Begotten one certain piece or Tract of Land being part of the Tract whereon I now Dwell beginning at a large White Oak by a Hole in the Ground it being a corner of the original Survey of the Whole Intire Tract and Running from the said oak South twenty one Degrees West two hundred and eight Poles then South forty two degrees west forty two Poles to a White Oak by a Mead on a corner of the Original Tract thence South forty two Degrees East Sixty Poles thence North Fifty four Degrees East three hundred and forty Poles until it Intersects the Line of the Intire Tract then with the same eighteen Degrees East Sixty five Poles to a Hickory Corner of the Original Tract thence North Thirty Degrees East eighty poles to the afs White Oak by Spring it being another Corner of the Original Tract then North Fifteen Degrees West Seventy Poles thence South Eighty three Degrees West Eighty Poles to a Black Oak then South ten Degrees West Fifty six Poles to a stake by a corner of a fence then East by the said fence to another stake then thirty Degrees then West one hundred and sixty four Poles to another stake then Northwest sixty six Poles to the Beginning containing by estimation three hundred and fifty acres of Land be it more less the same to be held and enjoyed under the same Restrictions and Limitations above mentioned in the Lands Willed and Bequeathed to my son *Abraham Van Metre* and his Heirs &c. Also, I give and Devise unto my said Daughter Mary wife to the said Robert Jones after my afsd Wife's Thirds of my Movable Estate and Legacies are paid an Equal Proportional Child's part arising therefrom as well of my Lands which are not to be disposed of if any there be as of all else, Provided, and it is my Soul Intent and meaning that *Robert Jones* With his wife *Mary* give Good and sufficient security unto my Executors for the sum of her proportional part of my Movable Estate, arising to be paid unto their Heirs equally divided amongst them when they arrive to the age of Twenty one years, and on Refusal of such security, the Proportional part so arising to remain in the hands of my Executors until the Heirs afs^d arrive af^sd.

Tenth, Item, I Devise Give and Bequeath unto my Daughter *Rebecca* wife to Solomon Hedges, Esq., and to her Heirs Lawfully Begotten of her body one parcel or Tract of land being part of the tract I now Dwell on Beginning at a corner marked Black Oak the lower most corner on the east side of the meadow and running with the lines of the Original Tract North Thirty three Degrees West One hundred & ten Poles to a Black oak then South Seventeen Degrees West one hundred and Fifty eight Poles to a Hickory then South Sixty Degrees West and Ninty five Poles to a Black Oak then South Fifteen Degrees West one hundred and thirty six Poles and in a corner of the other Tract then crossing the said Tract North seventy nine Degrees East one hundred and sixty Poles until it shall intersect the Line of the Intire survey then with the same North Twenty five Degrees East two hundred and forty four Poles to the Beginning Black Oak containing by estimation two hundred acres of Land and meadow be it more or less to be held and enjoyed by the Heirs of the said *Solomon and Rebecca* Lawfully begotten of her body under the same Restriction and Limitations as is mentioned to Abraham Van Meter's Heirs, &c. Also I give and devise unto my said Daughter *Rebecca* after my said wife's Thirds of my Movable Estate and Legacies are paid an Equal Proportional Child's part arising therefrom as well as of my Lands which are to be disposed of if any then be as of all else, &c. Provided, and it is my soul Intent and meaning that *Solomon Hedges and Rebecca his wife* give Good and sufficient security unto my Executor's for the sum of her Proportional Part of my Movable Estate arising to be paid unto their Heirs Equally Divided amongst them when they shall arrive to the age of Twenty one years and on Refusal of such Security, the Proportional part so arising to remain in the hands of my Executors until the Heirs afs^d arrive at the age afs^d &c.

Eleventh, Item, I give Devise and Bequeath unto my Daughter *Elizabeth* Wife to *Thomas Shepherd* and to the heirs of her body Lawfully Begotten

34

WILL OF JOHN VAN METRE

One Certain Tract or piece of Land being part of the Tract whereon I now dwell beginning at the South corner of the above Devised Land and running thence with the same North Fifty four Degrees East Three hundred and Forty Poles until it shall Intersect the Line of the Intire Tract thence Traversing the Lines of the Intire Tract round to the Beginning, containing by computation three hundred acres of Land. Also one other Tract of Land Lying situate and being in Prince George's County in the Province of Maryland known by the name of Pelmel. Beginning at a bounded Ash standing at the upper end of a Tract of land called Antetum Bottom on the Bank of Potomack River containing one hundred and sixty acres of Land according to the Certificate of Survey under the same Title Restrictions and Limitations as in afs^d Bequest and Devise unto my son Abraham Van Meter and his Heirs. Also if *Robert Jones* should be scarce of Water or his Heirs, or anyother the Devises or their Heirs into whose Hands the Lands shall come into, then it shall and may be Lawful for them to Digg a Trench to Convey the Water from the Run into the said Land with [out] Interruption of him the said *Thomas Shepherd* or his heirs afore^{sed}. Also I give and Devise unto my said Daughter *Elizabeth* wife to *Thomas Shepherd* after my afs^d wife's Thirds of my Movable Estate and Legacies are paid an equal Proportional Child's part arising therefrom as well of my Lands which are to be Deposed of if any there be as of all else &c. Provided, and it is my Soul Intent and meaning that *Thomas Shepherd* and *Elizabeth* his wife Give Good and sufficient security unto my Executors for the sum of her proportional part of my movable Estate arising to be paid unto their Heirs equally Divided amongst them when they shall arrive at the age of Twenty one Years, And on Refusal of such security the Proportional part so arising to Remain in the Hands of my Executors until the Heirs afs^d arrive at the age afsd &c.

Twelvth, Item, I Devise Give and Bequeath unto my Daughter *Magdalena* the sum of twenty shillings, as her full Legacy whereby when paid or tendered to her by my Executors is discharged and fully acquitted from any Right Title or Interest or in or to my Real or Personal Estate and I do Devise Will and Bequeath unto her Heirs Lawfully Begotten on her body a Certain Tract or piece of Land being part of the Tract whereon I now Dwell beginning at a marked Red Oak saplin being a corner of the original survey of the Intire Tract and Running thence North Thirty Degrees East Twelve Poles, then South Seventy one Degrees East two hundred and twenty four Poles then North sixty six Degrees East twenty four Poles then North Eighty two Degrees East Eighty four Poles then south Eighty Poles then south ten West fifty six Poles then East twenty Poles then North West sixtysix Poles to a white oak by a Hole being a corner of the survey of the Intire Tract then with the Line of the same to the beginning Black oak saplin Containing by estimation two hundred and fifty acres of Land be it more or less to be held and enjoyed by the heirs of my said Daughter under the Limitations and Restrictions according to the Devise made to my son Abraham van Meter's Heirs, &c. Also I give and Devise unto the Heirs of my said Daughter *Magdalena* after my wife's Thirds of my Movable Estate so arising to remain in the hands of my Executors until her heirs arrive to the age of Twenty one years and then equally between them and for want of such Heirs to be equally divided amongst the other Devisees &c.

Thirteenth Item, I will Devise Give and Bequeath to the son of Daughter *Rachael* deceased (viz) *John Leforge* a certain tract of land containing two hundred acres being part of four hundred acres of land which my son *Abraham Van Meter* hath Divided to him, which two hundred acres of Land are to be held and enjoyed under the same Restrictions and Limitations and Intails as aforementioned &c. as also two Breeding Mares, and if it so happen that he should die that then the said mares shall be given to his two cousins namely Johannes Van Meter son of Johanes Van Meter deceased and Joana daughter of the said Johanes deceased &c.

Fourteenth, Item, I will Devise and Bequeath unto my Grandson *Johannes Van Meter* son of my Eldest son Johannes Van Meter Deceased and to his Heirs Lawfully Begotten a certain parcel of Land being the uppermost part of the afs^d four hundred and seventy five acres of land which I purchased of *Jost Hite* Beginning at the afs^d Pine Trees mentioned in the second clause of my Bequest to my son *Abraham Van Meter* out of part of the same Tract and running thence with the same Division Line Between him and my son *Abraham* North sixty Degrees East sixty Poles to a small Hickory Saplin standing on the Line of the Survey of the whole Intire Tract then with the same South twenty three Degrees East two hundred and Fifty seven Poles to a White oak standing at a corner of the original survey and is the uppermost corner of the Land mentioned in *Jost Hite's* Deed then running with the Line of the said Deed to Opeckon Run and Down the same to the afs^d Pine Tree containing by estimation two hundred and thirty eight acres be it more or less. Provided the said Johanas Delivers an equal share of his Land at Monokasy or the value thereof to his sister Joana Daughter of Johannes Van Meter Deceased, then this Land Willed and Bequeathed to my Grand son Johannes Van Meter is to be held by him Under the same Restrictions and Limitations as aforementioned in *Abraham's* Bequest, Also I will that my said grandson Johannas have two Breeding Mares, &c.

Fifteenth, Item. I will that if any veins or any sort of mines should at anytime hereafter be Discovered on any part of my Lands herein mentioned, Given Willed Devised and Bequeathed, and that the same should arise amount or become of more value than Fifty Pounds that then such Mines to be equally divided amongst my Devisees and every of them to have equal share or proportion of the same with Liberty of Roads to and from the same for Transporting of such mine also Liberty to Digg and make search and Trail for such Mines in Co-Partnership with the rest of the Devisees, &c.

Sixteenth, Item, I also Will Devise Give and Bequeath the sum of Ten Pounds Virginia Money to be paid by my Executors to my grand-chidren to Johannes Van Meter and Joana Van Meter the sum of Fifteen Pounds when they arrive to the age of twenty one years of age.

Seventeenth, Item I do nominate, Constitute and Appoint my son-in-law Thomas Shepherd, Abraham Van Meter and Jacob Van Meter my sons joint Executors of this my last Will and Testament Impowering them to act and perform according to what is contained in every Clause being Contained in five Sheets of Paper Disannuling and making void all other Wills and Testaments by me in any wise by me heretofore confirming this and no other as my last Will and Testament.

In Witness Whereof I have hereunto set my hand and seal the Day and Year above Written.

signed JOHN METOR [SEAL]

Signed sealed Published and Pronounced and Declared by the said John Van Meter as his last Will and Testament in the Presence of us:

his
Edward   X   Morgan
mark
Andrew Corn
Joseph Carroll.

[Probated at Winchester Va. 3^d Sept. 1745].

DESCENDANTS OF JOHANNES VAN METRE

SARAH VAN METRE

I. SARAH VAN METRE (John[1]), eldest daughter of John Van Metre, born in Somerset Co., New Jersey, and baptized, according to the register of the Reformed Dutch Church at Somerville, N. J. (Records of the Holland Society, New York), on 30 Oct., 1706; died after 1745; married *circa* 1725 James Davis (probably of the family of James Davis of Pilesgrove, Salem Co., N. J.—Pilesgrove Church Record). A James Davis was killed by the Indians on one of their raids along the upper Potomac valley, in 1757 (Kercheval's History of the Valley). By the terms of her father's will Sarah was devised 220 acres of land out of his possessions in Frederick Co., Va., 1745. On July 9, 1754, James Davis conveys this property to his wife's youngest brother Jacob Van Metre (Frederick Co., Va., Records).

DESCENDANTS OF JOHANNES VAN METRE

II. JOHANNES VAN METRE (John[1]), eldest son of John and Sarah (Bodine) Van Metre was born on the Raritan, in Somerset Co., N. J., and was baptized at Somerville, N. J., 28 April, 1708 (Records of the Reformed Dutch Church), died in Maryland *circa* 1730; married Rebecca Powelson who was probably a descendant of Capt. Hendrick Pauelson, several of whose family were settled along the North Branch of the Raritan, between 1700–30.

John Van Metre having emigrated, *circa* 1725, to the Monacocy in Prince George's Co., Maryland, the son Johannes probably joined him there, after his marriage, accompanied by several friends and relatives. Here his two children were born: Johannes, Jr., and Joanna. Religeously venerated family tradition asserts that Johannes, Jr., was "the first white child born west of the Blue Ridge." But that statement can hardly be maintained since the Monacocy settlement is *east* of the Blue Ridge, unless this child was born in the valley of Virginia whilst his parents were with John Van Metre—the grandfather—when he was in Virginia to obtain the grant of lands from Governor Gooch. However, Johannes Van Metre remained a colonist in Maryland and probably died in Prince George's Co., during the prevalence of an epidemic which raged among the settlers on the Potomac in 1732–33, and which carried off many of the inhabitants in its fearful ravages. It is said that his widow, Rebecca, married a son of Jonas Hedges whose wife was Agnes Powelson, a sister of Rebecca, but these statements are univerified. Issue:

1, Johannes, Jr.; 2, Joanna.

37

THE VAN METRE GENEALOGY

1. JOHANNES, Jr. (John[1], Johannes[2]), son of Johannes and Rebecca (Powelson) Van Metre was b. *circa* 1730; d. *circa* 1818; *m.* 1st Josina Taylor; *m.* 2d *circa* 1790, "when in his 60th year," a young German woman and by whom he is said to have had nine children, several of whom were under age at the date of their father's death. His will does not mention his wife's name nor allude to her, and the inference is that he died a widower.

During the minority of Johannes and his sister Joanna they were under the care of their uncle Jonas Hedges and his wife Angelitje (Agnes). Their grandfather, John Van Metre, named them among legatees in his will (1745) and gave them personalty in his Deed of Gift (1744). Some difficulties having arisen in the distribution of the grandfather's estate, these children appealed to the Court of Prince George's Co., Md., and by it Jonas Hedges was appointed their guardian, 7 Oct., 1747. An action in chancery was taken by their guardian against Abraham and Jacob Van Metre, their uncles, and executors under the will of John Van Metre. Jonas Hedges filed his account in Court, as Guardian, in 1751; the wards having probably attained their majority prior to this time.

Johannes had an estate in Maryland called "Pipe Meadow"; it probably lay on Pipe Creek which emptied into the Monocacy in Price George's Co. Jointly, with his wife Josina's endorsement thereon, 22 acres of it was conveyed to Michael Raymer, 5 Aug., 1759. This particular piece of property was called: "End of Strife" (Book F, p. 837, Frederick Co., Md., Records). The original tract called "Pipe Meadow" was composed of 350 acres; and the elder Van Metre on July 18, 1745, had sold 150 acres of it to the above Michael Raymer, under power-of-attorney running to Baltis Foutz. A further conveyance was made of the remaining 178 acres which was described as located at the mouth of Carver's run—by young Van Metre—which did not bear the wife's endorsement—on 21 June, 1759 (29 Nov., 1759), to William Burns, the husband of his sister Joanna (Bk. F, p. 899). Having disposed of Pipe Meadow, Johannes removed into Berkeley Co., Md. (then Frederick Co.), and settled a property on the bank of the Opequon east of the present town of Martinsburg, W. Va.—while his sister and her husband, Wm. Burns, located near the present village of Kearneysville, Jefferson Co., W. Va. Johannes Van Metre was very fond of hunting. His death, it is said, was the result of having thrown himself upon the ground while heated, after one of these expeditions, thereby contracting pneumonia. His will is recorded at Martinsburg and was probated 12 Oct., 1818. In it his land is described as being on the road from Opequon to "Traveler's Rest," former residence of Gen. Chas. Lee, of the Revolution; and that it shall go to his male issue as a "Home in Common for all my children until the

38

youngest son attains the age of 21 years." His son Thornton is to have his dwelling plantation; and the three sons, Ezra, John and Thornton, "shall be chargeable with the clothing, schooling and support of my daughters: Catharine, Eliza, Josina, and Marie Van Metre." Then the instrument goes on to say: "Deeming it improper to hold a human creature in bondage during life I direct that my negro woman Hannah shall be emancipated when my son John arrives at age of 21 years, and at that period my executor pay her the sum of $5.00 for each of my children as a token for the attention she has shown toward my family." "Mulatto Mary" is to be emancipated when Thornton comes to age of 15 years. "All my younger slaves to be emancipated when they respectively arrive at age of 28 years and that all their descendants be emancipated when they arrive at same age." John Alburtis is named as Executor; but by a codicil of later date his eldest son Ezra is made a co-executor with Alburtis. Issue: 3, Nancy; 4, Ezra; 5, John; 6, Thornton; 7, Catharine; 8, Eliza; 9, Josina; 10, Marie; and 11, a child d. y.

2. JOANNA VAN METRE (John[1], Johannes[2]), dau. of Johannes and Rebecca (Powelson) Van Metre, was born on the Monocacy, in Prince George's Co., Md., *circa* 1732. The date of her birth and death are determined by the inscriptions found upon her tombstone in the burial plot on the homestead near Kearneysville, Jefferson Co., W. Va., which was, until recently, the property of the late John Baker Kerfott, Esq., one of her descendants. Joanna died 21 August, 1801," in the 69th year of her age." She *m.* William Burns, who was born 1718 and died 31 Dec., 1806. They were both buried, side by side, in the little graveyard on the Kearneysville farm.

The Burn's homestead, originally containing 350 acres, was granted to William Burns by patent from Lord Fairfax; and lay on the west side of Opequon Creek. This property was devised by his will to his grandson William Burns the eldest son of the testator's son George. In the event of William's death without issue the property was to pass to William's brother Joseph. Another property which the testator bought of the Hedges was bequeathed to testator's daughter Rebecca. It contained 300 acres of land and was situated on the Warm Springs road. The will also mentions testator's brother: "Robert Burns now of Pennsylvania"; Abraham Van Metre, Sr., and the latter's nephew, Abraham, son of Jacob Van Metre; and appoints son John Burns and Abraham Van Metre, Sr. (his son-in-law), Executors (Book 4, p. 123, Martinsburg Records). Issue: 12, George; 13, William; 14, John; 15, Robert; 16, Hannah; 17, Ruth; 18, Elizabeth; 19, Mary; 20, Isabella; 21, Margaret; 22, Rebecca.

3. NANCY VAN METRE (John[1], Johannes[2], Johannes[3]), dau. of Johannes and —— Van Metre, b. 29 June, 1794; d. ——; *m. circa* 1815, John Alburtis, who was b. 14 May, 1794.　Issue:
23, E. G. Alburtis, b. Berkely Co., Va., 6 July, 1817; d. 21 March, 1875; *m.* 20 Dec., 1842, Mary C. Swartz; issue, a son and seven daughters. E. G. Albertis was a captain in the Mexican War; was also a captain in the Wise Artillery and as such took part in the suppression of John Brown's raid upon Harper's Ferry, Va. He also served in the Civil War, and subsequently became clerk of the Berkeley Co., Va., Court. (Norris's History, Lower Shenandoah, Va.)

5. JOHN VAN METRE (John[1], Johannes[2], Johannes[3]), *m.* Mary Gorrell.

7. CATHARINE VAN METRE (John[1], Johannes[2], Johannes[3]), *m.* —— Pierce—em. to Ohio.

8. ELIZA VAN METRE (John[1], Johannes[2], Johannes[3]), *m.* 1, James Russell; *m.* 2, William McLean.

9. JOSINA VAN METRE (John[1], Johannes[2], Johannes[3]), *m.* John E. Van Metre.

10. MARIE VAN METRE (John[1], Johannes[2], Johannes[3]), *m.* Abraham E. Van Metre, son of "Colonel" Isaac Van Metre (IX. 12), which see.

12. GEORGE BURNS (John[1], Johannes[2], Joanna[3]), son of William and Joanna (Van Metre) Burns, b. ——; d.——; *m.* 10 July, 1799, at Martinsburg, Berkeley Co., Va., Agnes, dau. of Joseph and Elizabeth (Rawlings) Hedges.　Issue:
24, William Burns; 25, Joseph Burns.

13. WILLIAM BURNS (John[1], Johannes[2], Joanna[3]), *m.* Magdalena Van Metre.

14. JOHN BURNS (John[1], Johannes[2], Joanna[3]), *m.* Fanny Southwood.

15. ROBERT BURNS (John[1], Johannes[2], Joanna[3]), *m.* Rebecca Southwood.

16. HANNAH BURNS (John[1], Johannes[2], Joanna[3]), *m.* Abraham Van Metre.

17. RUTH BURNS (John[1], Johannes[2], Joanna[3]), *m.* Daniel Colgin.

18. ELIZABETH BURNS (John[1], Johannes[2], Joanna[3]), *m.* Abraham Van Metre.

19. MARY BURNS (John[1], Johannes[2], Joanna[3]), *m.* Isaac Van Metre.

20. ISABELLA BURNS (John[1], Johannes[2], Joanna[3]), *m.* James McDonald.

21. MARGARET BURNS (John[1], Johannes[2], Joanna[3]), *m.* Henry F. Whitnack. He was one of the pioneers who emigrated to the Valley from New Jersey. He served in the War of the Revolution as an officer in Gen. Daniel Morgan's regiment. Died at age of 92 years (see Cranmer's History of Wheeling, p. 830). Issue: 26, Hannah; 27, Eleanor; 28, Ruth; 29, John G.; 30, Sarah; 31, Margaret; 32, William; 33, Joseph; 34, Rebecca.

22. REBECCA BURNS (John[1], Johannes[2], Joanna[3]), *m.* William Van Metre.

26. HANNAH WHITNACK (or Whitney) (John[1], Johannes[2], Joanna[3], Margaret[4]), b. ——; d. ——; *m.* Samuel Roberts.

29. JOHN G. WHITNACK (John[1], Johannes[2], Joanna[3], Margaret[4]), son of Henry F. and Margaret (Burns) Whitnack, b. ——; d. ——; *m.* Mary A. Carl (or Carroll). He was born near Martinsburg, 1787, d. 1854. Was soldier in War of 1812. Issue: 35, Margaret; 36, John; 37, Eli Carroll; 38, John S.; 39, Samuel; 40, Eliza; 41, Mary V.; 42, David.

30. SARAH WHITNACK (John[1], Johannes[2], Joanna[3], Margaret[4]), dau. of Henry F. and Margaret (Burns) Whitnack, *m.* Robert Campbell.

31. MARGARET WHITNACK (John[1], Johannes[2], Joanna[3], Margaret[4]), dau. of Henry F. and Margaret (Burns) Whitnack; *m.* 1 Joseph Van Metre.

32. WILLIAM WHITNACK (John[1], Johannes[2], Joanna[3], Margaret[4]), son of Henry F. and Margaret (Burns) Whitenack; *m.* widow Sarah Mounts.

33. JOSEPH WHITNACK (John[1], Johannes[2], Joanna[3], Margaret[4]), son of Henry F. and Margaret (Burns) Whitenack; *m.* his cousin Ruth Southwood Burns, dau. of Robert Burns.

34. REBECCA WHITNACK (John[1], Johannes[2], Joanna[3], Margaret[4]), dau. of Henry F. and Margaret (Burns) Whitenack; *m.* Nicholas Strayer.

31. MARGARET WHITNAK (John[1], Johannes[2], Joanna[3], Margaret[4]), dau. of Henry F. and Margaret (Burns) Whitnak, b. Va., 1780; d. 7 Oct., 1865; *m.* Joseph Van Metre (John[1], Abraham[2], Abraham[3]), son of Abraham and Elizabeth (Burns) Van Metre, 18 Aug., 1800. He removed from Berkeley Co., Va., in the fall of 1809 and settled, with their family, at West Liberty in Ohio Co., Va. Issue: 43, Gabriel; 44, Robert; 45, Sarah; 46, Joseph W.; 47, Vincent; H. (For continuation of this line see IX., No. 23, *et. seq.*)

41

37. ELI CARROLL WHITNAK (John[1], Johannes[2], Joanna[3], John G.[4]), son of John G. and Mary A. (Carl) Whitnak; *m.* 1 Sophia Evans; *m.* 2 Elizabeth Martin.

38. JOHN S. (son of John S.), *m.* Amelia Morgan; 39, SAMUEL (son of John G.), *m.* —— Smith; 42, DAVID (son of John G.), *m.* Elizabeth Pollock.

Note: Among those settling in Ohio County was Joseph Van Metre, a great uncle of Vincent H. Van Meter, who built Fort Van Meter. John Van Meter, his brother, took up the land where West Liberty now stands and left a man in charge named Black, who built Black's Cabin; Abraham Van Meter afterward owned this land and sold 2 acres of it to Ohio County for £20. Joseph Van Metre, the father of Vincent H. Van Meter had 5 brothers: Abishua, Josiah, Ashahel, Abraham and Isaac; and three sisters: Ruth, Naomi and Elizabeth. Joseph was killed in crossing the Ohio River to hunt (Cranmer's History of Wheeling, p. 833).

NOTES

Johannes Van Metre, II. (son of John, first of Berkely), is credited, by Mrs. C. E. Van Metre, recently writing to a local Ohio newspaper, with being the grandfather of Jacob Van Metre who was living on the Hockhocking River near Lancaster, Ohio, about the year 1801. She supposes him to have been the son of Johannes, Jr. (sometimes called " Honce " and " Hannie " according to some old Virginia records the compiler has seen), who *m.* Josina Taylor and were living near Martinsburg, Va., between the years 1780 and 1800. According to this writer: Mr. Jap. Van Metre of Middletown, Indiana,—is of that descent. She adds that this Jacob Van Metre of Lancaster was an old fashioned gentleman; fond of stock and enterprising, and who lived to be 92 years of age. He had a dau. Josina who, while in Virginia *m.* a Rev. Hickman and finally removed to Indiana where the family became prominent. The following references may throw light on this subject:

1. Daniel Van Metre, living at Muddy Prairie, on the Hockhocking (or the Sciota), near Lancaster, O., in 1799 (see Trans. Alleghany Mag., Vol. I., p. 104).

2. Jacob Van Metre, living 4 miles east of Hocking River, where a town is laid off called West Lancaster, Fairfield Co., May 19, 1801. (See Trans. Alleghany Mag., Vol. I., p. 104).

3. Henry and Jacob Van Metre among the first settlers near Urbana, O., in Champaign Co., 42 miles from Columbus; 1807 (see Howe's Hist. Coll. of Ohio, p. 81).

4. John Van Metre among first lot purchasers at Lancaster, sale 1801–2 in Fairfield Co., Ohio (see Centennial Lancaster, O.).

DESCENDANTS OF REBECCA VAN METRE

MARY VAN METRE

III. MARY VAN METRE (John[1]), dau. of John and Sarah
(Bodine) Van Metre, b. in Somerset Co., N. J., and baptized
in the Reformed Dutch Church at Somerville (Raritan), N. J.,
26 April, 1709 (Records of Holland Society of N. Y.), d. after
1745; m. circa 1728-30, Robert Jones, probably the Robert
Jones who was a settler on the Perkiomen in Philadelphia Co.,
Penna., and who joined Jost Hite's Colony in the settlement of
the Valley of Virginia. By her father's will Mary is devised 350
acres of land "where I now dwell" in the vicinity of the forks
of Opequon Creek.

DESCENDANTS OF REBECCA VAN METRE

IV. REBECCA VAN METRE (John[1]), dau. of John and Margerat
(?) Van Metre, b. Somerset Co., N. J., circa 1711; d. circa 1770;
m. circa 1735, Solomon, eldest son of Joseph Hedges and his wife
Catharine Stalcop, daughter of John Stalcop, an early Swedish
settler of Salem Co., N. J., who afterward removed to New
Castle, Pa. (now in the state of Delaware). John Stalcop's
wife was Catharine, the daughter of John and Madelina Erick-
son who were among the earliest inhabitants in the Swedish
settlement at Lucas Point on the Delaware, near Salem, N. J.
Joseph Hedges was also in New Jersey, afterward in Chester
Co., Pa., whence, after his marriage, he emigrated to and located
on a plantation at Monocacy in the Province of Maryland where
he died in 1732. In his will he describes himself as of "Manacquacy." The return of his estate was made 17 February, 1732-3,
and was appraised by Robert Jones and Henry Ballinger (Book
1, p. 203; Prince George's Co., Md.). One of the descendants of
Joseph Hedges writes me that Joseph Hedges was either the son
of Samuel Hedges of the Province of West Jersey, or of Thomas
Hedges, Justice of Anne Arundel Co., Md., 1674; and of Baltimore
Co., Md., 1675; Clerk of Baltimore Co., 1689–1694-95; who signs
as Civil Officer of Baltimore Co., 1696.

Solomon Hedges was born 1710. He probably married Rebecca Van Metre at the Monocacy settlement circa 1735 and
immediately thereafter removed to Orange Co., Va., settling on
the South Branch of the Potomac—his residence afterward fell
within the limits of Frederick Co., when it was created 1748.
From his father's will it appears that Joseph Hedges died seized
of 400 acres of land on the Opequon in Virginia which are "to
be cleared and paid for out of my estate." 200 each of this
land are devised to testators two sons: Charles Hedges and Peter
Hedges; while to Solomon is devised "a tract of 285 acres lying

at Manacquacy Creek on the west side." The executor (Solomon) is instructed "to purchase —— acres of land on 'Opechan' which shall be equally divided between 'my two sons' Jonas Hedges and Joseph Hedges," and "to purchase 190 acres of land at Manacquacy" out of the estate for "my son Samuel" (Book 1, p. 203, Prince Geo. Co. Wills). This is evidence of the earliest purchase of land in the Valley of Monocacy in Frederick Co., Md., and was probably made by John Van Metre or Jost Hite.

The first recorded purchase of land by Solomon Van Metre was made 10 April, 1738 (Orange Co. Records, Book 1, p. 481) by Edward Davis late of Orange Co. to Solomon Hedges of same county who for the consideration of 5 shillings conveys a piece of land containing 275 acres lying on the west side of Sherundo (Shenandoah) River and Opequon Creek on a branch of the Hangaloota (Potomac) called Tullises Branch, it being a part of 875 acres granted unto said Edward Davis, 12 Nov., 1735, it adjoined lands of Peter Hedges. Witnesses were Peter and Joshua Hedges and Richard Morgan. On the same date as the preceding Peter Hedges also acquired by purchase from Davis 300 acres of the 875 acre tract—Solomon Hedges was one of the witnesses thereto.

The Court of Orange Co., Va., on 23 June, 1738, appointed Solomon Hedges and Jost Hite road-viewers.

In 1740 Solomon Hedges sold his patrimony in Maryland, two farms called "Hedges Hogg" and "Hedges Delight" and the conveyance was acknowledged by Rebecca Hedges before the Justices of Prince George's Co., Md., 8 May, 1740 (Lib. 7, fol. 170–171).

Frederick County having by this time, 1744, been established out of Orange Co., Solomon Hedges was appointed a Justice of the new county and was sworn 8 June, 1744 (Frederick County Court Journal) ; and on the 5th October, 1745, was commissioned the Coroner of Frederick Co. In this year also, Rebecca, his wife, received on the death of her father a legacy of 200 acres of his estate and a child's share in the personalty.

By the setting off of Hampshire Co. in 1753, from Frederick Co. the home of Solomon Hedges now lay in the new county; when the youthful surveyor George Washington was engaged in laying out lands in the Northern Neck for his patron Lord Fairfax, Solomon Hedges obtained and had surveyed to him, a farm on Patterson's Creek about 40 miles above its confluence with the Potomac. In later days when Washington made his "Journey over the Mountains to the Ohio," he stopped at Solomon Hedges for entertainment, and refers to him as "one of His Majesties Justices of the Peace" (Kercheval's History of the Valley ; Maxwell's History of Hampshire Co., Va.).

The Hedges gradually acquired other landed possessions among

44

DESCENDANTS OF REBECCA VAN METRE

Hampshire's hills; one tract containing 320 acres granted by the Proprietor of the Northern Neck 18 February, 1760, and another of 102 acres adjoining the first which was also granted by the Proprietor 16 February, 1760. These lands were situated on New Creek, Hampshire Co. (now Mineral Co., W. Va.) and were leased to Peter Sternberger 1 Aug., 1760. Solomon owned another piece of property on New Creek containing 250 acres which he sold to Thomas Dean 11th June, 1789.

The property in Frederick Co., Md., that was his wife's inheritance was disposed of to their son and heir-at-law Silas Hedges on 13th August, 1770, and to John Wilson of Frederick Co., Va. On 14 Oct., 1783, and on 5 July, 1786, Solomon Hedges was granted patents for lands on Buffalo Creek in Ohio County, Va. When David Shepherd, his brother-in-law, became High Sheriff of Ohio County, Va., 6th April, 1778, Solomon Hedges became his surety in the sum of £3,500. The bond is recorded at Wheeling, W. Va., 1778, April 8th. "In the former Commission of the Peace for Ohio County there must have been a mistake in the recomendation placing that of Silas (Hedges) prior to that of Solomon Hedges. Said Solomon having formerly acted as Jude (Judge) in the Court of Hampshire, this Court therefore would pray that Solomon aforesaid be inserted the first in the list of the new Commission." On the 2nd June, 1778, Solomon Hedges came into Court and took oath as Justice of the Peace. And it was "ordered that Solomon Hedges and Jno Williams, gentlemen,—distribute the public land consigned to this county upon proper and sufficient certificates to them presented." From this date to and including 7 Aug., 1780, Solomon Hedges and his son Silas were Justices of the Courts of Ohio Co., Va., sometimes the father and at other times the son was presiding Judge of the Court. At the latter date Virginia's jurisdiction over any part of Pennsylvania ceased. (Annals of Carnegie Museum, Vol. III., Pt. 1, Dec., 1904.) Solomon Hedges died in Dec., 1801. His will is recorded at Wheeling, W. Va.

The children of Solomon and Rebecca Hedges, were:
1, Silas; 2, Joseph; 3, Joshua, who emigrated to Marietta, O.; 4, Rachael; 5, Catharine, and 6, Rebecca.

1. SILAS HEDGES (John[1], Rebecca[2]) son of Solomon and Rebecca (Van Metre) Hedges was b. 2 Dec., 1736, on South Branch of Potomac in Frederick Co., Va., died at his homestead on Buffalo Creek, 6 miles west of Wellsburg, Brooke Co., Va., 17 May, 1811; m. 1, a Miss Mummy; 2, Margaret Hoagland, said to have been a sister of Capt. Henry Hoagland of Brooke Co., Va., and children of Capt. Derrick Hoagland. Margaret Hoagland was b. 16 Sept., 1751, and d. 24 March, 1837, at McConnellsville, Ohio. It is believed that Silas Hedges was one of Col. Zane's party to Redstone Old Fort (Brownsville, Pa.), on the

Monongahela River in the spring of 1765, where he lived for a short time before he married Margaret Hoagland (see Draper's Notes, Vol. 9, p. 132, at Madison, Wis.).

Silas Hedges was very active in the campaigning against the French and Indians, and is thought to have served as an officer with the levies. He settled on Buffalo Creek, Ohio Co., Va., in 1773. His name is frequently found in the Minute Book of the Virginia Court which was held at Fort Dunmore (Pittsburg) for the District of West Augusta, 1775–76 (see Virginia Hist. Mag., Vol. 4, p. 403), and at the organization of the first Court of Ohio County held at Black's Cabin, on Short Creek 6 Jan., 1777, the oath was administered to him as one of the Justices of that County, and at the same time was recommended to the Court as Colonel of the Militia (see American Pioneer, Vol. II., p. 377; Ann. of Carn. Museum, Vol. III., pt. 1, Dec., '04). Before this he was a member of the Committee of Safety, which was organized at the house of Ezekill Dewitt 27 Dec., 1776, and at its second meeting was appointed one of the inspectors of the troops enlisted by Capt. John Lemon for Continental establishment in the War of the Revolution (see Am. Pioneer, Vol. II., p. 396). He was chairman of the meeting of this Committee held 8 Feb., 1777, and at this time made his report on the inspection of Lemon's men. Governor Patrick Henry wrote him to proceed with a military organization in Ohio, Co., on Continental establishment and addressed him as Chairman. With Andrew Foutz he went down to Wheeling in 1777, to assist in burying the dead, after Capt. Forman's defeat. He was also enrolled at this time as a member of Capt. Ogle's company and took part in the siege of Fort Henry (Shepherd's Papers, Vol. IV., pp. 16–20). On June 7, 1777, he sold 607 lbs. bacon to Francis Duke, the Commissary of Fort Henry; and in August, 1777, received a store of ammunition for the use of the militia of Ohio County from Col. David Shepherd, the commandant of Fort Henry (see Draper's Notes). On 7 April, 1778, Lieut. Gov. John Page of Virginia appointed him Colonel of the Militia of Ohio Co. and the commission was read in open Court (Minute Book of the Ohio Co. Court); and at the same time was recommended by the Court, as High Sheriff of the County. Silas superseded, as Colonel of Militia, his cousin Col. David Shepherd, who had been advanced to the Lieutenantcy of the County. On the 25 of April, 1778, Silas Hedges served on a court martial that tried and honorably acquitted Col. Shepherd for proclaiming martial law in Ohio county without the order and authority of the court, when the safety of the settlers was jeopardized. At the organization of the court on January 7, 1777, Silas was appointed by the court to contract with Abraham Van Metre and obtain two acres of land for the county buildings [Minute Book of court of Ohio Co., Va.]. During the whole time that the courts were held at Black's Cabin in Ohio County, or until 1780, Silas was one of the county justices. His commission as colonel of the militia he resigned to Gov. Beverley Randolph, Sept. 7, 1789, because of old age and infirmities. Silas Hedges was tall in stature and slim, nearly six feet in height and very straight, and of dark complexion. He had ten children, all but two of whom were born on Buffalo Creek, in Ohio County. Issue:

7, Joseph, b. *circa* 1770; d. 1793, while on a scouting expedition against the Indians to recover stolen property.

8, Solomon, b. *circa* 1772, near Redstone, on Monongahela; d. 1817.

9, Catharine, b. 9 Sept., 1775; d. ——; *m.* Israel Robinson.

10, Silas, b. 18 Oct., 1777; d. ——.

11, Elizabeth, b. *circa* 1779; d. ——; *m.* 2 Nov., 1797, Joshua Meek.

12, Rebecca, b. *circa* 1781; d. ——; *m.* Ezekiel Huyett.

13, Isaac, b. 17 January, 1788; d. Mill Grove, Morgan Co., O., 9 May, 1876.

14, Ruth, b. May, 1791.

15, George, b. 22 Nov., 1793; d. Muskingum River, Ohio Co., ——, 1841.

16. Joanna, b. *circa* 1795; *m.* William Fouts.

2. JOSEPH HEDGES (John,[1] Rebecca[2]), son of Solomon and Rebecca (Van Metre) Hedges, b. in Virginia; d. 30 Sept., 1821; *m.* Margaret *Vanmetre*. She d. 19 Nov., 1823. They lived between Wellsburg and West Liberty, in Brooke Co., Va. Joseph donated the ground on a part of his farm upon which the Kentish Methodist Church stood, seven miles south of Wellsburg. They came about 1772. A Joseph Hedges served in the Indian campaign of 1758–59 in Capt. Rutherford's company of Rangers, for Berkeley (then Frederick) Co., Va. Land bounty certificate was granted him for land in 1763 (see Crozier's " Colonial Militia of Virginia," p. 38). Issue:

17, Ruth, b. *circa* 1767; d. *ante* 1820; *m.* —— Frazier.

18, Rebecca, b. *circa* 1769; d. 14 May, 1813.

19, William, b. 12 Nov., 1771; d. 22 May, 1839; *m.* Sarah Dunlap.

20, Rachael, b. *circa* 1773; d. ——; *m.* Isaac Meek.

21, Solomon, b. *circa* 1775; d. s.p. 25 April, 1815.

22, Abraham, b. *circa* 1777; d. 7 Jan., 1828 (drowned in Ohio River).

23, Catharine, b. *circa* 1779; d. 11 Oct., 1823; *m.* —— Storey.

24, Jemima, b. *circa* 1781; d. 25 Feb., 1833; *m.* Ninian Cash.

25, Samuel, b, 26 Dec., 1783; d. 17 Dec., 1865.

26, Silas, b. 1786; d. 16 Nov., 1834.

27, Joseph, b. 1789; d. 12 July, 1824.

3. JOSHUA HEDGES (John,[1] Rebecca[2]), son of Solomon and Rebecca (Van Metre) Hedges, b. in Frederick Co., Va., April,

47

1744; d. *circa* 1790; *m.* Elizabeth (Chapline of Washington Co., Md.). Issue:
  28, Elizabeth; 29, Mary, b. ——; d. *circa* 1797, s.p.; 30, Abigail; 31, Anne; 32, Joshua; 33, Samuel; 34, Solomon; 35, Jesse.

4. RACHEL HEDGES (John,[1] Rebecca[2]), dau. of Solomon and Rebecca (Van Metre) Hedges, b. Frederick Co., Va., *circa* 1745; d. ——; *m.* Capt. William Vause, a son probably of Wm. Vause, who emigrated from New Jersey to the Virginia settlements. Issue:
  36, William; 37, Theodosia; 38, Jemima; 39, Solomon; 40, Rebecca; 41, Susan; 42, Abraham; 43, Thomas.

5. CATHARINE HEDGES (John,[1] Rebecca[2]), dau. of Solomon and Rebecca (Van Metre) Hedges, b. Frederick Co., Va., *circa* 1748; d. *ante* 1801; *m.* George McCullough, of Hampshire Co., Va., whose first wife was sup. to have been Catharine, the dau. of Isaac Van Metre, of New Jersey, and brother of John Van Metre, of Virginia. George McCullough was one of the famous Mc-Cullough family who were noted scouts and Indian fighters of the Ohio border. George and his wife removed to Ohio County, where he became one of the justices. Their children are presumed to have been (see will of Thomas Newberry, Ohio County, 1777):
  44, George; 45, Rebecca; 46, Jane; 47, Silas, d. s.p. in War of 1812; 48, William, Capt., d. s.p. War of 1812.

6. REBECCA HEDGES (John,[1] Rebecca[2]), dau. of Solomon and Rebecca (Van Metre) Hedges, b. Frederick Co., Va., *circa* 1750.

7. JOSEPH HEDGES (John,[1] Rebecca,[2] Silas[3]), son of Silas and —— Hedges, b. *circa* 1770, near Redstone Old Fort (now Brownsville, Pa.); d. Dec., 1793, while on a scouting expedition against the Indians, who had stolen horses (Barber & Howe, Hist. Coll. of Ohio, pp. 202–3). The manner of his death is related in various ways by different writers, but it is recorded by L. C. Draper in his extensive notes (Vol. 9, p. 122). His death occurred on Bird's Run, a southern tributary of Mill Creek, and about twelve miles below Cambridge, Ohio Co., Va. (vide Vol. 10, p. 2). He, with other men, were scouting for Indians who had stolen horses and other plunder from the settlers along the waters of the Ohio. When found he had from five to seven shots through his body, and his death, according to the story of his brother Isaac and sisters, Mrs. Elizabeth Rowland and Ruth Meeks, was very tragic. At that time he was a member of the Ohio County militia and had been made ensign in a rifle company in that year, his name being in the roster of Capt. Henry Hoagland's company (see Draper's Notes, Vol. 10, p. 2, p. 126; Vol. 9, p. 122, p. 160).

8. Solomon Hedges (John,[1] Rebecca,[2] Silas[3]), son of Silas and Margaret (Hoagland) Hedges, b. *circa* 1772, near Redstone Old Fort (Brownsville, Pa.); d. *circa* 1817 in Arkansas; *m.* Susannah, dau. of Sarah Miller (who was the daughter of Andrew Fouts, of West Liberty, Brooke Co., Va.). They had no children. Solomon made his first trip against the Indians in Capt. Sam Brady's Co., in the Beaver Block House expedition in 1791. He then joined Capt. Faulkner's, or Capt. Ben. Lockwood's Co., and was out in St. Clair's defeat near Fort Jefferson, 4th Nov., 1791, at which time his company had to cut their way through the line of the savages. After St. Clair's defeat Solomon said he would never go to farming again " for the best farm in Brooke County." He was appointed lieutenant of the Rifle Co. of Ohio Co., 7th Jan., 1794. and was again with Brady in his expedition of 1794. He had served in 1793 in McCullough's scout and was in Linn's defeat, where " he had an arm broken, a shot in the breast and one in his belley," says Draper. He also spied with the Wetzells and other famous scouts. Solomon was with McMahon in his scout of 1792, and in February, 1794, he and Levi Morgan organized a scout and took some prisoners. In the War of 1812 he was out in the relief of Fort Meigs. Solomon was a large, stout man, weighing in his younger days about 175 lbs., always fond of hunting and kept a pack of dogs. For better hunting he went to Kentucky, where he killed many bears. While in Kentucky he also did some farming where he lived in Greenup County. From Kentucky he went to Arkansas, spending two years there; was there in 1816 and while there was robbed by the Osages. Returning to Kentucky with his wife and a little boy whom they took to raise; still unsettled they set their faces again toward Arkansas, meaning to go to Little Rock, but before going arranged for another hunting trip and before he could start upon it he was taken down with black jaundice and died. His widow remained in Kentucky and remarried (see Draper's Notes—*in extenso*).

9. Catharine Hedges (John,[1] Rebecca,[2] Silas[3]), dau. of Silas and Margaret (Hoagland) Hedges, b. 9 Sept., 1775, on Buffalo Creek; d. 19 Dec., 1845; *m.* 4 Feb., 1794, in Brooke Co., Va., Israel Robinson, who d. 12 May, 1845, was a son of Aaron Robinson, who came from the Forks of the Youghiogeny River, and his wife Mary, or Mercy, Pearce, who was b. 29 Jan., 1746, and d. 19 Nov., 1797. Israel Robinson belonged to the Ohio County militia and his name is found upon the Roll of Honor of Ohio Co. He was in the Hocking expedition with Capt. Sam Brady, who at that time, 1794, commanded the Pennsylvania spies. After his marriage he settled on the waters of Salt Creek, in Muskingum Co., O. In stature Israel Robinson was a little short of six feet, but heavily formed (see Draper's Notes at large). Issue:

49, Aaron; 50, Silas; 51, Mercy; 52, James, b. 3 March, 1804;
d. young and unmarried; 53, Israel; 54, Lewis, b. 18
Sept., 1806; d. in Muskingum Co., O.; 55, Isaac; 56,
Peggy, b. 26 March, 1811; d. ——; 57, Rebecca, b. 5
Feb., 1813; d. *unm.*; 58, Sarah, b. 22 April, 1815; d. 22
May, 1871, in Morgan Co., O., *m.* Wm. McIntire, lived
near New Athens, O.; 59, Elizabeth.

10. SILAS HEDGES (John,[1] Rebecca,[2] Silas[3]), son of Silas and
Margaret (Hoagland) Hedges, b. on Buffalo Creek, Va., 18 Oct.,
1777; d. after 1860; *m.* Mary Cox. They lived at Athens, Ohio.
His recollections of the Hocking expedition and Col. Wm. Crawford's campaign are noted by Draper (see his Notes). He was
with his brother Joseph when the latter was killed by the Indians
in 1793 on Bird Run. His name is on the muster roll of Capt.
John Elson's Co., who drew arms at Point Pleasant, and serving
in the 1st Virginia regiment in the War of 1812. During this
year he went to Fort Meigs on six month's service and left there
in April, 1813, going to Norfolk, Va.; in 1814 he was in the "three
month's service" (see Pan Handle History of Virginia).

11. ELIZABETH HEDGES (John,[1] Rebecca,[2] Silas[3]), dau. of Silas
and Margaret (Hoagland) Hedges, b. *circa* 1779, on Buffalo Cr.,
Va., d. ——; *m.* 2 Nov., 1797, by Rev. Joseph Doddridge, to
Joshua Meek, who was an ensign in the Rifle Co. of Ohio County
commanded by Capt. Wm. Connell. The Meeks lived in Guernsey Co., O.   Issue:
  60, Isaac Meek.

12. REBECCA HEDGES (John,[1] Rebecca,[2] Silas[3]), dau. of Silas and
Margaret (Hoagland) Hedges, b. on Buffalo Cr., Va., *circa* 1781;
d. ——; *m.* Ezekiel Huyett.   Issue:
  61, Silas; 62, Solomon; 63, Joseph; 64, Hezekiah; 65, Emman-
      uel; 66, Ruth; 67, Elizabeth; 68, Hetty; 69, Catharine;
      70, Rebecca.

13. ISAAC HEDGES (John,[1] Rebecca,[2] Silas[3]), son of Silas and
Margaret (Hoagland) Hedges, b. on Buffalo Cr., Va., 17 January, 1788; d. 9 May, 1876, at his residence Millgrove, Morgan
Co., O.; *m.* 3 Oct., 1809, Mary Fouts, dau. of Andrew and Nancy
(Lemon) Fouts. Mary Fouts was b. 2 Aug., 1791, and d. 3d
Nov., 1876. In 1816 Isaac removed to Morgan Co., O.   Issue:
  71, Solomon, *m.* Susan McGonigal, of Morgan Co., O.
  72, Charlotta.
  73, Joanna, b. *circa* 1814; d. ——; *m.* James A. Gillespie, of
      Morgan Co., O.
  74, Absalom, b. *circa* 1816; *m.* Elizabeth Barlow, of Oregon.
  75, Sarah, b. *circa* 1820; *m.* John Barrett, of Morgan Co., O.
  76, Margaret; 77, Nancy; 78, Joseph; 79, Ruth; 80, Isaac, b.
      circa 1830; d. 19 April, 1904; *m.* Satira A. Coburn, of
      McConnellsville.

81, William.

14. RUTH HEDGES (John,[1] Rebecca,[2] Silas[3]), dau. of Silas and Margaret (Hoagland) Hedges, b. on Buffalo Cr., Va., *circa* May, 1791; d. ——; *m.* 3 Oct., 1809, Samuel Rowland. The Rowlands lived and died at McConnellsville, O. They left issue.

15. GEORGE HEDGES (John,[1] Rebecca,[2] Silas[3]), son of Silas and Margaret (Hoagland) Hedges, b. Buffalo Cr., Va., 22 Nov., 1793; d. ——, 1841, on the Muskingum, in Morgan Co., O.; *m.* Elizabeth Koontz. George's name is on the muster roll of Capt. John H. Elson's Co., 1st Regt. of Va., that drew for arms at Point Pleasant for service in the "War of 1812" (see History of the Pan Handle of Virginia).

16. JOANNA HEDGES (John,[1] Rebecca,[2] Silas[3]), dau. of Silas and Margaret (Hoagland) Hedges, b. on Buffalo Cr., Va., *circa* 1795; d. —— at McConnellsville; *m.* 9 May, 1819, William Fouts, son of Andrew and Nancy (Lemon) Fouts, of West Liberty, and had issue.

17. RUTH HEDGES (John,[1] Rebecca,[2] Joseph[3]), dau. of Joseph and Margaret (Van Metre) Hedges, b. *circa* 1767; d. *ante* 1820; *m.* —— Frazier.   Issue:

82, William; 83, Rachael; 84, Ruth.

19. WILLIAM HEDGES (John,[1] Rebecca,[2] Joseph[3]), son of Joseph and Margaret (Van Metre) Hedges, b. 12 Nov., 1771; d. 22 May, 1839; *m.* 15 Aug., 1802, by Rev. James Hughes, Sarah Dunlap. They were living in Brooke Co., Va., but afterward removed to Morgan Co., O.   Issue:

85, Martha, b. 29 April, 1803; d. unm.
86, Margaret, b. 18 July, 1804; d. unm.
87, Prudence, b. 26 April, 1806; d. ——.
88, Rachael, b. 4 Nov., 1807; d. umn.; lived at McConnellsville, Morgan Co., O.
89, Jane, b. 25 Aug., 1810; d. unm.; lived at McConnellsville, Morgan Co., O.
90, Ruth F., b. 25 Sept., 1813; d. unm.; lived at McConnellsville, Morgan Co., O.
91, William, b. ——; d. 12 Aug., 1881, and is buried in Holmes Cemetery, near Cadiz, Ohio.
92, Daniel, b. ——.

20. RACHAEL HEDGES (John,[1] Rebecca,[2] Joseph[3]), dau. of Joseph and Margaret (Van Metre) Hedges, b. in Virginia *circa* 1773; d. ——; *m.* Isaac Meek, who was one of the prominent men of his time; was adjutant on Col. David Shepherd's staff in the Coshocton campaign of 1791 (see Shepherd Papers, Vol. IV., p. 3); sheriff of Ohio Co., June 20, 1792, to June 15, 1793; collector May 11, 1793, and served as one of the justices of Brooke Co., Va., at its first court held 23 May, 1797. In the latter years of

his life he lived about five miles from Mt. Pleasant, Jefferson Co., Ohio (see Draper's Notes; Pan Handle History of West Virginia).

22. ABRAHAM HEDGES (John,[1] Rebecca,[2] Joseph[3]), son of Joseph and Margaret (Van Metre) Hedges, b. *circa* ——; drowned in Ohio River, 7 January, 1828; *m*. Edith Carter.   Issue:
    93, Joseph; 94, Samuel; 95, Julia E., *m*. —— Smith; 96, Green-
        bury, W.; 97, Abraham Van Metre. All reared near
        West Liberty.

24. JEMIMA HEDGES (John,[1] Rebecca,[2] Joseph[3]), dau. of Joseph and Margaret (Van Metre) Hedges, b. *circa* 1781; d. 25 February, 1833; *m*. 1812 Ninian Cash.   Issue:
    98, William; 99, Susan, b. ——; d. 1890; *m*. Samuel Lewis;
        100, Sarah; 101, Daniel; 102, Drusilla.

25. SAMUEL HEDGES (John,[1] Rebecca,[2] Joseph[3]), son of Joseph and Margaret (Van Metre) Hedges, b. 26 Dec., 1783; d. 17 Dec., 1865; *m*. 26 October, 1809, Prudence Dunlap.   Issue:
    103, Abraham, b. 30 June, 1811; d. 21 May, 1813.
    104, Wm. Dunlap, b. 12 Dec., 1812; d. 4 June, 1867.
    105, Sarah, b. 4 Oct., 1814; d. 9 April, 1816.
    106, Martha D., b. 27 April, 1816; d. 20 Aug., 1870.
    107, Rachael Meek, b. 17 Oct., 1817; d. 28 Jan., 1897.
    108, Sarah Jane, b. 9 Nov., 1819; d. 8 Mar., 1841.
    109, Margaret, b. 4 Jan., 1820; d. 4 Sept., 1821.
    110, Prudence, b. 9 Nov., 1822; d. 21 Oct., 1823 (?).
    111, Samuel, b. 20 Jan., 1825; d. 29 May, 1886.
    112, Elizabeth, b. 2 Dec., 1827; d. ——.

28. ELIZABETH HEDGES (John,[1] Rebecca,[2] Joshua[3]), dau. of Joshua and Elizabeth (Chapline) Hedges; *m*. —— King. Issue:
    113, Elizabeth.

30. ABIGAIL HEDGES (John,[1] Rebecca,[2] Joshua[3]), dau. of Joshua and Elizabeth (Chapline) Hedges; *m*. —— Swain.   Issue:
    114, Elizabeth.

31. ANNE HEDGES (John[1], Rebecca[2], Joshua[3]), dau. Joshua and Elizabeth (Chapline) Hedges, b. ——; d. ——; *m*. —— Robertson.   Issue:
    115, Elizabeth.

32. JOSHUA HEDGES (John[1], Rebecca[2], Joshua[3]), son Joshua and Elizabeth (Chapline) Hedges, *m*. —— ——.   Issue:
    116, Elizabeth, b. ——; d. ——; *m*. —— Morgan.
    117, Phoebe, b. ——; d. ——; *m*. 21 Dec., 1820, William
        Lemon.

34. SOLOMON HEDGES (John[1], Rebecca[2], Joshua[3]), son Joshua and Elizabeth (Chapline) Hedges; *m*. —— ——.   Issue:
    118, Elizabeth.

DESCENDANTS OF REBECCA VAN METRE

49. AARON ROBINSON (John[1], Rebecca[2], Silas[3], Catharine[4]), son of Israel and Catharine (Hedges) Robinson, b. 22 Oct., 1796; d. 5 April, 1866, in Muskingum Co., Ohio, *m.* 21 Feb., 1821, Elizabeth Crumbaker.   Issue:
   119, Catharine; 120, Lucinda; 121, Louisa; 122, Jefferson; 123, Jacob M.; 124, Israel; 125, Lewis; 126, Aaron; 127, Benoni; 128, Isaac.

50. SILAS ROBINSON (John[1], Rebecca[2], Silas[3], Catharine[4]), son of Israel and Catharine (Hedges) Robinson, b. 13 Jan., 1798; d. in Hancock Co., Ill.; *m.* Polly Warne.   Issue:
   129, Allen; 130, Zill; 131, Abram; 132, Mergaline.

51. MERCY ROBINSON (John[1], Rebecca[2], Silas[3], Catharine[4]), dau. of Israel and Catharine (Hedges) Robinson, b. 26 June, 1800, in Guernsey Co., O., d. 29 Nov., 1894; *m.* 25 Nov., 1824, Jesse Warne, who was b. 29 June, 1801; d. 19 May, 1877.   Issue:
   133, Elizabeth Jane, b. ——.
   134, Amizet, b. 7 Dec., 1826; d. 5 Aug., 1854.
   135, Sarah R., b. 28 Mar., 1829; d. 30 Dec., 1905.
   136, Margaret, b. 16 July, 1831; d. 18 Nov., 1886.
   137, Zeambra, b. 28 Oct., 1834; d. ——.
   138, Catharine, b. 6 Jan., 1838; d. 9 Oct., 1890.
   139, Fernandez, b. 13 Nov., 1840.

53. ISRAEL ROBINSON (John[1], Rebecca[2], Silas[3], Catharine[4]), son of Israel and Catharine (Hedges) Robinson, b. 3 March, 1804; d. 23 Dec., 1872, in Ill.; *m.* Peggy Warne.   Issue:
   140, Jehu; 141, Warne; 142, Elbridge; 143, Sarah; 144, Lucinda; 145, Mahala.

55. ISAAC ROBINSON (John[1], Rebecca[2], Silas[3], Catharine[4]), son of Israel and Catharine (Hedges) Robinson, b. 28 Mar., 1811; d. in Muskingum Co., O.; *m.* Mary Ann Pierce. Issue:
   146, Rebecca.

59. ELIZABETH ROBINSON (John[1], Rebecca[2], Silas[3], Catharine[4]), dau. of Israel and Catharine (Hedges) Robinson, b. 2 Sept., 1817; d. 19 Sept., 1864; *m.* William Sims.   Issue:
   147, Israel; 148, Welcome; 149, Catharine; 150, Martha Jane.

60. ISAAC MEEK (John[1], Rebecca[2], Silas[3], Elizabeth[4]), son of Joshua and Elizabeth (Hedges) Meek. He filled many important public offices in Ohio Co., Va.; *m.* 3 Rachael Hedges; *m.* 1 —— Roberson. They lived 5 miles from Mt. Pleasant, Smithfield Twp., Jefferson Co., O., and were buried in the Holmes Cemetery, near Cadiz, O.   Issue:
   151, William, b. ——, 1808; d. 12 Aug., 1881.

76. MARGARET HEDGES (John[1], Rebecca[2], Silas[3], Isaac[4]), dau. of Isaac and Mary (Fouts) Hedges, b. *circa* 1822; d.——; *m.* Sept., 1843, George T. Turner, of Morgan Co., O.; they had 7 children.   Issue:

53

152, Ruth, b. 23 March, 1857; *m.* March 1886, Eugene A. Hawkins; 153, 154, 155, 156, 157, 158.

79. RUTH HEDGES (John[1], Rebecca[2], Silas[3], Isaac[4]), dau. of Isaac and Mary (Fouts) Hedges, b. 1828; *m.* 26 March, 1850, Alexander Rodgers, of Washington Co., O. He d. 24 Nov., 1899.　　　　　　　　　　　　　　　　　　　　　　　　　Issue:
159, Mary C.; 160, Isaac F.
161, Ella M., b. 30 July, 1864; d. 20 Jan., 1903; *m.* W. F. Deed.
162, Charles C., b. 25 Nov., 1870; *m.* Flo. Herryman, of Van Buren Co., Iowa.

80. WILLIAM HEDGES (John[1], Rebecca[2], Silas[3], Isaac[4]), dau. of Isaac and Mary (Fouts) Hedges, b. *circa* 1832; d. ——; *m.* Elizabeth Mills, of Millgrove, Morgan Co., O.　　　Issue:
163, Jessie S.

82. WILLIAM FRAZIER (John[1], Rebecca[2], Joseph[3], Ruth[4]), son of —— and Ruth (Hedges) Frazier, b. 10 Feb., 1810; d. 19 Sept., 1870, at Sparta, Ill.; *m.* 8 Feb., 1834, Margaret Nace, b. 23 April, 1813. In his earlier years Mr. Frazier was a tanner, then later a farmer. Both his wife and himself were devout Presbyterians.　　　　　　　　　　　　　　　　　　Issue:
164, Wm. Augustus, b. 10 Jan., 1832; d. 3 June, 1833.
165, Mary E.; 166, Joseph N.; 167, Wm. Henry; 168, Margaret Jane; 169, Samuel Creighton, b. 17 April, 1846; d. in Civil War, 16 June, 1864.
170, George A., b. 27 May, 1849.

87. PRUDENCE HEDGES (John[1], Rebecca[2], Joseph[3], William[4]), dau. of William and Sarah (Dunlap) Hedges, b. 26 April, 1806; d. ——; *m.* Samuel Campbell.　　　　　　　　　　　　Issue:
171, a son; 172, Lucinda, living, Rural Dale, Washington Co., O.

96. GREENBURY W. HEDGES (John[1], Rebecca[2], Joseph[3], Abraham[4]), son of Abraham and Edith (Carter) Hedges, b. ——; d. ——; *m.* —— ——.　　　　　　　　　　　　　　Issue:
173, Margaret; 174, Albert.

99. SUSAN CASH (John[1], Rebecca[2], Joseph[3], Jemima[4]), dau. of Ninian and Jemima (Hedges) Cash, b. ——; d. June, 1890; *m.* Samuel Lewis.　　　　　　　　　　　　　　　　　Issue:
175, Hattie, b. ——; d. ——; *m.* 1904, Frank Woodmansee.

100. SARAH CASH (John[1], Rebecca[2], Joseph[3], Jemima[4]), dau. Ninian and Jemima (Hedges) Cash, b. ——; d. 21 Jan., 1899; *m.* 16 Aug., 1833, John Gregory, who d. 27 Sept., 1876.　Issue:
176, William, b. 18 Sept., 1834; d. ——; *m.* Melissa Meeks, Bellaire, O.
177, Jemima, b. 4 May, 1836; d. 17 March, 1876; *unm.*

DESCENDANTS OF REBECCA VAN METRE

178, Ninian, b. 11 Dec., 1838; d. 16 April, 1888.
179, David, b. 2 June, 1841; d. 1866; lived at Milliken's Bend, Miss.
180, Samuel, b. 27 Aug., 1843; d. 13 Aug., 1872; emigrated to S. W. Texas.
181, Mary, b. 10 Sept., 1845; lives, Langford, S. Dakota.
182, Warner Rogers, b. 27 Sept., 1852; d. ——; m. 6 Dec., 1890, Eliza Johnson.
183, Sue, b. 11 Nov., 1856.

151. WILLIAM MEEK (John[1], Rebecca[2], Silas[3], Elizabeth[4], Isaac[5]), son of Isaac and Rachael (Hedges) Meek, b. —— 1809; d. —— 12 Aug., 1881; m. —— ——.   Issue:
184, a dau.; m. Geo. B. Holmes, Cadiz, Ohio.

152. RUTH TURNER (John[1], Rebecca[2], Silas[3], Isaac[4], Margaret[5]), dau. George T. and Margaret (Hedges) Turner, b. 23 March, 1857; m. March, 1886, Eugene A. Hawkins.   Issue:
185, Frank A., b. 6 Aug., 1887; 186, James H., b. 30 July, 1889.

159. MARY C. ROGERS (John[1], Rebecca[2], Silas[3], Isaac[4], Ruth[5]), dau. of Alexander and Ruth (Hedges) Rodgers, b. 25 Dec., 1850; d. 1896; m. John Miller, of Van Buren Co., Iowa.   Issue:
187, a son, b. 1895.

160. ISAAC F. RODGERS (John[1], Rebecca[2], Silas[3], Isaac[4], Ruth[5]), son of Alexander and Ruth (Hedges) Rodgers, b. 12 Feb., 1853; d. ——; m. Louisa Kitz, of Van Buren Co., Iowa.

165. MARY E. FRAZIER (John[1], Rebecca[2], Joseph[3], Ruth[4], William[5]), dau. of William and Margaret (Nace) Frazier, b. 16 July, 1835; d. 3 March, 1868; m. 1850, Thomas Orr.   Issue:
188, William; 189, Margaret; 190, Samuel; 191, Renwick[1]; 192, Millville; 193, Renwick[2]; 194, Thomas, of Roney's Point, W. Va.

166. JOSEPH NACE FRAZIER (John[1], Rebecca[2], Joseph[3], Ruth[4], William[5]), son of William and Margaret (Nace) Frazier, b. 24 May, 1837; d. Nov., 1897; m. Sarah A. Patterson, at Denver, Col., lives 1443 Cleveland Place, Denver, Col.   Issue:
195, William; 196, Mary; 197, Joseph; 198, Anna; 199, Fannie.

167. WM. HENRY FRAZIER (John[1], Rebecca[2], Joseph[3], Ruth[4], William[5]), son of William and Margaret (Nace) Frazier, b. 27 Jan., 1840; d. 10 Feb., 1904; m. June, 1866, at Citronelle, Ala., Mary Thompson. He was a merchant and a teacher.   Issue:
200, ——; 201, ——; 202, ——; 203, ——; 204, ——.

168. MARGARET JANE FRAZIER (John[1], Rebecca[2], Joseph[3], Ruth[4], William[5]), dau. of William and Margaret (Nace) Frazier, b. 26 Dec., 1843; d. ——; m. 11 Oct., 1864, Capt. S. B. Hood, who was b. 1834; Supt. City Schools, at Sparta, Ill., for 40 years.   Issue:

55

205, Sadie B., b. 25 Sept., 1869; d. ——.
206, Wm. Jos., b. 25 Dec., 1871; *m.* 1st June, 1898, —— ——.
207, John Alex., b. 13 March, 1873; Asst. Cashier, Armour
    Packing Co., St. Louis, Mo.
208, Samuel Bateman, b. 20 July, 1875.
209, George Alfred, b. 20 Nov., 1878.
210, Robert Davis, b. 7 April, 1881; *m.* —— ——.
211, Allen Carson, b. 25 May, 1886.

178. NINIAN GREGORY (John[1], Rebecca[2], Joseph[3], Jemima[4],
Sarah[5]), son of John and Sarah (Cash) Gregory, b. 11 Dec.,
1838; d. 16 Sept., 1892; *m.* 22 Jan., 1860, Rachael Sutton, who
d. 16 Sept., 1862; *m.* 2d Rachael Kirkendell. Issue:
    212, Samuel Pennell, b. 1860; d. 1864; 213, Charles.

205. SADIE B. HOOD (John[1], Rebecca[2], Joseph[3], Ruth[4], Wil-
liam[5], Margaret Jane[6]), dau. of Capt. S. B. and Margaret J.
(Frazier) Hood, b. 25 Sept., 1869; *m.* 28 Aug., 1897, Rev. J. G.
Kline, of Boulder, Col. Issue:
    214, Vivian; 216, Lorrain L.; 217, Mary Margaret.

206. WILLIAM JOSEPH HOOD (John[1], Rebecca[2], Joseph[3], Ruth[4],
William[5], Margaret Jane[6]), b. 25 Dec., 1871; d. ——; *m.* 1st
June, 1898, —— ——. Issue:
    218, Phyllis; 219, Josephine.

208. SAMUEL BATEMAN HOOD (John[1], Rebecca[2], Joseph[3],
Ruth[4], William[5], Margaret Jane[6]), b. 20 July, 1875; d. ——; *m.*
1897, Rose Starm. Issue:
    220, Thornton.

209. GEORGE ALFRED HOOD (John[1], Rebecca[2], Joseph[3], Ruth[4],
William[5], Margaret Jane[6]), son of Capt. S. B. and Margaret J.
(Frazier) Hood, b. 20 Nov., 1878; d. ——; *m.* —— Aug., 1902,
Ethel Brown.
    221, Ethel Brown.

DESCENDANTS OF ISAAC VAN METRE

V. ISAAC VAN METRE (John[1]), son of John and Margaret
Van Metre, b. *circa* 1713, probably in Somerset Co., N. J., called
in his father's will "my eldest son" (Johannes being deceased),
d. in Frederick Co., Va., *ante* 1748; *m.* Elsje (Alice) Scholl, of
Somerset Co., N. J. (Records Raritan Church at Somerville, N.
J.), *circa* 1736. John Van Metre in his will imposes upon his son
Isaac the condition precedent to receiving his legacy, that Isaac
shall sell his land on the Monocacy (Md.), etc. It is shown by
the records that Isaac and his wife subsequently conveyed a tract
of land called "Isaac's Inheritance," containing 200 acres, situate

at the mouth of Liganore Creek (which empties into the Monocacy) in Prince George's Co., Md., to Jacob Stoever, of same County, 2 Oct., 1744 (Prince Geo. Co., Md., Records). Alice Van Metre survived her husband and was granted letters of administration on her husband's estate, 7 February, 1748. She *m.* 2d Mr. Morgan *circa* 1751. Captain Richard Morgan, of Frederick Co., Va., was her bondsman. She filed her account in the name of Morgan "late Alice Van Metre," at a subsequent date (Frederick Co., Va., Records). It is significant, in this connection, and with the christian name of her second husband that the children of Thomas and Elizabeth Van Metre Shepherd, of Shepherdstown, should call Capt. William Morgan, son of Capt. Richard Morgan, "Cousin Wm. Morgan" in their references to him.

Isaac Van Meteren (for so the name is found upon the record) was received into membership of the Reformed Dutch Church at North Branch (Readington) on the Raritan, "on confession of faith" 6th Nov., 1731 (Records of Readington, N. J., Church).

By his father's will Isaac was given 250 acres of land situate on a drain of the Potomac known as Van Metre's Marsh; 120 acres of this tract was sold by Isaac's son John, 6th March, 1770, to a Mr. Dunn, in which transaction John is mentioned as "son and heir-at-law of Isaac Van Metre, deceased." (Berkely Co., W. Va., Records.) Issue:

1, Peter, bapt. 23 July, 1738, at Raritan Church, Ref. Dutch.
2, Johannes, bapt. 6 June, 1740; *m.* Elizabeth ——? at North Branch Ref. Dutch Ch.
3, Margaret, bapt. 6 June, 1740, at North Branch Ref. Dutch Ch.

The children were probably named: Peter, for his mother's father; Johannes and Margritje, for their father's parents, respectively. It is claimed that this Margaret Van Metre married one of her cousins, either Joseph Hedges, son of Solomon and Rebecca (Van Metre) Hedges; or, Joseph Van Metre, son of Abraham, who was b. 1740 and d. 1823. The will of Joseph Hedges, which was probated in Prince George's Co., Md., in 1753, mentions wife Mary (Book A, 1, p. 85). This, however, could not have been the Joseph meant, but Joseph, Jr., son of Joseph, and brother of Solomon.

ELIZABETH VAN METRE

VI. Elizabeth Van Metre (John[1]), dau. of John and Margaret Van Metre, b. probably, in Somerset Co., N. J., *circa* 1715; d. *circa* 1793, at Shepherdstown, Va.; *m. circa* 1733, probably in Maryland, Thomas Shepherd, the pioneer colonist at Mecklenburg (afterward Shepherdstown, Frederick Co., Va., incorporated in 1762 and so named in his honor). It is supposed that

Thomas and Elizabeth were married in Prince George's Co., Md., where Mary Shepherds lived, and immediately thereafter crossed the Potomac into the Colony of Virginia and settled upon the grant that Thomas Shepherd obtained from Jost Hite. For further data and descendants in this line see Shepherd Genealogy—Part II. of this book.

DESCENDANTS OF HENRY VAN METRE

VII. HENRY VAN METRE (John[1]), third son of John and Margaret —— Van Metre, b. Somerset Co., N. J., *circa* 1717, d. in Virginia *circa* 1793; *m.* 1st Eve ——; 2d *ante* 1757, Hannah ——; 3d Elizabeth Pyle, of Ohio Co., Va. License issued 8 April, 1777. Henry inherited, by the terms of his father's will, "400 acres of land where I now live." There is considerable documentary evidence regarding this Henry Van Metre and his migratory movements; the first of these is found recorded in the Journal of the Frederick Co., Va., Court, under date of "xi of 7ber, 1744," which states that Henry Van Metre is appointed overseer of the road from Noah Hampton's Mill, on the road to Cape Capon, near James Cody's.

On April 5, 1757, Henry Van Metre, jointly with his wife Hannah, transfer to Abraham Van Metre a tract of 150 acres of land which had been granted to said Henry and Abraham by Samuel Bryan, 12 Nov., 1747; on the same date Henry Van Metre conveys by deed another tract of land, containing 64 acres, which had been granted said Henry and Abraham Van Metre by Jacob Van Metre. This deed was unsigned, but is acknowledged by Henry Van Metre and his wife Hannah. (Records at Winchester, Va., and Obenchain, July–Aug., 1905.)

Henry Van Metre, Joseph Van Metre, John Lemon, Nicholas McIntyre and Edward Lucas, soldiers, of Frederick Co., Va., were paid 7 shillings each for services in resisting Indians; Sept., 1758 (Boogher's Gleanings of Virginia History, p. 81, and Virginia Colonial Militia, by Crozier, p. 72). They are rated as privates in Capt. Thomas Speak's Company, Virginia Colonial Militia.

While still remaining a resident of Virginia, Henry kept migrating westward, until he reached what is now southwestern Pennsylvania, the border land then in controversy between the Colony of Virginia and the Province of Pennsylvania. He took up his residence in this territory which later became Bedford, and afterward Washington, then Green counties of Pennsylvania. Here he took up land on Muddy Creek adjacent to his brother, Jacob Van Metre, and his name appears on the assessment roll of Springhill Township in 1772–1773, rated as a taxable. In the latter year some sort of disturbance of the peace occurred and Henry, Jacob and Abraham Van Metre were indicted by the

"Grand Inquest of Quarter Sessions," July 6, 1773, on two bills, for riot. These bills were found and presented to the Court of Yohogania Co., Va., which exercised jurisdiction over this part of Pennsylvania (see History of Washington Co., Pa., p. 152, Crumrine).

On 23 February, 1775, Henry Van Metre is recommended, among others, as a proper person to be added to the Commission of the Peace for the County of West Augusta (Virginia jurisdiction), and on the 18th of April, 1776, Henry Van Metre and Ebenezer Zane were appointed viewers, to view old road from Conrad Walter's to mouth of Wheeling; and again, on 20th August, 1776, Henry Van Metre was among those persons recommended to be added to the Commission of the Peace for Augusta Co., Va. (see Carnegie Museum Annals, Vol. I., pp. 533, 564, 565; 1902).

Henry Van Metre's name appears among those who received warrants for lands for military services; 400 acres were granted in Washington Co., Pa., 25th May, 1785, with 250 additional acres in the year 1786.

There is also found in the entries on the old mill books in possession of the Shepherd family at Shepherdstown, Va., a brief memorandum referring to "Henry Van Metre, Sr., £12. 3. 0 1785."

In his will, dated 3d March, 1790, and probated at ———, 1793, Henry Van Metre mentions his wife Elizabeth and children: Nathan, Joshua, Hester, Henry and Joseph, the latter then deceased at the date of the will, which recites: "My son Joseph Van Metre's estate which lies on the west side of the Ohio River in the Indian country." It is to be supposed that the above children, excepting Joseph, were the children of his second wife Hannah; the issue of his first wife, Eve, having already been provided for as they arrived at maturity. One of the executors of his will was William Gorrell, who *m*. a dau. of Jacob, brother of Henry. Issue:
1, John; 2, Joseph; 3, Henry, Jr.; 4, Isaac; 5, Jacob; 6, Hannah; 7, Ruth; 8, Nathan; 9, Joshua; 10, Hester.

1. JOHN VAN METRE (John,[1] Henry[2]), son of Henry and Eve (———) Van Metre, b. in Virginia, *circa* 1738; d. in Ohio, or Brooke Co., Va., *circa* 1803; *m*. 1st ——— ———; *m*. 2 Mrs. Jemima Bukey, widow of John, and mother of Zachariah Bukey. She was appointed administrator of the will of her former husband, 6 July, 1778; Joseph Van Metre was one of the appraisers of his estate. John Van Metre was granted land by his father, *ante* 1779, in Berkeley Co., Va., adjoining other lands owned by his brother Isaac and known as Flagg's Mill; the latter was erected at the mouth of the Tuscarara as it empties into the Potomac, two miles from Martinsburg, W. Va. When Bedford Co., Pa., was organized in 1771 it was of disputed Virginia territory.

John Van Metre was then living in Rosstraevor Township, near his uncle, Jacob Van Metre; here he was rated as a taxable. The Virginia-Pennsylvania boundary controversy was settled in 1783 and Washington Co., Pa., was erected out of Bedford County in that year. Rosstraevor Township fell within the limits of the newly created county and John Van Metre's domicile was located near where Waynesburg, Greene Co., Pa., now stands; he had at this time 300 acres of land and a family of nine persons A John Van Metre on view of road from Providence Mount's Mill at Augsburg Ferry to Catfish Camp (Augusta-town), was appointed by the Augusta Court 22 February, 1775 (Ann. Carnegie Mus., Vol. I., p. 527). During the period of his residence on the Pennsylvania frontier John Van Metre was very active in the military movements against the Indians. He was appointed ensign of militia of Yohogania Co. (Va.), 28 June, 1779 (Yohogania Court Journal). He commanded a company of Westmoreland Rangers and is variously mentioned in connection with the militia on the western waters between the years 1778–1783. Also a John Van Metre, Jr., was a member of the Stokeley Rangers during the same period (Penna. Arch., 3d Ser.; Draper's Notes; Wither's Chronicles, and Kercheval's History of the Valley, 2d ed., p. 204). The records of warrantees for land in Washington Co., Pa., show that John Van Metre, Sr., had 300 acres surveyed to him; and a similar amount to John Van Metre, Jr., in Bedford County, in 1784. John Van Metre later removed with his family to the Ohio country, settling near where Wellsburg, Brooke Co., W. Va., now stands, and is supposed to be identical with the Captain John Van Metre who was recorded as being at Beech Bottom, above Wheeling, in 1789. In 1783 occurred the murder of the wife and the infant child and the fifteen-year-old daughter of John Van Meter. The wife and child were butchered in the door of their dwelling. . . . The girl was washing at a spring and wore a sun bonnet which prevented her from seeing the approaching savage, who tomahawked her where she was bending over the spring. Three of Mr. Van Meter's children—sons, aged about eleven, eight and six years respectively—were playing in a field near the house, but discovering the Indians, all effected their escape, but John, the youngest, not so active as his brothers, was overtaken and carried away by them. While these events were transpiring Mrs. John Spahn, a niece of Mrs. Van Meter, was on her way to visit her aunt; upon nearing the house she observed the air to be filled with feathers, which caused her to suspect that something was wrong, which was confirmed by closer observation and convinced her of the presence of Indians. At once she grasped the clapper of the bell fastened to the neck of her horse, while she urged the animal to its utmost in an opposite direction and was the first to convey the intelligence of the presence of the redmen. The locality of this tragedy was on the farm now owned by Eugene Ridgeley (1902), situated on the waters of Short Creek, about four miles southwest of West Liberty.

In 1805 the young John Van Meter was found with a party of Wyandotte Indians in northern Ohio, where they were stopping at a trading post operated by Isaac Zane, the proprietor, in the neighborhod of Columbus. Mr. Zane discovered John Van Meter, now as much an Indian as the others, and learned that he was the one captured in 1783. Mr. Van Meter, the father, was still living in Virginia and was communicated with, who sent his two sons with instructions to bring John home and take up a civilized life. They came, saw and were convinced of John's identity. John consented to return and with six or seven squaws, one of whom was John's wife, went to Virginia. He visited his father for several weeks and was much gratified, but could not be persuaded to remain. Some years later he again visited Virginia, but in the meantime his father had died.

Several years after the murder of his wife John Van Meter, Sr., *m.* the widow of John Bukey, an early emigrant from New Jersey. One child was the issue of this marriage, Sarah, who *m.* the late Robert Patterson, of Wheeling, W. Va. (see Hist. and Biog. Ohio Co., W. Va., p. 32).

The following excerpt from the diary of Col. Isaac Van Metre, of Oldfield, Va., a descendant of Isaac, the brother of the progenitor of this line and one of the original Virginia grantees, is here given, as it probably relates to the young John Van Metre who was captured by the Indians and adopted their mode of life:

"Tuesday, April 28 [1801]. This day we passed an Indian Camp where I was introduced to John Van Metre, who was taken prisoner when a child and is so accustomed to the Indian habits that his firiends cannot prevail upon him to leave them. He shook hands with me and called me 'Captain,' and appeared to take more notice of me than of my companions. I bought a set of beaver stones of him for Aunt Rebecca. His wife was handsomely built, but rather old for him. She would not speak English. I asked him in her hearing how many children they had, he told me none. I told him he looked able to get children which caused her to smile modestly; but she attended to her skin dressing. We returned and lodged at Rankinson's" (Trans-Alleghany Magazine, p. 100). Rankinson's Bottom is on the Sciota, not far from Chillicothe, O.

John Van Metre at one time lived at Van Metre's Fort on Short Creek in Ohio County, but in 1789 he lived on a farm near it when the Indians attacked his home, killed his wife, a daughter and two small sons and took the three elder sons captive. Hannah was the name of the daughter that was killed; she was at the spring doing some washing—the place is still called Hannah's Spring. John Van Metre was at a neighbor's, but on hearing of the murder hurried home from Chas. Hedge's, where he was breaking flax with three or four men. The captured children were Abraham, Isaac and John, the two former finally making their escape, but John remained with the Indians and adopted

their mode of life, and though he sometimes visited his father, he could not be persuaded to return home. John Van Metre afterward married the widow of John Bukey, an early emigrant from New Jersey (see Doddridge's Border Narratives, Appendix, pp. 307-8).   Issue:
11, John; 12, Hannah, killed by the Indians; 13, Isaac; 14, Abraham; 15, Sarah.

2. JOSEPH VAN METRE (John,[1] Henry[2]), son of Henry and Eve (——) Van Metre, b. in Virginia, *circa* 1740; d. *ante* 1790; he was unmarried. He was killed by the Indians where Brandenburg, Meade Co., Ky., now stands. The locality was then in Hardin County; the town was founded by a man who is said to have married a Van Metre (W. A. O.). Brandenburg, capital of Meade Co., Ky., is on the Ohio River, sixteen miles below the mouth of Salt River and forty miles below Louisville; was founded by Col. Solomon Brandenburg (Collin's Kentucky, Vol. II., pp. 598-9).
Mrs. C. E. Van Metre, in correspondence recently with a local Ohio newspaper, says: " Abraham Van Metre, son of John, of Berkeley Co., Va., had a brother, Henry, whose son Joseph was the father of an Abraham, who was the grandfather of Mr. David Kilgore, of Anderson, Ind."

3. HENRY VAN METRE (John,[1] Henry[2]), son of Henry and Eve (——) Van Metre, b. Virginia, *circa* 1742; d. in what is now Greene Co., Pa., *circa* 1803; *m. Martha* or *Margaret* ——. He was probably the same Henry Van Metre who was granted land in Greene Co., Pa., on a Pennsylvania warrant 25 May, 1785, and patented to him in 1787. He had, however, warranted to him on 26 October, 1787, 393 acres of land in Washington Co. (record in office of Secretary of Internal Affairs at Harrisburg, Pa.), a part of which he sold to Azariah Davis, amounting to 625 acres. There appears also to have been patented to him 200 acres of land in Cumberland Township, in the same county, in 1781. One of his descendants is authority for the statement that he and his son Absalom, both of whom were living in Greene Co., Pa., in 1796, that they then owned considerable land in Mason Co. (W.) Va. (D. S. Van Metre Letters), and of having had surveyed to him in 1780 a tract of 400 acres on Cross Creek, in Ohio County, Va. (Pa. Arch., 2d Ser.). Henry Van Meter was assistant judge of Washington County Court under the Constitution of 1776; he was commissioned 11 February, 1785. He was also a commissioner of Washington Co., Pa., in November, 1788 (Crumrine's History of Washington Co., pp. 249, 469). Henry Van Metre laid claim, by tomahawk right, to all that beautiful and valuable valley known as the Randolph settlement on the south side of Pumpkin Run (the Swan Record). This settlement was in

Greene Co., Pa. From his will, probated in the latter county in 1803, the names of the following children are obtained: 16, Joseph; 17, Jesse; 18, Absalom; 19, Henry, Jr.; 20, Abraham; 21, John; 22, Alice; 23, Sarah; 24, Rachael; 25, Elizabeth; 26, Phœbe; 27, Rebecca; 28, Martha; 29, Mary. Also grandsons: Joab, Henry and William Thomas.

In the census of Washington County for 1790 the family of Henry Van Metre are enumerated: 2 in heads of family; 3 free white males; 6 free white females, with Joseph, Jesse and Absalom heading their own individual families.

At a Court held for Greene Co., Pa., 6th June, 1803, was heard the petition of William Thomas, a minor, asking the Court to appoint Martha Van Metre (his grandmother) his guardian; this woman was the widow of Henry Van Metre, deceased (see Hanna's History of Greene Co., Pa.).

4. ISAAC VAN METRE (John[1] Henry[2]), son of Henry and —— Van Metre, b. in Virginia 1750; d. 1798; m. circa 1775/6 Hester, daughter of Jacob and Lydia (Borden) Beck, the latter being the granddaughter of Benjamin Borden, Sr., one of the earliest settlers and largest grantees of land in the Valley of Virginia and an emigrant from New Jersey. Hester was b. in Rockbridge Co., Va., in 1760 (W. A. O.).

Henry, the father of Isaac, by deed of lease and release, dated 8th Dec., 1779, conveyed to his son the tract upon which Flagg's Mill was built. It was located on the Tuscarara, near Martinsburg, Va. Isaac Van Metre conveyed the Flagg's Mill property to John Snively in 1780. Isaac served as a private in Lewis and Clark's expedition and was allotted 108 acres of land in Clark's grant on the Ohio for his services (see English's Conquest N. W. Territory, Vol. II., p. 849). Issue:
30, Hannah; 31, Mary; 32, Elizabeth; 33, Placentia; 34, Jacob; 35, Joseph; 36, Sallie Hawkins.

5. JACOB VAN METRE (John,[1] Henry[2]), son of Henry and —— Van Metre, b. Frederick Co., Va., 1752; d. 12 April, 1838. He is said to have m. 1st a German woman by the name of Covenhoven, by whom he had issue. His first wife dying in Kentucky, he m. 2d Rebecca Rollings (or Rawlings), daughter of Rebecca V.-M. Rollings, who was the daughter of Jacob Van Metre (" Valley Creek Jake "). She is said to have been born in Kentucky in 1772; was drawing a pension as a soldier's widow in 1840, at which time her age was stated to be 63 years. There is record of a deed by Jacob and Catharine, his wife, of Bedford Co., Pa., to William Hanscher, for certain property, dated 21 August, 1772. There is a tradition that his first wife's name was Catharine Rhoades, but a contemporary annalist writes that her name was Covenhoven. Kentuckians called him " Miller Jake." He accom-

panied his uncle Jacob ("Valley Jake") from Virginia and settled near him in Severen's Valley, Ky. At a point about five miles below his uncle's location Jacob built a mill and a still and was known thereafter as "Miller Jacob." He also built a fort on his land located about five miles from Elizabethtown, Hardin County, which was known as Van Metre's Fort (Collin's Kentucky, Vol. II., p. 24). In 1832, in the application for a pension, he declared that he was born in Frederick Co., Va., and was then in his eightieth year; that in January, 1778, was commissioned an ensign at Fort Henry, Va., in the militia for Kentucky; in April, 1778, aided in recruiting the company, then marched under Capt. Harrod, descended the Ohio in company with Captains Leonard Helm and Joseph Bowman, all under Col. George R. Clarke. At the Falls of the Ohio (Louisville) they were joined by other troops from the western parts of Virginia and from Kentucky and then they took all villages and posts east of the Mississippi; was in service eight months. Returned home. Resided in Jefferson Co., Ky., was appointed by Governor Jefferson, 7 May, 1782, a captain and marched with Lewis and Clark's expedition that fall (Pension Statements, Part 1, Vol. V., p. 28, Draper's Notes). Ensign Jacob Van Metre was allotted 2,156 acres of land (same amount as a lieutenant) in Clark's grant on the Ohio (Collin's Kentucky, II., p. 738).

"On the north side of Barren River," says Collin's History of Kentucky, "about a quarter of a mile above the old Van Metre ferry and three miles from Bowling Green, some beech trees are still standing which indicates the camping ground in the spring of 1775 of an exploring party of thirteen from the new settlements of Harrodstown."

(A Rebecca Van Metre was a pensioner, Hardin Co., Ky., 1840; aged 63.)   Issue:
   37, Abraham; 38, William; 39, Henry; 40, Jacob, b. 1787; d.
      1872; 41, Ruth, b. 1789; 42, Washington; 43, John; 44,
      Hannah; 45, Rebecca; 46, Nancy; 47, Laetitia; 48, Mahala; 49, Edwin.

   6. HANNAH VAN METRE (John,[1] Henry[2]), dau. of Henry and —— Van Metre, b. Frederick Co., Va., *circa* 1755; d. ——; *m.* 1st —— Hite; *m.* 2d —— Jackman (probably of Washington Co., Pa.).   Issue:
   50, Thomas, and 51, Nancy Hite; 52, Samuel; 53, Polly; 54, Malinda Jackman.

   7. RUTH VAN METRE (John,[1] Henry[2]), dau. of Henry and —— Van Metre, b. in Virginia, 1758; d. 1840; *m. circa* 1779 Capt. Samuel Gill; he d. 1822. The marriage bond was signed by her brother, Isaac Van Metre, and Samuel Gill. Her father, Henry, was the proper person to have signed the bond, but Ruth, it is believed, took offense at her father's third marriage and had gone

to live in Isaac's family. After their marriage Capt. Gill and his wife removed to Botetourt Co., Va., where Isaac's family lived. The Gills afterward removed to Garrad Co., Ky., some time prior to 1790, where they were visited by Jacob, her brother, in 1833, while the latter was a member of the Kentucky Legislature (Obenchain Letters). Issue:

55, Cassandra; 56, Mary; 57, Samuel; 58, Elizabeth; 59, William; 60, Erasmus; 61, Joseph; 62, Patsey; 63, Emily.

8. NATHAN VAN METRE (John,[1] Henry[2]), son of Henry and —— Van Metre, b. in Virginia *circa* 1760; d. ——; *m. circa* 1780 Mary Ann Pyle, the dau. of Elizabeth Pyle, his father's third wife. Nathan lived in Virginia near his father in Berkeley County. By his father's will Nathan was bequeathed the Berkeley County homestead, with the bulk of the personal property, subject to his step-mother Elizabeth's dowry and certain legacies to be paid to other children named in the will. Nathan is presumed to have been the eldest son of Henry Van Metre by his second marriage to Hannah Pyle (the sister of his third wife Elizabeth Pyle?). There was probably no issue by the third marriage and the children of the first wife, Eva, being already provided for in the testator's lifetime. To Nathan's son Joseph was bequeathed the lands of Nathan's deceased brother Joseph, "lying on the west side of the Ohio." This grandson of Henry afterward went out to Ohio and took possession of the inheritance and was known as "Virginia Joe." Issue:

64, Joseph; 65, Daniel; *m.* ? 1798, Ruth Harp, of Berkeley Co., Va.

9. JOSHUA VAN METRE (John,[1] Henry[2]), son of Henry and Hannah (Pyle) Van Metre, b. in Virginia *circa* 1762; d. ——; *m.* ——. It was "to Joshua his heirs and assigns" that the father devised the land which was the property of his deceased son Joseph, lying in "Sufferin's" (Severn's) Valley, "District of Kentucky."

10. HESTER VAN METRE (John,[1] Henry[2]), dau. of Henry and Hannah (Pyle) Van Metre, b. in Virginia *circa* 1765; d. ——; *m.* ——. Her father required in his will that Hester was to live in Nathan's family "while she maintains her single state—or she shall have three negros in lieu of Nathan's care."

13. ISAAC VAN METRE (John,[1] Henry,[2] John[3]), son of John and —— Van Metre, b. ——; d. ——; *m.* Rachael ——. By the terms of his father's will, dated 2 March, 1797, and probated at Wellsburg, Brooke Co., W. Va., Isaac was devised one-half of the remainder of his estate, jointly with his brother Abraham, after the widow's 100 acres were taken out, leaving about 146 acres to be thus divided. It was part of a tract of 400 acres granted to John Van Metre by the Commonwealth of Virginia 14 July, 1786. According to the Land Tax records of Brooke

Co., W. Va., this land was on the waters of Short Creek and were held between the heirs until about 1815. Issue: 66, Mordecia.

14. ABRAHAM VAN METRE (John,[1] Henry,[2] John[3]), son of John and —— Van Metre, b. ——; d. ——; m. ——. He was living on Short Creek, Brooke Co., Va., and had 212 acres in 1815.

15. SARAH VAN METRE (John,[1] Henry,[2] John[3]), dau. of John and Jemima (Bukey) Van Metre, b. Brooke Co., Va., after 1789; d. ——; m. 1809 Robert Patterson. In 1809 Robert Patterson and his wife Sarah deeded her right of dower of 10 acres from her father John to her brothr Abraham Van Metre, 6 June, 1809.
Issue:
67, Col. Patterson, of St. Mary's.

16. JOSEPH VAN METRE (John,[1] Henry,[2] Henry[3]), son of Henry, Jr., and —— Van Metre, b. in Virginia; d. ——; m. *Elizabeth Aikens.* In the census of Washington Co., Pa., for 1790 (p. 248) Joseph Van Metre is rated as having two persons in the list of heads of families and four free white males under sixteen years of age and four free white females, including heads of family. His name is found among the warrantees for land in Cumberland Township, Washington Co., Pa., in 1781 for 200 acres; and again (township not named) for 300 acres, 25th May, 1785, and 250 acres, 20 February, 1786, all in Washington Co., Pa. Prior to this time a Joseph Van Metre name is recorded among others as being taxed on a small holding in Rosstraevor Township, Bedford Co., Pa., in 1773. Joseph Van Metre's death is related by Cyrus Van Metre, Esq., of New Castle, Ind. Joseph had gone back to Pennsylvania on horseback and on his return through Kentucky the horse got away from him, came on, swam the Ohio River and made his way home. When search was made for Joseph he was found dead on the Kentucky side of the river. It was believed by his family that his horse had thrown him off or had run under a leaning tree, or something like that, as there were no signs on his body that the Indians had killed him. " My mother remembered the story of his death very well." His son Absalom's dau. Maria *m.* David V. M., May 8, 1807. Issue: 68, Absalom, living in Adams Co., Ohio, *circa* 1804.

18. ABSALOM VAN METRE (John,[1] Henry,[2] Henry[3]), son of Henry and Martha Van Metre, b. in Virginia; was noted as a single man among the taxables of Cumberland Township, Washington County, in 1781. But in the census of 1790 he is noted with two in family, probably himself and wife. With his brothers, Henry and John, they emigrated to Mason Co., Va., in 1800, where they purchased lands and where some of their descendants resided for many years. Issue: 69, Rezin.

22. ALICE (or ELSIE) VAN METRE (John,[1] Henry,[2] Henry[3]), dau. of Henry and Martha Van Metre, *m. circa* 1780 Azariah Davis, probably a native of Chester Co., Pa., b. 12 February, 1756; d. Utica, Ohio, 1839, aged 83 years. Azariah Davis's name first appears in the list of taxables of Charlestown Township, Chester Co., Pa., for the years 1765–1766, in which he is stated to be a single man. This Azariah may have been the father of this subject. In 1781 Azariah Davis's name appears among the taxables in Washington Co., Pa., taxable in Rosstraevor Township, Westmoreland County, 1783; head of family and owning 350 acres of land in Washington County and warrantee in same for 400 acres, 16 Nov., 1784 (Penn'a Arch., 3d Series). Ensign 2d Company, 4th Battalion, Washington County militia, 1781–82; purchased tract of land from Henry Van Metre at an early date, which, by the erection of Greene Co., Pa., in 1796, fell within its limits; recorded as owning 125 acres of land in Cumberland Township, Washington County, under date of 1792; grantor of land in Jefferson Township called "Long Metre" in 1801. Was of Welsh ancestry; emigrated from Greene Co., Pa., to Knox Co., O., in 1811; died there and was buried at Newark, Licking Co., O. His wife Elsie died in Pennsylvania between 1794 and 1800; at the latter date he *m.* 2d Mary (Harrington) Smith, of Hagerstown, Md. She d. 1 Sept., 1839 (see Family Letters).   Issue:

70, Henry; 71, William; 72, Azariah; 73, Martha; 74, Rebecca; 75, Sarah; 76, Elizabeth; 77, Rachael, *m.* Uzzel Stevens; no issue. All born in Greene Co., Pa.

23. SARAH VAN METRE (John,[1] Henry,[2] Henry[3]), dau. of Henry and Martha Van Metre, b. Virginia, 1759, d. 1825; *m.* there 1772 Col. Charles Swan, son of John Swan, of Loudon Co., Va. He was born there 1749. In the removal of the Van Metre, Swan and Hughes families from the region of the Potomac, 1767, it is said that Charles was then but eighteen years of age. Sarah rode behind him on the same pillion during all that long and perilous journey and five years later they were married. Chas. Swan erected his cabin in Carmichael's Valley. During the Indian attacks and scares he frequently removed his family to the fort and participated in the scouting expeditions up the Youghiogheny, the Cheat or the Ten Mile Creek. He was a colonel in the Revolutionary War, an Episcopalian in religion and the founder of the Church of England chapel at Carmichaelstown, which edifice afterward became the well-known Greene Academy in 1809. Justice Henry Van Metre took his oath of affirmation, allegiance and fidelity on 16 Sept., 1777. He resided on the same farm in Greene County from the date of his marriage till his death in 1832. He was the owner of 1,300 acres of land bought from the government and located where the city of Lexington, Ky., now stands. After his marriage he tomahawked an area of 600 acres

near Carmichaelstown, and when his sons were married he built them each a home and gave them 100 acres of land apiece.

It is said that at the date of these pioneers from Virginia about 1767, the Swans, Hughes and Van Metre were middle-aged men and each had children nearly or quite grown (see the Swan Family Fecord).

78, Henry, b. Greene County, 12 March, 1774; d. Grave Creek, Va., 26 March, 1823; *m.* 1796 Elizabeth Bowen. Emigrated to Marshall Co., W. Va. Issue twelve children.

79, John, b. 5 Nov., 1776; drowned in a spring when a child.

80, Martha, b. 11 July, 1778; *m.* 17 Dec., 1795, Thomas H. Lucas. Fifteen children.

81, Elizabeth, b. 26 Dec., 1779; d. 30 Jan., 1860; *m.* 15 Oct., 1799, James C. Seaton. Ten children.

82, Thomas, b. 13 Nov., 1781; d. 11 April, 1845, in Fayette Co., Pa.; *m.* 1st Elenora Anderson and had 10 children; *m.* 2d 16 Nov., 1837, Harriet Barclay; 1 dau.

83, John, b. 10 Dec., 1783; *m.* Mary Barclay; emigrated to Tenn. and Mo.; left issue.

84, Mary, b. 6 Dec., 1785; *m.* Mr. Collins, who d., leaving one son; *m.* 2d Isaac Burson; no issue.

85, Charles, b. 9 Dec., 1787; *m.* 24 Jan., 1811, in Greene Co., Margaret Barclay; emigrated, 1856, to Knox Co., O.; she d. 1863; he d. 1873; 13 children.

86, Sarah, b. 5 Jan., 1790; *m.* 1st Elias Flennagan and had one son; *m.* 2d Rev. George Vannaman at Findley, Ohio.

87, Phoebe, b. 17 March, 1791; d. 16 March, 1856; *m.* 4 Sept., 1812, John F. McLain and had 9 children.

88, William, b. 17 April, 1794; d. 5 March, 1847; *m.* Mary Murdock in 1818; she d. 14 Oct., 1863; surviving family emigrated to Greene Co., Wis., and had issue, 10 children.

89, Richard, b. 14 Sept., —; d. Uniontown, Pa., 29 Dec., 1873; *m.* 1818, Susan Gregg, b. 22 May, 1795; d. 22 June, 1866; had issue, 7 children.

90, Jesse, b. 1 July, 1798; *m.* Phoebe Jennings; emigrated to Ohio, then to Peoria, Ill.; they had issue, 8 children.

91, Anne, b. 23 July, 1800; d. inf. (From Family Record of John Swan, of Greene Co., Pa., by Col. S. D. Swan, of Creston, Iowa).

30. HANNAH VAN METRE (John[1], Henry[2], Isaac[3]), dau. of Isaac and Hester (Beck) Van Metre, b. Virginia, *circa* 1778; *m.* —— McFerran, of Botetourt Co., Va.

31. MARY VAN METRE (John[1], Henry[2], Isaac[3]), dau. of Isaac and Hester (Beck) Van Metre, b. Virginia, *circa* 1781; *m.* Chas. Hedrick, of Charlestown, (W.) Va.

32. ELIZABETH VAN METRE (John[1], Henry[2], Isaac[3]), dau. of

Isaac and Hester (Beck) Van Metre, b. Virginia, *circa* 1784;
m. Benjamin Carper, of Botetourt Co., Va.   Issue:
   92, James; 94, George; 95, Joseph; 96, Mary Ann, *m.* Dr.
   Macajah Pendleton.

   33. PLACENTIA VAN METRE (John[1], Henry[2], Isaac[3]), dau. of
Isaac and Hester (Beck) Van Metre, b. Virginia, *circa* 1786; *m.*
—— Mr. McFerran.

   34. JACOB VAN METRE (John[1], Henry[2], Isaac[3]), son of Isaac
and Hester (Beck) Van Metre, b. Virginia, 24 Jan., 1788; d. 27
Feb., 1874; *m.* 24 Jan., 1816, Patsey Usher Shrewsbury, b. 9
Sept., 1792; d. 28 Feb., 1874. She was the granddaughter of
Col. John Dickinson and his wife, Mary Usher, who was a grand-
daughter of Counsellor Perry, of Dublin, Ireland; she died 27
Feb., 1874. Although apparently in her usual health, she passed
calmly away the following day. Jacob Van Metre was born at
White Stone Tavern, near the dividing line between Botetourt
and Rockbridge Counties. At the close of the War of 1812 he
went to Charlestown (now West), Va. In 1818 moved to Bowling
Green, Ky. In 1833 was elected to the Kentucky legislature.
Jacob Van Metre was a man of many excellent qualities. His
success in business attest his energy, his enterprise, and fine judgment. He was kind hearted and charitable; upright and sincere.
His motto, in a long, easy life, extending over half a century,
was: "Never give up."   Issue:
   97, William Steele, b. 29 April, 1817; d. 10 Jan., 1884; *m.*
      21 Dec., 1844, Mary E. Shrewsbury.
   98, Mary Jane, b. 29 Sept., 1819; d. ——.
   99, Julia Ann, b. 18 Oct., 1820; d. ——.
   100, Caroline Eve, b. 11 July, 1822; d. ——.
   101, Samuel Kirk, b. 26 March, 1824; d. ——.
   102, Charles Joseph, b. 22 May, 1826; d. ——; *m.* 1 Oct.,
      1878, Mrs. Kate Moss Overall, of Paducah, Ky.
   103, Sarah Frances, b. 25 Oct., 1828; d. Jan., 1883.
   104, Clinton Clay, b. 20 July, 1834; d. 30 Jan., 1875; was a
      Civil Engineer.

   35. JOSEPH VAN METRE (John[1], Henry[2], Isaac[3]), son of Isaac
and Hester (Beck) Van Metre, b. Fincastle Co., Va., 7 Sept.,
1790; d. Smyth Co., Va., 8 Nov., 1873; *m.* 15 Sept., 1815, Damaris
Lackland, who d. 8 Nov., 1879. Joseph was a soldier in the
War of 1812. He moved from Botetourt Co., to Marion, Smyth
Co., Va., in 1855, where he and his wife died and were buried.
                                                            Issue:
   105, Robert Logan, b. 1818; d. 15 Dec., 1862, in Arkansas; *m.*
      twice; no issue.
   106, Martha Hester, b. Oct., 1820; d. May, 1825; d. *unm.*
   107, Ellen Mary, b. March, 1822; d. April, 1895, *unm.*

THE VAN METRE GENEALOGY

108, Margaret Jennings, b. 26 Feb., 1824; d. July, 1832, *unm.*
109, William Alfred, b. Oct., 1825; d. Sept., 1854, *unm.*
110, Sarah Elizabeth, b. Aug., 1829; d. 3 June, 1908.
111, Ida Virginia, b. June, 1831; d. March, 1833.

36. SALLIE HAWKINS VAN METRE (John[1], Henry[2], Isaac[3]), dau. of Isaac and Hester (Beck) Van Metre, b. Virginia, 4 Aug., 1794; d. 13 April, 1881, in Greenup Co., Ky.; *m.* 20 Dec., 1814, Dr. Eleazer Sweetland, Capt. Chenango Co., N. Y., Militia; Justice of Peace in Botetourt Co., Va., and a Mason of high degree; d. 28 Oct., 1838, at Pattonsburg, Va.

112, Elizabeth, b. 12 Sept., 1815; 113, Mary Hester.
114, Charles Gould, b. 10 April, 1818; d. 24 Nov., 1858, *unm.*
115, Samuel McFerran; 116, Martha H., b. 27 Sept., 1823; d. 22 March, 1835; *m.* Elijah Walker.
117, Isaac Van Metre.
118, Henry Petit, b. 29 July, 1827; d. 1877; *m.* 1857, Augusta Ladd.
119, William Albert, b. 27 April, 1829; d. 1863; Capt. C. S. A., killed at Gettysburg, Pa.
120, Sallie E.; 121, James Otis; 122, Caroline; 123, Margaret.

51. NANCY HITE (John[1], Henry[2], Hannah[3]), dau. of —— Hite and Hannah (Van Metre) Hite, b. ——; d. ——; *m.* her 1st cousin Joseph Evans, Jr., son of Joseph and Mary (Van Metre) Evans.   Issue:
124, Martha A., b. ——; d. ——; *m.* —— Lusk, of Lancaster, Ky.

55. CASSANDRA GILL (John[1], Henry[2], Ruth[3]), dau. of Capt. Samuel and Ruth (Van Metre) Gill, b. ——; d. ——; *m.* —— Aldrich.   Issue:
125, Joshua; 126, John; 127, Emily, *m.* —— Andrews; 128, Eliza, *m.* —— Dunn; 129, Marie, *m.* —— Rainey; 130, Patsey, *m.* —— Tillot.

56. MARY GILL (John[1], Henry[2], Ruth[3]), dau. of Capt. Samuel and Ruth (Van Metre) Gill, b. ——; d. ——; *m.* —— Aldrich.   Issue:
131, Emily, *m.* —— Pettus; 132, Marie, *m.* —— Tillot; 133, Almira, *m.* —— Warren; 134, William; 135, Alexander; 136, Robert.

58. ELIZABETH GILL (John[1], Henry[2], Ruth[3]), dau. of Capt. Samuel and Ruth (Van Metre) Gill, b. ——; d. ——; *m.* William Owsley, who was Governor of Kentucky, 1844–1847 (Collin's Kentucky, Vol. I., p. 53).   Issue:
137, Amanda; 138, Amelia, *m.* —— Anderson; 139, Almira, *m.* —— Goodloe; 140, Elizabeth, *m.* Albert G. Talbot; 141, E. Boyle, living, Louisville, Ky.

60. ERASMUS GILL (John[1], Henry[2], Ruth[3]), son of Capt. Samuel and Ruth (Van Metre) Gill, b. ——; d. ——; *m.* Nancy Smith. Issue:
    142, Theresa, *m.* —— Worthington; 143, Martha, *m.* —— Drane; 144, Mildred, *m.* —— Sneed.

61. JOSEPH GILL (John[1], Henry[2], Ruth[3]), son Capt. Samuel and Ruth (Van Metre) Gill, b. ——; d. ——; *m.* Theresa Boyle. Issue:
    145, Boyle; 146, Samuel; 147, Joseph W., living Danville, Ky., 1890.

62. PATSEY GILL (John[1], Henry[2], Ruth[3]), dau. Capt. Samuel and Ruth (Van Metre) Gill, b. ——; d. ——; *m.* John Gill. Issue:
    148, Ruth; 149, John; 150, Malcolm.

63. EMILY GILL (John[1], Henry[2], Ruth[3]), dau. Capt. Samuel and Ruth (Van Metre) Gill, b.——; d. ——; *m.* —— George. Issue:
    151, William; 152, Theresa; 153, James.

64. JOSEPH VAN METRE (John[1], Henry[2], Nathan[3]), son of Nathan and Mary A. (Pyle) Van Metre, b. ——; d. (sup.) Hardin Co., Ky., *circa* 1870; *m.* —— ——, said by J. B. Kerfott to have married a Van Metre and removed to Hardin Co., Ky., in 1812, and was there known as "Virginia Joe." Issue:
    154, A. Morgan, b. ——; d. at Martinsburg, W. Va.

65. DANIEL VAN METRE (John[1], Henry[2], Nathan[3]), son of Nathan and Mary A. (Pyle) Van Metre. A Daniel Van Metre *m.* Ruth Harp, 1793 (Berkeley Co., W. Va., M. L.), and mention is made in numerous places upon the old store accounts of the Shepherd family at Shepherdstown. Issue:
    155, Joseph B., living at Van Clevesville, W. Va.

68. ABSALOM VAN METRE (John[1], Henry[2], Joseph[3]), son of Joseph and Elizabeth (Aikens) Van Metre, b. ——; located in Adams Co., Ohio, *circa* 1796. Issue:
    156, Maria, b. 7 Jan., 1804; *m.* David Van Metre, b. Highland Co., O., 18 July, 1805. They afterward removed to Fayette Co., Indiana. From thence they removed to Delaware Co., Ind., in 1824. (For continuation of this line, see IX. 164.)

69. REAZIN VAN METRE (John[1], Henry[2], Henry[3], Absalom[4]), son of Absalom and —— Van Metre; lived in Mason Co., Va.; *m.* —— ——. Issue:
    157, Oliver H. P., b. *circa* 1818; d. after 1891, in Mason Co.

70. HENRY DAVIS (John[1], Henry[2], Henry[3], Alice[4]), son of Azariah and Alice (or Elsie Van Metre) Davis, b. Greene Co., Pa., 1781; *m.* 1st Rachael ——, who d. 1848; *m.* 2d —— Anes.

In 1849 Henry was living near Homer, Vermillion Co., Ill. Issue: 158, Henry; 159, John; 160, Martha Hardin; 161, James Hayes; 162, Abraham; 163, Joseph.

71. WILLIAM DAVIS (John[1], Henry[2], Henry[3], Alice[4]), son of Azariah and Alice (Van Metre) Davis, b. Greene Co., Pa., 1783; d. 13 June, 1859; m. 1806, Lydia Fields whose parents formerly lived in Hamilton Co., O., but later emigrated to Spencer Co., Ind.   Issue:
164, David; 165, Sydney; 166, Lydia; 167, Azariah; 168, Mary Ann; 169, George; 170, Stephen; 171, John; 172, Amanda; 173, William.

72. AZARIAH DAVIS (John[1], Henry[2], Henry[3], Alice[4]), son of Azariah and Alice (Van Metre) Davis, b. Greene Co., Pa.; m. —— ——.   Issue:
174, John; 175, Hayes; 176, Polly Garsuch; 177, Rebecca Kidwell.

73. MARTHA DAVIS (John[1], Henry[2], Henry[3], Alice[4]), dau. of Azariah and Alice (Van Metre) Davis, b. Greene Co., Pa., 7 Dec., 1784; d. 19 Dec., 1828; m. 1st James Harrington Smith, of Hagerstown, Md., 1st Sept., 1804. Mr. Smith made a trip to Ohio as early as 1800, and in 1809 the couple emigrated and settled in Morgan Township, Knox Co., purchasing 125 acres of heavily timbered land located on the Martinsburg Road, four miles northeast of Utica. They cleared and improved their land by enduring the privations and hardships of pioneer days. They raised wool and flax from which they spun and wove their clothing. The settler learned blacksmithing and, being the only "smithy" in the neighborhood, made a profitable living. He was a soldier in the War of 1812. James H. Smith m. 2d 26 Jan., 1830, Margaret Honey. He d. while working in his sugar camp, 29 March, 1860; his second wife died 24 July, 1863. Both were members of the Owl Creek Baptist Church.   Issue:
178, Azariah; 179, Benjamin; 180, Mary, b. 15 Jan., 1809; d. 24 Feb., 1809; 181, John, b. Knox Co., O., 12 Jan., 1810; d. of yellow fever, 28 June, 1833, at New Orleans; 182, Sarah A.; 183, Rebecca; 184, James H.; 185, Henry D.; 186, Rachael; 187, Caroline C.; 188, Rees; 181½, Mary 2d, b. 5 Feb., 1812; d. 17 July, 1830; m. 30 Aug., 1828, Rees McClelland; 186½, Cornelia Smith, dau. of Jas. H. and Martha, 73 (Davis) Smith, m. Mr. Nemire, of Putnam Co., Ohio., and had issue: (1) Mary Ann Nemire, who m. Mr. Townsend, of Putnam Co., O.; a. a child. (2) Charity Nemire, who m. Thomas McDougle. They lived in Putnam Co., O., where she d. 1907. Issue, 6 children.

74. REBECCA DAVIS (John[1], Henry[2], Henry[3], Alice[4]), dau. of Azariah and Alice (Van Metre) Davis, b. Greene Co., Pa.; m.

1796, Jacob Hanger; they emigrated to Ohio in 1809 and settled in southeastern part of Morgan Township, Knox Co.   Issue: 189, Azariah; 190, Peter, d. single, aged 21; 191, Andrew; 192, Jackson; 193, Jacob; 194, Mary; 195, Rhoda, d. *unm.*; 196, Ellen; 197, Caroline, d. *unm.*; 198, Sarah; 199, Harriet.

75. SARAH DAVIS (John[1], Henry[2], Henry[3], Alice[4]), dau. of Azariah and Alice (Van Metre) Davis, b. Greene Co., Pa.; *m.* George Miller, who emigrated from Pennsylvania to the Licking, in Ohio.   Issue:
200, Lydia, *m.* Carmine Thrapp; 201, Ruth, *m.* —— Cox; 202, Mary, *m.* —— Jewel; 203, William; 204, John.

95. JOSEPH CARPER (John[1], Henry[2], Isaac[3], Elizabeth[4]), son of Benjamin and Elizabeth (Van Metre) Carper, *m.* Ann West.
    Issue:
205, Elizabeth, *m.* —— Echols; 206, Robert; served in C. S. A.; killed 1862; 207, Wyndham; 208, Ariana, *m.* 11 Sept., 1866, Wm. B. Bean.

98. MARY JANE VAN METRE (John[1], Henry[2], Isaac[3], Jacob[4]), dau. of Jacob and Patsey U. (Shrewsbury) Van Metre, b. 29 Sept., 1819; *m.* 23 Feb., 1837, William Cooke, of Bowling Green, Ky.   Issue:
209, John J., b. 30 Oct., 1839; d. 12 March, 1896; *m.* 1873, Lula Pevay.
210, Martha A., b. 11 Feb., 1842; *m.* 23 Nov., 1864, Capt. Daniel Kearney.
211, Charles L., b. 29 April, 1845; *m.* Jan., 1895, Ellen Dahl.
212, Samuel C., b. 20 Nov., 1848; d. 17 Jan., 1854.

99. JULIA ANN VAN METRE (John[1], Henry[2], Isaac[3], Jacob[4]), dau. of Jacob and Patsey U. (Shrewsbury) Van Metre, b. 18 Oct., 1820; *m.* 23 Nov., 1836, Atwood G. Hobson, of Bowling Green, Ky.   Issue:
213, Lucy U., b. 2 Oct., 1837; d. 19 March, 1838.
214, Mary Eliza, b. 5 Aug., 1840.
215, Ellen Francis, b. 31 March, 1842; d. 15 March, 1853.
216, Wm. Edward, b. 31 March, 1842; *m.* 5 March, 1863, Ida Thorn. W. E. Hobson, late Postmaster of Bowling Green, Ky., was formerly Colonel 13th Regt. Kentucky Volunteers, C. S. A.
218, Jonathan, b. 8 Dec., 1845.
219, Joseph V. M., b. 8 May, 1848.
220, George, b. 23 Sept., 1864.

100. CAROLINE EVE VAN METRE (John[1], Henry[2], Isaac[3], Jacob[4]), dau. of Jacob and Patsey U. (Shrewsbury) Van Metre, b. Va., 11 July, 1822; *m.* 23 June, 1841, George Bradley Adams.
    Issue:

221, Wm. Usher, b. 30 Jan., 1843; *m.* Mary Clarkson.
222, Mary Leland, b. 28 July, 1844; d. 2 March, 1893; *m.* 1st
    Feb., 1865, J. J. Hilburn, of Bowling Green, Ky.
223, Samuel Tyler, b. 12 July, 1846; d. 17 Dec., 1893; *m.* 5
    Nov., 1878, Sallie Porter. He was town marshal of
    Bowling Green, Ky.
224, Julia Woodbury, b. 2 Jan., 1849; *m.* 11 Dec., 1884, Wil-
    liam R. Carson.
225, Charles Joseph, b. 26 Oct., 1851; *m.* 14 Dec., 1873, Mary
    Z. Harrison.
226, George Bradley, b. 7 Oct., 1853; *m.* 16 Nov., 1882, Fannie
    P. Allen.

101. SAMUEL KIRK VAN METRE (John[1], Henry[2], Isaac[3],
Jacob[4]), son of Jacob and Patsey U. (Shrewsbury) Van Metre,
b. Va., 26 March, 1824; *m.* 5 March, 1860, Cessna J. Sharp.
                                                    Issue:
227, Martha U., b. 28 Feb., 1861; d. 1862; 228, Chas. Clinton,
    b. Sept., 1862.
229, Mary U., b. 1 Oct., 1865; *m.* Dec., 1884, Eugene Miller.
230, William Sharp, b. Sept., 1867; *m.* 2 Sept., 1891, Ella
    McGinnis.

102. CHARLES JOSEPH VAN METRE (John[1], Henry[2], Isaac[3],
Jacob[4]), son of Jacob and Patsey U. (Shrewsbury) Van Metre,
b. at Bowling Green, Ky., 22 May, 1826; *m.* 1 Oct., 1878, Mrs.
Kate (Moss) Overall, of Paducah, Ky. They have no issue.
After spending some years in the management of his father's
plantation, he, in partnership with his elder brother, William,
engaged in steamboating on the Green and Barren Rivers in 1856,
and continued in it until the breaking out of the Civil War in
1861. He then entered the Quartermaster's service of the Confederate States Army and continued in that duty until 1865.
After the close of the war he and his brother William resumed
steamboating, and, in connection with it, engaged in the lumber
business. In 1868 they joined a syndicate known as the Green
and Barren River Navigation Co., and leased from the State of
Kentucky the Green and Barren Rivers—that is, the State's improvements in the way of locks and dams—for thirty years.
Their franchise was sold to the Federal Government some ten
years before the expiration of the lease. In the same year, 1868,
he and his brother purchased Grayson Springs, in Grayson Co.,
and managed it themselves until 1884. Capt. Van Metre is now
residing on a farm near Bowling Green. He is a most estimable
man, hale and hearty, though now in his 83rd year, and kind
and charitable. He has always been a very active man, and no
one stands higher in the community than he does; a man of
sterling character; progressive and public spirited and much in-

CAPT. C. J. VAN METRE

By court sy of the Confederate Veteran.

MRS. E. A. OBENCHAIN

DESCENDANTS OF HENRY VAN METRE

terested in education. About three years ago he was elected Chancellor of the Western State Normal School, which was established in Bowling Green by the Legislature of 1906 (W. A. O.).

103. SARAH FRANCES VAN METRE (John[1], Henry[2], Isaac[3], Jacob[4]), dau. of Jacob and Patsey U. (Shrewsbury) Van Metre, b. 25 Oct., 1828; d. Jan., 1883; m. 14 Jan., 1856, Manoah P. Clarkson.   Issue:
    231, James V. M., b. 14 April, 1858; m. Nannie Clarkson;
        233, Clinton Clay, b. 18 Dec., 1859; d. 18 March, 1864.

110. SARAH ELIZABETH VAN METRE (John[1], Henry[2], Isaac[3], Joseph[4]), dau. of Joseph and Damaris (Lackland) Van Metre, b. Aug., 1829; d. 3 Jan., 1908; m. 6 Jan., 1880, Col. John E. Helms, of Morristown, Tenn., who d. 1906. Mrs. Helms was one of the best known and most successful teachers among the educators of western Virginia. For twenty years—from 1874 to 1894—she was the principal of the primary department of the Marion Female College, at Marion, Smyth Co., Va., and in that capacity had the shaping of the minds of her pupils and the moulding of their character at the most impressionable period of their lives; the result has been of enduring beneficence to them and a lasting honor to Mrs. Helms. Her great power and success are attributed, by a contemporary writer, to those cardinal qualities which she possessed: "her high conscientious conception of her life work; her purity of thought, of speech and of life; devotion to her friends, and in her consecration to her life-work." No issue.

112. ELIZABETH ANN SWEETLAND (John[1], Henry[2], Isaac[3], Sallie H.[4]), dau. of Dr. Eleazer and Sallie H. (Van Metre) Sweetland, b. 12 Sept., 1815; d. 1 July, 1892, in Botetourt Co., Va.; m. 14 Jan., 1840, Thomas Jefferson Obenchain, of Botetourt Co., Va.

VIRGINIA HEROINE, MRS. E. A. OBENCHAIN.

Mrs. Elizabeth Ann Obenchain, of Virginia, in whose veins ran good old Dutch, English and Norman, French Huguenot, and German blood, inherited the excellent qualities, and especially the courage, of her pioneer ancestors.

In the summer of 1864 Gen. Hunter marched with a large force up the Valley of Virginia to attack Lynchburg from the rear. Mrs. Obenchain's two older sons were in the Confederate army. Her husband was on duty with the Home Guard in the fortifications at Lynchburg. Her youngest son, then but fifteen years of age, to save it from capture had ridden to the country a horse she greatly prized, because a gift from her brother, Capt. William A. Sweetland, who was killed the year before at Gettysburg. Her oldest daughter was from home, at school. She was left alone, then, with her five younger children, all girls, ranging in age from four to thirteen years, and the youngest was at the time very ill.

Her eldest son had left at home some six or eight pounds of sporting powder. When Hunter's advance guard appeared on the hills on the

75

opposite side of James River from Buchanan, Mrs. Obenchain, fearing that her house would be searched by Federal soldiers when they entered the town, and wishing to save her son's powder, carried it over to St. John's churchyard, which adjoined her premises, and concealed it under some rank, matted grass near an old tombstone in the rear of the church, where, from the sacredness of the place, she supposed it would be secure.

During the day Federal soldiers had ransacked the house and taken many small articles of value and all her provisions. Later another squad of soldiers appeared at the front door in charge of a sergeant, who informed Mrs. Obenchain that he had orders to burn her house. Recovering quickly from this startling announcement, she calmly replied, "I am helpless, and at your mercy."—While standing in the door with her sick child in her arms pleading with the sergeant for the sake of her children, a Federal officer rode up. On learning the object of the squad he asked the sergeant to do nothing until he could communicate with General Hunter. Galloping at once to headquarters, he succeeded in getting the order countermanded and quickly returned with the welcome news.

The officer gave his name as Alexander and addressed Mrs. Obenchain as "Cousin Lizzie." Whether really related or not is not known. He knew that she had two sons in the Confederate Army. Learning that there were other Federal soldiers in the backyard he went out and ordered them to leave the premises at once.

After seeing that his order was obeyed, he came back into the house, manifested much interest, spoke words of sympathy and assurance, and promised her protection. Shortly after leaving he sent some provisions, and also a surgeon, who prescribed for her sick child and supplied the necessary medicine.

As has been said, Mrs. Obenchain supposed the powder would be safe where she had concealed it in the churchyard. How great, then, was her amazement when, on going out on the back porch at about ten o'clock at night, she saw several fires burning in that part of the churchyard and soldiers lying around them on the grass. She realized the situation at once. "Should fire get to that powder," she thought, "and in the explosion any injury be done, the soldiers, supposing it intentional, would become infuriated and burn the town." The mere thought of being the cause of such a calamity, however innocent, was more than she could bear. Immediately calling her housemaid, she said, pointing to the churchyard: "Hannah, look at those fires over there and the soldiers lying around them; you must go there at once and get that powder away."

"La! Miss Lizzie," said Hannah with a look of terror in her face, "I wouldn't go over dar among dem Yankees for de whole worl'."

"Then I'll go myself," said her mistress, starting at once.

"And I'll go with you," said the faithful Hannah, trembling in every limb.

Followed by the servant, Mrs. Obenchain went out through the garden and crept cautiously up to the dividing fence. Soldiers were stretched out on the ground, here and there, on the other side, fast asleep. Some of the fires were spreading slowly in the grass. Thinking only of what might happen to others, she whispered to the servant to remain where she was, climbed the fence noiselessly, crept lightly among the sleeping forms, secured the powder, and returned safely with it to the house.

When told afterwards that she was in great peril at the time; that if she had been detected when coming out with the powder in her possession, she would have been suspected of attempting to do what she had gone there to prevent, and would doubtless have been subjected to violence she smilingly said: "O, I never once thought of myself."

Like the Roman matrons of old, Mrs. Obenchain was a woman of remarkable fortitude and self-control. If she ever shed a tear when at

DESCENDANTS OF HENRY VAN METRE

any time her sons left home for the field of duty, she took care not to let them see it. It was only when they returned that she wept, as she tenderly threw her arms around them. But her tears then were tears of joy. And yet there was never a more affectionate and devoted mother. Her life was a life of constant solicitude and self-sacrifice for her children. She was ever watchful and patient; and to her repeated lessons, wholesome precepts, and noble example they are mainly indebted for all their higher aspirations.

Mrs. Obenchain was always kind and charitable to others, and ever ready to lend a helping hand in sickness or distress. During the war a hospital was established in her town, Buchanan, Va., for sick and invalid Confederate soldiers. To them she was a minstering angel. When told of a remark made about her by a convalescent soldier as one day he was slowly wending his way to her house to get some delicacy she had promised him—the remark that she was the best woman he had ever met—she modestly said: "I am only doing my duty, trusting in the Lord that some one will do the same for my sons should any misfortune befall them while they are away from home."

> "Kind hearts are more than coronets,
> And simple faith than Norman blood."

That simple faith Mrs. Obenchain had in the highest degree. She did what she could and trusted in the Lord, and in all the trials and troubles of this life her faith remained unshaken to the end.

Broken in health in her last years, she passed away peacefully in Wytheville, Va., July 1, 1892, in the seventy-seventh year of her age,

> "In the great history of the land,
> A noble type of good,
> Heroic womanhood."

Mrs. Obenchain's eldest son, Maj. William A. Obenchain, now President of Ogden College, Bowling Green, Ky., received an appointment in the artillery of the regular Confederate army in 1861, but served throughout the war in the engineer corps. He was promoted in 1864 for "skill and meritorious conduct," and was one of the staff engineers of the Army of Northern Virginia in the last year of the war.

Her second son, Capt. Francis G. Obenchain, now of Chicago, served also throughout the war in the Botetourt (Virginia) Artillery. At Port Gibson on May 1, 1863, this splendid battery of six guns, of which he was then orderly sergeant, was placed in the forefront to be sacrificed, if necessary, in the effort to hold Grant in check. It fired the first gun in that battle, bore the brunt of the engagement the greater part of the day, and suffered heavily in men, horses, and guns. At noon, all the lieutenants present for duty being killed and the captain disabled, the command of the battery devolved upon young Obenchain, then but twenty years of age. The last to leave the field with the two guns that could be brought off, he did excellent service in covering the retreat of the Confederate troops. He was conspicuous throughout the day for coolness and bravery, and was known afterwards in Pemberton's army as "the little fighting sergeant." Soon after he received promotion for "distinguished valor and skill" and commanded the Botetourt Artillery during the siege of Vicksburg. (From the *Confederate Veteran*, Nashville, Tenn., Feb., 1906.)

Issue:

234, William A.; 235, Francis Gardiner; 236, Martha Mary, b. March, 1845; d. 11 March, 1846.

77

237, James Thomas, b. March, 1849; d. 23 June, 1892; *m.* 4
May, 1884, Frances Lou. Collins; 238, Laetitia Ann,
b. 27 June, 1851.

239, Caroline, } *unm.*
240, Margaret S., } twins: b. 14 Oct., 1853; *m.* 20 Sept., 1906,
Nathaniel S. Dickenson, of Russell Co., Va.

241, Alice Virginia, b. 9 March, 1856; *m.* 10 Feb., 1903,
Zachary Taylor Atkins, of Marion, Smyth Co., Va.

242, Lura Borden, b. 13 Aug., 1860; *m.* 22 Dec., 1902, George
Barston Flint, of Anniston Alabama.

243, Florence Maffitt, b. 31 Aug. 1864; d. 31 May, 1881.

113. MARY HESTER SWEETLAND (John[1], Henry[2], Isaac[3], Sallie
H.[4]), dau. of Dr. Eleazer and Sallie H. (Van Metre) Sweetland,
b. 14 Sept., 1816; d. 30 June, 1846; *m.* 1 March, 1837, George
Walter Strickland.   Issue:
244, William E., b. 22 Feb., 1839; *m.* 23 Aug., 1863, Margaret
Rebecca Chinn.

245, Sallie Ann, b. 4 May, 1842; *m.* 5 June, 1862, Peter B.
Riffe.

246, Mary G., b. 1843; d. 17 April, 1870; *m.* 28 Oct., 1869,
Nash J. Evans.

115. SAMUEL MCFERRAN SWEETLAND (John[1], Henry[2], Isaac[3],
Sallie H.[4]), son of Dr. Eleazer and Sallie H. (Van Metre) Sweetland, b. 3 Feb., 1820; d. 17 April, 1856; *m.* 1st Martha V. Abernathy; *m.* 2d Mary Jane Abernathy.   Issue:
247, Venetia, b. 19 Aug., 1849; d. 27 Jan., 1850.

248, Samuel R., b. 15 Sept., 1856; *m.* 18 Dec., 1879, Maggie
Lowe, of Giles Co., Tenn.

117. ISAAC V. M. SWEETLAND (John[1], Henry[2], Isaac[3], Sallie
H.[4]), son of Dr. Eleazer and Sallie H. (Van Metre) Sweetland,
b. 24 April, 1826(?); *m.* 2d June, 1844, Martha Russell.   Issue:
249, John S., b. 20 April, 1846; 250, Mary H., b. 30 June,
1847; *m.* 18 March, 1846, T. A. Love.

251, Anne H., b. 11 July, 1848; *m.* March, 1870, William C.
Wiley.

252, Chas. R., b. 30 Jan., 1850; d. 17 March, 1850; 253, Elizabeth O., b. 21 March, 1851; *m.* 1873, James Hill; 254,
Maggie P., b. 22 Oct., 1855; *m.* 1874, Thos. J. Haile.

255, Carrie, V. M., b. 3 June, 1857; d. Sept., 1871; 256, Louis
R., b. 14 Feb., 1859.

257, Martha W., b. 11 Jan., 1861; *m.* Dec., 1886, Dr. Silas W.
Oxley.

258, Virginia W., b. 3 Aug., 1862; *m.* Feb., 1883, L. M.
Sanford.

259, Sallie R., b. 27 July, 1867.

DESCENDANTS OF HENRY VAN METRE

120. SALLIE E. SWEETLAND (John[1], Henry[2], Isaac[3], Sallie H.[4]), dau. of Dr. Eleazer and Sallie H. (Van Metre) Sweetland, b. 16 June, 1831; m. 25 April, 1861, Luke Powell.   Issue: 260, Henry, b. 21 Jan., 1862; 261, Mary, b. Feb., 1864; m. ―― Foster; 262, Lucy, b. 11 Jan., 1866; 263, Lilly, b. 5 Nov., 1867; 264, Luke, b. 15 May, 1873.

121. JAMES OTIS SWEETLAND (John[1], Henry[2], Isaac[3], Sallie H.[4]), son of Dr. Eleazer and Sallie H. (Van Metre) Sweetland, b. 14 June, 1833; m. 3 Jan., 1856, Martha V. Scott. James O. Sweetland was a member of the California Legislature.   Issue: 265, Jefferson D., b. 11 Febr., 1857; d. 16 June, 1857.
266, Laura V., b. 17 March, 1858; m. 31 Oct., 1875, Stephen R. Heath.
267, George Lee, b. 10 March, 1861; 268, Carrie, b. 20 Nov., 1864; d. 8 Feb., 1870.
269, Henry P., and 270, William A., twins, b. 13 June, 1866; Henry P. d. 5 March, 1885.
271, Laurence G., b. 9 July, 1871.

122. CAROLINE SWEETLAND (John[1], Henry[2], Isaac[3], Sallie H.[4]), dau. of Dr. Eleazer and Sallie H. (Van Metre) Sweetland, b. 12 Feb., 1835; d. 20 Oct., 1890; m. 26 Jan., 1860, Sylvanus H. Walcott.   Issue:
272, William L., b. 26 Dec., 1860; 273, Albert S., b. 6 Sept., 1863; d. 14 May, 1875.
273, Viola L., b. 29 June, 1865; m. 18 Feb., 1890, Martin B. Wilson.
274, Mattie W., b. 15 Sept., 1867; d. 29 Jan., 1890; m. 18 Jan., 1888, Emery W. Foreman.
275, Lura D., b. Dec., 1869; d. 25 Feb., 1870; 276, Alanson H., b. 26 July, 1872.
277, Ella V., b. 27 May, 1875.

123. MARGARET SWEETLAND (John[1], Henry[2], Isaac[3], Sallie H.[4]), dau. of Dr. Eleazer and Sallie H. (Van Metre) Sweetland, b. 17 Aug., 1837; m. 25 March, 1862, J. N. Powell.   Issue: 278, Charles E., b. 5 Dec., 1864; 279, Anna F., b. 2 July, 1866; m. 15 Jan., 1899, E. E. Chrisman; 280, Minnie B., b. 30 Sept., 1868; 281, Carrie E., b. 5 Aug., 1871.

137. AMANDA OWSLEY (John[1], Henry[2], Ruth[3], Elizabeth[4]), dau. of William and Elizabeth (Gill) Owsley, m. Clifton Rodes   Issue:
282, Robert, b. circa 1824.

157. OLIVER H. P. VAN METRE (John[1], Henry[2], Henry, Jr.[3]. Absalom[4], Reazin[5]), son of Reazin and ―― Van Metre, b. Mason Co., Va., circa 1818; m. Miriam Sayre.   Issue:
283, David S., who was an Attorney-at-Law, Parkersburg, W. Va.

79

THE VAN METRE GENEALOGY

164. DAVID DAVIS (John[1], Henry[2], Henry[3], Alice[4], William[5]), son of William and Lydia (Fields) Davis, b. Greene Co., Pa., 1809; d. 1882; *m.* Mary Coon. He served as 2d Lieut. in the Mexican War. Lived in Spencer Co., Indiana.   Issue.
284, William, b. 1828; *m.* 1st Dorcas McIntire; *m.* 2d Emma Egloff.
285, Frank, b. 1830; *m.* Ophelia Jones. Lives Clermont Co., Ohio.
286, Caroline, b. 1834; *m.* 1st Thos. McCoy; *m.* 2d John M. Jones.
287, Mary, b. 1839; *m.* Merion Jackson. Lives Spencer Co., Indiana.
288, Stephen, b. 1843; *m.* Emma Chase. Lives Warrick Co., Indiana.
289, Sydney, b. 1848; *m.* Adam Baum. Lives Spencer Co., Indiana.
290, John, b. *circa* 1852; *m.* 1st Orvilla McCoy; *m.* 2d Americus Turner.

165. SYDNEY DAVIS (John[1], Henry[2], Henry, Jr.[3], Alice[4], William[5]), dau. of William and Lydia (Fields) Davis, b. 1811; *m.* Benjamin Stites.   Issue:
291, Benton, *m.* Desdemonia Doolittle; 292, Olive, *m.* James Romine; 293, Emma, *m.* —— Johnson; 294, John, *m.* Elizabeth Johnson; 295, George.

166. LYDIA DAVIS (John[1], Henry[2], Henry, Jr.[3], Alice[4], William[5]), dau. of William and Lydia (Fields) Davis, b. 16 Feb., 1815; d. 8 Jan., 1878; *m.* George Nichols, b. 18 Sept., 1817; d. 2 Sept., 1905. They lived in Clermont Co., Ohio.   Issue:
296, Sydney Olive, b. 12 Jan., 1848; d. 28 Sept., 1906; *m.* —— ——.

167. AZARIAH DAVIS (John[1], Henry[2], Henry[3], Alice[4], William[5]), son of William and Lydia (Fields) Davis, b. 23 July, 1817; d. 8 Aug., 1876; *m.* 26 Nov., 1843, Ruth Patton, b. 3 March, 1823; d. 1 Nov., 1901.   Issue:
297, Lucien M., b. 24 April, 1845; *m.* 19 Oct., 1875, Miss Whitaker. He is a Methodist minister, living in Clermont Co., Ohio.
298, John W., b. 20 April, 1847; d. *unm.* 1889. Was a physician.
299, Alonza A., b. 13 Jan., 1850; d. 1852; 300, Wm. C., b. 29 Aug., 1852; d. 17 May, 1897.
301, Emma E., b. 27 Jan., 1855; 302, George W., b. 9 March, 1858.
303, Charles W., b. 18 June, 1862; 304, Edward C., b. 6 June, 1864.
305, Lillie M., b. 6 April, 1867; 306, Albert L., b. 2 Oct., 1869.

168. MARY ANN DAVIS (John[1], Henry[2], Henry, Jr.[3], Alice[4], William[5]), dau. of William and Lydia (Fields) Davis, b. 26 March, 1818; d. 20 Oct., 1886; m. 18 Oct., 1836, William B. Dunham, of Hamilton Co., O.; b. 8 Aug., 1811; d. 16 Feb., 1897. Issue:
307, Mary Drusilla, b. 14 Aug., 1837; d. 24 Sept., 1904; m. circa 1856, Samuel Pury.
308, W. Edwin, b. 12 Nov., 1843; d. 1 March, 1898; m. 12 Sept., 1866, —— ——.
309, Lydia, b. 26 Jan., 1850; m. —— Clark.

169. GEORGE DAVIS (John[1], Henry[2], Henry, Jr.[3], Alice[4], William[5]), son of William and Lydia (Fields) Davis, m. 1st Pauline Baldwin; m. 2d Phoebe Griffiths. Issue:
310, William, m. —— Dunham; 311, Sydnia, m. West Griffiths; 312, Viola; 313, George, m. Orvilla Crow.

170. STEPHEN DAVIS (John[1], Henry[2], Henry, Jr.[3], Alice[4], William[5]), son of William and Lydia (Fields) Davis, b. Hamilton Co., O., 1822; d. Chrisney, Spencer Co., Ind., 1882; m. 1846, Nancy Patton, b. 1824, the daughter of James Patton, of Brown Co., Ohio. Stephen Davis served in the Civil War. Issue:
314, Lydia; 315, Emma; 316, George, b. 1856, m. Sarah Wise; 317, Stephen.

171. JOHN DAVIS (John[1], Henry[2], Henry, Jr.[3], Alice[4], William[5]), son of William and Lydia (Fields) Davis, b. 1824; m. Calista Ward, of Withamsville, O. John Davis served as a captain in the Union army during the Civil War. Issue:
319, Nettie; 320, Arabell; 321, Fremont; all m. and living in Spencer Co., Ind.

172. AMANDA DAVIS (John[1], Henry[2], Henry, Jr.[3], Alice[4], William[5]), dau. of William and Lydia (Fields) Davis, b. 1826; m. Jonathan Pancoast; resided at El Paso, Tex. Issue:
322, Endora; living at El Paso, Tex.

173. WILLIAM DAVIS (John[1], Henry[2], Henry, Jr.[3], Alice[4], William[5]), son of William and Lydia (Fields) Davis, b. Hamilton Co., O., 1829; d. Cincinnati, O., 1896; m. Elizabeth Hahn, of Newtown, Hamilton Co., O. Issue:
323, Florence, b. 1850; m. Pharoah Chrisney, b. Alsace, France; brother of the founder of Chrisney, Spencer Co., Ind., John B. Chrisney.
324, Stephen C., b. 1853; d. 1894; m. 1874, Kitty Odour, who d. 1890.

178. AZARIAH SMITH (John[1], Henry[2], Henry, Jr.[3], Alice[4], Martha[5]), son of James H. and Martha (Davis) Smith, b. Greene Co., Pa., 20 Jan., 1805; d. 1847; m. 6 Oct., 1825, Charity Jewel, who d. 1880. They removed to Putnam Co., O., 1836. Issue:
325, Cornelia; 326, James; 327, William; 328, John Julian; 329, Leonidas; 330, Pheobe; 331, Leander.

179. BENJAMIN SMITH (John[1], Henry[2], Henry, Jr.[3], Alice[4], Martha[5]), son of James H. and Martha (Davis) Smith, b. Greene Co., Pa., 27 Jan., 1807; d. 9 March, 1900; m. 1833, Martha Brown, a native of Virginia; b. 4 March, 1809; d. 26 Sept., 1870. Benjamin Smith entered the last 125 acres of government land in Morgan Township, Knox Co., O. In his boyhood he attended school in a log cabin near his home; it had seats made of slabs, greased papers for windows and clay floor.   Issue:
332, Martha Jane, b. 31 March, 1834; d. 1855; 333, Sarah Ann, b. 16 Oct., 1836.

182. SARAH ANN SMITH (John[1], Henry[2], Henry, Jr.[3], Alice[4], Martha[5]), dau. of James H. and Martha (Davis) Smith, b. Knox Co., O., 5 Feb., 1814; d. 23 Feb., 1901; m. 4 Feb., 1841, John Wesley McCune, d. 14 June, 1892. They moved to Illinois in 1852, and in a few years later to Iowa, where they buried four children; the widow then returned in 1893 to Knox Co., O. Issue:
344, James H.; 335, Margaret R.; 336, Charles; 337, Henry; 338, Alexander; 339, Ettwina.

183. REBECCA SMITH (John[1], Henry[2], Henry, Jr.[3], Alice[4], Martha[5]), dau. of James H. and Martha (Davis) Smith, b. Knox Co., O., 28 Jan., 1816; d. 13 Nov., 1883; m. 26 Nov., 1844, Henry Crumley, who d. 188–; they lived in Van Wert Co., O.   Issue:
340, Oscar, m., lives in Defiance, O.; issue four children.
341, Sarah, m. —— Fair, lives at Rose City, Mich.; issue four children.
342, Margaret, m. —— Eagy, lives in Van Wert Co., O.   Issue three children.

184. JAMES H. SMITH (John[1], Henry[2], Henry, Jr.[3], Alice[4], Martha[5]), son of James H. and Martha (Davis) Smith, b. Knox Co., O., 28 Aug., 1818; m. April, 1844, Harriet Todd, of Putnam Co., O., where he went to reside in 1842. He held a number of county offices of honor and trust.   Issue:
343, Lafayette N.; 344, Louisa M.; 345, Kossouth; 346, Julia R.; 347, Annie C.; 348, Jefferson D. The three sisters live in Ottawa, O.

185. HENRY D. SMITH (John[1], Henry[2], Henry, Jr.[3], Alice[4], Martha[5]), son of James H. and Martha (Davis) Smith, b. Knox Co., O., 6 Dec., 1820; d. on the old Smith homestead, 1 June, 1887; m. 1848, Sarah McVey, who d. 14 Jan., 1854.   Issue:
349, Martha A.; 350, an infant b. 7 Jan., 1854; d. Jan., 1854. He m. 2d 30 Dec., 1858, Hannah Harris, b. 27 Sept., 1837; d. 30 Dec., 1893.
351, Elza H.; 352, Emma V.; 354, B. Franklin, b. 10 Jan., 1862; 355, S. Caroline; 356, George M.; 357, Rees, d. inf.; 358, Mary A.

DESCENDANTS OF HENRY VAN METRE

186. RACHAEL SMITH (John[1], Henry[2], Henry, Jr.[3], Alice[4], Martha[5]), dau. of James H. and Martha (Davis) Smith, b. Knox Co., O., 16 April, 1823; d. near Carthage, Mo., 1872; m. 1845, Newton McVey, who d. Carthage, 1904.   Issue:
359, Margaret; 360, Adaline; 361, Vorhees; 362, Rees Oscar; 363, Florence; 364, Flora; 365, Caroline, d. inf.

187. CAROLINE CAMPNET SMITH (John[1], Henry[2], Henry, Jr.[3], Alice[4], Martha[5]), dau. of James H. and Martha (Davis) Smith, b. Knox Co., O., 8 April, 1826; d. 16 March, 1906; m. 24 Oct., 1844, in Morgan Township, O., John James Tulloss, b. 11 Sept., 1820; d. 15 April, 1903. For sixty years this couple lived on their farm, located four miles northwest of Utica, O. Both received their early education in the subscription schools held in log cabins; both were members of the primitive Baptist Church and both were buried in Fairview Cemetery, not far from their old home.   Issue:
366, Emily, b. 1 Aug., 1845; d. 23 Oct., 1861; 367, Byram L.
368, John James, b. 27 Sept., 1848; d. 3 April, 1879; taught school at St. James, Nebraska, from 1874–1877.
369, Rees P.; 370, George W.; 371, Cynthia A., b. 3 April, 1858.
372, Caroline C., b. 22 Aug., 1861. These two sisters are both living in the old Tulloss homestead near Utica, a family home for ninety-seven years.
373, Benjamin F., b. 3 Oct., 1854, residing at Uralda, Veralda Co., Tex., 19 Sept., 1881. He went to Texas in 1877 and there taught schools in different towns of that State.

188. REES SMITH (John[1], Henry[2], Henry, Jr.[3], Alice[4], Martha[5]), son of James H. and Martha (Davis) Smith, b. 1 Dec., 1828; murdered by Mexicans in Arizona Territory in 1871; m. Alice Fly, a Spanish woman. Rees emigrated to California in 1849; represented California in State Legislature.   Issue:
374, Cornelia; 375, Camilious Rees; both lived in Nappa City, Cal., 1871.

189. AZARIAH HANGER (John[1], Henry[2], Henry, Jr.[3], Alice[4], Rebecca[5]), son of Jacob and Rebecca (Davis) Hanger, m. ——
——; died at age of 77 years.   Issue:
376, Elza; 377, Sarah Bell.

191. ANDREW HANGER (John[1], Henry[2], Henry, Jr.[3], Alice[4], Rebecca[5]), son of Jacob and Rebecca (Davis) Hanger, m. ——
——; had nine children and at age 74 years he was a minister of the Christian denomination.

192. JACKSON HANGER (John[1], Henry[2], Henry, Jr.[3], Alice[4], Rebecca[5]), son of Jacob and Rebecca (Davis) Hanger, m. ——
——; d. 1907 in Tennessee at home of his daughter, at the age of 76 (b. 1831). Had two children.

193. JACOB HANGER (John[1], Henry[2], Henry, Jr.[3], Alice[4], Rebecca[5]), son of Jacob and Rebecca (Davis) Hanger, *m.* ——; had nine children; d. in Illinois, aged 77. He also was a minister of the Christian denomination.

194. MARY HANGER (John[1], Henry[2], Henry, Jr.[3], Alice[4], Rebecca[5]), dau. of Jacob and Rebecca (Davis) Hanger, *m.* —— ——; had five children; d. in Iowa, aged 45 years.

198. SARAH HANGER (John[1], Henry[2], Henry, Jr.[3], Alice[4], Rebecca[5]), dau. of Jacob and Rebecca (Davis) Hanger, *m.* Elza Harris; d. 24 Sept., 1888.   Issue:
    378, Jacob; 379, Morgan; 380, Jackson; 381, Mary, *unm.*; 382, Elizabeth; 383, Rebecca.

199. HARRIET HANGER (John[1], Henry[2], Henry, Jr.[3], Alice[4], Rebecca[5]), dau. of Jacob and Rebecca (Davis) Hanger, d. in Illinois, aged 40 years; *m.* Daniel Boyd.   Issue:
    384, Mary; 385, Rebecca.

204. JOHN MILLER (John[1], Henry[2], Henry, Jr.[3], Alice[4], Sarah[5]), son of George and Sarah (Davis) Miller, b. 1 Sept., 1810; d. 11 Feb., 1884; *m.* 23 Feb., 1832, Cornelia Clutter; *m.* 2d 23 April, 1848, Elizabeth Helphrey, b. 23 May, 1827; d. 10 Feb., 1896.   Issue:
    384, William, b. 5 April, 1833; *m.* 1st Melissa King; *m.* 2d Mary Paul.
    385, Cinderella; 386, Rachael; 387, Calvin, b. 17 Jan., 1839; *m.* Elizabeth McClelland; 388, Charles; 389, John Franklin; 390, Mary Elsie; 391, Emma Alice; 392, Ira V.; 393, Lillian C.; 394, Ella, b. 5 April, 1866; *m.* 26 March, 1889, Charles S. Johnson, b. 22 Sept., 1864; no issue.

234. WILLIAM ALEXANDER OBENCHAIN (John[1], Henry[2], Isaac[3], Sallie H.[4], Elizabeth Ann[5]), eldest son of Thomas Jefferson and Elizabeth Ann (Sweetland) Obenchain, was born in Buchanan, Va., 27 April, 1841; *m.* 8 July, 1885, Eliza Hall Calvert, of Bowling Green, Ky., dau. of Thomas Chalmers and Margaret (Younglove) Calvert, and a descendant of James Hall, Scotch-Irish, who, on emigrating to America, settled in Derry, now Londonderry, Township, Dauphin Co., Pa., in the first quarter of the eighteenth century and moved with his family to Iredell County, North Carolina, in 1751. Mrs. Obenchain is the gifted writer of many poems, essays and short stories, which have appeared from time to time in leading magazines and is the author of "Aunt Jane of Kentucky," the exceptional merit of which attracted the attention and received the commendation of President Roosevelt. This book, depicting the quaintness and simplicity of character in certain phases of life in rural Kentucky, became at once widely popular and reached its fourteenth edition almost within two years of its publication. Copies of it have been printed in Braille for the use of the blind. Mrs. Obenchain

MAJOR W. A. OBENCHAIN

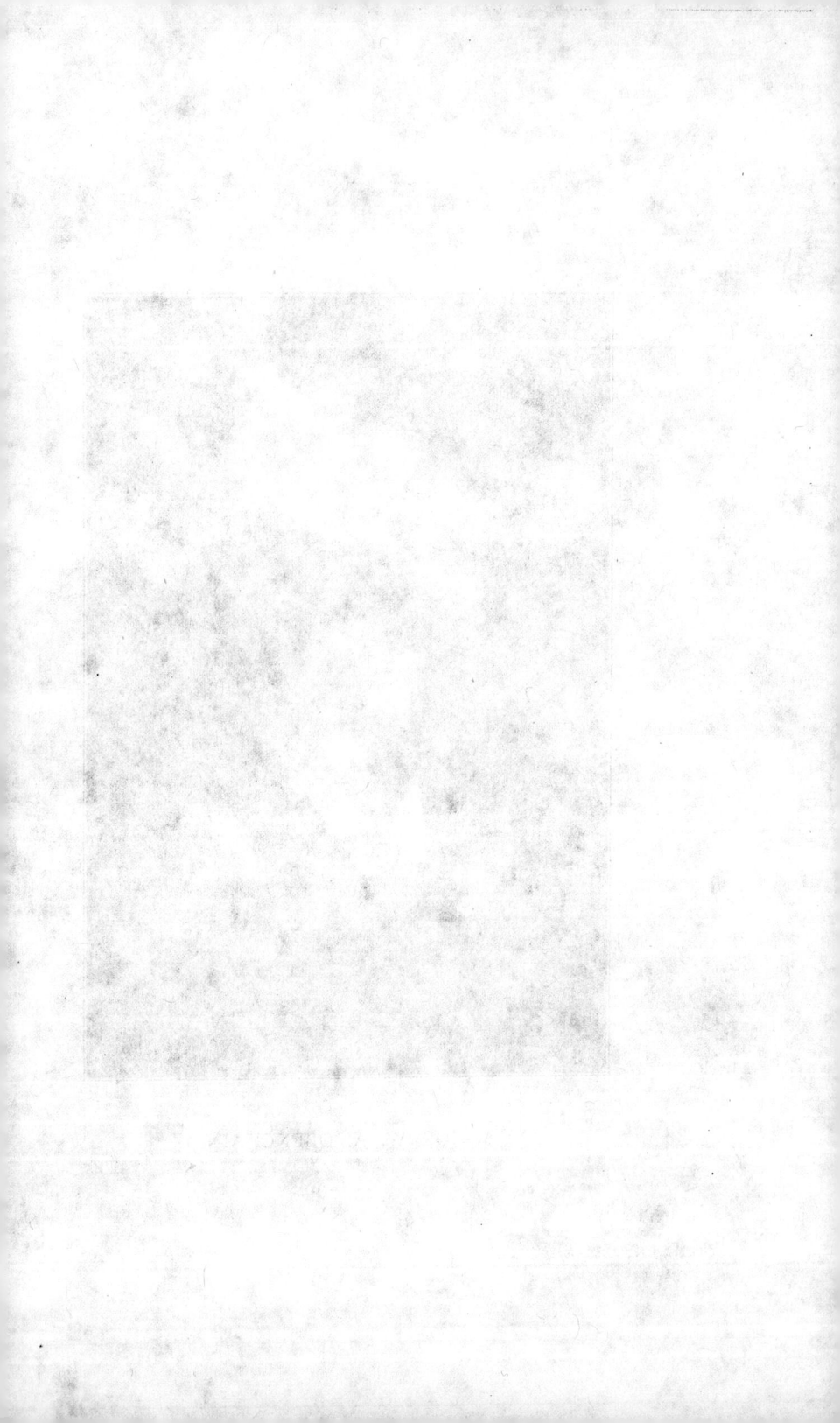

is prominent also in the equal rights and suffrage movements for women and has written and published, over her real name, many able and trenchant articles on these subjects. The father of W. A. Obenchain was of German and Welsh ancestry and a prominent and successful merchant up to 1861; was a man of great native ability and lofty character, commanding in appearance, pleasing in address, and of sterling integrity, which he preserved to the last. He was possessed of a fine judicial mind and actuated by a high sense of duty and he had the courage of his convictions with the firmness of an old Roman. As an official of the old Virginia type "he dignified the position of magistrate for more than a quarter of a century. His decisions were characteristic for their justice and equity to all litigants; and by his honesty and devotion to duty and his zeal in the enforcement of the laws, his reputation extended even beyond his own State." His was one of those rare cases in which the office seeks the man. Such was the esteem in which he was held by men of all political opinions, both as an official and as a man, and such was his popularity that even in his old age, and against his wishes, he was continually re-elected to office, and he died suddenly, in 1895, in Wytheville, Va., at the age of 81, while still in the harness. He was buried with Masonic honors, having been a member of that order for more than forty years. Major W. A. Obenchain graduated with the highest honors in his class at the Virginia Military Institute in 1861; was appointed second lieutenant of artillery in the regular army of the Confederate States, but was soon after transferred to the engineer corps, in which he served with distinction throughout the war. He was promoted captain for "skill and meritorious conduct" in 1864, and was one of the staff engineers of the Army of Northern Virginia the last year of the war. He was professor of mathematics and engineering in the Hillsboro (N. C.) Military Academy, 1866–1868; professor of mathematics and commandant of cadets in the Western Military Academy at New Castle, Ky., under Gen. E. Kirby Smith, 1868–70; professor of modern languages and commandant of cadets in the University of Nashville, 1870–1873; was elected professor of mathematics in Ogden College, Bowling Green, Ky., in 1878, and president of that institution in 1883. He ranks high as an educator, has been the recipient of many educational honors and has been elected a member of many learned and scientific societies. Issue:

395, Margery, b. 19 Sept., 1886; 396, Wm. Alexander, b. 21 Sept., 1888; 397, Florence Hall, b. 2 Nov., 1891; 398, Cecelia Calvert, b. 25 March, 1895.

235. FRANCIS GARDINER OBENCHAIN (John[1], Henry[2], Isaac[3], Sallie H.[4], Elizabeth A.[5]), second son of Thomas Jefferson and Elizabeth Ann (Sweetland) Obenchain, b. Buchanan, Va., 15

Feb., 1843; *m.* 25 Nov., 1875, Anna L. Brown, youngest daughter of Col. A. S. Brown, of Memphis, Tenn. Captain Obenchain made a good record in the private school of Wm. R. Galt, one of the ablest teachers in Virginia, but his education was cut short by the breaking out of the war. He immediately entered the Confederate service, at the age of 18, and served throughout the war. At the battle of Port Gibson, May 1, 1863, the splendid battery of six guns, the Botetourt (Virginia) Artillery, of which he was the orderly sergeant, was placed in the forefront, to be sacrificed, if necessary, in the effort to hold Grant in check. This battery fired the first gun in the battle about daylight, and soon attracted upon it the concentrated fire of two or more Federal batteries. It bore the brunt of the engagement, and, being in an exposed position, lost heavily in men, guns and horses. At noon all the lieutenants present for duty being killed and the captain disabled, the command of the battery devolved upon young Obenchain, then but twenty years of age. He was the last of his command to leave the field, late in the afternoon, and with two guns, all that could be brought off, he rendered excellent service in covering the retreat of the Confederate troops. He was conspicuous throughout the day for coolness and bravery, and was afterwards known in Pemberton's army as "the little fighting sergeant." He soon received promotion for "distinguished valor and skill," and commanded a force of infantry and artillery during the siege of Vicksburg. Such was his reputation for coolness and bravery, that, when a Federal gunboat grounded close to the shore near Vicksburg and it was decided to make an attempt to capture it at night, he was selected to command the attacking force. "In the early part of June, 1863, one of the Federal gunboats ran aground at shore on the east side of the Mississippi River, and at a point southeast of my part of the line of defense. The river bottom was quite wide then and covered with a dense growth of trees. On the fifth of June I received orders to make preparations to capture the vessel that night; and that I would be supported by Major W. H. Halsey, with part of the 42d Georgia Infantry. Major Halsey bore a reputation for bravery and coolness. At that time the enemy had possession of that part of the river bottom, but in what manner we had no means of knowing. All my men knew the conditions, and I could already see that at heart some of them did not relish the idea. My instructions were, if successful in capturing the vessel, to man it and fight it for all it was worth in destroying the vessels of the enemy! About sundown the gunboat succeeded in getting afloat and steaming away, making it impossible to capture her." He is a man of considerable culture, strong convictions and great force of character and has for many years been a broker in Chicago.　　　　Issue:

399, Jeannette Brown, b. 22 Aug., 1876; Fellow in Anthropology in the Chicago University, and member of the Phi Beta Kappa Fraternity.

400, Elizabeth Sweetland, b. 15 Aug., 1878; 401, Fannie Maude, b. 16 Jan., 1881; m. 26 Nov., 1902, John Cocke Abernathy, of Miami, Florida; 402, Alexandra Borden, b. 28 April, 1885.

237. JAMES THOMAS OBENCHAIN (John[1], Henry[2], Isaac[3], Sallie H.[4], Elizabeth A.[5]), third and youngest son of Thomas Jefferson and Elizabeth Ann (Sweetland) Obenchain, b. in Buchanan, Va., 8 March, 1849; d. Nashville, Tenn., 23 June, 1893; m. 4 May, 1884, Frances Lou Collins, of Nashville, Tenn. The war between the States beginning when he was but twelve years of age, his education was limited, but he had a native ability, a strong character and a winning manner. Though modest and unassuming, he possessed some of the elements of leadership, and had always at heart the good of his fellow-man. He was the promoter and one of the three founders of an association of retail clerks in Nashville, Tenn., known as the Retail Clerks' Union, which brought about their emancipation from long and trying hours of service. Prior to that time these clerks were required to be on duty from early in the morning until half-past ten and eleven o'clock at night. This organization compelled the proprietors to close their stores not later than seven in the evening. In recognition of his services he was elected vice-president of the union at its organization, and he held that position until his death. In May, 1875, while living in Dallas, Texas, he was shot in the breast and dangerously wounded by a drunken desperado, without any provocation whatever, while sitting on the front steps of his boarding house. The bullet could not be extracted, but his life was finally saved; it is doubtful, however, if he ever fully recovered from the effects of the wound. He died lamented by all who knew him. No issue.

283. DAVID SAMUEL VAN METRE (John[1], Henry[2], Henry, Jr.[3], Absalom[4], Rezin[5], Oliver H. P.[6]), son of Oliver Hazard Perry and Miriam (Sayre) Van Metre, b. 1849; m. 1878, —— Hoover. D. S. Van Metre was a lawyer, living in Parkersburg, W. Va.

He had a son: George Van Metre, painter, 201 Dorgenois Street, New Orleans, La., b. 1879, at Point Pleasant, W. Va. He left home in 1898, enlisted in the United States Army and was stationed at Jackson Barracks, near New Orleans; afterwards served in Cuba.

Brothers and sisters of David Samuel Van Metre and children of Oliver H. P. Van Metre, were:

a. William C., m. —— Crumb; resides Washington, D. C.

b. Oliver, m. —— Stuart; resides in Missouri.

c. Abner, m. Sarah Collins; resides Point Pleasant, W. Va.

d. Daniel W., *m.* —— Yeager; resides Point Pleasant, W. Va.
e. Ellen, resides Point Pleasant, W. Va.
f. Catharine, resides Point Pleasant, W. Va.
h. Anna, resides Middleport, O.

NOTE: My correspondent relates the story of a David Van Metre who lived about Middleport, O., who was then at the age of 105 years. Also tells of a Hoot Van Metre residing near Middleport, O., who in 1884 or 1885 was then 107 years of age and saw him pitch a sheaf of wheat to the thresher, though he had to be helped up to the wheat stack and taken down again after this performance. This man resembled an Indian in appearance and characteristics.

314. LYDIA DAVIS (John[1], Henry[2], Henry, Jr.[3], Alice[4], William[5], Stephen[6]), dau. of Stephen and Nancy (Patton) Davis, b. 1847; *m.* 1866, Isaac Strode. Issue:
  403, William, b. 1867; *m.* 1st Clara Lee; *m.* 2d Nellie Earl.
  404, Flora, b. 1869; *m.* Chas. Bays; 405, Etta, b. 1876; *m.* Rev. Ulysses Hartley, of Chrisney, Ind.; 406, John, b. 1881; *m.* Lily Doss, of Christian Co., Ky.

315. EMMA DAVIS (John[1], Henry[2], Henry, Jr.[3], Alice[4], William[5], Stephen[6]), dau. of Stephen and Nancy (Patton) Davis, *m.* Joseph Stoats. Issue:
  407, Mary Eva, b. 1870; *m.* Joseph Fella; 408, Nancy Josephine, *m.* Cornelius Harris, of Chrisney, Ind.

317. STEPHEN DAVIS (John[1], Henry[2], Henry, Jr.[3], Alice[4], William[5], Stephen[6]), son of Stephen and Nancy (Patton) Davis, *m.* 1st Addie Witherholt; *m.* 2d Martha Cockerell. Issue:
  409, Nancy Cockerell, *m.* Chas. Putnam; 410, Minnie, *m.* John Denton.

324. STEPHEN C. DAVIS (John[1], Henry[2], Henry, Jr.[3], Alice[4], William[5], William[6]), son of William and Elizabeth (Hahn) Davis, b. 1853; d. 1894; *m.* 1874, Kitty Odour, who d. 1890. Issue:
  411, Clarence, b. 1878, at Cincinnati, O.; resides in Oregon.
  412, Florence, b. Cincinnati, O., 1880; *m.* 1903, Meredith Sharp, of Central City, Ky.; he is a veteran of the Spanish-American War; resides Terre Haute, Ind.

328. JOHN JULIAN SMITH (John[1], Henry[2], Henry, Jr.[3], Alice[4], Martha[5], Azariah[6]), son of Azariah and Charity (Jewel) Smith, b. Knox Co., O., 9 Aug., 1830; *m.* 6 April, 1854, Mary Ann Nagle, of Putnam Co. They returned to Iowa in 1864. Issue:
  413, Melvina B.; 414, Mina; 415, Belle.

334. JAMES HARRINGTON McCUNE (John[1], Henry[2], Henry, Jr.[3], Alice[4], Martha[5], Sarah A.[6]), son of John Wesley and Sarah Ann (Smith) McCune, b. Knox Co., O., 1843; d. 7 April, 1892; *m.* 24 March, 1869, Mrs. Mary G. (Edwards) Ruble. He was a

soldier in the Civil War; was confined ten months in a Southern military prison at Camp Ford. Issue:
416, Alice Josephine.

335. MARGARET RACHAEL McCUNE (John[1], Henry[2], Henry, Jr.[3], Alice[4], Martha[5], Sarah A.[6]), dau. of John Wesley and Sarah Ann (Smith) McCune, b. 23 March, 1845; d. 14 Dec., 1884; m. 20 Aug., 1879, Charles E. Thompson. They reside at Woodburn, Iowa. Issue:
417, John Henry; 418, Merle Edward, b. 23 Aug., 1882; living in Minneapolis, Minn.

343. LAFAYETTE N. SMITH (John[1], Henry[2], Henry, Jr.[3], Alice[4], Martha[5], James H.[6]), son of James H. and Harriet (Todd) Smith, b. Oct., 1849; d. 19 Feb., 1905; m. Mary Rogers, of Toledo, O. Issue:
419, Bessie; 420, Carice; 421, Charles H.

348. JEFFERSON D. SMITH (John[1], Henry[2], Henry, Jr.[3], Alice[4], Martha[5], James H.[6]), son of James H. and Harriet (Todd) Smith; m. 1889, Mary Bone. They reside near Homer, O. Issue:
422, Earl; 423, Mable; 424, Harry; 425, Pearl; 426, John; 427, Floyd.

349. MARTHA A. SMITH (John[1], Henry[2], Henry, Jr.[3], Alice[4], Martha[5], Henry D.[6]), dau. of Henry D. and Sarah (McVoy) Smith, b. 14 Aug., 1850; m. 16 Dec., 1869, Wm. Spencer Eagle. They reside near Newark, O. Issue:
428, Ella M.; 429, Charles O.; 430, Daisey D., b. 11 June, 1875; m. 28 Nov., 1901, Clinton N. Bernhardt, of Columbus, O. Issue:
431, Bessie, b. 14 Aug., 1877; d. 20 Sept., 1877; 432, Roy Spencer, b. 9 May, 1890.

351. ELZA H. SMITH (John[1], Henry[2], Henry, Jr.[3], Alice[4], Martha[5], Henry D.[6]), son of Henry D. and Sarah (McVey) Smith, b. 10 Dec., 1859; m. 1892, Jenny Earlwine. They reside at Mansfield, O. Issue:
433, Basil; 434, Overna; 435, Guy; 436, Paul; 437, Susan; 438, Isaac; 439, a child.

352. EMMA V. SMITH (John[1], Henry[2], Henry, Jr.[3], Alice[4], Martha[5], Henry D.[6]), dau. of Henry D. and Sarah (McVey) Smith, b. 12 Jan., 1861; m. 1st Benjamin Clampet; m. 2d Mr. Hieronymus. Reside Monett, Mo.
440, Mary.

355. S. CAROLINE SMITH (John[1], Henry[2], Henry, Jr.[3], Alice[4], Martha[5], Henry D.[6]), dau. of Henry D. and Sarah (McVey) Smith, b. 29 Jan., 1863; m. 29 Jan., 1886, David Geisick; he d. March, 1892; m. 2d George Williams; he d. 1907. Widow lives in Denver, Colo. Issue:

441, Henry L., b. 1887; d. 1889; 442, Emma F.; 443, Mable H., d. 1890.

358. MARY A. SMITH (John[1], Henry[2], Henry, Jr.[3], Alice[4], Martha[5], Henry D.[6]), dau. of Henry D. and Sarah (McVey) Smith, b. 27 March, 1873; *m.* 1st Thomas Wright; *m.* 2d A. A. LaValle, deceased. Widow lives in Denver, Colo. Issue: 444, Marie.

360. ADELAIDE McVEY (John[1], Henry[2], Henry, Jr.[3], Alice[4], Martha[5], Rachael[6]), dau. of Newton and Rachael (Smith) McVey, *m.* 12 Oct., 1873, Marshall Earl, of Carthage, Mo. Issue: 445, Frank L.; 446, Orla M.; 447, Edna D. All reside Billings, Mont.

363. FLORENCE McVEY (John[1], Henry[2], Henry, Jr.[3], Alice[4], Martha[5], Rachael[6]), dau. of Newton and Rachael (Smith) McVey, *m.* Mr. Woods; have four children. They live in Lockwood, Mo.

364. FLORA McVEY (John[1], Henry[2], Henry, Jr.[3], Alice[4], Martha[5], Rachael[6]), dau. of Newton and Rachael (Smith) McVey, *m.* Samuel Stevens, of Garden City, Mo. They have three children and reside in Eureka, Kan.

367. BYRAM L. TULLOSS (John[1], Henry[2], Henry, Jr.[3], Alice[4], Martha[5], Caroline C.[6]), son of John James and Caroline C. (Smith) Tulloss, b. 1 Dec., 1846; *m.* 1st 4 Nov., 1869, Josephine R. Van Buskirk, who d. 16 May, 1879; *m.* 2d 1880, Sarah E. Dennis, who d. 18 March, 1885; *m.* 3d 1886, Mrs. Maggie Carpenter. He is a druggist and lives at 2098 Sullivant Ave., Columbus, O. Issue: 448, Clyde E.; 449, Nora; 450, Harry; 451, Josephine R., b. 23 March, 1881; 452, Dennis.

369. REES P. TULLOSS (John[1], Henry[2], Henry, Jr.[3], Alice[4], Martha[5], Caroline C.[6]), son of John J. and Caroline C. (Smith) Tulloss, b. 24 Oct., 1852; d. by accidental rifle shot, 29 Oct., 1886; *m.* in Putnam Co., O., 1880, Nina D. Weaver, of Leipsic, O. Issue: 453, Rees Edgar; 454, Decilina, b. 9 Sept., 1883, lives Leipsic, O.; 455, Fred. Wayne, b. 22 April, 1886, d. 3 Jan., 1893.

370. GEORGE W. TULLOSS (John[1], Henry[2], Henry, Jr.[3], Alice[4], Martha[5], Caroline C.[6]), son of John J. and Caroline C. (Smith) Tulloss, b. 21 March, 1856; *m.* 20 Sept., 1883, Avarilla Boner. Mr. Tulloss is a Baptist minister; they live on their farm west of Frederickstown, O.

379. MORGAN HARRIS (John[1], Henry[2], Henry, Jr.[3], Alice[4], Rebecca[5], Sarah[6]), son of Elza and Sarah (Hanger) Harris, *m.* Ella Salm, of Meadville, Pa. Issue: 456, Sylvester, b. 1890.

380. JACKSON HARRIS (John[1], Henry[2], Henry, Jr.[3], Alice[4], Rebecca[5], Sarah[6]), son of Elza and Sarah (Hanger) Harris, *m.* Mary Miller; he d. 11 June, 1886, aged 36 years. Issue: 457, Charles, killed in action in the Philippines while serving in the U. S. service, 19 April, 1900; buried at Utica, O., 1901.
458, Walter; 459, Elsie; 460, Herbert, d. aged 2 years (see 390).

382. ELIZABETH HARRIS (John[1], Henry[2], Henry, Jr.[3], Alice[4], Rebecca[5], Sarah[6]), dau. of Elza and Sarah (Hanger) Harris, *m.* —— ——. Issue:
461, —— ——; *m.* John Hayden, of Mt. Gilead, O.

383. REBECCA HARRIS (John[1], Henry[2], Henry, Jr.[3], Alice[4], Rebecca[5], Sarah[6]), dau. of Elza and Sarah (Hanger) Harris, *m.* Joseph Martin. She d. 19 April, 1889. Issue:
462, Mabel; 463, Ira.

384. WILLIAM MILLER (John[1], Henry[2], Henry, Jr.[3], Alice[4], Sarah[5], John[6]), son of John and Cornelia (Clutter) Miller, b. 5 April, 1833; *m.* 1st Melissa King and had:
464, Bettie Davis, *m.* 2d Mary Paul.
465, Henry; 466, Frederick; 467, John; 468, William.

385. CINDERELLA MILLER (John[1], Henry[2], Henry, Jr.[3], Alice[4], Sarah[5], John[6]), dau. of John and Cornelia (Clutter) Miller, b. 15 March, 1835; *m.* Dennis Bricker. Issue:
469, Clara; 470, Lorin.

386. RACHAEL MILLER (John[1], Henry[2], Henry, Jr.[3], Alice[4], Sarah[5], John[6]), dau. of John and Cornelia (Clutter) Miller, b. 1 April, 1837; *m.* Alexander Bell. Issue:
471, Sydney; 472, William; 473, Mellisa; 474, Mary.

388. CHARLES MILLER (John[1], Henry[2], Henry, Jr.[3], Alice[4], Sarah[5], John[6]), son of John and Elizabeth (Helphrey) Miller, b. 5 July, 1849; *m.* Lillian King. Issue:
475, Clyde; 476, Nellie; 477, King.

389. JOHN FRANKLIN MILLER (John[1], Henry[2], Henry, Jr.[3], Alice[4], Sarah[5], John[6]), son of John and Elizabeth (Helphrey) Miller, b. 10 June, 1851; *m.* Melissa Baughman. Issue:
478, Effie; 479, Myrta.

390. MARY ELSIE MILLER (John[1], Henry[2], Henry, Jr.[3], Alice[4], Sarah[5], John[6]), dau. of John and Elizabeth (Helphrey) Miller, b. 3 Dec., 1853; *m.* Jackson Harris. Issue:
480, Charles (see 380).

391. EMMA ALICE MILLER (John[1], Henry[2], Henry, Jr.[3], Alice[4], Sarah[5], John[6]), dau. of John and Elizabeth (Helphrey) Miller, b. 16 March, 1857; *m.* Eli J. Stickle. Issue:
481, Ralph; 482, Rollin; 483, Lillian.

THE VAN METRE GENEALOGY

392. IRA V. MILLER (John[1], Henry[2], Henry, Jr.[3], Alice[4], Sarah[5], John[6]), son of John and Elizabeth (Helphrey) Miller, b. 8 Feb., 1860; *m.* 12 Nov., 1885, Ida McClelland. Issue:
484, Lawrence V., b. 9 June, 1891.

393. LILLIAN C. MILLER (John[1], Henry[2], Henry, Jr.[3], Alice[4], Sarah[5], John[6]), dau. of John and Elizabeth (Helphrey) Miller, b. 29 Jan., 1863; *m.* Wm. A. Alsdorf. Issue:
485, Maxwell.

401. FANNIE MAUDE OBENCHAIN (John[1], Henry[2], Isaac[3], Sallie H.[4], Elizabeth A.[5], Francis G.[6]), dau. of Francis G. and Anna L. (Brown) Obenchain, b. 16 Jan., 1881; *m.* 26 Nov., 1902, John Cocke Abernathy, of Niami, Florida.
486, John Francis, b. 1903.

413. MELVIN B. SMITH (John[1], Henry[2], Henry, Jr.[3], Alice[4], Martha[5], Azariah[6], John J.[7]), son of John Julian and Mary A. (Nagle) Smith, *m.* —— ——. Lives in Rock Valley, Iowa.
Issue:
487, Zoe; 488, Pearl; 489, Jesse; 490, Cecil; 491, Mrs. Zella (Smith) Harless.

414. NINA SMITH (John[1], Henry[2], Henry, Jr.[3], Alice[4], Martha[5], Azariah[6], John J.[7]), dau. of John Julian and Mary A. (Nagle) Smith, *m.* —— Frame (or France). Issue:
492, Laura W.

415. BELLE SMITH (John[1], Henry[2], Henry, Jr.[3], Alice[4], Martha[5], Azariah[6], John J.[7]), dau. of John Julian and Mary A. (Nagle) Smith, *m.* —— Compton. Issue:
493, Cecil S.

416. ALICE JOSEPHINE McCUNE (John[1], Henry[2], Henry, Jr.[3], Alice[4], Martha[5], Sarah A.[6], James H.[7]), dau. of James H. and Mary G. (Ruble) McCune , b. 13 April, 1870; d. 18 June, 1896, at Woodburn, Iowa; *m.* 17 March, 1892, John C. Stewart.
Issue:
494, George Harrington, b. Woodburn, Iowa, 30 Dec., 1892; resides with Cynthia and Caroline C. Tulloss, at Utica, O., since 1896.

417. JOHN HENRY THOMPSON (John[1], Henry[2], Henry, Jr.[3], Alice[4], Martha[5], Sarah A.[6], Margaret R.[7]), son of Charles E. and Margaret R. (McCune) Thompson, b. 29 May, 1880; *m.* —— ——. Lives Des Moines, Iowa. Issue:
495, Merle.

428. ELLA M. EAGLE (John[1], Henry[2], Henry, Jr.[3], Alice[4], Martha[5], Henry D.[6], Martha A.[7]), dau. of Wm. S. and Martha A. (Davis) Eagle, b. 1 Dec., 1870; d. 6 May, 1898; *m.* 18 Oct., 1894, S. Wilkins Haas.

496, Laurence E., b. 4 Oct., 1895.

429. CHARLES O. EAGLE (John[1], Henry[2], Henry, Jr.[3], Alice[4], Martha[5], Henry S.[6], Martha A.[7]), son of Wm. S. and Martha A. (Davis) Eagle, b. 12 June, 1873; *m.* 23 Sept., 1897, Jessie G. Miller.   Issue:
    497, Forest L., b. 31 Dec., 1899; 498, Dorothy M., b. 7 Aug., 1904; d. 6 May, 1907; 499, Flossie J., b. 17 Nov., 1906.

442. EMMA F. GEISICK (John[1], Henry[2], Henry, Jr.[3], Alice[4], Martha[5], Henry D.[6], S. Caroline[7]), dau. of David and S. Caroline (Smith) Geisick, b. 1889; *m.* Dec., 1906, Rufus Hughes.   Issue:
    500, David, b. Sept., 1907.

448. CLYDE E. TULLOSS (John[1], Henry[2], Henry, Jr.[3], Alice[4], Martha[5], Caroline C.[6], Byram L.[7]), son of Byram L. and Josephine R. (Van Buskirk) Tulloss, b. 11 Jan., 1871; *m.* April, 1892, Margaret Huffman. He is a representative of the Columbus Pharmical Co., of Columbus, O.   Issue:
    501, Reginald B., b. 7 July, 1893; 502, Isabella R., b. 9 July, 1896.

453. REES EDGAR TULLOSS (John[1], Henry[2], Henry, Jr.[3], Alice[4], Martha[5], Caroline C.[6], Rees P.[7]), son of Rees P. and Mina D. (Weaver) Tulloss, b. 28 July, 1881; *m.* 18 June, 1908, Alpha Miller, of Springfield, Ohio. He is a graduate of the College and Theological Seminary of Wittemburg College, Springfield, Ohio, and is now serving, as a Lutheran minister, at Constantine, Mich.
                                                Issue:
    503, Frances Louisa, b. 27 March, 1909.

458. WALTER HARRIS (John[1], Henry[2], Henry, Jr.[3], Alice[4], Rebecca[5], Sarah[6], Jackson[7]), son of Jackson and Mary (Miller) Harris, *m.* Mandie Smith.   Issue:
    504, Charles Arthur, b. *circa* 1904.

459. ELSIE HARRIS (John[1], Henry[2], Henry, Jr.[3], Alice[4], Rebecca[5], Sarah[6], Jackson[7]), dau. of Jackson and Mary (Miller) Harris, *m.* Dwight Young, of Delaware, O.   Issue:
    505, Mary Roxanna, b. *circa* 1904.

462. MABEL MARTIN (John[1], Henry[2], Henry, Jr[3], Alice[4], Rebecca[5], Sarah[6], Rebecca[7]), dau. of Joseph and Rebecca (Harris) Martin, *m.* Martin Stetzer.   Issue:
    506, Gladys; 507, Joseph, b. 1908.

463. INA MARTIN (John[1], Henry[2], Henry, Jr.[3], Alice[4], Rebecca[5], Sarah[6], Rebecca[7]), son(?) of Joseph and Rebecca (Harris) Martin, *m.* ―― ――.   Issue:
    508, a son, b. 1904.

WILL OF HENRY VAN METRE

In the name of God, Amen. I Henry Van Mater, of Berkely County & Commonwealth of Virginia, feeling infirmity of body but of perfect mind and memory, and therefore reccolecting the mortality of human nature, do make and Constitute this my last Will and Testament. After my just debts and burial charges are paid, I do give and dispose of my wordly estate in manner and form following, that is to say I do give devise and bequeath unto my son *Nathan Van Mater* all my landed estate in the County of Berkeley and Commonwealth of Virginia, as well the plantation whereon I now live as all the tract or tracts of land which I have in said County of Berkeley, to him my said son *Nathan* and his heirs and assigns forever. I do give and bequeath unto my son *Henry Van Mater* five pounds Virginia currency, to be paid to him by my son *Nathan*. I do give and bequeath unto my son *Joshua* one hundred pounds Virginia currency to be paid to him by my son *Nathan* at the end of two years after my decease. I do further Will and bequeath unto my said son *Nathan Van Mater*, in addition to my Berkeley lands aforesaid, the following negroes namely: Sam, Gim (sic), Peter and Dinah, to him, his heirs and assigns, provided he takes his sister *Hester* into his family, or otherwise maintains her in a proper manner during her single state; and provided he fails or neglects to make such proper provision for her as aforesaid, then and in that case the three last mentioned negroes shall vest in her the said Hester forever. I do give and bequeath unto my wife *Elizabeth*, in addition to her third of my landed estate and in lieu of her part of my personal estate, the following legacy to wit; one negro girl to be purchased as soon as she may think it convenient, out of my estate, not exceeding eighteen nor under ten years of age; my two old negroes, viz: Beck and Jim, the feather bed and furniture whereon we now sleep together with her choice of six milch cows and one third of my dry cattle, her choice of two horses, a third of my sheep, and one third of all my household and kitchen furniture, together with all the movable estate which belonged to her when we were married, and of which I die possessed, to her, her heirs, and assigns, together with a full third part of my hogs and provisions and all the other moveable part of my estate, except the aforesaid four negroes bequeathed to my said son *Nathan*. It is also my earnest will and desire that she may have an uninterrupted home in my present dwelling house during her widowhood. The tract of land which did belong to my son *Joseph Van Mater* lying and being situate on the west side of the Ohio River, in the Indian country and which did devolve to me on his death, together with all the said *Joseph's* personal estate (my negro boy Gim only excepted) I do will devise and bequeath to my aforesaid son *Joshua* and his heirs and assigns forever. and the other tract of land lying and being situate in the Sufferer's Valley, in the District of Kentucky, Which was also the property of my said son Joseph, and at his death devolved to me by operation of law, I do give and devise to my Grandson *Joseph Van Mater*, the son of my aforesaid son Nathan, to him, his heirs and assigns forever. And the residue of my estate after the disposition and payment of the respective legacies above recited of every kind and of every determination, I do further give will devise and bequeath unto my aforesaid son *Nathan Van Mater*, his heirs and assigns forever, and he my said son *Nathan* is in consequence thereof is to pay unto my daughter also two hundred dollars specie within a twelvemonth of my decease. I do hereby make ordain, constitute and appoint my said son *Nathan Van Matre* and my friend *William Gorrell* my sole executors of this my last Will, interest for interest, for the intents and purpose in this my last will contained to take

DESCENDANTS OF HENRY VAN METRE

care to have the same performed according to my true intent (?) and meaning.

In Witness whereof, I the said Henry Van Matre have to this my last Will and testament set my hand and seal the third day of March, in the year of our Lord, seventeen hundred and ninty.

Signed sealed and delivered by the Said Henry Van Matre, as, and for his last Will and Testament in the Presence of us who were present at the signing and sealing thereof:
John McCulloch   William Allen
                              his
Jacob Vandever   Abraham **AM** Merlot
                              mark

(Sig.) HENRY **H** VAN METRE
            his   mark
           [SEAL]

This will was probated 17 December, 1793.

VAN METRE'S FERRY

This ferry was situated on Barren River, near Bowling Green, Ky. It was owned by Jacob Van Metre who came to Bowling Green in 1818, and was where the old " Salt River Road " from Louisville crossed Barren River. The ferry was just below an island, and in low water the river could be forded; notwithstanding this fact the ferry was very profitable—renting for $1,200 a year. This ferry is no longer used. The river is spanned by an iron bridge about a mile below—some 300 yards above the steamboat landing. The present road to Louisville—the old Louisville and Nashville pike, crosses Barren River on a wooden bridge at the foot of College Street—a few hundred yards above the L. & N. R. R. bridge. Owing to a big bend in the river, this bridge, while some four miles by water above the Van Metre ferry, is only about one mile from the steamboat landing [C. J. Van Metre Letter].

The first railroad in Kentucky was constructed about 1832 to Double Springs on Green River in Warren County. It was over a mile long and was built by Jacob Van Metre and Jacob R. Skiles [Collin's Hist. Ky., Vol. II., p. 747].

THE REAL SALT RIVER

It Flows Into The Ohio South of Louisville, Ky.

Salt river, sacred to defeated candidates, is a real stream. While not navigable, it is used every winter as an ice harbor by the towboats which go out of Pittsburg for the South.

Salt river empties into the Ohio about twenty-five miles south of Louisville. It is a small stream, which flows from the Kentucky hills to the great water, and is as tortuous, as crooked and as unpleasant to navigate as the mind can imagine. Yet it is navigated for a short distance from its mouth by steamers of light draft. Flatboats and rafts are floated down upon its bosom. Before the Civil War it was an important stream in the matter of bringing Kentucky whiskey down in the flatboats to a point where they could be unloaded to a river steamer. Refractory slaves were generally assigned to the task of bringing these boats down, as the work was arduous.

Salt river became a bugaboo among the negroes, and it was from the unplesant character of the work on this river that " a trip up Salt river " came to be used in politics to express the destination of a defeated candidate.

The name is supposed to have come from the salt springs which flow into it at its source. (Exchange.)

95

RACHAEL VAN METRE

VIII. RACHAEL VAN METRE (John[1]), dau. of John and Margaret Van Metre, b. probably in Somerset Co., N. J., *circa* 1719; d. *ante* 1744. Mentioned in her father's will as "deceased"; *m. circa* 1736, —— Leforge (or Lessige as is given in Deed of Gift) probably of the family of that name living in Middlesex Co., N. J.   Issue:

   1, John, b. ——; d. ——; mentioned in his grandfather, John Van Metre's will, as being under age (in 1744).

DESCENDANTS OF ABRAHAM VAN METRE

IX. ABRAHAM VAN METRE (John[1]), son of John and Margaret Van Metre, b. Somerset Co., N. J., *circa* 1721; d. in Berkeley Co., Va., *circa* 1783; *m.* 1st *circa* 1742, Ruth Hedges, daughter of Joseph and Catharine (Stallkop) Hedges, of Prince George's Co., Md., sister of Solomon Hedges, Esq., who *m.* Rebecca, the sister of Abraham Van Metre. When Ruth Van Metre died, he *m.* 2d Mrs. Martha Wheeler (*neé* Roberts). By his father's will Abraham was bequeathed a tract of 100 acres of land on Opequon Creek which was purchased from Francis Prichard; another tract, also on Opequon Creek and called "Allan's Hill," comprising 237 acres, purchased of Jost Hite, and still another half moiety of a property, equalling 200 acres, which Jost Hite had given his bond to purchase for John Van Metre, were also inherited by Abraham from his father. By a deed of conveyance, dated 3d May, 1768, it appears that Abraham secured the last mentioned land by patent from Lord Fairfax, under date of 28 Oct., 1754 (Frederick Co., Va., Records), and 100 acres of it was granted by Abraham Van Metre to Samuel Roberts (probably a brother of his (Abraham's) second wife) by the first mentioned conveyance.

Abraham Van Metre was appointed by the Court of Frederick Co., Va., 8 March, 1748, to be "overseer of road from Simon Linders to Old Sayds."

Abraham, like all of the Van Metres who were famous grazers and cattle traders, had extensive business relations with the frontier posts that were established along the borders during the advance of the settlers towards the Ohio Valley. With the pioneers who pressed farther into the wilderness and effected settlements in the most desirable localities, Abraham and his brothers were among them. Many emigrants from Virginia began to settle within the borders of southwestern Pennsylvania after the Indians had been dispersed and peace seemed to have restored confidence among the inhabitants. In looking over the

History of Washington Co., Pa., for the year 1772, it appears that when the grand inquest of the Quarter Sessions was held, on July 6 of that year, an indictment for riot was found against Abraham, Henry and Jacob Van Metre; and John, John, Jr., and Thomas Swan; the locality was then in what is now Greene Co., Pa. (History of Washington Co., Pa., p. 152).

The following is a record of one of his cattle-trading expeditions up the Ohio under date of 4 July, 1774.

"Then rec^d of Abraham Van Meeter Three Steers & one Cow; one Stear & one Cow mark^d a crop and half peny in ye neare Eare—half peny the of Eare. One Stear an mark^d the other mark^d half crop in the neare Eare and Slit in the of Eare. Being Appraised by Jacob Van Meetre & Edward Polke according to order of Capt. John Connolly Commander of Fort Dunmore. Being for the use of Government of Virginia & Appraisement to Sixteen Pounds ten Shillings. Rec^d by me" William Harrod [Documentary History of Dunmore's War, p. 68, Thwaites].

Abraham Van Metre acquired settlement rights to lands in Ohio Co., Va.; these were located on the waters of Short Creek, but some of it was not surveyed until 1786, long after he was deceased, but it became then the property of his heirs (Survey Book, No. 2, p. 48; Wheeling, W. Va.). A portion of this land, called Black's Cabin, and located on Short Creek, was the scene of the organization of Ohio County which was created out of the District of West Augusta, on Jan. 6, 1777, and afterwards established at West Liberty.

The following is a part of the record of the first Court held at

"Black's Cabin 6. January 1777; . . . & Forasmuch as the tract of land agreed upon for holding Coarts at in future doth of right appertain unto Abraham Van Meetre of Opeckan Creek in the County of Bartley, Ordered therefore, that Zachariah Sprigg, Silas Hedges, Esquires be appointed to Contract and Covenant with s^d Van Metre for not less than Two acres of sd tract Including the Cabbin and Spring. In behalf of this County, for the purpose of erecting and Building thereon a Coart-house, Prison and other necessary publick Building, for any sum not exceeding Twenty pounds, & Report make of their procedings therein as soon as may be to this Coart. signed, David Sheepherd" (See Ann. Carnegie Museum, Vol. III., No. 1, Dec., 1904).

"Know all men by these presents that I, Abraham Van Metre, of Bartley [Berkely] County, Colony of Virginia, do bargain and sell for the Consideration of Twenty pounds paid when Sur'y^d of the County current Money to the Court of Ohio County & Successors a Lott of Land Containing of Two acres which I claim lying on the Head of the Northerly Fork of Short Creek known by Black's Cabin, Boun'd as follows:— Beginning at a White Oak standing near the head of a spring & Running thence N. 56 W: 20 pole to a stake, South 34 W: 16 Pole to a stake thence S: E: 20: p. to a stake N: 34: E: 16: p. to the Beginning, Containing Two acres land for the use Publick of the sd County. I do Bind myself my Heirs & assigns and forever quit my claim for the above two acres as witness my hand & seal this day of March one thousand seven hundred and seventy-seven.

Abraham Vanmetre [SEAL]

Interlined before signing: ⎫
Witnesses: Andrew Fouts ⎬ Acknowledged in Open Court—
Conrad Stroup, John Spahn. ⎭ ordered to be recorded.

Test: James McMecken, C. C."

8 April, 1777: "Ordered that a Court house be erected and that John McCullogh High Sheriff,—be ordered to put the contract up at Publick auction to the lowest undertaker, on Abraham Van Metre's ground."

3 Nov., 1777: "Ordered that the Sheriff pay Abraham Van Metre 20 pounds for the lands which the County took to build Court house and prison on,—out of the money by him collected of the tithables in this county." (See Ann. Car. Museum, Vol. III., p. 1, Dec., 1904.)

A stockade was afterward erected on the Short Creek land a few miles above its juncture with the Ohio River, which became known as Van Metre's Fort. This property later fell to the possession of Abraham's son, Joseph Van Metre, and after his death the latter's eldest son, Morgan, inherited it (Washington-Irvine Correspondence, p. 302; Frontier Forts of Pennsylvania, Vol. II., p. 444). From 1777 to 1782 Major Samuel McCullough commanded at Fort Van Metre, styled the Court House Fort, from the circumstance of the first court of Ohio County in northwestern Virginia being held in it immediately after the organization of Ohio County from West Augusta. The Fort was one of the first erected in this part of Virginia and it stood on the north side of Short Creek, about five miles above its confluence with the Ohio (Pan Handle History of West Virginia, p. 134). The well-known Van Metre Fort was located in Richland Township (now) Brooke Co., W. Va. (vide p. 303). In this vicinity, were living at this time, John Duke, Francis Duke, Jr., Morgan Van Metre, John Van Metre, Wm. Dunlap, David McIntire, Wm. Shepherd, Hezekiah Thornburg, Charles Hedges and many others whose families came from the northern neck of Virginia, and all were in one way of another related.

It is probable that Abraham Shepherd was with Squire Boone at his station " Painted Stone " in now Shelby Co., Ky., in 1779 (Collin's Kentucky, Vol. II., p. 24), and is recorded as being with Capt. Wm. Harrod's party " at the Falls " (now in Jefferson and Shelby Counties, Ky.) in 1780 (Collin's Kentucky, Vol. I., p. 12).

In his will dated 21 Dec., 1780, and probated in Berkeley Co., Va., 18 Nov., 1783, no mention whatever is made of his wife and it may be presumed that his second wife was deceased at this date, 1780. There were ten children in his family and Jacob the only one not mentioned in his will as a legatee; the sons Jacob and Isaac, with son-in-law William Gorrell, were executors. It is said that of his children, Jacob, Abraham, Isaac, Joseph, Rebecca and Mary were by his first wife, Ruth Hedges (or Ruth Hedges Bentley, a widow as has been sometimes stated), and

98

John, Ruth, Daniel and Hannah were the issue of his second wife, Mrs. Martha Wheeler Van Metre (B. F. Van Metre, Biographical and Genealogical Sketches). The older set of children seem not to have participated in the provisions of the will, and in such case it is believed that he provided for them at the time of his second marriage, if we accept the theory that there were two sets of children. To Daniel was devised the father's present dwelling, on Opequon, containing 235 acres of land which came " by Patent from Governor Gooch's Office "; to son John certain land in Ohio; to Ruth and Hannah a tract of land in Ohio County containing 400 acres; to daughter Rebecca, wife of John Spahn, there is a bequest. In the sworn statement of account, filed by his executors, in Berkeley Co., and recorded 22 Sept., 1800, there is no mention made of Jacob, Rebecca and Daniel, but equal " legacies " were paid to Isaac, Hannah, Mary, John and Abraham; and to Reuben Forman and Drusilla Van Metre similar amounts, and Henry Van Metre, Jr. (probably a grand-nephew), a small bequest. I take it that Reuben Forman was probably the husband of Ruth; the basis of this opinion is found in a statement made by J. B. Kerfott, who was familiar with the Berkeley County family, and who wrote that "Ruth *married a Forman and went West.*" The *Drusilla* Van Metre who is charged in the account as having received a child's share in the cash distribution was probably the widow of Joseph Van Metre. The contention has been made that Joseph's wife was a Margaret Morgan whose parentage is as yet unascertained. This may have been, and he may have married a Drusilla Morgan whom he left his widow upon his death *circa* 1780/1. The fact that Drusilla and *not* Margaret receives an equal child's share in the cash distribution seems to give weight to the latter theory. In the account there appears also a charge made by the Executors of £12. 10. 0 " for expenses in going to West Liberty and conveying the Court House place " (Berkeley Co., Va., Records, Martinsburg, W. Va.). Issue:

1, Jacob; 2, Isaac; 3, Abraham; 4, Joseph; 5, Rebecca; 6, Mary; 7, Ruth; 8, Hannah; 9, Daniel; 10, John.

The present site of West Liberty was originally improved by Abraham Van Metre (IX.). His daughter Ruth *m.* Reuben Foreman; another daughter, named Hannah, *m.* Providence Mounts. Foreman and Mounts (or Mounce) laid out the town which was organized 20 Nov., 1787, and was the first in Ohio Valley. This section was known as the " Short Creek Country," and was principally settled by pioneers from Pennsylvania, Maryland and Virginia. Major Samuel, Major John, Abram and George McCullough were brothers. George was a farmer (" Ohio County History and Biography," pp. 15, 16, 17, and 787). Accounts of the deaths of Joseph Hedges and Wm. McCullough (Howe,

Hist. Coll. Ohio, p. 202), Gen. Hand's Expedition in the Squaw Campaign, winter of 1777–1778; Col. Wm. Crawford, commanding. This consisted of about 400 men; among its officers was Col. Providence Mounts, of Mounts Creek, which empties into the Youghiogheny River (Draper's Notes, Vol. III., No. 1, p. 27). John Van Metre, Morgan Morgan, Van Swearingen, and others, ordered by the Augusta Co., Va., Court, 22 Feb., 1775, to view a road from Providence Mounts's Mill, by Augsberg Ferry, to Catfish Camp (Washington, Pa.), Feb. 24, 1775; Court orders Providence Mounts, Wm. Crawford and Paul Froman to view the most convenient way for a road from Mounce's Mill to Froman's Mill.

May 17, 1775, Court orders Providence Mounts, and others, to view road from Major Crawford's to Indian Creek (see Ann. Carnegie Mus., Vol. II., 19—; pp. 527, 534, 539).

1. JACOB VAN METRE (John[1], Abraham[2]), son of Abraham and Ruth (Hedges) Van Metre, b. Va., 1745; d. Berkeley Co., Va., *circa* 1806; *m.* Isabella Evans who was probably of the family of John Evans, of Evans Fort, which was located at Big Spring about two miles from Martinsburg (see Kercheval, History of the Valley, p. 70). His will states that his sons Isaac and Abraham had already received their share in his lifetime, but that Joseph was to have part of the land upon which Jacob, the testator, then lived, which adjoined lands of Samuel Roberts. Issue:

> 11, Abraham, 12, Isaac; 13, Jacob, Jr.; 14, Magdalena; 15, Nancy (or Ann); 16, Ruth; 17, Isabel; 18, Mary; 19, Elizabeth; 20, Joseph.

3. ABRAHAM VAN METRE (John[1], Abraham[2]), son of Abraham and Ruth (Hedges) Van Metre, b. Virginia, Dec., 1751; d. 30 Dec., 1834; *m.* Elizabeth, b. 20 Oct., 1753, dau. of William and Joana (Van Metre) Burns. Issue:

> 21, Ruth; 22, Naomi; 23, Joseph; 24, Josiah, b. 21 Aug., 1781; d. 6 April, 1872(?); 25, Abraham; 26, Ashahel; 27, Abishua; 28, Isaac; d. *unm.*; 29, Elizabeth.

4. JOSEPH VAN METRE (John[1], Abraham[2]), son of Abraham and Ruth (Hedges) Van Metre; b. Virginia, *circa* 1743; d. *circa* 1780–81, on the Ohio River; *m.* either Margaret Morgan or Drusilla ——, or both, for it is difficult, in the absence of positive record of the fact, to reconcile the family traditions on the one hand that Margaret Morgan was his wife, with the record in the account of Joseph's father Abraham's estate filed, by his executors, in Berkeley Co., Va., 22 Sept., 1800. In this account, the executors, Jacob Van Metre (son) and William Gorrell (son-in-law) charge themselves with having paid, in settlement of the estate of Abraham Van Metre, as part of the legacies, to Hannah Van Metre, £50. 11. 1¾; to William Gorrell, in right of his wife

DESCENDANTS OF ABRAHAM VAN METRE

Mary, £52. 10. 0; to Reuben Forman and Drusilla Van Metre, £104. 2. 11. No mention is made of either Ruth (who is said, by J. B. Kerfott, "to have married a Forman and gone west), nor of Joseph or his widow Margaret, in which case they would have been named, or their heirs, if deceased; therefore, I am of opinion that the Reuben Foreman was the surviving son of Capt. William Forman who was killed at Grave Creek Narrows by the Indians, in 1777, with his two eldest sons, and that Drusilla Van Metre was the surviving widow of Joseph Van Metre—each entitled to a full child's part, the aggregate named in the settlement paid to them equalling, practically, the sum paid Hannah Van Metre and Mary Gorrell. There were a number of Morgans living in the Ohio settlements in the vicinity of Wheeling, Va., and it is claimed that Margaret Morgan was a near relative of Gen. Daniel Morgan, of Revolutionary fame, and it is also a fact that Drusilla was a common baptismal name among the Morgans. It is possible that Joseph Van Metre may have been twice married; first to Margaret Morgan to whom is credited the maternity of the several children, and at her death have married a sister Drusilla; but this is theorizing. He is frequently referred to as having married "his 1st cousin."

The death of Joseph Van Metre was, like others of the Van Metres, a tragic one; the condensed substance of the circumstances traditionally current in the family is that he lost his life while crossing the Ohio River, near Tiltonville; he was last seen, by a Mr. Hite, in a boat on the river and is supposed to have been either shot by the Indians, or lost his life by the capsizing of his boat. Nothing more was ever heard of him. The finding of his gun on a sand bar in the river, with his name upon it, many years afterward, only served to deepen the mystery. This event probably occurred about the year 1780.

Joseph Van Metre owned Fort Van Metre, on Short Creek, Va. (Washington-Irvine Correspondence, p. 302), and after his death it passed into the possession of his son Morgan Van Metre. During his later years he seems to have been very much in evidence in County Court affairs in the newly created County of Ohio, in Virginia. In the year 1778 he is frequently mentioned on the Court Journal as an appraiser in the estates of John McCullough, John Bukey, Francis Duke and Thomas Glenn. There was a hiatus in his activity of this character for the year 1779, but were renewed again in 1780 when he served as appraiser in Thomas Ryan's estate; and his last appearance on the records was as a juryman in the case of DeLong vs. Snediker, 5 June, 1780. The inventory of Joseph Van Metre's estate was filed in supplements between 2 March, 1782, and 19 Nov., 1784; the amount aggregated £135. 5. 16, as returned by Samuel McCulloug, John Mitchell and John Wilson, appraisers.　　　Issue:

30, Morgan; 31, Joseph; 32, William; 33, Abraham; 34, Ibba(?) John(?); 35, Isaac; 36, Margaret; 37, David; 38, Naomi.

5. REBECCA VAN METRE (John[1], Abraham[2]), dau. of Abraham and Ruth (Hedges) Van Metre, b. Virginia;——; d. Brooke Co., W. Va., ——; *m.* 1st John Spahn; he died *ante* 1796. She *m.* 2d Joseph Morgan, son of Edward Morgan, an immigrant to Richland Township, Ohio County, from Berkeley, W. Va. John Spahn was living in West Liberty in 1777 (see Pan Handle Hist. W. Va., pp. 304–5). Rebecca (V. M.) Spahn-Morgan had eight children, among whom:

    39, Josiah Morgan, b. 3 May, 1796; d. 1 Oct., 1860; *m.* 17 Oct., 1822, Susan S. Foreman; 40; 41; 42; 43; 44; 45; 46.

6. MARY VAN METRE (John[1], Abraham[2]), dau. of Abraham and Ruth (Hedges) Van Metre, b. Virginia, ——; d. ——; *m.* William Gorrell.
                                                Issue:

    47, Jacob, *m.* Isabella Evans; 48, James; 49, William; 50, Joseph; 51, Abraham; 52, Rachael, *m.* Joseph Chenowith; 53, Hannah, *m.* Jonas Quick; 54, Ruth, *m.* Tunis Quick.

7. RUTH VAN METRE (John[1], Abraham[2]), dau. Abraham and —— Van Metre, b. Virginia; *m.* Reuben Foreman; went west (J. B. Kerfott, Ohio County Biography and History). The whole of the land upon which West Liberty, Brooke Co., W. Va., now stands was owned by Reuben Foreman and William Mounce. Captain William Foreman, who was killed by the Indians at Grave Creek Narrows, 27 Sept., 1777, came from Hampshire Co., Va., or from near Martinsburg, Va., and at the time of his death was under orders from Col. David Shepherd at Fort Henry (Wheeling); with Capt. Foreman was killed his two sons. This was in Marshall Co., W. Va. Colonels Shepherd and Zane and Martin Wetzell buried the bodies (see History of the Pan Handle Counties of West Virginia, pp. 301, 363).

8. HANNAH VAN METRE, m. Col. Providence Mounce, of Youghania Co., Va.

9. DANIEL VAN METRE (John[1], Abraham[2]), son of Abraham and —— Van Metre, b. in Virginia, ——; d. ——; *m.* (sup.) 16 April, 1793, Ruth Harp. By his father's will Daniel inherited his father's homestead on Opecquon Creek in Berkeley Co., Va., containing 235 acres; was probably the youngest son. In an old account book kept by the Shepherds, of Shepherdstown, there is an entry under date of 1796: "Daniel Van Metre's note £91. 6. 3." A Daniel Van Metre was living, in 1801, at Muddy Prairie, near the Sciota, in Fairfield Co., O. (see Trans-Alleghany Mag., p. 104).

DESCENDANTS OF ABRAHAM VAN METRE

11. ABRAHAM VAN METRE (John[1], Abraham[2], Jacob[3]), son of Jacob and Isabella (Evans) Van Metre, b. Virginia, 27 Oct., 1773; d. ——; *m.* 1791, Hannah Burns, dau. of William and Joanna (Van Metre) Burns.   Issue:
55, Jonathan, b. 7 Jan., 1793; d. 3 July, 1823.
56, Jacob, b. 12 Nov., 1794; d. 30 April, 1845; *m.* Margaret Tabb.
57, Isabel, b. 2 Feb., 1797; d. ——; *m.* John Chenowith.
58, Rebecca; 59, William Burns, b. 1 July, 1801; d. ——.
60, Ailse, b. 25 March, 1804; d. 19 April, 1855; 61, Abraham.
62, Abner, b. 25 Oct., 1808; d. 25 March, 1864.
63, Ruth; 64, Elizabeth; 65, Daniel, b. 27 Sept., 1818; d. *unm.* 8 Feb., 1826.

12. ISAAC VAN METRE (John[1], Abraham[2], Jacob[3]), son of Jacob and Isabella (Evans) Van Metre, b. Virginia, ——; d. Berkeley Co., Va., *circa* 1828; *m.* Mary Evans (?). She was living in 1831.   Issue:
66, John Evans; 67, Jacob, *m.* after 1831, Emily Shepp.
68, Evans, *unm.* 1831; 69, William, *m.* after 1831, Lucy Shepp.
70, Isaac, Jr., d. *circa* 1831, *unm.*; 71, Abraham E.; 72, Joseph, *m.* after 1831 Miss Sowers.
73, Margaret (see IX., 30); 74, Isabel; 75, Mary, probably 2d wife Thos. Tabb (see IX., 19).

13. JACOB VAN METRE, JR. (John[1], Abraham[2], Jacob[3]), son of Jacob and Isabella (Evans) Van Metre, b. Virginia, ——; d. ——; *m.* Clarissa La Rue, dau. of James and Clara (Billups) La Rue (see Hist. Low. Shenadoah, p. 656).   Issue:
76, James L. Evans, b. ——; d. ——; *m.* 1854, Betty Keyser, who d. March, 1857.

14. MAGDALENA ("LENY") VAN METRE (John[1], Abraham[2], Jacob[3]), dau. Jacob and Isabella (Evans) Van Metre, b. Virginia, ——; d. ——; *m.* William Burns, her cousin, son of Wm. Burns and Joanna Van Metre (II., 2, 13).   Issue:
77, John, *m.* 1st Sarah Lemon; *m.* 2d Eliza Coles.
78, Isaac, *m.* Sarah Southwood; 79, William, *m.* Jane Marshall.
80, Jonathan, *m.* Nancy Williamson; 81, Caleb, *m.* Sidney Williamson; 82, Mary, *m.* her cousin, Ashahel Van Metre, son Abraham and Elizabeth (Burns) Van Metre.
83, Alice, *m.* Jacob Sharkle.
84, Elizabeth, *m.* Joseph Dust; 85, Rebecca, *m.* John Dust.
86, Joanna, *m.* Eli Bell, of Kentucky; 87, Isabel, *m.* 1st Jacob Gorrell, 2d Morgan V. Kline.
88, Ruth, *m.* Henry Furry; 89, Rachael, d. *unm.*

15. NANCY VAN METRE (John[1], Abraham[2], Jacob[3]), dau. of Jacob and Isabella (Evans) Van Metre, b. Virginia, ——; d. ——; *m.* 14 Aug., 1805 (see M. L. Berkeley Co., Va.), Abraham Van

Metre, her cousin, son of Abraham and Elizabeth (Burns) Van
Metre (IX., 3, which see). He was b. 4 Nov., 1783. They
lived on Opequon Creek about three miles east of Martinsburg,
Va. Nancy Van Metre was the first woman physician in the
Valley of Virginia (E. W. V. M. Letter). Issue:
  90, Isaac, b. 1805; 91, Elizabeth; 92, Ruth; 93, Isabel; 94,
  Abishua; 95, Abraham; 96, Ashahel; 97, Henry; 98,
  Anne; 99, Mary; 100, James.

16. RUTH VAN METRE (John[1], Abraham[2], Jacob[3]), dau. of
Jacob and Isabella (Evans) Van Metre, b. Virginia, ——; d.
——; m. 7 Aug., 1799 (M. L. Berkeley Co.), Joseph Gorrell, her
cousin, son of William and Mary (Van Metre) Gorrell (IX., 6,
50). Issue:
  101, Isabel, m. Van Gorrell; 102, Joseph, m. Eliza H. Burns;
  103, William.

17. ISABEL VAN METRE (John[1], Abraham[2], Jacob[3]), dau. of
Jacob and Isabella (Evans) Van Metre, b. Virginia, ——; d.
——; m. her cousin, Abraham Gorrell, son of William and Mary
(Van Metre) Gorrell. Issue:
  102, Van, m. Isabel (101) his first cousin.
  103, David; 104, Jacob; 105, Isabella, m. Benj. Boley.
  106, Abraham, m. Isabella Gorrell; 107, Mary, m. John Taylor
  Van Metre, son of John and Josina.
  108, William B., m. Isabella Henshaw; 109, Elizabeth, m. J. B.
  Wright; 110, Ruth, m. B. F. Burns.

18. MARY VAN METER (John[1], Abraham[2], Jacob[3]), dau. of
Jacob and Isabella (Evans) Van Metre, b. Virginia, ——; d.
——; m. 1797, John Evans. Issue:
  111, Abraham, m. Miss Vallen; 112, Jacob, m. Mary Walker.
  113, Tilletson, m. Mary A. Orr; 114, John, m. Mary Bell.
  115, Isaac V., m. Selena Dawson; 116, Hezekiah, m. Miss Bell.
  117, Westley H.

19. ELIZABETH VAN METRE (John[1], Abraham[2], Jacob[3]), dau.
of Jacob and Isabella (Evans) Van Metre, b. Virginia, ——; d.
——; m. Thomas Tabb, who m. 2d Mary Van Metre (?). Issue:
  118, Isabel, m. Abraham P. Van Metre; 119, Elizabeth, m.
  Jacob McQuilken; 120, James, d. unm.; 121, Jacob, m.
  Susan Jackson.

20. JOSEPH VAN METRE (John[1], Abraham[2], Jacob[3]), son of
Jacob and Isabella (Evans) Van Metre, b. Virginia, ——; m.
(M. L. 18 Sept., 1802) Nancy Evans. Issue:
  122, Joseph; 123, Isabel; 124, Nancy.

21. RUTH VAN METRE (John[1], Abraham[2], Abraham[3]), dau. of
Abraham and Elizabeth (Burns) Van Metre, b. 20 March, 1772;
d. ——; m. Robert Phillips. Issue:
  125, Elizabeth, m. Mr. Ramsey; 126, Fanny.

22. NAOMI VAN METRE (John[1], Abraham[2], Abraham[3]), dau. of Abraham and Elizabeth (Burns) Van Metre, b. 29 January, 1775; d. ——; m. Samuel Roberts; was his second wife.   Issue: 127, John; 128, Josiah; 129, Samuel; 130, Elizabeth. 131, Joseph; 132, Eliza, m. Samuel Van Cleve. 133, Naomi, m. Abraham Van Metre, her cousin, son of Abishua Van Metre.

23. JOSEPH VAN METRE (John[1], Abraham[2], Abraham[3]), son of Abraham and Elizabeth (Burns) Van Metre, b. Berkeley Co., Va., 5 Dec., 1778; d. Jan., 1822; m. Aug. 18, 1800, Margaret Whitenak, his cousin, dau. of John G. and Mary A. (Carl) Whitenak (I., 4, 35). His wife Margaret was b. 1780 and d. 7 Oct., 1865.   Issue: 134, Gabriel, b. 7 Aug., 1801, d. 1803; 135, Robert, b. 19 Nov., 1803; 136, Sarah, b. 14 March, 1808, m. 26 Nov., 1835, Robert Duncan; 137, Joseph W.; 138, Vincent H.

26. ASHAHEL VAN METRE (John[1], Abraham[2], Abraham[3]), son of Abraham and Elizabeth (Burns) Van Metre, b. 26 Nov., 1785; m. Mary Burns, his cousin, dau. of William and Magdalena (Van Metre) Burns.   Issue: 139, Abraham, m. Mary Chuppuck; 140, Elizabeth, m. J. Strider. 141, Naomi, m. J. H. Strider; 142, Rachael, m. Thomas Files. 143, Sarah, m. John B. Files; 144, Isabel, m. Asbury Tabler. 145, Mary, m. David Gorrell, her cousin, son of Abraham and Isabel V. M. Gorrell.

27. ABISHUA VAN METRE (John[1], Abraham[2], Abraham[3]), son of Abraham and Elizabeth (Burns) Van Metre, b. 29 Aug., 1788; m. Elizabeth Tabb, emigrated to Kentucky.   Issue: 146, Robert, m. Miss McClery; 147, Abraham, m. Naomi Roberts, his cousin. 148, Elizabeth, m. Joseph Roberts, son of Samuel and Naomi Roberts. 149, Isaac, m. Mary Abel; 150, Frances, m. John Avette. 151, Abishua, d. unm., was blind; 152, William, m. Miss English. 153, Jacob; 154, John; 155, Mary.

29. ELIZABETH VAN METRE (John[1], Abraham[2], Abraham[3]), dau. Abraham and Elizabeth (Burns) Van Metre, b. 25 Dec., 1795; d. July 28, 1820; m. John Evans Van Metre, son of Col. Isaac and Isabel (Evans) Van Metre. He m. 2d Josina, dau. of John ("Honce") Van Metre.   Issue: 156, John, m. Anne Alburtis (prob. dau. of John Alburtis). 157, Isaac Taylor.

30. MORGAN VAN METRE (John[1], Abraham[2], Joseph[3]), son of Joseph and Margaret, or Drusilla, Morgan Van Metre, b. ——; m. Margaret Van Metre, dau. of Isaac and Mary (Evans) Van

Metre. He died leaving issue. She *m.* 2d Wm. McDaniel. Issue:
158, Mary Ruth, b. *ante* 1831; *m.* Mr. Harlan.
159, Margaret, b. *ante* 1831; *m.* George McKown.
160, Rebecca, b. *ante* 1831; 161, James; 162, Anna; 163, Evangeline, *m.* Jos. Miller.

31. JOSEPH VAN METRE (John[1], Abraham[2], Joseph[3]), son of Joseph and Margaret or Drusilla (Morgan) Van Metre, b. 1770; d. in Ohio County, 1841; *m. circa* 1791-5, Mary Jolly. She was of Irish descent. They located in Highland Co., O., in 1796; while they were living in this county Joseph was wounded by the Indians. The Indians surrounded a squad of white men in a block house, on the west side of the Ohio River and fired through the door, the ball cutting a gash across the top of Joseph's head. About 1805 he removed with his family to Fayette Co., Ind., settling near Alquina, from whence they removed, about 1824, to Delaware Co., Ind., where Joseph died near Yorktown.   Issue:
164, David; 165, Alsey; 166, ——; 167, ——.

32. WILLIAM VAN METRE (John[1], Abraham[2], Joseph[3]), son of Joseph and Margaret or Drusilla (Morgan) Van Metre, b. ——; d. ——; *m.* Sarah Bell.   Issue:
168, Dr. Milton; 169, Newton; 170, Laetitia, *m.* Abraham Suman; 171, Harrison; 172, Perry.

33. ABRAHAM VAN METRE (John[1], Abraham[2], Joseph[3]), son of Joseph and Margaret or Drusilla (Morgan) Van Metre, b. 1778; d. ——; *m. circa* 1798, Sarah Morgan.   Issue:
173, Jacob; 174, Morgan; 175, Hannah; 176, Catharine.

35. ISAAC VAN METRE (John[1], Abraham[2], Joseph[3]), son of Joseph and Margaret or Drusilla (Morgan) Van Metre, b. ——; d. 4 July, 1835; *m.* 9 March, 1797, Mary Caldwell, dau. of William and Mary (McCune) Caldwell, both of Scotch-Irish lineage. Isaac crossed the Ohio into Indiana, where all his children except Margaret were born on a farm near Anderson. He finally disposed of his homestead and emigrated with two or three of his brothers to Bourbon Co., Ky. (Goodwyn). Isaac is said to have died near Chesterfield, Madison Co. (C. V.).   Issue:
177, Margaret; 178, Joseph; 179, William; 180, Agnes; 181, Morgan; 182, Sarah; 183, Elizabeth; 184, Isaac; 185, Mary Ann.

36. MARGARET VAN METRE (John[1], Abraham[2], Joseph[3]), dau. of Joseph and Margaret or Drusilla (Morgan) Van Metre, b. ——; d. ——; *m.* John Van Metre.   Issue:
186, Cynthia; 187, Henry; 188, Joseph; 189, Wm. Jackson, *m.* Margaret Johnson.
190, Mary, *m.* Jacob Chismond; 191, Peter, d. 1865, *m.* Sophia Miller.

DESCENDANTS OF ABRAHAM VAN METRE

37. DAVID VAN METRE (John[1], Abraham[2], Joseph[3]), son of
Joseph and Margaret or Drusilla (Morgan) Van Metre, b. ——;
d. ——; *m.* Marie Van Metre.   Issue:
 192, Henry Jolly; 193, Mary J.; 194, Elma; 195, Samantha.
 196, Joseph, b. ——; d. 10 May, 1862, *unm.,* Marine Hospital,
      St. Louis, Mo.
 197, Absalom, b. ——; d. aged 12; 198, Abner; 199, Osee Bell.
 200, Edwin, b. ——; d. ——; *m.* ——; soldier in Cuban War;
      editor Legor "Times," Portsmouth, Legor Co., Okla-
      homa.
 201, Agnes, *m.* Samuel Rotan, Holden, Miss.
 202, David, *unm.,* editor newspaper at Velasco, Texas.
 203, Cyrus.

38. NAOMI VAN METRE (John[1], Abraham[2], Joseph[3]), dau.
of Joseph and Margaret or Drusilla (Morgan) Van Metre; b.
——; d. ——; *m.* Joseph D. Van Metre.   Issue:
 204, William Wallace, *m.* Sallie ——; lives Kingsville, Mo.
 205, John D., d. *unm.*
 206, Joseph Josephus, *m.* Ann Jackson; 207, Peter Lewis, *m.*
      Lucy Colven.
 208, Mary Elizabeth, d. *unm.;* 209, Marie Emmeline, *m.* Mr.
      Lester.
 209, Margaret, *m.* Mart Dodd.

48. JAMES GORRELL (John[1], Abraham[2], Mary[3]), son of William
and Mary (Van Metre) Gorrell, b. ——; d. ——; *m.* Nancy
Boley.   Issue:
 211, Benjamin; 212, Mary, *m.* —— Shammell; 213, William.
 214, Elizabeth, *m.* —— Witt; 215, Fanny, *m.* —— Pitman, of
      Martinsburg, W. Va.
 216, John B.; 217, F. F.

49. WILLIAM GORRELL (John[1], Abraham[2], Mary[3]), dau. of
William and Mary (Van Metre) Gorrell, b. ——; d. ——; *m.*
Nancy Van Metre.   Issue:
 218, Van, *m.* Catharine Miller; 219, Joseph, *m.* Priscilla Blue.
 220, William, *m.* Sarah Johnson(?); 221, Anthony, *m.* Malvina
      Estill.
 222, Mary, *m.* Thomas Gorrell; 223, Susan, d. *unm.*
 224, Jacob, *m.* Sarah Johnson(?); 225, Ann, *m.* Luther Van
      Metre.
 226, John, killed by Indians; 227, Rachael, d. *unm.*

50. JOSEPH GORRELL (John[1], Abraham[2], Mary[3]), son of William and Mary (Van Metre) Gorrell, b. ——; d. ——; *m.* Ruth
Van Metre. dau. of Jacob and Isabella (Evans) Van Metre.

51. ABRAHAM GORRELL (John[1], Abraham[2], Mary[3]), son of
William and Mary (Van Metre) Gorrell, b. ——; d. ——; *m.*
Isabel Van Metre.   Issue:

107

228, Joseph C., *m.* Mary Turner; 229, Mary B.
230, Isabella E., *m.* Chris L. Tabb, of Martinsburg, W. Va.

58. REBECCA VAN METRE (John[1], Abraham[2], Jacob[3], Abraham[4]), dau. of Abraham and Hannah (Burns) Van Metre, b. 2 May, 1797; d. 26 April, 1831; *m.* John Schell.   Issue:
231, Hannah, *m.* —— Shaner; 232, Isabel, *m.* —— Wellshance.
233, John; 234, John.

61. ABRAHAM VAN METRE (John[1], Abraham[2], Jacob[3], Abraham[4]), son Abraham and Hannah (Burns) Van Metre, b. 25 Oct., 1805; d. 25 May, 1864; *m.* Marie Van Metre.   Issue:
235, Henry Clay; 236, Isaac; 237, Mary Eliza, *m.* Hugh Campbell; 238, John.

63. RUTH VAN METRE (John[1], Abraham[2], Jacob[3], Abraham[4]), dau. of Abraham and Hannah (Burns) Van Metre, b. 12 May, 1811; d. 15 Jan., 1855; *m.* Jacob Stepp.   Issue:
239, Abraham; 240, Isaac; 241, Margretta.

64. ELIZABETH VAN METRE (John[1], Abraham[2], Jacob[3], Abraham[4]), dau. of Abraham and Hannah (Burns) Van Metre, b. 14 June, 18—; d. Dec., 1843; *m.* Frederick Deck.   Issue:
242, Susan; 243, Rebecca; 244, Ruth; 245, a son, *m.* Ellen Butler.

66. JOHN EVANS VAN METRE (John[1], Abraham[2], Jacob[3], Isaac[4]), son of Isaac and Mary (Evans) Van Metre, *m. ante* 1831, Josina Van Metre, his cousin, dau. of John and Josina (Taylor) Van Metre.   Issue:
246, Isaac Taylor, b. *ante* 1831.

71. ABRAHAM E. VAN METRE (John[1], Abraham[2], Jacob[3], Isaac[4]), son of Isaac and Mary (Evans) Van Metre, *m.* Marie, dau. of John and Rebecca (Powelson) Van Metre.   Issue:
247, Isaac, b. *ante* 1831.

75. MARY VAN METRE (John[1], Abraham[2], Jacob[3], Isaac[4]), dau. of Isaac and Mary (Evans) Van Metre (was probably second wife of Thomas Tabb). (See IX., 19.)   Issue:
248, Nancy, *m.* Thomiah Boley; 249, Mary, *m.* John B. Gorrell.
250, Nathan; 251, John; 252, Susan; 253, Susan, *m.* Samuel W. Strider.

80. JONATHAN BURNS (John[1], Abraham[2], Jacob[3], Magdalena[4]), son of William and Magdalena (Van Metre) Burns, *m.* Nancy Williamson.   Issue:
254, John, *m.* Miss Foch; 255, Catharine; 256, Mary.

91. ELIZABETH VAN METRE (John[1], Abraham[2], Jacob[3], Nancy[4]), dau. of Abraham and Nancy Van Metre, b. 30 Nov., 1807; d. ——; *m.* John S. Files.   Issue:

257, John Burns; 258, Thomas, *m.* Rachael Van Metre, his cousin; 259, Elizabeth.

92. RUTH VAN METRE (John[1], Abraham[2], Jacob[3], Nancy[4]), dau. Abraham and Nancy Van Metre, b. 4 Dec., 1809; *m.* Henry Rutherford *circa* 1830 and emigrated to the Miami River Valley, "making their journey on horseback and crossing the Ohio River at Wheeling." Issue:
260, Abraham, *m.* Eliza Ridgway; 261, Isaac, *m.* 1st Miss Worth; 2d Miss Morrell.
262, Archibald, *m.* Eliza Ray; 263, Elizabeth, *m.* Frank Hall.
264, Mary, *m.* Mr. Hesse; 265, Eliza.

93. ISABEL VAN METRE (John[1], Abraham[2], Jacob[3], Nancy[4]), dau. Abraham and Nancy Van Metre, b. 30 April, 1811; d. 22 Nov., 1885; *m.* Colbert Anderson. Issue:
266, Ceracy, *m.* Wm. Bealor; 267, Mary Catharine; 268, Jane Staten; 269, James.

94. ABISHUA VAN METRE (John[1], Abraham[2], Jacob[3], Nancy[4]), son of Abraham and Nancy Van Metre, b. 4 Dec., 1813; d. ——; *m.* Nancy Morris. Issue:
270, Abraham; 271, Smith; 272, Ashahel, *m.* Miss Pitzer; 273, John, b. 1835; d. 14 Oct., 1860.

95. ABRAHAM VAN METRE (John[1], Abraham[2], Jacob[3], Nancy[4]), son of Abraham and Nancy Van Metre, b. 15 April, 1816; d. ——; *m.* Eliza Russell. Issue:
274, Scott; 275, Barney; 276, Martin, *m.* Miss Bradshaw; 277, Sarah; 278, Mary, *m.* John Honest; 279, Martha, *m.* —— Stanley.

96. ASHAHEL VAN METRE (John[1], Abraham[2], Jacob[3], Nancy[4]), son of Abraham and Nancy Van Metre, b. 16 April, 1818; d. 24 Dec., 1897; *m.* 1844, Mary M. Willhelm. Issue:
280, Isabel; 281, Ruth E.; 282, Ellen Jane; 283, James Henry.

97. HENRY VAN METRE (John[1], Abraham[2], Jacob[3], Nancy[4]), son and Abraham and Nancy Van Metre, b. 26 April, 1820, on the Opequon, about three miles from Martinsburg, W. Va.; d. 17 June, 1894; *m.* Mary Whitson. Issue:
284, Elijah W.

98. ANNE VAN METRE (John[1], Abraham[2], Jacob[3], Nancy[4]), dau. Abraham and Nancy Van Metre, b. 11 April, 1822; d. 12 Dec., 1888; *m.* James Collahan.

99. MARY VAN METRE (John[1], Abraham[2], Jacob[3], Nancy[4]), dau. of Abraham and Nancy Van Metre, b. 7 July, 1825; d. ——; *m.* Foster Rutherford. Issue:
285, Ruth, *m.* John Kendall; 286, Eliza R., *m.* Chas. Hollis; 287, Ella R., *m.* Asbury Troxell.

100. JAMES VAN METRE (John[1], Abraham[2], Jacob[3], Nancy[4]), dau. Abraham and Nancy Van Metre, b. 7 June, 1828, living 1907; *m.* Catharine Hoorne, 18 Dec., 1855. Issue:
288, Mary Ann, b. 6 Oct., 1856; d. 27 May, 1886; *m.* Aaron Funderbush, of Columbia, S. C.
289, George Wm., b. 31 Aug., 1858; d. ——; *m.* Nov., 1891, Rose Alice Farrell. He was surveyor of Berkeley Co., W. Va., and lived at Martinsburg, W. Va.
290, James M., Jr., b. 5 Dec., 1860; d. ——; *m.* 19 Aug., 1886, Mary Riley, lives in Columbia, S. C.
291, Abraham Henry, b. 2 March, 1865; d. Sept., 1894; *m.* Mary Myers.
292, Ruth Isabel, b. 13 Nov., 1867; d. ——; *m.* 5 April, 1889, Philip Myers.
293, Eliza K., b. 13 May, 1875; d. 16 April, 1886.
294, Isaac David, b. 8 July, 1878.

101. ISABEL GORRELL (John[1], Abraham[2], Jacob[3], Ruth[4]), dau. of Joseph and Ruth (Van Metre) Gorrell, b. ——; d. ——; *m.* her cousin, Van Gorrell. Issue:
295, Joseph; 296, Jacob; 297, Isabel; 298, Ruth.

102. JOSEPH GORRELL (John[1], Abraham[2], Jacob[3], Ruth[4]), son of Joseph and Ruth (Van Metre) Gorrell, b. ——; d. ——; *m.* Eliza H. Burns. Issue:
299, Lanny, *m.* Alex. Newcomer; 300, Lucy Louise, *m.* J. Walper Snyder.
301, Jennie Virginia, *m.* John Blue; 302, Washington, *m.* Mary A. Miller.
303, John Burns, *m.* Rebecca Miller; 304, Joseph Baker, *m.* Mary Norris.
305, Benjamin F., *m.* Virginia Herndon; 306, George W., *m.* Drusilla Gainhurst.
307, ——, a son, who *m.* Catharine Moore.

103. DAVID GORRELL (John[1], Abraham[2], Jacob[3], Isabel[4]), son of Abraham and Isabel (Van Metre) Gorrell, *m.* Mary B., his cousin, dau. of Ashahel and Mary B. Van Metre. Issue:
308, Ruth, *m.* Seaton Magruder.

104. JACOB GORRELL (John[1], Abraham[2], Jacob[3], Isabel[4]), son of Abraham and Isabel (Van Metre) Gorrell, b. ——; d. ——; *m.* 1st Miss Bols; *m.* 2d Hannah Burns; *m.* 3d Mrs. Thomas Tabb. Issue:
309, Mary Bols, *m.* George Newcomer; 310, Weaverford Bols, *m.* Daniel Burns.
311, Abraham Burns, *m.* Miss Gorrell; 312, Jacob Tabb, *m.* ——.

112. JACOB EVANS (John[1], Abraham[2], Jacob[3], Mary[4]), son of John and Mary (Van Metre) Evans, *m.* Mary Walker. Issue:
313, Henry; 314, Clarissa; 315, Mary.

118. Isabel Tabb (John[1], Abraham[2], Jacob[3], Elizabeth[4]), dau. of Thomas and Elizabeth (Van Metre) Tabb, *m.* Abraham P. Van Metre (a desc. of Henry[1]). Issue: 316, Mary Martha.

130. Elizabeth Roberts (John[1], Abraham[2], Abraham[3], Naomi[4]), dau. of Samuel and his second wife Naomi (Van Metre) Roberts, *m.* Samuel Van Cleve. Issue: 317, Benjamin; 318, Frances, *m.* William Van Cleve.

131. Joseph Roberts (John[1], Abraham[2], Abraham[3], Naomi[4]), son of Samuel and Naomi (Van Metre) Roberts, *m.* his cousin, Elizabeth, dau. of Abishua and Elizabeth Tabb Van Metre. Issue: 319, D. W.; 320, Alfred; 321, Melvina; 322, Elvira, *m.* —— Van Metre; 323, Rorilla, *m.* —— Sisson; 324, Oregon; 325, Julia, *m.* —— Tabb; 326, Isaac.

135. Robert Van Metre (John[1], Abraham[2], Abraham[3], Joseph[4]), son of Joseph and Margaret (Whitnack) Van Metre, b. 19 Nov., 1803; *m.* 1822, Mahala, dau. of John Henson Wheeler, who was b. 1778; d. 1849. She was b. 5 Feb., 1805. Robert Van Metre lived and died on the old Van Metre homestead at West Liberty, W. Va. Issue: 327, Henrietta; 328, Margaret; 329, Anna; 330, Samuel Roberts; 330½, Joseph Whitnack, *m.* —— Spark.

137. Joseph W. Van Metre (John[1], Abraham[2], Abraham[3], Joseph[4]), son of Joseph and Margaret (Whitnack) Van Metre, b. in Ohio Co., Va., 25 June, 1812; d. — Jan., 1858; *m.* 1837, Eliza, dau. of William and Margaret Ray. 332, Margaret; 333, Sarah; 334, Catharine, d. aged 10 years. 335, Joseph Vincent, living in Scott Co., Ill., *m.* his cousin, Sallie Ray, dau. of Thomas and Julia (Curtis) Ray.

138. Vincent H. Van Metre (John[1], Abraham[2], Abraham[3], Joseph[4]), son of Joseph and Margaret (Whitnack) Van Metre, b. in Ohio Co., Va., 7 June, 1817; *m.* 6 March, 1845, Margaret A. Whitnack, dau. of John G. and Mary A. (Carroll) Whitnack, of Berkeley Co., Va. (see II., 29). No issue. He d. 24 April, 1901.

139. Abraham Van Metre (John[1], Abraham[2], Abraham[3], Ashahel[4]), son of Ashahel and Mary (Burns) Van Metre, *m.* Mary Chappuck. Issue: 335, Elizabeth; 336, Jennie.

143. Sarah Van Metre (John[1], Abraham[2], Abraham[3], Ashahel[4]), dau. of Ashahel and Mary (Burns) Van Metre, *m.* her cousin, John Burns Files, son of John Snowden and Elizabeth (Van Metre) Files. Issue: 337, Mary Elizabeth; 338, Sarah; 339, Jennie, *m.* Ronald Alpert; 340, John; 341, William.

146. ROBERT VAN METRE (John[1], Abraham[2], Abraham[3], Abishua[4]), son of Abishua and Elizabeth (Tabb) Van Metre, b. ——; d. ——; m. Miss McClary. Issue:
342, Alice, m. Mr. Ambrose; 343, Mary, m. Mr. Watkins; 344, Elizabeth; 345, Sheridan; 346, Eliza; 347, Darby; 348, Charles.

164. DAVID VAN METRE (John[1], Abraham[2], Joseph[3], Joseph[4]), son of Joseph and Mary (Jolly) Van Metre, b. in Highland Co., O., 18 July, 1805; d. Delaware Co., near Middletown, Ind., 20 Dec., 1882; m. ——. David was farming in Richwood in February, 1827. (This correspondent, Mr. Cyrus Van Metre, of Middletown, Ind., in his letter, February, 15, 1908, says that Margaret (Morgan) Van Metre, widow of Joseph Van Metre, m. 2d John Seaman, and had three children, John, Jeremiah and Elizabeth; the latter m. 1st Bazil Neely and had John and Bazil Neely; she m. 2d —— Gouldin, and surviving him, died at the home of her son John Neely and was buried in Mount Pleasant Cemetery, near Yorktown, Delaware Co., Ind. Issue:
349, Cyrus; 350, a dau., living in Missouri.

165. ALSEY VAN METRE (John[1], Abraham[2], Joseph[3], Joseph[4]), dau. of Joseph and Mary Jolly, b. Highland Co., O., m. 1st —— McCullough, who emigrated to Delaware Co., then to Wabash Co., Ind., where he died; m. 2d —— Cusick and had issue:
351, Nancy, m. Thomas Windsor; 352, Rebecca, m. Abner Van Metre.
353, Elizabeth, m. —— Daniels; 354, Margaret, m. Samuel Clevinger, who lived near Windsor, near the line of Delaware and Randolph Counties, Ind. It is also stated by above correspondent that Alsey Van Metre m. William Curry and had five children, among whom a dau. m. Mr. Phiol and removed to Kentucky.

168. DR. MILTON VAN METRE (John[1], Abraham[2], Joseph[3], William[4]), son of William and Sarah (Bell) Van Metre, m. in Delaware Co., Ind., Nellie ——. Issue:
355, a dau., who m. Reuben Thompson; resides Muncie, Ind.

171. HARRISON VAN METRE (John[1], Abraham[2], Joseph[3], William[4]), son of William and Sarah (Bell) Van Metre, m. Martha Brandon. Issue:
356, a dau., who m. Arthur Franklin, of Dalesville, Ind.

172. PERRY VAN METRE (John[1], Abraham[2], Joseph[3], William[4]), son of William and Sarah (Bell) Van Metre, m. Amelia Brandon; live at Dalesville, Ind. Issue:
357, John; 358, Charles A. (probably Supt. of Public Schools of Delaware Co., Ind.); 359, Williard.

173. JACOB VAN METRE (John[1], Abraham[2], Joseph[3], Abraham[4]), son of Abraham and Sarah (Morgan) Van Metre, b. ——; d.

; *m.* Mary Black, dau. of Capt. Adam Black, of Black's
Fort in W. Va., who was a soldier of the Revolution.   Issue:
360, Abraham, d. *unm.*; 361, Henry; 362, Morgan; 363, Jacob
James; 364, John; 365, Joseph; 366, Robert; 367, Polly,
d. *unm.*; 368, Sarah, *m.* Mr. Dennison, of Oxford,
England.

174. MORGAN VAN METRE (John[1], Abraham[2], Joseph[3], Abraham[4]), son of Abraham and Sarah (Morgan) Van Metre, b.
——; d. ——; *m.* Rebecca Knott.   Issue:
369, Hannah, *m.* Henry Lupher; 370, Sarah, *m.* Henry, son
of Jacob Van Metre.
371, John; 372, Abraham; 373, Elsie; 374, Drusilla, *m.* ——
Brandt, of Kilgore, Carroll Co., O.; 375, Morgan, *m.*
—— Polly, lives Magnolia, O.

175. HANNAH VAN METRE (John[1], Abraham[2], Joseph[3], Abraham[4]), dau. of Abraham and Sarah (Morgan) Van Metre, *m.*
William Knotts.   Issue:
376, William; 377, John; 378, Rebecca, *m.* —— Wibb.

176. CATHARINE VAN METRE (John[1], Abraham[2], Joseph[3],
Abraham[4]), dau. of Abraham and Sarah (Morgan) Van Metre,
b. ——; *m.* —— ——.   Issue:
379, Rebecca; 380, Harriet.

177. MARGARET VAN METRE (John[1], Abraham[2], Joseph[3],
Isaac[4]), dau. of Isaac and Mary (Caldwell) Van Metre, b. 29
May, 1798, in Bourbon Co., Ky.; d. June, 1835, in Anderson,
Ind.; *m.* 1821, James W. Brown, major Indiana Militia.   Issue:
381, Mary, b. 1822; d. ——; *m.* —— Chapman.
382, Isaac V., b. 12 July, 1826; d. 15 May, 1863; *m.* Elizabeth Carroll, of New Jersey.
383, Wm. Josephus, b. 1828; d. 1862; 384, Sarah, b. 1830;
d. 1895; *m.* 1st —— Ward; *m.* 2d —— Martindale;
m. 3d James Guy.
385, Samuel Lafayette, b. 1832; d. 1849.

186. CYNTHIA VAN METRE (John[1], Abraham[2], Joseph[3], Margaret[4]), dau. of John and Margaret (V. M.) Van Metre, b. ——;
m. Simon Summers.   Issue:
386, John V.; 387, William; 388, Dr. Henry; 389, Ferriby;
390, Jane Davis.

187. HENRY VAN METRE (John[1], Abraham[2], Joseph[3], Margaret[4]), son of John and Margaret (V. M.) Van Metre, b. ——;
m. Elizabeth Summers.   Issue:
391, Margaret Moore; 392, Jasper; 393, William.

188. JOSEPH VAN METRE (John[1], Abraham[2], Joseph[3], Margaret[4]), son of John and Margaret (V. M.) Van Metre, b. ——;
m. Julia McCalister.   Issue:

394, Lewis; 395, Margaret, *m.* L. P. Shoemaker, Middleturn, Ind.

192. HENRY JOLLY VAN METRE (John[1], Abraham[2], Joseph[3], David[4]), son of David and Marie (V. M.) Van Metre, b. ——; *m.* Eliza Miller. Issue:
396, David P.; 397, Laetitia; 398, Richard T.; 399, Joseph, d. *unm.*
400, Mary, *m.* Samuel Summers, of Yorktown, Ind.
401, Jane, *m.* 1st —— Fountain; *m.* 2d —— Bowyer, of Anderson, Ind.

193. MARY J. VAN METRE (John[1], Abraham[2], Joseph[3], David[4]), dau. of David and Marie (V. M.) Van Metre, b. ——; *m.* Mathias Pitzer, Magnolia, Ind. Issue:
402, Cyrus; 403, Warren; 404, Vileta; 405, Joseph; 406, David; 407, Jasper; 408, Laura; 409, Morton.

195. SAMANTHA VAN METRE (John[1], Abraham[2], Joseph[3], David[4]), dau. of David and Marie (V. M.) Van Metre, b. ——; *m.* David. Nation. Issue:
410, Mary Jane, *m.* —— Whitson; 411, Sophia, *m.* Wm. Riddle, Iberia, O.
412, Josephine, *m.* —— White; Columbia, Mo.; 413, Oscar O., *unm.*, Velasco, Tex.
414, Cassius, Velasco, Tex.; 415, Lowly(?), *m.* —— Williams, Richmond, Tex.

198. ABNER VAN METRE (John[1], Abraham[2], Joseph[3], David[4]), son of David and Marie (V. M.) Van Metre, b. ——; *m.* Elizabeth A. Stewart; she d. 1898. Issue:
416, Lilian, *m.* —— Whitlow; 417, Peter Cyrus, b. ——; d. Dec., 1904; *m.* and had issue. Was editor "Herald" and Postmaster, Warrensburg, Mo.

199. OSEE BELL VAN METRE (John[1], Abraham[2], Joseph[3], David[4]), dau. of David and Marie (V. M.) Van Metre, b. ——; *m.* John Snider, Holden, Mo. Issue:
418, Will, T. S., in city mail service, Warrensburg, Mo.

203. CYRUS VAN METRE (John[1], Abraham[2], Joseph[3], David[4]), son of David and Marie (V. M.) Van Metre, b. ——; d. ——; *m.* 1st Sarah C. Sayford, d. 27 Jan., 1901; *m.* 2d Laura V. Sayford, 19 March, 1905; lives near Middletown, Ind. Issue:
419, Dr. Cassius Emmet, b. ——; *m.* 16 Sept., 1895, Minnie May MacFarland.
420, Augustus Abner, b. ——; *m.* 27 Dec., 1894, May Lois Davis.
421, Naomi J., *m.* Wm. A. Painter; 422, Joseph.
423, Chas. Cyrus, *m.* Margaret Rinker; 424, Marie, *m.* Chas. S. Shedron.

229. MARY B. GORRELL (John[1], Abraham[2], Mary[3], Abraham[4]), dau. of Abraham and Isabel (V. M.) Van Metre, b. ——; d. ——; m. J. Baker Kerfott, of Martinsburg, W. Va. Issue: 425, Clarence P., m. Rebecca Kratz; 426, Hetty Bell, m. Milton S. Miller; 427, Mary Baker, m. J. Henry Bogert; 428, Joseph Gorrell, m. —— ——; 429, Fanny Quick, m. C. M. Siebert, of Martinsburg, W. Va.

259. ELIZABETH FILES (John[1], Abraham[2], Jacob[3], Nancy[4], Elizabeth[5]), dau. of John S. and Elizabeth (V. M.) Files, b. ——; m. William Orndorff. Issue: 430, Florence; 431, Harriet; 432, Julia; 433, Fannie; 434, Robert; 435, Nettie, m. —— Sigler, of Shepherdstown, W. Va.

267. MARY CATHARINE ANDERSON (John[1], Abraham[2], Jacob[3], Nancy[4], Isabel[5]), dau. of Colbert and Isabel (V. M.) Anderson, m. George Henry. Issue: 436, Clara Bell, m. John Henry; 437, Doll, m. Henry Bayless.

268. JANE STATEN ANDERSON (John[1], Abraham[2], Jacob[3], Nancy[4], Isabel), dau. of Colbert and Isabel (V. M.) Anderson, b. ——; m. Wm. Riddelberger. Issue: 438, Lou; 439, Jennie; 440, Charles.

270. ABRAHAM VAN METRE (John[1], Abraham[2], Jacob[3], Nancy[4], Abishua[5]), son of Abishua and Nancy (Morris) Van Metre, b. ——; m. Sarah Fisher. Issue: 441, Allen; 442, Smith.

271. SMITH VAN METRE (John[1], Abraham[2], Jacob[3], Nancy[4], Abishua[5]), son of Abishua and Nancy (Morris) Van Metre, b. ——; m. Miss Pitzer. Issue: 443, Anne.

275. BARNEY VAN METRE (John[1], Abraham[2], Jacob[3], Nancy[4], Abraham[5]), son of Abraham and Eliza (Russell) Van Metre, b. ——; m. Sarah Wolf. Issue: 444, Ernest.

277. SARAH VAN METRE (John[1], Abraham[2], Jacob[3], Nancy[4], Abraham[5]), dau. of Abraham and Eliza (Russell) Van Metre, b. ——; m. —— Price. Issue: 445, Abraham.

280. ISABEL VAN METRE (John[1], Abraham[2], Jacob[3], Nancy[4], Ashahel[5]), dau. of Ashahel and Mary A. (Willhelm) Van Metre, b. 11 Nov., 1848; d. 13 July, 1880; m. 24 Dec., 1867, Joseph Strine. Issue: 446, Mary Ella, b. 20 Feb., 1869; m. 6 March, 1888, John, son of John B. and Sarah V. M. Files; he was b. 28 Dec., 1859.

THE VAN METRE GENEALOGY

281. Ruth Elizabeth Van Metre (John[1], Abraham[2], Jacob[3], Nancy[4], Ashahel[5]), dau. of Ashahel and Mary A. (Willhelm) Van Metre, b. 16 Sept., 1850; d. ——; m. 6 June, 1878, Rev. Wm. Hesse, D.D., of Lutheran Church at Brookeville, Pa.   Issue: 447, Mary Agatha, b. 8 July, 1880; 448, Luella Virginia, b. 23 Nov., 1882.
449, Chas. F. V., b. 9 Feb., 1885; 450, Margaret Jane, b. 3 June, 1887.
451, William Nelson, b. 16 Oct., 1890.

282. Ellen Jane Van Metre (John[1], Abraham[2], Jacob[3], Nancy[4], Ashahel[5]), dau. of Ashahel and Mary A. (Willhelm) Van Metre, b. 25 Sept., 1852; d. ——; m. 26 July, 1877, Peter E. Strine.   Issue:
452, Margaret, b. 22 Oct., 1878; d. 18 July, 1879; 453, Philip, b. 14 Oct., 1897.

283. James Henry Van Metre (John[1], Abraham[2], Jacob[3], Nancy[4], Ashahel[5]), son of Ashahel and Mary A. (Willhelm) Van Metre, b. 1 Nov., 1862; d. ——; m. Sept., 1895, Ora Jones.
Issue:
454, Margaret Susan, b. 9 April, 1896.

284. Elijah W. Van Metre (John[1], Abraham[2], Jacob[3], Nancy[4], Henry[5]), son of Henry and Mary (Whitson) Van Metre, b. ——; m. Mary Byers. Resides at Washington, D. C.
Issue:
455, Earl, at Naval Academy, Annapolis, Md.; 456, Louisa, at Womans College, Baltimore, Md.

291. Abraham Henry Van Metre (John[1], Abraham[2], Jacob[3], Nancy[4], James[5]), son of James and Catharine (Hoorne) Van Metre, b. 2 March, 1865; d. Sept., 1894; m. 3 Feb., 1886, Mary Myers.   Issue:
457, a dau.; 458, a dau.; both live at Pittsburg, Pa.

308. Ruth Gorrell (John[1], Abraham[2], Jacob[3], Isabel[4], David[5]), dau. of David and Mary B. (V. M.) Gorrell, b. ——; d. ——; m. Seaton Magruder.   Issue:
459, David L.; 460, Robert; 461, William; 462, Thomas; 463, Edward; 464, Allen.

316. Mary Martha Van Metre (John[1], Abraham[2], Jacob[3], Elizabeth[4], Isabel[5]), dau. of Abraham P. and Isabel (Tabb) Van Metre; b. ——; m. Samuel W. Strider.   Issue:
465, Virginia Ann, m. Benjamin F. Harrison, of Shepherdstown, W. Va.

318. Frances Van Cleve (John[1], Abraham[2], Abraham[3], Naomi[4], Elizabeth[5]), dau. of Samuel and Elizabeth (Roberts) Van Cleve, b. ——; d. ——; m. William Van Cleve.   Issue:
466, William; 467, Lucy; 468, Frances.

SAMUEL ROBERTS VAN METRE

DESCENDANTS OF ABRAHAM VAN METRE

327. HENRIETTA VAN METRE (John[1], Abraham[2], Abraham[3], Joseph[4], Robert[5]), dau. of Robert and Mahala (Wheeler) Van Metre, b. 15 April, 1823; *m.* 2 Feb., 1842, Jacob Fowler, who d. 17 April, 1867.   Issue:
  469, Robert, b. 1 Sept., 1843; *m.* 1863, Sarah Hamilton.
  470, Eliza, b. 13 Jan., 1846; d. inf.
  471, Mary J., b. 18 April, 1855; d. 2 Jan., 1876; *m.* — May, 1873, Dr. D. Hughes.
  472, Flora, b. 21 Feb., 1857; *m.* 1st 30 Aug., 1857, A. F. Lane; *m.* 2d 22 Oct., 1884, Henry O. Hiser.

328. MARGARET VAN METRE (John[1], Abraham[2], Abraham[3], Joseph[4], Robert[5]), dau. of Robert and Mahala (Wheeler) Van Metre, b. 1 Dec., 1825; d. 18 May, 1872; *m.* 21 Dec., 1843, Othey E. Price. He d. 5 Sept., 1853.   Issue:
  473, Mahala, b. 19 Jan., 1845; *m.* 11 April, 1867, B. B. Tarman.
  474, Isaac, b. 19 Nov., 1847; d. 11 Nov., 1906; *m.* 29 Feb., 1869, Mary Cunningham.
  475, Joseph V., b. 3 Dec., 1850; *m.* 30 Jan., 1881, Charlotta Naomi South.
  476, Amarilla, b. 4 Oct., 1852; d. inf.; 477, Francis, b. 5 Jan., 1854; d. inf.
  478, Vincent, b. 22 Aug., 1856; *m.* 25 Nov., 1883, Anna Bershares.
  479, Sarah A., b. 21 June, 1859; d. 15 July, 1891; *m.* 30 Aug., 1877, Merrick Cox.
  480, Emma Augusta, b. 3 April, 1864; d. inf.
  481, Mason O., b. 5 Sept., 1865; *m.* 21 Jan., 1891, Maggie A. Price.
  482, Mary C., b. 2 March, 1870; *m.* 27 May, 1890, William W. Baker.

329. ANNA VAN METRE (John[1], Abraham[2], Abraham[3], Joseph[4], Robert[5]), dau. of Robert and Mahala (Wheeler) Van Metre, *m.* Webster D. Wallbridge; they live in Appleton City, Mo.
                                                                Issue:
  483, Maggie, *m.* 1886, Chas. Duffy; 484, Willis P., *m.* 1886, Ella Long.
  485, Frances C., *m.* 1888, Ed. C. Gird; 486, Ruby Ellen, *m.* 1885, Wm. McElheney.
  487, Robert E., *m.* 1899, Gussie Smith; 488, Frank M., *m.* 1902, Lydia Schrinke.
  489, M. Jean, *m.* 1896, Bert Rogers; 490, Henrietta, *m.* 1900, Willis B. North.

330. SAMUEL ROBERTS VAN METRE (John[1], Abraham[2], Abraham[3], Joseph[4], Robert[5]), son of Robert and Mahala (Wheeler) Van Metre, was born on the Old Van Metre homestead near West Liberty, Va., where his grandfather, Joseph Van Metre,

located over one hundred years ago. Mr. Van Metre's birth occurred 8 Aug., 1836. He remained on the farm until eighteen years of age then he began teaching school, but later his occupation was steamboating. He finally settled down to mercantile life in which he has continued for nearly fifty years; he *m.* 22 Aug., 1861, Miss Josephine, dau. of Isaac and Laura (Stanton) Johnson. He helped to organize the Citizens' National Bank, and Board of Trade of Marietta; also the Farmers' Mutual Insurance Co. of Washington County, Ohio, and was president of same for twelve years, and treasurer and director of the former. He also helped to organize and wrote the By-Laws of the Mutual Cyclone and Windstorm Association of Columbus, Ohio, and is a director and the vice-president of the same; and also of the Federation of Mutual Insurance Associations of Ohio; and of the Co-Operative Mutual Fire Associations of the United States. Until recently he owned a three hundred acre farm upon which he raised fine grades of cattle and sheep. Mr. Van Metre is still in the mercantile business and owns one of the finest residences in the beautiful pioneer city of Marietta, where he loves to entertain his relatives and friends.   Issue:

491, Laura, b. 17 Oct., 1862, *unm.*; 492, Mary; 493, Wyllis, b. 23 Oct., 1869, *m.* 5 June, 1895, Grace Applegate. No issue. They reside in Marietta, O.

331. ELIZABETH VAN METRE (John[1], Abraham[2], Abraham[3], Ashahel[4], Abraham[5]), dau. of Abraham and Mary (Choppuck) Van Metre, *m.* Wirt Tabler.   Issue:

483, Naomi; 484, Matilda; 485, Laura; 486, Bessie; 487, Cora; 488, Clayton.

332. JENNIE VAN METRE (John[1], Abraham[2], Abraham[3], Ashahel[4], Abraham[5]), dau. of Abraham and Mary (Choppuck) Van Metre, *m.* Corbin Tabler.   Issue:

489, Ernest; 490, Lillie; 491, Ray; 492, Henry; 493, Mildred; 494, Edith.

333. MARY ELIZABETH FILES (John[1], Abraham[2], Abraham[3], Ashahel[4], Sarah[5]), dau. of John B. and Sarah (V. M.) Files, b. ——; *m.* David Pitznagle.   Issue:

494, Cora; 495, Sarah; 495½, John Wilbur.

336. JOHN FILES (John[1], Abraham[2], Abraham[3], Ashahel[4], Sarah[5]), son of John B. and Sarah (Van Metre) Files, b. 28 Dec., 1859; *m.* 6 March, 1888, Mary E. Strine (No. 442), dau. of Joseph and Isabel (V. M.) Strine.   Issue:

496, Mabel, b. 18 Aug., 1892; 497, Thomas, b. 11 Sept., 1894. 498, Ella, b. 6 July, 1896; 499, Chas. James, b. 20 Sept., 1898. 500, Virginia Bell, b. 15 May, 1901; 501, Theodore, b. 27 Sept., 1903.

337. WILLIAM FILES (John[1], Abraham[2], Abraham[3], Ashahel[4], Sarah[5]), son of John B. and Sarah (Van Metre) Files, b. ——; m. Anna Bell Knight. Issue:
506, Eliza; 507, John S.; 508, Anna.

357. HENRY VAN METRE (John[1], Abraham[2], Joseph[3], Abraham[4], Jacob[5]), son of Jacob and Mary (Black) Van Metre, b. ——; m. his cousin, Sarah, No. 366, dau. of Morgan and Rebecca (Knott) Van Metre. Issue:
509, William; 510, John; 511, Isaac; 512, Rebecca.

358. MORGAN VAN METRE (John[1], Abraham[2], Joseph[3], Abraham[4], Jacob[5]), son of Jacob and Mary (Black) Van Metre, b. ——; m. Jennie Sheriff, dau. of Jennie Sheriff (neé Black) a sister of Morgan's mother, Mary Black. Issue:
513, William; 513½, James; both living in western Pennsylvania; 513¾, Mary Ann.

359. JACOB JAMES VAN METRE (John[1], Abraham[2], Joseph[3], Abraham[4], Jacob[5]), son of Jacob and Mary (Black) Van Metre, b. ——, 1815; d. ——; m. Mary Dean. Issue:
514, John Newton, killed in army, unm., 1864; 515, Amanda Jane.
516, Eleanor Dean, m. Dewitt Clinton Moore; no issue; resides at Berkeley, Cal.
517, Hannah Marie; 518, Matilda Aramintha; 519, Mary Frances; 520, Leah Steel; 521, Sylvester Fremont.

360. JOHN VAN METRE (John[1], Abraham[2], Joseph[3], Abraham[4], Jacob[5]), son of Jacob and Mary (Black) Van Metre, m. —— ——. Issue:
522, Josephine; 523, Lula.

361. JOSEPH VAN METRE (John[1], Abraham[2], Joseph[3], Abraham[4], Jacob[5]), son of Jacob and Mary (Black) Van Metre, b. ——; d. ——; m. —— ——. Issue:
524, Alice; 525, Addie; 526, Frederick.

362. ROBERT VAN METRE (John[1], Abraham[2], Joseph[3], Abraham[4], Jacob[5]), son of Jacob and Mary (Black) Van Metre, b. ——; m. —— ——. Issue:
527, Emma, m. —— Derby; 528, a dau.

371. MORGAN VAN METRE (John[1], Abraham[2], Joseph[3], Abraham[4], Morgan[5]), son of Morgan and Rebecca (Knott) Van Metre, m. —— Polley; living in Magnolia, O. Issue:
529, Rebecca, m. —— Swenk; resides in Magnolia, O.

379. ISAAC V. M. BROWN (John[1], Abraham[2], Joseph[3], Isaac[4], Margaret[5]), son of James W. and Margaret (Van Metre) Brown, b. 12 July, 1826; d. 15 May, 1863; m. 24 Dec., 1846, Elizabeth Drummond Carroll, of New Jersey, granddaughter of Loudon

Carl, a soldier of the Revolution. Isaac was a tanner, farrier and a circuit rider.   Issue:
> 530, James W., b. Sept., 1847; d. Oct., 1847.
> 531, Anna Louise, b. Logansport, Ind., 9 Jan., 1849; *m.* 1874, Watson Thompson; resides at Clinton, Ia.
> 532, Mary Eleanor, b. 16 Oct., 1851; d. Aug., 1853.

413. PETER CYRUS VAN METRE (John[1], Abraham[2], Joseph[3], David[4], Abner[5]), son of Abner and Elizabeth A. (Stewart) Van Metre, b. ——; d. —— ; *m.* —— ——.   Issue:
> 533, Elizabeth.

416. AUGUSTUS ABNER VAN METRE (John[1], Abraham[2], Joseph[3], David[4], Cyrus[5]), son of Cyrus and Sarah (Sayford) Van Metre, *m.* 27 Dec., 1894, Mary Lois Davis.   Issue:
> 534, Herschel D.; 534½, Julia C.; 535, Mary E.; 536, Benjamin Cyrus, of Middletown, Ind.

417. NAOMI VAN METRE (John[1], Abraham[2], Joseph[3], David[4], Cyrus[5]), dau. of Cyrus and Sarah (Sayford) Van Metre, b. ——; d. ——; *m.* James A. Painter.   Issue:
> 537, James O., *m.* Flo. Wishart; resides at Middletown, Ind.

420. MARIE VAN METRE (John[1], Abraham[2], Joseph[3], David[4], Cyrus[5]), dau. of Cyrus and Sarah (Sayford) Van Metre, *m.* Chas. C. Shedron.   Issue:
> 538, Arthur; 539, Osee Bell; 540, Elroy; 541, Charles, *m.* Mattie Sykes; 542, Josie; 543, Lowly.

421. CLARENCE P. KERFOTT (John[1], Abraham[2], Mary[3], Abraham[4], Mary[5]), son of J. Baker and Mary (Gorrell) Kerfott, b. ——; *m.* Rebecca Kratz.   Issue:
> 544, Clarence R.; 544¼, J. Conrad; 544½, Mary Louise; 544¾, Ruth; 545, Robert R.

422. HETTY· KERFOTT (John[1], Abraham[2], Mary[3], Abraham[4], Mary[5]), dau. of J. Baker and Mary (Gorrell) Kerfott, b. ——; *m.* Milton S. Miller.   Issue:
> 546, Mabel Lee; 547, Florence S.; 548, Mary `Baker; 549, Charles J.; 550, Anna Ruth; 551, Fred.

423. MARY BAKER KERFOTT (John[1], Abraham[2], Mary[3], Abraham[4], Mary[5]), dau. of J. Baker and Mary (Gorrell) Kerfott, b. ——; *m.* J. Henry Bogert.   Issue·
> 552, Mary Kerfott; 553, Eleanor Bird.

433. DOLL HENRY (John[1], Abraham[2], Jacob[3], Nancy[4], Isabel[5], Mary C.[6]), dau. of George and Mary C. (Anderson) Henry, *m.* Henry Bayless.   Issue:
> 554, Margaret; 555, Lottie; 556, Boyd; 557, Ella; 558, Jesse.

492. MARY VAN METRE (John[1], Abraham[2], Abraham[3], Joseph[4], Robert[5], Samuel R.[6]), dau. of Samuel R. and Josephine (Johnson) Van Metre, b. 5 Nov., 1864; *m.* 4 Sept., 1884, Capt. O. J.

DESCENDANTS OF ABRAHAM VAN METRE

Stowe; they reside at Ventura, California, where Capt. Stowe is engaged extensively in fruit growing and shipping.   Issue:
559, Josephine Johnson, b. Jan., 1886; *m.* at Santa Barbara, Cal., Edward Wileman, Sept., 1907.

513. ANNA LOUISE BROWN (John[1], Abraham[2], Joseph[3], Isaac[4], Margaret[5], Isaac[6]), dau. of Isaac V. M. and Elizabeth D. (Carroll) Brown, b. 9 Jan., 1849; *m.* 1874, Watson Thompson, of Syracuse, N. Y.   Issue:
560, Ralph; 561, Eleanor Foster, twins, b. 9 Nov., 1874; Ralph d. 23 Oct., 1876; Eleanor d. 9 Nov., 1874.

515. AMANDA JANE VAN METRE (John[1], Abraham[2], Joseph[3], Abraham[4], Jacob[5], Jacob J.[6]), dau. of Jacob J. and Mary (Dean) Van Metre, *m.* David Porter.   Issue:
562, Preston.

517. HANNAH MARIE (John[1], Abraham[2], Joseph[3], Abraham[4], Jacob[5], Jacob J.[6]), dau. of Jacob J. and Mary (Dean) Van Metre, *m.* John Kaser.   Issue:
563, Kyle K.; 564, Avelrose; 565, Lorin; 566, Aramintha; 567, Esther; 568, Elmo; 569, Clarence.

519. MARY FRANCES VAN METRE (John[1], Abraham[2], Joseph[3], Abraham[4], Jacob[5], Jacob J.[6]), dau. Jacob J. and Mary (Dean) Van Metre, *m.* —— Miller.   Issue:
570, Brunetta Frances, *m.* Mr. Wetmore; no issue.
571, Charles Emmet, *m.* Ruby Thomas.

520. LEAH STEEL VAN METRE (John[1], Abraham[2], Joseph[3], Abraham[4], Jacob[5], Jacob J.[6]), dau. of Jacob J. and Mary (Dean) Van Metre, *m.* —— ——.   Issue:
572, a son; 573, a son.

521. SYLVESTER FREMONT VAN METRE (John[1], Abraham[2], Joseph[3], Abraham[4], Jacob[5], Jacob J.[6]), son of Jacob J. and Mary (Dean) Van Metre, *m.* —— ——.   Issue:
574, a son.

537. JAMES O. PAINTER (John[1], Abraham[2], Joseph[3], David[4], Cyrus[5], Naomi[6]), son of James A. and Naomi (Van Metre) Painter, *m.* Flo. Wishart.   Issue:
575, Carl.

538. ARTHUR SHEDRON (John[1], Abraham[2], Joseph[3], David[4], Cyrus[5], Marie[6]), son of Chas. C. and Marie (Van Metre) Shedron, *m.* —— ——.   Issue:
576, a child.

559. JOSEPHINE STOWE (John[1], Abraham[2], Abraham[3], Joseph[4], Robert[5], Samuel R.[6], Mary[7]), dau. of Capt. O. J. and Mary (Van Metre) Stowe, *m.* at Santa Barbara, Cal., Sept., 1907, Edward Wileman.   Issue:
577, Richard Stowe, b. Oct., 1908.

571. CHAS. EMMETT MILLER (John, Abraham, Joseph, Abraham, Jacob, Jacob J., Mary F.), son of —— and Mary (Van Metre) Miller, *m.* Ruby Thomas.   Issue: 578, Lorin; 579, Eleanora.

DESCENDANTS OF JACOB VAN METRE

JACOB VAN METRE (John[1]), youngest son of John and Margaret Van Metre, b. in Somerset or Salem Co., N. J., 1723; d. near Elizabethtown, Hardin Co., Ky., 16 Nov., 1798 (see Wither's Chronicles, p. 123; Collins' History of Kentucky, II., p. 312); *m.* 1738, Letitia Strode, probably a daughter of James Strode, an early settler of Frederick Co., Va., who lived, *circa* 1770, near Mecklenburg, Va. Letitia died in Kentucky, 25 Dec., 1789.

By the terms of his father's will Jacob received a devise of 233 acres of land; it was a portion of the land upon which his father had lived and adjoined that inherited by his brother Isaac, "together with all houses and orchards on the said parcel or tract of land." Jacob acquired otherwise certain grants of land in Virginia by patent. With his wife they conveyed 170 acres of the latter to his brothers, Henry and Abraham, 31 March, 1755, "being part of the patent upon which said Henry lives."

Jacob and his wife "Lettice" conveyed on 4 June, 1764, 16 acres to Thomas Thornburgh; it was a part of tract devised by his father's will to James Davis, husband of his sister Mary. This was reconveyed to Jacob again.

Jacob and Lettice made a lease of some land in Frederick Co., Va., to Jacob Vandever, 17 March, 1769.

Jacob Van Metre is mentioned in Major Carlyle's reports for a "waggonage" account, 20 Dec., 1754 (Governor Dinwiddie's Letters).

About 1768–9 Jacob deemed it desirable to move farther west, as many of the inhabitants of the Valley of Virginia were then doing, and after disposing of much of his property, accompanied John Swan, Thomas Hughes and others in a tour of the southwestern parts of Pennsylvania, then claimed as a part of Virginia territory. "They reached the vicinity of the present Carmichaelstown and tomahawked such enclosures as they desired. The place of settlement was on Muddy Creek. Returning to Virginia they brought back their families and household effects on pack horses, the slaves walking and driving the stock, and the whole train, aggregating about fifty persons, followed the route cut out by Braddock's army as far as it lay in their course, after which they cut a way for themselves." Swan and Van Metre located near each other on some bottom land not far from the mouth of Muddy Creek, a tributary of the Monongahela, in Cumberland Township, where, it appears, Jacob Van Metre had acquired a grant of 400 acres in 1759 (see Hale's Trans-Alleghany Pioneer, p. 259; Trans-Alleghany Mag., Vol. II., pp. 9, 11), and is credited with settlement made thereon in 1770 (Pa. Archives, 3d Series, Bedford Co., Tax Transcripts). Here the two neighbors erected a strong stockade which was known on the frontier as Fort Swan and Van Metre (see Frontier Forts of Pennsylvania, Vol. II., p. 441). Certificates for settlement were granted them by the Commissioners "in the fifth year of the Commonwealth." The region was known among Virginians in those days as Monongalia County, in the District of West Augusta. The records of Washington Co., Pa., evidence the fact that an application No. 2405, dated 3 April, 1769, a tract of land called "Burgundy," situated on the west side of Monongahela, containing 211 acres, 3 perches, was granted to Jacob Van Metre; it was surveyed 13 Oct., 1769 (Dept. Int. Affairs, Harrisburg, Pa.).

Jacob Van Metre and Lettice are among the names of signers for the organization of The Regular Baptist Church of Jesus Christ at Uniontown (Fayette Co.), Pa., which was constituted at Great Bethel, 7 Nov., 1770. A stream called Van Metre's Run is in Perry Township, and a Peter Van Metre was the owner of a saw mill near its mouth. This stream probably emptied into Jacob's Creek, which is in its vicinity (see History of Fayette Co., Pa., pp. 316, 713). In 1773 Jacob's name was enrolled among the taxables of Rosstraevor Township, and on the 6th July of the same year, he, with one of his brothers and several others, were indicted by the grand inquest of the county for "inciting to riot" (History of Washington Co., Pa.).

Jacob Van Metre and Lettice Strode, his wife, and Abraham, son and heir of Jacob and Lettice, his wife, of the Province of Pennsylvania, and settlement of Muddy Creek, waters of Ohio, 232 acres in Van Metre's marsh, part of 1,785 acres granted to John and Isaac Van Metre as part of 40,000 acre grant. 1773. Deed Bk. No. 2, Martinsburg. (W. W. Van Metre.)

On the 6 Dec., 1774, Joseph Hill was appointed constable "in room of Jacob Van Metre" (see Ann. Carnegie Museum, Vol. I., p. 526).

It is noted that Jacob Van Metre was one of "the Committee from Augusta County, Va., which met at Pittsburg, 16 May, 1775." And on the minutes of the Court of Yohoghania Co., Va., 23 March, 1779, which met at Andrew Heath's farm near West Elizabeth, it is recorded that "Jacob and Abraham Van Metre and others have produced recommendations from the Court of Monongalia Co., Va., to pass unmolested to the falls of the Ohio (Louisville, Ky.), which was read and approved." It is recited in Collins' History of Kentucky, Vol. II., that Jacob Van Metre moved from the waters of Muddy Creek in south-western Pennsylvania, where he had resided several years, to what afterward became Hardin County, Ky. A tradition exists in the family that Jacob took boat at Fort Pitt in 1779, and went down the Ohio, landing at Bear Grass, now Louisville, Ky. The foregoing record from the minutes of the Yohogania County Court seems to confirm this tradition. The last documentary evidence of his residence in what is now Pennsylvania is found in an item in the Journal of the Washington County Court, under the date of 1781, which states that Jacob Van Metre is appointed one of a jury of view "to view a road from Washington's Mill to Capt. Van Swearingen's ferry on the Monongahela, and thence to Catfish Camp" (Washington, Pa.). General Washington's mill was located where Perryopolis, Fayette Co., Pa., now stands; and Van Swearingen's ferry was at Greenfield (see History of Washington Co., Pa.).

As new counties were erected in southwestern Pennsylvania, the region about the Forks of the Yohogania fell first in one county and then in another, which accounts for the apparently different localities with which Jacob's name is associated.

Capt. Abraham Shepherd, nephew of Jacob Van Metre, when writing to his brother, Col. David Shepherd, Lieutenant of Ohio Co., Va., who was then living on Wheeling Creek, tells him, Nov., 1778, that he stopped at his Uncle Jacob's "on the Creek." This refers to the Monongahela trail which lay between the Potomac and the Ohio Rivers. From the head of Muddy Creek to the head of the south fork of Wheeling Creek was only a few miles westward across country.

In the fall or winter of 1780, Capt. James Helm, Col. Andrew Hynes and Samuel Haycroft, with others from Virginia, settled where Elizabethtown (capital of Hardin County), Ky., now stands. The spot was in Severen's Valley, forty odd miles from Louisville, and was then in Nelson Co., Ky., from which Hardin County was set off in 1792. These pioneers erected three forts or block houses about a mile apart and were the only settlements, at that day, between Green River and the Ohio (see Hale's U. S. Wars, p. 217; Shepherd Papers, Vol. IV., p. 3; Collins's Kentucky, Vol. II., p. 307).

Among those who joined this colony at this time were Jacob Van Metre, his wife, three sons and seven daughters, viz., Mrs. Margaret Haycroft (wife of Samuel), Susan and her husband, Rev. John Gerrard; Mary and her husband, David Hinton (who was drowned in the Ohio River while on the way); Jacob, Jr.; Isaac; John; Rebecca; Rachael; Ailcey and Elizabeth Van Metre, and a family of slaves; most of them opened farms in Severen's Valley. Rev. John Gerrard was installed the first pastor of the second Baptist Church established in Kentucky. The church was organized 17 June, 1781, near Hyne's Station with eighteen members. Gerrard was afterward captured by the Indians and never heard of again (see Collins's Kentucky, II., p. 308).

DESCENDANTS OF JACOB VAN METRE

Jacob Van Metre was active in military operations along the Ohio; served under Gen. George Rogers Clark in Kaskaskia campaign of 1778; he commanded a company in Clark's expedition against the Indian renegades under Girty in 1782; and was on the Coshocton campaign in Capt. William Crawford's company under command of his nephew, Col. David Shepherd in 1791 (see Wither's Chronicles, p. 133; Shepherd Papers, Vol. IV., p. 3). In his younger days Jacob served in Capt. Richard Morgan's company from Mecklenburg, Va., in the French and Indian War, 1756–1758 (see Shepherdstown Register, 14 Jan., 1903).

When he located on Severen's Valley Creek, about two miles above the present site of Elizabethtown, Jacob erected a fort, as other settlers had done; it was known as Van Metre's Fort; it was the scene of an Indian scare, 13 Oct., 1790 (Collins's History of Kentucky, Vol. II., pp. 307–308).

Fom the fact that Jacob Van Metre and his nephew Jacob, the son of Henry, came together from the Muddy Creek settlements, and both locating on Severen's Valley Creek, not far apart and each having mills, the elder man was distinguished by the style of "Valley Creek Jake" and the nephew as "Miller Jake," because of his milling pursuits.   Issue:

1, Abraham; 2, Isaac; 3, John; 4, Rachael, *m.* —— Pritchett; 5, Margaret; 6, Jacob; 7, Elizabeth; 8, Rebecca, *m.* 1st —— Rollinger, *m.* 2d —— McKenzie; 9, Susan; 10, Mary; 11, Alcinda; 12, Ellen, *m.* —— Kline; 13, William.

1. ABRAHAM VAN METRE (John¹, Jacob²), son of Jacob and Letitia (Strode) Van Metre, *m.* —— ——. He, it is said, was killed by the Indians about sixty miles from his father's home, and to have left surviving four sons and four daughters (see J. C. Van Metre's and W. W. Van Metre's Letters). The names of the husbands of the daughters were Messrs. Swank, Edlin, Ashby and Goodwin; and a son, supposed to have been Abraham, Jr., *m.* Mary, or Nancy, Evans (see Mrs. Mary Ann Wale's Letters).

2. ISAAC VAN METRE (John¹, Jacob²), son of Jacob and Letitia (Strode) Van Metre, b. Frederick Co., Va., 2 Feb., 1759; d. 4 June, 1808, in Grayson Co., Ky.; *m.* 1st Mrs. Martha (Hubbard) Hoagland, widow of Capt. (Henry?) Hoagland; *m.* 2d Jane Carson, by whom there was no issue. Isaac was the first circuit rider and the first Clerk of Grayson Co., Ky.; was a Revolutionary soldier and a pensioner in Grayson Co., Ky. In the minutes of the County Court of Augusta, Va., 17 April, 1776, the record is made of the probate of the last will of Larkin Pierpoint, deceased, in which the name of Isaac La Meetre appears as a witness.   Issue:

THE VAN METRE GENEALOGY

14, Frances, b. 16 Oct., 1784, *m.* her first cousin, James Haycroft; 15, Abraham; 16, Jacob, b. 2 April, 1789, d. Otter
Creek, Ky., 30 Sept., 1832.
17, Nancy, b. 9 July, 1791, *m.* 1st John Porter. Isaac Van
Metre and John Porter were of the number who formed
the settlement at Losantiville (Cincinnati), 28 Dec.,
1788. Porter was a member of the Kentucky House of
Representatives from Logan County, 1802, 1806; and
from Bath Co., 1817, 1824–25, 1829 (Collins's Kentucky, Vol. II., pp. 433, 733).
18, Elizabeth, b. 15 Aug., 1794; *m.* Joel Morrison.
19, Isaac Hoagland, b. 1 Jan., 1796; 20, Polly, b. 9 July, 1798.
21, Letitia, b. 1 March, 1800; 22, Hubbard, b. 6 Aug., 1802.
23, Matilda, b. 28 Aug., 1807; was second wife of John Porter.

3. JOHN VAN METRE (John[1], Jacob[2]), son of Jacob and Letitia
(Strode) Van Metre, b. Frederick Co., Va., *circa* 1761; *m.* a
Miss Strode, probably a daughter of Samuel Strode, who erected
Strode's Station on Strode's Run in Kentucky. John Van Metre
lived for a time in southwestern Pennsylvania.   Issue:
24, Ottersee; 25, Moses; 26, Strode; 27, Cyrus; 28, Zillie, *m.*
circa 1808, John Kellar; 29, Cynthia, *m. circa* 1810,
Fred. Kellar; they lived at Glendale, Hart Co., Ky.; the
Kellars were sons of George and Sarah (Hedges)
Kellar, who were probably settled at Kellar's Station
on Bear Grass Creek in Jefferson Co., Ky., *ante* 1780.
Catharine Kellar is said to have *m.* Wm. Van Metre.
30, John, said to have *m.* a Kellar also; 31, Nathan, b. 1790.

5. MARGARET VAN METRE (John[1], Jacob[2]), dau. of Jacob and
Letitia (Strode) Van Metre, b. Frederick Co., Va., *circa* 1760;
m., at Fort Pitt, *circa* 1779, Samuel Haycroft. He was born in
Virginia 11 Sept., 1752; d. Kentucy, 15 Oct., 1823. The Hay-
crofts accompanied Jacob Van Metre and others into Kentucky
in 1780 and settled in Hardin Co. He built a station and soon
became prominent in county affairs; was sheriff in 1802; Judge
of Court of Quarter Sessions, 1803; Assistant Judge of the Circuit Court of Elizabethtown and later a member of the Legislature. He served in the War of the Revolution and his widow
Margaret is recorded as drawing a pension while living in Hardin
County in 1840; her age at that time was given as eighty years.
"Judge Haycroft was a farmer, an honored and useful citizen"
(Collins's Kentucky, II., p. 311).   Issue:
32, Samuel; 33, James, *m.* his first cousin, Frances, dau. of
Isaac Van Metre.

6. JACOB VAN METRE (John[1], Jacob[2]), son of Jacob and Letitia
(Strode) Van Metre, b. Frederick Co., Va., 4 Oct., 1762; d.
Meade Co., Ky., 27 February, 1852 (Collins's Kentucky, Vol. II.,

p. 311); *m.* 16 Nov., 1786, Elizabeth Rhodes (probably dau. of Henry Rhodes, Sr., named as supervisor in Brother's Valley Township, Bedford Co., Pa., 18 July, 1771). Elizabeth Rhodes, at her marriage, was of Hardin Co., Ky.; b. 1770; d. 1852. Jacob is said to have succeeded to the Muddy Creek, Pa., homestead on the death of his father. In Kentucky he was known as "Valley Jake." Issue:

34, Sarah; 35, Abraham; 36, John, who lived and died in Meade Co., Ky.

37, Joseph, called in Kentucky "Virginia Joe," *m.* Elizabeth Evans; 38, Thomas; 39, Susan; 40, Jacob, who d. in Washington, Ill.; 41, Henry; 42, Daniel; 43, Nathaniel, *m.* a Miss Doney, sister of his brother Abraham's wife; 44, Elizabeth; 45, Mary, who *m.* —— Leevis, and lived in Bedford, Taylor Co., Ia.; 46, David.

47, Rebecca *sup.*), *m.* Jacob Van Metre, son of Henry[1] Van Metre. A Rebecca Van Metre was a Revolutionary soldier's widow, drawing pension in Hardin Co., in 1840, at which time her age was given as 63 years (b. 1777) (Collins's Kentucky, Vol. II., p. 321). A Rebecca Van Metre, of Hardin Co., is said to have *m.* Robert Harris, 1 Dec., 1806. Cynthiana, Ky., is claimed to have been named for two Van Metre women (O. O. Nation). This town is the capital of Harrison Co., Ky., was founded on the Licking by Robert Harris in 1793, and named for his two daughters, Cynthia and Anna (Family tradition, Collins's Kentucky, Vol. II., p. 321).

7. ELIZABETH VAN METRE (John[1], Jacob[2]), dau. of Jacob and Letitia (Strode) Van Metre, *m.* 1st John Swan, Jr., son of John Swan, of Loudon Co., Va.; *m.* 2d —— McNeil; *m.* 3d —— Vantner, or Vertrees.

10. MARY VAN METRE (John[1], Jacob[2]), dau. of Jacob and Letitia (Strode) Van Metre, *m.* 1st David Hinton, who was drowned while crossing the Ohio while the family were emigrating to Kentucky; *m.* 2d —— Chenowith. Issue:

48, John Hinton; 49, Hetty Hinton, *m.* Walter Briscoe. They had a son William.

11. ALCINDA VAN METRE (John[1], Jacob[2]), dau. Jacob and Letitia (Strode) Van Metre, *m.* 1st James (or Jacob) Rhodes; *m.* 2d —— McIntyre.

13. WILLIAM VAN METRE (John[1], Jacob[2]), son of Jacob and Letitia (Strode) Van Metre, *m.*(?) Phoebe Hart in Monongalia Co., Va., 1795 (Trans.-Alleghany Mag., Vol. II., p. 57). A Nathaniel Hart settled in Kentucky. He came from Pennsyl-

vania. William Van Metre *m.* Catharine Kellar, of Kentucky, *circa* 1805 (Mrs. W. S. Goodwyn's Letter).

15. ABRAHAM VAN METRE (John[1], Jacob[2], Isaac[3]), son of Isaac and Martha (Hoagland) Van Metre, b. Hardin Co., Ky., 17 Aug., 1786; d. *circa* 1850. He was engaged in the Indian wars in Indiana and contracted phthisis while foraging for beeves in the swamps of Indiana during the time he was fighting Indians (W. W. Van Metre Letters); *m.* 1807, his first cousin Sarah, dau. of Jacob and Catharine Van Metre. Issue:

    50, Miles Haycroft; 51, Isaac; was poisoned by eating wild parsnips, a deadly vegetable, looking so much like the table variety as to sometimes even deceive the frontiersman (W. W. Van Metre Letters).

    52, Jacob; 53, Joseph, *m.* —— Lawson; d. 1845; 54, Jeremiah, d. aged 20 years.

    55, Hubbard, d. 1845; 56, Elizabeth, *m.* —— Carlton; 57, Matilda; 58, Sarah P., *m.* —— Wortham; lives in Leitchfield, Ky.

30. JOHN VAN METRE (John[1], Jacob[2], John[3]), son of John and —— (Strode) Van Metre, *m.* —— Kellar. John met a tragic fate while riding his horse, in being thrown against a tree and killed. The scene of the accident was in the neighborhood of Rock Creek, in Grayson Co., Ky., where John was then a resident (J. C. Van Metre's Letter). Issue:

    59, Samuel, a physician; d. at Charlestown, Ill., 1872.
    60, John; 61, a dau.

31. NATHAN VAN METRE (John[1], Jacob[2], John[3]), son of John and —— (Strode) Van Metre, b. 1790; *m.* —— ——.
    62, John, b. 1820.

35. ABRAHAM (W.) VAN METRE (John[1], Jacob[2], Jacob[3]), son of Jacob and Elizabeth (Rhodes) Van Metre, b. 1790; *m.* Miss Dorsey. Abraham flatboated on the Mississippi until 1814–1815. He offered his services to General Jackson and served in the Battle of New Orleans, Jan. 8, 1815. Afterward settled in Washington, Ill. Issue:

    63, Rhodes; 64, Jacob; 65, William C.; 66, Endemile; 67, Mary; 68, Edward Abraham; and probably, 69, Joseph, a lawyer of New Orleans.

    69, A Joseph Van Metre *m.* Mrs. Cynthia Latin, a widow of New Orleans, *circa* 1861. He was a lawyer; but went to Texas, at close of war, and bought a sheep ranch. He sold this out later and returned to New Orleans; while on the voyage back he was taken sick and d. in 1865 (Family Tradition). "Josephs Vans Meater, died 25 Nov., 1865, at Lousiane Hotel; aged about 63 years. (Signed) Declaration of a friend" (From

Minute Book, City Board of Health, New Orleans, 1865). Joseph Van Metre, lawyer, living at New Orleans 1842–1846, at No. 14 Exchange Place (N. O. City Directory), was consulted by Miles H. Van Metre in reference to some legal matters, in 1845. His dying at a hotel indicates no home circle; "declaration by a friend" implies absence of very intimate associates, and lack of entry or record in wills, or "succession" books between 1865–1870, indicates his decease in modest, or probably humble circumstances. The Hotel Lousiané of that day cannot be at present located (W. W. Van Metre's Letters).

37. JOSEPH VAN METRE (John[1], Jacob[2], Jacob[3]), son of Jacob and Elizabeth (Rhodes) Van Metre (sometimes called Virginia Joe?), m. and settled in Petersburg, Ind., and had:
   70, Grotias; 71, Henry, who were the ancestors of an influential family of Van Metres in Iowa.

39. SUSAN VAN METRE (John[1], Jacob[2], Jacob[3]), dau. of Jacob and Elizabeth (Rhodes) Van Metre, b. 9 April, 1796; d. 1872; m. 1820, Joseph Woolfolk. Issue:
   72, Mary Jane, b. 10 Sept., 1820; m. 1840, Henry K. Wale. They lived in Jasper Co., Mo., where he d. 24 Jan., 1878.

50. MILES HAYCROFT VAN METER (John[1], Jacob[2], Isaac[3], Abraham[4]), son of Abraham and Sarah Van Metre, b. in Kentucky, 1810; emigrated to Kendall Co., Ill., 1836, and in 1850, to shores of Lake St. Croix, N. W. Wisconsin. Was captain in Illinois militia, 1847, when there was some local trouble with the Irish settlers. Lived in Wisconsin till his death, 1898. He m. 1829, Mary Pirtle Litsey. Issue:
   73, Davis Rhodes; 74, Marion Lafayette; 75, James Herbert, b. 1834; d. 1 May, 1908. Was a lieutenant in the Union Army.
   76, John H., formerly a captain in the Union Army, now living at Kincaid, Kan.
   77, Mary Ellen, b. 15 Feb., 1844, in Kendall Co., Ill., unm., lives at Hudson, Wis.; 78, Cassander Palestine, m. ——— Dyer, living at Hudson, Wis.; 79, Henry, killed at Chickamauga, Tenn.
   80, Abraham Chenowith, d. at Hudson, Wis., 1897; 81, Edward, b. 1853; m. 1883, Anna McLeod. He d. at Hudson, Wis., 14 Nov., 1908.

57. MATILDA VAN METER (John[1], Jacob[2], Isaac[3], Abraham[4]), dau. of Abraham and Sarah Van Metre, m. James W. Conklin, who was a son of David Conklin, one of the first settlers of Grayson Co., Ill. Issue:
   82, Abraham Van Meter, m. Elizabeth Butler, dau. of Miner

Butler. Abraham d. 15 Dec., 1906, leaving two sons and five daughters.

83, Palestine, *m.* —— Wortham. Resides at Leitchfield, Grayson Co., Ky.

62. JOHN VAN METER (John[1], Jacob[2], John[3], Nathan[4]), son of Nathan and —— Van Meter, b. *circa* 1820; *m.* —— ——.

Issue:

84, Jackson C., b. 1857; living at Bowling Green, Ky.

70. WILLIAM BRISCOE (John[1], Jacob[2], Mary[3], Hetty[4]), son of Walter and Hetty (Hinton) Briscoe, *m.* Miss Slaughter, dau. of Robert Slaughter, of Hardin Co., Ky. Issue:

85, Abbie; 86, Nannie; 87, a son.

73. DAVIS RHODES VAN METER (John[1], Jacob[2], Jacob[3], Abraham[4], Miles H.[5]), son of Miles H. and Mary P. (Litsey) Van Metre, b. at Falls of Rough Creek, Grayson Co., Ky., 7 July, 1830; resides at Washington, Ill.; *m.* 1856, at Washington, Ill., Susan Baker. Issue:

88, Ida, b. 4 July, 1857; *m.* 22 Feb., 1877, John Drury; resides in Nebraska.

89, Lettie, b. 30 May, 1859; *m.* 5 April, 1906, Chas. Puffer; resides at Chicago.

90, Nellie, b. 1 Sept., 1861; *m.* 1st 27 Dec., 1882, Jeremiah Riegel; *m.* 2d 12 Dec., 1905, A. W. Pinkney; resides Peoria, Ill.

91, John Wesley, b. 15 Oct., 1863; *m.* 5 June, 1890, Ona Randolph; resides at Oklahoma.

92, Elizabeth, b. 25 May, 1865; *m.* 3 Sept., 1896, John Chas. Roberts; resides at 103 High Street, Peoria, Ill.

93, Estina, b. 9 Jan., 1867; *m.* 30 Oct., 1888, Lester Birkett; resides at Washington, Ill.

94, Chas. Henry, b. 5 Sept., 1868; *m.* 19 May, 1902, Hattie Cardwell; resides at Chicago, Ill.

95, Geo. Williams, b. 23 April, 1871; *m.* 4 Aug., 1898, Bertha Lehman; resides Oklahoma.

74. MARION LAFAYETTE VAN METER (John[1], Jacob[2], Isaac[3], Abraham[4], Miles H.[5]), son of Miles H. and Mary P. (Litsey) Van Meter, b. "Falls of the Rough," Grayson Co., Ky., 1 Oct., 1832; *m.* 12 Feb., 1857, in Illinois, to Marian Julia Wallace Bell, who was the great-great-granddaughter of Col. James Slaughter; and great-great-great-granddaughter of Major Philip Clayton; both officers in the War of the Revolution. Marion L. Van Meter was taken by his father to Kendall Co., Ill., in 1836, and to Wisconsin in 1852, returning to Illinois in 1854 where he was married. He was a bridge-builder and mill superintendent. Moved to Tolone, Champaign Co., Ill., in 1871; farmed there for six years.

Removed to El Paso, Ill., in 1877, and took up the work of a building contractor. Retired and moved to Urbana, Ill., in 1893. Mother died there 10 July, 1904. He was not in Civil War nor held any political office, but was well-to-do.   Issue:
  96, Mary Telva; 97, Anna Roberta, b. 22 May, 1860; resides at Urbana, is professor of Household Science, University of Illinois. B.A. and M.A. degrees.
  98, Luella Bell; 99, Arthur Lee, b. 21 July, 1867; *unm.*; owner of Tolono Light and Power Works, Tolono, Ill.
  100, William Wathem, b. 8 Aug., 1871; *m.* 11 May, 1899, Catharine Caborn. General contractor; Vice-president Contractors' and Dealers' Exchange, New Orleans. No issue.
  101, Margaret J., b. 26 Sept., 1873; d. 6 Dec., 1880.
  102, Helen J., b. 13 Oct., 1875; *m.* 1896, C. J. Alyea, with the North American Insurance Co.; lives at Urbana, Ill.; no issue.

75. JAMES HERBERT VAN METER (John[1], Jacob[2], Isaac[3], Abraham[4], Miles H.[5]), son of Miles H. and Mary P. (Litsey) Van Meter, b. at Falls of Rough Creek, Ky., 7 March, 1834; d. 1 March, 1908; *m.* 5 Nov., 1855, his cousin, Mary E. Van Meter, of Washington, Ill. James H. served as lieutenant in the Union Army, 1862–65.   Issue:
  103, Emma, *m.* Rodney Hurlburt; lives at Minneapolis, Minn.
  104, Hattie, *m.* George Williams; lives at St. Paul, Minn.
  105, William S., d. Nov., 1906; 106, Howard C.; lives at St. Paul.
  107, Victor, decd.; 108, Clifford C.; lives at Hudson, Wis.

78. CASSANDRA PALESTINE VAN METER (John[1], Jacob[2], Isaac[3], Abraham[4], Miles H.[5]), dau. of Miles H. and Mary P. (Litsey) Van Meter, b. in Grayson Co., Ky., 22 April, 1836, in the year that her father emigrated to Illinois; *m.* —— Dyer, at Hudson, Wis., 1860; he is deceased.   Issue:
  109, Celesta; 110, Henry M.; lives at San Antonio, Texas.
  111, John, b. 1863; d. 1880; 112, Bertha; 113, Ambrose; living in Mexico; 114, Max; with Quarter-Master's Department on Isthmus of Panama; 115, Mary V.; living in Connecticut.

80. ABRAHAM CHENOWITH VAN METRE (John[1], Jacob[2], Isaac[3], Abraham[4], Miles H.[5]), son of Miles H. and Mary P. (Litsey) Van Meter, b. Kendall Co., Ill., 2 Jan., 1842; d. 29 Jan., 1899; *m.* —— ——.   Issue:
  116, Frank; 117, Claude; 118, Carl; 119, Guy.

85. ABBIE BRISCOE (John[1], Jacob[2], Mary[3], Hettie[4], William[5]), dau. of William and —— (Slaughter) Briscoe, *m.* Benjamin Helms Bristow, son of Francis M. and Emily (Helms) Bristow,

who was the daughter of Benjamin Helms, of Elizabethtown, Ky. Hon. Benjamin H. Bristow was Secretary of the Treasury during President Grant's administration (W. A. O.).

96. MARY TELVA VAN METER (John[1], Jacob[2], Isaac[3], Abraham[4], Miles H.[5], Marion L.[6]), dau. of Marion L. and Marian J. W. (Bell) Van Metre, b. 1 March, 1858; *m.* 1882, Daniel I. Durfey. They live retired at Tolono, Ill.   Issue:
   120, Jeanette, *m.* John Leslie; lives at Tolono Ill.
   121, Franc; 123, Dorothy; 124, Donald.

98. LUELLA BELL VAN METER (John[1], Jacob[2], Isaac[3], Abraham[4], Miles H.[5], Marion L.[6]), dau. of Marion L. and Marian J. W. (Bell) Van Meter, b. 2 March, 1862; *m.* 1889, William C. Warwick. They live in Laurel, Miss., where Mr. Warwick is connected with the M. J. & K. C. R. R.   Issue:
   125, Robert; 126, Margaret.

100. WILLIAM WATHEM VAN METER (John[1], Jacob[2], Isaac[3], Abraham[4], Miles H.[5], Marion L.[6]), son of Marion L. and Marian J. W. (Bell) Van Metre, b. 1871; member Contractors' Exchange, New Orleans, La.; *m.* 11 May, 1899, Catharine Caborn, of Mt. Vernon, Ind., dau. of Jas. L. Caborn, of Boston, Lincolnshire, England. On her maternal side she is related to the Neals and McDowels, of Virginia and Kentucky.   No issue.

MAGDALENA VAN METRE

MAGDALENA VAN METRE (John[1]), dau. of John and Margaret Van Metre, b. probably in Somerset Co., N. J., *circa* 1725; d. after 1745; *m. circa* 1742–45, Robert Pewsey. In her father's Deed of Gift Magdalena is styled "my youngest daughter." Nothing respecting this branch of the family has been found, excepting the following brief memoranda from the Journal of the Frederick Co., Va., Court.

"7th May, 1745, Robert Pewsey files an action *vs.* Jacob Van Metre." The case was continued from court to court and finally decided in favor of plaintiff, 6 Aug., 1745, and on 4 Oct., 1745, the court orders that Robert Pewsey pay Jacob Van Metre 100 lbs. of tobacco for attending court four days as an evidence in case of Pewsey *vs.* Ann Lilburn.

THE VAN METRES IN MARYLAND, VIRGINIA AND PENNSYLVANIA

While an inhabitant of Orange Co., Va., John Van Metre, "yeoman," gives bond to Joseph and Thomas Palmer, of Westchester Co., N. Y., agreeing to convey to them a tract of land

W. W. VAN METER, ESQ.

called "Metre" lying on the Monocacy River in Prince George's Co., Md., containing 300 acres. This bond was dated 9 Nov., 1739; the transaction seems to have been consummated on 5 Aug., 1741, when Van Metre made deeds to Thomas Palmer for 138 acres, for three parcels of land; and to Joseph Palmer for 162 acres, also in three parcels, all being parts of the aforesaid tracts called "Metre," in Prince George's Co., Md. Only a short time before his death, which occurred in 1745, in Frederick Co., Va., John Van Metre gave power of attorney to "my well-beloved friend, Baltis Fouts," of Prince George's Co., Md., to make a deed for 150 acres of land in the latter county, called "Meadow," to Michael Raymer. John Van Metre made other purchases of land in Frederick Co., Va., besides those heretofore noted, principally a grant obtained from Lord Fairfax, of 1,786 acres under date of March 24, 1736, and located in Orange County; another of 100 acres on Opequon Run, bought of Francis Prichard; another, also on the Opequon, of 475 acres, called "Allen's Hill," purchased of Jost Hite; and still another from Hite, of 400 acres. By the terms of his will the aggregate of 3,338 acres are bequeathed to his children. A draft, in the possession of the writer, shows that much of this devise was in a solid area located near the headwaters and about the forks of the Opequon, in Frederick Co., Va. One parcel, however, lay in Prince George's Co., Md. This tract, containing 162 acres and called "Pelmel," was situate at or near "Antetum" bottom on the Potomac River. This particular property was bequeathed to his daughter, Elizabeth, the wife of Thomas Shepherd. It has been asserted that much of the land upon which Shepherdstown, W. Va., is built, was part of Van Metre's original holding. This is questioned by Col. J. T. Holmes who has made much study of the matter and writes me that "the land was granted to Thomas Shepherd by the Royal Governor of Virginia some ten years, as I remember dates, before Shepherd laid out the town of Mecklenburg (subsequently Shepherdstown). He did not find a town there when he bought, but caught some of the German drift from the Colonies of New York and New Jersey, and more especially from Pennsylvania, in those days, toward the Shenandoah and the valley of the South Branch of the Potomac, and otherwise, through that region, and carried and courted it by conferring the German name on the village— Mecklenburg. *John Van Metre never owned land upon which Shepherdstown stands*" (see his letters, 27 Jan., 1905).

Writers on the early history of the western Virginia borders have mentioned four Van Metres as the original emigrants to the Valley, *i. e.,* John, Isaac, Abraham and Jacob, supposedly brothers. This may be questioned, as only two Van Metres came into the valley originally—John, 1728–1730; and Isaac, 1744. The former died in 1745; the latter was murdered by Indians in 1757. In

John's family were his sons, Abraham and Jacob; in Isaac's were his sons, John, Isaac and Henry; these were probably confused by earlier writers and alluded to by Mr. B. F. Van Metre (see his Genealogies and Biographies, p. 48), where he says:

"Four of his [John Van Metre's] sons came to Virginia about the year 1740 (?) viz: Abraham, Isaac, Jacob and John. Abraham and John settled in Berkeley Co., on the east side of the Allegheny Mountains. Jacob settled at lower end of the South Branch Valley, and Isaac in the beautiful valley of the South Branch, known as 'Indian Old Fields.'"

There is no doubt that those mentioned by Mr. Van Metre were, John Van Metre, from Maryland, his two sons, Jacob and Abraham, and John's brother Isaac, of "Old Fields," and his son, Henry. Foote mentions: "among settlers in the immediate vicinity of Shepherdstown, on the Cohongorooten (the Iroquois name for the Potomac), in 1734, were Jacob Van Metre and brothers" (see Sketches of Virginia, 2d Series, p. 15). Neither Kercheval nor Doddridge refer to four brothers, but to two only.

As to Henry Van Metre, there is this to be said: George Washington, in "My Journey over the Mountains," states that

"Henry Van Metres is on ye branch and was living on 'ye Trough,' Old Fields. Ye Trough is a couple of ledges of mountains impassable running side by side together for eight miles and ye river down between them, ye must ride round ye back of ye mountain for to get below them."

Colonel Washington stopped at Henry Van Metre's for two days in April, 1747–48. Henry Van Metre also entertained Leonard Schnell and John Brandmuller, two Moravian missionaries who were making a tour of the settled parts of Virginia from October to December, 1749 (see Va. Hist. Mag.; also W. Va. Hist. Mag., Vol. IV., No. 3, p. 230).

Among memoranda left by John Duke, of Frederick Co., Va., appear the following notes: "4 June, 1757, John Vermeter owes me 21 shillings paper money for 6½ yards linen cloth." This was probably John's son John who was living then in Duke's neighborhood.

Another interesting fact in connection with the Van Metre family, of Frederick Co., relates to their participation in the election of George Washington to the Virginia House of Burgesses at the election held in Winchester 24 July, 1758. Washington received the votes of Isaac's sons, John and Henry, and of John's sons, Abraham and Jacob; but the Van Metres were divided, however, on the vote for Washington's colleagues (two Burgesses being then voted for), John and Abraham voting for Captain Swearingen, and Jacob and Henry voting for Mr. West.

1736, March 23. Jost Hite sells to John Van Metre for £205, 475 acres on Opequon Creek, "part of a tract on which John Selbour lives," Orange Co., Va., DB. 1, p. 21 (see "The German Element in the Shenandoah Valley," p. 62).

"1736, July 20. Ordered that Morgan Morgan, Morgan Bryant, John Petilis, and John Van Metre, or any three of them, being first sworn before a Justice of the Peace of this County—do meet and value and appraise the money and estate of Robert Whorlington and make report on their finding" (Journal, Orange Co., Va., Court).

1737, March 24. Jost Hite acknowledged his deed of lease and release to John Van Metre and same is admitted of record (*vide* same).

1738, Aug. 24. John Van metre appointed road receiver at this court. Deed of lease and release of Richard Morgan to John Van Metre confirmed at this court (*vide* same).

1745, Sept. 3. Probate of John Van Metre's will; and appointment of Richard Morgan, Peter Van Cleve, John Hite and Thomas Hart, or any three of them, as appraisers (Frederick Co., Va., Journal of Court).

For many years a dispute existed between Virginia and Pennsylvania as to the ownership of the territory embraced in the northern part of the present state of West Virginia, and western Pennsylvania. This dispute was not infrequently accompanied by violence. On June 15, 1776, the Virginia Convention proposed a temporary dividing line. The matter was finally decided by commissioners appointed by the two states. Rev. James Madison and Robert Andrews on the part of Virginia, and George Bryan, George Ewing and David Rittenhouse for Pennsylvania; in 1779 they reached an agreement which was confirmed by the two states. The final report, however, of the commissioners appointed to run the line, was not made until 23 Aug., 1785.—Hening: X., 519–537 (see Va. Mag. of History, July, 1908, p. 48, footnote).

Some of the children of John Van Metre, in their movements westward from the Valley of Virginia, followed the upper course of the Potomac to Will's Creek (Cumberland, Md.), thence crossing the Alleghanies by Nemacolin's Path or Braddock's Road, reached the headwaters of the Yohoghany and Monongahela on the other side of the mountains and then gained communication with the valley of the Ohio River, that great highway of the pioneers and the gateway into our western empire. The great wilderness into which they penetrated was still within the jurisdiction of Virginia, a part of her, as yet, undefined District of West Augusta, a territory of which the counties bordering the upper Ohio named Yohogania, Monongalia and Ohio formed the entire southwestern section of Pennsylvania and by that Province claimed as part of her county of Cumberland—disputed soil. Its area extended into Pennsylvania as far north as the junction of the Alleghany and Kiskiminetas Rivers and eastward to the summit of the Laurel Hill Range, a section to-day represented by the Pennsylvania counties of Westmoreland, Washington, Fayette and Greene, with parts of Bedford and Alleghany, and with Pittsburg (then Fort Pitt) as the dominant center. The contention for the possession of this territory between "the Old Dominion" and the Province of Pennsylvania was finally settled in the latter's favor about 1783. In the meantime the Virginia counties of Monongalia, Yohogania and Ohio had been effaced and in their place came the Pennsylvania counties recited in the foregoing.

During the period of disputation the Penns sold land in these western counties at £5 the 100 acres and Virginia at ten shillings for the same amount. Each government allowed a preëmption right by improvement or actual settlement when and where there was no interference with a prior claim, official grant or survey. The settlers had the privilege of deferring payment for their grants until their claims were perfected. These privileges were confined to southwestern Pennsylvania, and while the majority of the settlers in the Forks of the Yoghoghany and other streams tributary to it were held under Virginia, rights were granted in the triangle on the opening of the land office in Pennsylvania in 1769, which included grants by the Penns, along Chartier's Creek (see History of Westmoreland (Pa.) County).

Jacob Van Metre, as it appears by the records, was the first of the younger generation to make settlement on any of the western waters; he acquired a tract of 400 acres, called Burgundy, on Muddy Creek, a tributary of the Monongahela River, near where Carmichaelstown now stands and about fourteen miles east of the present town of Waynesboro, in Greene Co., Pa. The date of his settlement is given as 1769. In the following year he added another 400 acres by certificate from the Commission "in the Fifth year of the Commonwealth," which was assigned to David Duncan in 1770. Three years later, among the taxables of Rosstraevor Township, Bedford County, are found the names of John, Jacob and Joseph Van Metre. Rosstraevor Township was then in Westmoreland County. In the same year, 1773, among the taxables in Springhill Township, Westmoreland County (but now in Fayette County), were Jacob, Henry and Abraham Van Metre. These were probably sons of Henry Van Meter, son of John, of Virginia. Four hundred acres were surveyed to Henry Van Metre, Jr., in Washington County, 25 May, 1785; 300 acres were surveyed to John Van Metre, Sr., and 400 acres to Jacob Van Metre in Washington County, 17 Dec., 1784. Also, on the same date and in the same county, 300 acres were warranted to Joseph Van Metre, surveyed 20 Feb., 1786; and to John Van Metre, Jr., in Bedford County, 300 acres. On the 17 May, 1780, Abraham Van Metre applies, on a Virginia entry, for 400 acres on the waters of Cross Creek in Ohio County, upon which was built the court house of that county. In a list of the inhabitants of Cumberland Township, Washington Co., Pa., who were rated for the Effective Supply Tax in 1781 appear the names of Henry and Absalom Van Metre.

The Indians along the Ohio kept up a predatory and brutal warfare upon the settlers of these western counties. Their raids became so frequent and destructive that companies of "frontier rangers" were raised and organized for the protection of the inhabitants. Westmoreland and Washington Counties were the principal ones covered by the operations of the rangers. Among the officers of this military establishment were Captains John, Thomas and James Van Metre, between the years 1778 and 1783 (Pa. Arch., 3d Series).

"At a court continued and held for Berkeley County, Va., the 18th day of October, 1780, John Van Metre formally appeared in Court and the oath prescribed by a Resolution of the General Convention, and was sworn as a Major in the Militia of the County" (see Minutes of Berkeley Co., Va., 1779–1782).

For some breach of laws or usages of the royalist government an indictment "by the King" was found against Henry Van Metre at the first court held for Westmoreland Co., Pa., 6 April, 1773 (see History of Westmoreland County, p. 53).

Among the gentlemen chosen members of the Committee for the District from the inhabitants of that part of Augusta County that lies west of Laurel Hills, at a meeting held at Pittsburg, the 16th day of May, 1775, were Jacob Van Meteren, David Shepherd and John McCullogh (*vide,* p. 451).

PART II

THOMAS SHEPHERD

THE CREST OF THE SHEPHERDS OF DEVONSHIRE,
ENGLAND

THE CREST OF THE SHEPHERDS OF SHEPHERDSTOWN,
VIRGINIA

THE SHEPHERDS OF WASHINGTON COUNTY, MARYLAND

BEING AN ARGUMENT FAVORING THAT LOCALITY AS THE EARLY
HOME AND PLACE OF NATIVITY OF THOMAS SHEPHERD,
FOUNDER OF SHEPHERDSTOWN, W. VA.—BY S. G. SMYTH

Prince George's County, prior to 1748, was the westernmost county: the wild and mountainous frontier of the Province of Maryland. In that year all the territory lying west of the mouth of the Monocacy Creek and extending northerly along the Potomac to the fartherest limits of the Province, was erected into a new county called Frederick. Virginia, likewise, about the same time, created on the south side of the Potomac, with an area co-extensive with that of the Maryland County, a new county also named Frederick, so that the Potomac River was not only the dividing line between the Province of Maryland and the Colony of Virginia, but was also the line of demarcation between the two counties of Frederick; each of them, by growth, development and political conditions, became in turn divided and subdivided until at this time the scenes of interest in the history of the Shepherd family are concentrated within the borders of the present counties of Jefferson, in West Virginia, and Washington, in Maryland, the Potomac, scarcely more than a stone's throw wide, separating them.

Among the earliest settlers in the distant parts of Prince George's County and taking up their abode along the Potomac and its tributaries were the Spriggs, Bealls, Chaplines, Cresaps, Shepherds and others no less notable in the early annals of provincial Maryland. They were granted large tracts of land, which tracts, by a unique custom fostered and still prevalent in that State, were given peculiar designations, at once stamping upon these plantations individuality and distinction. Instances are: "Skipton on Craven," "Dutch Folly," "Sprigg's Delight," "Shepherd's Discovery," "Shepherd's Purchase," "Chursley Forest," "Antietam Bottom," and a thousand others of like character. The earliest of these grants were obtained by colonists who advanced westward from the tidewater counties on Chesapeake Bay to the mountains long before the venturesome Scotch-Irish and the Dutch elements found the valley trail leading from the northerly Province of Pennsylvania, an Indian highway to the fords of the Potomac, and thus into the heart of Virginia.

Documentary evidence, which furnishes the basis of the argument, is found first in the Land Record Office at Annapolis; they show that Shepherd families were among the earliest in Anne Arundel, Calvert, Baltimore and Prince George's counties. In the first Inventory Book of the latter county the initial presence of a Shepherd is revealed; it states that on 16 March, 1698, James Beall was appointed administrator, Thomas Sprigg and Will Offutt, appraisers of the estate of Thomas Shepherd, deceased. The return of same, filed 6 April, 1699, gives the valuation of his estate at £3 2s. 8½d.

William Shepherd, of Prince George's Co., Md., carpenter, conveyed, 12 Oct., 1717, to Philip Gitting (son-in-law of Thomas Cresap) his plantation called "Mt. Arraras," at the head of Beaver Dam Run, and running out at the Eastern Branch (near Washington, D. C.), containing 140 acres (F. 16); and on the same day Shepherd took title from John Bradford to a tract of land containing 150 acres, situate in the western part of Prince George's County, designated as "Shepherd's Purchase," the same being a part of a tract called "Chursley Forest" (F. 45). Whether or not William Shepherd held title to the remainder of "Chursley Forest" does not appear; evidently he did, for on the 18 Dec., 1721, he became the grantor of a part of "Chursley Forest," containing 150 acres, to John Bradford, merchant, the consideration being £143 18s. 9d. (I. 243); and the parcel called "Shepherd's Purchase" (containing 150 acres) was conveyed by William Shepherd to James Brooke, 27 Oct., 1739, for about the same consideration as that obtained and mentioned in the conveyance to John Bradford in 1721. This deed bears the endorsement of Sarah Shepherd, wife of said William Shepherd, and the witnesses were Joseph Chapline, John Gold, Peter Brentijo and John Shepherd (who made his mark) (Y. 147).

William Shepherd, now styled "Senior," becomes grantee, by a deed dated 16 April, 1741, from John Moore, "Planter," and both of Prince George's County, "to all that tract of land called 'Shepherd's Purchase,' containing 50 acres, and being a part of 'Antietam Bottom,' situate in Prince George's Co., on the bank of the Potomac River, and adjoining a tract called 'Sprigget's Delight.'" This deed was witnessed by Thomas Cresap and Joseph Chapline (Y. 300); with this item the land operations of William Shepherd disappear from the records.

NOTE: A Mary Shepherd is witness to the baptism of Theodora, daughter of James Moore, on 21 June, 1735. This baptism and several others was performed in this neighborhood by Rev. Johannes Casper Stoever, an itinerating Evangelical minister.

John Bradford, who figures in the Shepherd grants, held title to lands also, on Rock Creek (now in the District of Columbia). In 1719, when a church was organized, the chapel was erected in what was called Rock Creek Hundred; not only did John Bradford contribute 100 pounds of tobacco towards its erection, but he also gave the 10 acres of ground upon which it was built, and this was the beginning of the famous old Rock Creek Church of Prince George's Parish.

In 1728 the Governor of the Province was petitioned to divide this parish and create a new one in the western part of the county; among the petitioners were Thomas and William Shepherd. Thus All Saint's parish came into existence with its church at Rockville (now in Montgomery County), twelve miles farther west. In 1742 there were districts in this parish and that one in which the Shepherds lived was called Antietam Hundred, and among the communicants of All Saint's at this time was William Shepherd, Sr., and William Shepherd, Jr., Thomas Shepherd not being among those mentioned. Query: Was it not because he reappeared in Frederick County (or Orange, as it then was), Va., in 1733/34?

As to John Shepherd: record is found of a transfer of land by him to John Penson, both of Prince George's County, under date of 3 June, 1715 (I, 686); and on the 24th May, 1726, the administration bond of Charles Digges, in the estate of John Shepherd, deceased, of Prince George's County, is approved by the court.

By a deed of conveyance dated 22 Nov., 1752, John Shepherd takes title from Thomas Shepherd, both of Frederick Co., Md. (Frederick erected 1748), to a tract of land called " Shepherd's Purchase," being part of a tract called "Antietam Bottom," lying on the Potomac River and containing 50 acres. Witnesses were: William Griffitts and Joseph Chapline (B. 662). It is evident that this is the John Shepherd who *made his mark* as witness to one of William Shepherd's land transfers. Query: Was Thomas Shepherd, the grantor, in this instance, the son and heir-at-law of William Shepherd and was he conveying the homestead to a brother, he himself having interests in Virginia? It may be safely presumed, I think, that William Shepherd left at least four children: Thomas, John, William and Mary.

NOTE: A Mary Shepherd, sponsor at a baptism at Monocacy, Md., in 1734 with John Hillis. (Fletcher.)

John Shepherd (the man who "made his mark") conveys to Mattias Ulrich Hopman, by deed dated 9 April, 1762, a tract of land called "Tichneck," or "Richneck," containing 54 acres (G. 466). Query: Was this "Shepherd's Purchase" renamed and resurveyed and thus increased to 54 acres? A few weeks later John Shepherd takes title from Thomas Mills (probably father of Lieutenant John Mills, who m. David Shepherd's daughter Ruth), on 14 June, 1762, to a tract of land called "Shepherd's Discovery"; it was part of "Resurvey of Antietam Bottom," containing 64 acres, situate on the north side of the Potomac River in Frederick Co., Md. In both deeds in which John Shepherd appears in the capacities of grantor and grantee the witnesses were Peter Bainbridge and Moses Chapline (brother of Joseph) (H. 28).

In the will of John Shepherd, of Frederick Co., Md., dated 9 Dec., 1764, probated 13 Feb., 1765 (A. 1, p. 228), he names his wife Sarah, his children: Nathan, Thomas, William, Sarah, Drusilla and a child unborn (afterward Margaret). To Nathan the homestead in Maryland is devised; to Thomas and William are bequeathed lands which the testator owned on Back Creek, in Frederick Co., Va., while the daughters inherited personal property. All the children, except Nathan, are stated to be under age.

This reference to Shepherd possessions in Virginia reveals, upon further investigation, an interesting piece of information and lends a significant phase in its relation to the Maryland Shepherds. A group of Shepherds are found located in Frederick Co., Va., who were civilly prominent in the period 1744–50.

Thomas Shepherd, of Prince George Co., Md., d. *circa* 1698,
   m. —— —— ——

William Shepherd, of Pr. Geo. Co., John Shepherd, of Pr. Geo. Co., Md., d. 1726,
   d. *circa* 1741/45,
   m. Sarah ——   *m.* —— ——   Issue :
                                      John ⎫ *m.* Jane left issue
                                      Nathan ⎬ all of Frederick Co., Va.
                                      William ⎭ [see Winchester, Va., Record].

Thomas, of Shepherdtown, William, Jr., of Rock Creek, John, of Frederick Co., d. 1765,
   b. 1705, d. 1776,   *m.* Sarah
   m. Elizabeth Van Metre.   all of Washington Co., Md.

David	b. *1734*	William,	Thomas, Nathan, Sarah, Drusilla, Margaret.
Sarah	1736?	*m.* —— ——	*m.* Leah ——
Elizabeth	*1738*	John, who	John
William	1741 ?	speaks of	Joseph
Thomas	1745 ?	" Unkle Thomas,"	David
John	1750 ?	1797.	Sarah, *m.* Matthias Spong, June, 1817.
Mary ⎫	Twins		
Martha ⎭	1752		
Abraham	*1754*		
Susanna	*1758*		

John Shepherd and Thomas Shepherd were overseers in 1745; John Shepherd had a suit *vs.* Nathan Shepherd, 1745; John Shepherd is deceased in 1746, leaving a wife Jane and children unnamed; Thomas Shepherd, appraiser, 1746; suit John Shepherd *vs.* Fitzimmons, 1748; William Shepherd under-sheriff, 1748; surveyor, 1750; and Nathan Shepherd tithable, 1748. Of the foregoing, Thomas Shepherd was the settler at Mecklenburg, and John Shepherd lived, one of them—perhaps the earlier one—at the head of Bullskin Creek, which ran into the Shenandoah beyond Charlestown, Va. The John Shepherd who d. in Frederick Co., Md., 1765, left lands on Back Creek, near the North Mountain and about nine miles from the Potomac.

The query naturally arises, in view of the similarity in Christian names and the circumstances in connection with these property matters: Was there not blood kinship between these respective families of Maryland and Virginia? In the absence of family records, traditions or other personal data to afford a clue to its solution, the writer hazards a genealogical analysis such as this:

In a suit instituted by David Shepherd, eldest son and heir-at-law of Thomas and Elizabeth Shepherd, in the year 1764, which was meant to determine and perpetuate the metes and bounds of "Pell Mell," the testimony of Joseph Chapline, who made the survey for John Van Metre (father of Elizabeth Shepherd) in 1743, states "that it lay on the Potomac river above Swearingen's ferry, and adjoined a tract called 'Antietam Bottom.'" Jacob Van Metre, son of John and brother of Elizabeth Shepherd, who was a witness to the survey, gave similar evidence. Mecklenburg is said to be only three miles above the mouth of the Antietam Creek, and as Packhorse ford was just below Mecklenburg and "the only fordable crossing for miles above or below," and as Thomas Shepherd was given permission by Act of Assembly of Virginia in October, 1765, to establish a ferry "*from his land in the town of Mecklinburg, in the County of Frederick, Va., over Potomac to his land opposite thereto in the Province of Maryland, etc., etc.,*" it can readily be seen that either "Pell Mell" was "*his land*" referred to, or else he owned other lands at that point and wanted further convenience for himself and the public, instead of continually resorting to the Packhorse ford some distance below. Swearingen's ferry probably intervened between these points, for in 1766 the General Assembly revoked its grant to Shepherd "because the same being but a small distance from a ferry already established from the lands of Thomas Swearingen over Potomack in Maryland" (History Lower Shenandoah, pp. 319–371).

It is recorded that David Shepherd and his wife Rachael, by deed dated in 1767, conveyed "Pell Mell," containing 162 acres, to Jacob Vandiver, of Salem, N. J.; and by the will of the latter, dated 1772, this land was devised to Vandiver's granddaughter Phoebe, afterward the wife of Dr. Clarkson Freeman, of Somerset Co., N. J. In whatever way the transaction may have occurred, it is a matter of record in Washington Co. (erected 1776), Md., that title to "Pell Mell" at a later date became vested in Abraham Shepherd, brother of David, the grantor to Vandiver, so that before the close of the century Abraham Shepherd began disposing of "Pell Mell" piecemeal in the following way:

1797, Nov. 18, release 20 acres woodland to George Batson (L. 47).

1797, Nov. 27, deed 70¾ acres to John Blackford (Z. 286).

1797, Nov. 27, deed 9¾ acres, with dwellings, to Abram Myers (Z. 284).

1813, Nov. 24, deed 70¾ acres to Henry Thomas Swearingen and Benoni Swearingen Blackford (Z. 282).

Making a total of the divisions of "Pell Mell" aggregating 171¼ acres (which probably included a gain of about 9¾ acres in the resurvey of "Pell Mell"). Thus that plantation passed into alien hands.

In the descriptions of the tracts thus variously conveyed, those to Batson and to Blackford particularly recite that these lands adjoin the "Resurvey of 'Pile's Delight.'" Now "Pile's Delight" was a neighboring plantation bordering the Potomac, which in the period 1743-50 belonged to Col. Edward Sprigg (History Western Maryland, Vol. II., p. 985), and in 1814 was in the ownership of Philip Ground (Z. 679). "Pile's Delight" and part of "Addition to Pile's Delight," the former containing 157¾ acres, the latter 114 acres, were sold by George Ground, the son and executor of his father, Philip Ground, to Thomas Shepherd ("Unkle Thomas" of the chart), of Washington Co., Md., as will appear by deed dated 16 April, 1814 (Z. 697). According to further records the conditioned payments of the purchase money not, apparently, having been made by Thomas Shepherd, the grantee, he gives the property, some months later, as security to John Blackford for the balance of the conditioned payments (A. A., 61), the deed reciting that the land is part of two tracts lying on the Potomac River called "Antietam Bottom Resurveyed," or "Antietam Bottom," and "One Husband" and "Addition to One Husband," the latter section being the late dwelling place of Philip Ground, deceased, and adjoining lands of Benoni Swearingen, Jacob Bedinger, Sarah Chapline and others (A. A., 61). Thomas Shepherd, the (supposed) owner of this land, by his will (Liber C, 9), dated 24 March, 1817, probated 9 April, 1817, names his wife Leah and children John, Joseph, David and Sarah Shepherd. This agrees with the census report of Washington Co., Md., for 1790, which gives information that Thomas Shepherd, of that county, had a family at that date of wife, three sons and a daughter above sixteen years of age then living.

John Shepherd, of Washington Co., Md., is also enumerated in the census of 1790 for himself, five sons and four daughters above sixteen years of age. Query: What John Shepherd was this?

John Blackford and Abram Myers were executors of the will of the foregoing Thomas Shepherd.

In a deed dated 5 April, 1819, John Blackford and Abram Myers, executors, John, Joseph and David Shepherd, Mathias Spong and Sarah, his wife, children and heirs of Thomas Shepherd, deceased, jointly convey to John Youtsey, also of Washington Co., a tract of 122¾ acres, being parts of a tract composed of "Pile's Delight" and "Addition to Pile's Delight," situate in Washington Co., and adjoining lands of John Shepherd (D. D.,

693). This latter John Shepherd was probably one of the heirs mentioned above.

John Youtsey, jointly with David Bowles, of Frederick Co., Md., reconvey the same parcels to Joseph and David Shepherd and Mathias Spong, Jr. (who had *m.* Sarah Shepherd, 10 June, 1817), by deed dated 11 May, 1822 (F. F., 961), the brother John eliminated from this deal was the owner of an adjoining property containing 93 acres called "Three Springs," purchased from the heirs of Amos Eakle, deceased (G. G., 890).

The foregoing Sarah Spong is believed to have been buried in the Shepherd family burying ground at Shepherdstown, W. Va., where, it is said, none but those of Shepherd blood are allowed interment.

Thomas Shepherd, 3d, grandson of Thomas 1st, died 9 Nov., 1832, at the home of one of his children (Sarah, who *m.* George R. Weber) in Washington Co., Md. *His* son, Thomas C. Shepherd, was living at Blackford's Ferry, where his first child was born, and in 1836 the family removed to Illinois.

Col. John Blackford, of Washington Co., Md., was a prominent man in his day and was living in the county as late as 1830.

Among accounts in the old books of Abraham Shepherd which are in possession of his descendants at Shepherdstown, there are to be found several memoranda, such as: "1799—Thomas Shepherd *of Maryland,* to Clark's notes: £3. 12. o" and "£15. 5. o." etc., etc., these showing, at least, business relations, if not those of family ties, between these families.

THOMAS SHEPHERD'S LAND GRANT

"George, the Second. To all men knowe ye that for the Consideration mentioned in an Order of our trusty and well beloved William Gooch Esqʳᵉ our Lieut Genˡ and Commander-in-chief of our Colony and Dominion of Virginia in our Council of the said Colony the Twelvth day of June, One thousand Seven hundred and thirty four. We Have given granted and confirmed and by these Presents for us our Heirs and Successors— Do give grant and confirm unto Thomas Shepherd one certain Tract or Parcel of land containing Two hundred and twenty-two acres lyeing and being on the West side of Sherrando River and designed to be included in a County to be called the County of Orange being part of Forty thousand acres purchased by Jost Hite from Isaac and John Vanmatre who had obtained orders of our said Lieut. Govʳ. in Council to take up the land upon certain conditions therein expressed which were made the Seventeenth day of June one thousand seven hundred and thirty and bounded as followeth (to wit) Beginning at a White Oak marked T.S. on a hill on the south side of Cohongaluta and on the east side of a branch called the Falling Spring below a fall in said run and running thence South eight degrees westerly six Poles south twenty degrees west Forty-four Poles thence southwest seventy-two Poles to a hickory saplin thence south thirty degrees west Forty Poles to a White-oak by a meadow thence north seventy degrees west crossing the said meadow one hundred and eighty poles to a double red oak on a hillside thence south seventy-three degrees east two hundred and twelve Poles to the first station—

Witnesseth to Have and to Hold and to beholden yielding and paying, Provided &c., &c.

In Witness—witness our trusty and well-beloved William Gooch, Esq' our Lieut. Gov' and Commander in chief of our said Colony and Dominion of Virginia at Williamsburg under the seal of our said Colony the third day of October one thousand seven hundred and thirty-four in the eighth year of our reign.

(sig) WILLIAM GOOCH.

(Book of Grants, No. 15, p. 306, in Register of Land's Office, Richmond, Va.)

THOMAS SHEPHERD, HIS CHILDREN AND HIS WILL

Captain Thomas Shepherd, founder of Shepherdstown (formerly Mecklenburg), West Virginia, settled there *circa* 1732; was born *circa* 1705; died 1776; married, *circa* 1733, Elizabeth, daughter of John Van Metre, "the Indian Trader," grantee of extensive tracts of land in Spottsylvania Co., Va., from Governor Gooch in 1730. Elizabeth Van Metre Shepherd was born, probably in New Jersey, *circa* 1715; died at Shepherdstown, W. Va., 1792–3. Issue:

I, David, b. Jan., 1734; d. Ohio Co., Va., 2 Feb., 1795.

II, Sarah, b. *circa* 1736; d. Shepherdstown, 18 Oct., 1780.

III, Elizabeth, b. 3 Oct., 1738; d. Shepherdstown, Va., 1788.

IV, William, b. *circa* 1740; d. Wheeling, Va., 1824.

V, Thomas, b. 1743; d. Shepherdstown, Va., 1792.

VI, John, b. 1749; d. Red Oak, Ohio, 31 July, 1812.

VII, Mary, VIII, Martha, twins, b. *circa* 1752; Martha d. Brooke Co., Va., *circa* 1825.

IX, Abraham, b. 10 Nov., 1754; d. Shepherdstown, Va., 7 Sept., 1822.

X, Susannah, b. 1 Sept., 1758; d. Wheeling, Va., 13 April, 1835.

OFFICIAL RECORDS REFERRING TO THOMAS SHEPHERD

1734, Oct. 3. Grant from Governor Gooch and Council of Virginia of 222 acres of land on west side of Sherrand [Shenandoah] River, in Orange Co., Colony of Virginia, being part of the original grant of 40,000 acres made to John Van Metre, the father-in-law of Thomas Shepherd, by order of Council, 17 June, 1730 (No. 15, Book of Grants, p. 306, Richmond, Va.).

—. Settled upon his grant, which was located near a crossing of the Potomac known afterward as the Packhorse ford and was the only crossing of the Potomac for many miles east or west of it (History of Lower Shenandoah, p. 319).

1738, Oct. 26. Payment made to Thomas Shepherd for one

wolf's head, by certificate of Richard Morgan, "gent"—o. 14. o (Frederick Co., Va., Court Journal).

1739, June. "Thomas Shepherd having attended court one day as a witness for Daniel Chancey *vs.* Wm. Williams, desires to be allowed for same. Be it therefore ordered that we pay him for the same according to law" (Orange Co. Court records).

—, April 6. View of road to Thomas Shepherd's Mill ordered (Frederick Co., Va., Court Journal, Bk. 1, p. 77).

1744, Oct. 12. Thomas and wife Elizabeth Shepherd, beneficiaries in Deed of Gift from John Van Metre (Frederick Co., Va., Deed Bk., 1, p. 211).

1745, 9ber 7. Thomas Shepherd appointed overseer of road in place of Van Swearingen, gent (Frederick Co. Court Journal, No. 2, p. 2).

1746, June 3. Thomas Shepherd, Richard Morgan, Van Swearingen and Wm. Chapline, or any three of them, to appraise estate of Edw. Chambers (Frederick Co. Court Journal, Bk. 2, p. 103).

1757, March 1. Thomas Shepherd to be overseer of road from Swearingen's Ferry to Jacob Hite's, in room of Abraham Teague (Frederick Co., Va., Court Journal, No. 7, p. 180).

1762, Nov. Act of Assembly of Virginia authorizing Thomas Shepherd to erect the town of Mecklenburg (Hening's Statutes, Vol. 7, p. 600).

1765, July 25. Thomas and Elizabeth Shepherd convey lot No. 50 in Mecklenburg to David Shepherd (Frederick Co., Va., Court Journal, No. 9, p. 425).

—, Oct. Act of Assembly authorizing Thomas Shepherd to establish a ferry at Mecklenburg (Hening's Statutes, Vol. 8, p. 146).

1766. Act of Assembly repealing the foregoing privilege (Hening's Statutes, Vol. 8, p. 262), "because the same being at a very small distance from a ferry already established from the land of Thomas Swearingen over Potomac in Maryland" (History of Lower Shenandoah, p. 371).

1772, Aug. Thomas Shepherd obtained permission to erect a mill on a stream of water runnning through the town of Mecklenburg (History of Lower Shenandoah, p. 227).

SHEPHERD'S FERRY AT SHEPHERDSTOWN

Established by Act of Assembly of Virginia, October, 1765. "Be it enacted by the Governor, Council and Burgesses of the present General Assembly and it is hereby enacted by authority of the same—That a ferry be established and constantly kept, from the land of Thomas Shepherd in the town of Mecklinburg, in the County of Fredrick, over Potomack River, to his land opposite thereto in the Province of Maryland; the price of a man, three pence; and for a horse the same; and for the transportation of wheel carriages, tobacco, cattle and other beasts, the ferry

THE SHEPHERD GENEALOGY

keeper may demand and take the following rates, to wit: For every coach, chariot, or waggon, and the driver thereof, the same as six horses; and for every cart, or four-wheeled chaise and the driver thereof, the same as for four horses; and for every two-wheeled chaise, or chair, the same as for two horses; and for any hogshead of tobacco, the same as for one horse; and for every sheep, goat, hog or lamb, one fourth part the ferriage of one horse, according to the price hereinbefore settled at the said ferry." [Hening's Statutes at Large [Va.] Vol. 8, pp. 146–147]. This grant was revoked by the Assembly in November, 1766.

WILL OF THOMAS SHEPHERD

In the name of God, Amen.—I. Thomas Shepherd, Senr of the town of Mecklinburg, County of Berkeley, and Colony of Virginia, being sick and weak of body but of sound and perfect sense and memory, thanks be given to God, and considering the uncertainty of life, do make publish and declare this my last will and testament in manner and form following

Item I give and bequeath to my son *William* Shepherd a certain tract of land in the aforesaid County and Colony, being part of a tract of land granted to me by the Right Honourable Thomas, Lord Fairfax, by deed dated June 12, A. D. 1751 and bounded as follows: Beginning at a hickory standing near a sink hole, a corner of the original, and running thence with the same, west one hundred and eighty poles to two black oaks, a corner between me and William Morgan, the 2nd thence with Morgan's line S. 16 degrees E. 112 poles to a double White oak, being a corner to the said Morgan; then N. 63 degrees E. 23 poles to a white oak, then S. 83 degrees E. 63 poles to a hickory, then S. 77 degrees E. 50 poles to a stake to a marked black oak on the original line, then leaving the original line and running across the tract N. 10 degrees E. 120 poles to the beginning tree, laid out for one hundred and four acres more or less to him and his heirs and assigns forever.

Item I also give and bequeath unto my said son William three lots in the town of Mecklinburg known by No. 83 No. 84 and No. 85 to him and his heirs forever. *Item* I also give and bequeath unto my said son William my saw mill in the town of Mecklinburg and all the utensils and appurtenances thereunto belonging to him and his assigns forever. *Item* I give and bequeath unto my son Thomas Shepherd a certain tract of land in the said county and Colony being a part of the same tract as that is that I have devised to my son William and bounded as follows: Beginning at a hickory, the beginning to the land devised to my son William, and running across the tract with his line reversed S. 10 degrees W. 120 poles to a stake, Williams' corner, standing on the line of the land of the original running thence with the same S. 77 degrees E. 120 poles to a locust stake near a marked hickory sapling on a line of the original, then leaving the original line and running across the tract N. 16 degrees E. 162 poles to a stake on the first line of the original, thence with the same S. 80 degrees W. 102 poles to a red oak an original corner, thence N. 72 degrees W. 41 poles to the beginning, containing 104 acres more or less, to him and his heirs and assigns forever. *Item* I give and bequeath unto my said son Thomas a lot in the town of Mecklinburg known by No. 63 to him and his heirs and assigns forever. Also I give and bequeath to my said son Thomas my grist mill standing on the said lot No. 63 and also the utensils thereuntobelonging to him and his heirs and assigns forever. *Item* I give and bequeath unto my son John Shepherd a certain tract of land in the said County and Colony being a part of the aforesaid tract and also a part of another tract for which I have

150

the King's patent and bounded as follows: Beginning at a stake near a marked hickory sapling on the first mentioned original line, it being the corner to that devised to my son Thomas and running thence with the original line S. 77 degrees E. 51 poles to a black oak, a corner to that tract for which I have the King's patent then reversing the lines of the same S. 70 degrees E. 180 poles to a White oak, an original corner, then No. 30 degrees E. 40 poles to a hickory, an original corner then leaving the original line and running across the tract, No. 68½ degrees W. 45 poles to an apple tree planted by a rock, thence N. 56 degrees W. 206 poles to a small hickory sapling standing on the division line between this devised to my sons John and Thomas, then with the said division line to the beginning, containing 104 acres, more or less, to him and his heirs and assigns forever. Also I give and bequeath to my said son John a piece of land adjoining the town of Mecklinburg, beginning at a marked rock, the beginning of that tract of land that I have conveyed to my son Abraham and running thence with his line S. 19 degrees E. 1 pole through the middle of a spring in the mill branch, then crossing the same the same course continued 22 poles to a hickory bush on a line with Mill street, thence with the said Street S. 26 degrees W. till it intersects with the original of the entire tract then S. 73 degrees E. to a locust stump a corner to Nicholas McIntyre and William Brown, thence by a straight line to the beginning to him and his heirs and assigns forever. I. also give and bequeath to my said John my new mill standing on the above land to him devised with all the utensils and appertenances thereunto belonging to him and his heirs and assigns forever. But if my said sons William Thomas and John all or either of them die without lawful heirs of their own body, lawfully begotten, then it is my devise that the lands and other legacies so devised be after his or their decease be sold and the money so arising be equally divided among my surviving sons *Item* I will and bequeath unto my son *Abraham* all my lands that remain to him and his heirs and their heirs forever. It is my will and devise that my son Abraham or his heirs allow my beloved spouse the free use of two acres of my meadow in any part she pleases of the same and the dwelling house and Garden and ten pounds a year during her natural life. Also I will and bequeath unto my said son *Abraham* all the yearly rents that shall arise from the town of Mecklinburg both from out lots and in lots to him and his heirs and their heirs, forever. But under this restriction that he the said *Abraham* and his heirs at any time hereafter shall not debar his brothers *William, Thomas* or *John* or either of them or either of their heirs, but not their assigns from making draws on his land for the use of their mills provided he is not damaged thereby. It is also my Will and devise that what part of Lots No. 62 and 82 remains now unsold shall always remain in the hands of my son *Abraham* and of his heirs and shall not by him nor them be sold nor improved but be open for the use of the mills, they, my sons, *William, Thomas* and *John,* and their heirs and assigns, paying him the said *Abraham* and his heirs yearly twelve shillings sterling as a ground rent forever. I will and bequeath unto my said son Abraham the one half of my personal estate after my funeral charges and just debts are paid. It is my Will and devise that my son *Abraham* and his heirs may add any number of lots to the town of Mecklinburg, that he or them thinks proper out of the lands hereby to him and them devised and to grant deeds in fee simple to the purchasers of them. It is my positive order that my said son *Abraham* or his heirs pay or cause to be paid unto my daughter *Susannah* or her heirs or assigns in the following manner—twenty five pounds on her marriage day or when she arrives to the age of eighteen years, and twenty-five pounds yearly for three years thence next ensueing making up in the whole one hundred pounds. It is also my positive order that my son *John* or his heirs pay or cause to be paid unto my daughter *Mary* or to her heirs and assigns one hundred pounds in the following manner: twenty five pounds twelve months after my decease and twenty five pounds yearly for three years thence next ensuing. It is also my desire that my son *William* or his heirs pay or cause to be paid unto my daughter Martha or to her heirs or assigns fifty pounds in the following manner; twelve pounds ten shillings twelve months after the time of my decease and twelve pounds ten shillings yearly for three years thence next ensueing making up the whole fifty pounds. It is also my desire that my son Thomas, his heirs executors administrators pay or cause to be paid unto my daughters *Sarah* and *Elizabeth* one hundred pounds in the following manner, twenty five pounds in twelve months after the time of my decease and twenty five pounds yearly for three years thereafter to them and to their heirs. *Item* I give and bequeath to my wife *Elizabeth* one good feather bed and furniture and her choice of the milch cows and her choice of a riding horse and saddle. It is my express Will and devise that my sons William, Thomas and John or their heirs do each of them pay or cause to be paid unto my beloved spouse ten pounds yearly during her natural life making up thirty pounds yearly. I will and bequeath to my son *David* and to his heirs and assigns one half of my personal estate after my just debts and funeral charges are paid also a bond of sixty pounds which I have of my son *Abraham.* I will and bequeath to my grandson *Thomas Thornburg* and unto his heirs and assigns forever a lot in the town of Mecklinburg known by No. 53. I will and bequeath to my daughter *Martha* or to her heirs or assigns forever a lot of ground in the town of Mecklinburg known by No. 3. I will and bequeath to my daughter *Mary* and to heirs and assigns forever, a lot in the town of Mecklinburg, known by No. 2, also a feather bed and furniture and a cow and calf. I will and bequeath to my daughter *Susannah* and to her heirs and assigns forever a lot in the town of Mecklinburg known by No. 37, also a feather bed and furniture and a cow and calf. It is my Will and positive order that the sums of Money left to be divided among my children by their grandfather *John Van Metre* deceased, be included in these legacies by me devised and if any of my legatees shall refuse to give receipts to the executors for their part of that sum when they shall be capable of receiving it then it shall be lawful for my executors to retain so much out of their respective legacies as shall be sufficient to discharge the said *John Van Metre's* legacies aforesaid. As I have left several lots in the town of Mecklinburg to my children and grandchildren it is my positive Will that while they or their heirs possess them they shall be clear of ground rents but if any or all of them should sell their lots or any part of them then the person or persons so purchasing shall pay or cause to be paid to my son *Abraham* or to his heirs such quit rents as are paid by the other inhabitants of the said town. It is my desire that the lot in the town of Mecklinburg on which the English Church stands known by No. 40 be the sole use of the Parish of Norbonne free from Ground rent and my heirs to give to the vestry a deed for it if required as I have left several sums of money to be paid by my sons unto my daughters, it is my positive order that my executors at the time of my decease take bonds of my sons to secure the payment of such sums to my daughters when they become due and if any or all of my sons shall refuse to give such bonds then it shall be lawful for my executors to seize—a part of the legacies that—devised to either or all of them so refusing as shall be of value sufficient to discharge the sum or sums. As my son *William* is gone abroad if he should never return home then it is my will and desire that after my decease that the said mill we rented out by my executors till *Thomas,* his eldest son comes of age and the rents made use of to dis-

APPRAISAL OF THOMAS SHEPHERD'S PERSONAL ESTATE

charge his just debts and to pay his sisters the sums of money that I have devised to them to be paid by him and to pay for the education of his children and what is over of the rents to be equally divided among his three children and the other lands that I have devised to him is to be for the use of his children and widow during her widowhood but if she marries she is then to have no more benefit from anything that I have devised to my son *William* and it is my desire that when my son *William's* son *Thomas* comes of age I will and bequeath him the saw mill and lots No. 83 and No. 84 to him and his heirs and assigns forever and when my son *William's* son *William* comes of age I will and bequeath him the land formerly devised to his father to him and his heirs and assigns forever and when my son *William's* daughter *Sarah* comes of age I will and bequeath her Lot No. 85 to her and her heirs and assigns forever. I constitute and appoint my sons *Abraham* Shepherd, *John* Shepherd and my wife *Elizabeth,* Executors of this my last Will and Testament. In Witness whereof I have hereunto set my hand and seal this twenty-third day of March in the year 1776.

THOS. SHEPHERD (LS)

Signed Sealed and Delivered by the Testator as his last Will and Testament in presence of
Edward Lucas, Junr.
Henry Cookus, Junr.
Thomas Worley
Henry Scheets
Robert Coshburh.

At a Court held for Berkeley County, the 20th day of August, 1776. The last Will and Testament of Thomas Shepherd deceased was presented in Court by Abraham Shepherd one of the executors therein named who made oath thereto according to law and the same being proved by Edward Lucas, Jun[r], Henry Cookus, Jun[r]. and Thomas Worley, the same is admitted to record and on the motion of the said executors who entered into bond together with William Morgan and Martin Woolford his securities in the penalty of one thousand pounds conditioned for his true and faithful administration of the said estate. Certificate is granted him in due form.

Teste.   Will Drew, C. C. Court.
[From " The Shepherdstown [W. Va.] Independent," Wednesday, January 12th, 1898.]

APPRAISAL OF THOMAS SHEPHERD'S PERSONAL ESTATE

In Obedience to an Order of Berkely Court to us the Subscribers directed we have met this 9th day of September 1776, and appraised the estate of M[r]. Thomas Shepherd as was brought to our view.

5 Horn Cattle year old	6.10.0	Scales
Big brown steer	3.10.0	Large steelyards
White backed steer	2.15.0	small steelyards
Brindle steer	2. 0.0	frying pan
a red heifer	2. 0.0	grid iron
brown cow with white face	3.10.0	shovel & Tongs
bell cow	2. 0.0	Brass mortar & pesell
little black cow	3. 0.0	Brass hatchet
red brown cow	3. 0.0	old box of iron
2 yr old red steer		Hand saw

153

and Red year old
a plough & Irons & Clevis
a harrow and teeth
cross cut saw
grindstone & axletree
4 wagon hoops
New iron—2 bars, 2 peices spindle
pewter—4 plates, 2 dishes, 3 basins
1 porringer—2 spoons
4 Knives—4 forks, Tea kettle
tin halfgallon and quart
pewter halfgallon & quart
stew pot and old pot
Dough trough
Tubs, Big wheel (Mothers)
piece of cloth (Abrahams)
a closet
bed and furniture
bed and furniture
parcel wheat
parcel Barley
Cutting box

Big Augur
half bushel & old Lumber
2 Brass clocks
sheep shears
padlock
4 bottles
money scales
parcel of books
Grubbing hoe
Old iron & Lumber
big pot
broken-edge pot [Mother's]
a case of drawers
a trunk
½ doz chairs
a table
parcel of wheat in the barn
old wheat stack
parcel rye
stack Hay
stove

12 September

a Brown Horse	15.0.0	Wagon and gears
a White Horse	2.0.0	Bay Horse
a White Mare	17.0.0	Bay & sorrell horses, black horse.

17 October

Sledge hammer & crowbar
pair maul & rings
12 sheep.
a jug
a watering pot

part of Lock chain
six sheep (Mothers)

sum total £258.4.9

Witnesses: Martin Woolford, Edward Lucas Jr., William Morgan.
At Court, Berkely Co. 1777, 19 August.

THOMAS SHEPHERD, OF SHEPHERDSTOWN

It has never been established by the writer after exhaustive
study and research, nor has it been brought to light in any of the
correspondence with his descendants, nor from the various traditions concerning him, as to who were the ancestors of Thomas
Shepherd; whence he came, when or where he married, nor anything concerning the youth and antecedents of the progenitor of
the extensive line of descendants of this most worthy of Virginia
patriarchs. The one dominant tradition which has been handed
down through the generations is:

"Three brothers: Thomas, John and William—came to this country
from Shropshire [Wales] and landed at Annapolis, Md., Thomas settled
at Shepherdstown; John in Maryland, in what is now Washington County
and William went to the West." [Family correspondence; W. Va. Hist.
Mag., Oct. '02, p. 28.]

THOMAS SHEPHERD, OF SHEPHERDSTOWN

John Shepherd, Esq., of Chicago, Ill., writes:

"Thomas Shepherd may have been descended from Thomas Shepherd who was a member of the London Virginia Company, and one-sixth owner of the Virginia grant. As the latter was a London Merchant and a Director in the Colony, he furnished a lot of the money to forward the enterprise. He evidently sent many of his relatives to the Virginia colony who occupied positions as parish priests, collectors, Justices of the Peace, &c."

Another view is projected by one of the descendants of Thomas Shepherd which involves a comparison between the crest used by the Shepherd families of Kingston and Devonshire, in England, with the one engraved upon a piece of ancestral plate in possession of Mrs. Abraham Shepherd, of Shepherdstown; there is but a slight difference in the design of the two devices, and strongly supports the presumption that the family was of English origin, a branch probably of one of the Devonshire houses. That a scion of the latter stock did emigrate to this country is determined by the fact that the will of a Thomas Shepherd, of Cecil County, Maryland, which was probated 1 Sept., 1756, contains this item: "to my cousin Thomas Shepherd, son of John Shepherd of Columpton, in Devonshire, in the Kingdom of Old England the sum of £50." Now Columpton is in that district of Devonshire where many Shepherd families lived at that period and in a part of the county which contributed so many brave and hardy mariners to the fleets of Drake, Raleigh, Davy and Gilbert.

The arms borne by the Devonshire family referred to are described: "Sa a fesse ar.; in chief three pole axes of the second." Crest: "on a mount vert. a stag lodged reguard ar. vulned. on the shoulder, gu" (Burke's General Armory, Ed. 1878, p. 20; also Fairbairn's Crests, Plate 51, crest 9). In the crest in possession of the Virginia family an arrow protrudes from the wounded shoulder, while in the English crest the wound alone is shown, "which," writes another of the descendants, "verifies the statement always made by my grandmother, that the family was originally English."

The compiler of this genealogy, in the course of his investigations, found the record of a group of Shepherd brothers, bearing the names of Thomas, David, John and James that had come to the Province of East Jersey about 1683, from County Tipperary, Ireland. There was also a Moses Shepherd living in the Shrewsbury settlement, in East Jersey, at the same time, but his connection with the four brothers above named is undetermined. The four first named, after a short residence in East Jersey, removed to West Jersey and severally settled on both banks of the Cohansey Creek, in Salem County. These brothers were Baptists, but later identified themselves with the Quakers, and many of their descendants so remain. Nothing has been found, however, to connect these families with those of the Virginia

Valley; but there is some significance in the similarity of family names and in the fact that a number of East Jersey families from Salem County about the time of the youth of Thomas Shepherd emigrated to the Potomac region and settled along the small tributaries of what was then Prince George's County, Md. Among those pioneers were the Morgans, Hedges, Hardins, Nevilles, Holmes, Van Metres and others whose names became more or less prominent in the colonization of the Valley of Virginia. Richard Morgan and the Van Metres in particular were the original patentees of land in about Shepherdstown (West Virginia Historical Magazine, April, 1903, pp. 125 *et seq*).

In Scharf's History of Western Maryland (Vol. 1, p. 501) reference is made to the erection of certain parishes in the western parts of the Province (Maryland). It is there stated that St. John's Parish, in 1719, was co-extensive with Prince George's County, a vast territory reaching from the settlements at the head of Chesapeake Bay into the heart of the Alleghanies. In 1726 St. John's Parish was divided; all the region lying beyond the eastern branch of the Potomac, including Rock Creek and Potomac Hundreds, and the section which afterwards became the District of Columbia, was allowed to retain the old name, while the new parish, which included the western remainder of the county, was called St. George's Parish. Upon the petition of a number of the inhabitants living in the western portion of St. George's Parish permission was granted in February, 1728, for the erection of a new chapel for their greater convenience. Among those subscribing funds for the building of the new place of worship were Thomas and William Shepherd. This is the only instance where Thomas Shepherd's name is mentioned by Scharf, and deducing from the fact that Thomas Shepherd was then living in the uppermost part of the parish, he had only to cross the Potomac to possess the virgin lands where he afterward established his home. William Shepherd remained in Maryland, for his name is found among the petitioners of 1740 praying for a division of St. George's Parish and the creation of All Saint's Parish, which was to extend northward and westward from Great Seneca Creek, and to include within its limits Antietam Hundred. At about this period there were several Shepherd families living in that part of Prince George's County, as the county records at Upper Marlboro will bear ample evidence; and that particular part of the Province where they lived formed a part of Frederick County after its creation in 1748, and so again, in 1776, another change brought the locality within the limits of Washington County and it so remains.

When Jost Hite began to dispose of his lands in Spottsylvania Co., Va., which had been assigned to him by John and Isaac Van Metre, among the first to procure desirable parcels was Thomas Shepherd, who purchased 222 acres on the south side of the

Cohongoluta (Potomac). The record of the grant was dated 3 October, 1734, the same year in which Orange County was set off from Spottsylvania County. The grant thus fell within the bounds of the former. Shepherd made his selection at a point on the bank of the Potomac near the crossing afterward called "Packhorse ford" by the settlers. An additional grant of 450 acres by Lord Fairfax, 12 June, 1751 (Land Grants, Bk. G, p. 457, Richmond), increased Shepherd's possessions. These were supplemented by a purchase from Capt. Richard Morgan, 5 Aug., 1762, of 50 acres; and again, on 15 Jan., 1768, when Lord Fairfax conveyed to him 222 acres, so that the combined acreage which Thomas Shepherd owned in the vicinity of "Packhorse ford" aggregated about 1,000 acres; and the settlement which followed, due no doubt to some German influence, became known as Mecklenburg.

In the meanwhile (1745) Thomas Shepherd's father-in-law, John Van Metre, had died and in his will had bequeathed to his daughter Elizabeth, the wife of Thomas Shepherd, a plantation of 162 acres called "Pell Mell," which lay on the opposite side of the river in Maryland adjacent to the Antietam Creek, which had been surveyed for John Van Metre in 1743 by Joseph Chapline. Subsequently this property became the property of David Shepherd, the eldest son of Thomas and Elizabeth Shepherd.

On the beautiful wooded bluff overlooking the sinuous windings of the Potomac, and beyond it, the low slopes of the Maryland shore; and on both sides of a small, but swift, run that tumbled down over the rocky ledges of a defile leading to the river, Thomas Shepherd founded the settlement, which, in years to come, was destined to honor his name. Less than a mile below was the old "Packhorse ford" marking the main trail—the path, which, from time immemorial, the savages had worn deep into the soil from intercourse between the tribes of the north and those of the souṭṇ—but now absorbed by the constantly increasing volume of pioneers passing down and through to the settlements of Maryland and Pennsylvania to be distributed, at this point, over the various Indian highways toward the south. Thomas Shepherd was shrewd enough to realize the importance of the location and its strategic advantages for trade and barter with the Indians and with the emigrants that flowed, like a stream, over his land.

It is said that his first settlers were thrifty German mechanics. Whoever they may have been, they were encouraged by the enterprising energy of Thomas Shepherd, and an industrious community was soon developed. Then a fort was erected, for the times were full of menace, and the Indians were growing more restless and troublesome under the influence of the French parties who sought to control the commercial and territorial advantages along the Ohio. To Shepherd's Fort came the settlers in times of danger, for protection, and it is no doubt due to these circumstances that Thomas Shepherd received the title of Captain which Kercheval, and some other writers of border history, gave him. "The Fort" was built of stone and erected in the centre of the village, and there remained until 1812 when it was demolished and a brick building erected on its site (W. Va. Hist. Mag., Oct., 1902, p. 31).

As Mecklenburg grew in population, its proprietor resourcefully met the expansion by enlarging its bounds. Mills were erected; a ferry projected, and other inducements followed the laying out of the town. The disposition of lots was made upon the terms recited in an old document, now in the possession of one of the proprietor's descendants, which reads:

"The said Thomas Shepherd executed an article in writing wherein he covenanted and agreed with the subscribers thereto to lay off 20 lots, ½ an acre in each lot; to let each subscriber have one lot during the continuance of the Indian war free and clear from rent or any encumbrance; and at the end of the then Indian war each subscriber should pay fourty shillings current money of Virginia; and on payment of the said fourty shillings each subscriber, his heirs or assigns, should receive a sufficient title for his lot, subject to the yearly rent after the then Indian war, of five shillings sterling, and for making the said titles and complying with the covenants and agreements above mentioned the said Thomas Shepherd bound himself, his heirs, executors and administrators in the penal sum of one thousand pounds like current money of Virginia, to be paid to the subscribers in his non performance" [West Va. Hist. Mag., Oct. '02, p. 30].

Samuel Washington is said to have received one of these lots. The Act of Incorporation of the town, in 1762, reads in part, as follows:

"Whereas it is represented that Thomas Shepherd of Frederick Co., hath laid off some 50 acres of his lands—on the Potomac in said county, with lots and streets for a town, and has disposed of many of said lots, the purchasers thereof have made their humble application that the said land may be established a town, being pleasantly and commodiously situated for trade; that the same be established a town by name of Mecklinburg, and when the free holders shall have built upon and saved their lots, according to the conditions of their deeds, it shall be entitled to all the rights of other towns" [Hening's Statutes of Va., Vol. VIII, p. 600; West Va. Hist. Mag., July, 1901, p. 31, &c.].

After the death of Thomas Shepherd the name of the town was changed from Mecklenburg to Shepherdstown.

In the establishment of the ferry over the Potomac—which was located just below the present bridge over the river, and at the mouth of a ravine through which flows the water power for Shepherd's several mills (fed from copious springs above the town) and crossing the deep pool in the river as it sweeps around the curve at Shepherdstown—there seems to have been strenuous

WILL OF ELIZABETH SHEPHERD

rivalry with Thomas Swearingen, a landed proprietor of Maryland, who was operating a similar public conveyance a little
farther down the stream. Swearingen's ferry, established by law,
in 1755, was more recently known as Blackford's ferry, both
families having intermarried; the ferry was long continued by
these families.

Thomas Shepherd was granted ferry privileges by the General
Assembly of Virginia, in 1765, only to have them revoked the
following year (Hening's Statutes of Va., Vol. VIII., pp. 146,
263). His son, Abraham, succeeded again, in 1778, and met with
a repeal in 1779 "because it was at a very short distance from the
lands of Thomas Swearingen in Maryland" (Hening's Statutes
of Va., Vol. X., p. 197; Virginia Historical Society Collections).
Which of these proprietors was the victor, eventually, the compiler is unable to say.

Thomas Shepherd died in 1776; his wife, Elizabeth, in 1793.
They had a family of ten children, all of whom grew to maturity,
married, and left a host of worthy descendants.

WILL OF ELIZABETH SHEPHERD

In the name of God Amen. I Elizabeth Shepherd of Berkely County
and Commonwealth of Virginia being poorly in health but of perfect
mind & memory, thanks be given unto God Calling unto mind the mortality of my body knowing that it is appointed for us all once to die, do
make and ordain this my last Will and Testament that is to say principally and first of all I give and reccomend my soul unto the hand of
Almighty God who gave it and my body I reccomend to the earth to be-
buried in a decent manner by the one hereafter appointed nothing doubt-
but at the General ressurrection I shall receive the same again by the
mighty power of God, and as touching such worldly estate wherewith it
hath pleased God to bless me in this life I give devise and dispose of the
same in the following manner and Form. Firstly I give and bequeath to
my son David Shepherd, my Bible in full for his part of my estate, Also,
I give and bequeath to my daughter Susannah Eoff all my estate viz; as
to legacies, back rents &c. all [and] every part of my estate to the said
Susannah Eoff and her heirs forever, whom I request my body to be
decently buried by—out of my said estate. I do hereby utterly revoke
and disannul all and every other former Testament Wills and Legacies
bequests and executors by me in any wise before named willed and bequeathed ratifying and confirming this and no other to be my last Will
and Testament. In Witness Whereof I have hereunto set my hand and
seal this tenth day of July one thousand seven hundred and eighty-six.
Signed sealed and delivered and acknowledged in the presence of Thos.
White, Thomas Thornburg and Nicholes Shill
                              her
              (sig) ELIZABETH E SHEPHERD [L S].
                             mark

Proved by the oaths of Thomas White and Necoles Shall two of the
subscribing witnesses thereto, at a Court held for Berkely Co. 12 June
1793, and on the motion of John Eoff who made oath according to

law certificate is granted him for obtaining letters of administration of the estate of said Elizabeth Shepherd deceased—with the Will annexed no executor being named therein. &c &c. Abraham Shepherd bondsman in the sum of £1000. &c &c

Teste   MOSES HUNTER.

CUSTOMS AND DRESS OF THE PIONEERS

Most of the frontier cabins of those early days were fashioned in a rude style. The furniture consisted of a few pewter dishes and spoons; but mostly of wooden bowls, trenchers and naggins; or of gourds and hard-shell squashes. Iron pots, knives and forks were brought from the east, along with salt and wire, on pack-horses. "Hog and hominy" were the chief food, "Johnny Cakes" and pone being the only bread at supper; mush and milk was the standard dish; when milk was scarce, molasses, bear's oil, or ham gravy were the substitutes. The "truck patch" attached to every cabin supplied the roasting ears, squashes, pumpkins, beans and potatoes and these were well cooked with pork, venison and bear's meat.

The frontier dress for the men was partly Indian; the chief article being the hunting shirt, which was a loose frock, open before, with large sleeves, reaching half way down the thighs and lapping over the waist-belt a foot or more. The cape was large and handsomely fringed with ravelled cloth; the belt had suspended on one side the bullet-bag and tomahawk, and on the other side the scalping knife in a leathern sheath. A pair of drawers, or breeches, and fringed "leggins" covered the legs, while moccasins, of dressed deer-skins, served much better than shoes. They were neatly made of a single piece, with a gather seam along the top of the foot and another from the bottom of the heel, without gather, as high as the ankle joint. Flops neatly tied to the ankles and lower parts of the legs by thongs of doe-skin, so as to exclude dirt, snow and sand, were left on each side. Each hunter made his own moccasins, in a few hours, with a moccasin awl, which, together with a roll of buckskin and thongs or whangs for mending, was part of the regular trappings. In cold weather the moccasins were well stuffed with deer's hair or dry leaves, but in wet weather moccasin-wearing was only a decent way of going barefoot—due to the spongy nature of the leather. Owing to this, Indians, as well as whites, were much afflicted with rheumatism, and this was the reason why, at night, all slept with their feet to the fire. Very frequently young frontiersman became so enamoured of the Indian dress that drawers were laid aside, and the leggings made to come well up on the thigh, and the breeches-clout adopted, which last was a piece of linen, or cloth, nearly a yard long, and eight or nine inches wide.

This passed under the belt, before and behind, leaving the ends for flops with ornamental ends hanging over the belt. Where this belt passed over the hunting shirt, the upper part of the thigh and part of the hips were naked. Doddridge asserts that the young hunter, instead of being abashed by his nudity, was proud of his Indian dress, frequently entering houses of worship thus clad. Their appearance did not, however, according to the veracious chronicler, "add much to the devotion of the young ladies."

The linsey petticoat and bed gown formed the universal dress of the women, with a small hand-made kerchief about the neck. They went barefoot in warm weather, while in cold their feet were covered with moccasins, or coarse shoe packs.

The garments of both men and women were hung aroung the cabin on wooden pegs. The young women of those days knew nothing of curls, ruffles, rings, jewels, or other modern adornments. Instead of the toilet they had to handle the distaff, or shuttle, the sickle or weeding hook, contented if they could obtain their linsey clothing and cover their heads with a sun bonnet.

Doddridge gives an interesting account of the manner in vogue in these rude times of settling a young couple for life. Their cabin was built by neighbors. First were the choppers, then those who hauled or sorted the logs on the chosen spot. The best axemen searched the woods for a straight-grained tree, from three to four feet thick, for making clapboards for the roof. These were split four feet long with a large iron, and wide as the timber would allow, and were used without hewing. Others still got out puncheons for the floor, by splitting young trees and hewing the faces with a broad axe. They were half the length of the floor they were intended to make. The second day was alotted for the raising. Four cornersmen were first selected, whose business was to notch and place the logs. The rest raised the timbers to their places. When the cabin was raised a few rounds high the sleepers and floor began to be laid. Next a door was made by cutting the logs on one side so as to make an opening about three feet wide; a wider opening was made for the chimney, which was built of logs and made large to admit a back and jambs of stone. The roof was formed by making the end logs shorter until a single log formed the "comb" of the roof. On these the clapboards were placed, the ranges of them lapping some distance over those next before, and kept in their places by logs resting on them. A third day was spent levelling off the floor, furnishing up, making a rude floor table, bedstead and three-legged stools. Then the masons made billets for chinking up the cracks between the logs, which were plastered over with mud mortar. The cabin being thus finished and furnished, the house warming took up a whole night—and consisted of a vigorous dance, made up of the bride and groom's relations, and all the neighbors. On the following day the young couple took possession of their new house (see McKnight's Old Fort Duquesne).

THE OHIO COMPANY AND ITS OBJECT

The Ohio Company was organized in Virginia, in 1748, under a royal grant. Thomas Lee, of Virginia, formed the design, and twelve other persons were associated with him, among whom were Lawrence and Augustine Washington, brothers of George.

The purpose of the Ohio Company was to divert the trade of the Indians, north of the Ohio and its headwaters, southward, by the Potomac route, and to settle the country around the head of the Ohio with English colonists from Virginia and Maryland. To this end the king granted the Company 500,000 acres of land " west of the mountains," to be taken chiefly on the south side of the Ohio, between the Monongahela and the Kanawha, but with privileges to take part of the quantity north of the Ohio. 200,000 were to be taken up at once, free of quit-rents, or taxes to the king, for ten years, upon condition that the Company would, within seven years, seat 100 families on the lands; build a fort; maintain a garrison and protect the settlement.

Many settlements were made on lands supposed to be in Virginia but were afterwards disclosed to be within the charter limits of Pennsylvania. This provoked the French and Indian traders and stirred up the Indians to hostility. Christopher Gist was the Company's agent to select the lands and conciliate the Indians. The Company imported large quantities of goods for trade with the Indians and established posts for trade. Among the posts established were Wills Creek, Redstone (Brownsville, Pa.), on the way to the forks of the Ohio (Frontier Forts of Pennsylvania, Vol. II., p. 162).

Governor Dinwiddie, to encourage enlistments to prevent the French settling on the Ohio, grants 200,000 acres (Dinwiddie Papers, Vol. I., p. 97).

NEMACOLIN'S PATH

What is called " Nemacolin's Path " was a great Indian trail which led east from the " forks of the Ohio " (Pittsburg) through southern Pennsylvania. At the instance of the Ohio Company, Nemacolin, a well-known Delaware, who resided at the mouth of Dunlap's Creek, Fayette Co., Pa., " blazed " the forest path from Wills Creek (Cumberland) to the Ohio, which was the original tracing of that great highway now known as the National, or Cumberland Road. In 1753 it was well marked and cleared of bushes and fallen timber, so as to make it a good pack-horse road. "Gists's Plantation" was located on this road which afterwards became Braddock's Road. This, says Judge Veech, was a misnomer, it should have been called Washington's Road for he made it to Gists; from Gists's to Turtle Creek it was Braddock's (Appendix to Old Fort Duquesne, pp. 482-3).

"MEMORANDA OF JOURNEY OF WM. BROWN AND THOS. SHEPHERD—SHEPHERDSTOWN TO WHEELING"

"April the 28th 1786, Wm Brown and Thomas Shepherd set out for Wheeling.

[going out]		[returning]
About 4 o'clock Opekon	o=o=8.	May 8 Lodged at Catfish—McNeals
and lodged at Cauffmans	o=1=4.	9 Lodged at Christians Gap
29 Boyd's ferry	o=1=6.	10 and Crossed Monongahela
and lodged at Kings at		Lodged at Levi Springers
fifteen	=5=5.	12 loddged at Mountains
30 lodged at Griers	o=	13 Griers
May 1 Lodged at Mountains	o=5=10.	14 at Wm. Grays
Charaty or alms	o=1=10.	15 at J. Spongs at Bath Town
2 Thos Wills	1=11=10.	16 at Shepherdstown.

Route out: Opequon, Cauffmans, Boyds's Ferry, Kings, Griers, the Mountains and Thos. Wills.

Returning: Catfish (Washington, Pa.), Christians Gap, Monongahela, Levi Springers (Uniontown, Pa.), Mountains, Griers, Wm. Grays, Springs (Berkeley Springs, W. Va.) and Shepherdstown.

Wheeling to Catfish, Pa., 25 miles, to Springers, to Blue Ridge. The route of the National Road to Uniontown and Braddock's Road to Cumberland.

THE ROUTE TO THE OHIO COUNTRY

"In relation to the road taken by Thomas Shepherd and William Brown in 1786 when they visited the region west of the Alleghany Mountains, where John Grove and his wife Mary Brown Grove had settled,—I will give you such information as may be at my command.

"The original road was nothing more than an Indian trail, which was known as Nemacolin's trail, until Washington came over it in his campaign of 1754. At that time he cut his way through the forest and made it possible for General Braddock the following year to convey his munitions of war over the old trail to what is now Fayette Co., Penna. when he was on his way to Fort Duqusne [now Pittsburg] to attack the French and their Indian allies. You will remember that Braddock's army was ambushed at the Monongahela, near where the city of Braddock stands, and the General mortally wounded, and many of his men slain on the field.

"Had it not been for Washington and his Virginians, none of Braddocks' army would have escaped, as they knew nothing of Indian warfare. After the disastrous defeat of the army and the fatal wounding of General Braddock, the army protected by the Virginia frontiersmen under Washington retreated to what is now known as Dunbar's Camp on the summit of the Alleghany Mts., about 5 miles east of the present site of Uniontown, Pa. Here Braddock died and his remains were carried to a point on the Braddock Road about 10 miles east of Uniontown, where he was buried in honors of war and the wagon train ran over the newly-made grave to destroy all marks of his burial so that the body would not be disinterred and the head scalped by the Indians. The old Braddock Road was located on the course of Nemacolin's Path, and led from Winchester, Va. by way of Wills Creek [now Cumberland, Md.] to Great Crossing of the Youghiogheny River [now Somerfield, Pa.], thence across the Chestnut and Laurel Ridges of the Alleghany Mountains to Washington's Spring on the summit of Laurel Ridge. From Washington's Spring the Braddock Road took a course north westerly toward Mt. Braddock, or Col. Gist's plantation. From Wills Creek to Great Crossing was a distance of 41 miles, and thence to the site of Uniontown, a distance of 22 miles, or 63 miles from Cumberland to Uniontown. The road taken by Brown and Shepherd was no doubt identical with that of Braddock and Washington thirty one years previous.

"At Washington's Spring on the top of Laurel Ridge, a road known as Nemacolins, or Dunlap's—bore westward and came down the western slope of the Mountains through what is known as Lick Hollow, to the town (now of Hopwood), passing through its southern part, and thence on to Brownsville, 12 miles, thence to Catfish [Washington, Pa.] 24 miles additional, and thence to Fort Henry [Wheeling] 31 miles further. This seems to have been the terminus of the Journey of Brown and Shepherd.

Levi Springer spoken of in record of their trip, lived about 1 mile northwest of Uniontown, and there is now a Levi Springer, an old bachelor, living on the old farm, which is located in North Union township. The Springers were very early settlers, having moved from near Winchester, Va. Many of the early settlers were Virginians, and came from the frontier in the Shenandoah Valley near Winchester.

"The Scotch Presbyterians [Scotch-Irish] were natural born frontiersmen and fighters. They seem chosen for the duty of preparing the border county for those who were to follow and assist in developing the wilderness." (Letter M. M. Hopwood, Apl. 19, 1907.)

CHRONOLOGICAL RECORD OF DAVID SHEPHERD AS A PIONEER ON THE WESTERN WATERS

Ohio County, Va., as originally created (1776) extended northward to the mouth of Cross Creek, southward to the mouth of Middle Island Creek and from the Ohio River, eastward, so as to include the present Townships of Hopewell, Independence, Buffalo, Blaine, Donegal, the East and West Finleys, and parts of Canton and Franklin, in Washington Co., as well as the western one-third of Greene Co., Pa.

Black's Cabin, where the first courts of Ohio County were held, was on the north fork of Short Creek, about eleven miles northeast of Fort Henry (now Wheeling, W. Va.), and about six or eight miles northwest from Fort Alexandria, in Washington Co.,

Pa. There was Van Metre's Fort, and not far away was Rice's Fort, on Buffalo Creek, in Washington Co., Pa., and Beeman's and Ryerson's Stations in Greene Co., Pa., and Fort Jackson, now Waynesboro.

Its southern part has been made into a number of new Virginia (now West Virginia) Counties, and its northern part, above the mouth of Short Creek has been divided into Brooke and Hancock Counties (W. Va.), while, by the actual running of the western boundary of Pennsylvania, in 1784-5, it lost all its old possessions in Pennsylvania.

The Court of Ohio County was removed from West Liberty on Short Creek to Wheeling in 1796 and its records are to be found in the office of the county clerk in the court house for Ohio County, in that city. Black's Cabin is now West Liberty, W. Va. (see Annals Carnegie Museum, Vol. III., Dec., 1904).

1755. David Shepherd married *circa* 1755-1757, Rachael Teague, who, it is believed, was the daughter of William Teague, a landowner of Frederick Co., Va., who, about 1751, disposed of his landed possessions and emigrated to the Carolinas. His sons were Edward, Abraham, Elijah and Moses.

1758. In the election held throughout Virginia in 1758 for representatives to the House of Burgesses, George Washington, then a young militia officer stationed at Fort Loudon (Winchester, Va.), was one of the candidates and for him Thomas and David Shepherd, father and son, voted (see West Virginia Hist. Mag., Vol. I., Part I., 19).

1761. David Shepherd soon became a land owner and an active man of affairs in Frederick County; a record is found of taxes on his land and paid by him to William Hatch on June 25, 1761.

1763, March 4. David Shepherd, one of the justices of the Frederick Co., Va., Court, held this day (Frederick Co., Va., Order Bk., No. 11).

1763. He had become, at the age of thirty years, one of the " gentlemen Justices " of Frederick County and was present at a court held 4th of March in that year at Winchester (see Court Journal, Frederick Co.), and on the 3d of April following it is also recorded that he paid his county and parish levies for that year to Wm. Nelson.

1764. David Shepherd entered suit 26 April, 1764, to establish and perpetuate the bounds of a tract of land in Washington Co., Md., called " Pell Mell," to which he then held title, the land in question being the inheritance of his mother, Elizabeth Shepherd, from her father, John Van Metre (see Frederick Co., Va., and Frederick Co., Md., records).

" Pell Mell " was located on the bank of the Potomac River at a point probably opposite, or nearly so, to the present town of Shepherdstown, W. Va. It adjoined lands of Thomas Swearingen, who later established a ferry from his property to the Virginia side of the Potomac. The "Pell Mell" tract contained about 162 acres; it had been surveyed for John Van Metre in 1743 by Joseph Chapline, according to his testimony and that of Jacob Van Metre, a brother of David's mother, who was a youth at the time, and the property lay between Swearingen's lands and a larger tract called "Antietam Bottoms," which flanked the westerly side of Antietam Creek and was largely owned by a Maryland family of Shepherds. Having established the metes and bounds of "Pell Mell," David Shepherd sold it 4 June, 1769, to Jacob Vandever, of Salem, N. J. The transfer was endorsed by Rachael Shepherd 24 June, and the deed recorded 11 July, 1769 (see Frederick Co., Md., records).

In this year, also, he paid £5 to Samuel Oldham for taxes on his Virginia lands.

In this year David Shepherd had some dispute with Thomas Swearingen and was brought before the Court of the Province of Maryland, held at Annapolis, 27 Oct., 1769. Col. Thomas Prather was summoned to Annapolis to testify in this case as a witness, under penalty of £5. Shepherd and Prather accordingly appeared before Judge Stewart, one of the Justices of the Provincial Court at Annapolis, on the date named (see Shepherdstown Register, Jan., 1903).

1764, July 25. Thomas and Elizabeth Shepherd convey lot No. 50 in Mecklenburg to David Shepherd (Court Order, Bk. 9, p. 425, Frederick Co., Va.).

1765, August 8. David Shepherd and Hugh Stephenson give bond to the King for a faithful keeping of a ferry from the land of Thomas Shepherd at the town of Mecklenburg to the opposite shore in Maryland, and the said David Shepherd hath undertaken to keep the same.

Acknowledged in open court by David Shepherd and Hugh Stephenson (Frederick Co. Order Book, No. 10, p. 460).

1767. David Shepherd is allowed 50 pounds of tobacco for his services as witness at the May term of Court of Frederick Co., Va. He is also credited with having paid £5 for yearly dues (see Shepherd Mss.).

1770, Nov. 9. The old order book of Frederick Co., Va., Court (No. 15) records that Van Swearingen was ordered to pay to David Shepherd 50 pounds tobacco for attending court two days as a witness to prove William's will.

1770. David Shepherd left Shepherdstown with his family and settled near Wheeling, which was established in 1769, at the forks of Big and Little Wheeling creeks, where he built a blockhouse (see Shepherd MSS., Madison, Wis.).

1772. David Shepherd and Rachael, his wife, of Norbonne Parish, in Berkeley Co., Va., convey to Samuel Washington (brother of Col. George Washington) a half-acre lot in Mecklenburg (Shepherdstown, Va.), being part of a tract of 222 acres patented to Thomas Shepherd, 3 Oct., 1734 (see County Records, Martinsburg, W. Va.).

1772. In an interview with Mrs. Lydia Cruger, the daughter-in-law of Col. David Shepherd, she said that David Shepherd purchased from Silas Zane land, of which he had "tomahawked" 1,000 acres, at the Forks of Wheeling Creek. The Zanes and others came overland from Redstone (Brownsville, Pa.) by way of Catfish (Washington, Pa.) and Scotch Ridge, thence down the same path afterward taken for the National Road, to the Forks. Zane went down Wheeling Creek (June, 1772) and with others occupied the fine lands along the Wheeling, Buffalo and Short Creeks. Among those persons were David Shepherd, the Mitchells, Van Metres, Millers and others. Many of the settlers of this part of West Virginia were from the upper counties of Virginia and Maryland (see DeHaas, pp. 82–83).

When David Shepherd settled on Wheeling Creek he brought with him from Shepherdstown region three blacksmiths, a horse-shoer and several mechanics for the new settlement (see Preston Papers, Vol. XXI., p. 203, at Madison, Wis.).

The sources of the main stem of Wheeling Creek, which empties into the Ohio River, are found in three tributaries which rise in Washington Co., Pa., Big Wheeling in East Finley Township, Middle Wheeling in West Finley, and Little Wheeling in Donegal Township; Little Wheeling and Middle Wheeling unite at Triadelphia and empty into Big Wheeling at Shepherd's Mills, near Elm Grove, near City of Wheeling (Creigh's History of Washington Co., Pa., p. 47). Travelers to Wheeling probably used the old Catfish Path (later Cumberland National Road) from Brownsville (see Washington and the West, p. 123).

1772, April 17. At about the first session of the Court of Berkeley Co., Va., Robert Worthington and David Shepherd were appointed coroners for the county and sworn in (Norris's History of Lower Shenandoah, p. 226).

——, May 19. David Shepherd appointed coroner (*vide*, p. 296).

——, June 16. David Shepherd paid quit rents to Robert Stephens for land in Berkeley Co., Va., for years 1768, 1769, 1770 and 1771 (see Shepherd MSS.).

1772, Aug. 18. David Shepherd appointed a road viewer from Mecklenburg to Key's Ferry (Berkeley Co. Order Book).

——. "Wm. Morgan, cousin," is appointed overseer of the road from Robert Lemon's to Mecklenburg in the room of —— ——(Berkeley County records).

——, 17. David Shepherd for one old wolf's head, 1—5—0.

1773, March 17. David Shepherd, Wm. Shepherd and Nicholas McIntire: jurymen.

1773. Among the certificates granted to settlers on western waters by Commissioners Francis Peyton, Philip Pendleton and Joseph Holmes, sitting at Redstone Old Fort in 1779 was one to David Shepherd for 400 acres of land on the upper side of the Little Kanawha in Monongalia Co., Va., about five miles from its mouth, to include his settlement made in 1773 (see Trans-Alleghany Magazine, Oct., 1902, p. 24). This certificate was granted according to a clause in Section IV. of the Act of General Assembly of Virginia, May, 1779, to wit:

"That all persons who at any time before the first day of January, in the year 1778, have really and *bona fide* settled themselves, or their families, or at his, her, or their charge, have settled others upon any waste or unappropriated lands on said western waters, to which no other person hath any legal right or claim, shall be allowed for every family so settled, four hundred acres of land, or such smaller quantity as the party chooses, to include such settlement." . . . "And if any such settlers shall desire to take up a greater quantity of land than is hereby allowed them, they shall on payment to the treasurer of the consideration money required from other purchasers, be entitled to pre-emption of any greater quantity of land adjoining to that allowed them in consideration of settlement, not exceeding 1000 acres, and to which no other person hath any legal right or claim." (Trans. Alleghany Mag., Vol. I., p. 63.)

Under the above conditions Moses Shepherd, the youngest son of David Shepherd, was also granted by the Commissioners of Monongalia Co., Va., at the same time and place:

"400 acres on a small drain of the Ohio river, about 2 miles below Bull Creek, to include his settlement made in 1773, with a pre-emption to 1000 acres adjoining." (Vide Vol. II., p. 24.)

1774. David Shepherd receives warrant from Lord Dunmore for 1,063 acres of land under the King of Great Britain's proclamation of 1763, lying in the Forks of Wheeling, in the County of Augusta. This warrant was afterward confirmed and signed by Governor Benjamin Harrison, 18 March, 1784 (H. McI. F.).

———. Col. William Crawford took up lands on the Wheeling, in 1774, for Col. David Shepherd (see Draper's Notes, Madison, Wis.).

In the spring of 1774 David Shepherd moved to the Forks of Wheeling, where he purchased the settlement right of Silas Zane. Dunmore's War breaking out, Col. Shepherd removed to the crossing of the Yohoghany, near now Connellsville. In the fall of 1774 he returned to Wheeling. Col. Shepherd made a fort on his place to which the up-creek people resorted, erected a mill in 1775, a single-geared wheel; commanded at the siege of Wheeling in 1777, and commanded some men in the Tuscarawas campaign (Draper's Notes, Vol. II., No. 4, p. 37, 1845).

1774. Col. Crawford writes Col. Washington, 13 May, 1774: "We this day received some news from Wheeling, and several inhabitants of that place have gone back and are planting their corn. David Shepherd, who lives at Wheeling, moved his family up to my house; he has gone back himself to plant his corn" (Shepherd Papers, Vol. XV., p. 84).

——, May 25. Neighbors are building a stockade fort at Crawfords.

——. Among those called (by Court of West Augusta District) by Lord Dunmore to serve on the Commission of Oyer and Terminer for the County Court of West Augusta to December, 1774, was "David Shepherd, living west of the mountains" (History of Washington Co., Pa., p. 204).

1774, August. Resolves of Lord Dunmore's army, in which they say:

"We will exert every power within us for the defense of American Liberty, and for the support of her just rights and privileges . . . when regularly called forth by the unanimous voice of our countrymen."

This event occurred at Pittsburg (Fort Dunmore) on the return of the army from their attack on the Shawnees on the Sciota, in August, 1774 (see Howe's Historical Collections of Ohio, p. 408).

1775. Shepherd's Fort was erected in 1775 by David Shepherd at the Forks of Wheeling (now Triadelphia), upon the spot now occupied by Mrs. Crugar. It was almost an exact square, with block houses two to of the corners, so as to command the walls either way. Cabins were arranged the inner side and the place perhaps was one of the most complete and safe in the west (see Wills DeHaas, p. 311).

——, 20 March–16 May. David Shepherd at Fort Pitt as member of Augusta Co., Va., Executive Committee of Safety (H. McI. F.).

——, 16 May. David Shepherd's name appears among those appointed as a Committee for Augusta Co., Va., on this date, and at which meeting Resolutions were adopted approving the action of their New England brethren declaring for the Colonies, etc., and taking stand against the tyranny of England (see American Archives, 4th Series, Vol. II., p. 614).

"Among those called into a meeting of the inhabitants of that part of Augusta Co. that lies on the west side of Laurel Hill, at Pittsburg the 16 day of May, 1775,—were George Croghan, Jacob Van Metre, William Vance, David Shepherd, John Swearingen and others. At this meeting Resolves were made approving the spirited action of their New England bretheren and proposing to follow their example, and voting money to be used by the Deputation to the General Congress" [Hist. Washington Co. Pa. p. 74]. [Hist. Westmoreland Co., Pa., p. 451.]

——, May 17. David Shepherd applies for 1,600 acres of land through Wm. Crawford, surveyor: 400 acres on Peter's Run; 400 adjoining the Great Wheeling; 400 on west side Middle Island, and 400 adjoining same on east side Middle Island, to include his improvements and erect a mill.

———, 19 Sept. Fort Dunmore. David Shepherd (of near present Wheeling) took the usual oath to his Majesty's person and government and subscribed the ab (juriatum) oath and test, and then took the oath of a J. P. and a Justice of the County Court in Chancery and of a Justice of Oyer and Terminer. President Judge, David Shepherd (History of Washington Co., Pa., p. 209).

1776, April. Colonel George Morgan was appointed Indian Agent for Middle Department with headquarters at Pittsburg (see Frontier Forts of Pennsylvania, Vol. I. or II., p. 18).

1776. David Shepherd was appointed Lieutenant of Ohio County by Governor Patrick Henry of Virginia.

In early New England each town had its train-band or company of militia, and the companies in each county united to form the County Regiment. In Virginia it was just the other way. Each county raised a certain number of troops and because it was not convenient for the men to go many miles from home in assembling for purposes of drill, the county was subdivided into military districts, each with its company, according to rules laid down by the Governor. The military command in each county was vested in a *County Lieutenant,* an officer answering in many respects to the Lord Lieutenant of the English shire at that period. Usually he was a member of the Governor's Council and as such exercised sundry judicial functions. He bore the honorary title of "Colonel," and was, to some extent, regarded as the Governor's deputy; but in later times his duties were confined entirely to military matters (see Fiske's Virginia and Her Neighbors, pp. 41-42).

Ohio County was a military colony formed out of the District of West Augusta, Va., by Act of Legislature.

David Shepherd was directed by Charles Simms, Secretary of Virginia, to raise a company of militia, under instructions from the Convention of 1776, and to administer the oath (H. McI. F.).

1776, 20 Aug. David Shepherd and John Carmen, gentlemen, appointed by the Court held at Pittsburg, this date, to contract with persons to build a house 14 feet by 24 feet with a " petition " in the middle, " to be used for a gaol at Augustatown " (History of Washington Co., Pa., p. 210).

———, Sept. 4. Letter dated at Wheeling, addressed to David Shepherd, informing him of his appointment, on that day, as commissary of the troops on the Ohio. Letter was approved by the Council of the County, signed by Dorsey Pentecost, County Lieutenant (see Shepherd Papers, Vol. I., p. —).

The Ohio frontier reached from the Alleghany Mountains to Kittatinny on the Alleghany River, forty-five miles above Pittsburg, then on the west side thereof down that river and the Ohio to the mouth of the Great Kanawha. The only posts of importance below Fort Pitt at this date were Forts Henry and Randolph. The former was built at the commencement of Lord Dunmore's War (then called Fort Fincastle) in 1774, and the latter was erected by Virginia in 1775 (Frontier Forts, Vol. I. or II., p. 18).

1776, Sept. 4. At a council held on this date Dorsey Pentecost writes David Shepherd that he has been appointed commissary for the stations along the Ohio from Grave Creek to Fort Pitt. Foot-note adds that David Shepherd was chosen County Lieutenant in January, 1777, for the newly erected county of Ohio, and acted in that capacity till his death in 1795; that he commanded Fort Henry during its siege in 1777, and led a regiment on Broadhead's Coshocton expedition (1781). During 1783-85 served in the Virginia Legislature and during the Indian wars was efficient in guarding the borders (Thwaites, The Revolution on the Ohio, pp. 195-196).

1777. January 6. At a court for Ohio County, Va., held at Black's Cabin on Short Creek (the following is taken from the court proceedings): "Sworn in as J. P. of Ohio Co., by John McCullogh, High Sheriff—David Shepherd, who administered the oath to the other Justices." The Court recommended that David Shepherd be recommended to his honor, the Governor, as County Lieutenant for this county. Proceedings signed by David Shepherd, who presided at court held the following day (Annals Carnegie Museum, Dec., 1904).

Black's Cabin, the scene of the convening of the first court of Ohio Co., Va., is now called West Liberty and lies at the head of Short Creek, Ohio Co., about six miles from the Ohio River. Beech Bottom Fort was erected on Buffalo Creek, Ohio County, twelve miles above Wheeling and three miles below Wellsburg (the present county seat of Brooke Co., W. Va.). Here fifteen or twenty families forted in 1776 (Draper's Notes, ——).

——, Jan. 29. At a meeting of council of war held at Catfish Camp in the District of West Augusta: among those present was David Shepherd, Esq., County Lieutenant. Among the Resolutions adopted was one designating the house of David Shepherd, of Ohio County, as a proper place for a magazine. It was also resolved that Thomas Jones, or some other person, be appointed by the County Lieutenant to open shop for the making of arms and the repairing of tomahawks, scalping knives, etc., at the house of Col. David Shepherd (History of Washington Co., Pa., p. 187).

——, March 4. David Shepherd is appointed by Council of Virginia to be Colonel of Ohio County and David Rogers Lieutenant (Journal of Executive Council of Virginia).

1777, March 24. David Shepherd notifies Governor Patrick Henry of the situation on the Ohio and says that he has eighty miles of frontier and his militia consists of only 350 effective men; he had ordered fifty militiamen to Wheeling; fifty to Grave

Creek, and fifty to Beech Bottom.   Foot-note adds: Beech Bottom Fort stood about three miles below Wellsburg and twelve miles above Wheeling, in what is now Buffalo District, Brooke Co., W. Va.   It was occupied in 1777 and protected the settlement of the Hedges family (see Thwaites, The Revolution on the Ohio, p. 242).

——.   On the same date Colonel Shepherd applies for supplies, to which Governor Henry responds later and adds that he wants Shepherd to do nothing to offend the Delaware Indians, but to protect and give them assistance when necessary, because they are friendly (see Thwaites, The Revolution on the Ohio, pp. 243–244).

1777, April 12.   Governor Patrick Henry of Virginia addresses David Shepherd as Colonel of Ohio.

——, June 2.   David Shepherd takes the oath as Colonel of Ohio County in open court (Annals of Carnegie Museum, Dec., 1904).

——, June 28.   David Shepherd appointed Lieutenant of Ohio County in place of David Rogers, resigned (Mrs. H. McI. F.).

The Indians leagued with the English having become quite active and sanguinary along the Ohio border, much correspondence in relation thereto ensued between Governor Patrick Henry and Colonel David Shepherd.   In a letter dated at Fort Pitt, 29 July, 1777, the Governor instructs Colonel Shepherd to supply Wheeling with provisions and ammunition, suggesting also that he appoint a Deputy (which he probably did in the person of Francis Duke, his son-in-law).   A letter from the agent, Geo. Morgan, about this time says:

"I shall depend on you alone to supply all the Stations in Ohio County; 'neither money or anything in my power shall be wanting to assist you, &c.'—Aug. 19. Col. Shepherd at Fort Henry [Wheeling] issues to Silas Hedges, 10 lbs powder for use of the Ohio militia.—Sept. 1. Historic siege of Fort Henry by a large body of Indians. Among the slain were: William Shepherd, the Colonel's eldest son, and Francis Duke, his son-in-law, who was the Commissary at Fort Henry. For 23 hours, under command of Col. Shepherd, 35 settlers and militia assisted by their wives and daughters in loading guns and moulding bullets,—successfully resisted the attacks of the savages. Colonel Shepherd's report of the affair is as follows: '1 Lieut. and 14 privates killed; 1 captain and 4 privates wounded.' By the best judges here who have seen the plans laid by the Indians, and their breast-works and blinds in the last action, it is thought their number must have been between two and three hundred, . . . the destruction of cattle is not yet ascertained. A number of distressed families have moved off—yet a number remain for want of horses."

Such is the terse account of an encounter, by the commander, who lost among the rest his son and son-in-law! (Shepherd Papers). Foremost on the list of brave defenders was Col. David Shepherd, whose good conduct on this occasion gained for him the appointment of County Lieutenant from Patrick Henry (Lewis's History of West Virginia, p. 167).

——, Sept. 3. Colonel Shepherd appeals to Fort Pitt for aid (Hand Papers, Vol. III., p. 97, Madison, Wis.).

——, Sept. 8. David McClure writes to General Hand at the instance of Colonel Shepherd, "the people of Wheeling Fort are in sore need of men and provisions" (Frontier Wars MSS., Vol. I., p. 93).

——, Sept. 15. Reporting to General Hand, Colonel Shepherd writes: "1 Lieut. and 20 men rank and file fit for duty—sick and wounded: 1 Capt. and 4 rank and file." He appeals for troops, saying that the times of some of the men have expired, while others are protecting Beech Bottom (Frontier Wars MSS., Vol. I., p. 94).

Major Chew was sent in response to the urgent needs of Colonel Shepherd.

In consequence of the great loss of men at Wheeling in September, 1777, and the loss of his son William and son-in-law Francis Duke, it was determined in the fall of that year to abandon the place and send the families to Redstone. The fort was accordingly evacuated, 27 Sept., 1777, and soon after the Indians burned it to the ground (DeHaas, p. 311).

It appears from Colonel Shepherd's note-book that Shepherd's Fort at the Forks of Wheeling broke up about the 3d or 4th of September, Capt. David Williamson escorting the people away (Hand Papers, Vol. IX., p. 55).

——, Oct. 3. Col. David Shepherd writes General Hand: "Your timely relief by Major Chew was very acceptable as we could not bury the dead before he came." Major Chew writes General Hand, same date, and says: "Since my arrival Col. Shepherd and myself have buried those unfortunate men in the late action—a moving sight! cruelly butchered soon after death" (see DeHaas, and H. McI. F.).

——, Nov. 15. Colonel Shepherd is ordered to draw fifty men, who, with one hundred from interior of the State, will garrison Ohio County. While so doing he will receive Continental pay for a Colonel (Hand Papers, Vol. III., p. 97).

1778, April 4. Col. David Shepherd writes General Hand that he "has 21 men at Fort Henry, 15 at Beech Bottom, and 12 at forks of Wheeling; that the men are better than former soldiers and [he] does not need to use so much compulsion" (Frontier Wars MSS., Vol. II.).

——, April 6. Colonel Shepherd present at court. Ordered that David Shepherd, Esq., officiate in the office of High Sheriff for this county, in the stead of Jno. McCullogh, deceased, agreeable to an Act of Assembly in that case made and provided. David Shepherd executed his bond of office for 500 pounds and produced Solomon Hedges, Samuel Mason, Joseph Ogle and Andrew Fouts as sureties, who were accepted by the Court.

Likewise one other bond of 3,000 pounds conditioned for his faithful collecting and duly accounting for all office fees by him received, etc., and produced Samuel Mason, Joseph Ogle, Solomon Hedges and Andrew Fouts as sureties, who were likewise accepted. Ordered that the same be recorded (Annals Carnegie Museum, Dec., 1904).

———, April 7. David Shepherd produced a Commission from his honor, John Page, Esq., Lieutenant-Governor of this State, appointing him Lieutenant of Ohio Co., same was read and sworn to in open court.

David Shepherd, appointed by the court to appraise the estate of Walter Colhoon, decd., was sworn and ordered to make return to next court, and was also appointed appraiser of the estate of Rogers McBridge, decd. Upon the motion of George McCullogh to this court, wherein he has exhibited certain instances of David Shepherd having acted out of the line of his office as Commanding Officer of the Militia, by commanding certain officials of militia without the recommendation of this court; whereupon this court has thought that information be made to his Excellency, the Governor, praying that he may take cognizance thereof as to him shall seem meet. Whereupon David Shepherd came into court and produced sundry commissions of certain gentlemen that he had commissioned in the time of the courts' recess and prayed that the court would regulate the said commissions as to them shall seem meet, as he acknowledges that he had no intention to detract from the prerogative of this court, as he was conscious that the urgent necessity of the times compelled him to act thus, and further prays that this court would proceed to recommend suitable officers to fill up the sundry vacancies in the militia. Colonel Shepherd came into court and prays the opinion of the court as to whether he, in the case of his commissioning certain militia officers, of the County Militia, within the recess of the court for that purpose, was intentionally to detract from the prerogative of this court in that case, or not. 8 April. The court are of opinion that *he did not*. Two members ignoramus. David Shepherd surrenders to this court the appointment of Isaac Meeks as Lieutenant of Militia, and Isaac Taylor as Deputy Sheriff (Ann. Car. Museum, Dec., 1904).

1778, June 1. David Shepherd continued in the Commission of the Peace, and took the oath as a Justice. His commission, by the Governor, appointing him High Sheriff was read and sworn to in open court. Rezin (Virgin), Joseph Ogle and Andrew Fouts, bondsmen (*vide*).

———, June 2. David Shepherd was ordered by the court, as Sheriff of the County (Ohio Co., Va.), to advertise to the lowest undertakers the building of the " Publick Building " of the County according to the dimensions therein contained. A recognizance

against Samuel Mason for disposing of and exchanging some of
the Continental stores at Fort Henry, was exhibited by David
Shepherd, whereupon the defendant came into court and asked
the charge in part; whereupon the court have considered that
Samuel Mason, aforesaid, be fined 5 pounds; return into the
hands of Colonel Shepherd an equally good gun, or the value
thereof, valued by Reazin Virgin, and Joseph Hoge, sworn for
that purpose, valued at 17 pounds. Furthermore, it appears to
this court that Samuel Mason, aforesaid, had exchanged his own
property for the stores aforesaid with a certain V. Doulton, D. Q.,
in the Continental service.

Upon Colonel David Shepherd's motion, ordered that requisi-
tion be made to the Justices of Yohogania County to call upon the
Commissioners for adjusting the boundary line between the
County of Yohogania and Ohio as soon as possible, and report
their proceedings, so the militia in the disputed territory may
forthwith be called upon, if required.

Upon motion of David Shepherd, ordered that his mark, a crop
in the right and swallow fork in the left, be recorded.

David Shepherd protests against the sufficiency of the jail of
this County (Ann. Car. Mus., Dec., 1904).

———, June 24. The court ordered that Colonels David Shepherd and Wm. Crawford lay out the prison bounds for the County
of Yohoghania and report to the court (Hist. Wash. Co., Pa.,
p. 16).

———, Aug. 4. David Shepherd, an evidence in the case of
John Huff assaulting the court.

———, Nov. 3. David Shepherd, as Sheriff, ordered by the
court, to pay Abraham Van Metre 20 pounds for the land the
County took to erect the public buildings on. Administration
upon the estate of Francis Duke (his son-in-law), decd., is
granted to Colonel David Shepherd, he having complied with
the law.

David Shepherd is allowed by the court, for extra services,
310 lbs. tobacco.

David Shepherd, "gent." with secretary, acknowledge their
bond for his collection of the County Levy, which include these
items:

David Shepherd's account presented to court:

Extra services for 1 year	28.14.0
for expenses to Winchester or	
Rather Zane's work	100. 0.0
for balance of last year's acct.	14. 6.6

David Shepherd appointed a viewer for the nearest and best
way for a road from Jacob Wolf's to the County line leading

toward Redstone, and make report to next court (Ann. Car. Mus., Vol. III., pt. 1, Dec., 1904).

1778, 24 June. At Court held 24 June, 1778: Ordered that William Crawford and David Shepherd, gent., do lay out the prison bounds of this County agreeable to law.

Whereupon, Wm. Crawford and David Shepherd made report as follows: " Beginning at a black oak standing Easterly from the Court house and marked with 6 notches and extending thence southerly, by a line of marked trees to a white oak near and including a Spring thence northerly by a line of marked trees including the house of Paul Matthew, to a white oak, thence by a line of marked trees to the beginning." Same is ordered to be recorded (see Minutes of Court of Yohogania County, Va., held at Augusta-town (now Washington, Pa.), and afterwards on the Andrew Heath farm, near West Elizabeth, Pa., 1776–1780 (Reprint of Ann. Carnegie Mus., Vol. II., p. 245).

1779, July 17. General Daniel Broadhead, commanding at Fort Pitt, invites Colonel Shepherd to go with him on an expedition up the Alleghany (Draper's Notes).

——, Nov. 8. Colonel Shepherd issues orders to captains who failed to appear with proper muster rolls; . . . certifies, as magistrate to —— offices in classing men for military service (Shepherd Papers, Vol. V., p. 94).

——, Dec. General Irvine, commanding the Department of the West, in reorganizing the regular army, finds a garrison at Fort Wheeling, of one Continental officer and fifteen privates (Butterfield's Crawford Exp. against Sandusky).

1780, March 6. Court ordered that Wm. Scott, Silas Hedges, " gent," be recommended to his Excellency, to appoint one of them to serve as a Sheriff in room of David Shepherd.

——, April 5. Colonel David Shepherd and Major McCullogh were in attendance at the Convention at Fort Pitt, to propose plans for a general defense of the frontier. Shepherd said he could not aid, as nearly all in his district were enrolled in Pennsylvania. Ohio County sent about 200 men on Crawford's Expedition (Butterfield's Crawford's Expedition against Sandusky).

David Shepherd himself was carried on the rolls of the Washington Co. (Pa.) Frontier Rangers (Penn. Archives, 3d Ser., Vol. XXIII., 199, and 4th Ser., Vol. V., p. 421).

——, Sept. 17–18. Colonel David Shepherd present at a conference with the Delaware Indians at Fort Pitt (Shepherd MSS., H. McI. F.).

——, Oct. 17. F. W. Johnson addresses Colonel Shepherd in a memorial praying for the opening of a new state west of the Alleghanies (Shepherd Papers).

——, Nov. ——. Colonel Daniel Broadhead organizes an expedition against the disaffected Delawares. The forces were to rendezvous at Fort Wheeling. They were mostly volunteers and numbered about 300. They crossed the Ohio and marched by the nearest route to the principal Delaware villages on the Muskingum (now Coshocton, O.) (Butterfield's Crawford's Expedition against Sandusky).

1781, April 7. General Broadhead (succeeding General McIntosh in command at Fort Pitt), in command of the 8th Pennsylvania Regiment, set out from Fort Pitt with 150 regulars; at Wheeling he picked up Colonel David Shepherd, Lieutenant of Ohio Co., Va., with 134 militia, including officers; beside these were five friendly Indians eager for Delaware scalps (Withers's Chronicles of the Border, pp. 77, 78).

———, April 10. Colonel David Shepherd's name appears among field officers on pay rolls of Coshocton Campaign (Draper's Notes; H. McI. F.).

1782, Sept. 14. Ebenezer Zane, writing from Wheeling, on this date, to General Irvine, refers to Fort Henry then being surrounded by the enemy and British "cullars" (colors), and demanding surrender. Being refused they attacked the fort and were repulsed, and so again for four times, till the enemy retired, Sept. 13, having begun the siege on Sept. 11, 1782 (Butterfield's Crawford's Expedition against Sandusky, p. 277).

———. A daughter of Colonel Wm. Crawford was raised by Colonel Shepherd, of Wheeling Creek. She married a Mr. Thornburg. At her marriage, Colonel Shepherd gave her 100 acres of land at the village of Triadelphia. This was after her father had been burned at the stake (DeHaas, p. 380; Preston Papers, Vol. XXIX., p. 12).

1783, Feb. 6. "There are not more than two companies of Militia at this time, in the County, and they all live in forts during the summer season and are very much distressed" (Draper's Notes, Vol. XI., p. 178).

———, March 3. Col. David Shepherd, writing to the Governor of Virginia, says: "the Indians have done no mischief this Spring, as yet; people are moving back to their plantations very fast and if no mischief is done our country will soon be settled again (Draper's Notes, Vol. XI., p. 178).

———, June 23. David Shepherd entered 1,000 acres of land on the Ohio River, three miles above the mouth of the Middle Island Creek; the grant to include the improvements made in 1771 (Shepherd MSS., and H. McI. F.). Middle Island Creek rises in Doddridge Co., W. Va., enters the Ohio at Pleasants, about 25 miles below Fishing Creek, the latter being about 26 miles below Grave Creek (see Thwaites, The Rev. on the Ohio, p. 213).

1784, Sept. 28. Philadelphia, 28 Sept., 1784; In council: The Comptroller-General's accounts were read and approved. Among the items was one for provisions furnished the Washington Co. (Pa.) militia, by David Shepherd (History of Washington Co., Pa., p. 68.)

1785 April. David Shepherd mentioned as Sheriff of Ohio Co., Va., also as Member of Virginia Legislature for years, 1783–85 (Draper).

——, June 23. Governor Randolph writes, advising Col. David Shepherd to provide for trouble with the Indians. Letter from Edmund Randolph dated from the Constitutional Convention and addressed to David Shepherd, refers especially to the formation of a new state west of the Alleghany Mountains—a matter in which Colonel Shepherd was interested (Draper's Notes).

1786. Colonel Shepherd deeming it safe to bring back his family, rebuilt his fort (DeHaas, p. 311).

1787, April 30. Colonel Shepherd writes Governor Randolph asking for arms and ammunition "as the Indians have begun depredations and the country is in a very defenceless state" (Draper's Notes, Vol. XII., p. 141).

——, Oct. 22. David Shepherd exchanged 500 acres of land on treasury warrant, for 1,000 acres of land granted to Benjamin Johnston, 29 June, 1782, who assigned same to David Shepherd. The 1,000 acres were situated in Ohio Co., Va., on the waters of Little Grave Creek, adjoining Joseph Tomlinson and Dorsey Pentecost. Wm. Shepherd, Agent, to Robert Woods, Surveyor Ohio Co. (Survey Book, No. 2, Wheeling, W. Va.).

——, Nov. 10. Colonel Shepherd informs the Governor of Virginia that Indians have killed about forty people on the frontier of the County (Draper's Notes, Vol. XII., p. 54).

1788, May 15. Colonel Shepherd again writes that the Indians have become quiet again (Draper's Notes, Vol. XII., p. 181).

1788, Oct. ——. David Shepherd, George McCullogh, and others, appointed Oct., 1788, by Act of Assembly, Trustees of Randolph Academy (Hening's Statutes, Vol. 12, p. 661).

Randolph Academy was established at Clarkesburg, on the Monongahela River, in Harrison Co., Va.. in 1787. It has a prominent position as an influential center of learning among a highly intelligent class of pioneers. It was succeeded by the Northwestern Academy in 1843 (Trans-Alleghany Magazine, p. 128).

1789, June 1. Governor Beverley Randolph writes Col. David Shepherd an extract from a letter he received from Gen. George Washington (then President), to the effect that the United States will take up the Government west of the Alleghanies, thus relieving Virginia of the same, and requesting Colonel Shepherd to discharge all officers connected with the County government, and act for the United States instead of for Virginia.

1790. Colonel Shepherd reconstructed his fort at forks of

Wheeling. This time it was built of sycamore logs three inches in thickness and twelve feet long. They were placed in mortised logs, one plank resting upon the other. There were bastions on the corners and port-holes along the sides (DeHaas, p. 311).

——. Colonel Shepherd reports 50 persons killed by the Indians in Ohio County, in 1790; among them Captain Boggs's son (Draper's Notes).

1791, March 10. Colonel Shepherd receives documentary authority from Henry Knox, Secretary of War, to protect the frontier.

——, March 25. Governor Beverley Randolph writes Colonel Shepherd requesting discharge of Shepherd's men who are employed by Virginia, as the protection of the frontier is now in the hands of the general government.

——, April 10–28. Col. David Shepherd commands a force in the Coshocton Campaign; this was most important and far-reaching in its results, as it pushed the Delawares back to the Muskingum and Tuscarawas Rivers and they never returned (Shepherd Papers, Vol. IV., p. 3).

Pay-roll of Staff Officers of Coshocton Expedition for State of Virginia, commanded by Colonel David Shepherd. Expedition lasted from April 10 to 28, 1791. The officers were: David Shepherd, Colonel ($575.00 per month); Samuel McCulloug, Major; Isaac Meeks, Adjutant; Wm. McIntire, First Major; James Lemon, Second Major; Jonathan Zane, Spy (Shepherd Papers, Vol. IV., p. 3).

——, May 6. Col. David Shepherd applies to the Secretary of War for arms and ammunition "on account of attacks on the frontier and its defenceless condition" (Draper's Notes, Vol. XIII., p. 15).

——, May 31. Secretary of War ordered 100 arms, 2 barrels of powder, and 400 lbs. of lead to be delivered to Colonel Shepherd out of the magazine at Fort Pitt.

1792, Aug., 12. Col. David Shepherd certifies to service of George McCullogh, Jr., as spy for Ohio Co. (Shepherd Papers, Vol. III., p. 102).

1793, Jan. 3. Same record as preceding (vide 109).

——, Jan. 17. Colonel Shepherd writes General Wayne in reference to instructions concerning the spies to be employed (Shepherd MSS.).

——, Feb. 23. He pays George McCullogh, Ja., $107.12 for services as spy, in the year 1792 (Shepherd Papers, Vol. III, p. 103).

——, Col. David Shepherd said to have commanded an expedition in the Tuscarawas Campaign.

——, June 7. Colonel Shepherd certifies, as Co. Lieut., to services of Jeremiah Williams, James Smith, and George Mc-

Cullogh, as scouts for Ohio Co., and on Sept. 21 James Smith and George McCullogh made oath before Colonel Shepherd, Co. Lieut., that they had faithfully served as scouts (Shepherd Papers, Vol. III., p. 110).

1795, Feb. 2. Col. David Shepherd died on his old plantation at Fort Shepherd, and was buried in the graveyard by the Old Stone Church, at Elm Grove, on Wheeling Creek (H. McI. F.). David Shepherd was an Episcopalian. He stood a little short of six feet. Good sense, brave, honest, liberal and benevolent; cheerful and good natured, and greatly beloved. He spent much of his later time on Wheeling Creek, and Catfish, tending his mills. His old houses were burnt, but his mill was unmolested, except, sometimes the Indians would set it running and leave it. (From interview with Mrs. Lydia Crugar, daughter-in-law of Colonel Shepherd, by L. C. Draper: Draper's Notes, Vol. II., No. 4, p. 37, 1845.)

—, Oct. 10. Moses Shepherd, executor of estate of David Shepherd, decd., credited by cash received of He. Thornburg, £85. 0. 0.

1799, April 5. Power of attorney of David Shepherd, formerly of Berkeley Co., Va.—at present (?) of Chillicothe, Ross Co., Ohio—to transfer his lands in Virginia, found of record at Martinsburg, Va.

IN COMMAND OF THE PLUGGY'S TOWN EXPEDITION

JOURNAL OF THE EXECUTIVE COUNCIL OF VIRGINIA, 1776–1777.

"Tuesday the 4th day of March, 1777.
Present:
His Excellency, the Governor, &c. &c.
Ordered that commissions issue, appointing David Shepherd Colonel, David McClure, Lieut Colonel, and Samuel McCullough Major of the County of Ohio."
Wednesday the 12th day of March, 1777.
Present:
His Excellency the Governor. &c &c.
The Board having from time to time received undoubted intelligence of repeated Hostilities Committed on the subjects of this Commonwealth, by the Indians of Pluggy's town; and notwithstanding the just Remonstrances, made to them on the subject by our Agents for Indian affairs they have not been brought to a sense of their duty, but from the repeated injuries, there is the greater reason to believe an increased insolence instead of that good neighborhood we wish to cultivate with all the Indian tribes. And whereas the obstinate and wicked disposition of the said indians of Plugg's town have been represented to Congress, and they seem to have no prospect of concilation, but have referred to this Board the propriety of making war upon them if it can be done without exciting Jealousy and Discord with the neighboring nations. Resolved that George Morgan esquire, superintendent of Indian affairs, and Col. John Neaville, or in the case of his absence, Robert Campbell,

esquire, do confer with such Chiefs of the Delawares and Shawnese Indians as may be relied on for secrecy and fidelity, and represent to them the necessity of Chastiseing the said Indians, and in case the said Gentlemen shall find that the said Shawnese and Delawares do not give Reason to apprehend discord with them by reason of such proceedings, that three hundred men of the militia, commanded by a Colonel, Major, six captains six Lieutenants, six ensigns and a proper number of non-commissioned officers be ordered to make an expedition to the said Pluggy's Town in order to punish that people for their unprovoked cruelties committed on the Inhabitants of Virginia. That the officers commanding this Expedition have it charge at their peril and that of all those concerned that no Injury, provocation or ill treatment of any kind be done or suffered to the Delawares and Shawnese Indians through whose country the pass. But on the other Hand that the said officers strictly charged and commanded to conduct themselves toward them, as our faithful friends and Bretheren Government being determined to avenge the least injury done.

That the officers commanding this expedition apply to George Morgan, esquire, for ammunitions, provisions and stores necessary for the party, who is requested to give every assistance in his power to forward the undertaking, that the commanding officer ought to be directed to show to women, children, and such of the men as surrender themselves, and to send all prisoners taken by his Party, belonging to the said Pluggy's-town to this city, and as the success of this expedition will depend the dispatch with which it is conducted.

Resolved that if a majority of the field Officers and Captains who are to be engaged in it, shall judge best that the men shall be directed to march on Horseback, finding their own horses, and carrying their own provisions, and that they out (?) to receive a reasonable allowance for so doing.

Resolved that Colonel David Shepherd of Ohio County be Commander in Chief of this Expedition, That Major Taylor of Yohogania County be Major; and that they nominate the Captains and subalterns officers out of those commissioned in the counties of Monongalia, Yohoghania and Ohio or either of them.

Letters on the above subject were written to Messieures Morgan and Neville, and Colonel David Shepherd. Copies filed and ordered to be recorded."

I, W. G. Stanard, do hereby certify that the foregoing are true copies from the original Journal, now in the Virginia State Library.

(sig) W. G. STANARD.

Richmond, Va., 22d January, 1902.

Pluggy was a noted Mingo chief, killed in an attack on McClelland's Station, at Royal Springs (now Georgetown, Ky.), 29 Dec., 1776 (Collins's History of Kentucky, Vol. I., p. 178).

Pluggy was a Mohawk Indian, who, with a band of unorganized and undisciplined followers, had migrated westward about 1772, and settled upon the present site of Delaware, Ohio (see Thwaites, The Revolution on the Ohio, p. 56).

WILLIAMSBURG, April 12, 1777.

Sir:—The expedition against Pluggy's Town is to be laid aside by a Resolution of Congress. I am sir, your Hbble servt.
Col° David Shepherd, Ohio P. HENRY.

THE SHEPHERD GENEALOGY

This Resolution of Congress was adopted 25 March, 1777, upon the receipt of a letter from Col. George Morgan, dated 15 March, in which he deprecates any expedition into the Indian country "which involve us in a general and unequal Quarrel with all the nations who are at present quiet but extremely Jealous of the least encroachment on their lands" (see Thwaites, The Revolution on the Ohio, p. 247).

SOME OFFICIAL AND OTHER CORRESPONDENCE

COL. SHEPHERD TO GEN. HAND.

FORT HENRY, 22 Aug. 1777

Sir:

In obedience to your order I have called all the men to this place that is under pay and have removed my family likewise, but there seems to be a great confusion in this county concerning it. I have ordered Capt. Ogle to keep up a scout between this fort and Beech Bottom. Likewise Capt. Mason to send a party to scout between this and Grave creek. I shall order such scouts and spies over the river as our strength will admit of. Captain⁸ Shannon, Leach and Merchant arrived here on the 20ᵗʰ. inst. and seem very well behaved and obliging. Our Captains is making up their Companies as fast as possible . . . we are preparing the fort as fast as possible and *I shall soon have it Indian proof.*

I am sir, with respect,
Your humble servant

DAVID SHEPHERD.

To General Hand.

COL. SHEPHERD TO GEN. HAND.
[Frontier Wars *MSS.*, Vol. II, p. 7.]

FORT HENRY, March 10, 1778.

Dear Sir:

I received your favor by John Green which informed me of your safe arrival at Fort Pitt. I am glad to hear that our neighbors is spirited enough to turn out on the last occasion, and for my part, I partly concur with you in the scheme proposed, all the people I spoke with concerning it join in sentiments in favor of the scheme. I cannot as yet give you an exact account what numbers of men I can [supply] you with, but I have summoned all the Captains in the County to meet on Friday next in order to send men to the stations and other purposes, when I expect to give you a better account. But at this time I expect to furnish you with 30 men if possible against the day appointed. I have sent by Lieut. Berry 53 rifles, 8 muskets, likewise 915 lbs lead and there remains in store 390 lbs. The state of the store I shall attend to and do all in my power to secure the provisions as soon as I can collect some men. Our brave Beefeater's time is out and they are all returning home to tell of the great exploits they have done on the Ohio, but I hope they will send us better men the next time. As for news I have none, but the people are well pleased with our last trip.

Sir, I am, with respect,
Your humble servant,

DAVID SHEPHERD.

182

SOME OFFICIAL AND OTHER CORRESPONDENCE

ABRAHAM SHEPHERD TO DAVID SHEPHERD.

MECKLINBURG, May 22ᵈ 1778.

Honorable Brother:

It is with infinite pleasure I inform you of my safe arival home to my affectionate Mother, which perhaps may tend something to soothe her unhappy situation. I find many things not according to my wish, but live in hopes [of] seeing them better. I condoll with you for your misfortunes and hope your manly fortitude may ever support you in the most distressing misfortunes and to live in hopes of seeing better. I am on parole. No time limited for that reason you cant expect news. My health is not perfect, but not dangerously ill. I left my friends well on Long Island. Mother is well with all friends here. Remember me to all friends there. Sally has arrived safe here. . . . never let Hope, the sole Comfort of the wretched, forsake you. And believe [me] Dear Sir, I am, with Due respect

Your most dutiful
& affectionate
ABRAᴹ SHEPHERD.

I arrived yesterday.

(Draper's Notes, Vol. II., No. 6.)

ABRAHAM SHEPHERD TO DAVID SHEPHERD.

MECKLENSBURG, Jan. 18, 1779.

. . . Believe me—Mankind is not to be trusted—I am sorry to inform you I have some apprehensions of being called to the British, as I am not confident of my being exchanged—I have likewise the pleasure of informing you the ferry is established in my name. Mother, since you were here, has been almost "delerious" but since this affair has asserted in my favor she appears in as good spirits and as hearty as I ever saw her in my life. I do every thing I can to make her happy, which I shall ever esteem my greatest duty and happiness. . . .

ABRAᴹ SHEPHERD.

CAPT. Wᴹ. McMAHON, A MAGISTRATE OF OHIO CO. VA. TO CAPT. HUTCHINS.

21 Sept. 1786.

Sir:

The difficulty of securing hands, occasioned by the late alarms, is beyond conception; several have engaged and disappointed me. Wheeling is become a garrison. The inhabitants to a man, as high up as Zanes' have fled, except Tomlinsons and Shepherds, and a few about the Mingo bottom who are building blockhouses . . . Alarm came by a certain William Newland . . . he was under oath not to inform, or spread the alarm, except to tell Zane and Shepherd to be on their guard. Zane has made every necessary preparation, Shepherd has made none, rests assured they (the Indians) cannot spare their men in such numbers as Clarke's Expedition is now in their County. (Shepherd Papers, Vol. XV., p. 29.)

COL. SHEPHERD TO GOVERNOR BEVERLY RANDOLPH.

OHIO COUNTY, 13 May 1789.

Sir:

The continued depredations of the savages on our frontier under our situation is truly alarming, and of consequence increases when we find that a proclamation has been issued by Governor Mifflin of Pennsylvania offering reward of one thousand dollars to any person who will apprehend some men or any of them who killed some Indians at the mouth of Big Beaver Creek, Alleghany Co., west of Ohio (calling it an atrocious act), and as some of that party were under my command from this county, I conceive it my duty to inform your Excellency of the facts which induced our men to attack the enemy in their quarters.

About the 16th February last a party of Indians murdered in a most cruel manner, five persons near the mouth of Buffaloe Creek; plundered the houses of all that were valuable, and made off. Upon this I thought it expedient to send out four spies for our better security who soon returned with intelligence of the enemy's approach. Upon this a party from the different companies assembled at the mouth of the Buffaloe, where they were joined by a party from Washington County, crossed the Ohio, and under the direction of the spies went to meet the enemy, who, finding they were discovered, made off, and kept along the lower hills, that it was with great difficulty our men could follow their tracks, into a place known by the name of Big Buffaloe Licks,—where a council was held by the officers, in which Capt. Brady, being one of the spies, well knowing the subtlety of Indians, informed them that they would retire to some distance until the return of our men, or probably go to their usual place of rendezvous, at the mouth of Big Beaver, a block house erected by A. Wilson & Co. who were notoriously known to supply them with ammunition and arms of all kinds ever since war has been declared against them. Under these considerations, twenty six volunteers from the party proceeded on the trail, and soon found by their movements that the blockhouse was their intention upon which they crossed the hills, and fell upon the trail about three miles distant from that place. They sent forward spies, who returned with intelligence of the enemy's having encamped opposite the block house; upon this our men left their horses with two men and defeated the enemy; killed four men and one woman who was not known from a man by the dress until too late. This is a true statement of the facts as they were communicated to me by persons which were present and whose veracity I can confide in. For further particulars I shall refer you to the bearer, Capt. Connel, who is acquainted with every circumstance of what there happened, likewise those which have lately taken place.

During the last year 29 persons have been most cruelly murdered, yet, upon the authenticity of A Wilson & Co. does Gov. Mifflin send out his proclaimation. His government, it appears, is not confined to Pennsylvania and his information is from those who have feasted upon the blood of our fellow citizens by supplying the savages with every instrument necessary for our destruction.

If we have erred in being avenged of our enemy, we are willing to be corrected by your Excellency, upon whom we, at this dangerous period, rely, in hopes you will if possible, make provision to relieve us from distress,   I remain, your Excellency's most

Obedient and humble servant

(Sig) DAVID SHEPHERD.

To His Excellency,
Beverly Randolph.

WILLIAM DUKE TO COL. SHEPHERD.

BERKELEY Co., October 18, 1791.

Honorable Col.

I embrace this Opportunity to let you know I am in good health at this present time, hoping these few lines will find you and your family in good health too.

SOME OFFICIAL AND OTHER CORRESPONDENCE

I intend to be out to see you in a short time if I am spared, and to see if you will let me have the land which you promised to secure for me, and as you promised before Capt. M'Intire and my Father. I therefore hope your Honor will be as good as your word. If you intend not to let me have the Land, I hope you will send me word by first opportunity you can get, in order that I may then know how to manage concerning the land. For as I have my Brother Francis' Obligation and a Bill of Sale of the Land for the making of it good to me, I intend to make my Brother's Estate pay me the money that I paid for the Land and the lawful Interest due upon said money, and I hope, to prevent any trouble between your Daughter and me, that you will fulfill your promise as a man of Honor should do, and in so doing you will much oblige your Honour's Obedient and very humble servant

WILLIAM DUKE.

To the Hon. Col. David Shepherd
living in Ohio County—favored by Mr. Moses Shepherd.

PHILADELPHIA, FEBRUARY 25, 1792.

Sir:

I thank you for the information respecting the intention of the Tomlinsons' and others to dispute my title to a tract of land called the Round Bottom.

I wish these persons and many others who may be disposed to dispute my title to that land to be informed in the most explicit and pointed manner, that it is my fixed determination to defend, at all events every inch of that land which is within the lines of my patent. If, therefore, any encroachments are made thereon, the person or persons by whom they are made may depend upon being prosecuted as long as there shall be a shadow of right or justice in so doing.

I have nothing to say respecting any surveys which may be made without the lines of my patent, but let them beware of the consequences of coming *within* them.

I am sir

With very great esteem
Your most Obed^t ser'nt
GEO: WASHINGTON.

To Coll. David Shepherd.
[Shepherd Papers, Vol. III, p. 61.]

Pound (or Round?) Bottom became the property of General Washington through allotment for services in the French and Indian War, and by purchases from other grantees he assembled 587 acres in the tract. It was of exceedingly rich fertility and located on the banks of the Ohio River opposite Pipe Creek, about fifteen miles below Wheeling, with a frontage on the river of two and one-half miles. Thompson, Marshall Co., O., is the present postoffice on the tract which was sold by George and Martha Washington to Archibald McLean, of Alexandria, 8 Aug., 1798, for a consideration of $5,870, and when surveyed it was found to contain nearly twice the acreage called for in the patent of Governor Harrison and the deed of General Washington (see West. Va. Hist. Mag., Jan., '02, pp. 73-75).

WILL OF DAVID SHEPHERD

In the name of God Amen. I David Shepherd of Ohio County and State of Virginia being [sick] in body but of sound and perfect mind, and memory, blessed be Almighty God for the same do make and publish this my last Will and Testament in manner and form following (that is to say) I will and bequeath to my beloved wife Rachael Shepherd all the plantation Whereon I now dwell in the forks of Wheeling Creek during her life and Also her feather bed and furniture likewise her Choice of three Cows, and two work Horses and a plow and Tackle. And also I will bequeath to my wife one Mulato Girl named Nance and one Negro man named Tymothy as also all her common and Tea Table furniture. I also will and bequeath to my daughter Elizabeth Lee during her life time all that tract or parcel of Land lying and bounded as follows, that is to say beginning at the old Grist Mill dam then running with the line of Moses Shepherd to the Sugar tree, Corner as mentioned in his,—thence with the line of the Original Across Peter's run unto Craig's fork, thence down the said Creek unto the beginning, more or less, to hold during her Natural life and then to descend to the heirs of William McIntire, deceased, I likewise Will unto my three daughters, viz. Elizabeth Lee, Sarah Springer and Ruth Mills all the remaining part, of my Estate after my just debts & Legacies and Funeral Expenses are paid to be equally divided among them, my will is that the "presbiterian" Church have free privilidge to build places for public worship and the purpose of burying their dead on the lot laid out for them but for no other purpose. I also will and bequeath unto my son Moses Shepherd all that part or tract of land with all the appurtenances that lies below Little Wheeling and up as far as the old Grist Mill dam, thence with a straight line near a N. W. course to a Sugar tree Corner, Corner to the original Tract, thence down the Original Tract, to the Beginning at the Saw Mill, likewise after the death of his Mother to have the whole of the Old plantation he paying to his three sisters each one hundred pounds Virginia Currency, to be paid in three years after he shall enter on the premises but in case he should die without an heir the old plantation is to be sold so as to be equally divided between my three daughters or their Surviving heirs. I likewise will and bequeath unto my grand daughter Elizabeth Shepherd twenty-five pounds Virginia Currency to be paid out of the money arising from the sale of my personal property. I hereby appoint sole executors of this my Last Will and Testament Moses Shepherd and John Mills hereby revoking all former wills by me made. In Witness Whereof I have hereunto set my hand & Seal the 20th day of January in the year of our Lord 1795.

(sig) DAVID SHEPHERD [SEAL].

Signed sealed published and declared by the above named David Shepherd as his last Will and Testament in the presence of us who have hereunto subscribed our names, as Witnesses, in the presence of the testator

William Flahaven   Abner Springer
Francis Drake [Duke]   William McIntire.
A copy

Teste: Moses Chapline, Clk.
(W. B. L., p. 31—Wheeling Records.)

"A INVENTORY OF THE GOODS & CHATTELS OF DAVID SHEPHERD, LATE OF OHIO COUNTY, AND STATE OF VIRGINIA, DECEASED, APRIL 27, 1795."

Nineteen head of cattle	123.50
Five head horses	173.
Ten head sheep & 1 ram	15.
One waggon & plow	29.50
1 Bed and Bedstead 16 & 12	28.
1 Bedstead Cord	2.
2 Coverleads	4.
3 Lettis and 2 steel naps	8.
1 Hand vise & sundry iron tools	7.
3 sickles and 2 sets horse gears	6.
3 books	3.50
4 yards Broadcloth	24.
One man's sadle	2.50
Eleven head Hogs	33.
1 ax, ten cut saw and bit	2.66
1 Surveyor's Compass and instruments	30.
1 pair stillyards & 1 gold weight	1.83
	493.49

Executors: Moses Shepherd and John Mills.
Appraisers: George Sticker, Moses Williams, Lewis Bonnett.
A true copy; Moses Chapline, Clerk.

(From Settlement Book No. 1
p. 83, 1795; Wheeling, W. Va.)

WILL OF MOSES SHEPHERD

In the Name of God Amen.

I Moses Shepherd of Ohio County, in the State of Virginia, do make and constitute this my last will and testament in manner and form following, that is to say: 1st I will and direct that all my just debts be paid 2d I give and bequeath to my wife my lands lying above big Wheeling Creek and adjoining the same and little Wheeling Creek being divided from the estate on which I now live, by both the said creeks together with the improvements thereon, including the grist and saw mills, the tavern-house now occupied by Mrs Gooding, to have and to hold the same, with the appurtenances to her and heirs and assigns forever.

3d All the household and kitchen furniture remaining in my possession, at the time of my decease, I devise and bequeath to my said wife and her assigns.

4th my negro man Jack and his wife Susan and their family, children or other descendants—I give to my said wife and her assigns.

5th all my other lands except my home plantation including those I claim in a suit with persons of the name of Larue, and those I claim in a suit with a person of the name of Richelos, if recovered, I devise to my executrix to be sold and the proceeds thereof together with the proceeds of such part of my personal estate as she may think proper to sell after payment of just debts to be by her vested in Bank stock. 6th And whereas I have sold some tracts of land which I have not conveyed and on some of which the whole, and on some, part of the purchase money is due. I do therefore, hereby authorize and empower my executrix to execute all such contracts to all interests [intents?] and purposes as I could do if in life, and if any such lands should fall back to my estate for want of payment by or without suit, I do devise and direct that they be sold and the proceeds after payments of just debts be vested as aforesaid. 7ᵗʰ I do devise and bequeath my home estate whereon I now live, to my said wife for and during her natural life, the same being my estate lying between the forks of Wheeling Creek. 8ᵗʰ After the payment of just debts when the proceeds of the sale aforesaid and of the sale of such personal estate as my executrix may dispose of, shall be vested as above, and also the proceeds of the sale of all my slaves except those above mentioned, which I hereby direct to be made and vested as aforesaid I give and bequeath the same to my said wife together with the use, dividends or profits of all the monies aforesaid so to be vested to hold the same so as to be vested to her and her assigns.

9ᵗʰ After the decease of my said wife my will is that my said home plantation or estate be sold and the proceeds of such sale to be equally divided between the children of my sisters Elizabeth Lee, Ruth Mills and Sarah Springer so that if any of them be dead the issue of such deceased are to take part of his, her or their parcel.

Hereby revoking all others I do make, ordain, publish and declare this to be my only last will and testament and I do appoint my said wife Lydia Shepherd to be the whole and sole executrix thereof and so declare that she shall not, by the Court, be held to give security.

Witness my hand and seal this first day of January 1830.

(sig) MOSES SHEPHERD.

signed, sealed, published and
declared in presence of us:

Archie Wood	John Good
John Carter	Thos Thornburg
[Wheeling, W. Va., Records.]	

Notes from "A Tour to the Western Country Through the States of Ohio and Kentucky, &c, &c, 1807-1809," by F. Cuming.

"At two miles from Wheeling I passed a very handsome house, a fine farm and a mill of a Mʳ. Woods, on the left. . . . A mile further I passed Mr. Chapline's fine merchant mill; and a mile and a half beyond that, where the valley narrows, I observed on the left some very remarkable loose rocks. . . . Half a mile beyond this I stopped at a Mʳ. Eoff's neat cottage and good farm where everything had [evidence?] of plenty and comfort. Four or five genteel looking young women were all engaged in sedentary domestic avocations, and an old lady served we with some milk and water which I had requested, after which I resumed my walk. A mile up the side of a creek brought me to Mʳ. Shepherds Mill and elegant house of cut stone. Here the creek forks and the road also; one of the forks called Big Wheeling coming from the southeast, and the right-hand road leading along it from Morgantown; the left fork called Little Wheeling, which forms the Shepherd mill-race, coming from the eastward and the road toward Washington (Pa.) leading along it through a narrow valley with small farms wherever a bottom or an easy declivity of the hills would permit. . . . From here I proceeded to McKinley's Tavern, four miles from Shepherd's."

[See Cranmer's Hist. and Biog. Ohio Co. (W. Va.), p. 141.]

NOTES ON THE TEAGUES

Persons of this name were located at an early date in the Northern Neck of Virginia, whence they probably came from the adjacent counties of Maryland. In Cecil County, Md., where some of the family lived, the tombs of several may be seen, it is said, in the graveyards of old St. Mary Ann's Parish, in the vicinity of Rising Sun and at Northeast. Among those that lie in the churchyard of St. Mary Ann's are tombs dating back to 1720, of William and Elijah Teague, one of whom may or may not have been the ancestor of William Teague, a record of whom is found in the Frederick Co., Va., court house. He was a settler on the Hite-Van Metre lands; the date of his grant has not been ascertained, but his property was a part of a 300 acre tract, then in Orange County, granted to Richard Pendall, 3 Oct., 1734; 88 acres of it was conveyed by Pendall to William Teague, 20 June, 1742. Subsequently Teague acquired several other parcels of land in Frederick County: 145 acres from Richard Pendall, 121 from James Brown, "lying on the south side of the Cohongo-luta river" (Potomac River above its confluence with the Shenandoah), and another 145 acres granted by Thomas, Lord Fairfax, 11 Oct., 1750. The property from Pendall is described as being on a branch of the "Shenandore" River, called the "Cattail branch," etc., while the one from Brown was situate on the Potomac, probably between Martinsburg and Mecklenburg, and it is uncertain upon which, if either of them, he resided. A small stream, called "Teague's Run," empties into the Potomac in the vicinity of Shepherdstown, which may have acquired its name from the circumstance of having its headspring on one of the old Teague properties.

In 1751 William Teague prepared to emigrate to the Carolinas and began to dispose of his properties. The conveyances, according to the Frederick Co., Va., records, were as follows: June 13, 1751, to Benjamin Sebastian, 88 acres; to Elijah Teague, his son, 17 Aug., 1751, 145 acres; on same date, to Robert Fulsham, 121 acres; and on 3 Oct., 1751, 145 acres to Abraham Teague (perhaps another son). Thus his entire holdings, approximating 500 acres, were relinquished. Elijah Teague and his wife Alice transferred to Wm. Crawford adjoining tracts of 64 and 128 acres respectively on 4 Aug., 1753, for which certificates of deeds of lease and release were made to Elijah and Abraham Teague by William Teague, and recorded 12 Feb., 1752. The sale to William Crawford of the preceding two tracts aggregating 192 acres was confirmed to Crawford by the bond of Edward Teague, recorded 10 Oct., 1753. Edward Teague is described as the eldest son and heir-at-law of William Teague, late of Frederick County, but lately removed to some part of Carolina. The recitation in the bond reads: "Whereas the above named William Crawford purchased from Elijah Teague part of the said tracts which said Elijah Teague, who is a brother of the said Edward, had formerly purchased from his father William Teague before he removed to Carolina, etc."

The tract of 145 acres which Abraham acquired was reconveyed by him and Ann, his wife, 2 Oct., 1753, to Margaret McKee, widow, and (her sons?) William and James McKee.

Edward Teague, who is described as the eldest son of William Teague, was, prior to 1747, grantee of a portion of the Hite-Van Metre lands lying on the west side of the Sherando (Shenandoah) River. He conveyed a part of it to Richard Mercer, 3 Sept., 1745. He obtained by grant from Lord Fairfax, 13 March, 1751, a tract of 400 acres lying near the river Cohongo (Potomac) in Virginia, 100 acres of which was disposed of by him to William Morgan, 31 Jan., 1756. This tract is supposed to have been in the immediate vicinity of Mecklenburg (head of Teague's Run?). Moses Teague was a witness to the deed to Wm. Morgan and William Shepherd was a witness to the conveyance from Wm. Teague to Robert Fulsham, 17 Aug., 1751.

On July 13, 1744, William Teague was assignee of Jno. Baldwin. Moses Teague was appointed constable vice James Thurston.

7 Feb., 1748. Edward Teague was appointed by the Court one of the appraisers of the estate of Isaac Van Metre, deceased (son of John Van Metre, Jr., and grandson of John 1st of Berkeley), whose widow Alice was the administratrix (she afterward married a Morgan). This estate lay in the neighborhood of Opequon Creek, near its confluence with the Potomac.

Edward Teague appointed arbiter in the case of Fitzimmons vs. John Shepherd, 7 June, 1748; Abraham Teague, grantor to Thomas Mayberry, 11 Sept., 1749. (The first will probated in Ohio Co., Va., was that of Thomas Mayberry, who probably emigrated thence, with other pioneers, from the Potomac.)

7 March, 1754. Edward Teague, overseer of road from Jacob Hite's to Swearingen's Ferry, and prior to March, 1757, Abraham Teague performed like service at same place and was succeeded by Thomas Shepherd in March, 1757. (All the preceding records are from county records at Winchester, Va.)

A William Teague polled his vote for Major Blackburn for Burgess, in King William Co., Va., election of 1741 (Boogher's Gleanings of Virginia History, p. 116).

It is evident that the Teagues, Shepherds, Morgans, Crawfords, Van Metres, Hites and others were identified with the Mecklenburg locality, and there is reasonable grounds for a presumption that Rachael Teague, the wife of David Shepherd, was a daughter of either Abraham or Moses Teague, or, perhaps, of William Teague. She had two sons: William, the eldest, and Moses, the youngest child, with a daughter intervening.

DESCENDANTS OF DAVID SHEPHERD

I. DAVID SHEPHERD (Thomas[1]), son of Thomas and Elizabeth (Van Metre) Shepherd, b. at Mecklenburg, Va., Jan., 1734; d. at Forks of Wheeling, Va., 2 Feb., 1795; *m. circa* 1752/3, Rachael Teague. Issue:
1, William, b. Mecklenburg, Va., d. Sept., 1777, in siege of Fort Henry; 2, Elizabeth, b. Mecklenburg, Va.; 3, Ruth, b. Mecklenburg, Va.; 4, Sarah, b. Mecklenburg, Va., d. 25 Oct., 1832, at Uniontown, Pa.; 5, Moses, b. Mecklenburg, Va., 11 Sept., 1763; d. 29 April, 1832, at Wheeling, Va.

1. WILLIAM SHEPHERD (Thomas[1], David[2]), son of David and Rachael (Teague) Shepherd, b. Mecklenburg, Va., *circa* 1753; killed in the siege of Fort Henry (Wheeling), Va., 1 Sept., 1777; *m.* Rebecca McCullough, sister of Hugh McCullough, *circa* 1776. Issue:
6, Elizabeth, b. Wheeling, Va., 1777; was living in 1795.

2. ELIZABETH SHEPHERD (Thomas[1], David[2]), dau. of David and Rachael (Teague) Shepherd, b. Mecklenburg, Va., *circa* 1755; d. 1792; *m.* 1st *circa* 1774, William McIntire, son of Nicholas McIntire, formerly of Mecklenburg, Va.; killed by Indians at Limestone, Ky., 1792; *m.* 2d John Lee. Issue of William McIntire:
7, David; 8, Eleanor; 9, Sarah; 10, Rachael; 11, Harriet; 12, Ruth; 13, Joseph, b. at Triadelphia, Ohio Co., Va., 2 March, 1779, d. 14 May, 1842; 14, William, b. on Wheeling Creek, Va., 1773; 15, Thomas Lee.

3. RUTH SHÉPHERD (Thomas[1], David[2]), dau. of David and Rachael (Teague) Shepherd, b. Mecklenburg, Va., *circa* 1757; d. ——; *m.* John Mills, lieutenant, afterward a captain, in the Continental Army. He settled, about 1793, at Elm Grove, Forks of Wheeling, and was still living in Ohio Co., Va., at the close of 1833 (see Saffell's Soldiers of the Revolution, p. 551, and History of Pan Handle Counties of Virginia). Issue:
16, Juliet, b. ——, *m.* John Feay; 17, Moses, b. ——, living in Ohio Co., Va., 1879; 18, Lydia, b. ——, *m.* Francis Melton; 19, David, S., b. ——; 20, Elizabeth, b. ——; 21, William, b. ——; 22, Sarah, b.

4. SARAH SHEPHERD (Thomas[1], David[2]), dau. of David and Rachael (Teague) Shepherd, b. Mecklenburg, Va.; d. Uniontown, Fayette Co., Pa., 25 October, 1832; *m.* 1st 1773, Francis Duke, son of John Duke, of Berkeley Co., Va., and was killed at the seige of Fort Henry (Wheeling, Va.), 1 Sept., 1777; *m.* 2d 1780, Levi Springer, of Uniontown, Pa., who was b. 4 May, 1744, and d. 23/26 March, 1823. Issue by Francis Duke:
23, John, b. 1774/5; 24, Francis, b. 1777; for descendants of Nos. 23 and 24 see Duke Genealogy, Part III.

25, Sarah, b. 9 Dec., 1782; 26, David, b. 3 Jan., 1785; 27, Dennis, b. 3 March, 1787; 28, Rachael, b. *circa* 1789/90; 29, Job, b. 15 Aug., 1792; 30, Elizabeth, b. 23 Feb., 1794; 31, Lydia, b. *circa* 1798; 32, Hannah, b. 15 Dec., 1801.

5. MOSES SHEPHERD (Thomas[1], David[2]), son of David and Rachael (Teague) Shepherd, b. (sup.) Shepherdstown, Va., Nov., 1763; d. Wheeling, Ohio Co., Va., 29 April, 1832; *m.* Lydia Boggs, who resided near Redstone Old Fort in 1784. "Lydia Boggs became quite famous for her courage in times of danger, as well as for her narrow escape from death. During the siege at Wheeling she moulded bullets until her arms were blistered, and once, when captured by the Indians and carried down the Ohio River, she effected her escape by compelling her horse to swim the river" (Crumrine's History of Washington Co., Pa., p. 674). She was b. 26 Feb., 1766; d. Wheeling, Va., 26 May, 1867, in her 102d year. She *m.* 1st *circa* 1785, Moses Shepherd, and upon his death, *m.* 2d a former partner of Mr. Shepherd, General Daniel Crugar, a native of New York State. She had no issue by either marriage. Col Moses Shepherd was a very wealthy and influential resident of Ohio Co., Va., and had much prominence in national affairs after the organization of the government. While yet a boy he served in the Revolution in Capt. Lewis Bonnett's company of militia, and as aid to his father, Col. David Shepherd, who was the commandant at Fort Henry and Lieutenant of Ohio County, Va. He took up large tracts of land in the river valleys of western Virginia and also inherited much of his father's large estate in the vicinity of Wheeling. In 1798 he erected upon the site of Fort Shepherd, in the forks of Wheeling Creek, a handsome colonial mansion which is still standing in excellent preservation and known as "Monument Place." Moses Shepherd also constructed large sections of the National Road, which extends from the city of Cumberland, Md., to St. Louis, and through which his fame and fortune was largely augmented. Many of the famous men of his day were visitors to his fine home and he in turn was a notable and familiar figure in Washington during sessions of Congress. He is buried at the "Old Stone Church," on the hill at Elm Grove, overlooking the Forks of Wheeling and the great national highway (see also West Virginia Historical Magazine for January and July, 1903).

7. DAVID McINTIRE (Thomas[1], David[2], Elizabeth[3]), son of Major William and Elizabeth (Shepherd) McIntire, b. ——; *m.* ——; lived on Big Wheeling Creek, near Wheeling, Va. Issue: 33, David Shepherd; 34, William; 35, George, b. ——; 36, Silas C., b. ——; 37, Charlotte, b. ——, *m.* Jos. Welsh; 38, Elizabeth, b. ——; 39, Lydia, b. ——, *m.* Calvin Hendershott; 40, Sarah, b. ——, *m.* Jas. M. Dillon; 41, Jane, b. ——, *m.* Nelson Mallory.

COL. MOSES SHEPHERD

MRS. LYDIA B. SHEPHERD-CRUGAR

8. Eleanor McIntire (Thomas[1], David[2], Elizabeth[3]), dau. of William and Elizabeth (Shepherd) McIntire, b. *circa* 1777; d. ——; *m.* Zadoc Springer (probably son of Levi and Sarah (S. Duke) Springer). Issue:

42, Levi, b. ——; 43, Job, b. ——; 44, Hervey, b. ——; 45, Jonathan, b. ——; 46, Dennis, b. ——; 47, Elizabeth, b. ——, *m.* Ellis Bailey; 48, William S., b. ——; 49, Jacob, b. ——; 50, Ann, b. ——, *m.* Noah Morrison; 51, Morgan, b. ——.

9. Sarah McIntire (Thomas[1], David[2], Elizabeth[3]), dau. of William and Elizabeth (Shepherd) McIntire, b. ——; d. ——; *m.* 1st John Martin; *m.* 2d George Feay, d. *circa* 1815; *m.* 3d John Seaman. The Feays, who came from the upper Potomac region in Virginia, settled on the Wheeling Creek about 1775, Joseph Feay living there in 1879 (History of Pan Handle Counties of Virginia). Issue:

52, Joseph Feay; 53, Eliza Feay, *m.* Moses Creighton; 54, George Feay, *m.* Sarah ——; a, Thomas.

10. Rachael McIntire (Thomas[1], David[2], Elizabeth[3]), dau. of William and Elizabeth (Shepherd) McIntire, b. ——; d. ——; *m.* William McClelland. Issue:

55, George Dawson, b. ——.

11. Harriet McIntire (Thomas[1], David[2], Elizabeth[3]), dau. of William and Elizabeth (Shepherd) McIntire, b. ——; d. ——; *m.* William Templeton. Issue:

56, Joseph, b. ——, *m.* Ellen ——; 57, Samuel, b. ——; 58, Thomas, b. ——; 59, Harriet, b. ——, *m.* Joseph Woods.

12. Ruth McIntire (Thomas[1], David[2], Elizabeth[3]), dau. of William and Elizabeth (Shepherd) McIntire, b. ——; d. ——; *m.* John Collins. Issue:

60, Thomas, b. ——; 61, Mary, b. ——, *m.* Noble Woodward; 62, Sarah, b. ——, *m.* Joseph Lee; 63, James, b. ——; 64, John, b. ——; 65, Elizabeth, b. ——, *m.* John McCracken; 66, Ellen, b. ——, *m.* Hillary Austin.

13. Joseph McIntire (Thomas[1], David[2], Elizabeth[3]), son of William and Elizabeth (Shepherd) McIntire, b. at Triadelphia, Ohio Co., Va., 2 March, 1779; d. near Reynoldsburg, Fairfield Co., Ohio, 14 May, 1842; *m.* 21 Oct., 1798, Jane, dau. of James and Martha (Dickey) Crawford; she was b. at Bridgeport, Conn., 6 May, 1779, and d. in Ohio, 17 Nov., 1865. She was a sister of David and Dr. Isaac Crawford, founders of Crawfordsville, Washington Co., Iowa. Joseph McIntire held large land possessions near Columbus, O., where he lived and raised a large family. Issue:

67, William, b. 29 Dec., 1803, d. 28 Dec., 1886, *m.* Mary Longshore; 68, Martha, b. 10 April, 1805, *m.* Nathaniel

Painter; 69, Elizabeth, b. 21 Oct., 1806, m. James Collins; 70, James, twin, b. 13 Sept., 1809; 71, Sarah, twin, b. 13 Sept., 1809; 72, David, b. 11 Aug., 1811, d. 9 Jan., 1891, m. Margaret Sloan; 73, Margaret, b. 2 Jan., 1813, m. Abraham Morferd; 74, Thomas, b. 25 Dec., 1815, d. 25 Sept., 1885, m. Mary E. Barr; 75, Ruth, b. 6 June, 1816; 76, Joseph, b. 12 Dec., 1817, m. Mary Howard, b. 31 Oct., 1828, d. 29 May, 1901; 77, Shepherd, b. 2 March, 1822, d. inf.; 78, John, b. 16 Jan., 1823, d. 24 Jan., 1884, m. in Philadelphia, Pa., 1 April, 1852, Elizabeth Louisa McDonald.

14. WILLIAM McINTIRE (Thomas[1], David[2], Elizabeth[3]), son of William and Elizabeth (Shepherd) McIntire, b. —; d. —; m. — —.
Issue:
80, Jane, m. George Adams; 81, David; 82, Marjory, m. John Terhune; 83, James; 84, Dorinda, m. Jas. B. McIntire; 85, George; 86, Elizabeth, m. C. Brown; 87, Joseph; 88, Mary.

15. THOMAS LEE (Thomas[1], David[2], Elizabeth[3]), son of John and Elizabeth (Shepherd-McIntire) Lee, b. —; d. —; m. Friend.
Issue:
89, Elizabeth; 90, William; 91, Joseph.

16. JULIET MILLS (Thomas[1], David[2], Ruth[3]), dau. of Capt. John and Ruth (Shepherd) Mills, b. —; d. —; m. John Feay.

20. ELIZABETH MILLS (Thomas[1], David[2], Ruth[3]), dau. of Capt. John and Ruth (Shepherd) Mills, b. —; d. —; m. Joseph Shaw.
Issue:
92, Harriet; 93, John; 94, Thomas; 95, Ruth, m. Alex. Gaston; 96, Margaret, m. Joseph Gibbons; 97, Joanna, m. John Rynhart; 98, Eleanor, m. William Stewart; 99, Sarah, m. — Scott; 100, Elizabeth, m. Hugh Walker.

21. WILLIAM MILLS (Thomas[1], David[2], Ruth[3]), son of Capt. John and Ruth (Shepherd) Mills, b. —; d. —; m. — —.
Issue:
101, William; 102, John; 103, James; 104, Sarah J.; 105, Minerva; 106, Cardine; 107, Catharine, b. —; m. John Hall Gassoway; 108, Ruth, m. James Nixon.

22. SARAH MILLS (Thomas[1], David[2], Ruth[3]), dau. of Capt. John and Ruth (Shepherd) Mills, b. —; d. —; m. George McCreary.
Issue:
109, George; 110, Jane; 111, Elizabeth; 112, Henry; 113, John.

25. SARAH SPRINGER (Thomas[1], David[2], Sarah[3]), dau. of Levi and Sarah (Shepherd-Duke) Springer, b. 9/12 Dec., 1782; d. —; m. 1799–1800, in Uniontown, Pa., William Harbaugh, of Pittsburg, who emigrated to New Lisbon, Columbiana Co., O.,

in 1803, a saddler by trade; merchant at New Lisbon, 1809–1819; farmer till his decease in 1833. William Harbaugh was the first postmaster in Columbiana Co., O.; one of the justices of the peace of that county, and was a Representative in the Ohio Legislature for several terms. When the State was divided into military districts he was appointed by the Legislature Quartermaster-General of the Fourth District. This district was the theater of war at the time of Commodore Hull's surrender. Harbaugh supplied the troops with tents, forage and provisions. It is said that he built the first flouring mill in his county and his product was sent down the Ohio to New Orleans.   Issue:
   114, Lila, b. 7 Dec., 1801, *m.* DeLorme Brooks, issue ten children; 115, Susan, b. 3 July, 1804, *m.* David Whitacre, issue four children; 116, Jacob, b. 18 Jan., 1806; 117, Rachael, b. 16 Nov., 1810, *m.* Warrick Martin, issue seven children; 118, Sarah, b. 13 June, 1812, *m.* William Cocks; 119, Dennis, b. 18 July, 1814, d. *unm.* 1856; 120, Springer, b. 16 March, 1816, *m.* Roxa. Brooks, dau. of Thos. Brooks, of Montpelier, Vt.; 121, Elizabeth, b. 16 Nov., 1817, d. 1845; 121½, William, b. 23 Mar., 1818.

26. DAVID SPRINGER (Thomas[1], David[2], Sarah[3]), son of Levi and Sarah (Shepherd-Duke) Springer, b. 3 Jan., 1785; d. ——; *m.* his cousin, Elizabeth, dau. of Dennis and Ann (Fricket) Springer. David removed to the west about 1835, his two eldest sons remaining in Pennsylvania.   Issue:
   122, Shepherd, b. 21 Sept., 1805, d. 1853; 123, Marshall; 124, Isaiah; 125, Nathan; 126, Jacob; 127, Oliver; 128, Albert; 129, Lafayette; 130, Rachael; 131, Levi.

27. DENNIS SPRINGER (Thomas[1], David[2], Sarah[3]), son of Levi and Sarah (Shepherd-Duke) Springer, b. 3 March, 1787; d. at Uniontown, Pa., 1 March, 1866; *m.* 22 March, 1821, Sally Brownfield at Winchester, Va.; she was b. 26 Sept., 1797; d. 17 Jan., 1871.   Issue:
   132, Mary Ann, b. 25 Dec., 1821; 133, Elizabeth B., b. 12 Dec., 1823; 134, Lydia J., b. 4 Feb., 1827, *m.* Albert J. Rizzer; 135, Sarah J., b. 9 July, 1829; 136, Levi B., b. 22 Jan., 1832; 137, Catharine, b. 28 Dec., 1838, *m.* P. P. Craig.

29. JOB SPRINGER (Thomas[1], David[2], Sarah[3]), son of Levi and Sarah (Shepherd-Duke) Springer, b. 15 Aug., 1792; d. ——; *m.* Mary Lewis, of Fayette Co., Pa.   Issue:
   138, Daniel, *m.* Ella J. Walker; 139, Ewing B., b. 16 July, 1826; 140, Ruth A.; 141, Eliza; 142, Jacob L., killed while serving in Union army.

30. ELIZABETH SPRINGER (Thomas[1], David[2], Sarah[3]), dau. of Levi and Sarah (Shepherd-Duke) Springer, b. 28 Feb., 1794; d. 15 Oct., 1828; *m.* William Hibben, of Wilmington, O.   Issue:

143, Anna M., *m.* John McLean; 144, Sallie M., *m.* Abraham Hiveling; 145, Rebecca J., *m.* Franklin Conover; 146, William; 147, George E., *m.* Patience ——; 148, Alpheus; 149, David.

32. HANNAH SPRINGER (Thomas[1], David[2], Sarah[3]), dau. of Levi and Sarah (Shepherd-Duke) Springer, b. 15 Dec., 1801; d. ——; *m.* —— Wright. Issue:
150, Mary E., *m.* Jas. H. Collins, Pittsfield, Mass.

40. SARAH McINTIRE (Thomas[1], David[2], Elizabeth[3], David[4]), dau. of David McIntire, b. ——; d. ——; *m.* James M. Dillon. Issue:
151, Marie; 152, David; 153, Harriet.

41. JANE McINTIRE (Thomas[1], David[2], Elizabeth[3], David[4]), dau. of David McIntire and —— ——, b. ——; d. ——; *m.* Nelson Mallory. Issue:
154, Harriet, *m.* Wm. McDougal; 155, Jane Anne, *m.* Daniel Shepherd; 156, Jeanette.

48. WILLIAM SPRINGER (Thomas[1], David[2], Elizabeth[3], Eleanor[4]), son of Zadoc and Eleanor (McIntire) Springer, b. ——; d. ——; *m.* —— ——. Issue:
157, Zadoc; 158, Ellen J., *m.* Geo. C. Martin; 159, Virginia.

49. JACOB SPRINGER (Thomas[1], David[2], Elizabeth[3], Eleanor[4]), son of Zadoc and Eleanor (McIntire) Springer, b. ——; d. ——; *m.* —— ——. Issue:
160, Job; 161, Caroline.

50. ANN SPRINGER (Thomas[1], David[2], Elizabeth[3], Eleanor[4]), dau. of Zadoc and Eleanor (McIntire) Springer, b. ——; d. ——; *m.* Noah Morrison. Issue:
162, Eliza; 163, William; 164, Ellen; 165, Elizabeth.

52. JOSEPH FEAY (Thomas[1], David[2], Elizabeth[3], Sarah[4]), son of George and Sarah (McIntire) Feay, b. ——; d. ——; *m.* Barbara King. Issue:
166, William G.; 167, Sarah, *m.* Edwin Roe, 1861/5; 168, Annie King, *m.* John S. Creighton; 169, Mary, d. *unm.* at Elm Grove, Ohio Co., Va.; 170, Francis.

54. WILLIAM (or GEORGE) FEAY (Thomas[1], David[2], Elizabeth[3], Sarah[4]), son of George and Sarah (McIntire) Feay, b. ——; d. ——; *m.* Sarah ——. Issue:
171, Jennie E., *m.* Thomas Gist; 172, Margaretta, *m.* 1st —— Binkham, *m.* 2d Bennie Feay.

57. SAMUEL TEMPLETON (Thomas[1], David[2], Elizabeth[3], Harriet[4]), son of William and Harriet (McIntire) Templeton, b. ——; d. ——; *m.* —— ——. Issue:
173, Alice Olivia, *m.* —— Middleton.

REV. THOMAS McINTIRE, Ph.D.

59. HARRIET TEMPLETON (Thomas[1], David[2], Elizabeth[3], Harriet[4]), dau. of William and Harriet (McIntire) Templeton, b. ——; d. ——; m. Joseph Woods.   Issue:
174, Olivia.

67. WILLIAM MCINTIRE (Thomas[1], David[2], Elizabeth[3], Joseph[4]), son of Joseph and Jane (Crawford) McIntire, b. 29 Dec., 1803; d. 28 Dec., 1886; m. Mary Longshore.   Issue:
a, Susan; b, Albert; c, Rosetta.

70. ELIZABETH CRAWFORD MCINTIRE (Thomas[1], David[2], Elizabeth[3], Joseph[4]), dau. of Joseph and Jane (Crawford) McIntire, b. 21 Oct., 1806; d. ——; m. James Collins.   Issue:
174, Mary Jane, m. Jacob Adams; 175, David; 176, Minerva, m. E. D. Gonelly; 177, Joseph; 178, Charlotta, m. Asa Sanders; 179, Louisa; 180, Robert.

72. DAVID MCINTIRE (Thomas[1], David[2], Elizabeth[3], Joseph[4]), son of Joseph and Jane (Crawford) McIntire, b. 11 Aug., 1811; d. 9 Jan., 1891; m. in Monmouth, Ill., 8 May, 1834, Margaret Sloan, b. 13 April, 1816; d. 17 April, 1900.   Issue:
a, Samuel, b. 26 May, 1835; m. 20 Aug., 1870, Anna Arthur.
b, Joseph, b. 1 Sept., 1837; d. 24 Jan., 1885; m. 13 Feb., 1862, —— ——.
c, Jane, b. 14 Oct., 1839; m. 22 March, 1861, James Parks, d. 1 Aug., 1899.
d, George, b. 26 March, 1843; d. 27 April, 1883.
e, David C., b. 28 June, 1846; m. 25 Oct., 1881, Helen Ingram.
f, Andrew, b. 17 Feb., 1850; m. 28 Feb., 1873, Ida May Boyce.
g, Mary, b. Feb. 8, 1853; m. 19 Feb., 1870, Robert Newbank, d. 24 Jan., 1891.
h, Esther Lee, b. 6 March, 1856; resides at Monmouth, Ill.
i, Margaret, b. 7 June, 1857; m. 29 April, 1877.

75. THOMAS MCINTIRE (Thomas[1], David[2], Elizabeth[3], Joseph[4]), son of Joseph and Jane (Crawford) McIntire, b. 25 Dec., 1815, at Reynoldsburg, O.; d. in Indianapolis, Ind., 25 Sept., 1885; m. 26 Sept., 1843, Mary Elizabeth Barr, dau. of John and Nancy (Nelson) Barr, of Columbus, O. She was b. 15 July, 1825, and d. 21 June, 1899. Rev. Dr. Thomas McIntire, Ph.D., was two years at Hanover College, Ind.; graduated from Franklin College, New Athens, O., 1840; from Princeton Theological Seminary, 1842; instructor Ohio Deaf and Dumb Institute, 1842–45; founder and superintendent Tennessee Deaf and Dumb Institute, Knoxville, Tenn., 1845–50; book store in Columbus, O., 1850–52; supt. Indiana Deaf and Dumb Institute, 1852–79; supt. Michigan Deaf and Dumb Institute, Flint, Mich., 1879–82; founder Western Pennsylvania Institute for Deaf and Dumb, 1883–85, Wilkinsburg, Pa.   Issue:
181, Harriet Newell, b. Barr Homestead, 30 July, 1844.

182, Alice, b. Knoxville, Tenn., 1 Dec., 1847; d. 28 Jan., 1863.
183, Susan Van DeMan, b. Barr Homestead, 28 Oct., 1850; d. 9 March, 1899.
184, Martha Livingston, b. Indianapolis, 30 July, 1853; m. Charles Martindale, 10 July, 1878.
185, Frances, b. Indianapolis, Ind., 23 Jan., 1856; m. at Flint, Mich., 11 Jan., 1882, Moses Ross.

78. JOHN McINTIRE (Thomas[1], David[2], Elizabeth[3], Joseph[4]), son of Joseph and Jane (Crawford) McIntire, b. 16 Jan., 1823; d. 24 Jan., 1884; m. 1 April, 1852, at Philadelphia, Pa., Elizabeth Louise McDonald. She was born in London, England; came to America while an infant.

Issue:
a, Charles Thomas, b. 4 July, 1853, has a Cuban record; b, La Salle Vandeman, b. 30 Jan., 1855; c, Wm. Newell, b. 13 May, 1857; d, Frank Shepherd, b. 7 Dec., 1859, d. 26 Oct., 1886; e, Harry Ellsworth, b. 7 May, 1862, d. 12 July, 1863; f, Henry, b. 8 Sept., 1863, d. 7 Nov., 1863.

87. JOSEPH McINTIRE (Thomas[1], David[2], Elizabeth[3], William[4]), son of William and —— McIntire, b. ——; d. ——; m. ——.

Issue:
186, Eleanor; 187, Matilda; 188, Jane.

88. MARY McINTIRE (Thomas[1], David[2], Elizabeth[3], William[4]), dau. of William and ——, b. ——; d. ——; m. Roger Duffey.

Issue:
189, William A.

98. ELEANOR SHAW (Thomas[1], David[2], Ruth[3], Elizabeth[4]), dau. of Joseph and Elizabeth (Mills) Shaw, b. ——; d. ——; m. William Stewart.

Issue:
190, William; 191, Thomas; 192, Armstrong, b. ——; m. ——; issue: a, Nancy; b, Ellen.

99. SARAH SHAW (Thomas[1], David[2], Ruth[3], Elizabeth[4]), dau. of Joseph and Elizabeth (Mills) Shaw, b. ——; d. ——; m. —— Scott.

Issue:
193, Harriet.

100. ELIZABETH SHAW Thomas[1], David[2], Ruth[3], Elizabeth[4]), dau. of Joseph and Elizabeth (Mills) Shaw, b. ——; d. ——; m. Hugh Walker.

Issue:
194, John; 195, Emmaline, m. —— Mayhew; 196, Virginia, m. James Meeks; 197, Cecelia.

116. JACOB HARBAUGH (Thomas[1], David[2], Sarah[3], William[4]), son of William and Sarah (Springer) Harbaugh, b. 18 Jan., 1806, at New Lisbon, O.; d. ——; m. 5 July, 1832, Elizabeth Converse.

Issue:
198, Porter William, b. 17 July, 1833; 199, M. Josephine, b. 6 Sept., 1836.

198

118. SARAH HARBAUGH (Thomas[1], David[2], Sarah[3], William[4]), dau. of William and Sarah (Springer) Harbaugh, b. 13 June, 1812, at New Lisbon, O.; d. ——; *m.* William Cocks; emigrated to Oregon. Issue:
  200, Sarah, *m.* William Rinehart and removed to Oregon; 201, Henry; 202, Caroline, *m.* Caleb M. Sickler; 203, Annie, *m.* Jared S. Hinds; 204, Roxa S.; 205, Elisha B.

122. SHEPHERD SPRINGER (Thomas[1], David[2], Sarah[3], David[4]), son of David and Elizabeth Springer, b. 21 Sept., 1805; d. ——, 1856; *m.* Eliza Clements, of Fayette Co., Pa. She died in 1891. Issue:
  206, Athilla, b. 6 Sept., 1828, *m.* D. Gillespie; 207, Josiah, b. 29 May, 1830; 208, Isaac, b. 9 Sept., 1833, *m.* A. Brown; 209, David, b. 2 Feb., 1835, *m.* Elizabeth Cruse; 210, Elizabeth, b. 29 May, 1837, d. 30 Oct., 1871, *m.* J. O. Todd; 211, *John,* b. 1840; 212, Sarah E., b. 1843, d. 1847; 213, Rebecca, b. 1845, d. 1845; 214, Margaret, b. 1847, *m.* S. Martin; 215, Rebecca[2], b. 30 Sept., 1852, d. single.

123. MARSHALL SPRINGER (Thomas[1], David[2], Sarah[3], David[4]), son of David and Elizabeth Springer, b. ——; d. Birmingham, Pa., ——; *m.* Susan Thompson. Issue:
  216, James T.; 217, John C.; 218, Charles A.; 219, Rachael; 220, Hannah F.; 221, David M.; 222, William E.; 223, Emma G.

134. LYDIA J. SPRINGER (Thomas[1], David[2], Sarah[3], Dennis[4]), dau. of Dennis and Sally (Brownfield) Springer, by 4 Feb., 1821; d. 21 March, 1865; *m.* Albert J. Rizzer, of Cumberland, Md., 25 Sept., 1845. He d. 5 Dec., 1869. Issue:
  224, George S., b. 6 July, 1846, *m.* Emmaline Rice; 225, Florence M., b. 22 Aug., 1847, *m.* John H. Kunst; 226, Mary F., b. 9 Oct., 1849; 227, Henry Benj., b. 25 Jan., 1852, *m.* Mary Kelso; 228, Albert A., b. 1 Nov., 1854.

137. CATHARINE SPRINGER (Thomas[1], David[2], Sarah[3], Dennis[4]), dau. of Dennis and Sally (Brownfield) Springer, b. 28 Dec., 1838; *m.* 24 Feb., 1864, P. P. Craig. Issue:
  229, Albert R., b. 2 Jan., 1865; 230, Charles H., b. 9 Sept., 1867; 231, Walter C., b. 3 June, 1869.

138. DANIEL M. SPRINGER (Thomas[1], David[2], Sarah[3], Job[4]), son of Job and Mary (Lewis) Springer, b. ——; d. — July, 1882; *m.* 23 Sept., 1841, —— ——. Issue:
  a, Mary R., b. 8 Jan., 1843; *b,* Thomas W., b. 3 Sept., 1844, d. 30 Aug., 1864, in Salisbury Prison; *c,* John S., b. 14 March, 1846, d. 1 June, 1864, in Andersonville Prison; *d,* Elizabeth, b. 15 March, 1848; *e,* William, b.

19 Feb., 1850; *f*, Ruth, b. 6 May, 1852; *g*, Sarah, b. 15 Oct., 1854; *h*, Julia, b. 7 April, 1857.

139. EWING B. SPRINGER (Thomas[1], David[2], Sarah[3], Job[4]), son of Job and Mary (Lewis) Springer, b. ——; d. ——; *m.* —— ——, and settled in Ohio. Issue:
a, Jacob, b. 1 May, 1848; *b*, James L., b. 27 Sept., 1849; *c*, Mary D., b. 10 July, 1851; *d*, John W., b. 15 Jan., 1853; *e*, Elva E., b. 19 Oct., 1859.

181. HARRIET NEWELL McINTIRE (Thomas[1], David[2], Elizabeth[3], Joseph[4], Thomas[5]), dau. of Rev. Thomas and Mary E. (Barr) McIntire, b. Columbus, O., 3 July, 1844; *m.* 16 July, 1873, Chapin C. Foster, on Indianapolis. He served in the Union Army, enlisting 18 May, 1864, in 132d Regiment Indiana Volunteers; mustered out 17 Sept., 1864; was aid-de-camp to General Milroy during Morgan's Raid through Indiana. Mrs. Foster is a prominent member of the Daughters of The American Revolution —National number, 1999; State Regent, 1892–1898; First Honorary State Regent since 1898. Issue:
232, Mary McIntire, b. 6 Aug., 1874; d. 13 June, 1905.
233, Robert Sanford, b. 10 June, 1876; 234, Martha Martindale, b. 12 Nov., 1880.

183. SUSAN VAN DEMAN McINTIRE (Thomas[1], David[2], Elizabeth[3], Joseph[4], Thomas[5]), dau. of Rev. Thomas and Mary E. (Barr) McIntire, b. Columbus, O., 28 Oct., 1850; d. March 9, 1899; *m.* 11 Sept., 1872, Merrick E. Vinton, of New York City, N. Y. Issue:
235, Thomas M., b. 5 Oct., 1874, at Indianapolis, Ind.; *m.* June, 1902, Mary Toffrey Wheeler.
236, Stallo, b. 19 Dec., 1876; 237, Almus, b. 31 July, 1878; *m.* 24 Feb., 1904, Anne Mary Hurty.
238, Merrick, Jr., b. 17 Aug., 1883, in St. Paul, Minn.; d. 7 May, 1907, in San Francisco, Cal.

192. ARMSTRONG STEWART (Thomas[1], David[2], Ruth[3], Elizabeth[4], William[5]), son of William and Eleanor (Shaw) Stewart, b. —— ——; d. —— ——; *m.* —— ——. Issue:
239, Nancy; 240, Ellen.

209. DAVID SPRINGER (Thomas[1], David[2], Sarah[3], David[4], Shepherd[5]), son of Shepherd and Eliza (Clements) Springer, b. 2 Feb., 1835; *m.* Elizabeth Cruse. Issue:
241, Eliza, b., 23 Oct., 1858, d. —— 1858; 242, Sarah(?), b. ——.

210. ELIZABETH SPRINGER (Thomas[1], David[2], Sarah[3], David[4], Shepherd[5]), dau. of Shepherd and Eliza (Clements) Springer, b. 29 May, 1837; d. 30 Oct., 1871; *m.* J. O. Todd, 1855. Issue:
243, Ross M., b. 15 Dec., 1856; 244, Catharine C., b. 31 March,

MRS. HARRIET McINTIRE FOSTER

1858; 245, Mary L., b. 24 Aug., 1860; 246, John H., b. 7 Jan., 1863; 247, Eliza E., b. 26 Nov., 1864; 248, Thomas, b. ——; 249, John S., b. Sept., 1868; 250, Sally G., b. 8 July, 1870.

214. MARGARET SPRINGER (Thomas[1], David[2], Sarah[3], David[4], Shepherd[5]), dau. of Shepherd and Eliza (Clements) Springer, b. —— 1847; d. ——; m. 28 Jan., 1868, Lucius Martin, of Uniontown, Pa.   Issue:
251, Minnie, b. 21 March, 1869; 252, William, b. 21 June, 1872; 253, Annie E., b. 21 June, 1876.

224. GEORGE S. RIZZER (Thomas[1], David[2], Sarah[3], Dennis[4], Lydia J.[5]), son of Albert S. and Lydia J. (Springer) Rizzer, b. 6 July, 1846; d. ——; m. 19 Feb., 1868, Emmaline Rice, of Cumberland, Md., and settled in Springfield, Ohio.   Issue:
254, Louis R., b. Jan., 1869; 255, Chas. W., b. Sept., 1870; 256, Lucy A., b. July, 1873.

225. FLORENCE M. RIZZER (Thomas[1], David[2], Sarah[3], Dennis[4], Lydia J.[5]), dau. of Albert S. and Lydia J. (Springer) Rizzer, b. 22 Aug., 1847; m. 2 March, 1871, Louis H. Kunst.   Issue:
257, Sarah L., b. 16 Sept., 1872; 258, George H., b. 16 May, 1874.

227. H. BENJAMIN RIZZER (Thomas[1], David[2], Sarah[3], Dennis[4], Lydia J.[5]), son of Albert S. and Lydia J. (Springer) Rizzer, b. 25 Jan., 1852; d. ——; m. 5 Aug., 1875, Mary Kelso, of Cumberland, Md.   Issue:
259, Lydia F., b. 30 April, 1876.

232. MARY MCINTIRE FOSTER (Thomas[1], David[2], Elizabeth[3], Joseph[4], Thomas[5], Harriett M.[6]), dau. Chapin C. and Harriet N. (McIntire) Foster, b. 6 Aug., 1874; d. 13 June, 1905; m. 19 April, 1904, at Indianapolis, Ind., Chas. H. Morrison. Issue:
260, Robert Foster, b. 10 June, 1905.

233. ROBERT SANFORD FOSTER (Thomas[1], David[2], Elizabeth[3], Joseph[4], Thomas[5], Harriet M.[6]), son of Chapin C. and Harriet N. (McIntire) Foster, b. 10 June, 1876; m. 10 Oct., 1896, Edith Lucille Gray dau. of Rev. W. H. and Elsie (McFairn) Jeffries, of Indianapolis. Mr. Jeffries d. 22 Dec., 1894.   Issue:
261, Mary Edith, b. 31 July, 1907.

DESCENDANTS OF SARAH SHEPHERD

II. SARAH SHEPHERD (Thomas[1]), dau. of Thomas and Elizabeth (Van Metre) Shepherd, b. Mecklenburg, Va., *circa* 1736; d. Shepherdstown, Va., 18 Oct., 1780; m. *circa* 1751-2, Thomas Thornburgh, who d. at Shepherdstown, 1789. His will is re-

THE SHEPHERD GENEALOGY

corded at Martinsburg, W. Va. (Bk. 2, p. 44); dated 30 July, 1787; probated 21 Oct., 1789, and his wife is not mentioned therein; children recited:

    1, Thomas, b. 1752 (only one mentioned in his grandfather, Thomas Shepherd's will); 2, John; 3, Hezekiah; 4, Josiah; 5, William; 6, Azariah; 7, Mercy; 8, Sarah (will probated at Martinsburg, Va., 1795).

    1. THOMAS THORNBURG (Thomas[1], Sarah[2]), son of Thomas and Sarah Thornburgh, b. — Sept., 1752; d. 10 May, 1793, and is buried in the Shepherd family burying-ground at Shepherdstown, W. Va.; *m.* 1772.   Issue:

    9, Thomas, b. 1773; 10, John, mentioned in his grandfather's (Thomas Thornburgh) will, 1789; 11, Ephraim; 12, William.

    2. JOHN THORNBURGH (Thomas[1], Sarah[2]), son of Thomas and Sarah (Shepherd) Thornburgh, b. *circa* 1755; d. ——; *m.* —— ——. He is mentioned in the settlement of the estate of Thomas Shepherd, Jr., 1793, and in old Shepherd papers, 1793–98; trustee of Shepherdstown, 1796.   Issue:

    13, Thomas, b. ——; *m.* Margaret Millar.

    3. HEZEKIAH THORNBURGH (Thomas[1], Sarah[2]), son of Thomas and Sarah (Shepherd) Thornburgh, b. ——; d. ——; *m.* —— ——. (History Pan Handle Counties of Virginia.) He is mentioned as one of two brothers who emigrated from the vicinity of Shepherdstown, Va., and settled about the forks of Wheeling Creek, in Ohio Co., Va., where his relatives, the Shepherds and the Dukes, were already seated. He was a witness to a deed from Col. David Shepherd to the latter's grandson, Francis Duke, dated 29 Jan., 1795, and is credited on the old books at Shepherdstown as having remitted to Moses Shepherd £85, being part of David Shepherd's estate, in 1795. His first wife was a niece of Capt. Wm. Crawford, who was so barbarously martyred at the stake in Wyandotte Co., O. (Howe's Hist. Coll. of Va., p. 117), while on the ill-fated Sandusky Expedition in 1782. After which the niece was taken into the family of Col. Shepherd, and upon her marriage to Thornburgh was granted 200 acres of land in Triadelphia Township, Ohio Co., Va., by Col. Shepherd. His second wife is not recalled.   Issue:

    14, John; 15, Thomas; 16, David; 17, Moses; 18, Ephraim, settled in Iowa; 19, Sarah, *m.* Wm. Martin, no issue.

    6. AZARIAH THORNBURGH (Thomas[1], Sarah[2]), son of Thomas and Sarah (Shepherd) Thornburg, b. ——; d. ——; *m.* 18 Aug., 1793, Drusilla Morgan, by Rev. Moses Hoge, at Shepherdstown, Va. (Berkeley Co., Va., M. L.).

9. THOMAS THORNBURGH (Thomas[1], Sarah[2], Thomas[3]), son of Thomas and —— Thornburgh b. 13 July, 1773; d. 4 Nov., 1861, married three times:
Married 1st, Dec., 1813, Barbara Byers, b. 8 Dec., 1795; d. 5 July, 1828.   Issue:
    21, Sarah Ellen, b. Oct., 1814, d. 9 Dec., 1818; 22, John Conrad, b. 31 Oct., 1816, d. 25 Jan., 1817; 23, Prudence Elizabeth, b. 14 Dec., 1817, d. *unm.*; 24, Solomon, b. 26 April, 1820; 25, Mary Shepherd, b. 2 July, 1822, d. 23 Nov., 1857; 26, Rebecca Ripply, b. 17 Oct., 1824; 27, Samuel Thomas, b. 14 Dec., 1826, d. 19 Oct., 1831.
Married 2d, 9 Oct., 1828, Maria Barbara Swingle, b. 18 Jan., 1804, d. 23 Oct., 1831.   Issue:
    28, Jacob Smith, 18 June, 1829, d. 5 Nov., 1831; 29, Margaret Catharine, b. 2 Feb., 1831.
Married 3d, 13 Nov., 1832, Maria Myers, b. 25 Feb., 1804; d. 29 Feb., 1876.   Issue:
    30, Isaac Newton, b. 18 Aug., 1833; *m.* Ellatta T. Rockwell, of Washington, D. C.
    31, Collins Unseld, b. 16 Jan., 1835; *m.* Nora C. Millar, 1860, Cabell Co., W. Va.
    32, Wm. Henry, b. 19 Nov., 1836, d. 14 April, 1837; 33, Geo. Fouk, b. 19 March, 1838; *m.* Mary Frances Griffin, Cattlettsburg, Ky.
    34, Uriah Millar, b. 12 Nov., 1840; 35, Maria Coe, b. 23 Dec., 1848; d. 31 Jan., 1856.
Note: Thomas Thornburgh *m.* Sarah Ellis 30 May, 1806. Thomas Thornburgh *m.* Margaret Martin 25 June, 1812.

13. THOMAS THORNBURGH (Thomas[1], Sarah[2], John[3]), son of John and —— Thornburgh, b. ——; d. ——; *m.* 12 Dec., 1837, Margaret, dau. of John and Sophia (Clendinin) Millar, of the Kanawha Valley. She was b. 25 Nov., 1813; d. 19 Aug., 1859. Thomas Thornburgh was a successful farmer and merchant of Cabell Co., Va. Beginning in 1857 he represented that County in the Virginia Legislature; in 1872 he was a member of the Constitutional Convention of West Virginia. He was a Master Mason and for forty-six consecutive years was the Secretary of Cabell Lodge, No. 13, F. & A. M.   Issue:
    36, John (Lieut. C. S. A.), *m.* Mary Long, of Mason Co., W. Va.; 37, George, *m.* Nannie Millar; 38, Bayley, *m.* Nettie Samuels; 39, Elizabeth, *m.* Dr. A. R. McGuiness; 40, Ellen, *m.* Capt. Will Hovey, U. S. A.; 41, Mary; 42, Margaret (see W. Va. Hist. Mag., Oct., 1901, p. 27).

14. JOHN THORNBURGH (Thomas[1], Sarah[2], Hezekiah[3]), son of Hezekiah and —— Thornburgh, b. —— 1796; d. ——; *m.* Jane Abernathy. She was b. 1793, d. 1843. John Thornburgh

settled with his father at the forks of Wheeling Creek and on his father's death succeeded to the homestead property and was still living, in 1879, one of the oldest inhabitants in that section of the country. Issue:

43, Rachael, *m.* Jeptha Thornburgh; 44, Elizabeth, *m.* Henry Shepherd Thornburgh.

15. THOMAS THORNBURGH (Thomas[1], Sarah[2], Hezekiah[3]), son of Hezekiah and —— Thornburgh, b. ——; d. 1871; *m.* Ann Lunsford, and lived near the Forks of Wheeling. Issue:

45, Rachael, living 1879 on the Old National Road, Elm Grove, *unm.*; 46, Sarah, *m.* —— Millar; 47, Wm. C.; 48, a dau. *m.* —— Waddell.

16. DAVID THORNBURGH (Thomas[1], Sarah[2], Hezekiah[3]), son of Hezekiah and —— Thornburgh, b. ——; d. ——; *m.* 1st Sarah Martin, who was born in Pennsylvania, in 1812. Issue:

49, Daniel; 50, Henry Shepherd, *m.* his cousin Elizabeth Thornburgh; 51, Jeptha, *m.* his cousin Rachael T.; 52, William; 53, John; 54, Thomas; 55, Martha.

Married 2d, Rachael, dau. of John Feay, his cousin, and a descendant of John Feay, who *m.* Mary Shepherd, dau. of Thomas[1] Shepherd. No issue.

24. SOLOMON THORNBURGH (Thomas[1], Sarah[2], Thomas[3], Thomas[4]), son of Thomas and Barbara (Byers) Thornburgh, b. 26 April, 1820; d——; *m.* Mary Staley (or Stanley), dau. of Stephen Staley. They soon afterward removed to Cabell Co., Va., and settled at Barboursville. The Thornburgs were Welsh and the Staleys German. Solomon was a farmer and merchant, and represented Cabell Co. in the Virginia Legislature. The Thornburgs came from Shepherdstown (W. Va. Hist. Mag., Oct., 1901, p. 27).

43. RACHAEL THORNBURGH (Thomas[1], Sarah[2], Hezekiah[3], John[4]), dau. of John and Jane (Abernathy) Thornburgh, b. ——; d. ——; *m.* her cousin Jeptha Thornburg (son of David Thornburgh). Issue:

56, Morgan; 57, Isaac; 58, Sarah.

44. ELIZABETH THORNBURGH (Thomas[1], Sarah[2], Hezekiah[3], John[4]), dau. of John and Jane (Abernathy) Thornburgh, b. ——; d. ——; *m.* her cousin Henry Shepherd Thornburgh (son of David). Issue:

59, Martin.

48. A daughter of Thomas Thornburgh (Thomas[1], Sarah[2], Hezekiah[3], Thomas[4]), b. ——; d. ——; *m.* —— Waddell. Issue:

60, Sarah E.

52. WILLIAM THORNBURGH (Thomas[1], Sarah[2], Hezekiah[3], David[4]), son of David and —— Thornburgh, b. ——; d. ——; *m.* Hattie Bush, of Ohio.

DESCENDANTS OF ELIZABETH SHEPHERD

59. Martin Thornburgh (Thomas[1], Sarah[2], Hezekiah[3], John[4], Elizabeth[5]), son of Henry Shepherd and Elizabeth (Thornburgh) Thornburgh, b. 1865, now living at Thornburgh Place, Triadelphia, Ohio Co., W. Va. Was formerly associated with James Pursell in a grocery business at Elm Grove, established by Moses Shepherd in the eighteenth century.

DESCENDANTS OF ELIZABETH SHEPHERD

III. Elizabeth Shepherd (Thomas[1]), dau. of Thomas and Elizabeth (Van Metre) Shepherd, b. Mecklenburg, Va., 2 or 3 Oct., 1738 O. S.; d. 1788; m. 3 May, 1762, William Brown, of Mecklenburg, Va., who was b. 13 Sept., 1724 O. S.; d. 24 July, 1801. (Probably son of Thomas Brown who d. *circa* 1756.) Issue:
    1, John, b. 16 Feb., 1763; 2, Elizabeth, b. 27 Dec., 1764; 3, Thos. Abraham, b. 25 Feb., 1767, d. Nov., 1768; 4, Mary, b. 15 Sept., 1768; 5, Sarah, b. Sept., 1771, d. 24 Jan., 1845; 6, William, b. 24 March, 1774, d. 29 May, 1774; 7, Shepherd, b. 14 April, 1775-6, d. 1817; 8, George W. (or Barry), b. 22 Oct., 1777, called " Barry Washington," living 1801; 9, Hannah Matilda, b. 11/22 Nov., 1781, m. Dr. Evans.

1. John Brown (Thomas[1], Elizabeth[2]), son of William and Elizabeth Shepherd Brown, b. Mecklenburg, Va., 16 Feb., 1763; d. ——; m. —— ——. According to a note in his father's day book, John was living on General Stephens's land in 1786. He is again mentioned in his father's books in 1794. His cousin, Moses Shepherd, writes, in 1778: "I am on my way to Williamsburg with my uncle Abraham."

4. Mary Brown (Thomas[1], Elizabeth[2]), dau. of William and Elizabeth (Shepherd) Brown, b. 15 Sept., 1768; d. —— 1812; m. 6 Feb., 1785, John Grove, a descendant of Hans Groff, sometime Baron Von Welden, of Switzerland, who fled to America in 1696 and some years later settled in the beautiful Pequea Valley in Lancaster Co., Pa. It was his son Jacob who became the ancestor of the numerous Grove families of Washington Co., Md. (History of Washington Co., Md., and Scharf's Western Md., Vol. II., p. 1218).
John Grove and his wife, Mary Brown, settled in western Pennsylvania, and reared a large family, where many of their descendants now live. Issue:
    10, Sarah, b. 13 Dec., 1785, m. Lemuel Hall; 11, Jacob, b. 29 Aug., 1787; 12, Elizabeth, b. 24 Sept., 1789, m. John Spark; 13, Catharine, b. 26 Jan., 1791, m. —— Auld; 14, Shepherd, b. 14 March, 1793; 15, John, b. 1 Feb.,

1795, *m.* Anna McGuilliams; 16, Parry, b. 2 Feb., 1797, *m.* Mary Sprinkle; 17, Levi, b. 6 Dec., 1798; 18, Hannah M., b. 1 Dec., 1800; *m.* Elias Parshall; 19, William Brown, b. 12 April, 1802, *m.* Nancy Allendar; 20, Stephen, b. 15 Feb., 1804, *m.* Ann Coldron; 21, Harvey, b. 19 Feb., 1806, *m.* Elizabeth Lackey; 22, Mary, b. 6 Jan., 1808; *m.* John Ground.

5. SARAH BROWN (Thomas[1], Elizabeth[2]), dau. of William and Elizabeth (Shepherd) Brown, b. 6/16 Sept., 1771; d. 24 Jan., 1845; *m.* 1795, William Eaty (supposed son of Rev. Henry and Christina (Lemon) Eaty; he was a soldier in the War of 1812; was wounded on Lake George; died 24 Jan., 1845. He is credited on William Brown's store books: Dec., 1800, for wheat delivered; and on 26 Feb., 1802, for expenses incurred in proving William Brown's will.   Issue:
23, Elizabeth, b. 25 Sept., 1797; 24, Henry, b. 23 Feb., 1800, d. 2 Aug., 1832, d. s.p.; 25, Hannah M., b. 5 Jan. or June, 1803, d. April, 1839; 26, Shepherd B., b. 25 Feb., 1805, d. 24 Dec., 1835/45, d. s.p.; 27, Susannah, b. 20 Dec., 1807, d. 2 April, 1865; 28, Abraham 'S., b. 5 Jan., 1811, d. s.p.

7. SHEPHERD BROWN was a merchant in New Orleans about 1825. Coming to Baltimore to buy goods he somehow fell out of a window and was killed (L. K. Hall, Greensboro, Pa., 1907).

10. SARAH GROVE (Thomas[1], Elizabeth[2], Mary[3]), dau. of John and Mary (Brown) Grove, b. 13 Dec., 1785; d. ——; *m.* Lemuel Hall, of Fayette Co., Pa.   Issue:
29, John, b. *circa* 1805, d. *circa* 1827; 30, Martha, b. 1807, *m.* Fred. Mestrezett; 31, James S., b. 1809, *m.* Elizabeth Steigner; 32, William, b. 1811, *m.* Isabella Graham; 33, Elizabeth, b. 1814, *unm.*, living 1907, age 93; 34, Mary, b. 1817, *m.* David Jenkins; 35, Matilda, b. 1820, *m.* Jacob Cove; 36, Leroy K., b. 22 Nov., 1824, *m.* Valinda A. Hennen.

11. JACOB GROVE (Thomas[1], Elizabeth[2], Mary[3]), son of John and Mary (Brown) Grove, b. 29 Aug., 1789; d. ——; *m.* —— ——.   Issue:
37, Rachael, *m.* —— Wilson; 38, Mary, *m.* —— Kelso, a Dunkard preacher; 39, John; 40, Kessia F.; 41, Hannah M., *m.* —— Allender.

12. ELIZABETH GROVE (Thomas[1], Elizabeth[2], Mary[3]), dau. of John and Mary (Brown) Grove, b. 24 Sept., 1789; d. ——; *m.* 1st John Sparks; *m.* 2d Thomas Schreyer.   Issue:
42, John Sparks; 43, Adaline Sparks; 44, Elizabeth Schreyer, *m.* Rev. —— Henderson, a Cumberland Presbyterian

minister, removed to Oregon; 45, Rebecca Schreyer, *m.* Dr. Miller, removed to Illinois; 46, Harvey Schreyer, *m.* —— ——, left family of girls.

13. CATHARINE GROVE (Thomas[1], Elizabeth[2], Mary[3]), dau. of John and Mary (Brown) Grove, b. 26 Jan., 1791; d. ——; *m.* James Auld. Issue:
47, John; 48, Mary, *m.* —— Sprinkle; 49, Adelaide, *m.* —— Nixon; 50, Elizabeth, *m.* —— Parshall; 51, Martha, *m.* —— Kelso; 52, James; 53, William; 54, David, *m.* Rhoda Jennings; 55, Hannah Coffman; 56, Catharine, *m.* —— Leidy; 57, Jane, *m.* —— Thompson.

16. PARRY GROVE (Thomas[1], Elizabeth[2], Mary[3]), son of John and Mary (Brown) Grove, b. 2 Feb., 1797; d. ——; *m.* Mary Sprinkle and removed to Ohio. Issue:
58, Melvina, *m.* —— Biery; 59, Elizabeth, *m.* —— Bryan; 60, Sarah; 61, Harvey, *m.* —— Bixler; 62, John, *m.* —— Gettig.

18. HANNAH MATILDA GROVE (Thomas[1], Elizabeth[2], Mary[3],). dau. of John and Mary (Brown) Grove, b. Masontown, Pa., 1 Sept., 1800; d. at McClellandstown, Pa., 28 April, 1881; *m.* 1817, Elias Parshall, Jr., who was b. *circa* 1796 and d. at McClellandstown, Pa., 4 July, 1882. Issue:
63, Vincent, b. 12 Dec., 1817, d. 25 May, 1898; 64, Harvey, b. 19 July, 1819, d. 5 June, 1822; 65, William Grove, b. Sept., 1821, d. 4 July, 1883; 66, Reuben, b. 9 Nov., 1823, d. 26 April, 1884, *unm.*; 67, Emily, b. 25 Sept., 1825, d. 12 June, 1902; 68, Mary, b. 30 Aug., 1827, d. 10 July, 1906; 69, James M., b. 12 Aug., 1829, d. 11 Feb., 1903; 70, Maria, b. 7 May, 1831, d. 16 Sept., 1873, *m.* Wm. Porter, no issue; 71, Hamilton, b. 10 Jan., 1833, d. 2 Oct., 1833; 72, Nelson, b. 23 Feb., 1834, d. 2 July, 1834; 73, Elizabeth, b. 9 March, 1836; 74, Caroline, b. 27 Jan., 1838; 75, Hannah M., b. 2 Feb., 1840, d. 28 Oct., 1844; 76, Stephen Colvin, b. 13 Feb., 1842, d. 9 Nov., 1844; 77, Sarah Helen, b. 11 Oct., 1844, *m.* 4 Jan., 1882, Melancthon J. Crow, no issue; 78, Louretta, b. 17 Aug., 1845.

20. STEPHEN GROVE (Thomas[1], Elizabeth[2], Mary[3]), son of John and Mary (Brown) Grove, b. 15 Feb., 1804; d. —— *m.* Elizabeth Ann Coldron, of German Township, Fayette Co., Pa. Stephen Grove was auditor of German Township, in 1842. Family moved to Ohio, thence to Indiana. Issue:
79, Mary; 80, Hannah M.; 81, Emma; 82, John; 83, Eleanor; 84, William; 85, Calvin; 86, Miles.

21. HARVEY GROVE (Thomas[1], Elizabeth[2], Mary[3]), son of John and Mary (Brown) Grove, b. 19 Feb., 1806, d. ——; *m.* Eliza-

beth Leckey, dau. of Thomas Leckey, of German Township.
Harvey was school director from 1857-62; and two terms assessor, *circa* 1843. Issue:
87, Mary Louise, *m.* Geo. W. Hess; 88, Hannah M.; 89, Naomi,
m. Aaron Moore; 90, Reuben, *m.* Hettie C. Higgen-
botham; 91, Rhoda; 92, Elizabeth, *m.* 1st William
Jeffreys, 2d Henry Coonley; 93, Mary.

22. MARY GROVE (Thomas[1], Elizabeth[2], Mary[3]), dau. of John
and Mary (Brown) Grove, b. 6 Jan., 1808; d. ——; *m.* 1st John
Grund; *m.* 2d —— Immell. The family moved first to Ohio and
later to Indiana. Issue:
94, Hannah M.; 95, Mary; 96, Jefferson; 97, George; 98, James.

23. ELIZABETH EATY (Thomas[1], Elizabeth[2], Sarah[3]), dau. of
William and Sarah (Brown) Eaty, b. 25 Sept., 1797; d. ——; *m.*
15 Aug., 1816, Peraquin Greenwood, b. 22 July, 1790, son of
Benjamin and Elizabeth Greenwood, of Shepherdstown, Va. Issue:
99, Benjamin H., b. 20 Oct., 1819, d. ——, 1851; 100, James
W., b. 28 Jan., 1821, d. 21 June, 1903; 101, Sally Ann,
b. 30 April, 1823, d. 21 Jan., 1888, *m.* —— Loshorn;
102, Sebastian E., b. 10 Aug., 1825, d. 1 June, 1869; 103,
Matilda, b. Feb., 1828, d. 13 May, 1889; 104, Shepherd
MacDonald, b. 13 Nov., 1831, d. s.p.

25. HANNAH MATILDA EATY (Thomas[1], Elizabeth[2], Sarah[3]),
dau. William and Sarah (Brown) Eaty, b. 5 June, 1803, d. April,
1839; *m.* —— Gommerd and moved to western Pennsylvania.

27. SUSANNAH EATY (Thomas[1], Elizabeth[2], Sarah[3]), dau. of
William and Sarah (Brown) Eaty, b. 20 Dec., 1807; d. 2 April,
1865; *m.* 11 Dec., 1832, John George Unseld, son of John and
Mary (Haines) Unseld, of Shepherdstown, Va. Issue:
105, Henry, b. 9 Oct., 1833; 106, George Montgomery,
d. in childhood; 107, John George, Jr., b. 17 March,
1838, living 1904; 108, Benjamin Collins, b. 18 Oct.,
1843; d. ——.

36. LEROY K. HALL (Thomas[1], Elizabeth[2], Mary[3], Sarah[4]), son
of Lemuel and Sarah Grove Hall, b. 22 Nov., 1824; d. ——; *m.*
3 July, 1851, Valinda A. Hennen, b. 1829. Issue:
109, E. Grove, b. 26 March, 1853; 110, Emma F., b. 8 Nov.,
1854; 111, Ella Virginia, b. 14 Nov., 1856; 112, Catharine Hennen, b. 28 Nov., 1858; 113, Sarah E., b. 23
Jan., 1865; 114, William Lee, b. —, 1866, d. *unm.*,
resided in Chicago, Ill.; 115, Fred A., b. 22 Feb., 1869;
116, George B., b. 8 Feb., 1871.

54. DAVID AULD (Thomas[1], Elizabeth[2], Mary[3], Catharine[4]),
son of James and Catharine (Grove) Auld, b. ——; d. 3 April,
1887; *m.* 28 Oct., 1841, Rhoda Jennings, b. ——; d. 8 June, 1883.
Issue:

117, Porter, b. ——, d. 19 Dec., 1906, *m.* and left issue; 118, Vincent P., b. ——, d. 9 June, 1851; 119, Amanda S.; 120, Hannah M., b. ——, d. 2 July, 1884.

63. VINCENT PARSHALL (Thomas[1], Elizabeth[2], Mary[3], Hannah M.[4]), son of Elias, Jr., and Hannah M. (Grove) Parshall, b. 12 Dec., 1817; d. 25 May, 1898; *m.* 23 Feb., 1843, Ann Eliza Crow, of Berryville, Va.   Issue:
    121, Hannah M., b. 14 May, 1844, *unm.;* 122, Laura, b. 10 May, 1846, *m.* Silas F. Baughman; 123, Nancy Louise, b. 16 June, 1847, *unm.;* 124, Elias Calvin, b. 15 Oct., 1849, d. 16 Dec., 1901; 125, Isaac Hamilton, b. 22 Sept., 1851, *m.* Francis Palmer, 7 Feb., 1878; 126, Mary E., *unm.;* 127, James Worthington.

65. WILLIAM GROVE PARSHALL (Thomas[1], Elizabeth[2], Mary[3], Hannah M.[4]), son of Elias, Jr., and Hannah M. (Grove) Parshall, b. Sept., 1821; d. 4 July, 1883; *m.* April, 1864, Martha A. Hawks.   Issue:
    128, Wm. Worthington, b. 18 June, 1866, *m.* 11 June, 1902, Amelia Baldwin; 129, Louise P., d. inf.; 130, Delafield, d. inf.; 131, Emily, b. 8 Nov., 1875, d. ——, *m.* 11 Oct., 1899, Frank R. Crow; 132, Vesta, d. aged 12 years.

67. EMILY PARSHALL (Thomas[1], Elizabeth[2], Mary[3], Hannah M.[4]), dau. of Elias, Jr., and Hannah M. (Grove) Parshall, b. 25 Sept., 1825; d. 12 June, 1902; *m.* 11 Dec., 1845, John T. Worthington.   Issue:
    133, Hannah M., b. 1849, *m.* 22 Aug., 1883, George E. Pomeroy, Toledo, O.

68. MARY PARSHALL (Thomas[1], Elizabeth[2], Mary[3], Hannah M.[4]), dau. of Elias, Jr., and Hannah M. (Grove) Parshall, b. 30 Aug., 1827; d. 10 July, 1906; *m.* 27 Dec., 1849, Thomas W. Lyons, of Uniontown, Pa.   Issue:
    134, Oliver Grove, b. 18 April, 1851, d. 14 Aug., 1864; 135, Ella Caroline, b. 8 Nov., 1854, d. 10 April, 1896; 136, Hannah M., b. 12 May, 1861, *m.* Frank Snider; 137, Elizabeth Lee, d. inf.; 138, William John, b. ——, d. 29 Oct., 1868, *m.* Emma Lynn.

69. JAMES M. PARSHALL (Thomas[1], Elizabeth[2], Mary[3], Hannah M.[4]), son of Elias, Jr., and Hannah M. (Grove) Parshall, b. 22 Aug., 1829; d. 11 Feb., 1903; *m.* 22 Dec., 1865, Mary Higginbotham.   Issue:
    139, William James, b. 22 June, 1867; 140, Robert Vincent, *m.* Annie McCain.

73. ELIZABETH PARSHALL (Thomas[1], Elizabeth[2], Mary[3], Hannah M.[4]), dau. of Elias, Jr., and Hannah M. (Grove) Parshall; b. 9 March, 1836; *m.* 9 May, 1861, George Porter, of Uniontown, Pa.   Issue:

141, Elizabeth, b. 23 May, 1862; 142, Edward Tiffen, b. 3
April, 1866, *m.* Julia McShane; 143, George, *m.* 28 May,
1900, Mary Moore.

74. CAROLINE PARSHALL (Thomas[1], Elizabeth[2], Mary[3], Hannah
M.[4]), dau. of Elias, Jr., and Hannah M. (Grove) Parshall, b. 27
Jan., 1838; *m.* 9 April, 1856, Thomas N. Wiltner, of McKeesport,
Pa.   Issue:
    144, John Seaton, b. 24 Jan., 1857, *m.* Cordelia Ramage; 145,
    Reuben Parshall, b. 6 April, 1859, *m.* Tenona Alle-
    baugh; 146, Florence, b. 15 Dec., 1865; *m.* Wm. A.
    Applegate; 147, Frank, b. 15 Sept., 1870, *m.* Jennie Mc-
    Combs; 148, Wm. Worthington, b. 24 March, 1873, *m.*
    Maud Morris; 149, Helen, b. 14 April, 1877, *m.* 1st
    Samuel Gwynne, 2d William Wirt.

78. LOURETTA PARSHALL (Thomas[1], Elizabeth[2], Mary[3], Hannah
M.[4]), dau. of Elias, Jr., and Hannah M. (Grove) Parshall, b. 17
Aug., 1845; *m.* 14 Nov., 1872, Dr. George W. Neff, of Mason-
town, Pa.   Issue:
    150, Robley P., b. 21 Jan., 1874, d. 6 Aug., 1874; 151, Hannah
    M., b. 12 Feb., 1875, *m.* 26 June, 1906, Norman Powell;
    152, Mary Anne, b. 5 June, 1877, d. ——; *m.* William
    White; 153, Louretta Parshall, b. 11 Nov., 1879, *m.*
    Chester Lingle; 154, Elizabeth Porter, b. 21 March,
    1882; *m.* Harold Stevens.

87. MARY LOUISE GROVE (Thomas[1], Elizabeth[2], Mary[3], Harvey[4]), dau. of Harvey and Elizabeth (Leckey) Grove, b. ——; d.
——; *m.* George W. Hess. He was prominently identified with
stock-raising, mercantile business and banking. At the time of
his death he was the holder of much valuable real estate and coal
lands.   Issue:
    155, Laura Bell, *m.* Monroe M. Hopwood; 156, John Ellsworth,
    m. Lida Jeffries.

89. NAOMI GROVE (Thomas[1], Elizabeth[2], Mary[3], Harvey[4]),
dau. of Harvey and Elizabeth (Leckey) Grove, b. ——; d. ——;
m. Aaron Moore, of Redstone Township, Fayette Co., Pa. He
was a farmer and stock-breeder.   Issue:
    157, Mary, *m.* George Porter, Jr.; 158, Harry; 159, Charles,
    unm.

90. REUBEN GROVE (Thomas[1], Elizabeth[2], Mary[3], Harvey[4]),
son of Harvey and Elizabeth (Leckey) Grove, b. ——; d. ——;
m. Hettie C. Higginbotham, of Redstone Township, Fayette Co.,
Pa. He was assessor of German Township, Fayette Co., Pa.,
1868.   Issue:
    160, William E., *m.* Martha McShane; 161, Annie, *m.* Joseph
    Acklin; 162, Ettie C., *m.* Frank Jamison; 163, Minnie
    A., *m.* Robert McLaughlin; 164, Corena B.; 165, Reuben

O., Jr., *m.* Maud Vernon; 166, Harvey E.; 167, Frank
L.; 168, Uriah H.; 169, Bertha.

92. ELIZABETH GROVE (Thomas[1], Elizabeth[2], Mary[3], Harvey[4]),
dau. of Harvey and Elizabeth (Leckey) Grove, b. ——; d. ——;
m. 1st William Jeffries, of German Township, Fayette Co., Pa.
They removed to Dwight, Ill. After her first husband's death
she *m.* 2d Henry Coonley (no issue).   Issue (Jeffries):
170, Ettie; 171, Lonnie; 172, William; 173, Norvel.

100. JAMES W. GREENWOOD (Thomas[1], Elizabeth[2], Sarah[3],
Elizabeth[4]), son of Peraquin and Elizabeth (Eaty) Greenwood,
b. 28 Jan., 1821; d. 22 June, 1903; *m.* [Betsey Eaty(?)]. Issue:
  174, James W.; 175, Shepherd L., *m.* 1870, Ellen L. Byers,
  resides at Bedington, Va.; 176, Thomas C.; 177, Benjamin E.; 178, C. Frank, *m.* 14 June, 1887, Mary C.
  Trayman; 179, Margaret.

101. SALLY ANN GREENWOOD (Thomas[1], Elizabeth[2], Sarah[3],
  Elizabeth[4]), dau. of Peraquin and Elizabeth (Eaty)
Greenwood, b. 30 April, 1823; d. 21 Jan., 1888; *m.* 1st —— Bill-
myer; *m.* 2d —— Orndorff.   Issue:
  180, Thomas Billmyer; 181, Charles Billmyer; 182, William
  Billmyer; 183, Shepherd Orndorff.

107. JOHN GEORGE UNSELD, JR. (Thomas[1], Elizabeth[2], Sarah[3],
Susannah[4]), son of John George and Susannah (Eaty) Unseld,
b. 17 March, 1838; *m.* 3 Feb., 1881, Emma Jane Ronemous.
                                                    Issue:
  184, George Peterlain, b. 12 Nov., 1881, *unm.*, living at Shepherdstown, W. Va.

109. EUGENE GROVE HALL (Thomas[1], Elizabeth[2], Mary[3],
Sarah[4], Leroy K.[5]), son of Leroy K. and Valinda A. (Hennen)
Hall, b. 26 March, 1853; *m.* 1st Flora Yeager, 25 Sept., 1879; *m.*
2d Kate Springer; resides at Connellsville, Pa.   Issue:
  185, Charles S., cashier Broad Street National Bank, Scottdale,
  Pa.; 186, Eugene G., Jr.

110. EMMA F. HALL (Thomas[1], Elizabeth[2], Mary[3], Sarah[4],
Leroy K.[5]), dau. of Leroy K. and Valinda A. (Hennen) Hall,
b. 8 Nov., 1854; d. ——; *m.* 26 Sept., 1875, Samuel Blackburn,
of Woodstock, Ill.   Issue:
  187, Ethel; 188, Chester.

111. ELLA VIRGINIA HALL (Thomas[1], Elizabeth[2], Mary[3], Sarah[4],
Leroy K.[5]), dau. of Leroy K. and Valinda A. (Hennen) Hall, b.
14 Nov., 1856; *m.* William Edgar Moore, Dec., 1880. Resides
at Fairchance, Fayette Co., Pa.   Issue:
  189, A. Harmer Grove, b. ——; assistant cashier and director
  Fairchance National Bank; 190, Flora, *m.* —— Har-
  stead, of Fairchance, Pa.; 191, Susie, *unm.*, teacher;
  192, Fannie; 193, Bertha; 194, Arthur.

112. CATHARINE HALL (Thomas[1], Elizabeth[2], Mary[3], Sarah[4], Leroy K.[5]), dau. of Leroy K. and Valinda A. (Hennen) Hall, b. 28 Nov., 1858; m. 14 July, 1881, Rev. Thomas I. Collings, of Spokane, Washington.   Issue:
195, Ira V.; 196, Leroy Collins.

113. SARAH ELIZABETH HALL (Thomas[1], Elizabeth[2], Mary[3], Sarah[4], Leroy K.[5]), dau. of Leroy K. and Valinda A. (Hennen) Hall, b. 23 Jan., 1865; m. 1st Frederick A. Hallock, 7 Oct., 1890; 2d E. W. Mills.   Issue:
197, Florence E. Hallock.

115. FRED A. HALL (Thomas[1], Elizabeth[2], Mary[3], Sarah[4], Leroy K.[5]), son of Leroy K. and Valinda A. (Hennen) Hall, b. 22 Feb., 1869; m. 14 May, 1891, Ella Sue Palmer. Resides at Minneapolis, Minn.   Issue:
198, Gertrude; 199, Helen.

116. GEORGE B. HALL (Thomas[1], Elizabeth[2], Mary[3], Sarah[4], Leroy K.[5]), son of Leroy K. and Valinda A. (Hennen) Hall, b. 8 Feb., 1871; m. Alice Donifer (now deceased), 3 July, 1896. Resides at Rose Hill Cemetery, Chicago, Ill. Issue two children:
200, 201.

117. PORTER AULD (Thomas[1], Elizabeth[2], Mary[3], Catharine[4], David[5]), son of David and Rhoda (Jennings) Auld, b. ——; d. 19 Dec., 1908.   Issue:
202, David; 203, Vincent P.; 204, Arthur.

119. AMANDA S. AULD (Thomas[1], Elizabeth[2], Mary[3], Catharine[4], David[5]), dau. of David and Rhoda (Jennings) Auld, m. Alexander D. Foster.   Issue:
205, Bertie M., m. Ed. P. Junker; 206, David A., m. Elva Coon;
     207, Samuel D., m. Charlotta Adams; 208, Edwin A.,
     unm.

125. ISAAC HAMILTON PARSHALL (Thomas[1], Elizabeth[2], Mary[3], Hannah M.[4], Vincent[5]), son of Vincent and Ann E. (Crow) Parshall, b. 22 Sept., 1851; m. 7 Feb., 1878, Frances Palmer. Issue:
209, Ralph; 210, Vernon; 211, Leo; 212, Mabel; 213, Blanche;
     214, Raymond.

128. WILLIAM WORTHINGTON PARSHALL (Thomas[1], Elizabeth[2], Mary[3], Hannah M.[4], William G.[5]), son of William Grove and Martha A. (Hawke) Parshall, of Uniontown, Pa., b. 18 June, 1866; m. 11 June, 1902, Amelia Baldwin.   Issue:
215, William; 216, Louisa.

131. EMILY PARSHALL (Thomas[1], Elizabeth[2], Mary[3], Hannah M.[4], William G.[5]), dau. of William Grove and Martha A. (Hawks) Parshall, b. 8 Nov., 1875; m. 11 Oct., 1899, Frank R. Crow. Issue:
217, Martha; 218, Francis.

DESCENDANTS OF ELIZABETH SHEPHERD

135. ELLA CAROLINE LYONS (Thomas¹, Elizabeth², Mary³, Hannah M.⁴, Mary⁵). dau of Thos. W. and Mary (Parshall) Lyons, b. 8 Nov., 1854; d. 10 April, 1896; *m.* 25 Dec., 1878, Daniel P. Morgan.   Issue:
219, Alice, b. 28 Oct., 1879, *m.* E. S. Browne; 220, Etta, b. 23 July, 1881; 221, Howard W., b. 16 July, 1883; 222, Thos. W., Jr., b. 25 Aug., 1885; 223, Daniel S., b. 10 June, 1900; 224, George Neff, b. 29 March, 1896.

136. HANNAH MATILDA LYONS (Thomas¹, Elizabeth², Mary³, Hannah M.⁴, Mary⁵), dau. of Thomas W. and Mary (Parshall) Lyons, b. 12 May, 1861; d. ——; *m.* 3 Sept., 1890, Frank Snider.
                                                          Issue:
225, Joseph L., b. 25 Aug., 1894; 226, Mary L., 227, Marguerite L., twins, b. 20 Dec., 1895; 228, Thomas W., b. 13 June, 1897; d. 24 July, 1898; 229, Frank L., b. 30 Aug., 1898.

138. WILLIAM JOHN LYONS (Thomas¹, Elizabeth², Mary³, Hannah M.⁴, Mary⁵), son of Thos. W. and Mary (Parshall) Lyons, b. 29 Oct., 1868; b. ——; d. ——; *m.* 11 July, 1895, Emma Lynn.   Issue:
230, infant; 231, Mary, b. 21 June, 1897; 232, Etta, b. 27 Oct., 1898; 233, Gertrude, b. 16 May, 1900; 234, Hannah, b. 27 Aug., 1902; 235, Thomas, b. 9 July, 1904; 236, James Lynn, b. 8 July, 1906.

139. WILLIAM JAMES PARSHALL (Thomas¹, Elizabeth², Mary³, Hannah M.⁴, James M.⁵), son of James M. and Mary (Higginbotham) Parshall, b. 22 June, 1867; d. ——; *m.* —— ——, Uniontown, Pa.   Issue:
237, James M.; 238, Mary; 239, Cox.

140. ROBERT VINCENT PARSHALL (Thomas¹, Elizabeth², Mary³, Hannah M.⁴, James M.⁵), son of James M. and Mary (Higginbotham) Parshall; b. ——; d. ——; *m.* 21 March, 1898, Carrie McCain.   Issue:
240, Robert; 241, a dau.

141. ELIZABETH PORTER (Thomas¹, Elizabeth², Mary³, Hannah M.⁴, Elizabeth⁵), dau. of George and Elizabeth (Parshall) Porter, b. 23 May, 1862; d. ——; *m.* June, 1888, —— ——.   Issue:
242, Geo. Ewing Porter, b. 9 March, 1889; 243, Mildred Elizabeth, b. 9 March, 1891; 244, Sara Constance, b. 23 Feb., 1893; 245, Mary Caroline, b. 26 March, 1897; 246, Alice Trevor, b. April, 1899; 247, Cecil William.

142. EDWARD TIFFIN PORTER (Thomas¹, Elizabeth², Mary³, Hannah M.⁴, Elizabeth⁵), son of George and Elizabeth (Parshall) Porter, b. 3 April, 1866; d. ——; *m.* 21 March, 1894, Julia McShane.   Issue:
248, George, b. 2 Feb., 1896; 249, Edward Tiffin, Jr., b. Jan., 1900.

144. JOHN SEATON WILTNER (Thomas[1], Elizabeth[2], Mary[3], Hannah M.[4], Caroline[5]), son of Thomas N. and Caroline (Parshall) Wiltner, b. 24 Jan., 1857; d. ——; *m.* 9 April, 1878, Cordelia Ramage. Issue:

250, Helen; 251, Wayne; 252, George, deceased.

145. REUBEN PARSHALL WILTNER (Thomas[1], Elizabeth[2], Mary[3], Hannah M.[4], Caroline[5]), son of Thomas N. and Caroline (Parshall) Wiltner, b. 6 April, 1859; d. ——; *m.* Terrona Allebaugh. Issue:

253, Louretta; 254, George; 255, Caroline.

146. FLORENCE WILTNER (Thomas[1], Elizabeth[2], Mary[3], Hannah M.[4], Caroline[5]), dau. of Thos. N. and Caroline (Parshall) Wiltner, b. 15 Dec., 1865; d. ——; *m.* 1893, William A. Applegate, of McKeesport, Pa. Issue:

256, Corrine; 257, Florence; 258, Caroline; 259, William.

147. FRANK WILTNER (Thomas[1], Elizabeth[2], Mary[3], Hannah M.[4], Caroline[5]), son of Thos. N. and Caroline (Parshall) Wiltner, b. 15 Sept., 1870; d. ——; *m.* 18 Sept., 1895, Jennie McCombs. Issue:

260, Guy Carlton; 261, Ernest Rupert; 262, Clifford; 263, 264, 265.

148. WILLIAM WORTHINGTON WILTNER (Thomas[1], Elizabeth[2], Mary[3], Hannah M.[4], Caroline[5]), son of Thos. N. and Caroline (Parshall) Wiltner, b. 24 March, 1873; d. ——; *m.* 6 March, 1893, Maud Morris. Issue:

266, Nina Davis; 267, Edgar Pomeroy; 268, Harold.

149. HELEN WILTNER (Thomas[1], Elizabeth[2], Mary[3], Hannah M.[4], Caroline[5]), dau. of Thos. N. and Caroline (Parshall) Wiltner, b. 14 April, 1877; d. ——; *m.* 1st 2 Feb., 1899, Samuel Gwynne; *m.* 2d William Wirt. Issue:

269, Marion Wirt; 270.

152. MARY ANN NEFF (Thomas[1], Elizabeth[2], Mary[3], Hannah M.[4], Louretta[5]), dau. of Dr. George W. and Louretta (Parshall) Neff, b. 5 June, 1877; d. ——; *m.* William White. Issue:

271, Mary Harriet.

153. LOURETTA PARSHALL NEFF (Thomas[1], Elizabeth[2], Mary[3], Hannah M.[4], Louretta[5]), dau. of Dr. George W. and Louretta (Parshall) Neff, b. 11 Nov., 1879; d. ——; *m.* Chester Lingle. Issue:

272, Louretta; 273, Gertrude.

154. ELIZABETH PORTER NEFF (Thomas[1], Elizabeth[2], Mary[3], Hannah M.[4], Louretta[5]), dau. of Dr. George W. and Louretta (Parshall) Neff, b. 21 March, 1882; d. ——; *m.* Harold Stevens. Issue:

274, Elizabeth.

155. LAURA BELL HESS (Thomas[1], Elizabeth[2], Mary[3], Harvey[4], Mary L.[5]), dau. of George W. and Mary L. (Grove) Hess, b. ——; d. ——; m. Monroe Moreland Hopwood, attorney-at-law, Uniontown, Pa. Issue: 276, Harold Ellsworth; 277, Eleanor Mary.

156. JOHN ELLSWORTH HESS (Thomas[1], Elizabeth[2], Mary[3], Harvey[4], Mary L.[5]), son of George W. and Mary L. (Grove) Hess, b. ——; d. ——; m. Lida Jeffries. Issue: 278, Walter M.; 279, Laura M.; 280, George W.

157. MARY MOORE (Thomas[1], Elizabeth[2], Mary[3], Harvey[4], Naomi[5]), dau. of Aaron and Naomi (Grove) Moore, of Redstone, Pa., b. ——; d. ——; m. George Porter, Jr., of Uniontown, Pa., electrical mining engineer.

159. CHARLES MOORE (Thomas[1], Elizabeth[2], Mary[3], Harvey[4], Naomi[5]), son of Aaron and Naomi (Grove) Moore, b. ——; d. ——; m. Mary Seaton. Issue: 281, Wendell.

160. WILLIAM E. GROVE (Thomas[1], Elizabeth[2], Mary[3], Harvey[4], Reuben[5]), son of Reuben and Hettie C. (Higginbotham) Grove, b. ——; d. ——; m. Martha McShane. Issue: 282, Mary; 283, Grace; 284, Porter; 285, Carl.

174. JAMES W. GREENWOOD (Thomas[1], Elizabeth[2], Sarah[3], Elizabeth[4], James W.[5]), son of James W. and —— —— Greenwood, b. ——; d. ——; m. 19 Dec., 1871, Mary Unseld. Issue: 286, Harry S., b. 14 Nov., 1872; 287, Harvey H., b. 30 Dec., 1876; 288, Clara B., b. 25 April, 1880.

176. THOMAS C. GREENWOOD (Thomas[1], Elizabeth[2], Sarah[3], Elizabeth[4], James W.[5]), son of James W. and —— —— Greenwood, b. ——; d. ——; m. Sept. 2, 1884, Catharine Waters; resides at Roanoke, Va. Issue: 289, Milford, b. 2 July, 1887, d. 11 Nov., 1894; 290, Anna M., b. 11 July, 1889; 291, Laura, b. 4 March, 1892; 292, H. Lawrence, b. 7 Oct., 1896; 293, H. Wellman, b. 4 April, 1898.

177. BENJAMIN E. GREENWOOD (Thomas[1], Elizabeth[2], Sarah[3], Elizabeth[4], James M.[5]), son of James W. and —— —— Greenwood, b. ——; d. ——; m. 23 Dec., 1889, Rosa V. Lumbert; living at Portsmouth, Va. Issue: 294, Lillian M., b. 18 Oct., 1890, d. 15 Aug., 1894; 295, Edna L., b. 4 Nov., 1893, d. 28 July, 1894; 296, Raymond R., b. 26 July, 1895.

179. MARGARET E. GREENWOOD (Thomas[1], Elizabeth[2], Sarah[3], Elizabeth[4], James W.[5]), dau. of James W. and —— —— Greenwood, b. ——; d. ——; m. 27 Sept., 1881, T. B. Miller; lives at Roanoke, Va. Issue: 297, Edward S., b. 2 Jan., 1882.

219. ALICE LYONS MORGAN (Thomas[1], Elizabeth[2], Mary[3], Hannah M.[4], Mary[5], Ella Caroline[6]), dau. of Daniel P. and Ella Caroline (Lyons) Morgan, b. 28 Oct., 1879; d. ——; *m.* July, 1898, E. D. Browne.   Issue:
297, Morgan; 298, Louretta.

WILLIAM SHEPHERD

IV. WILLIAM SHEPHERD, third son of Captain Thomas and Elizabeth (Van Metre) Shepherd, born in Mecklenburg, 1737, married Mary Clark (who was probably a daughter of the sister of William Clark, schoolmaster at Shepherdstown, 1793). In his father's will dated 1776, William is referred to as "being abroad," meaning doubtless that he was absent from home with the militia then in active duty along the western frontiers of Virginia. It was probably to this William Shepherd that a warrant was issued, dated Feb. 24, 1776, at Williamsburg to a William Shepherd for £3. 13. 0. express hire (Am. Hist. Reg., Vol. II., p. 858). This probably reveals the cause of his "being abroad" and the line of duty upon which he was engaged. Thomas Shepherd bequeathed to his son William a tract of 104 acres of ground out of the Fairfax grant of 1751, and three towns lots in the town of Mecklenburg, Nos. 83, 84 and 85. The first official record referring to William Shepherd is that of his appointment as a juryman by the Berkeley County Court, March 17, 1773, and also as one of the viewers of a road to be laid out from Robert Buckle's to Hall's Mills. I take this to mean a highway from the Rattling Springs property on the Potomac above Harper's Ferry to the Shenandoah, where Hall's rifle works subsequently were located. In the same year he is found in company with his uncle, Henry Van Metre (6 April, 1773), in the disputed territory of Pennsylvania and Virginia—Westmoreland County. Both their names appear upon the court records of that county (History of Westmoreland Co., Pa., p. 58). After his father's decease he removed to the Indian country, as the western shores of the Ohio were then called, and settled among his friends on Wheeling Creek, one mile above where his nephew, Moses Shepherd, afterward lived. In the new country he became a surveyor and was often engaged in this line of work. Like his brother, he was an earnest participant in the military affairs of the border and at various periods his name appears on the militia rosters of Ohio County. In 1778 he was fined 54 pounds of flour (Shepherd Papers, Vol. IV., p. 63). In Dec., 1779, his name appears as a private on the roll of Col. Benjamin Flower's regiment and connected with the department of Military Stores (Pa. Arch., 2d Ser., Vol. XV., p. 383), and is rated among the taxables of Ohio County, Va., for 1784 (History Pan Handle Counties of West

Virginia, p. 161). At some period during the progress of the Indian troubles along the Ohio he obtained from, and receipted to his brother, Col. David Shepherd, for "Rifle No. 66 and a shot bag" (Shepherd Papers).

In 1787 William Shepherd's name appears upon the muster roll of Captain Lewis Bonnett's company of militia, and on Dec. 22d of that year David Shepherd makes him the assignee for 1,000 acres of land by virtue of a Pre-emption Warrant No. 2487 granted to said Shepherd 23 June, 1783, assignee of David Duncan, who was assignee of Jacob Van Metre, lands situated in Ohio County on waters of Little Wheeling. Two days later, 24 Dec., 1787, there was granted to William Shepherd 925 acres of land, by virtue of an entry on a Pre-emption Certificate No. 2507, granted Robert Woods for 1,000 acres situate in Ohio County, on waters of Wheeling where a small branch falls into Wheeling Creek, and corners to lands of John Feay and David Shepherd (see Survey Book No. 2, pp. 87 et seq., Wheeling, W. Va.).

In 1779 William Shepherd reappears in Mecklenburg, a fact mentioned by his brother Abraham in a letter to another brother, Col. David Shepherd; and while there William signed deeds for a transfer of some property which was recorded at Martinsburg. In 1791 his name again appears on the pay rolls of the militia of Ohio County under date of October 21. By indenture dated 6 Nov., 1794, William Shepherd, of Ohio Co., Va., conveys to William Stephenson, also of Ohio County, Va., a tract of 112 acres situate in Ohio Co., Va., part of a larger tract granted to William Shepherd, 27 Oct., 1785. The witnesses thereto were: Solomon and Elizabeth Nighswanger and John Clark. William Shepherd is a witness to deed of conveyance dated 29 Jan., 1795, from David Shepherd to his grandson, Francis Duke, for 42 acres of land on Short Creek; and on the tax list for 1802 in Ohio County this item is found: "Wm. Shepherd Dr. to Flour 108 lbs. £6. 6. 8."

DESCENDANTS OF WILLIAM SHEPHERD

IV. WILLIAM SHEPHERD, son of Thomas and Elizabeth (Van Metre) Shepherd, b. sup. Mecklenburg, Va., 1739; d. —, 1824, at Wheeling, Ohio Co., Va., aged 87 years; m. Mary Clark (sup. dau. of William Clark, of Mecklenburg, Va., schoolmaster). This family later (after 1776) removed to Ohio River.   Issue:
   1, Thomas; 2, William, b. March 1769 (in Sussex Co., N. J.?), d. 4 June, 1833, in Putnam Co., Ind.; 3, Sarah, d. inf.; 4, Sarah, b. 25 Dec., 1777, d. 23 Oct., 1822; 5, Elizabeth, m. Mr. Willitts and lived in Chillicothe Co., O., in 1827; 6, Ruhamah, b. 23 Oct., 1778, d. 23 Nov., 1831.

1. THOMAS SHEPHERD (Thomas[1], William[2]), son of William and Mary (Clark) Shepherd, b. ——, d. ——; m. —— ——. They emigrated to Ross Co., O.; he died in Shepherdstown, Va.

Issue:

7, Joseph, b. 10 July, 1786, d. 2 Aug., 1858, m. Polly Betz (or Bates); 8, David, m. Elizabeth Bates, 1802; 9, James, m. Frances Daily, 1804; 10, John, d. Galliopolis, m. Betsey Van Metre; 11, Sarah, m. John Mills; 12, Mary, m. James Wiley.

2. WILLIAM SHEPHERD (Thomas[1], William[2]), son of William and Mary (Clark) Shepherd, b. (sup.) Sussex Co., N. J., March, 1769; d. Putnam Co., Ind., 4 June, 1833; m. 15 Oct., 1792, " at House of William Shepherd on Patterson's Creek, Va." He served in Corps of Artificers, Continental troops of New Jersey, as a private, from 1 April, 1780, to 1 Aug., 1782, granted pension in 1819; m. 1st Eleanor Peck, b. 15 May, 1771, d. 29 Aug., 1829 (?); m. 2d Mary Henthorne. Issue:

13, Jonathan, b. 12 Oct., 1794; 14 Lewis, b. 27 Dec., 1797; 15, Thomas, b. 26 Feb., 1799; 16, Lewis, b. 15 Jan., 1800; 17, John, b. 18 Oct., 1801, m. 25 Dec., 1832, Harriet Bonnet (Wheeling Records); 18, David, b. 14 Oct., 1803; 19, William, 20, Eleanor, twins, b. 11 May, 1806; 21, Elizabeth, b. 16 Nov., 1812, m. —— Paul; 22, Mary, b. 10 March, 1813; m. —— Ming; 23, Sarah, b. 15 July, 1815, m. —— Newhall; 24, Henry, b. 16 June, 1817 (see Wheeling Records); 25, Eleanor, b. ——. Among those who were pioneers in Wirt Co., Va., he came from the South Branch of the Potomac in 1796 (?) and settled where the town of Elizabeth now stands (Lewis' History of West Virginia, p. 698).

From sworn statement of Lewis Cheney, J. P., Clinton Co., Ind., 18 Oct., 1850.

4. SARAH SHEPHERD (Thomas[1], William[2]), dau. of William and Mary (Clark) Shepherd, b. 25 Dec., 1777; d. 23 Oct., 1822; m. Benjamin Mills, of Wheeling, son of Levi and Elizabeth (Dunn) Mills, 25 April, 1796. They lived first at Wheeling, but later removed to Morgan Co., Ind., where Benjamin and Sarah Mills are buried. In William Brown's account books there is this entry: " 1789, Aug. 26, Received of Wm. Brown 10 gold rings and 10 coverlids for Sally Shepherd a cording to order of her father William Shepherd, and I say received of me:" (signed) John Eoff. Issue:

26, Elizabeth, b. 17 Feb., 1797; d. 19 July, 1803.
27, William, b. 8 March, 1799; d. 20 Oct., 1822 or 1832(?).
28, Rebecca, b. 3 June, 1801; d. 28 March, 1872.
29, Elizabeth, b. 10 Nov., 1803; d. 17 Oct., 1864 (or 1874?), at Waverly, Ind.

DESCENDANTS OF WILLIAM SHEPHERD

30, Thomas, b. 3 July, 1806; d. 24 Feb., 1887.
31, Benjamin, b. 25 July, 1809.
32, Ruhamah, b. 1 June, 1812; d. 29 Aug., 1865.
33, Gabriel-Jacob, b. 11 April, 1815; d. 3 Jan., 1856.
34, Sarah, b. 5 Aug., 1818; d. 30 May, 1894, at Cowley, Kan.

6. RUHAMAH SHEPHERD (Thomas[1], William[2]), dau. of William and Mary (Clark) Shepherd, b. 23 Oct., 1778; d. 23 Nov., 1831; m. 8 Dec., 1795, Jacob Wetzell, who was b. 16 Sept., 1765; d. 2 July, 1827, who removed from Wheeling, Va., with his family 1819; settled near the site of Indianapolis, where six generations of his descendants have succeeded to the old homestead. Jacob was the son of John and Mary (Bonnet) Wetzell. Issue:
35, Sabra, b. 22 Feb., 1798, d. 20 Jan., 1822; 36, Cyrus, b. 1 Dec., 1800, d. 16 Dec., 1871; 37, Maria, b. 2 July, 1803, d. 18 Jan., 1843; 38, Eliza, b. 1 July, 1806; 39, Sarah, b. 28 Sept., 1809; 40, Hiram, b. 27 May, 1813, d. 20 Dec., 1855; 41, Emily, b. 2 May, 1816, d. 4 March, 1899.

7. JOSEPH SHEPHERD (Thomas[1], William[2], Thomas[3]), son of Thomas and —— —— Shepherd, b. 10 July, 1796; d. 2 Aug., 1858; m. 21 April, 1819, Polly Betz (or Bates). Issue:
42, William; 43, Amanda; 44, Ophelia; 45, Orlando; 46, James; 47, John; 48, Margaret; 49, Joseph.

8. DAVID SHEPHERD (Thomas[1], William[2], Thomas[3]), son of Thomas and —— —— Shepherd, b. ——; d. ——; m. 1803, Elizabeth Bates.

11. SARAH SHEPHERD (Thomas[1], William[2], Thomas[3]), dau. of Thomas and —— —— Shepherd, b. ——; d. ——; m. John Mills. They removed to Perry Co., O, 1812. Issue:
50, Thomas; 51, Adaline; 52, Mary Ann; 53, Rebecca; 54, Warner; 55, Emily; 56, Ashford; 57, Sarah.

15. THOMAS SHEPHERD (Thomas[1], William[2], William[3]), son of William and Eleanor (Peck) Shepherd, b. 26 Feb., 1799; d. at Wheeling, Va.; m. Elizabeth McHenry, b. 27 March, 1806. Issue:
58, William; 59, Ruhamah; 60, Mary Jane; 61, Francis M.; 62, John; 63, James L.; 64, George W.; 65, McDonald; 66, Henry Edward; 67, Mary; 68, Sarah.

16. LEWIS SHEPHERD (Thomas[1], William[2], William[3]), son of William and Eleanor (Peck) Shepherd, b. 15 Jan., 1800; d. ——; m. 24 April, 1827, Sarah Fleming, of Indiana. Issue:
69, Mary J., b. 27 July, 1829; 70, Drusilla, b. 6 Jan., 1831; 71, Melinda, b. 29 Oct., 1833; 72, Emily, b. 14 Jan., 1836; 73, Martin V., b. 9 July, 1838; 74, Martha, b. 23 Oct., 1840.

20. ELEANOR SHEPHERD (Thomas[1], William[2], William[3]), dau. of William and Eleanor (Peck) Shepherd, b. 11 May, 1806 (or 1809); d. ——; *m.* James Renforth. Issue: 75, Mary.

28. REBECCA MILLS (Thomas[1], William[2], Sarah[3]), dau. of Benjamin and Sarah (Shepherd) Mills, b. 3 June, 1801; d. 28 March, 1872; *m.* Levi Rench. Issue:
    76, Sarah, b. 7 Nov., 1822; 77, Otto, b. 14 Jan., 1825; 78, Catharine, b. 16 July, 1828; 79, Cassandra, b. 14 Feb., 1830; 80, Mary Naomi, b. 3 Sept., 1832; 81, Levi, b. 5 Oct., 1838; 82, Eli K., b. 3 Sept., 1840; 83, Ulysses, b. 26 Jan., 1844.

29. ELIZABETH MILLS (Thomas[1], William[2], Sarah[3]), dau. of Benjamin and Sarah (Shepherd) Mills, b. 10 Nov., 1803; d. 17 Oct., 1864/74, at Waverly, Ind.; *m.* 13 April, 1828, her first cousin, Cyrus Wetzell. Issue:
    84, Sabra Malvina, b. 16 Jan., 1829, d. 26 Aug., 1830; 85, Sarah M., b. 10 Sept., 1831, d. 23 March/Sept., 1886; 86, Elizabeth Missouri, b. 29 Aug., 1836, d. 29 April, 1847; 87, Francis Marion, b. 6 Oct., 1839, d. 27 July, 1899; 88, Gabriel Jacob, b. 4 June, 1843, d. 24 April, 1879.

30. THOMAS MILLS (Thomas[1], William[2], Sarah[3]), son of Benjamin and Sarah (Shepherd) Mills, b. 3 July, 1806; d. 24 Feb., 1887; *m.* Sallie Tull. Issue:
    89, Wm. Shepherd; 90, Milton; 91, Andrew J.; 92, Sarah; 93, Elizabeth; 94, Thomas.

31. BENJAMIN MILLS (Thomas[1], William[2], Sarah[3]), son of Benjamin and Sarah (Shepherd) Mills, b. 25 July, 1809; d. ——; *m.* Dolly Aldrich. Issue:
    95, Benjamin; 96, Sarah.

32. RUHAMAH MILLS (Thomas[1], William[2], Sarah[3]), dau. of Benjamin and Sarah (Shepherd) Mills, b. 1 June, 1812; d. 29 Aug., 1865; *m.* David Howe. Issue:
    97, Thomas; 98, Emmanuel; 99, Benj. Franklin; 100, Sarah; 101, Gabriel.

34. SARAH MILLS (Thomas[1], William[2], Sarah[3]), dau. of Benjamin and Sarah (Shepherd) Mills, b. 5 Aug., 1818; d. 30 May, 1894, at Cowley, Kansas; *m.* 1st Allan McLane; *m.* 2d John Harrow. Issue:
    102, Sarah Jane McLane; 103, John Harrow, b. 12 Jan., 1854; 104, Annie Harrow, b. 5 March, 1858.

35. SABRA WETZELL (Thomas[1], William[2], Ruhamah[3]), dau. of Jacob and Ruhamah (Shepherd) Wetzell, b. 22 Feb., 1798; d. 20 Jan., 1822; *m.* Dr. Charles Newton. Issue:

105, Amanda, b. 9 Nov., 1819; 106, Sabra, d. 17 Oct., 1822.

37. MARIA WETZELL (Thomas[1], William[2], Ruhamah[3]), dau. of Jacob and Ruhamah Wetzell, b. 2 July, 1803; d. 18 Jan., 1843; *m.* David Allen. Issue:
107, Correna; 108, Elena; 109, Thurza.

38. ELIZA WETZELL (Thomas[1], William[2], Ruhamah[3]), dau. of Jacob and Ruhamah (Shepherd) Wetzell, b. 11 July, 1806; d. ——; *m.* James S. Kelley. Issue:
110, Nancy; 111, Amanda; 112, William; 113, Oscar.

39. SARAH WETZELL (Thomas[1], William[2], Ruhamah[3]), dau. of Jacob and Ruhamah (Shepherd) Wetzell, b. 28 Sept., 1809; d. ——; *m.* Thomas Low. Issue:
114, Caroline; 115, Adaline.

40. HIRAM WETZELL (Thomas[1], William[2], Ruhamah[3]), son of Jacob and Ruhamah (Shepherd) Wetzell, b. 27 May, 1813; d. 20 Dec., 1855; *m.* Alzedah Aldrich. Issue:
116, Cyrus Oscar, b. 11 Feb., 1838; 117, Sabra Shepherd, b. 9 Nov., 1839; 118, Olive Ruhamah, b. 28 Sept., 1841; 119, Jacob Hiram, b. 16 March, 1847.

85. SARAH MELVINA WETZELL (Thomas[1], William[2], Ruhamah[3], Elizabeth[4]), dau. of Cyrus, Jr., and Elizabeth (Mills) Wetzell, b. 10 Sept., 1831; d. 23 Sept., 1886; *m.* 26 Aug., 1852, William Nelson McKenzie, of Glasgow, Scotland. Issue:
120, Cyrus W., 3d, b. 23 Aug., 1853; 121, Elizabeth J., b. 21 Feb., 1856; 122, Lewis, Jr., b. 4 Dec., 1858; 123, William Wilson, b. 28 June, 1861; 124, Sarah, b. 21 Feb., 1864; 125, Wm. Donald, b. 12 Feb., 1869, *m.* Emma Vaders; 126, Kenneth Seaforth, b. 20 Feb., 1874.

120. CYRUS WETZELL MCKENZIE (Thomas[1], William[2], Ruhamah[3], Elizabeth[4], Sarah M.[5]), son of Wm. N. and Sarah M. (Wetzell) McKenzie, b. 23 Aug., 1853; d. ——; *m.* Molly Park. Issue:
127, Kenneth Seaforth; 128, Wm. Nelson; 129, Sarah Melvina; 130, Dorie May.

121. ELIZABETH JANE MCKENZIE (Thomas[1], William[2], Ruhamah[3], Elizabeth[4], Sarah M.[5]), dau. of Wm. N. and Sarah M. (Wetzel) McKenzie, b. 21 Feb., 1856; d. ——; *m.* Horace Hines Fletcher, resides at Indianapolis, Ind. Issue:
131, Elizabeth Malvina, b. 17 June, 1882.

122. LEWIS WETZELL MCKENZIE (Thomas[1], William[2], Ruhamah[3], Elizabeth[4], Sarah M.[5]), son of Wm. N. and Sarah M. (Wetzell) McKenzie; b. 4 Dec., 1858; *m.* Mary Ann Councilman. Issue:
132, Frank McKenzie.

DESCENDANTS OF THOMAS SHEPHERD

V. THOMAS SHEPHERD (Thomas[1]), son of Thomas and Elizabeth (Van Metre) Shepherd, b. *circa* 1743; d. Shepherdstown, Va., 1793; *m.* 1773, Susannah, dau. of Richard and Sarah (Shepherd-Williams) Hulse; she afterward *m.* —— Brooke; she d. at Shepherdstown, Va., 17 Nov., 1839, and is buried in the Shepherd burial ground.   Issue:

    1, Thomas, b. 3 Nov., 1774, d. 9 Nov., 1832; 2, David; 3, John, *m.* Elizabeth Van Metre; 4, Joseph, *m.* Mary Bates; 5, Sarah, *m.* James Wiley or Anthony Kearney; 6, Elizabeth, d. 11 Oct., 1804; 7, James; 8, Mary, *m.* Francis Daly.

    1. THOMAS SHEPHERD (Thomas[1], Thomas[2]), son of Thomas and Susannah (Hulse) Shepherd, b. 3 Nov., 1774, d. 9 Nov., 1832; *m.* 15 Oct., 1805, at Shepherdstown, Va., Mary Byers (probably dau. of Joseph or Conrad Byers, of Shepherdstown, Va.). She was b. there 13 Dec., 1779; d. 25 Nov., 1870, at the home of her son-in-law, Philip Weber, in Sangamon Co., Ill.
                                                    Issue:

    9, Thomas C., b. 28 June, 1806, *m.* Ella Miller; 10, Henry, b. 3 Dec., 1807, d. 1850; 11, Susan, b. 1809, *m.* Geo. R. Weber, April 25, 1832; 12, Amanda M., b. 8 Nov., 1812, *m.* Philip W. Weber; 13, Mary, b. 31 Oct., 1813, *m.* S. B. Smith, b. Nov. 14, 1833; 14, Joseph, b. 11 July, 1816; 15, John J., b. — 1821, *m.* 1st Susan Pettus, d. s.p., *m.* 2d Mrs. Annie Lewis, no issue, live Lincoln, Ill.; 16, Sarah C., b. 5 July, 1823; 17, James. This family lived at Blackford's Ferry, Washington Co., Md., till 1836, then removed to Sangamon Co., Ill. Administration on the estate of his father, Thomas 3d, was granted to Thomas C. Shepherd, 27 Feb., 1833, and accounts were filed on 4 March, 1834, and 2 April, 1835 (Wash. Co., Md., Lib. C, Fol. 9).

18, (Henry, named in administrator's account as an heir).

2. DAVID SHEPHERD (Thomas[1], Thomas[2]), son of Thomas and Susannah (Hulse) Shepherd, b. Shepherdstown, Va.; d. ——; *m.* 1823, Elizabeth Betz (or Bates).

4. JOSEPH SHEPHERD (Thomas[1], Thomas[2]), son of Thomas and Susannah (Hulse) Shepherd, b. 10 July, 1786; d. 2 Aug., 1858; *m.* 21 April, 1809, Mary (Polly) Bates.   Issue:
    19, William; 20, Amanda; 21, Ophelia; 22, Orlando; 23, James; 24, John; 25, Margaret, *m.* Henry Osborn, Oct. 31, 1832; 26, Joseph.

DESCENDANTS OF THOMAS SHEPHERD

6. ELIZABETH SHEPHERD (Thomas[1], Thomas[2]), dau. of Thomas and Susannah (Hulse) Shepherd, b. ——; d. 11 Oct., 1804; *m. circa* 1803, Captain John Leland Tabb, son of William and Joanna (Tompkins) Tabb, of Gloucester Co., Va., and a descendant of Robert Tabb and Elizabeth Elliott, formerly of Gloucester Co., Va. Captain John Leland Tabb served as Lieutenant in Captain Van Bennett's company of light infantry, attached to the 57th regiment (Lieutenant-Colonel Mason's) of Virginia militia in War of 1812. He d. 14 July, 1839, and is buried, with his wife, in the Episcopal churchyard, at Shepherdstown, W. Va. Issue:

    27, Elizabeth, b. 11 Oct., 1804, d. 14 Oct., 1863, *m.* 23 Jan., 1823, Nathaniel Mitchell, of Mitchell's Gardens, Cambridge, Dorchester Co., Md.

7. JAMES SHEPHERD (Thomas[1], Thomas[2]), son of Thomas and Susannah (Hulse) Shepherd, b. ——; d. ——; *m.* 1st Julianna Catharine ——. Issue:

    28, Louisa Eleanor, b. 12 July, 1810; 29, Eliza Catharine, b. 25 Aug., 1817; 30, Mary Henrietta, b. 24 Aug., 1819; *m.* 2d 5 May, 1828, Amelia Humphreville, of Lancaster, Pa., b. 21 Dec., 1801; 31, Amelia Henrietta, b. 2 July, 1829; 32, William Beecher, b. 24 April, 1831, d. 31 March, 1832; 33, Robert Douglass, b. 21 April, 1833, d. 12 May, 1835; 34, Edward Clarence, b. 24 July, 1835; 35, Henry Smith Mayer, b. 25 Sept., 1836; 36, Susan Randolph, b. 6 Aug., 1838, d. 23 Sept., 1872; 37, Ann Hammond, b. 7 Aug., 1841, d. 14 Jan., 1868.

8. MARY SHEPHERD (Thomas[1], Thomas[2]), dau. of Thomas and Susannah (Hulse) Shepherd, b. ——; d. ——; *m.* —— ——.

9. THOMAS C. SHEPHERD (Thomas[1], Thomas[2], Thomas[3]), son of Thomas and Mary (Byers) Shepherd, b. 28 June, 1806; d. ——; *m.* 3 July, 1834, Ella Miller, of Shepherdstown, Va., b. 24 June, 1813; d. —— (both living 1876). This family "lived at Blackford's Ferry, Washington Co., Md., until after their first child was born, then they removed to Illinois, 17 Nov., 1836," to a farm six miles south of Springfield which had been purchased the previous spring. Issue:

    38, Thomas B., b. 28 Sept., 1835, at Blackford's Ferry, Md.; 39, John H., b. 2 Feb., 1838; 40, William B., b. 6 June, 1840; 41, Charles M., b. 18 Nov., 1841; 42, Mary E., b. 5 Jan., 1849.

10. HENRY SHEPHERD (Thomas[1], Thomas[2], Thomas[3]), son of Thomas and Mary (Byers) Shepherd, b. 3 Dec., 1807; d. in Sangamon Co., Ill., 1860; *m.* 1833, Mary Peaff, after which date they moved to Chillicothe, and to Sangamon Co. in 1838; in 1849 went to California during the gold excitement. Issue:

43, Jeanne; 44, Harriett, *m.* Geo. Metler who d. 1872, and had issue one daughter. Mother and daughter live at Petersburgh, Monard Co., Ill.

11. SUSAN SHEPHERD (Thomas[1], Thomas[2], Thomas[3]), dau. of Thomas and Mary (Byers) Shepherd, b. — 1809; d. ——; *m.* 1 May, 1832, George R. Weber, who was b. in Baltimore, 29 May, 1808, but removed with his parents to Shepherdstown, W. Va. After their marriage Geo. R. Weber and his wife removed to New York City, where Mrs. Weber soon died. The widower returned to Shepherdstown and later removed to Springfield, Ill., where he was married, 1836, to Catharine Welsh.

12. AMANDA M. SHEPHERD (Thomas[1], Thomas[2], Thomas[3]), dau. of Thomas and Mary (Byers) Shepherd, b. 8 Nov., 1812; d. ——; *m.* 18 June, 1839, Philip W. Weber, who was b. Shepherdstown, Va., 28 Jan., 1812. He went south in 1835, where he built a mill, with other parties, at Raymond, Miss.; sold out and came to Springfield, Ill., 1837, where he married in 1839. He went to California in 1849 and returned in 1859 and afterward engaged in farming with his brother, John B. Weber, near Pawnee, Sangamon Co., Ill. Issue:

45, John P., b. 19 March, 1840; 46, Mary E., b. — 1842; 47, William B., b. 11 March, 1844, d. ——; *m.* 1 Jan., 1867, Henrietta Lough; 48, Amanda, b. 3 March, 1846, *m.* 9 May, 1869, John W. Blakey; 49, Sarah C., *m.* 12 Dec., 1867, Balaam M. Brown; 50, Emma S.

13. MARY SHEPHERD (Thomas[1], Thomas[2], Thomas[3]), dau. of Thomas and Mary (Byers) Shepherd, b. 31 Oct., 1813; d. ——; *m.* 15 Nov., 1833, at Sharpsburg, Md., S. B. Smith, who was b. Martinsburg, Va., 10 June, 1810. He was four times sergeant at arms—as assistant and as principal—in Illinois Legislature 1850 to 1854. He and his wife were living three miles south of Rochester, Sangamon Co., Ill. Issue:

51, Andrew, b. in Pickway Co., O., 3 Aug., 1837. He is a merchant; married and lives in Boise City, Idaho. Andrew Smith was in Berkeley Co., Va., at the beginning of the Rebellion and voted against the Ordnance of Secession. He was forced into the Confederate Army by receiving a severe bayonet wound, but refused to take the oath of allegiance or perform military duty. Some whisky was offered him which he could not be induced to drink; it was carelessly left in the way of some of their own men, one of whom drank it, not knowing that it was poisoned, and he died in two hours. Andrew Smith escaped from the Confederates and joined the Union Army in Washington, D. C., and after a brief term of service was discharged on account of

physical disability (see History of Sangamon Co., Ill.).
52, William, b. 5 Jan., 1839, in Alleghany City, Pa., *m.* 5 Sept., 1866, Lou Ray.
53, Henry H., b. 10 Oct., 1840, in Pittsburg, Pa., *m.* 14 Nov., 1864, Mrs. Lavinia Wakeley.
54, Joseph H., b. 23 Jan., 1844, in Alleghany City, Pa., *m.* Mary I. Craig.
55, Thomas C., b. 31 March, 1848, *m.* Anne Craig.
56, Amanda L., b. 31 March, 1848, d. 19 Nov., 1869.
57, Mary P., b. —, 1853, d. 4 Oct., 1869.

14. JOSEPH SHEPHERD (Thomas[1], Thomas[2], Thomas[3]), son of Thomas and Mary (Byers) Shepherd, b. 11 July, 1816; d. —; *m.* 1st 16 March, 1848, Fanny Smith, b. Franklin Co., Pa., 25 Oct., 1818; d. 19 Feb., 1863; *m.* 2d Mrs. Lydia (Byers) Haggard. Issue first wife:
52, J. Thomas, b. 18 Jan., 1849; d. —; *m.* 4 Sept., 1872, Amanda Whitecraft, Pawnee, Ill.
53, James H., b. 19 Oct., 1853; d. —; *m.* 10 Sept., 1874, Jessie F. Winchester, b. 3 Oct., 1856, in New Jersey, lived near Springfield, Ill.
54, Fanny A., b. —, d. 14 Dec., 1869; 55, Salome C.; 56, Joseph F.; 57, Amanda E.
Issue second wife:
58, William C.; 59, Lydia.

16. SARAH C. SHEPHERD (Thomas[1], Thomas[2], Thomas[3]), dau. of Thomas and Mary (Byers) Shepherd, b. 5 July, 1823; d. —; *m.* 1837, Dr. E. C. Williams. Dr. E. Clagget Williams, of Martinsburg, Va., son of Dr. Edward O. and Elizabeth Williams, was born on what is known as the Swan Pond Place, in Berkeley Co., Va., in 1815. His mother was Miss Elizabeth Claggett. Dr. E. C. Williams, graduated from Jefferson Medical College, Philadelphia, 1839.   Issue:
60, Edward C.; 61, Louis M,, *m.* Miss Grey; 62, Thomas S., *m.* Anna Byers, dau. of Wm. Byers; 63, Frank C., d. Jan., 1889, *m.* 1878, Miss Small, of Martinsburg; 64, Mary Elizabeth, *m.* Abraham Shepherd; 65, Richard H., d. young, thrown from horse at age of 12; 66, Richard K. C., b. —, 1848; d. —, 1861; 67, Millard, F., b. —, 1855, d. —, 1877.

27. ELIZABETH TABB (Thomas[1], Thomas[2], Elizabeth[3]), dau. of Capt. John L. and Elizabeth (Shepherd) Tabb, b. 11 Oct., 1804; d. 14 Oct., 1863; *m.* 23 Jan., 1823, Nathaniel Mitchell, of Mitchell's Gardens, Dorchester Co., Md., son of Reuben and Ruth (Lee) Mitchell, of Maryland; a Revolutionary patriot. Nathaniel Mitchell was a soldier in the War of 1812. The family removed to New Lisbon, Ohio.   Issue:

68, John L., b. 24 Nov., 1823; d. 11 Dec., 1879; *m.* Caroline
Swift.
69, Charles Henry, b. 18 Aug., 1827, living in California; 70,
Edward Lee, b. and d. inf.; 71, Virginia Lelia, b. 20
Oct., 1831, d. 27 May, 1888, *m.* Col. Chas. Benjamin
Stephenson, C. S. A., great-grandson of Lieut. Wm.
Stephenson, of Harper's Ferry.
72, Elizabeth Ruth, b. 26 July, 1834; d. 11 Aug., 1885; *m.*
Judge Oliver H. P. Shiras.
73, Wm. Kempe, b. 29 Oct., 1836, d. 24 April, 1881; 74, Ellen
Jane, b. 17 March, 1839, lives in California; 75, Ann
Harriett, b. 15 Dec., 1841, d. 16 March, 1900; 76, James
Lee, d. s.p.

31. AMELIA HENRIETTA SHEPHERD (Thomas[1], Thomas[2],
James[3]), dau. of James and Amelia (Humphreville) Shepherd,
b. 2 July, 1829; d. ——; *m.* 29 March, 1853, James Finley.
Issue:
77, Robert; 78, Rosalind; 79, William Short.

34. EDWARD CLARENCE SHEPHERD (Thomas[1], Thomas[2],
James[3]), son of James and Amelia (Humphreville) Shepherd,
b. 24 July, 1835; d. 5 Sept., 1907, at Frederick City, Md.; *m.* 17
Aug., 1870, Amelia Shock.   Mr. Shepherd was professor of
mathematics for twenty-five years in Frederick College, and for
several years past was the efficient tax collector and register of
the city of Frederick, Md.   Issue:
80, Edward Clarence, b. 24 Jan., 1876, *m.* —— ——, issue,
E. C. Shepherd 3d; 81, Anna Isabel; 82, Clinton Webb;
83, George Randolph.

38. THOMAS B. SHEPHERD (Thomas[1], Thomas[2], Thomas[3],
Thomas C.[4]), son of Thomas C. and Ella (Miller) Shepherd, b. at
Blackford's Ferry, Md., 28 Sept., 1835; d. ——; *m.* 26 Oct., 1859,
Araminda Pyle.   Issue:
84, Thomas A.; 85, Ann; 86, Mary E.

39. JOHN H. SHEPHERD (Thomas[1], Thomas[2], Thomas[3],
Thomas C.[4]), son of Thomas C. and Ella (Miller) Shepherd, b. 2
Feb., 1838; *m.* 6 Oct., 1869, Ann Pyle.   Issue:
87, Araminda.

40. WILLIAM B. SHEPHERD (Thomas[1], Thomas[2], Thomas[3],
Thomas C.[4]), son of Thomas C. and Ella (Miller) Shepherd, b. 6
June, 1840; *m.* 22 Oct., 1867, Elizabeth K. Brown, b. 20 Oct.,
1848, near Wheeling, Ohio Co., Va., living near Woodside, Ill.
Issue:
88, Alice Virginia.

41. CHARLES M. SHEPHERD (Thomas[1], Thomas[2], Thomas[3],
Thomas C.[4]), son of Thomas C. and Ella (Miller) Shepherd, b. 18

Nov., 1841; *m.* 11 Nov., 1869, Sarah E. Ford. Chas. M. Shepherd enlisted for the Union Army at Springfield, Ill., 20 July, 1861, Company B, 11th Regiment Missouri Infantry, serving three years. Issue:
89, Charles Raymond, b. 26 Sept., 1875.

42. MARY E. SHEPHERD (Thomas[1], Thomas[2], Thomas[3], Thomas C.[4]), dau. of Thomas C. and Ella (Miller) Shepherd, b. 5 Jan., 1849; d. ——; *m.* Lawson Pyle. Issue:
90, Mildred.

47. WILLIAM B. WEBER (Thomas[1], Thomas[2], Thomas[3], Amanda M.[4]), son of George R. and Amanda M. (Shepherd) Weber, b. 11 March, 1844; d. ——; *m.* 1 Jan., 1867, Henrietta Lough. They reside at Pawnee, Sangemon Co., Ill. Issue:
91, Frank; 92, Andrew.

49. SARAH C. WEBER (Thomas[1], Thomas[2], Thomas[3], Amanda M.[4]), dau. of George R. and Amanda M. (Shepherd) Weber, b. ——; d. ——; *m.* 12 Dec., 1867, Balaam N. Brown. Issue:
93, Ida Belle; 94, Fanny May.

52. WILLIAM SMITH (Thomas[1], Thomas[2], Thomas[3], Mary[4]), son of S. B. and Mary (Shepherd) Smith, b. 5 Jan., 1839, in Alleghany City, Pa.; *m.* 5 Sept., 1866, Lou Ray. Issue three daughters, living in Champaign Co., Ill.:
95, Lillian; 96, Grace; 97, Jessie.

53. HENRY H. SMITH (Thomas[1], Thomas[2], Thomas[3], Mary[4]), son of S. B. and Mary (Shepherd) Smith, b. 10 Oct., 1840, in Pittsburg, Pa.; d. ——; *m.* 14 Nov., 1864, Mrs. Lavinia Wakeley, at Three-Mile Creek, Utah. These children live in Box Elder Co., Utah:
98, Mary P.; 99, Francis A.; 100, George W.

54. JOSEPH H. SMITH (Thomas[1], Thomas[2], Thomas[3], Mary[4]), son of S. B. and Mary (Shepherd) Smith, b. 23 Jan., 1844, in Alleghany Co., Pa.; d. ——; *m.* 15 Feb., 1872, Mary J. Craig, at Springfield, Ill. Issue:
101, —— (a child).

60. EDWARD B. WILLIAMS (Thomas[1], Thomas[2], Thomas[3], Sarah C.[4]), son of Dr. E. Claggett and Sarah C. (Shepherd) Williams, b. ——; d. ——; *m.* Miss Laura Henshaw, dau. of Levi Henshaw, Esq., of Berkeley Co., Va. Issue:
102, Edith Claggett; 103, Sallie C.; 104, Levi Edward.

61. LOUIS M. WILLIAMS (Thomas[1], Thomas[2], Thomas[3], Sarah C.[4]), son of Dr. E. Claggett and Sarah C. (Shepherd) Williams, b. ——; d. ——; *m.* Miss Grey. He was in Sangemon Co., Ill., when the Civil War began and enlisted on the first call for men in the Seventh Illinois Regiment of Infantry for three months,

then again in Twenty-ninth Illinois Infantry for three years. Again he enlisted in 1864, as a veteran, and was honorably discharged at the close of the war. He *m.* Miss Grey and removed to Texas.

66. RICHARD KEENE CLAGGETT WILLIAMS (Thomas[1], Thomas[2], Elizabeth[3], Elizabeth[4]), son of Dr. E. Claggett and Sarah C. (Shepherd) Williams, b. ——, 1848; d. ——, 1861; *m.* Mary V. Chapline, dau. of Abraham and Ann (Adler) Chapline, of Prince George's Co., Md.   Issue:
105, Nannie Claggett, *m.* Jos. S. Bragonier; 106, Otho, *m.* Florence Rowan Kearney.

68. JOHN L. TABB MITCHELL (Thomas[1], Thomas[2], Elizabeth[3], Elizabeth[4]), son of Nathaniel and Elizabeth (Tabb) Mitchell, b. 24 Nov., 1823; d. 11 Dec., 1879; *m.* Caroline Smith.   Issue:
107, Catharine; 108, Edward; both live in California.

71. VIRGINIA LELIA MITCHELL (Thomas[1], Thomas[2], Elizabeth[3], Elizabeth[4]), dau. of Nathaniel and Elizabeth (Tabb) Mitchell, b. 20 Oct., 1831; d. 27 May, 1888; *m.* Colonel Chas. Benjamin Stephenson, C.S.A., of Harper's Ferry, Va., great-grandson of Lieutenant William Stephenson of the Revolution.   Issue:
109, Ella Isabella; 110, South Carolina; 111, Edward Lee; 112, Charles Tabb; 113, Elizabeth Mitchell; 114, Roberta Lee; 115, Andrew Pickens.

73. WILLIAM KEMPE MITCHELL (Thomas[1], Thomas[2], Elizabeth[3], Elizabeth[4]), son of Nathaniel and Elizabeth (Tabb) Mitchell, b. 29 Oct., 1836; d. 24 April, 1881; *m.* Mary Harris, a niece of Rear-Admiral J. N. Miller, U. S. N., who was the grandson of Mary Tabb and Samuel Hedges.   Issue:
116, William Kempe, Jr.; 117, Virginia; 118, Alice, *m.* Louis Dorsey.

75. ANN HARRIET MITCHELL (Thomas[1], Thomas[2], Elizabeth[3], Elizabeth[4]), dau. of Nathaniel and Elizabeth (Tabb) Mitchell, b. 15 Dec., 1841; d. 16 March, 1900; *m.* Frederick Doolittle. Issue:
119, Oliver; 120, Carl; 121, Elizabeth; 122, Frances.

105. NANNIE CLAGGETT WILLIAMS (Thomas[1], Thomas[2], Elizabeth[3], Sarah C.[4], Richard K. C.[5]), dau. of Richard K. C. and Mary V. (Chapline) Williams, b. ——; d. ——; *m.* Joseph S. Bragonier.   Issue:
123, Dr. Richard K. C. Bragonier; lives in Shepherdstown.

106. OTHO WILLIAMS (Thomas[1], Thomas[2], Elizabeth[3], Sarah C.[4], Richard K. C.[5]), son of Richard K. C. and Mary V. (Chapline) Williams, b. ——; d. ——; *m.* Florence Rowan Kearney, a descendant through another branch, from Thomas Shepherd, founder of Shepherdstown, Va.   Issue:
124. Nannie Claggett.

DESCENDANTS OF JOHN SHEPHERD

113. ELIZABETH MITCHELL STEPHENSON (Thomas[1], Thomas[2], Elizabeth[3], Elizabeth[4], Virginia L.[5]), dau. of Col. Charles B. Stephenson and Virginia Lelia Mitchell, b. ——; d. ——; m. Dr. Campbell Caldwell Fite, of Tennessee.   Issue: 125, Frank; 126, Northcote.

JOHN SHEPHERD

VI. JOHN SHEPHERD, in 1785, is charged with wheelwright material upon old account books at Shepherdstown, Va. In 1787 he removes to Ohio County, Va. On 22 Feb., 1802, Nathan Shepherd and Mary, his wife, convey to John McConnell lands on waters of Buffalo Creek, Ohio Co., Va., lying at a small beech drain adjoining lands of Beal Plumer, Joseph Hedges and *John Shepherd,* being 100 acres of a tract granted to Derick Hoagland, who conveyed same to *John Shepherd,* and by said Shepherd was conveyed, 6 April, 1795, to Nathan Shepherd (Wellsburg, Brooke Co., Va., Deed Bk., No. 2, p. 507).

From 1802 to 1815, inclusive, his name is found upon the list of taxables in Brooke Co., Va., for land situate on Buffalo Creek, 96 acres; and in the latter year his holdings were increased to 376 acres (Tax Lists Brooke Co., Va., at Wellsburg).

His name is also found among the list of privates in the Westmoreland County militia (Pa. Arch., Ser. IV., Vol. V., p. 455).

DESCENDANTS OF JOHN SHEPHERD

VI. JOHN SHEPHERD (Thomas[1]), son of Thomas and Elizabeth (Van Metre) Shepherd, b. Mecklenburg, Va., *circa* 1749; d. at Red Oak, O., 31 July, 1812; m. *circa* 1773, at Mecklenburg, Va., Martha Nelson. John Shepherd lived in Shepherdstown, Va., till 1787, and from thence removed to Buffalo Creek, and from thence to Maysville, Ky.; remaining there but a short time, he removed to Red Oak, O., where he lived at the date of his death. He served in Capt. William Cherry's company, 4th Va. Regt. Inf., April, 1777, to March, 1778; was a member of a Masonic Lodge at Ripley, O., a Presbyterian in religion and a miller and millwright by occupation. All his children, except John, the youngest, were born in Shepherdstown; John was born on Buffalo Creek.

Issue:

1, Elizabeth, b. 14 Feb., 1774; d. in Illinois, 17 Feb., 1858; m. Andrew Moore.

2, Abraham, b. 13 Aug., 1776; d. in Illinois, 16 Jan., 1847; m. Margaret Moore.

3, Isaac S., b. 13 Sept., 1777; d. Red Oak, O., 19 Feb., 1811.

4, Mary, b. 19 April, 1779; d. Red Oak, O., 7 June, 1846; *m.* Wm. Dunlap.

5, Jacob, b. 19 Nov., 1780; d. Red Oak, O., 8 Oct., 1868(?).

6, Sarah, b. 15 Dec., 1786; d. Red Oak, O., 11 July, 1832; *m.* Wm. Mills.

7, John, b. 31 Aug., 1788; *m.* Nancy Baird.

1. ELIZABETH SHEPHERD (Thomas[1], John[2]), dau. of John and Martha (Nelson) Shepherd; b. Shepherdstown, Va., 14 Feb., 1774; d. in Illinois, 17 Feb., 1858; *m.* Andrew Moore.   Issue:
8, Sarah, *m.* John Denny; 9, Martha, *m.* James McClung; 10, Shepherd, *m.* Margaret Hawthorne; 11, Robert, *m.* Fanny Luper; 12, Andrew, d. at age of 16; 13, John, b. 18 Feb., 1809, d. 10 May, 1899; 14, Polly; 15, Reggy; 16, Alexander; 17, Amanda.

2. ABRAHAM SHEPHERD (Thomas[1], John[2]), son of John and Martha (Nelson) Shepherd, b. Shepherdstown, Va., 13 Aug., 1776; d. in Illinois, 16 Jan., 1847; *m.* 1st Margaret Moore, 1799. He was a captain of a company in the First Brigade, Second Division, Ohio militia, in War of 1812; in service from 2 Sept., 1812, to 22 Aug., 1813 (Adams Co., O., History).   Issue:
18, William, b. 16 June, 1800; d. Georgetown, O., 1806.
19, John H., b. 10 Oct., 1801; d. 20 April, 1832.
20, Nancy, b. 18 May, 1803; d. 27 Dec., 1878.
21, Polly, b. 11 April, 1805; d. 4 Aug., 1837.
22, Isaac, b. 14 Jan., 1808; d. 10 Nov., 1836; *m.* Betsey Poage.
23, Campbell A., b. 10 March, 1810; d. 6 Nov., 1882.
24, Amanda, b. 9 Dec., 1811; d. Dec., 1837.
25, Margaret, b. 21 Dec., 1813; d. 3 Oct., 1820.
26, Elizabeth, b. 30 April, 1815; d. 11 April, 1842; *m.* Bartemus Stephenson.
27, Sarah, b. 5 April, 1818; d. 30 Jan., 1838.
Abraham Shepherd *m.* 2d 1819, Harriet Kincade.   Issue:
28, Andrew Kincaid, b. 15 Nov., 1820; 29, Martha Ann, b. 1 March, 1823.

4. MARY SHEPHERD (Thomas[1], John[2]), dau. of John and Martha (Nelson) Shepherd, b. 19 April, 1779; d. 7 June, 1846; *m.* William Dunlap.   Issue:
30, Amanda; 31, James (Rev.), b. 6 Sept., 1804, d. 31 March, 1883; 32, Milton (Dr.); 33, Nancy, b. 25 May, 1809, d. 19 May, 1846; 34, Alexander (Dr.), b. ——, d. 16 Feb., 1894, at Springfield, O.; 35, Shepherd; 36, Betsey Ann; 37, William, *m.* Grace Hopkins.

5. JACOB SHEPHERD (Thomas[1], John[2]), son of John and Martha (Nelson) Shepherd, b. 19 Nov., 1780; d. 8 Oct., 1868(?); *m.* 3 June, 1802, Agnes Johnston.   Issue:
38, Smiley, b. 9 March, 1803; d. 4 April, 1882.

39, Nelson, b. 6 Dec., 1804; d. 22 Oct., 1888.
40, Johnston, b. 27 Feb., 1807; d. 5 Aug., 1874.
41, Isaac N. (Rev.), b. 29 May, 1809; d. 3 July, ——.
42, Keziah, b. 5 March, 1812; d. 3 Sept., 1873.
43, Sarah, b. 10 April, 1814; d. 3 March, 1835.
44, Reazen, b. 3 Aug., 1813; d. 31 Dec., 1893.
45, Albert, b. 13 Jan., 1819; d. 2 April, 1824.
46, Harvey, b. 22 April, 1822; d. 3 April, 1824.
47, Nancy A., b. 10 Oct., 1824; d. 31 March, 1876.

6. SARAH SHEPHERD (Thomas[1], John[2]), dau. of John and Martha (Nelson) Shepherd, b. 15 Dec., 1786; d. 11 July, 1832; *m.* 1 June, 1805, William Mills. Issue:
48, Amasa; 49, Susannah, *m.* Thomas Parnell; 50, Margaret Jane, *m.* Robert Leedom, of Manchester, O.; 51, Sarah May, *m.* Samuel Moore; 52, John, *m.* Polly Devoe; 53, James, *m.* Polly Ellis; 54, Willis, *m.* Hester Bassett; 55, Shepherd, *m.* Nancy McDaniels; 56, Campbell, *m.* Eliza Jane Glaze.

7. JOHN SHEPHERD (Thomas[1], John[2]), son of John and Martha (Nelson) Shepherd, b. 31 Aug., 1788; d. ——; *m.* Nancy Baird. Issue:
57, Martha Ann, *m.* —— Pearson; 58, Harvey (Dr.), d. 1867, at Lawrence, Kan.; 59, Eliza Jane; 60, Sarah Amanda, *m.* Darwin Bowen; 61, J. Milton, *m.* Miss Dale, of Virginia; 62, Albert, *m.* Ann Dale, of Virginia (sister of Miss Dale); 63, Mary, *m.* a Methodist minister, of Warrenburg, Mo.; 64, Worcester; 65, William.

18. WILLIAM SHEPHERD (Thomas[1], John[2], Abraham[3]), son of Abraham and Margaret (Moore) Shepherd, b. 16 June, 1800; d. ——, 1806, at Georgetown, O.; *m.* Hannah Newkirk. Issue:
66, Marshall; 67, Marie Antoinette.

19. JOHN H. SHEPHERD (Thomas[1], John[2], Abraham[3]), son of Abraham and Margaret (Moore) Shepherd, b. 10 Oct., 1801; d. 20 April, 1832; *m.* Caroline Butt. Issue:
68, John; 69, Allen.

20. NANCY SHEPHERD (Thomas[1], John[2], Abraham[3]), dau. of Abraham and Margaret (Moore) Shepherd; b. 18 May, 1803; d. 27 Dec., 1878; *m.* 1st Robert Coulter. Issue:
70, Alfred.
Nancy Shepherd *m.* 2d Alexander Wishner. Issue:
71, Harriet; 72, Jacob; 73, Adrian.

21. POLLY SHEPHERD (Thomas[1], John[2], Abraham[3]), dau. of Abraham and Margaret (Moore) Shepherd, b. 11 April, 1805; d. 4 August, 1837; *m.* George Southerland. Issue:
74, Harvey; 75, Elijah.

22. ISAAC SHEPHERD (Thomas[1], John[2], Abraham[3]), son of Abraham and Margaret (Moore) Shepherd; b. 14 June, 1808; d. 10 Nov., 1836; *m.* Betsey Poage.

23. CAMPBELL A. SHEPHERD (Thomas[1], John[2], Abraham[3]), son of Abraham and Margaret (Moore) Shepherd, b. 10 March, 1810; d. 6 Nov., 1882; *m.* Mary Ann Johnston. Issue:
76, John Horatio, U. S. A., b. 13 May, 1839, d. 27 June, 1872, *m.* Caroline Rose Schutt; 77, Mary Johnston, b. 21 March, 1841; 78, Margaret Butt, b. 7 May, 1843; d. 6 March, 1888; 79, Adrian Campbell.

24. AMANDA SHEPHERD (Thomas[1], John[2], Abraham[3]), dau. of Abraham and Margaret (Moore) Shepherd, b. 9 Dec., 1811; d. Dec., 1837; *m.* Dr. —— Robinson. Issue:
80, Adonijah.

26. ELIZABETH SHEPHERD (Thomas[1], John[2], Abraham[3]), dau. of Abraham and Margaret (Moore) Shepherd, b. 30 April, 1815; d. 11 April, 1842; *m.* Bartemus Stephenson.

30. AMANDA DUNLAP (Thomas[1], John[2], Mary[3]), dau. of William and Mary (Shepherd) Dunlap; *m.* 1st Dr. Henry Foster. Issue:
81, Nancy Ann.
Amanda Dunlap *m.* 2d William McCague, leaving no issue; *m.* 3d Rev. Samuel Crother. Issue:
82, Mary; 83, Willie.

31. JAMES DUNLAP (Rev.) (Thomas[1], John[2], Mary[3]), son of William and Mary (Shepherd) Dunlap, b. 6 Sept., 1804; d. 31 March, 1883; *m.* Mary Stewart. Issue:
84, Archibald; 85, George S., d. 27 Jan., 1885, at Chattanooga, Tenn.; 86, Margaret Mary; 87, Nettie S.; 88, Amanda S.; 89, Alice S.; 90, Chas. James S.

32. MILTON DUNLAP, Dr. (Thomas[1], John[2], Mary[3]), son of William and Mary (Shepherd) Dunlap, b. ——; d. ——; *m.* Frances Kincaid. Issue:
91, Mary; 92, Nancy; 93, Matilda; 94, William; 95, Shepherd; 96, Caroline; 97, Robert (Dr.); 98, David; 99, Arthur; 100, Charles; 101, Fanny; 102, Samuel.

34. ALEXANDER DUNLAP, Dr. (Thomas[1], John[2], Mary[3]), son of William and Mary (Shepherd) Dunlap, b. ——; d. 16 Feb., 1894, at Springfield, O.; *m.* Elizabeth Bell. Issue:
103, Charles; 104, Shepherd; 105, Mary Elizabeth.

38. SMILEY SHEPHERD (Thomas[1], John[2], Jacob[3]), son of Jacob and Agnes (Johnston) Shepherd, b. 9 March, 1803, d. 4 April, 1882; *m.* Elizabeth Paul. Smiley served in Indian war, 1832, under Capt. Willetts. Issue:

106, Augustus, b. 7 Feb., 1830; *m.* 1863, Ellen B. Shepherd; 107, Nancy Jane, b. 2 Feb., 1833; d. 1 Feb., 1852; 108, Sarah Ann, b. April, 1835, d. Oct., 1836.

39. NELSON SHEPHERD (Thomas[1], John[2], Jacob[3]), son of Jacob and Agnes (Johnston) Shepherd, b. 6 Dec., 1804; d. 22 Oct., 1888; *m.* Mary Baird. Nelson Shepherd, served in Indian war, 1832, in Capt. Geo. B. Willett's Co., under Col. J. Straun. Issue: 109, Milton, b. 2 July, 1832, d. 7 April, 1852; 110, Cyrus, b. 20 Dec., 1833, d. 20 Nov., 1864; 111, Lyle, b. 21 Jan., 1835, d. ——; *m.* 3 Feb., 1869, Caroline King; 112, Albert, b. 15 Aug., 1840, d. —— 1900; 113, William; 114, John B., b. 3 Aug., 1844; 115, James H., b. 22 Sept., 1846; 116, Austin N., b. 24 Nov., 1848; 117, Mary A.

40. JOHNSTON SHEPHERD (Thomas[1], John[2], Jacob[3]), son of Jacob and Agnes (Johnston) Shepherd, b. 27 Feb., 1807; d. 5 Aug., 1874; *m.* 1st 1831, Melinda Livingston. Issue: 118, William Wiley, b. 24 Oct., 1832, d. ——; *m.* Mary A. Moore; 119, Ellison Livingston, b. 1 April, 1835; d. ——; *m.* Priscilla Robinson.
Johnston Shepherd *m.* 2d, 1837, Mary Henry. Issue: 120, Sarah Ann, b. 2 June, 1839, d. 14 Jan., 1896; 121, Henry Baring, b. 21 March, 1841; 122, Mary Elizabeth, b. 4 Dec., 1844, d. 11 Sept., 1878; 123, Margaret Agnes, b. 19 Sept., 1845.

41. ISAAC N. SHEPHERD (Rev.) (Thomas[1], John[2], Jacob[3]), son of Jacob and Agnes (Johnston) Shepherd, b. 29 May, 1809; d. 3 July, 18—; *m.* 1839, Hannah Barker. Issue: 124, Ellen, b. 2 Oct., 1840; 125, Jacob Henry, b. 29 Sept., 1842; 126, Julius Buckner, b. 27 Jan., 1845; 127, Edwin Hopkins, b. 12 Aug., 1847; 128, Chas. Melville (Rev.), b. 24 Feb., 1853; 129, Herbert, b. 8 Jan., 1856.

42. KEZIAH SHEPHERD (Thomas[1], John[2], Jacob[3]), dau. of Jacob and Agnes (Johnston) Shepherd, b. 5 March, 1812; d. 3 Sept., 1873; *m.* Edwin Hopkins. Issue: 130, Alonzo Albert, b. 17 Nov., 1837; 131, Melinda Shepherd, b. 2 June, 1841, d. Feb., 1886; 132, Luther Shanklin, b. 4 July, 1844, d. 21 Oct., 1865.

44. REAZON SHEPHERD (Thomas[1], John[2], Jacob[3]), son of Jacob and Agnes (Johnston) Shepherd, b. 3 Aug., 1816; d. 31 Dec., 1893; *m.* 29 Dec., 1852, at Greenfield, O., Sarah Amanda Wilson. Issue: 133, Edwin Arthur, b. 29 Dec., 1853; 134, Cora Wilson, b. 20 April, 1855; 135, Franklin Crothers, b. 14 July, 1858; 136, Wilson Nelson, b. 9 June, 1861, d. 2 April, 1891.

76. JOHN HORATIO SHEPHERD (Thomas[1], John[2], Abraham[3], Campbell A.[4]), son of Campbell A. and Mary A. (Johnston) Shepherd, b. 13 May, 1839; d. 27 June, 1872; *m.* Caroline Rose Schutt. Issue:
137, Edwin Avery, b. ——.

85. GEORGE S. DUNLAP (Thomas[1], John[2], Mary[3], James[4]), son of James and Mary (Stuart) Dunlap; d. Chattanooga, Tenn., 27 Jan., 1885; *m.* Fanny Alexander. Issue:
138, Jessie; 139, Margaret; 140, Grace.

87. NETTIE S. DUNLAP (Thomas[1], John[2], Mary[3], James[4]), dau. of James and Mary (Stuart) Dunlap, b. ——; d. ——; *m.* —— Kurtz. Issue:
141, Carrie, *m.* —— Fisher, Springfield, O.; 142, William; 143, Harrod.

106. AUGUSTUS SHEPHERD (Thomas[1], John[2], Jacob[3], Smiley[4]), son of Smiley and Elizabeth (Paul) Shepherd, b. 7 Feb., 1830; *m.* 1863, —— Ellen B. Shepherd. Issue:
144, Henry Lawrence, b. 17 Nov., 1863; 145, Jessie, b. 5 June, 1865; 146, Cyril P., b. 7 Nov., 1876; 147, Ethel Claire, b. 31 Jan., 1878; 148, Jennie Bailey, b. 25 Dec., 1879; 149, Bertha Hanna, b. 16 March, 1865.

111. LYLE SHEPHERD (Thomas[1], John[2], Jacob[3], Nelson[4]), son of Nelson and Mary (Baird) Shepherd, b. 21 Jan., 1835; *m.* 3 Feb., 1869, Caroline King. Issue:
150, Alma K.; 151 Maggie.

118. WILLIAM WILEY SHEPHERD (Thomas[1], John[2], Jacob[3], Johnston[4]), son of Johnston and Melinda (Livingston) Shepherd, b. 24 Oct., 1832; d. ——; *m.* Mary A. Moore. Issue:
152, L. Vernon, b. 21 March, 1863; 153, Harry Lincoln, b. 3 April, 1865; 154, Sarah May, b. 2 March, 1868.

135. FRANKLIN CROTHERS SHEPHERD (Thomas[1], John[2], Jacob[3], Reazon[4]), son of Reazon and Sarah A. (Wilson) Shepherd, b. 14 July, 1858; *m.* 1891, Nellie McKibben, living at Freeport, Ill. Issue:
155, Wilbur Leon, b. 8 Oct., 1895; 156, Cora Jeanette, b. 28 June, 1897; 157, Elinor Alice, b. 23 Aug., 1892.

DESCENDANTS OF MARY SHEPHERD

VII. MARY SHEPHERD (Thomas[1]), dau. of Thomas and Elizabeth (Van Metre) Shepherd, b. (sup.) Mecklenburg, Va., *circa* 1752; d. Brooke Co., Va., *m.* 1st John Feay, who emigrated to the vicinity of Wheeling Creek, *circa* 1780, and was living on the creek in 1787 where his lands adjoined those of his brother's-in-

law, David and William Shepherd. She *m.* 2d Samuel Buchanan. Issue:
1, John; 2, Thomas; 3, Eliza, *m.* Moses Creighton; 4, George, *m.* Sarah ——; 5, Joseph, *m.* Barbara King.

1. JOHN FEAY (Thomas[1], Mary[2]), son of John and Mary (Shepherd) Feay, b. ——; d. ——; *m.* —— ——. Issue:
6, Rachael, b. ——; d. ——; *m.* Henry Shepherd Thornburg, of Elm Grove, Ohio Co., Va.

4. GEORGE FEAY (Thomas[1], Mary[2]), son of John and Mary (Shepherd) Feay, b. ——; d. ——; *m.* Sarah ——. Issue:
7, Jennie E., b. ——; d. ——; *m.* Thomas Gist; 8, Margaret, b. ——; d. ——; *m.* 1st —— Beckham, *m.* 2d Bennie Feay.

5. JOSEPH FEAY (Thomas[1], Mary[2]), son of John and Mary (Shepherd) Feay, b. ——; d. ——; *m.* Barbara King. Issue:
9, Sarah, *m.* 1881, Edwin Roe; 10, Annie King, *m.* John S. Creighton; 11, Mary; 12, Francis.

DESCENDANTS OF MARTHA SHEPHERD

VIII. MARTHA SHEPHERD (Thomas[1]), dau. of Thomas and Elizabeth (Van Metre) Shepherd, b. Mecklenburg, Va., 1752; d. *circa* 1825; *m.* Oct., 1771, George McNabb, of Chester Co., Pa., who was b. *circa* 1746; d. 1/4 May, 1818, on his farm three miles southwest of Clairsville, Belmont Co., O. Issue:
1, Elizabeth, b. 24 July, 1772; d. 15 Nov., 1857; *m.* 28 Oct., 1794, Isaac Holmes, b. 29 April, 1764; d. 9 June, 1851.
2, Mary, b. 28 Feb., 1779; d. 26 Feb., 1858; *m.* 1795, Samuel Holmes, b. 26 March, 1776; d. 1 Jan., 1856.
3, John, b. 1780; d. Dec., 1851; *m.* 1803, Sarah Parrish, of Maryland.
4, Sarah, b. 26 Aug., 1783; d. 5 March, 1862; *m.* 26 Feb., 1799, Joseph Holmes, b. 27 Jan., 1771; d. 20 April, 1868.
5, Susannah, b. 12 Dec., 1789; d. 6 July, 1867; *m.* 14 Dec., 1809, Joseph Milnor, b. 31 June, 1786; d. 25 Dec., 1861.
6, George, Jr., b. 1792; d. Oct., 1868; *m.* 1821, Polly Hoge, of Belmont Co., Ohio, d. Oct., 1868.

1. ELIZABETH MCNABB (Thomas[1], Martha[2]), dau. of George and Martha (Shepherd) McNabb, b. 24 July, 1772; d. 15 Nov., 1857; *m.* 28 Oct., 1794, Isaac Holmes, b. 29 April, 1764; d. 9 June, 1851. Issue:
7, Martha, b. 1795; d. a widow, 1883; *m.* 1st 1815, Joseph Wilson; *m.* 2d Wm. Leeper.
8, Clunn, b. 1797, d. *unm.* 1820; 9, Sarah, b. 1799; d. 1884; *m.* Jacob Millisack, 1822.

10, Mary, b. 1801; d. 1864; *m.* 1822, James Price.

11, Nancy, b. 1803, d. 1805; 12, Susannah, b. 1806, d. 1893, *m.* 1823, Joseph Masters.

13, George W., b. 1807; d. 1887; *m.* 19 Jan., 1837, Mary Cripliver.

14, Samuel, b. 1811; d. 17 May, 1900; *m.* 8 Dec., 1841, Emily E. Pumphrey.

15, Elizabeth, b. 1815; d. 1891; *m.* 1837, Samuel Jenkins.

16, John McNabb, b. 1817; d. 1883; *m.* 1st 1839, Miss Jenkins; *m.* 2d 1851, Emily Stratton, who d. 190—.

2. MARY MCNABB (Thomas[1], Martha[2]), dau. of George and Martha (Shepherd) McNabb, b. Mecklenburg, Va., 28 Feb., 1779; d. 26 Feb., 1858; *m.* 1795, Samuel Holmes.   Issue:

17, Nackey, b. 1796; d. May 21, 1839; *m.* Daniel Huffman.

18, Elizabeth, b. 1797; *m.* Joseph Lanning.

19, Obadiah, b. 1799; d. *unm.*, 2 April, 1849; captain in the Mexican War.

20, Martha, b. 1802; d. ——; *m.* Samuel Osborn.

21, Mary, b. 1804; d. 24 Feb., 1843; *m.* John Dille.

22, Huldah, b. 1806; d. 22 Aug., 1837; *m.* Cephas Dille.

23, Margaret, b. 1809; d. ——; *m.* Isaac E. Osburn.

24, Phoebe, b. 1811; d. ——; *m.* James Taylor.

25, Sarah, b. 1813; d. ——, 1815; 26, Susannah, b. 1815; d. ——, *m.* George Tipton; 27, Nancy, b. 1816, d. ——, *m.* George Roberts; 28, Charlotte, b. 1819, d. ——, *m.* Francis Ward, living in 1905; 29, Sally, b. 1821, d. ——, *m.* William Ashton, living in 1905; 30, Rebecca, b. 1823, d. ——, *m.* Hiram King, living in 1905.

3. JOHN MCNABB (Thomas[1], Martha[2]), son of George and Martha (Shepherd) McNabb, b. Mecklenburg, Va., 4 July, 178·; d. Dec., 1851; *m.* 10 Nov., 1803, Sarah Parrish, of Maryland, b. 7 June, 1785, d. after 1831.   Issue:

31, Joseph, b. 4 Dec., 1804; *m.* 26 July, 1827, Jemima Horton.

32, Isaac, b. 16 July, 1806; *m.* Sept., 1831, Mahala Bush.

33, Elizabeth, b. 14 Jan., 1808; *m.* 5 Jan., 1828, George Cox.

34, Addison, b. 22 Jan., 1810; *m.* 9 May, 1835, Winney Thomas.

35, George, b. 27 Sept., 1811; d. 28 Sept., 1828.

36, Martha, b. 21 May, 1813; *m.* 7 Sept., 1837, John Sharples.

37, Sarah Ann, b. 12 Sept., 1815; *m.* 9 March, 1837, John Bradley.

38, Maria, b. 12 Oct., 1817; *m.* William Thomas.

39, Mary, b. 19 April, 1820; *m.* 12 April, 1869, James Copeland.

40, Susannah, b. 1 Oct., 1821; *m.* 24 May, 1846, Edward Wright.

41, John, b. 5 March, 1824; d. 17 April, 1904; *m.* 1849, Susannah Adams, b. 1830, d. 12 Aug., 1896.

42, Obadiah Holmes, b. 17 May, 1826; d. *circa* 1892.

DESCENDANTS OF MARTHA SHEPHERD

43, Margaret Jane, b. 8 Feb., 1831; *m.* 1st Dr. Sheldon; *m.* 2d
Wm. A. Oliver was living in 1909; 43½, John, b. 5 March,
1824, d. 190–, *m.* 1849, a Miss Adams, b. 1830, d. 1896.

4. SARAH MCNABB (Thomas[1], Martha[2]), dau. of George and
Martha (Shepherd) McNabb, b. 26 Aug., 1783; d. 5 March, 1862;
m. 26 Feb., 1799, Joseph Holmes, who with Isaac and Samuel,
were the sons of Obadiah and Mary (Clunn) Holmes, natives of
Monmouth Co., N. J. They emigrated in 1763 to Virginia and
removed later to Chartier's Creek, Strabane Township, Washington Co., Pa., where their home lay about 2½ miles from Catfish
Camp (Washington, Pa.). Joseph Holmes and Sarah McNabb
were married near St. Clairsville, O., and on the same day they
proceeded to their new home at Emerson, near Mt. Pleasant, O.
The place where Joseph Holmes lived, died and was buried from
is on Buffalo Creek, but in full sight of Beech Bottom and the
Ohio River at that point. The homestead is seventeen miles
north-northwest of Wheeling.   Issue:

44, George, b. 24 Oct., 1799; d. 29 June, 1886; *m.* 1st 8 March,
1822, Hannah Lynn; *m.* 2d 23 Aug., 1824, Tacy Thom-
son; *m.* 3d 7 Jan., 1834, Hannah Mansfield.

45, Mary, b. 25 April, 1801; d. Nov., 1882; *m.* 22 April, 1829,
John Glasener, who d. *ante* 1882.

46a, Elizabeth, b. 26 Dec., 1803; d. 22 June, 1851; *m.* 1st 7
Jan., 1818, Wm. Dickerson; *m.* 2d 20 Dec., 1822, Isaac
Thomas, b. 2 June, 1795, d. 21 May, 1876.

46b, Cynthia, b. 6 Jan., 1805; d. 26 Nov., 1844; *m.* 13 Jan.,
1821, John Stiers.

47, Asa, b. 4 Dec., 1806; d. 3 Jan., 1891; *m.* 2 Feb., 1837, Mary
McCoy, b. 12 May, 1814, d. 18 March, 1901.

48, Abraham, b. 1 Dec., 1808; d. 3 May, 1880; *m.* 1st 10 March,
1836, Rachael Mansfield, b. 14 Jan., 1814, d. 12 Feb.,
1854; *m.* 2d 15 May, 1856, Phoebe Ekey; still living.

49, Martha, b. 8 Jan., 1811; d. 9 Sept., 1893; *m.* 13 Nov., 1830,
John Webb, b. 5 Feb., 1806, d. 15 Jan., 1893.

50, Joseph, Jr., b. 12 May, 1815; d. 7 March, 1891; *m.* 1st 10
Feb., 1842, Mary J. Heberling, b. 18 April, 1816; d. 16
March, 1856; *m.* 2d *circa* 1860, Sarah Moore; still living.

51, Sarah, b. 27 Aug., 1817; d. ——; *m.* 3 Nov., 1841, James
Haverfield.

52, Susannah, b. 19 Feb., 1820; d. 4 Aug., 1878; *m.* 1st 16 Jan.,
1838, Joseph Webb, who died and was buried at sea
thirty miles off Acapulco, in May, 1850. He was one
of the argonauts bound for California. "He was attacked with fever while crossing the isthmus and suc-
cumbed as the vessel was going up the coast. He left a
wife, three nice children, and a fine farm, to go away off

there on an uncertainty." Susannah, *m.* 2d, *circa* 1854. Joseph Dunlap.

53, John, b. 6 Dec., 1821; d. 20 July, 1829.

5. SUSANNAH McNABB (Thomas[1], Martha[2]), dau. of George and Martha (Shepherd) McNabb, b. 12 Dec., 1789; d. 6 July, 1867; *m.* 14 Dec., 1809, Joseph Milner, b. 31 June, 1786; d. 25 Dec., 1861.   Issue:

54, George, b. 14 Dec., 1810; 55, Edward, b. 22 Aug., 1812, d. 30 Dec., 1831, *m.* Jane ——.

56, Sarah, b. 17 July, 1817; *m.* 3 Sept., 1857, Aquila Cowgill.

57, John, b. 3 June, 1816, d. ——, *m.* Miss Hoge; 58, Rezin, b. 16 Jan., 1818, d. ——; 59, Isaac, b. 25 Feb., 1820, d. ——, *m.* Isabella McCullogh; 60, Martha, b. 1 Nov., 1821, d. ——, *m.* John Lynn.

61, Jesse, b. 8 Aug., 1823; d. 1 April, 1895; *m.* 16 Oct., 1866, Mary Barry, b. 24 Dec., 1840, d. 2 March, 1899.

62, Joseph W., b. 14 Oct., 1825, d. *unm.,* 2 Feb., 1863; 63, Jane, b. 15 Feb., 1828, d. ——, *m.* Joseph Morton; 64, Asa, b. 23 Oct., 1831, d. ——, *m.* Jane Hair.

6. GEORGE McNABB, JR. (Thomas[1], Martha[2]), son of George and Martha (Shepherd) McNabb, b. 4 April, 1795; d. 21 Jan., 1868; *m.* 6 Dec., 1821, Polly Hoge, of Belmont Co., O.   Issue:

65, Martha, b. 20 Sept., 1822; still living; *m.* 21 Dec., 1859, John E. Davis, b. 8 April, 1825, d. 19 Oct., 1895.

66, Elizabeth, b. 20 Sept., 1826; d. 31 Jan., 1908; *m.* 14 April, 1849, Washington Norris, b. Aug., 1824, d. 19 Dec., 1900.

67, Isaac, b. 8 Jan., 1829; *m.* 1st, 1854, Deborah Devinney, d. Jan., 1887; *m.* 2d Cassandra Murray.

68, Hannah, b. 11 July, 1831; d. 20 Nov., 1906; *m.* April, 1876, Samuel Haskins, b. in England.

69, Susannah, b. 18 April, 1838; d. Feb., 1873; *m.* April, 1860, Edward Burchfield, d. Oct., 1905.

70, Solomon Hoge, b. 14 Oct., 1838; d. *unm.* 7 Sept., 1901.

71, William, b. 15 Aug., 1840; *m.* 14 July, 1870, Josephine Parish.

47. ASA HOLMES (Thomas[1], Martha[2], Sarah[3]), son of Joseph and Sarah (McNabb) Holmes, b. 4 Dec., 1806; d. 3 Jan., 1891; *m.* 2 Feb., 1837, Mary McCoy, b. 12 May, 1814; d. 18 March, 1901.   Issue:

74, James Taylor; 75, a dau.; 76, a dau.; 77, a dau.; 78, a son; 79, a dau.; 80, a son; 81, a dau.; 82, a son; 83, a son, b. 29 Sept., 1856.

74. JAMES TAYLOR HOLMES (Thomas[1], Martha[2], Sarah[3], Asa[4]), son of Asa and Mary (McCoy) Holmes, who was the daughter of Thomas and Hannah McCoy (pioneers from western Pennsylvania, at the close of the War of 1812); born in Short Creek

Township, Harrison Co., O., 25 Nov., 1837; lawyer; residing at Columbus, O.; *m.* 28 Dec., 1871, Lucy Kelley Bates, b. 9 Dec., 1850; dau. of Judge James L. Bates, who, from 1851 to 1866, was Judge of the Common Pleas Court in the Fifth Judicial District of Ohio; and granddaughter of the Hon. Alfred Kelley, late of Columbus, widely known and prominent in connection with the public works and railroad enterprises of Ohio. James T. Holmes received his elementary education in the public schools of his home district which was the only preparation he had received, when, in his seventeenth year, he left the farm and entered upon a classical course of study in Franklin College, New Athens, Ohio. His studies were characterized by zealous and indomitable industry; he achieved success as an essayist and debater; and received his A.B. in 1859. He tutored six classes at his alma mater 1858–59; in the latter year, was elected to the presidency of Richmond College, in Jefferson Co., O., where he remained until he was elected to the chair of mathematics in Iowa Wesleyan University, at Mount Pleasant, Iowa, July 1862; A.M. from Franklin College, 1862.

The Civil War being now in progress, the professorship in the university was declined to accept a call to a larger and higher duty—that of service to his state, in the Union Army. Commissioned as Second Lieutenant of Ohio Volunteers by Governor Tod, 11 Aug., 1862, he recruited, within four days thereafter, a company of 110 men, and upon the organization of the company was unanimously elected its captain. On the twenty-second day of the same month Company G was mustered into, and made a part of the 52d Regiment Ohio Volunteer Infantry, under the command of Colonel Daniel McCook, who was one of the famous family of "Fighting McCooks." Upon the 31 of August, following, this regiment entered upon the vigorous campaign which marked its career to the end of the war, and participating in some of its most important engagements; notably those of Chickamauga, 1863, Kenesaw Mountain, Siege of Atlanta, The March to the Sea, and Savannah, 1864; and in Averysboro and Bentonville on the march from Savannah to Raleigh, in 1865. At Kenesaw the gallant McCook, commanding the brigade, fell on the enemy's works. Major Holmes had been promoted prior to Chickamagua in which, and at Kenesaw, he commanded the regiment. In this famous assault of June 27, 1864, the 52d Regiment went into action with 450 men and in the "maelstrom" of shot and shell lost 108 men, more than 80 of them at the climax of the engagement, in the brief space of eight minutes—almost 25 per cent. of its force. Major Holmes was commissioned a lieutenant-colonel after this event by Governor Brough and was subsequently brevetted to that rank by the President "from the 13th of March, 1865." After the "muster-out" Colonel Holmes turned his attention to the choice of a profession; he read law with Francis Collins, Esq., of Columbus, and was admitted to the bar of the state, in that city, 8 May, 1867, where he has ever since resided and practised. Was admitted to the Federal Bar at Cincinnati, O., 1870; one of the organizers and the Secretary of the Ohio State Bar Association, 1880–1890; President of the same, 1890–1891; in the latter year received the degree of LL.D. from Franklin College.

Mr. Holmes is said to possess one of the largest and finest private libraries of law and literature to be found in the state. His researches in the lines of history and biography are frequently published, and the manuscript results of his investigations and collections are contained in nearly fifty bound volumes, aggregating more than 40,000 pages.   Issue:

84, Mabel; 85, Constance; 86, Lawrence Asa, b. 23 Oct., 1881, m. 19 July, 1909, Dolena MacIvor, South Cove, Cape Breton, N. S. She was b. 25 Dec., 1881; 87, Helen, b. 10 April, 1887; d. 8 May, 1887; 88, Eleanor, b. 14 March, 1892.

81. MARY ELLEN HOLMES (Thomas[1], Martha[2], Sarah[3], Asa[4]), dau. of Asa and Mary (McCoy) Holmes, b. 2 Feb., 1849; m. 8 March, 1870, Samuel McCleary Dickerson, b. 13 April, 1844, son of Joseph and Mary (Jones) Dickerson, and grandson of Thomas and Mary (Curry) Dickerson.   Issue:

89, Lucy Bates, b. 30 Sept., 1871; m. Rev. Geo. R. Grose, of the M. E. Church.

90, Oliver Hamline, b. 19 Nov., 1873, unm. C. E.; 91, Gertrude.

84. MABEL HOLMES (Thomas[1], Martha[2], Sarah[3], Asa[4], Jas. T.[5]), dau. of James T. and Lucy K. (Bates) Holmes, b. 13 Oct., 1874; m. 27 April, 1897, John Dudley Dunham, b. 23 Aug., 1873. Issue:

92, Lucy Bates, b. 9 Feb., 1898; 93, John Milton, b. 11 May, 1901; 94, Theodore Chadbourne, 2 Oct., 1906; 95, Alfred Bates, b. 16 April, 1908.

85. CONSTANCE HOLMES (Thomas[1], Martha[2], Sarah[3], Asa[4], James T.[5]), dau. of James T. and Lucy K. (Bates) Holmes, b. 20 Sept., 1877; m. 2 April, 1901, Alonzo Hathaway Dunham, b. 30 Aug., 1874.   Issue:

96, Taylor Holmes, b. 4 June, 1902; 97, Harold Hathaway, b. 1 Sept., 1903; 98, Elizabeth Gilmour, b. 13 Oct., 1907; 99, Marshall Bates, b. 4 Dec., 1908.

91. GERTRUDE DICKERSON (Thomas[1], Martha[2], Sarah[3], Asa[4], Mary E.[5]), dau. of Samuel M. and Mary E. (Holmes) Dickerson, b. 23 Jan., 1878; m. 28 Nov., 1901, Rev. Harry Franklin Kerr, of the Presbyterian Church.   Issue:

100, Marcus Kerr.

CAPTAIN ABRAHAM SHEPHERD

IX. ABRAHAM SHEPHERD, the youngest son of Capt. Thomas and Elizabeth (Van Metre) Shepherd, *m.* 27 Dec., 1780, Eleanor Strode, dau. of Capt. James Strode, an early settler of Frederick Co., Va., whose lands were located on the waters of the Opequon a few miles east of the present site of Martinsburg, W. Va. James Strode was one of the first justices of Berkeley Co. (in 1772) ; a commissioner of revenue; a committee to let the contract for the building of the County court house, and one of the town trustees of Martinsburg. His son-in-law, Abraham Shepherd, afterward became the owner of the Strode homestead, and it is claimed that on this estate, in the days of James Strode, Andrew Jackson was born, 1765, who, in the course of time, became one of the presidents of the United States. It is said that Jackson was born on the Strode farm in 1765 and shortly after was taken by his parents on their emigration to the Waxhaw Settlements in North Carolina (West Va. Hist. Mag., Oct., 1902, pp. 7-8).

Abraham Shepherd was just of age when the War of the Revolution began, and he, like his eldest brother, was an ardent patriot and joined the ranks when the call to arms rang through the Valley of Virginia and her sturdy bordersmen hastened to join the militia—Berkeley Co., Va., gave the cause of the colonies her ablest men and many who were destined to be great; out of her free soil sprang no less than five generals of the Revolution, besides lesser officials, who gained their laurels in the great liberty-giving epoch. Two companies were recruited in the little settlement behind the Blue Ridge; they were riflemen whose name brought fear upon the ranks of the enemy: Morgan's and Stephenson's. Abraham Shepherd became a lieutenant of Hugh Stephenson's company when it was recruited at Morgan's Spring, near Shepherdstown, and from thence, with its crimson banner bearing the device of the Culpepper Minute-men—that company started east on its famous " bee-line-for-Boston" March, 17 July, 1775. The company after a rapid journey reached Boston and joined Washington's Army at Cambridge, 10 Aug., 1775—two days ahead of Daniel Morgan's company of riflemen, and several days in advance of Cresap's Marylanders—all of whom started from their rendezvous at the same time, but each taking different routes (Am. Arch., Vol. III., p. 1, 2).

From that day of the muster at Morgan's Spring Abraham Shepherd's military career was an active one, and he, brave, hardy, enduring—with, at times, perilous service in engagements and battles—came out of them unscathed. At the battle of Kingsbridge, New York, Nov., 1776, where his superior officers, Colonel Rawlins and Major Otho Williams, were wounded, Abraham

Shepherd commanded the regiment of Maryland and Virginia riflemen during the remainder of the engagement with great courage and credit; and for their valorous conduct on that occasion General Washington, only a short time before his fatal illness, wrote Captain Shepherd a highly complimentary letter (History of Lower Shenandoah, and Lee of Virginia, p. 471). After the Kingsbridge engagement Congress appointed Lieutenant Shepherd to the command of a company and gave him a captain's commission in a Virginia regiment (Am. Arch., 5th Ser., Vo. I., p. 1570).

He served with Col. Daniel Morgan in September and October of 1777 in the Burgoyne campaign; and was a witness to the surrender of the British general at Saratoga. The Hessian prisoners taken at the surrender were sent to the Valley of Virginia under Morgan's escort and were cantoned near Winchester, and here many of them preferred to remain after the war was over. In passing, it will be interesting to note that the fine old home of General Morgan, which he later erected in Winchester, was by him, called "Saratoga" and it is said that some of his former Hessian prisoners assisted in its construction.

Some time after the Burgoyne surrender, Abraham Shepherd was taken prisoner by the British and was sent to Long Island; he was however paroled and permitted to return to his home in Virginia. Upon this subject I quote the following extracts from letters to his broher, Col. David Shepherd, of Ohio Co., Va. "Mecklinburg, 22 May, 1778; I am on parole; no time limited for that reason you can't expect news. My health is not perfect. I left my friends well on Long Island. I arrived yesterday." Another "Fredericksburg, October, 1778"; and "On Creek, 28 Nov., 1778" (meaning, perhaps, "on Opequon Creek where his expected father-in-law lived, and which letter was carried west by his uncle, Jacob Van Metre, whose wife was also a Strode), "Am still enjoying unlimited liberty." Writing again: "Mecklinburg, 18 June, 1779," reiterates his "apprehension of being called to the British, as I am not confidant of being exchanged," adding that "the ferry is now established in my name" (Shepherd Papers, Vol. I., p. 117, at Madison, Wis.). It is evident that he was either released or exchanged before the summer of 1779, for he was with the Continental Army of the North and in the vicinity of the Hudson River about this time. But before this period he was again with Gen. Daniel Morgan's regiment, now attached to General Woodford's brigade.

"Friday, May 6, 1779; Captain Shepherd and myself set off for headquarters. Had a most fatigueing journey over the mountains to New Windsor [on the Hudson, 6 miles above West Point] and a tedious rainy passage down the river to Light Infantry. We passed headquarters and West Point and arrived at the Light Infantry about 1 o'clock.

CAPTAIN ABRAHAM SHEPHERD

"Saturday, 7th, Capt. Shepherd and myself dined at Headquarters and lodged at New Windsor" (Memoirs of Gen. John Cropper).

In August of 1779 he returned to Virginia permanently. A number of letters passed from him to his brother David dated from various points in the neighborhood of his home, and indicating, by their tenor, his retirement from service. In December, 1780, he was married. For his services in the Revolution Captain Shepherd, in 1784, was granted 5,000 acres of land by the State of Virginia (Saffell's Revolutionary Soldiers, p. 506).

Settling down to private life, Abraham Shepherd now devoted his attention to the development of his personal estate, and for the exploitation and well-being of Shepherdstown. His was the energetic spirit in the formation of its government and his initiative advanced its resources, fostered its industries and invested the little town on the bank of the Potomac with such dynamic progressiveness that it become a place of real importance. Here Rumsey the inventor, and with the village blacksmith, perfected the steamboat and, ably supported by Abraham Shepherd, achieved his first success when its trial took place upon the waters of the Potomac, 3 Dec., 1787, in the presence of some of the most distinguished citizens of the country. Then Shepherdstown became nationally known. Following in the steps of this important event came the agitation for the location of the seat of the national government. Many, and strongly urged, were the claims put forth for its establishment at Shepherdstown. The Shepherds strenuously advocated it; the newspapers of that section rallied to its support and subscriptions were solicited for the erection of the Federal buildings—but eventually all these efforts failed (Lewis's History of West Virginia, p. 614). *Sic transit gloria mundi!*

Abraham Shepherd was an influential, consistent member of the Episcopal church (of Norbonne Parish), at Shepherdstown, which his father had generously endowed; and in this connection Bishop Meade thus speaks of him: "He was a true friend of the church in its darkest days" (Meade's Historic Churches of Virginia; Lee of Virginia, and History of Lower Shenandoah). "He was a thin-visaged, little man of prominent features, full of energy, a first-rate farmer, and an unfailing friend of the church, traits which have been literally transmitted to some of his descendants" (History of Lower Shenandoah, p. 413).

SOME ABRAHAM SHEPHERD RECORDS

1778, Oct. Act of Assembly authorizing and granting privilege of operating a ferry to Abraham Shepherd from his land, over the Potomac, to Thos. Swearingen's land in Maryland (Hening's

Statutes, Va., Vol. X., p. 197). This was repealed by the Assembly, 1779.

———. Regulating, by Act of Assembly, Oct., 1778, price of ferriage, "1 man, 6 pence," over Abraham Shepherd's ferry to Thomas Swearingen's land in Maryland (*Vide*, Vol. IX., p. 546).

1787, Dec. 20. Record of survey of 1,000 acres of land on Turkey Run, Ohio Co., Va., and for 700 acres granted 5 April, 1783, on Gillespy's and Turkey Run (Survey Bk., No. 2, pp. 81–83, Wheeling),

1788, Oct. Act of Assembly authorizing Abraham Shepherd to build tobacco warehouse at Mecklenburg (Hening's Statutes, Vol. XII., p. 778).

1791, Dec. 11. Surveyed for Abraham Shepherd 200 acres of land on two military warrants, nos. 1915 and 1919, on the waters of Brush Creek. (Sig.): Nath. Massie; Wit.: John Scott, Duncan McKendrick and John Youkhana, chain bearers (Abr. Shepherd's Note-book).

1792, Oct. Act of Assembly in reference to the establishment of a system of tobacco inspection; among these places mentioned that of "at Shepherd's Warehouse, Mecklinberg" (Hening's Statutes, Vol. XIII., p. 481).

1793, Oct. 26. Surveyed for Abraham Shepherd, warrant no. 290, 1,000 acres on Backfork, Brush Creek, Ohio County.

Warrant no. 290. 1,000 acres on East Fork, Brush Creek, Ohio County.

———, Oct. 28. Warrant no. 3432, 4,000 acres on waters, East Fork, Brush Creek.

———, Nov. 3. Warrant no. 290 (Military Warrant), 1,000 acres on the waters of Red B(ud?) Creek, northwest of Ohio River. (Sig.): Nath. Massie. Wit.: Duncan McKendrick, Robert Smith, and Thomas Short, chain bearers.

DESCENDANTS OF ABRAHAM SHEPHERD

IX. ABRAHAM SHEPHERD (Thomas[1]), son of Thomas Shepherd and Elizabeth (Van Metre) Shepherd, b. 10 Nov., 1754, at Mecklenburg, Va.; d. 7 Sept., 1822, at same; *m.* by Rev. Daniel Sturgis, first rector of the Episcopal Church at Shepherdstown, 27 Dec., 1780, Eleanor Strode, dau. of Capt. James Strode, of Shepherdstown; she was b. 27 June, 1760; d. 23 Sept., 1853.

Issue:

1, James Strode, b. 19 June, 1782; d. 5 May, 1789.

2, Rezin Davis, b. 1 Aug., 1784; d. 10 Nov., 1865; *m.* Lucy Gorham.

3, Abraham, Jr., b. 13 June, 1787; d. 9 Oct., 1853; *m.* Helen or Eleanora Peck.

4, James Hervey, b. 5 May, 1790; d. 27 July, 1837, *unm.*
5, Henry, b. 4 Jan., 1793; d. 12 Oct., 1870.
6. Annie, b. 13 June, 1796; d. 16 Sept., 1866; *m.* Dr. Thomas Hammond.
7, Eliza, b. 26 July, 1799; d. 25 Aug., 1833; *m.* Edmund Jennings Lee.
8, Charles Moses, b. 11 April, 1800; d. Oct., 1851; *m.* Margaret Hook.

2. REZIN DAVIS SHEPHERD (Thomas[1], Abraham[2]), son of Abraham and Eleanor (Strode) Shepherd, b. 1 Aug., 1784; d. 10 Nov., 1865; *m.* Lucy Gorham, of Massachusetts. She was b. 1789; d. at Sweet Springs, Va., 23 Aug., 1814.   Issue:
    9, James Henry; 10, Anne; 11, Eliza; 12, Charles Moses; 13, Ellen; 14, a child, d. Sweet Springs, Va., 4 Aug., 1814.

3. ABRAHAM SHEPHERD, JR. (Thomas[1], Abraham[2]), son of Abraham and Eleanor (Strode) Shepherd, b. 13 June, 1787; d. 9 Oct., 1853; *m.* Helen Peck, of Staunton, Va.   Issue:
    15, James Hervey, b. —, 1823, *m.* Florence Hamtranck; 16, Catharine, *m.* Robert A. Lucas; 17, Frances R., *m.* Robert McMurran; 18, Ellen, *m.* —— ——; 19, Henry St. John; 20, William Meade; 21, Robert F., d. in Civil War; 22, Valeria, *m.* Mr. Carter; 23, Alexander H., d. in Civil War; 24, Lucy; 25, Mary.

5. HENRY SHEPHERD (Thomas[1], Abraham[2]), son of Abraham and Eleanor (Strode) Shepherd, b. 4 Jan., 1793; d. 12 Oct., 1870; *m.* 7 May, 1822, Fanny E. Briscoe, b. 7 May, 1800, dau. of Dr. John and Eleanor (Magruder) Briscoe, of " Piedmont, Jefferson Co., W. Va."   Issue:
    26, Mary Eleanor, b. 18 July, 1824, d. 18 Aug., 1825; 27, Rezin Davis, b. 7 July, 1826, d. 2 Nov., 1862; 28, Ann Elizabeth, b. 25 Aug., 1828, d. 30 Nov., 1833; 29, Henry, b. 13 June, 1831, d. 1891; 30, John, b. 9 June, 1833, d. 20 June, 1879, *unm.*; 31, Abraham, b. 21 March, 1836, was a soldier in the Confederate Army, was captured and sentenced to death, but finally exchanged; 32, James Truro, b. 21 Aug., 1838.

6. ANN SHEPHERD (Thomas[1], Abraham[2]), dau. of Abraham and Eleanor (Strode) Shepherd, b. 13 June, 1796; d. 16 Sept., 1866; *m.* Dr. Thomas Hammond.   Issue:
33, Mary.

7. ELIZA SHEPHERD (Thomas[1], Abraham[2]), dau. of Abraham and Eleanor (Strode) Shepherd, b. 26 July, 1799; d. 25 Aug., 1833; *m.* Edmund Jennings Lee, a descendant of Col. Richard Lee, of Virginia; a graduate of Princeton College; and a lawyer,

of Shepherdstown, W. Va., b. Alexandria, Va., 3 May, 1797; d. at "Leeland," Shepherdstown, W. Va., 10 Aug., 1877. He was the author of "Lee, of Virginia." Issue:

34, Ellen, b. 23 Sept., 1824, d. at "Leeland" 25 Aug., 1865; 35, Chas. Shepherd, b. 17 Sept., 1826, lives at Berryville, Va.

8. CHARLES MOSES SHEPHERD (Thomas[1], Abraham[2]), son of Abraham and Eleanor (Strode) Shepherd, b. 11 April, 1800; d. Oct., 1851; m. Margaret Hook, of Louisiana. Issue:

36, Harriett; 37, Richard; 38, Charles.

13. ELLEN SHEPHERD (Thomas[1], Abraham[2], Rezin D.[3]), dau. of Rezin D., and Lucy (Gorham) Shepherd, b. ——; d. ——; m. Gorham Brookes, of Boston, Mass. Issue:

39, Peter Gorham; 40, Shepherd; 41, Fannie, m. Mr. Allen, of Pittsburg.

27. REZIN DAVIS SHEPHERD (Thomas[1], Abraham[2], Henry[3]), son of Henry and Fannie E. (Briscoe) Shepherd, b. 7 July, 1826; d. 2 Nov., 1862; m. Elizabeth Stockton Boteler, of Shepherdstown, W. Va. Issue:

42, Fanny; 43, Alexandria; 44, Davis.

29. HENRY SHEPHERD (Thomas[1], Abraham[2], Henry[3]), son of Henry and Fannie E. (Briscoe) Shepherd, b. 13 Jan., 1831; d. ——, 1891; m. Azemia McLean, of New Orleans. Issue:

45, Rezin Davis, an actor; 46, Henry; 47, William J.; 48, Augustus M.

31. ABRAHAM SHEPHERD (Thomas[1], Abraham[2], Henry[3]), son of Henry and Fanny E. (Briscoe) Shepherd, b. 21 March, 1836; m. 1871, his cousin, Elizabeth, dau. of Dr. E. Clagett and Sarah C. (Shepherd) Williams, of Shepherdstown, W. Va. Abraham was in the Confederate service during the Civil War; was captured and sentenced to death, but was finally exchanged. Issue:

49, Edward C., b. 17 Jan., 1872; unm.; Martinsburg, Va.

50, James Truro, b. 27 March, 1873; 51, Henry Abraham, b. 8 Jan., 1875, d. 13 Jan., 1875.

52, Elizabeth Briscoe, b. 15 Dec., 1875(?); 53, Sallie C., b. 4 Dec., 1878, m. Chas. Butler, of Shepherdstown, 22 Aug., 1900.

54, Mary Fanny, b. 16 March, 1884; 55, Louisa V. (or Laura), b. 16 March, 1888.

34. ELLEN LEE (Thomas[1], Abraham[2], Eliza[3]), dau. of Edmund J. and Eliza (Shepherd) Lee, b. 23 Sept., 1824; d. at "Leeland," 25 Aug., 1865; m. 17/18 Sept., 1844, John Simms Powell, son of Cuthbert Powell, of Va. Issue:

56, Eliza Shepherd, b. ——, d. 1854; 57, Cuthbert, b. Salisbury, Fairfax Co., Va., 29 April, 1849.

58, Katharine Simms, b. "Salisbury," Fairfax Co., Va., 18 March, 1851.

59, Edmund Lee, b. "Salisbury," Fairfax Co., Va., 16 May, 1852.

60, Simms, b. "Salisbury," Fairfax Co., Va., 3 Sept., 1854.

61, Eleanor Strode, b. "Salisbury," Fairfax Co., Va., 14 May, 1857.

62, Laura Stewart, b. "Salisbury," Fairfax Co., Va., 31 May, 1859.

63, Sally Lee, b. "Bedford," Jefferson Co., W. Va., 5 Aug., 1861.

64, Charles Lee, b. Lexington, Va., 19 March, 1868.

35. CHARLES SHEPHERD LEE (Thomas[1], Abraham[2], Eliza[3]), son of Edmund J. and Eliza (Shepherd) Lee, b. 17 Sept., 1826; d. ——; m. 16 May, 1849, Margaret H., dau. of Mann H. and Margaret (Beale) Page. Issue:

65, Eliza Shepherd; 66, Margaret Page; 67, Charles Randolph; 68, Edmonia Louise; 69, Ellen Byrd; 70, Phillips Fitzgerald; 71, Edwin Grey; 72, Mann Randolph Page; 73, Eliza Holmes; 73a, Rezin Davis.

45. REZIN D. SHEPHERD (Thomas[1], Abraham[2], Henry[3], Henry[4]), son of Henry and Azemia (McLean) Shepherd, b. ——; d. ——; m. 1st Marie Prescott, who d. 1893; m. 2d, 2 April, 1897, Odette Tyler. Rezin D. Shepherd was known in theatrical circles as "R. S. McLean"; lived on the "Wild Goose Farm," on the Potomac, near Shepherdstown, W. Va.

46. HENRY SHEPHERD (Thomas[1], Abraham[2], Henry[3], Henry[4]), son of Henry and Azemia (McLean) Shepherd, b. ——; d. ——; m. Miss Rinehart. Issue:

74, Henry.

57. CUTHBERT POWELL (Thomas[1], Abraham[2], Eliza[3], Ellen[4]), son of J. Simms and Ellen (Lee) Powell, b. 27 April, 1849, at Salisbury, Fairfax Co., Va.; d. ——; m. 27 July, 1886, at Kansas City, Mo., Lucie Sidney, dau. of Wash. and Mary (Dill) Davis. Issue:

75, Lucie Beverly, b. Kansas City, Mo., 13 Jan., 1889; 76, Cuthbert, b. Kansas City, Mo., 6 Sept., 1890.

60. SIMMS POWELL (Thomas[1], Abraham[2], Eliza[3], Ellen[4]), son of J. Simms and Ellen (Lee) Powell, b. 3 Aug., 1854; d. ——; m. 2 Dec., 1882, at Richmond, Va., Marie Eustace, dau. William and Caroline P. Brent. Issue:

77, Caroline B., b. Parkersburg, W. Va., 9 April, 1884.
78, John Simms, b. Parkersburg, W. Va., 5 April, 1886.
79, William B., b. Parkersburg, W. Va., 20 Aug., 1887.
80, Ellen Lee, b. Parkersburg, W. Va., 2 Nov., 1889.

81, Edmund Lee, b. Parkersburg, W. Va., 9 July, 1892.
82, Lucy Ludwell, b. Parkersburg, W. Va., 29 Sept., 1894.

61. ELEANOR STRODE POWELL (Thomas[1], Abraham[2], Eliza[3], Ellen[4]), dau. of J. Simms and Ellen (Lee) Powell, b. "Salisbury," Fairfax Co., Va., 14 May, 1857; d. ——; *m.* 27 Sept., 1881, at Shepherdstown, W. Va., Henry W. Potts, son of Joseph and Annie (Clay) Potts, of Pottstown, Pa.; b. there 4 Jan., 1847, and a descendant of the original Joseph Potts, the pioneer ironmaster of the Schuylkill Valley, Pa. Issue:

83, Eleanor Lee, b. Shepherdstown, W. Va., 11 Nov., 1884.
84, Joseph Henry, b. Shepherdstown, W. Va., 28 Dec., 1887.
85, Margaret Anna, b. Shepherdstown, W. Va., 10 May, 1890.
86, Llewellyn Powell, b. Jamesville, S. C., 9 Feb., 1895.

62. LAURA STEWART POWELL (Thomas[1], Abraham[2], Eliza[3], Ellen[4]), dau. of J. Simms and Ellen (Lee) Powell, b. "Salisbury," 31 May, 1859; d. ——; *m.* 4 May, 1886, at Shepherdstown, W. Va., Rev. W. T. Roberts, rector of Old Bruton Parish Church, at Williamsburg, Va. Issue:

87, Ellen Lee, b. at Culpeper, Va., 7 April, 1888.
88, William Saunders, b. at Harrisonburg, Va., 24 Jan., 1891.
89, Laura Powell, b. in Mecklenburg Co., W. Va., 13 April, 1893.

90, Edward Lee, b. at Williamsburg, Va., 6 Dec., 1894.

64. CHARLES LEE POWELL (Thomas[1], Abraham[2], Eliza[3], Ellen[4]), son of J. Simms and Ellen (Lee) Powell, b. Lexington, Va., 19 March, 1868; d. ——; *m.* 25 June, 1893, at Los Angeles, Cal., Laura Crane Haughawat, dau. of Wm. J. and Ada M. She was b. 7 Feb., 1869, at Neosha Falls, Kansas (see Lee of Virginia).

DESCENDANTS OF SUSANNAH SHEPHERD

X. SUSANNAH SHEPHERD (Thomas[1]), dau. of Thomas and Elizabeth (Van Metre) Shepherd, b. in Virginia, 1 Sept., 1758; d. in Wheeling, W. Va., 13 April, 1835; *m.* in Shepherdstown, Va., 15 April, 1777, John Eoff, who was b. 14 Feb., 1752; d. at Wheeling, Ohio Co., Va., 13 Feb., 1831. John Eoff is said to have been a resident of the Shenandoah Valley at the time of Thomas Shepherd's arrival there in 1733, and later was associated with Lord Fairfax in sundry land transactions in and about Shepherdstown. Evidence of these business relations were found in many curious parchments, documents, deeds and papers, which were in the possession of Mr. Beverley M. Eoff, at Wheeling, about the year 1858. These papers have disappeared entirely since that time, otherwise they would at this time have likely thrown much light on the obscurity which envelops the American origin or beginning of the Shepherd family.

DESCENDANTS OF SUSANNAH SHEPHERD

About the year 1789 John Eoff removed from Shepherdstown to Wheeling, where he continued in the accumulating of land. He was probably a son of Jacob Eoff, Sr., a German Palatine, who emigrated to New York, *ante* 1742; settled in Somerset Co., N. J.; vestryman of Zion Lutheran Church at New Germantown, 1767; took oath of allegiance in Somerset Co., N. J., 22 July, 1777; was of the Pluckamin settlement; will probated in Somerset Co., N. J., 10 Sept., 1780; and is said to have been over 100 years old at time of his death. Issue:

1, Elizabeth, *m.* Robert Woods; issue, a son and a daughter.
2, Susan, *m.* John White; issue, a son and five daughters.
3, Eleanor, *m.* Andrew White; issue, two sons and three daughters.
4, Naomi, *m.* 1st John Williams; issue, two daughters; *m.* 2d Chas. Cecil; issue, one son and two daughters.
5, John.

5. JOHN EOFF (Thomas¹, Susannah²), son of John and Susannah (Shepherd) Eoff, b. Shepherdstown, Va., 2 Oct., 1788; d. Wheeling, Va., 28 Jan., 1859; *m.* 17 Oct., 1812, at Kanawha, Va., Helen Starke Quarrier, b. Richmond, Va., 27 Sept., 1793; d. Wheeling, Va., 8 Oct., 1876.

John Eoff was a famous physician of Wheeling, Va.; educated at Jefferson College, Philadelphia, under the supervision of the celebrated Dr. Benjamin Rush, and graduated in 1809. Dr. Eoff soon became an authority in medicine and acquired an extensive reputation and practice. He had an inventive faculty in his own domain as a physician, as well as in the general field of physics, formulating prescriptions and remedies which were found in every household, and the knowledge and use of these formulas extended far beyond his native state. In the realm of physics he was equally at home. In 1855, he built the first cement houses; they are still standing. His most famous experiment was his attempt to manufacture sugar from the juices of sorghum cane, but it proved an utter failure, because he could not granulate the juices by the various processes he devised. The problem remains unsolved to the present day.

It was about 1849, that he placed black bass, taken from the Ohio River and its tributaries, in the tank of a locomotive and sent them to the Smithsonian Institution at Washington, where they were used to stock the Potomac. He was a close observer and student of the habits of fishes. As an authority in piscatorial sport, his advice was sought by all classes. His passion for hunting was keen and his excursions frequent through his native streams and forests in quest of their habitants. He owned, practically, all of the lower half of the city of Wheeling, and had control of the water front of the Ohio on the Virginia side. He built mills, warehouses, houses, tenements and a theatre. He lived, as did the gentlemen of his day, without ostentation, but in a large and commodious mansion, with slaves, horses and equipages at his command. In habits and manners he was a simple, kindly gentleman, easily approached, and greatly beloved by his neighbors and the citizens generally.   Issue:

6, John Quarrier, b. Charleston, Va., 5 Aug., 1813; d. Wheeling, Va., 5 April, 1856.

7, Elizabeth Susannah, b. Charleston, Va., 18 April, 1815; d. Philadelphia, Pa., 5 Feb., 1885.

8, Margaret Alexander, b. Wheeling, Va., 28 May, 1817; d. Charleston, Va., 26 Dec., 1884.

9, Virginia Southgate, b. Wheeling, Va., 15 Oct., 1819; d. Washington, D. C., 13 April, 1897.

10, Beverley McKree, b. Wheeling, Va., 13 Dec., 1822; d. Wheeling, W. Va., 2 Jan., 1887.

11, Caroline Mary, b. Wheeling, Va., 27 Sept., 1827; d. Santa Barbara, Cal., 25 Aug., 1896.

12, Alexander Quarrier, b. Wheeling, Va., 26 Mar., 1828.

13, Helen Corrina, b. Wheeling, Va., 27 Nov., 1830; d. Wheeling, W. Va., 24 Sept., 1897.

14, Charles William, b. Wheeling, Va., 21 Feb., 1833; d. New York City, 31 Jan., 1854.

15, Henrietta Miller, b. Wheeling, Va., 20 May, 1836; d. Bethlehem, Pa., 12 April, 1894.

6. JOHN QUARRIER EOFF (Thomas[1], Susannah[2], John[3]), son of John and Helen (Quarrier) Eoff, *m.* Mary Ann ——.   Issue:
16, William Chapline.

7. ELIZABETH SUSANNAH EOFF (Thomas[1], Susannah[2], John[3]), dau. of John and Helen S. (Quarrier) Eoff, *m.* James S. Stout, of Wheeling, Va.; no issue.

8. MARGARET ALEXANDER EOFF (Thomas[1], Susannah[2], John[3]), dau. of John and Helen S. (Quarrier) Eoff, *m.* Charles S. Whitteker, of Charleston, Va.   Issue:
17, Helen Danbury; 18, Virginia C.; 19, Emily S.; 20, Caroline T., d. young; 21, Henry T.; 22, Corrina S.

9. VIRGINIA SOUTHGATE EOFF (Thomas[1], Susannah[2], John[3]), dau. of John and Helen S. (Quarrier) Eoff, *m.* Roderick S. Moodey, of Steubenville, O.   Issue:
23, John S., *m.* May E.; 24, David, *unm.*; 25, Helen Q.; 26, Chas. E.; 27, James S.; 28, Virginia; 29, Beverley E.; 30, Roderick S.; 31, Edward McC.; 32, Margaret W., *unm.*

10. BEVERLEY MCKREE EOFF (Thomas[1], Susannah[2], John[3]), son of John and Helen S. (Quarrier) Eoff, *m.* Harriet Laidley, dau. of Robert C. Woods, of Wheeling, W. Va. She d. 10 April, 1904, at Christiansburg, Va.   Issue:

33, Robert Woods; 34, Elizabeth Stout; 35, John Ravencroft; 36, Margaret Roberta; 37, Chas. William; 38, Josephine McCabe; 39, Virginia Southgate; 40, Beverley Mc-Kree, Jr.

11. CAROLINE MARY EOFF (Thomas[1], Susannah[2], John[3]), dau. John and Helen S. (Quarrier) Eoff, *m.* Henry Tallant, of Santa Barbara, Cal.   Issue:
    41, Drury, J.; 42, William F.; 43, Beverley E.; 44, Walter S.; 45, Edward C.; 46, Henry K.; 47, Caroline L.; 48, Alfred; 49, Chas. L.; 50, Elizabeth B.

12. ALEXANDER QUARRIER EOFF (Thomas[1], Susannah[2], John[3]), son of John and Helen S. (Quarrier) Eoff, of Columbus, O.; *m.* Lavinia C——.   Issue:
    50*a*, Mary L. J., d. inf.; 50*b*, John Q., d. *unm.*; 50*c*, Thomas Delaplaine. Alexander Q. Eoff d. at Columbus, O., 2 Feb., 1906, aged 78 years. His wife d. at Carnegie, Pa., 9 April, 1906, aged 77 years.

13. HELEN CORRINE EOFF (Thomas[1], Susannah[2], John[3]), dau. of John and Helen S. (Quarrier) Eoff, *m.* John P. Gilchrist, of Wheeling, W. Va.   Issue:
    51, Margaret J.; 52, John Eoff; 53, Caroline T.; 54, Minnie Eoff; 55, Charles Eoff; 56, Henry D.; 57, Robert A.

15. HENRIETTA MILLER EOFF (Thomas[1], Susannah[2], John[3]), dau. of John and Helen S. (Quarrier) Eoff, *m.* Adams Dodson, of Bethlehem, Pa.
    58, James S.

16. WILLIAM CHAPLINE EOFF (Thomas[1], Susannah[2], John[3], John Q.[4]), son of John Q. and Mary Ann Eoff, *m.* 1st Fannie ——; *m.* 2d Ella ——.   Issue:
    59, Louise Garrett; 60, Sadie, d. y.; 61, Laura Maude, *unm.*; 62, Ella McCausland; 63, Oscar Edgerly, d. y.
    William C. Eoff d. St. Louis, Mo., Dec., 1903, in his 63d year.

17. HELEN DANBURY WHITTEKER (Thomas[1], Susannah[2], John[3], Margaret A.[4]), dau. of Chas. S. and Margaret A. (Eoff) Whitteker, *m.* Geo. W. Harrison, of Piedmont, W. Va.   Issue:
    64, Chas. W., d. inf.; 65, Virginia W.; 66, Helen; 67, Victoria; 68, John H. F.; 69, George W.

18. VIRGINIA C. WHITTEKER (Thomas[1], Susannah[2], John[3], Margaret A.[4]), dau. of Chas. S. and Margaret A. (Eoff) Whitteker, *m.* John Dryden, of Charleston, W. Va.   Issue:
    70, Chas. W.; 71, Henry A.

19. EMILY S. WHITTEKER (Thomas[1], Susannah[2], John[3], Margaret A.[4]), dau. of Chas. S. and Margaret A. (Eoff) Whitteker, *m.* David S. Smithers, of Charleston, W. Va.   Issue:

72, Benjamin S.; 73, Rose C.; 74, Margaret Eoff.

21. HENRY T. WHITTEKER (Thomas[1], Susannah[2], John[3], Margaret A.[4]), son of Chas. S. and Margaret A. (Eoff) Whitteker, *m.* Emma L. ——. Issue:
75, Edith May; 76, Robert Eoff.

22. CORRINE S. WHITTEKER (Thomas[1], Susannah[2], John[3], Margaret A.[4]), dau. of Chas. S. and Margaret A. (Eoff) Whitteker, *m.* Dee C. Smoot, of Kanawha, W. Va. Issue:
77, Helen L.

25. HELEN Q. MOODEY (Thomas[1], Susannah[2], John[3], Virginia S.[4]), dau. of Roderick S. and Virginia S. (Eoff) Moodey, *m.* James A. Coolidge, of Washington, D. C. Issue:
78, Helen M.

26. CHARLES EOFF MOODEY (Thomas[1], Susannah[2], John[3], Virginia S.[4]), son of Roderick S. and Virginia S. (Eoff) Moodey, of Steubenville, O.; *m.* Emma T. ——. Issue:
79, Roderick S.; 80, Chas. Eoff.

27. JAMES S. MOODEY (Thomas[1], Susannah[2], John[3], Virginia S.[4]), son of Roderick S. and Virginia S. (Eoff) Moodey, of Steubenville, O.; *m.* —— ——. Issue:
81, Virginia S.; 82, Mary; 83, Helen Q.; 84, Charles.

28. VIRGINIA MOODEY (Thomas[1], Susannah[2], John[3], Virginia S.[4]), dau. of Roderick S. and Virginia S. (Eoff) Moodey, *m.* J. J. Norris, of Jersey City, N. J. Issue:
85, Henrietta; 86, Thomas.

29. BEVERLEY EOFF MOODEY (Thomas[1], Susannah[2], John[3], Virginia S.[4]), son of Roderick S. and Virginia S. (Eoff·) Moodey, of Charlotte, N. C.; *m.* Lida H. ——. Issue:
87, Beverley R.; 88, Stella H.

30. RODERICK S. MOODEY (Thomas[1], Susannah[2], John[3], Virginia S.[4]), son of Roderick S. and Virginia S. (Eoff) Moodey, of Chicago, Ill.; *m.* Elizabeth ——. Issue:
89, Florence; 90, Irene Dora; 91, William S.

31. EDWARD McC. MOODEY (Thomas[1], Susannah[2], John[3], Virginia S.[4]), son of Roderick S. and Virginia S. (Eoff) Moodey, of Alleghany, Pa.; *m.* Florence B. ——. Issue:
92, Florence.

33. ROBERT WOODS EOFF (Thomas[1], Susannah[2], John[3], Beverley McK.[4]), son of Beverley McK. and Harriet (Woods) Eoff, of Chicago, Ill.; *m.* Lily Agnes ——. Issue:
93, Harold Rufus.

35. JOHN RAVENSCROFT EOFF (Thomas[1], Susannah[2], John[3], Beverley McK.[4]), son of Beverley McK. and Harriet (Woods) Eoff, of Ashland, Va.; *m.* Rosamunda Hale, deceased. Issue:

94, Beverley McK.; 95, John Ravenscroft, *m.* Helen Junkin, 24 Jan., 1906, at Christiansburg, Va.; 96, Matthew Hale Huston; *m.* 2d Eloise H.; 97, Anne Hepburn; 98, Harriet Woods; 99, Robert Grimshaw; 100, William Tallant.

36. MARGARET ROBERTA EOFF (Thomas[1], Susannah[2], John[3], Beverley McK.[4]), dau. of Beverley McK. and Harriet (Woods) Eoff, *m.* Harry Caldwell, of St. Paul, Minn.   Issue:
101, Alex. Woods, *m.* St. Paul, Minn., 21 Nov., 1900, Minnie G. Haggerty; 102, Harriet; 103, George Baird; 104, Margaret Roberta; 105, Josephine Eoff.

37. CHARLES WILLIAM EOFF (Thomas[1], Susannah[2], John[3], Beverley McK.[4]), son of Beverley McK. and Harriet (Woods) Eoff, of Kansas City, Mo.; *m.* Henrietta H. ——.   Issue:
106, Helen Woods; 107, Maude Roemer.

38. JOSEPHINE MCCABE EOFF (Thomas[1], Susannah[2], John[3], Beverley McK.[4]), dau. of Beverley McK. and Harriet (Woods) Eoff; *m.* Friend Cox, of Moundsville, W. Va.   Issue:
108, Roberta May; 109, Cresap Brent; 110, Josephine Ruth.

41. DRURY J. TALLANT (Thomas[1], Susannah[2], John[3], Caroline Mary[4]), son of Henry and Caroline M. (Eoff) Tallant, of Great Falls, Mont., *m.* —— ——.

42. WILLIAM F. TALLANT (Thomas[1], Susannah[2], John[3], Caroline M.[4]), son of Henry and Caroline M. (Eoff) Tallant, of Christiansburg, Va.; *m.* Elizabeth ——.   Issue:
111, Helen Kyle, d. inf.; 112, Wm. Henry, d. inf.; 113, Walter Montague.

44. WALTER S. TALLANT (Thomas[1], Susannah[2], John[3], Caroline M.[4]), son of Henry and Caroline M. (Eoff) Tallant, of Butte, Mont.; *m.* Jennie S. ——.   Issue:
114, Harry S.

45. EDWARD C. TALLANT (Thomas[1], Susannah[2], John[3], Caroline M.[4]), son of Henry and Caroline M. (Eoff) Tallant, of Santa Barbara, Cal.; *m.* Martha D. ——   Issue:
115, Edward; 116, Charles H.

46. HENRY K. TALLANT (Thomas[1], Susannah[2], John[3], Caroline M.[4]) son of Henry and Caroline M. (Eoff) Tallant, of Christiansburg, Va.; *m.* Caroline ——.   Issue:
117, John Hampton, d. inf.; 118, Hoge; 119, Alfred.

47. CAROLINE L. TALLANT (Thomas[1], Susannah[2], John[3], Caroline M.[4]), dau. of Henry and Caroline M. (Eoff) Tallant, *m.* Ralph K. Stevens, of Santa Barbara, Cal.   Issue:
120, Ralph T.; 121, Kinton B.; 122, Barbara E.

49. CHARLES L. TALLANT (Thomas[1], Susannah[2], John[3], Caroline M.[4]), son of Henry and Caroline M. (Eoff) Tallant, of Junction City, Kan.; *m.* Gertrude ——.   Issue:
123, Kinton.

51. MARGARET J. GILCHRIST (Thomas[1], Susannah[2], John[3], Helen C.[4]), dau. of John P. and Helen C. (Eoff) Gilchrist, m. William McCoy, of Wheeling, W. Va.   Issue: 124, Helen; 125, Bertha.

53. CAROLINE T. GILCHRIST (Thomas[1], Susannah[2], John[3], Helen C.[4]), dau. of John P. and Helen C. (Eoff) Gilchrist, m. A. P. Tallman, of Wheeling, W. Va.   Issue: 126, Helen.

58. JAMES S. DODSON (Thomas[1], Susannah[2], John[3], Henrietta[4]), son of Adams and Henrietta M. (Eoff) Dodson, of Bethlehem, Pa.; m. Martha A. ——.   Issue: 126a, Adams.

59. LOUISE GARRET EOFF (Thomas[1], Susannah[2], John[3], John Q.[4], William C.[5]), dau. of William C. and Nannie, or Ella, Eoff; m. Edward L. Graham, of Lexington, Va.   Issue: 127, Thomas W.; 128, Edward L.; 129, John A.; 130, Samuel M.; 131, Mary L.

62. ELLA McC. EOFF (Thomas[1], Susannah[2], John[3], John Q.[4], William C.[5]), dau. of William C. and Nannie, or Ella, Eoff; m. at St. Louis, Mo., 2 July, 1901, William D. Lawton.   Issue: 131a, William D., Jr., b. Topeka, Kan., 2 Aug., 1903.

65. VIRGINIA W. HARRISON (Thomas[1], Susannah[2], John[3], Margaret A.[4], Helen D.[5]), dau. of George W. and Helen D. (Whitteker) Harrison, m. Paul D. Milholland, of Reading, Pa.   Issue: 132, James H.; 133, George H.; 134, Mary Ann.

66. HELEN HARRISON (Thomas[1], Susannah[2], John[3], Margaret A.[4], Helen D.[5]), dau. George W. and Helen S. (Whitteker) Harrison, m. Robert F. Bopes, of Cumberland, Md.   Issue: 135, Charles; 136, Victoria H.

67. VICTORIA HARRISON (Thomas[1], Susannah[2], John[3], Margaret A.[4], Helen D.[5]), dau. of George W. and Helen D. (Whitteker) Harrison, m. Doddridge F. Graham, of Luke, Md.   Issue: 137, Klein H.; 138, Helen Q.; 139, Robert D.

68. JOHN H. F. HARRISON (Thomas[1], Susannah[2], John[3], Margaret A.[4], Helen D.[5]), son of George W. and Helen D. (Whitteker) Harrison, of Piedmont, W. Va.; m. Edith ——.   Issue: 140, Margaret K.; 141, Frank W.; 142, Helen W.

69. GEORGE W. HARRISON, JR. (Thomas[1], Susannah[2], John[3], Margaret A.[4], Helen D.[5]), son George W. and Helen D. (Whitteker) Harrison, of Piedmont, W. Va.; m. Anna B. ——.   Issue: 143, Helen H.; 144, George.

107. MAUDE ROEMER EOFF (Thomas[1], Susannah[2], John[3], Beverley McK.[4], Chas. W.[5]), dau. of Chas. W. and Harriet L. (Woods) Eoff, m. at Kansas City, Mo., 22 Aug., 1898, Robert M. Williams.   Issue: 145, Beverley Eoff, b. 3 May, 1903.

PART III

ARMS OF THE DUKES OF SUFFOLK, ENGLAND

THE DUKES

DERIVATION OF THE FAMILY NAME

In genealogy much speculation and not a little thought and study is given to the subject of the origin of the surname a person bears, and it generally becomes a more difficult matter to determine than the mere collecting and compiling of data which the investigator for the historic and chronologic part of the work finds in existing records.

It is deemed necessary at the outset of this work to give, by way of introduction, some consideration to this phase of the genealogy before we take up its development from earlier times to those of the present.

In the medieval era, and in England especially, when the population was small and more generally scattered, when the village by the wayside contained but few inhabitants, and large cities congested with humanity did not exist, as compared with the examples of concentration observed to-day, a man bore but one name, and that, a personal one, all that then was needed.

After the Conquest, in the eleventh century, when the Norman followers of William I., son of Robert, le Duc of Normandy, overran the subjugated isles, it became impossible longer to continue the single designation, and for such a one to maintain a current identity, without some further distinction, hence the adoption of surnames came into vogue as the simple result of necessity and peculiar conditions. From such beginnings it became a fixed practice, so that to-day the distinguishing sobriquet each one of us owns has become an hereditary thing, "as much a part and parcel of man's property as any other of his possessions that can be passed on to his direct descendants."

The earliest changes from the personal to the addition of a surname appears, therefore, to have been the outgrowth of conditions following the Conquest. A later and similar development occurred during the Reformation; and these are said to have been the two revolutionary crises in English nomenclature.

Investigation develops five general sources from which English surnames were derived: those from property designation, or local peculiarities; vocations which the owner followed; those of patronymical origin from personal names of father or mother; from rank, title and office; and those from some mental or physical characteristic of its owner (English Surnames, pp. 3, 6, 7, 11, 12).

The surname of *Duke,* like that of King, Prince, Knight, Baron, etc., is derived from the titular class, the nobility; and one authority from whom we have liberally drawn says: "There is no reason, however, why our *Dukes,* Dooks, or Ducs, as they are more generally found, should not be what they represent, or rather, then represented. A Duke was, of course, anything but what we now understand by the term, being then, as it more literally signifies, a leader, or chieftain, or head" (English Surnames, p. 174) ; or, as another authority expresses it: "The name *Duke* signifies Leader, and is also, according to some writers, a nickname for Marmaduke." And *"Dukes* is another form of Duke" (Patronymica Brittanica, p. 96). Barker gives still another source: "Dug," "Tuc," "Tucca," from the Anglo-Saxon word *Dugan,* "to be doughty" (British Surnames, p. 133).

Scriptural warrant for the antiquity of the title: *Duke* is found in the Book of Genesis (36–15, 18, 40–43), where it is recorded by the sacred writer that "the sons of Esau who dwelt in Mount Sier were 'dukes' in the land of Edom." One thousand eight hundred and forty years before Christ! In the Revised Version they are called *chiefs.* Thus, by the highest and most sacred authority, its earliest use as a biblical term was to denote family leadership.

The first recorded use of the word *Duke* as a family surname appears in Domesday Book, Vol. IV., where an entry is found under the head of "Summerset" in Hunderpret division, stating that one *Walfinus de Duaco* (the equivalent of Duke) is a landholder (Rev. S. Ferguson). Its use becomes more common in the reign of Richard "the Lion-hearted," and especially in the time of King John frequent reference is made to persons of that name (Burke's Extinct Peerages, Vol. I.). In Queen Elizabeth's long reign it often occurs among the rolls of her ennobled subjects who were prominently mentioned in the annals of her time (XXII. Report of the Deputy-Keeper of Public Records, at Dublin).

Duke families are found very early in Ireland. Some were residing in County Westmeath in the fifteenth century (O'Hart's Irish Pedigrees, Vol. II., pp. 686–8). The will of one William Duke, of Kyllenagh Co., Kildare, recorded 1551, is found at Dublin. After this early date the family name appears with more or less variation in form, and with increasing frequency upon the pages of the Irish Public Records. Hanna, in his "Scotch-Irish Families of Ulster," estimates that there were in 1890 within the Province of Ulster 268 persons bearing the name of Duke.

Thus the Dukes were one of the ancient families of England and of Ireland. They are among the earliest recorded by Burke in his pedigrees of the nobility and of the landed gentry. The first mention made of them by this eminent authority is that of Roger Duke (Burke's Extinct Peerage, Vol. I.), or, as he is called by Bardsley (English Surnames), " Roger le Duc." This person was Sheriff of London in the early part of the reign of Richard I. (1190), the great-grandson of William the Conqueror, and it is stated that Roger is supposed to have come from France during the Norman period with others of his countrymen in the century following the Conquest. Burke also notes one Peter Duke, of London, who was granted the right to bear arms in 1620 (*temp* Charles II.). This Peter was probably the same who accompanied Sir Francis Drake in his enterprise against the Spanish West Indies in 1586. His descendants, who settled near Saxmundham, Suffolk, were known as the Dukes of Benhall. Sir Edward Duke of this line was the father of Elizabeth Duke, wife of Nathaniel Bacon, the leader of Bacon's Rebellion in Virginia, in 1676. The father objecting to this marriage resulted in her disinheritance. It was from this line also that many of the Dukes of tidewater Virginia, so prominent in the early days of that colony and of subsequent periods, were descended.

Other Dukes mentioned in early English history were: Adam le Duc (Writs of Parliament), William le Duck (English Surnames, p. 174), Nicholas Duke (The Hundred Rolls), and Thomas Duke (Calendarium Inquisitorum Post-mortem).

Among the numerous Dukes mentioned by Burke were those of Brampton, Power Hayes, Otterton and Aylesford, in Devonshire, from each of whom sprang many branches (History of the Commoners, Vol. III.). In the reign of Queen Mary, daughter of Henry VIII., 1553–8, one Michael Duke established an ancestral seat at Power-Hayes in Devonshire. Michael had three grandsons, children of his son John; they were John, George and Andrew. John succeeded his father to the title and estates as head of the Devonshire line, while George, in 1578, purchased the estate and manor of Lake, in Wiltshire, and became the head of the branch known as the Dukes of Lake. Andrew, the third son, was progenitor of still another line, the Dukes of Bulford (Burke's General Armory, p. 304). It was John, the grandson of Michael of Power-Hayes, who, with his son George, that afterward became involved with certain other Royalists in an attempt to restore the exiled Charles II. to the throne of England. In the disastrous defeat which befell the Royalist forces at Salisbury in 1655, some of the leading supporters of the king surrendered to Cromwell; among these were John Duke, his son George, Colonel Penruddock and several others, all of whom were tried and sentenced. Eight were accordingly executed, but the Dukes, however, were pardoned on condition that they withdraw to Virginia, then a general term for the West Indies, and make no further attempt against the government of Cromwell (William and Mary Quarterly Magazine, Vol. II., p. 275; Economic History of Virginia, Vol. I., p. 610). It is now believed that neither of them ever came to Virginia as Burke records George's death in England in 1655, the year of the uprising, and his father's in 1671 (Burke's History of the Commoners, Vol. I., pp. 285–6). Colonel Penruddock is stated by one authority to have been hung and by another writer to have been pardoned in company with the two Dukes (William and Mary Quarterly Magazine, Vol. II., p. 275).

The downfall of the monarchy under Charles I. and the success of the army of the Commonwealth became a fruitful opportunity for Cromwell to reward his friends and victorious followers by giving them grants of land in Ireland. By Acts of Parliament beginning in 1642 and ceasing in 1646 liberal advantages had been offered to Englishmen to "plant" in Ireland, particularly in the Province of Ulster, where it had been proposed to propagate a settlement of English and Scotch to offset the native Irish on land formerly held by the Irish chieftain O'Neil, but had now been confiscated by the Crown for the treasonable practices of the Ulster earl in 1641. In the period 1642–1646 subscriptions for "adventures" for land in Ireland were opened. The conditions were easy. Upon payment of £200 one thousand acres of land were to be alloted to every subscriber who would comply with the terms and conditions. The portents of war coming on delayed this scheme, but it did not altogether stop its operation, for in 1653 preparations were made for setting out these lands to the satisfaction of the subscribers under the Acts of 1642–1646. By this time, 1653, and in consequence of the war, many of the original subscribers had died, disappeared, or had assigned their rights, titles and claims to other parties, who subsequently enrolled, so that by this year these Irish lands were divided between the remaining original subscribers, the "adventurers," or their successors, the English army and the State, so that the provisions of the Acts of Parliament referred to were carried out under somewhat changed conditions than originally contemplated (O'Hart's Irish Pedigrees, Vol. II., p. 698), and many of the Cromwellian soldiers were given land debentures which were largely bought up, or otherwise passed into the possession of their officers and others interested in the absorption of Irish plantations (Prendergast's "Cromwellian Settlement of Ireland," 2d ed., pp. 204–5, 251, 403–4).

Oliver Cromwell had fought in Ireland during the monarchy and among his troopers disbanded in County Sligo, in 1643, was one of the name of Duke, said to have been a cadet of the house of Benhall, in Suffolk, England (O'Hart's Landed Gentry When Cromwell Came to Ireland, p. 18). This Duke was granted a tract of land at New-Park County Sligo, for which he paid one thousand marks; here he settled and established a family—the Dukes of New-Park. John Duke, a son of this trooper, was a "titulador," meaning a person liable for poll- or head-tax on their title as gentleman, esquire, etc. (men and women over fifteen years of age were liable for poll-tax in Ireland, and there were other forms of taxation: for hearth-money, chimney, etc., in the period 1660–1669). He died in 1679, leaving a son Robert, who died in 1731.

Let us revert for a moment to the Elizabethan era. Following the defeat of Gerald, Earl of Desmond and head of the Geraldine League in Munster, on November 11, 1584, came the confiscation of his vast estate, amounting to about 570,000 acres and spreading over several counties in Ireland. This was all afterward distributed, according to proclamation, to "undertakers" who were "conditioned to be younger sons of good families of England" and who would "obligate themselves 'to plant' a certain number of families thereon." Some who thus obtained Irish grants were: Sir Christopher Hatton, Sir Peter Carew, Sir Walter Raleigh, Sir Samuel Hubert, Colonel Francis Cosby and others (Magee's History of Ireland, Vol. I., p. 411). In this group of "planters," some of whom located in County Cavan, was one Henry Duke, later Sheriff of Cavan, and one of the Queen's valiant officers whom she subsequently knighted (Report Deputy-Keeper of Public Records, Dublin).

Ireland was in a foment of rebellion. The subjugated Irish chiefs were on the one hand and their English conquerors on the other hand. The Ulster Confederacy, which grew out of this warring condition, was intended to unify the chieftains of the north in a compact to wrest the land from the English invaders. At its head was the once powerful Lord of Ulster, Henry O'Neil, Earl of Tyrone, and Art O'Donnell. After O'Neil, by way of reprisal, abducted the sister of Sir Henry Bagnall, Marshal of Ireland, and though he married her, it nevertheless fanned the hatred of both parties and a conflict was precipitated in 1593.

In August of that year Sir Richard Bingham, Governor of Connaught, and one of the Royal Commissioners to Ireland, with a force of followers, was attacked by Sir Brian O'Rurare and the Maguires, who had invested Enniskillen. Sir Henry Duke and Sir Edward Herbert hastened to relieve the beleaguered Bingham, but they were met and repulsed with great loss by the Irish, Sir Henry Duke barely escaping alive. Hearing of this unfortunate situation, the Lord Deputy, Sir William Fitzwilliam, in person, supported by others of the Privy Council, led a superior force against the enemy and succeeded in relieving Enniskillen on August 18, 1593 (Magee's History of Ireland, Vol. I., p. 421).

Sir Henry Duke, of Castle Jordan, died 12 February, 1595. There were other Dukes in Ireland in the latter part of Queen Elizabeth's reign, among whom were James, Richard and Henry Duke, each of whom, according to the records at Dublin Castle, appears to have been granted royal pardons (22d Report of Deputy-Keeper of Public Records, Dublin "Index of Fiants").

In the lists of original " Adventurers " for land in Ireland in the period 1642–1646, subscriptions for which were opened in England during the reign of the first Charles, is found the name of " ffrancis Duke of Westminster " [London] " gent. £200, No. 33." This entry indicates a grant to that person of 1,000 acres in the Province of Ulster. Search has failed to reveal whether or not Francis Duke exercised his rights by taking possession of the Irish land, or if he assigned them to another. It is significant, however, in this connection that in an early record at Annapolis, Md., of the will of Henry Duke, of Baltimore County, who died in 1712, the testator bequeaths to his wife Susannah his plantation on Patapsco Neck, called " Westminster."

The state documents in the Public Record Office at Dublin give the name of Andrew Duk found on the list of Protestant householders residing in Ballymoney Parish, Dunluce Barony, County Antrim, in 1740; Hugh Dook and Adam Dook, living in County Down in 1691 and 1752 respectively. Several of the name of *Duck* were among the " English " inhabitants in the Baronies of Dunluce and Kilconrie, on the demesne of Alexander Hamilton, Sr., a Scotch " planter," who recovered this great estate by suit, in 1740, from the Earl of Antrim; and as recently as 1847 the will of one Francis Duke, of Moyad, County Down, is recorded at Dublin Castle.

Certain of the Duke family in England seem to have taken prominent interest in the early enterprise of William Penn in this country, as it appears from the records contained in the Colonial Archives of New Jersey. One Edward Duke, of Aylesbury, County Kent, gentleman, and Thomas Duke, of London, draper, became owners of 6,000 acres of land in the Province of West Jersey, through some business connection with John Fenwick, Edward Wade, John Eldridge and others, of London, original patentees of the large tract of land in Salem County, which was afterwards known as Fenwicks Colony. The Dukes received their grant 7 June, 1675, and it was afterward conveyed by them, in 1677, to " Edward Gibbon, late of Benenden, County Kent," at this time a merchant in New York.

In the land records of Pennsylvania it is found that Bartholomew Duke, of St. Giles Parish, County Middlesex, London, a baker, figures, through his wife Ann Clarke, who had inherited 500 acres from her mother in the Province of Pennsylvania. Her mother was Jane Clarke, wife of Robert Clarke and daughter of Ann O'liffe, a widow, residing at Oxon, England, in 1681. Bartholomew Duke disposed of this land in 1716 to James Robins, also of London, " meal ffactor," for £10.

The name of James Duke appears in an account of lands granted by William Penn in Pennsylvania " to several purchasers in England, Ireland and Scotland." It occurs in an order sent by Penn's deputy, Philip Ford, to Thomas Holme, Surveyor-

General, under date of 22d 3 mo., 1682. The purchase was for 250 acres in Township plot No. 41.

ENGLISH AND IRISH SOURCES

Many of the principal Duke families in England and Ireland appear to have descended from what is, apparently, the parent stock—the Dukes of Otterton Parish, in Devonshire.

The ancient estate, still retained by the representative branch of the family, lies in one of the loveliest regions of genial south-eastern England where, on the river Otter, near the village of East Budleigh, and within a mile or so of the famous Devon coast, may yet be seen portions of the venerable edifice reared by the patriarchal forefathers. The parish in which Otterton park is situated was granted by William the Conqueror to the Monastery of Mont St. Michel, in Normandy; here a priory was soon after established by John Lackland; but, in Henry VIII.'s time, when, by his acts, the dissolution between the Church and the State was effected, the monastic manor was bought by one Richard Duke, who, according to an early chronicler, "built a fair house upon an ascent over the river Otter which driveth his mills underneath his house" (Pole; see S. Baring Gould's Devon, 1907). Since that time Otterton has remained the seat of successive Dukes and from whom have sprung various branches known as the Dukes of Otterton, of Pinne, and of Colaton Raleigh, in Devonshire; of Lake, and of Bulford, in Wiltshire; of Cosenton, and Maidstone, in Kent; of Richmond, in Surrey; of Applesham, in Hampshire; of Castle Jordan, in County Meath, Ireland, and of other families bearing the name in different parts of Great Britain.

Representatives of this stock were prominently identified in many of the great historical events in the kingdom. Being Devonshire men bred in the blasts of the sea they sailed its trackless waters and shared in the spoils and glories of the great Elizabethan age with Drake, Hawkins, Gilbert and Raleigh; as royalists they fought and bled for the Stuart and barely escaped the puritanical condemnation of Cromwell, who banished, rather than executed, some of them; but they came into their own again upon the restoration of Charles II. to the throne.

They intermarried with the leading families of the shires— with Carew, Rolle, Yonge, Bartlett, Channons, Raleigh and others. Lord Chief Justice Coleridge, of England, was of this blood; and another, the prototype of Sir Roger de Coverley whom Joseph Addison, of *The Spectator,* made famous in portraying—was Richard Duke, a quaint old gentleman whose seat at Bulford was near Milstone, in Wiltshire, and in the neighborhood of the birthplace of the great philosopher.

It was one of the earlier Richard Dukes, of Otterton, who owned Hayes Barton, the birthplace of the brave and gallant Sir Walter Raleigh, and to whom the famous captain, when in the zenith of his prosperity, wrote in 1584, "but for the natural disposition I have to that place, being born *in that house,* I had rather seat myself there than anywhere, etc."

In running through the genealogies of these ancient families one is at once impressed with the persistency by which hereditary Christian names have been passed down from generation to generation; even to this day, and after the lapse of centuries. Such are found in widely separated American families and include such baptismal names as Richard, Basil, William, Francis, John, George, Robert and James; all peculiarly significant ancestrally.

The eldest sons generally inherited these entailed estates and resided upon them, leaving the cadets, or younger sons, a small bequest and the prospect of a career in the church, the army, or the wider and wilder field of adventure in an adventurous age. Thus the professions received some scions of the family, but in those days when the resources of the new world were attracting, by golden dreams, the ambitious youth of Great Britain, doubtless many of the Dukes were beguiled to serve and share with the sea dogs of Devon in the conquest of a new empire beyond the sea.

THE DUKES OF COLONIAL VIRGINIA

The earliest manuscript records of the presence of the Duke family in America are found in the Colonial Land Grants of Virginia and refer, chiefly, to the conferring of land under "head rights" to planting adventurers who had "imported" or brought into the colony a certain number of colonists some of whom are named, but many only enumerated, upon the land grant records. The first of such grants to one of the Duke name occurs under date of 13 May, 1673, by Sir William Berkeley to John Duke for 486 acres in James Cittie Co., situated on the Chickahominy River. This grant was followed by other grants to him for land under similar conditions, varying proportions, and in divers locations, by Berkeley and succeeding governors. And it not only appears that John Duke became possessed of great quantities of land in this way, but also that Richard, Thomas, Henry, Francis and other Dukes profited in the same manner, at slightly later periods of the early colonial era.

From a study of the names of the men who came into the colony, whether as grantees or those "imported," there is an

AN EARLY HOME OF THE DUKES IN DEVONSHIRE, ENGLAND

BIRTHPLACE OF SIR WALTER RALEIGH

apparent probability that the larger number of these came from the coast counties of southeastern England: Devonshire and Wiltshire. The Devonshire men were predominately a sea-faring folk and it is reasonably certain that the land that produced such renowned navigators as Drake, Raleigh, Hawkins and Gilbert, would also contribute their brave and hardy supporters, recruited from the manorial families and yeomenry of the shire.

It may then be assumed that, as the ancient houses of the Dukes of Otterton and Bulford were situated in these counties, that the younger sons (and those of the hereditary retainers of those houses) preferred to cast their lots with the great captains to whom some were related as kinsmen—and participate in the adventurous enterprises of their sea-roving chiefs—rather than remain at home and follow an idle and portionless existence upon the ancestral estates. Moreover, it was an age when exploration and colonization attracted attention and engrossed the minds of the daring, and offered an opportunity for, at least, a career of excitement, if not one of profit, to the youth of England.

A learned contributor to the Virginia Historical Magazine has stated that "the Carys intermarried with the family of Richard Cocke about 1690. This was a Devonshire family as were the Brays and Dukes" (Va. Hist. Mag., Vol. III., p. 285).

The John Duke mentioned in the foregoing was evidently of York Co., Va., a land owner there in 1670, and a man of some prominence in the colony. On 19 July, 1670, he was assignee of the property of Bryan Smith and his wife Dorothy Tucker (York County Records).

John Duke *m.* Jane, eldest daughter of Lt.-Col. John Scarsbrooke and his wife, who was Elizabeth Bushrod, the daughter of Elizabeth Bushrod, Sr., a sister of Elizabeth Scarsbrook— Lydia *m.* Thos. Harwood. In the will of Lieutenant-Colonel Scarsbrook, he mentions, without naming them "the children of my dau. Jane Duke" (see will of John Scarsbrook, d. 1679, York County Records).

It is evident that John Duke enjoyed a prominent civil relation to the community in which he lived, as his name frequently appears upon the records: juryman, 1677; was appointed one of a commission to divide the estate of Wm. Allen, Sept. 24, 1678; one of the appraisers of the estate of William Major, 27 Aug., 1678; and appointed attorney by Thos. Raynor, probably in same year; a resident of York Co., 1679 (see York Co., Va., Records), and probably removed later to James City Co.

John Duke, a son (?) of the preceding, *m. ante* 1664, Susannah Goodwin, daughter of James Goodwin (who d. *circa* 1678/9), and his first wife Rachael Porter who was said to be of the Porters of Warwick, England. The will of James Goodwin's second wife, who d. 22 Sept., 1701, names dau. Susannah Duke

and grandchildren: James and Elizabeth Duke (see William and
Mary Quarterly, Oct., 1897, p. 7; and April, 1894, p. 275; and
York County Records). James Duke, the son of John Duke, Jr.,
was sheriff of James City Co. in 1719 (Va. Hist. Mag., Vol. II.,
p. 6).

It seems well to note, in passing, that Elizabeth Duke was the
wife of Nathaniel Bacon, the instigator and leader of "Bacon's
Rebellion"; he died in 1675; she lived and remarried, and was
a contemporary of John and Henry Duke, and was probably
related to them.

Henry Duke, thought to have been another son of John Duke,
Jr., was a justice of Prince George Co., Va., in 1712, and d. there,
Jan., 1718 (Va. Hist. Mag., Vol. VII., p. 400).

The Ludwell MSS. states that Elizabeth, widow of Henry
Duke, and James Duke, "gent," were surviving executors of the
estate of Henry Duke, Esq. (see William and Mary Quarterly,
Vol. II., p. 275). A James Duke was Justice of the Quorum in
James City Co., in 1714 (Va. Mag. of Hist., Vol. II., p. 6).

Henry Duke, sometimes called "Captain" Henry Duke, and
often styled "gent," appears to be the next name found upon the
roll of grantees of "head rights"; he was probably the most
conspicuous of the Duke name in early Virginia history, largely
for his connection and participation with Nathaniel Bacon, who,
by his boldness, became "the first martyrs to the principles of
American liberty," the chief figure in "Bacon's Rebellion." Of
his devotion to Bacon and his cause against the arbitrary rule of
Berkeley there can be no question.

"Mr. Duke was one of Bacon's good Justices in hastening, forwarding,
taking and giving of Bacons oathes, and because Bacon's Capt. Nevet
Wheeler should not want force to fight and destroy the Governor's soldiers, sends two of his own servants that shed the first christian blood, and
alsoe before that sent me to goe with Bacon the Oceanuchel march! Hill's
own words, in his defence against charges of scandal by James Minge."

From 1680 to 1702 Henry Duke was officially connected with
the government at Jamestown, as Justice, Sheriff, Burgess and
Member of the King's Council (see Va. Hist. Mag., Vol. III.,
p. 249).

Henry Duke's wife was Lydia Hansford, a daughter of Chas.
Hansford, one of the chief supporters of Nathaniel Bacon (see
William and Mary Quarterly, Vol. II., p. 275). Henry Duke
was of the council and sat in judgment at the trial of Grace Sher-
wood, who was charged by the authorities of Nansemond Parish,
of being a witch (Va. Hist. Mag., Vol. VII., p. 400). In an
affidavit taken at the time, in reference to the "barring out" of
students at William and Mary College, May 2, 1705, he was a
member of the council. He d. circa 1713-14 (Va. Mag. Hist.,
Vol. VII., pp. 371, 400).

From 23 Oct., 1690, to April, 1710/11, his name frequently appears in the list of grantees of land in James City Co. and New Kent Co., for locations along the Chickahominy River, Darroy Creek, and other waters, tributaries of the James; the aggregate of which, according to the land records, amounted to many thousand acres (see Land Office Records, State House, Richmond, Va.). Henry Duke had at least one son, Henry Duke, Jr., who *m.* Elizabeth —— and d. in 1724.

The probabilities are that the above mentioned John and Henry Duke were brothers; and it may be reasonably assumed that Richard and Thomas Duke, who were also grantees—the former for 400 acres on the King's Road to Piscataway in New Kent Co., granted in 1679; and the latter for 430 acres in the Upper Parish of Nansemond, granted in 1681—were also brothers or closely related to John and Henry. Richard Duke received head rights for himself, his wife, " Ma. Duke " and his son (prob.) George Duke; while Thomas's grant included head rights for himself and his son Thomas Duke, Jr. In the description of a subsequent grant of land in Nansemond made by Governor Spottswood, the relationship is more clearly defined, as the record reads: "to Thomas Duke, Jr., and his brother, John Duke," the land-mark standing at " their father Thomas Duke's line " next to land of Francis Mace (Mace was " imported " by the elder Thomas Duke and had obtained head rights from him in the previous year). Francis Duke obtained a grant of land in Nansemond Co. of 231 acres in 1718; this grant adjoined Thomas Duke's land. The presence of Francis Duke's name in the colony and the repetition of the hereditary family names, as those above, indicate the origin of this line among the Dukes of Devonshire, England.

Henry Duke d. in Prince George Co., Va., in 1718.

Inventory of Capt. Henry Duke was recorded in Prince George Co., Va., Jan. 18, 1718, and Elizabeth Duke was named as his administratrix.

With this introduction relative to the beginnings of the Duke family in tidewater Virginia we shall now come to the next stage in their geographical expansion.

Henry Duke, called " brother " in will of Cliveures Duke I., of Louisa Co., Va., was living on Indian Creek, in Louisa Co., in 1789, on land adjoining his brother Cliveures Duke; and in that year made title to certain lands in that locality, to *his* son Henry Duke, Jr. His wife, Ann, joins in the conveyance. The wife of Henry, Jr., appears to have been Susannah. Henry Duke, Sr., had another son whose name was John. Henry apparently disposed of the balance of his land to Cliveures Duke after having served in the Revolution and then removed, presumably, to North

Carolina and there established, it is thought, the line of Dukes famous as the tobacco factors of Durham.

Dorothy Orum who seems to have joined in some of the land transactions in which Cliveures Duke was interested may possibly have been a sister of Cliveures as the name of Dorothy appears frequently among the baptismal names of the Dukes in Devonshire and in Virginia.

The following line of Dukes are descendants of George and Catharine (Barham) Duke, of Wandsworth, Surrey, England.

Arms: Azure, a chevron between three birds close argent membered gules.

Crest: On a plume of five ostrich feathers two argent three azure a sword argent hilt or.

Motto: In adversis idem.

Cliveures Duke, Sr., is held to have been, according to the traditions of his descendants, the son of Henry Duke, of James City Co., Va., King's Councillor, and his wife, —— Cliveures, who was the daughter of an early Huguenot emigré. Cliveures Duke was probably born *circa* 1718, and therefore a son of Henry Duke, Jr., as Henry the elder, was deceased not later than 1714, according to the evidence in the preceding pages. It is likely he was the son of Captain Henry who d. in Prince George Co., Va., in 1718, and Elizabeth, his wife, whose name may have been Elizabeth Cliveures. Cliveures Duke was a justice of Lousia Co., Va., 1764.

Cliveures Duke, whose name frequently appears in the records of Hanover and Lousia Counties, Va., *m. circa* 1740. He is described in old documents as of Little Rivers, in the Parish of St. Martin's and County of Lousia, Virginia. He became an extensive land owner by the purchase of many thousand acres in the two counties mentioned. The following schedule represents a part of his realty transactions:

8 Dec., 1742, from Benjamin Brown, 423 acres; 7 June, 1744, from Joseph Swift; 7 Dec., 1750, from John Wright and Wm. Birket; 2 May, 1752, from James Yancey, 280 acres; 4 May, 1752, from John Mervine and wife, and Wm. Mervine, of Amelia Co., 420 acres; Feb., 1761, from M. Chinn, 200 acres; 13 May, 1765, from Robert Yancey; 11 Aug., 1766, from John Fox, 400 acres; 28 March, 1774, from Cosby Duke and wife, 423 acres; 11 Jan., 1776, from John Cosby, 400 acres, near Wash's plantation 30 Sept., 1776, from Richard Terrill, from Capt. Wm. Terrill, from Robert Dabney, also; 4 Nov., 1777, from Cosby Duke, 143 acres.

Some time before his death, in 1784, Cliveures Duke began to dispose of a great deal of his possessions to his numerous children and others, among which these are noted:

14 Aug., 1765, to his son Cosby Duke, 800 acres and 9 negroes.

11 Aug., 1767, to his grandchild Ann, daughter of his son John Duke, of Hanover Co.

13 Feb., 1769, to his grandchild Amediah, daughter of his son James, a negro.

14 May, 1769, appoints his son Cosby Duke, his attorney-in-fact.

4 Oct., 1769, convey to his son James Duke, of Hanover, the Fox lands on Little Rivers.

In the same year he was grantor with Cosby Duke and Dorothy Orum of 133 acres "on both sides of the Great Mountain Road."

6 Sept., 1770, conveys to Cosby Duke the land upon which Cliveures Duke, Jr., now lives.

9 April, 1773, gives negroes, etc., to John and Mary Garland Duke, children of his son Cosby Duke.

17 Jan., 1778, conveys 400 acres to George Lumsden, husband of his daughter Elizabeth.

6 March, 1778, gift to his granddaughter Mary, of a negro girl.

12 Nov., 1783, grantor, with Mary his wife, to John Gunnell.

1784, contributes to his son-in-law Thomas Swift, a negro.

30 Dec., 1784, his will is dated and 14 Feb., 1786, date of probate of will.

Cliveures Duke is said to have been at least five times married; the names of his wives in their order are supposed to have been: Cosby, Eggleston, Barbara; was *m.* to Lucy Smith 12 Oct., 1772; to Mary Wash, who survived him, 7 April, 1783. The issue from these several marriages are said to have been very numerous. Some of them were: John, James, Thomas, Cosby, Amy, Henry, Dorothy, Elizabeth, Cliveures, William, Hardin, Susannah, and a daughter who is supposed to have *m.* a Cosby, and another daughter who *m.* Henry Clivera(?).

I. JOHN DUKE, son of Cliveures, b. *circa* 1738, m. Nancy or Ann —— and had issue: Mary, Martha and Ann; all b. *ante* 1767. (The will of this John Duke names his wife Ann and sister Elizabeth Lumsden.)

II. JAMES DUKE, son of Cliveures, Sr., b. *circa* 1740; *m. circa* 1758, Keziah Burnley, who after her husband's death, *m.* 2d Samuel Redd. She d. after 1822. Issue of James and Keziah Burnley Duke:

1, Cliveures Duke, III., b. *circa* 1760; d. in Albemarle Co., Va., in 1818.

2, James, Jr., b. *circa* 1762; *m.* (Mary Munkas, in Henrico Co., 7 Dec., 1789).

3, Amediah, b. *circa* 1764; *m.* Samuel O. Pettus.

The issue of Cliveures (III.) Duke who *m. circa* 1780, Ann Overton Pettus:

a, Lucy, b. *circa* 1781; *m.* Nelson Burrus.

b, Archibald B., b. *circa* 1782; *m.* Sarah Dickerson.

c, James, Jr. (3), b. *circa* 1784; d. 1844; *m.* Mary Biggars.

d, Richard, b. 1786; d. ——; *m.* 1806, Maria Walker.

The issue of Amidiah Duke and Samuel O. Pettus:

a, Hugh Pettus (adm. of the est. of his mother Am. D. Pettus), *m.* Barbara Price, and had issue: Samuel O. Pettus, killed at San Jacinto, 1836.

The issue of Lucy Duke and Nelson Burrus:

a, Richard; *b,* James; *c,* John, and *d,* Nelson, Jr.

The issue of Archibald B. Duke and Sarah Dickerson who was the daughter of Wiley Dickerson and his wife Mary, daughter of John Carr and Barbara Overton.

a, Emily; *b,* Cornelia; *c,* Cliveures; *d,* Richard; *e,* Amanda, who *m.* Benj. Johnson; *f,* Hardenia; *g,* Lucy, *m.* —— Trevallian; *h,* Caroline; *m.* —— Wheeler; and *i,* Archibald, Jr.

The issue of James Duke, Jr., and Mary Biggars, *m. ante* 1795. He is described as of Henrico, and owner of 200 acres of land on Beaver Creek, which was disposed of in 1795. He was associated with his brother, Richard, in the management of Rivanna Mills. They had a stone mill at Millington and later established a mill on Rocky Creek. Appointed to County Bench (Albemarle), 1838. Issue:

a, Richard Duke, of Nelson Co., Va., *m.* Virginia Williams. Issue: Charles; Denie, *m.* —— Whitehead; and Marie, *m.* —— Coles.

b, Lucy, *m.* Thomas Ballard and had issue: James; Ann, *m.* —— Thompson; Dr. T. Edgar, *m.* Nannie M. Pannell.

c, Horace, *m.* and removed to Mississippi; his dau. Charlotta, *m.* Dr. Wm. Garland Carr, and had issue: James, Terrill, Nannie, Charlotta, Lucy, Emily, Patty and Daniel Carr, of Scooba, Miss.

Richard Duke, *m.* Maria Walker, dau. of Capt. Thomas Walker, and granddaughter of Dr. Thomas Walker, of "Castle Hill," Albemarle Co., Va. Issue:

a, William J., *m.* Emily Anderson, who d. Charlottesville, Va., 18 Nov., 1905, aged 87 years; issue: Laura, Florence, and R. W. Duke, who *m.* Kate H. Hedges, and has issue: Charles, Emily, Kate, Elizabeth and Mattie.

b, Lucy, *m.* 1st David Wood, who left issue; *m.* 2d John H. Bills, who removed to Hardman Co., Tenn. They had one dau. who d. s.p.

c, Mary J., *m.* Wm. W. Smith, removed to Texas; no issue.

d, Mildred W., *m.* George C. Gilmer, brother of Governor Gilmer, of Virginia. She d. 1900; issue: Frank; Maris, *m.* Cunningham, now decd.

e, Elizabeth, *m.* Gen. Robert E. Rodes, C. S. A., who fell at Winchester, Va., in 1864; issue: Mary, who *m.* —— Anderson.

HON. R. T. W. DUKE, Sr.

HON. R. T. W. DUKE, Jr.

f, Richard T. W., b. 1822; d. 1898; lived at Charlottesville;
m. 1846, Elizabeth Scott, b. 1820; d. 1896; dau. of Wm.
Scott and Margaret Frances (Brown) Eskridge, of
Staunton, Va. R. T. W. Duke was Colonel of 46th
Virginia Regiment, C. S. A.; Member 41st and 42d
Congress, U. S. A.; and had issue:
W. R., *m.* May Coleman; issue: Cammen Coleman, and
W. R., Jr.
R. T. W., Jr., *m.* Edith Ridgeway, dau. of John Flavel
and Mary Haines (Harker) Slaughter, of Lynch-
burg, Va.—1 Oct., 1884. Mr. Duke graduated
from University of Virginia, 1784; Judge Corpora-
tion (Hustings) Court of Charlottesville, Va.,
Grand Master of Masons in Virginia, and an Attorney and Counsellor at Law; born at Charlottesville, Va., 27 Aug., 1853. Resides there; issue:
Mary W.; R. T. W., 3d, b. 19 June, 1887; John F.
S., b. 11 Feb., 1889; William Eskridge, b. 23 Feb.,
1893, and Helen Risdon. Mary Willoughby Duke
m. Dr. Chas. Slaughter; she had one dau.; Mary
W. D., who *m.* 1905, Dr. Claude M. Lee, medical
missionary to China.
g, Mattie L., d. *unm.*
h, Margaret, d. *unm.*
i, Sarah, *m.* Harvey Deskins; issue: Nannie, *m.* R. A. Robinson.
j, Charles C., *m.* Hattie W. Walker, who d. in Texas, leaving
several sons and daughters.

III. THOMAS DUKE, of Hanover Co., Va., b. 1742; d. 1826; *m.*
Jane Tilman and had issue:
1, John Tilman Duke, b. 1789; d. Hanover, 1863; *m.* 1810,
Miss Cox; issue:
a, Thomas, *m.* Miss Shacklefoot; *b,* Edwin P., *m.* Mary
Newton; *c,* Frederick Cox, *m.* Miss Page.
d, Albin Gilpin, b. Hanover, Va., 1827; d. 1902; *m.* 1st
1863, Elizabeth Gilman, and had issue; *m.* 2d Mary
Vass; no issue.
Richard Cliveures Duke, b. Hanover Co., Va., 1869;
m. 1893, Miss Callie Davis, and had issue:
Maud H., Richard T., Cornelia T., and John L.
f, Richard, d. *unm.*; *g,* Mary *m.* Isaac Perrin, of Hanover.
h, Amelia, m. John Turner, of Hanover Co., Va.

IV. COSBY DUKE, son of Cliveures Duke, Sr., b. *circa* 1745; d.
circa 1778; *m.* Elizabeth (Garland?), who was still living in 1810.
On August 14, 1765, Cliveures Duke, the father, conveys to his
son 800 acres of land and nine negroes, and about the same time

joins with his father Cliveures and Dorothy Orum in the conveyance of 133 acres of land on both sides of the road from Great Mountain to Hanovertown. On 5 Dec., 1766, Cosby gets a deed for land from Wm. Blackwell. His father appoints him attorney-in-fact 14 May, 1769. Cliveures Duke deeds land to Cosby upon which Cliveures lives. On 6 Sept., 1770, and on 9 April, 1773, receives a gift of negroes. Cosby transfers 143 acres of land to Cliveures, 4 Nov., 1777, but on 28 March, 1774(?), Cosby and his wife reconvey to Cliveures Duke 423 acres of the land he once conveyed to them. Cliveures's wife, Lucy, was interested in this transaction. Cosby Duke's will is dated 7 Dec., 1777, and by it his estate is devised to his wife Elizabeth and children: John and Mary Garland Duke.   Issue:

1, John Duke, b. *circa* 1762; *m. circa* 1780, Jane Roy.   Issue:
> *a,* Cosby Duke, b. 1783; d. 1853; served in the War of 1812; *m.* 1st Martha Mallory and had issue, ten children; *m.* 2d Miss Martin; issue, three children, among whom:
>> i, John Duke, of Negro Foot, Hanover, who d. 1893; *m.* —— ——, and had a dau., b. 1845, who *m.* P. H. Lowry, of Bracket, Va., and L. T. Duke, of Johnson City, Tenn.
>> ii, Thomas Taylor Duke, b. Goochland Co., 1813; d. 1874, in Henrico Co., Va.; *m.* 1838, Mary Ann Netherland and had issue:
>>> *a,* Frances Elizabeth, b. 1839; d. 1840.
>>> *b,* Francis Johnston, b. 11 July, 1842, in Hanover Co., d. 31 Dec., 1905; he was Secretary and Treasurer of the Richmond, Fredericksburg and Potomac Railroad. He *m.* 25 May, 1869, Lucy Barton Williamson and had issue: Frank W., b. 1871, *m.* June, 1901, Rosa Pleasants Cocke and had issue: William Dabney, b. 1872; Gen. Mgr. Richmond, Fredericksburg and Potomac R. R.; *m.* 1904, Jane E. Taylor, of Wake Forest, N. C., dau. of President Taylor, of Wake Forest, Coll., and had issue: Francis Johnston Duke, b. 6 March, 1906. Elizabeth, b. 1874, d. 1874; Thomas Taylor, b. 1875, lieutenant U. S. A.; James Netherland, b. 1877, d. 1891; Cora de Jarnette, b. 1878, and Lucy Williamson, b. 1880, living in Richmond, Va.
>>> *c,* Robert Edward Duke, b. 1845; d. 1903; *m.* 1867, Mattie Smith, who d. 1903, and left surviving: Oolah Duke, b. 1868.

d, Clementine Ann Duke, b. 1847; d. 1880; *m.* 1874, Alex. Clay Evans and had Norma, b. 1874; d. 1875.

e, Victoria Juliet Duke, b. 1849; d. 1880; *m.* 1868, Henry Hill Doggett, who d. 1870, and left issue: Harry Hill, b. 1869; *m.* Alice Barnes, of Richmond, and had: Lenora Anderson, b. 1900; Victoria Juliet, b. 1902.

f, Louis Napoleon Duke, b. 1853; d. 1891; *m.* 1878, Barbara ———, who d. s.p.

g, Matthew Garrett Duke, b. 1851; d. 1873.

h, Alice Duke, b. 1857; d. 1859.

2, Mary Garland Duke, b. *circa* 1765; *m.* Jan., 1782, John Hawkins.

V. Amediah (Amy) Duke, dau. of Cliveures Duke, *m.* Thomas Swift. Amy was b. *circa* 1747. She had issue Rebecca and Amediah (both mentioned in their grandfather Duke's will); Thomas, and Mary, who *m.* Gabriel Poindexter *ante* 1784, and is mentioned in the will of her grandfather also.

VIII. Elizabeth Duke, dau. of Cliveures Duke, b. *circa* 1753; *m.* Oct. 12, 1773, George Lumsden, and to whom his father-in-law conveys 400 acres of land, 17 Jan., 1778. Not only was Cliveures Duke, Sr., and his son Cliveures, Jr., on George Lumsden's marriage license bond, but he performed the same gracious office for the elder Cliveures when he espoused Mary Wash, 7 April, 1783. George Lumsden was one of the executors of the will of Cliveures Duke, probated 14 Feb., 1785.

IX. Cliveures Duke, Jr., son of Cliveures Duke, Sr., b. 1755, as he states in his pension application, made in 1820, for service rendered during the Revolution. He d. in 1847. He may have *m.* 1st Elizabeth Burnley, sister of John Burnley, and *m.* 2d Ann Armstrong, widow of Thomas Armstrong, who was b. 1742. The supposition of the compiler is that Cliveures Duke, Jr., if having *m.* 1st Elizabeth Burnley, may have been legally separated from her, as in 1818 he does not appear as one of the litigants in Duke *vs.* Burnley suit, and in 1820 in his pension application states that his wife's name is Ann Armstrong, and there is no evidence of his having any issue by her, while the issue of Elizabeth Burnley Duke are found named in the papers of the famous Duke-Burnley case. They were: Burnley, Ann, Elizabeth, Mary, Patsey, Lucy and Nancy. In his will the father of Cliveures mentioned the son Cliveures as living on his (the father's) land, which he bought of Robert Dabney. In a document dated 5 May, 1784, Cliveures, Jr., is mentioned as having given his daughter, Lucy Burnley Duke, a negro girl; and later acknowledges an obligation to James Burnley of £1,600. On the 15th Nov., 1800, Henry Clivears(?) receipts him and Ann, his wife, for a negro boy, Nathan: "for my wife's share in her father's Estate." 7 Feb., 1807, he gives to his daughter Nancy certain slaves; and having, it is said, ran through his fortune in one way or another, he makes acknowledgment of his poor estate in his pension application in 1820. Issue:

1, Burnley Duke, b. ——; m. Huldah Brown, sister of Benjamin Brown, of Amherst Co., Va., and Dr. Edmund Brown, of Georgia, and had issue:

a, Dr. John Burnley Duke, of Kentucky; member Kentucky Legislature, 1825.

b, General Benjamin B. Duke, m. Mary P. Winston, dau. of Dr. John Winston. General Duke lived and died in Louisa Co., Va., April 12, 1819; he is noted in a transaction had with Burnley Duke, of Hanover Co., Va.

c, Alfred Duke, b. 1806; d. 1890; m. Ann Elizabeth Goodwin, dau. of William Doswell Goodwin and Mary Winfield Cosby, his wife, of Hanover Co., Va., and had issue (see Supplement, William and Mary Quarterly, Oct., 1907): William Burnley Duke, Mary Goodwin Duke, who m. John A. Garratt; Elizabeth Ann Duke, d. unm.; Sarah Wingfield Duke, m. D. Rihon; Philip St. John Duke, who m. —— —— and had: Alfred Duke, of Howletts, Hanover Co., Va., graduate U. of Pa., 1907.

d, Orlando Duke, emigrated to Natchez, Miss.; e, George W. Duke, emigrated to Missouri; f, Lewis Duke, emigrated to Kentucky.

g, Alfred Nelson Duke, b. 1810(?); d. 1852; m. Mary E. Timberlake, b. 2 March, 1812; d. 4 March, 1906; dau. of Granville and Mary (Richardson) Timberlake. They had issue:

i, Carolina Fredonia, b. 1840; m. 1862, John C. Millar, of Goochland Co., Va., and had Ada, b. 1863, m. 1886, Joy Fogg; Florence, b. 1865, m. 1884, Lewis Duke, issue six children; Blanche, b. 1867, d. 1874; George, b. 1870, m. 1894, Jane Duke; John C., b. 1879, killed 1899.

ii, Emma Duke, b. June, 1842, m. 1858, Minor McLaughlin, of Caroline Co., Va., and had issue: Ridgeway, b. 1859, m. 1890, Miss Rolfe and had Minor, Jr., and Mary; Olive, b. 1862, m. 1887, —— Sanders and had issue six children; Virginia, b. 1864, m. 1883, —— Harrison; Morton, b. 1866, m, 1894, —— Smith; Conway, b. 1871,

   unm.; *Alma,* b. 1875, *m.* 1895, —— Joyner;
   James, b. 1878, *unm.*; Maude, b. 1880, *m.* 1901,
   Willis Duke; *Minnie,* b. 1884.
 iii, Burnley Duke, b. 1844; d. 1844.
 iv, George Duke, b. 1845; d. 1885; *m.* —— ——;
   issue: Mary, b. 1868, d. 1882; Albert, b. 1871;
   Willis, b. 1877, *m.* 1901, Maude McLaughlin;
   Everetta, b. 1879, *m.* 1903, —— ——.
 v, John Duke, b. 1848; *m.* 1869, Laura Fogg and had
   issue: Emma, b. 1869, d. 1894, *m.* 1889, C.
   Jones, issue *Laura Mabel,* b. 1872, *m.* 1897,
   —— McGherin and had Willis and Ellwood;
   Burnley, b. 1876; *Maude* (?), b. 1881, *unm.*
 vi, Lewis Duke, b. 1850; d. 1854.
 vii, Alberta Nelson Duke, b. 1852 (see Richardson-
   Du Priest Family).
 h, Elizabeth B. Duke, *m.* —— Hogue, of Rockingham
   Co., Va.; issue three daughters.
 i, Sarah Duke, d. *unm.*; *j,* Emma Duke, d. *unm.*
 k, Alexander Duke, *m.* 1835, Elizabeth K. Garratt, dau. of
   Alexander and Evalina (Bolling) Garratt; she was
   the dau. of John Bolling, of North Garden, and a
   descendant of the Princess Pocahontas. For some
   years Alexander Duke was connected with the Rev.
   Pike Powers in conducting a high school at Midway, Albemarle Co., Va. Issue: (*i*) Susan, who
   m. ante 1875, Col. Horace W. Jones.
 l, Mildred Duke, who *m.* George McLaughlin. On her
   death he *m.* 2d Patsey Duke.
2, Ann Duke, dau. of Cliveures, Jr., *m.* William Smith.
3, Elizabeth Duke, dau. of Cliveures Duke, Jr., *m.* Reuben
  Smith.
4, Mary Duke, dau. of Cliveures Duke, Jr., *m.* Richard Keeling
  Tyler.
5, Patsey Duke.

XI. HARDIN DUKE, son of Cliveures Duke, Sr., b. 1759; d.
circa 1855; *m.* 7 April, 1783, Elizabeth Swift, both of Louisa Co.,
Va. Hardin was a soldier of the Revolution and served seven
years in that war.   Issue:
 1, Thomas Duke, his son, *m.* Jane O. (or Mary) Halliday and
   had issue:
   a, Thomas A.; *b,* Anne; *c,* Sarah Lewis; *d,* Jemima, *m.*
    H. S. Lowry; *e,* Catharine, *m.* W. B. Cocke; *f,*
    Mildred; *h,* Frederic; *i,* Luther W.
 2, William Duke, *m.* Sarah L. Richardson, and d. s.p.
 3, James F. Duke, *m.* —— Sharp and had issue:

a, Sarah, who *m.* William Richardson; b. ——; *m.* Tom
Richardson.

4, Garland Duke, b. 16 March, 1790; d. 27 Sept., 1875; *m.* 14
Jan., 1812, Frances Gibson, b. 28 May, 1795, dau. of
Gen. Wm. Gibson, who fought in the Revolution, and
whose wife was Miss Terry, a near relative of General
Terry, who lived near Fredericksburg.   Issue:

a, John E., b. 29 Nov., 1812; d. 16 March, 1837.

b, William Garland, b. Jan. 18, 1815; d. 31 July, 1878; *m.*
Elizabeth Blades and had Elizabeth.

c, Richard Hardin, b. Louisa Co., Va., 24 July, 1817; d.
Richmond, Va., 27 Jan., 1887; *m.* 24 Feb., 1853,
Salena Nieblung, of Baltimore.   Issue:

  i, Frank Morris, b. 5 Dec., 1853, d. 10 July, 1876;
  ii, Lena M., b. 10 Oct., 1855; iii, Charles R.
  H., b. 31 March, 1860; iv, Walter Garland, b.
  24 Jan., 1864; v, Florence, b. 7 Sept., 1865.

d, Barbara Anne, *m.* —— Reynolds and had: Kate, who
m. Sidney Beckwith and had Gladys Beckwith.

e, George W. Duke, b. 12 Nov., 1825; d. ——, 1900; *m.*
Dorothy Swift.   Issue:

  i, Emma, who *m.* —— Tiller, of Louisa Co., Va.
  ii, Ida, who *m.* —— Gore, of Williamsburg, Va.

f, Benjamin F. Duke, b. 30 Sept., 1823; d. 5 June, 1866;
m. —— —— and had:

  i, Isabel; ii, Lewis; iii, Frank.

g, Mary E. Duke, b. 12 Dec., 1825; d. ——, 1905; *m.* J.
Thomas Bumpass, of Bumpass Station, on C. & O.
R. R., and have issue: C. W. Bumpass and others.

h, Alfred, d. *unm.*

i, James B. Duke, b. 17 March, 1830; d. in Pueblo, Col.,
1896; *m.* —— ——.   Issue:

  i, Melville; ii, Ellen; iii, William; iv, Frank; living
  in Pueblo, Col.

j, Lunsford, b. 17 Feb., 1832; d. 7 Jan., 1833.

k, Patrick Henry, b. 3 May, 1834; living at Soldiers'
Home, Hampton, Va.; *m.* Georgie Wood, of City
Point, Va., and had:

  i, Rosa, who *m.* —— Galpin; ii, James B., of Memphis, Tenn.

l, Frances Ellen Duke, b. 18 Aug., 1836; d. Feb., 1862; *m.*
—— Pindall, of Anne Arundel Co., Md.

m, Julia R. Duke, b. 17 Jan., 1839; d. 27 Oct., 1869; *m.*
Walter Leake, a nephew of Judge Leake, and had
issue:

  i, Mary, who *m.* —— Dietrich and lives in Manchester, Va.

5, Richard S. Duke, *m.* Elizabeth L. Halliday and had issue:

  a, Thomas H.; *b*, William A.; *c*, Sarah C.; *d*, Walter L.;
  e, James L.
6, Hardin Lunsford Duke, *m.* Betsey Richardson.   Issue:
  a, Jabez; *b*, John, who *m.* Eliza Swift and had Lavinia,
    who *m.* —— Nuckols.
7, Mary Duke, *m.* —— Nuckols and had issue:
  a, Hardin, who *m.* —— Jones; *b*, Eliza, who *m.* 1st Wm.
    Cocke; *m.* 2d W. Nuckols; *c*, Louisa.
8, Elizabeth Duke, *m.* —— Nuckols and had:
  a, Ponce; *b*, Mary, who *m.* —— Willhite.
9, Ann Duke, *m.* —— Armstrong and had:
  a, Henry; *b*, Mary, *m.* Robert Sharp; *c*, Miranda; *d*,
    Margaret; *e*, Amy.
  10, Louisa Duke, *m.* —— Sharp.
4, C, IV. WALTER GARLAND DUKE, son of Richard Hardin and
Salena (Nieblung) Duke, b. Richmond, Va., 24 Jan., 1864; *m.*
27 Nov., 1894, Jane, dau. of Joseph Henderson and Hannah
(Irving) Terrill and have Irving Terrill Duke, b. 9 Jan., 1901.
Fontaine Duke, of Hanover, or Louisa, Co., Va., *m.* Judith
N. Pryor.

I. THOMAS D. DUKE, b. Virginia; d. McNary Co., Tenn., 1856;
m. 1825, his fourth cousin, Elvira Duke.   Issue:
  1, John Hughes Duke, of Jackson, Tenn., b. 2 Feb., 1830, in
    Louisa Co., Va., removed with parents to western Ten-
    nessee in 1834; *m.* Dec., 1858, Miss Wisdom.   Issue:
    a, Ella; *b*, Grace; *c*, John Burns.

II. JANE E. DUKE.

III. LOWRY M. DUKE.

IV. FONTAINE PRYOR DUKE.

COLONIAL DUKES IN THE CAROLINAS

Down in the eastern corner of Devonshire in England, about
three miles from the village of Otterton, the seat of the Dukes
of Otterton and but a short distance from Budleigh-Salterton, a
noted watering place on the Devon coast, will be found the birthplace of Sir Walter Raleigh, the great Elizabethan admiral.   It
is situated on what is known as Barton-Hayes farmstead.   A
low quadrangular house, quaintly esconsed in a flowery bower,
indicates the place where he first saw the light.   For a long time
after this event took place it was owned by the Duke family, and
when the great captain, surfeited with the pleasures, the gayeties,
and weary of the gilded grandeur of the court which surrounded
him, turned for repose to the scene of his nativity.   It was then
that he wrote Richard Duke, in 1584, of his desire to purchase

it. In that letter he says: "But for the natural disposition I have in that place, being born in that house, I had rather seat myself there than anywhere else." This letter was preserved for a long time by the Duke family at Otterton House, but is now, I am told, lodged in the museum at Exeter.

Richard Duke, a descendant of the one to whom Raleigh wrote, was of the Otterton line; he was a Westminster boy and was educated at Trinity College. In later years he became a noted clergyman, and also wrote some good verse, and of such merit that Dr. Johnson included them among the classics. Richard Duke died in London, 10 Feb., 1710–11. The family traditions say that he had two sons, Richard and Raleigh, for the Raleighs and the Dukes intermarried and Raleigh was the younger brother and father of William Duke, who was born at Hayes Farm in 1709 and came to Virginia, as a boy, under the patronage of his kinsman, Col. William Byrd, who seated "Westover," on the James. At "Westover" young Duke spent the early years of his life preparing himself for future citizenship under the precept and example of Colonel Byrd, accompanying him on many of his expeditions on the public business and explorations into the fastnesses of southern Virginia. It is claimed also that when Byrd was one of the commissioners to run the dividing line between Virginia and the Carolina province, William Duke was with him; at least it is credited to Colonel Byrd that it was through his persuasion and influence, and to the glowing description that he gave of the land of Eden, which induced young Duke to settle later over the border in the Carolina country; and there he chose a fine plantation near what is now Ridgeway, in Bute Co., N. C., called the "Purchase Patent," where he settled about 1735.

On the Land Grant books at Richmond are records which tend to show the presence of William Duke in Virginia at an early date.

Governor Gooch, on the 28th Sept., 1728, granted to William Duke 317 acres of land in Brunswick County, situated on the south side of the south fork of Reedy Creek. On the same date a grant of 195 acres was made by Governor Gooch to John Duke; it also was located in Brunswick County, on the outward fork of Reedy Creek. In the description of the metes and bounds of this tract one of its corners is defined as adjoining William Duke's land, etc. (see L. G. book, No. 14, pp. 31, 59).

The presumption is that this William Duke referred to in the foregoing grants was identical with Colonel Byrd's protege.

William Duke married Mary Green, daughter of Thos. Edward Green, of Bute Co., N. C., and removed beyond the Roanoke about 1735. He built a house on his plantation modelled from "Westover," the home of his friend and patron, and furnished it with glass windows, said to have been the first introduced into that section of the province of North Carolina. The old Duke home was destroyed by fire many years ago, but the remains of much of its old-time grandeur is found to-day in the beauty and arrangement of the surroundings.

William Duke and Mary Green had several children, among whom were: Green, Sally, Tamar, Winifred and Nannie.

1, Mary Duke, *m.* Isaac Howze.

2, Winifred Duke, *m.* Jonathan Davis and are said to have been the ancestors of Jefferson Davis, former President of the Confederacy. Jefferson Davis was the son of Samuel Davis, a soldier of the Revolution, who after the war removed to Christian Co., Ky., where Jefferson was born, 3 June, 1808. He was appointed to West Point where he graduated. On 30 June, 1835, he *m.* Sallie Knox, dau. of Zachary Taylor, who was then Colonel of the First U. S. Infantry and afterward the famous general of that name. Jefferson Davis was survived by a widow and a daughter, Winnie.

3, Green Duke, *m.* —— ——.

4, Tamar Duke, *m.* 1st Mr. Wortham; *m.* 2d Edward Jones, son of Edward and Abigail (Shugan) Jones. Her descendants are numbered among the Tannahills, Whites, Pritchards, Hayes, Greens and others.

5, Nannie Duke, *m.* 1st (John?) Christmas; *m.* 2d Robert Jones, son of Edward and Abigail (Shugan) Jones, a descendant of Judge Jones, one of the judiciary who sat in judgment on Charles I. of England. His parents emigrated from King and Queen Co., Va., about 1732. Abigail Shugan is said to have been the first white woman to cross the "Shocco Creek country." After the death of Edward Jones she *m.* 3d Thomas Cook, and although there was no issue by this marriage she was long and affectionately known throughout the family as "Grandmother Cook." Of the children of Edward Jones and Abigail (Shugan) Jones, I. Priscilla *m.* 1st William Macon; *m.* 2d James Ransome, whose son, Seymour Ransome, had a dau., Mary Ransome, who *m.* Lewis Duke, and their dau., Indiana L. Duke, *m.* Hon. Daniel R. Goodloe. Nannie Duke and John (?) Christmas lived at Melrose, near Warrenton, N. C. They had issue; surname Christmas.

6, Sallie Davis; 7, Lewis Duke.

8, Henry, an officer in the American navy, who died at sea.

9, Mary, who *m.* General Philomel Hawkins, of North Carolina; issue eleven children.

10, Patsey, who *m.* Allison Williams.

11, Elizabeth Swann Jones, b. 1783; *m.* Robert Jones, of the Halifax line.

12, Sarah Jones, b. 1785, *m.* Rev. John C. Glenn; moved to

Tennessee in 1804; an ancestor of Col. Thomas Allen Glenn, of Philadelphia, Pa.; historian and genealogist.

13, Thomas Cook Jones, b. 1787; *m.* Tempie Williams and had son, Thomas Jones, of Arkansas. She *m.* 2d Dr. Calvin Jones, of Massachusetts, founder of Wake Forest College, North Carolina.

14, William Duke Jones, b. 30 Sept., 1788; *m.* Mary Ann Speed, dau. of Joseph Speed, of Mecklenburg, Va.

15, Ann Winnifred Jones, b. 1790; d. 1820; *m.* 1815, Rev. John Early, one of the pioneer bishops of the Methodist Church in the South. They lived at Lynchburg, Va.

16, Abigail Henry Jones, b. 1792; d. *unm.*

6. SALLIE DAVIS (William[1], Winnifred[2]), dau. of Jonathan Davis and Winnifred (Duke) Davis, *m.* Henry Fitts (see Fitts' Family History).

7. LEWIS DUKE (William[1], Green[2]), son of Green and —— Duke, *m.* Mary Ransome.

10. PATSEY CHRISTMAS (William[1], Nannie[2]), dau. of John(?) and Nannie (Duke) Christmas, *m.* Allison Williams. Issue: 17, James; 18, Mary.

11. ELIZABETH SWANN JONES (William[1], Nannie[2]), dau. of Robert and Nannie (Duke-Christmas) Jones, b. 1783; *m.* Robert Jones, of the distinguished Jones family of Halifax, N. C. From these are descended, among others: Rev. John N. Cole, of Raleigh, who *m.* Elizabeth Marshall Jones, of Virginia. Mr. Cole is a member of the North Carolina Methodist Conference, and superintendent of the Methodist Orphanage at Raleigh. They have several children. His sister, Lucy Cole, *m.* Wm. H. Burwell and left a large family.

14. WILLIAM DUKE JONES (William[1], Nannie[2]), son of Robert and Nannie (Duke-Christmas) Jones, b. 30 Sept., 1788; *m.* 1st Mary Ann, dau. of Joseph Speed, of Mecklenburg, Va. Joseph Speed was a man of exalted character, cultured and accomplished, and one of the most trusted and influential citizens in the section in Virginia in which he lived. He was a descendant, in a direct line, from Sir Joseph Speed, of England, b. 1552; historian, geographer, antiquarian; a contemporary of Sir Walter Raleigh. Speed's History of England, in its day, was considered a most remarkable production. At the age of twenty-six Joseph Speed, of Virginia, was a member of the celebrated Virginia Convention which proclaimed the Rights of Man. An ancestor of Mary Speed(?) was Col. Robert Bignall, of Tarboro, an attorney, and secretary of the colony. He was a member of the Committee of Safety with two former governors of North Carolina and rendered efficient service until his death in 1776 (Colonial Records

of North Carolina). Wm. Duke Jones, *m.* 2d Mrs. Angelina
Fennell (*neé* Peete), widow of Dr. Fennell, of Virginia, and
daughter of Edwin Peete and Anne Bignall and the niece of Mary
Ann Speed Jones. Issue of first uxor:
>19, Joseph Speed, b. 7 Oct., 1814, d. May, 1900; 20, Anne
>Bignall; 21, Minerva Temperance; 22, Mary Eliza;
>23, John Edwin.

Issue of second uxor:
>24, Pattie, d. *unm.*; 25, Ella Speed; 26, Elizabeth Anne; 27,
>Emma Peete; 28, Mary Williams.

17. JAMES WILLIAMS (William[1], Nannie[2], Patsey[3]), son of
Allison and Patsey (Christmas) Williams, *m.* Miss Pat Lou.
They lived near Ringwood, Halifax Co., N. C. They had four
children:
>29, Pat Lou, *m.* Col. Thomas Jones, of Woodley, Warren
>Co., N. C.
>30, Sallie, *m.* John Jones, of Warren Co. They resided at
>Henderson.

18. MARY WILLIAMS (William[1], Nannie[2], Patsey[3]), dau. of
Allison and Patsey (Christmas) Williams, *m.* William Burwell,
of the noted Spottswood-Burwell line of Virginia. He also was
a descendant of William Duke, of Devonshire.   Issue:
>31, William Henry Burwell.

19. JOSEPH SPEED JONES (William[1], Nannie[2], William D.[3]),
son of William Duke and Mary A. (Speed) Jones, b. 7 Oct.,
1814; d. 17 May, 1900; *m.* 1st Miss Lucy Pettway, dau. of Mark
H. Pettway, of Halifax Co.; *m.* 2d Mrs. Mary Fort, of Baltimore, dau. of William and Harriet (Wilson) Fort, both of ancient
Yorkshire (England) families recorded in the Yorkshire Visita-
tions. Mary Fort, at sixteen years of age, graduated from the
Patapsco Institute of Baltimore, then under the auspices of Mrs.
Myrd Linden Phelps. Losing her father, her home devastated
by the horrors of war, Mary, with her widowed mother and
sisters, sought refuge in Virginia and Carolina. In the latter
state she met and married Joseph Speed Jones, then a man of
great wealth and of high social position. War swept away his
fortune, but to his aid came this noble woman. Gathering together
the children of her own household and those of the country about
her, she opened, at " Shocco Hill," her home school and educated
all within her reach. She looked well to the ways of her own
household and kept all things in perfect order, while every day
giving lessons in English, Latin, French, music and mathematics,
and finding time also, with her class in botany, to search out and
analyze the flowers of the fields and gardens, and to scan the
heavens with her class in astronomy. Uncomplaining and serene
in the midst of the conditions of the time she fulfilled her duty

to her neighbors and her own family.   Issue by first uxor:
32, Mary Speed, decd.; 33, Mark Pettway; 34, Marina Williams; 35, William Robert; 36, Pattie Clark; 37, John Buxton Williams; 38, Lucy Barker; 39, Joseph Speed, Jr.; 40, Edwin Early; 41, Tempie W., d. inf.
Issue of second uxor:
42, Mary Speed; 43, Howard Field; 44, Peter D.; 45, Nathan Wilson, who resides at the ancestral home "Shocco Hill," Warren Co., N. C. The Warren White Sulphur Springs, which is part of the estate, has long been a health resort of national reputation and is located in a very beautiful region. It was owned and developed by Wm. Duke Jones. Nearby is the home once occupied by Robert Jones, his father, in the colonial days, with its fragrant bowers and undimmed memories.

20. ANNE BIGNALL JONES (William[1], Nannie[2], William D.[3]), dau. of William Duke and Mary A. (Speed) Jones, *m.* John E. Boyd, of Roanoke. He was of the well-known Boyd-Armistead family, distinguished in the colonial history of Virginia.   Issue:
46, Mary Speed; 47, John; 48, Parthenia Anne; 49, Henry Armistead; 50, Walter Blaire, *m.* Miss Bettie Hawkins. He was president of the Warrenton R. R. Co., and now extensively identified with many other enterprises in Warrenton and vicinity; 51, William.

21. MINERVA TEMPERANCE JONES (William[1], Nannie[2], William D.[3]), dau. of William D. and Mary A. (Speed) Jones, *m.* Henry Fitts.   Issue:
52, James.

22. MARY ELIZA JONES (William[1], Nannie[2], William D.[3]), dau. of William Duke and Mary A. (Speed) Jones, *m.* Joseph Brehon Somerville, of Warren Co. They removed to Haywood Co., Tenn.   Issue:
53, William J., dec'd; a former attorney at Memphis, Tenn.
54, Catharine Vant, dec'd; 55, Mary Speed, dec'd; 56, Rosa Claiborne; 57, Tempie J.; 58, Sallie Gilmer; 59, Walter E., attorney, dec'd; 60, Eliza; 61, Nannie Boyd.

23. JOHN EDWIN JONES (William[1], Nannie[2], William D.[3]), son of William D. and Mary A. (Speed) Jones, *m.* 1st Marina Pettway, no issue; *m.* 2d Millie Pettway; *m.* 3d Miss India Royster, no issue:
62, Millie P., d. y.

25. ELLA SPEED JONES (William[1], Nannie[2], William D.[3]), dau. of William D. and Angelina (Peete-Fennell) Jones, *m.* Francis Marion Hyman, of Martin Co., N. C.; member of firm of Hyman & Dancy, of Norfolk, Va.   Issue:
63, Maggie, d. in early womanhood.

26. ELIZABETH ANNE JONES (William[1], Nannie[2], William D.[3]), dau. of William D. and Angelina (Peete-Fennell) Jones, *m.* Col. W. S. Davis, of Warren Co. Mrs. Davis d. 1907.   Issue:
   64, Wm. Jones, *m.* Miss Hannah Barham, of Louisburg, N. C.; had issue.
   65, John B., *m.* Miss Bennie Williams whose mother was a Miss Kearney, of the well-known family of that name in Warren Co.; had issue.
   66, Mary Ella; 67, Robert Lee, *m.* Miss Marioll Betts, dau. of Rev. A. D. Betts, of the North Carolina Methodist Conference, and a noted leader in the prohibition movement of 1908. They reside at Wilson, N. C., and have several children.
   68, Elizabeth Speed, missionary to Brazil; 69, Richard, residing at Chicago, Ill.; 70, Frank M., *m.* Margaret Clark, of Wilson, N. C., and has issue: 71, Emma H., *m.* Mr. Stafford, of Virginia; 72, Joseph Speed, d. y.; 73, Julian C., resides at Warrenton, N. C.; 74, Angelina Peet, deceased.

27. EMMA PEETE JONES (William[1], Nannie[2], William D.[3]), dau. of William D. and Angelina (Peete-Fennell) Jones, *m.* Henry B. Hunter, of Warren Co., a citizen of prominence; residing at Afton, Warren Co., N. C.   Issue:
   75, Frank P.; 76, Willie Jones, d. 1906, *m.* Ernest M. Goodwin; 77, Carrie; 78, Lulu, *m.* L. Jones, of Durham, N. C., have issue; 79, Harry Blount, of Norfolk, Va.; 80, Edwin D.; 81, Emma Jones; 82, Robert K.

28. MARY WILLIAMS JONES (William[1], Nannie[2], William D.[3]), dau. of William D. and Angelina (Peete-Fennell) Jones, *m.* Wesley Irby, of Virginia.   Issue:
   83, Henry H.; 84, Frank M.; 85, Ella Hyman; 86, Willie Jones.

31. WILLIAM HENRY BURWELL (William[1], Nannie[2], Patsey[3], William[4]), son of William and Mary (Williams) Burwell, *m.* 1st Laura Pettway.   Issue:
   87, William H., Jr., of Warrenton, *m.* 1st Olive Burton, dau. of Rev. R. O. Burton, a prominent Methodist clergyman of Virginia; *m.* 2d Mary Watson. Reside in Warrenton.
   88, Mark Pettway, *m.* Anne Taylor of Virginia. Reside in Warrenton.
   89, Tempie, *m.* R. B. Boyd, of Virginia, and have several children.

33, MARK PETTWAY JONES (William[1], Nannie[2], William D.[3], Joseph S.[4]), son of Joseph S. and Lucy (Pettway) Jones, *m.* Miss Nannie P. Jones, of Wake Co., N. C.   Issue:

90, Alfred Speed, dec'd; 91, Mark Harwell, dec'd; 92, William Duke, deputy sheriff of his County, d. at age of 21 years; 93, Elizabeth Price, *m.* Geo. W. Davis, of New York; 94, Lucy Pettway.

34. MARINA WILLIAMS JONES (William[1], Nannie[2], William D.[3], Joseph S.[4]), dau. of Joseph S. and Lucy (Pettway) Jones, *m.* Charles Alston Cook, graduate of Princeton College; attorney, afterward district attorney of Warren Co., under President Harrison; member of many state and national conventions; a judge of the Supreme Court of North Carolina. In 1903 removed to Muskogee, Okla., "that his family might grow up in the great west," but always a loyal son of Carolina, and a typical southern gentleman. He is a descendant from the Marshalls, Branches, Le Noirs, Alstons, Macons and Jones families; among these ancestors were former governors of North Carolina, and statesmen. He was a member of the first Legislature of Oklahoma. Mrs. Cook is a woman of rare gifts and both are highly esteemed in their adopted home. Issue:

95, Branch Alston, decd.; 96, Lenoir; 97, Bignall Speed, who *m.* Miss Pearl Stuart, of N. Y. They have several children. Reside at Glen Hazel, Pennsylvania.

98, Josephine Henry; 99, Barker Pettway, dec'd; 100, Charles Alston, in United States Army; 101, Marshall Edward, assistant postmaster at Muskogee, Okla.; 102, William Jones, financier; 103, Marina Williams, d. y.; 104, Benjamin Edwards at the University of North Carolina; 105, Mary Speed Mercer.

36, PATTY CLARK JONES (William[1], Nannie[2], William D.[3], Joseph S.[4]), dau. of Joseph S. and Lucy (Pettway) Jones, *m.* Jonas Carr Williams, son of John Buxton Williams, of Warren Co., N. C. She is dec'd. Issue:

106, Eva Thornton; 107, Joseph Speed, *m.* Hattie Hill, of Louisburg; 108, Lucy Pettway; 109, Tempie Dameron; 110, Marina Cook, *m.* Edward S. Paddison, manager Carolina T. & T. Co., of Wilson, N. C.

111, Mark Pettway, manager Henderson Tele. Co.; resides at Rocky Mount, N. C.

112, F. Graham, electrician Oxford, N. C.; 113, Mary A.; 114, Pattie Jonas, d. 1909, aged 20 years.

37. JOHN BUXTON WILLIAMS JONES (William[1], Nannie[2], William D.[3], Joseph S.[4]), son of Joseph S. and Lucy (Pettway) Jones, *m.* Mrs. Nannie P. Jones, widow of Mark P. Jones, who d. 1898. Issue:

115, Nancy Peters Saunders; 116, Alpheus; 117, Joseph Speed.

38. LUCY BARKER JONES (William[1], Nannie[2], William D.[3],

Joseph S.[4]), dau. of Joseph S. and Lucy (Pettway) Jones, *m.*
Samuel S. Reeks.   Issue:
118, Samuel Soule, dec'd; 119, Josephine Speed.

39. JOSEPH SPEED JONES, JR. (William[1], Nannie[2], William D.[3],
Joseph S.[4]), son of Joseph S. and Lucy (Pettway) Jones; *m.*
Estelle McKinney, of Texas.   Issue:
120, Mattie Nobles; 121, Lucy Pettway; 122, Willie Estelle;
123, Helen; 124, Tillet Nobles; 125, Josephine Speed.

42. MARY SPEED JONES (William[1], Nannie[2], William D.[3],
Joseph S.[4]), dau. of Joseph S. and Mary (Fort) Jones, *m.* William Mercer, of Edgecombe, N. C. He is descended from the
Mercers of "Aldie," Scotland, and from the Rouths of England.
He represented his county twice in the Senate of North Carolina,
and has repeatedly refused office; graduate of Trinity College,
N. C., 1876; studied medicine at the University of Virginia and
graduated from the University of the City of New York; located
and practices in his profession at the home of his ancestors, West
End, Edgecombe Co., N. C.   Issue:
126, Margaret E.; 127, Mary Fort; 128, John Routh; 129,
Routh Speed; 130, Lenoir Cook.

43. HOWARD FIELD JONES (William[1], Nannie[2], William D.[3],
Joseph S.[4]), son of Joseph S. and Mary (Fort) Jones, *m.* Estelle
Brodie, of Wilson, N. C. He is one of the most popular men in
Warren Co.; optimistic, talented, and a firm believer in the future
of his state. He is editor of the *Warrenton Record*.   Issue:
131, Walter Brodie; 132, Bignall Speed; 133, William Duke;
134, Ella Brodie; 135, Howard F., Jr.

44. PETER D. JONES (William[1], Nannie[2], William D.[3], Joseph
S.[4]), son of Joseph S. and Mary (Fort) Jones, *m.* Miss Susan
M. Daughtry.   Issue:
136, Sallie Mercer; 137, Mary Speed, dec'd; 138, Susan Mercer,
of Rocky Mount, N. C.

46. MARY SPEED BOYD (William[1], Nannie[2], William D.[3], Anne
B.[4]), dau. of John E. and Anne (Bignall) Boyd, *m.* Joseph Ware,
of Tennessee.   Issue:
139, Anne Boyd; 140, Grace Arrington, *m.* Colonel Sanford,
of Tennessee; 141, William S.

48. PARTHENIA A. BOYD (William[1], Nannie[2], William D.[3],
Anne B.[4]), dau. of John E. and Anne (Bignell) Boyd, *m.* William P. Massenburg, of Louisburg, a member of one of the old
families of that town.   Issue:
142, John, *m.* 1908, Nannie White; 143, Mary Speed.

49. HENRY ARMISTEAD BOYD (William[1], Nannie[2], William D.[3],
Anne B.[4]), son of John E. and Anne (Bignall) Boyd, *m.* Miss

Bettie Norwood. He is an attorney and practices and resides at Warrenton.

Issue:

144, William Norwood, m. Elizabeth Burwell; 145, Annie Jones, m. Prof. William A. Graham, principal of the Graham High School at Warrenton. Their home is at the old Willcox Institute, once famous in the South as a school for young ladies.

146, Marian Massenburg.

51. WILLIAM JONES BOYD (William[1], Nannie[2], William D.[3], Anne B.[4]), son of John E. and Anne (Bignall) Boyd, m. 1st Miss Mollie Bachelor, of Halifax; m. 2d Miss Cornelia Mills, of Halifax. They reside at Ringwood, N. C.

Issue:

147, Anne Bignall; 148, Pattie B.

52. JAMES FITTS (William[1], Nannie[2], William D.[3], Minerva T.[4]), son of Henry F. and Minerva T. (Jones) Fitts, m. Miss Fannie Bird, of Petersburg, Va.

Issue:

149, Millie, d. y.; 150, Henry Bird; 151, James H.

56. ROSA CLAIBORNE SOMERVILLE (William[1], Nannie[2], William D.[3], Mary E.[4]), dau. of Joseph B. and Mary E. (Jones) Somerville, m. James Gibson, of Tennessee.

Issue:

152, Nathan, attorney, living at Muskogee, Okla., m. Florence ———.

153, Joseph S.; 154, James R.; 155, Rosa; 156, Mary S.; 157, Thomas.

57. TEMPIE J. SOMERVILLE (William[1], Nannie[2], William D.[3], Mary E.[4]), dau. of Joseph B. and Mary E. (Jones) Somerville, m. Judge Henry J. Livingston, of Brownsville, Tenn.; a descendant of a long line of distinguished ancestry.

Issue:

158, Mary S.; 159, Rosa G., m. Mr. Sherman, of Brownsville, Tenn.; 160, Genevieve; 161, Henry J., Jr.

60. ELIZA J. SOMERVILLE (William[1], Nannie[2], William D.[3], Mary E.[4]), dau. of Joseph B. and Mary E. (Jones) Somerville, m. James S. Ment, of Staunton, Tenn.

Issue:

162, George, graduate of University of the City of New York, practiced for a while there as a physician, but now of Memphis, Tenn.

163, Tempie, graduate of Randolph-Macon Woman's College, Lynchburg, Va.

61. NANNIE BOYD SOMERVILLE (William[1], Nannie[2], William D.[3], Mary E.[4]), dau. of Joseph B. and Mary E. (Jones) Somerville, m. W. B. Nash, of Staunton, Tenn.

Issue:

164, Will Brehm.

66. MARY ELLA DAVIS (William[1], Nannie[2], William D.[3], Elizabeth A.[4]), dau. of Col. W. S. and Elizabeth A. (Jones)

286

Davis, *m.* W. H. McCabe, banker of Durham, N. C.   Issue:
165, W. H. McCabe, Jr.

96. LENOIR COOK (William[1], Nannie[2], William D.[3], Joseph S.[4], Marina W.[5]), dau. of Chas. Alston and Marina W. (Jones) Cook, *m.* George Egbert McLaurine, of Tennessee, a descendant of the Haywoods, of Carolina and Tennessee.   Issue:
166, Chas. Alston Cook; 167, Margaret Haywood.

106. EVA THORNTON (William[1], Nannie[2], William D.[3], Joseph S.[4], Patty C.[5]), dau. of Jonas C. and Patty Clark (Jones), *m.* C. D. Tharington.   Issue:
168, Marion Speed; 169, Tempie Zollicoffer.

113. MARY A. WILLIAMS (William[1], Nannie[2], William D.[3], Joseph S.[4], Patty C.[5]), dau. of Jonas S. and Patty C. (Jones) Williams, *m.* Benj. Tharington.   Issue:
170, Ellen.

126. MARGARET E. MERCER (William[1], Nannie[2], William D.[3], Joseph S.[4], Mary S.[5]), dau. of Dr. William and Mary S. (Jones) Mercer, *m.* Theodore Clyde Tilghman, of Maryland.   Issue:
171, Theo. Clyde, Jr.; 172, Rosa Lynwood.

127. MARY FORT MERCER (William[1], Nannie[2], William D.[3], Joseph S.[4], Mary S.[5]), dau. of Dr. William and Mary S. (Jones) Mercer, *m.* Ernest M. Tilghman, of Salisbury, Md.   Issue:
173, Wm. Mercer; 174, Ernest M., Jr.

150. HARRY BIRD FITTS (William[1], Nannie[2], William D.[3], Minerva T.[4], James[5]), son of James and Fannie (Bird) Fitts, *m.* Miss Bugby, of New York. Dr. Fitts is a naval surgeon now in charge of the Naval Recruiting Station at Indianapolis, Ind.; a man of unusual gifts and a charming personality of manner and conversation; a pleasing writer, and very popular in naval society circles.   Issue:
175, George, residing in Richmond, Va.; 176, Nadja; 177, Margaret Chandler Remey; 178, Virginia.

151. JAMES H. FITTS (William[1], Nannie[2], William D.[3], Minerva T.[4], James[5]), son of James and Fannie (Bird) Fitts, *m.* Miss Mary Blair, of Richmond, Va. He also was a naval officer, and immediately after his wedding was ordered on a three year's cruise, which rather than do, he resigned his commission in the navy and accepted a professorship in the college at Blacksburg, Va. While en route to the Chicago Exposition where he expected to join his brother, Dr. H. B. Fitts, from whom he had been separated for many years, a railway collision occurred in which he lost his life. His widow afterward *m.* Mr. Hawes, of Richmond, Va. (see Fitts Family History).   Issue:
179, James H.; 180, Moylan Bird.

THE DUKE GENEALOGY

There is, in connection with the records of the Duke family, an item of historic but pathetic interest, and the facts of which are eminently worthy a place in these pages.

During the progress of the Civil War, in the year 1862, and while William Duke Jones was the proprietor of the White Sulphur Springs in Warren Co., N. C., Gen. Robert E. Lee sent his daughter, Miss Annie Carter Lee, to that famous southern resort to regain her waning health; in spite, however, of all that loving hearts and hands could do to check the advance of her malady, she lingered awhile and died while at the springs. With tender care they laid her remains in what was once the rose-garden of Nannie Duke Jones, and here among the tombs of departed generations of the Duke family, and the ashes of some of the famous patriots of Warren and the old North State, rest those of Annie C. Lee. Under the initiative of Mr. Joseph Speed Jones, the citizens of Warren County, with loving devotion to the memory of the daughter of their great chieftain, now doubly afflicted, erected a monument of native granite over her grave. The following lines sent by her grief-stricken father form part of the inscription on the shaft.

> "Perfect and true are all thy ways
> Whom earth adores and Heaven obeys."

The following letter, in reference to this subject, written by Stephen B. Weeks, Esq., of Greensboro, N. C., appeared in the *Warren Sentinel* under date of 15 Aug., 1866.

"Honor to whom Honor is Due"

"*Messrs Editors:*—

"Your editorial request for some friend to furnish your paper with an account of the erection of the monument to Miss Anne C. Lee, late daughter of Gen. R. E. Lee, by the citizens of Warren County, N. C., was subsequent to that event, but, as one of the committee of arrangements and your friend, I nevertheless would have most promptly responded but for the knowledge of the fact that two or three newspaper reporters were present, and that a communication from me at that period would have been a work of supererogation. Nor would I trouble you or your readers now with any remarks upon the subject, but for the reason that the honor of erecting this monument has been unintentionally, I am sure, given to those who neither claim nor desire it, while the name of Joseph Speed Jones, Esq., who alone is entitled to all the honor, is entirely ignored by the correspondent of the Petersburg Index. M^r. Jones petitioned to Gen. Bragg, two or three years ago to detail M^r. Z. Crowder, the patriotic artist, for the special purpose, urging, as an additional reason that Mr. Crowder had volunteered in the regular army after he had passed the then conscript age, and not 'conscripted,' as reported, that he had participated in all the hard fought battles in Virginia up to that time, and was then in feeble health. Gen. Bragg promptly consented.

"Mr. Jones whose patriotism is only equalled by his philanthropy, projected and erected this monument, through the aid of Mr. Crowder.

"Col. Heck and a few of the prominent citizens of the neighborhood then proposed to Mr. Jones to allow the citizens of Warren to share its

TOMBS OF NANNIE DUKE JONES AND MISS ANNA C. LEE

honors, to which he most cheerfully consented, but stated to the meeting of those neighbors that he had calculated to defray the whole expense of it himself, and had purchased the iron railing to enclose the cemetery, which they positively refused to let him do, though he still refuses to accept any remuneration for the railing and claims the right to share in the expenses of the monument.

"I am perfectly cognizant of all these facts, and they are well known by all of his neighbors; and hence, as a token of gratitude to him, and as an act of Justice to his accomplished wife, the Committee of Arrangements elected her President of The Ladies Aid Society by acclamation. How well she deserved that distinguished honor, you may judge, when I inform you, that the letter of invitation to Gen. Lee to attend the erection was indited by her in a few hours and without previous notice. For its sublime devotion and patriotism, its elegance, harmony and perfection of language, for its soul stirring allusion to the modesty, greatness and goodness of this illustrious chieftain under the vicissitudes of fortune, it is not surpassed, in my humble opinion, by any record of epistolary belles-lettres.

"The locality of this monument is within the cemetery of the Jones family of this County, on Shocco Creek, near White Sulphur and Shocco Springs, in full view of Gen. Jethro Sumner's monument—one of the first generals appointed by Congress, and one of the heroes of '76. The surrounding country is highly picturesque, and its inhabitants educated and refined. It was settled by Edward Jones who emigrated from Virginia in 1740, and his wife whose maiden name was Abagail Shugan. Tradition informs us that she was the first white lady that crossed the Roanoke River. Mr. Jones left a large family of children, and his widow married Thomas Cook. She is known to posterity as 'Grandmother-Cook.' She was said to have been a remarkable woman for the strength of her intellect, and for the firmness and energy of her character. In the wilderness surrounded by savages and wild beasts, and left a widow at an early age with a house full of children, by her indomitable energy she raised and educated them all to become the leading and most useful citizens of the country—five of whom were at one and the same time members of our Legislature, and two of them in Congress. Beneath the sacred shades of this cemetery once gambolled in girlhood, her daughters—the mothers of the Hon⁸ Nathaniel Macon, Willis Alston, M. T. Hawkins and Judge Sewell; the Hills, the McLemores,—with their compasses and hatchets opened the way for civilization in Georgia and Tennessee. The Joneses, Eatons, Martins and Greens have left their civic, legal and legislative services as a legacy to their country. The Pegrams, and those noble brothers,—Major Robert and Matt Ransom, beside many others in the Southern and Western States are descendants of 'Grandmother Cook.'

"When I was a boy the aged father and mother of our venerable citizen, William Duke Jones, resided hard by the Cemetery. Their commodious and spacious dwelling was on a level plot of ground, gently undulating from the yard to a pebbled brook, in front and in the centre of several acres of ground clad with verdant sward and adorned with the original forest trees, grand and hoary with age. It was literally the seat of hospitality, refinement and religion. Bishop Early's first wife was a member of this family and sleeps in this Cemetery, and the Rev. Messrs Glenn and Jones married two of her sisters. What a history this sacred spot could unfold, if it had a tongue to speak! Not a solitary tree or stone is left to tell the joys and sorrows of its former inhabitants. 'Sic transit gloria mundi.'

"I would give you a description of this exquisitely wrought monument, and the highly interesting ceremonies that attended its erection if it had not been so graphically done by abler hands. It was eminently proper for the citizens of North Carolina to pay this tribute of affection and respect to the daughter of that great and grand man, who so often led our sons to Victory against such unequal numbers—and likewise, an indispensible debt of gratitude they are under to the ladies of Virginia for their munificent kindness to our citizen soldiers in sickness and health, as well as for their pious care in collecting the remains of our hero dead into cemeteries and bedecking their graves with floral offerings."

INVENTORY OF ESTATE OF WILLIAM DUKE

Inventory of the Personal Estate of William Duke taken 29th November 1793, viz: 1 walnut desk and book case; 1 walnut desk; 1 walnut chest of drawers; 3 dining tables; 1 dressing table with small glass; 1 tea table; 1 square walnut dressing table; 2 kitchen tables; 1 candle stand; 1 doz. walnut chairs; 1 walnut arm chair; 1 doz. parlor chairs; 2 doz common chairs; 1 large looking glass; 1 dressing glass; 1 old dressing glass; 1 eight-day clock; 1 bed with four sheets, bed cover and two pillows; 3 beds; two sheets, 4 counterpanes, 2 pillows, 1 blanket, 2 bed quilts; 2 beds, 2 pr. sheets, 2 blankets, 4 table covers; 10 counterpanes; 1 china press; 2 pr. bed curtains (calico) 1 pr. bed curtains home spun; 1 large walnut chest; 1 large leather trunk; 1 small trunk; 5 prs Andirons; 4 Queens China dishes and pudding pans; 25 cups; 26 saucers; 2 delft bowls; 12 large bowls; 1 tumbler; 23 small tumblers; 1 tureene; 12 dram glasses; 3 wash 6 earthen dishes; 15 earthen plates; 7 pewter dishes; 3 pewter basins; 1 porringer; 29 knives and forks; 12 cups and saucers; 1 milk pot; 25 teaspoons; 19 tablespoons; 1 coffee mill; 1 coffee pot; 1 pepper mill; 1 spice mortar; 2 brass candlesticks; 1 lanthorne; 1 pepper box; 1 knife box; 2 jugs; 2 churns; 1 butter pot; 1 willow pot; 1 blue-and-white China Mug; 2 delft mugs; 2 decanters; 6 deep earthern plates; 2 doz. white saucers; 1½ doz. cups 1 white water pot; a parcel of lumber in the cuddy; 2 useless saddles; 64 head of cattle; 52 hogs; 37 sheep; 13 geese; 17 horses; 2 wagons; with gears; 1 ox cart; 1 carriage; 2 whip saws; 1 X cut saw; 4 shovels; 18 plow horses; a parcel of wheat; 1 parcel of oats; 1 set Smith's tools; 2 looms with gears; some old tire; 3 wash bowls; 1 butter pot; 1 jug; 3 jugs with same set; 1 brass corn (?); 5 pots; 3 Dutch ovens; 1 frying pan; 1 skillet; 1 gridiron; 1 cotton gin; 1 water pail; 2 piggins; 1 tub; 5 bu. hair; 1 still; 7 jugs; 1 pickle pot; the crop of fodder and tobacco; 2 barrels with some brandy; a carriage with harness for four horses ("coach and four"); 19 hoes; 7 axes; 3 augers; 2 chisels; 1 drawing knife; 1 single chaise; 1 parcel of collars; The Negroes; Squire, Alsey, Sidney, Mingo, Lucy, Abram, Seal, Will, Frank, Stephen, Anny, Doctor, Tempy, Tona, Sr., Morina, Anthony, Cloe, Essie, Sr. Dilcey, Delph, Ball, Annaday, Sandy, Alsey, Jr., Adam, Sitter, Burston, Edom, Aaron, Fed, Patience, Essie, Jr., Grace, Alfred, John, Tom, Jr., Mollie, Pat, Dinah, Harvey, Charlotta, Glasgow, Ephraim, Phil, Dye, Visey, Phil-nick-nick, David, Jerrie, Tim, Brittan, Phil-glasgow, Jr. Holly—52 Negroes. A number of Bonds the amount of which cannot now be ascertained, but which the administrator is always ready to make a division of, as soon as the parties concerned can attend. Several are of an old date and as the deceased left no books, it will require some time to ascertain how much may be due on them. On the whole it is impossible at this time, considering the shortness of the notice that an exact inventory of the Bonds could be returned.

GREEN DUKE, *Administrator.*

Supplementary Inventory to be added to the Inventory of 29th Nov. 1793 Amount of Bonds £1040.0.0 (among other things are 8 panes of window glass, 4 bladders of putty and some old continental money).
Supplemental Inventory of Nov. 1794,
old notes, many judgements, Virginia money, 1079 lbs. Tobacco—lent to Jonathan Davis (his son-in-law).
Division of Negroes belonging to the estate of Wm. Duke, dec^d. made 21 day of January 1793 (?).

Lot No.	1.	To Mrs. Duke widow of deceased (naming each)	£608. 6.8
"	" 2.	To Edward Jones on behalf of his wife,	645.16.8
"	" 3.	To Thomas Christmas on behalf of his wife,	616.13.4
"	" 4.	To Robert Jones on behalf of his wife Nancy,	595. 0.0
"	" 5.	To Green Duke,	637.10.0
"	" 6.	Isaac House on behalf of his wife, dec^d.,	620.16.8
" Furniture for Mrs. Duke,			83. 9.0
"	"	" Mrs. Green Duke,	100. 6.8

JOHN DUKE, THE PIONEER, AND HIS FAMILY

The tradition in respect to the earliest ancestor of our particular branch of the Duke family of Virginia, as it is recalled by one of the oldest living members, is: "That one Colonel William Duke, of English origin, came over to Ireland with the army of William of Orange in 1691, in command of a troop of horse, and that when the war was over Colonel Duke remained in Ireland, finally settling in the Province of Ulster. One of his descendants was William Duke, of County Down, father of James Duke, who came to this country from Warren Point, near Newry, County Down, in 1774; served in the American Revolution and married Judith Crane in Philadelphia, 11 Nov., 1779."

Mrs. Margaret Ann Dukesmith, of Charlestown, W. Va., a granddaughter of the foregoing James Duke, is my authority for this statement, as it was related to me in the summer of 1906. She further stated, and this additional information has been confirmed by Mrs. John McFaden, of Harper's Ferry, W. Va., who is one of the eldest representatives of the line of John Duke, Jr., the emigrant ancestor whom we have under consideration, that her parents and grandparents, as well as the children of her own generation, recognized and spoke of the children of John Duke, Jr., as *cousins;* and not only exchanging visits and family gossip concerning their respective households, but in other ways acknowledging kinship of that degree.

Accepting this statement and its confirmation as substantially correct, it then becomes necessary to trace the connection between their respective families and establish the basis upon which it is founded.

Inasmuch as James Duke was born in 1755 and John Duke, Jr., was born *circa* 1720, it is evident that the former belonged to a generation younger; and if James Duke and *his* children were cousins to the children of John Duke, Jr., who was of the generation corresponding to that of William, the father of James, then the proposition argues to the conclusion that John Duke, Sr., must have been the father of both John, Jr., and William Duke, and he the son of Colonel William Duke, the English officer. Now to carry the argument farther: James Duke was a youth of nineteen when he came to this country in 1774, and after serving in the patriot army from 1779 to 1780 married, and naturally seeking the society of his kindred, proceeded to the Valley of Virginia by way of Cumberland Co., Pa., and in the vicinity of Charlestown, Va., set up his own establishment near that of his uncle, John Duke, Jr. Moreover, if there is any significance in the transmitting of family hereditary names, it is found in the cases of these two men: John Duke, Jr., naming his eldest son William and his second son John, and James Duke naming *his* eldest son William and his second son James.

There were other Dukes about this time in the same neighborhood in Virginia: George, John and Andrew Duke, whose names are perpetuated among descendants of James Duke. All of these men served in the American army; George was killed at the Battle of Brandywine, John served through the war and was pensioned, and Andrew was lost sight of. Leaving these speculations and now to come to the patent facts.

In the year 1749, living upon the remnant of a vast estate in the north of Ireland, were two John Dukes, father and son. Both were of the Protestant, farmer class, occupying their holdings jointly near Ballymoney, County ——, Ireland, under a lease from Felix O'Neil, a descendant of that ancient and once powerful family of O'Neil, Lords of Ulster.

The linen industry was flourishing throughout Ulster about this time and the Dukes, in common with their neighbors, were actively engaged in this industry in addition to farming. The father and son appear to have operated the land together at that date and until 1751, when a separation seems to have taken place and John Duke, Sr., drops out of sight altogether, and his son John Duke, Jr., appears again in Virginia shortly after and where he became a landholder in 1764.

In the decade between 1750 and 1760 a great wave of emigration swept over the north of Ireland, carrying thousands of its sturdy and industrious people toward a land of better conditions. The Province of Pennsylvania attracted by far the greater number of these settlers, and it was to this part of the New World that John Duke, Jr., with his family of wife and four small children came, supposedly, between 1751 and 1755.

It is believed that he landed at New Castle and from thence made his way into western Pennsylvania, and from thence into Maryland, and finally crossed the Potomac into Frederick Co., Va., where we definitely find him established upon a plantation of his own in 1764. Certain passages in his diary indicate that he was a trader for a time along the emigration trails. These trails, leading south from Pennsylvania and the east, were filled with pioneers making their way to the borders and pushing the lines of civilization further westward, and for their protection chains of trading posts guarded the frontiers of Pennsylvania, Maryland and Virginia and stretched away into the Carolinas from the northwest passes in the Alleghanies.

From the note-book or diary already mentioned it is evident that he was familiar with the route and the characters which traversed them, as frequent mention is made of Captain Pearis and other traders of the time.

Captain Pearis was a famous frontiersman and Indian leader; he was a fearless character and an active figure in border history, and with a strong and undisputed influence which he wielded over the Southern Indians. At the head of bands of Catawbas and Cherokees, he led his Indian contingent to the service of Governor Dinwiddie of Virginia, in 1755–1756. He was given a command under Colonel George Washington, then at Fort Loudon (Winchester), to assist the Virginia militia in the campaign against the French and their hostile allies that were at the time driving the borderers back to the shelter of the fortified posts in the Valley of Virginia. Pearis, while in charge of his friendly tribesmen, also rendered aid to Governor Sharpe of Maryland; so, too, he performed similar service for the Province of Pennsylvania in 1755–56, in which he commanded a body of new levies from the lower counties (Delaware), in Colonel William Clapham's provincial forces. He was in Virginia in 1761, at which time, it appears, John Duke sold him supplies.

Captain Richard Pearis was a remarkable character and the events of his strenuous career are full of interest and excitement. After a stormy experience with the military authorities of Virginia he removed to an island in the Holston River, which had been granted him in 1754, and later established a trading post among the Indians of that section, who loved him so well. That post is now Greenville, S. C.

Among other transactions which are recorded in John Duke's note-book, it shows that he furnished quantities of salt, wheat and other commodities to John Van Metre, also a famous trader, and son of the Dutch pioneer of the same name; and to William Morgan, a relative of General Daniel Morgan of the Revolution; and to Edward Lucas, into whose family one of his grand-daughters married; and there were many others of prominence in the valley with whom he had commercial relations and among whom he disposed of his linen cloth and received in return Virginia currency, worth about $3.33 to the pound.

In his account book are entries of loans made to Edward Lucas, Charles Burk, John Watson, Henry Pettigrew, William

THE DUKE GENEALOGY

Morgan, John and James Wright and to others; and it will be comforting no doubt to descendants of these persons to know that there are also records of the repayments of these loans.

The note-book, so often referred to in this narrative, is the one tangible link left us by which our kinship is determined and its record binds us to this early ancestor. It is the only register of that early time which enables us to discover our relationship, containing, as it does, the names and dates of birth of his children and grandchildren. This interesting relic is a small parchment covered book, about three inches wide, five inches long and a half inch thick, and is more or less shrivelled by the heat from a fire which threatened its destruction several years ago. It contains about fifty pages of heavy, hand-made paper, which show plainly the lines and water-mark of strange and ancient design. This book was used by our forefather for his memorandum and accounts. On the inside of the cover is this inscription: "May the first day 1745 John Duke his book," and was evidently started about the time of his marriage and life was opening up for him its responsibilities. In it our ancestor has recorded, in a clear round hand and in the peculiar spelling and phraseology of the period, notes as are of a business character; receipts from his landlord in Ireland, receipts for quit-rents paid to Lord Fairfax in Virginia, for taxes and county levy, and many domestic happenings. It is the family register of the births and deaths of his children and grandchildren and jottings of interest, historical and genealogical.

On the death of John Duke the book passed into the possession of his eldest son, William, who used it similarly; and so on down the succeeding generations, each family so acquiring it adding some of their own vital statistics and in that respect it is to-day the only reliable record of at least the first three generations. From a study of its pages light is thrown upon persons and incidents of pioneer days, of comrades and experiences in the wilds, for when these items of fact were placed upon its pages life along the forest frontiers of Virginia must have been anything but favorable in opportunities for recording, at length, the events transpiring about them.

The registration of the births of John Duke's children is recorded in the following quaint language:

I. "July the 14th day at 10 in the morning Betty Duke was born the 14th day of the New Moon the moon was full that night 1747 (dide 1773)."

II. "March the 17th day at 9 in the morning William Duke was Born the 10th day of the New Moon 1749."

III. "February the 11th day Francis Duke was Born at two in the morning the moon was in the wan 3 days to come 1751."

IV. "August the 20th day John Duke was born at three in the morning 1753."

294

July the 19 day at
10 in the morning
Betty Duke was born
the 19 day of the new
moon the moon was
first at 12 that day
night 1777 (in) 4775

Mark the 17 day
at 9 in the morning
William Duke was
born this 10 day of
the new moon —
1779
1779 Matthew

September the 24 1777
Frances Duke was
killed by the Ingans

October the 4 1791
John Duke was
Killed by the
Ingans about
Sun riseing
at the saddle of
Jacobs Jonbotem

JOHN DUKE, THE PIONEER

V. "May the 4th day at two in the afternoon Robert Duke was born 1755."

VI. "June 30th day at 1 in the morning Mary Duke was born the moon was 15 days ould She was full at 12 the next day 1757."

VII. "July the 5th day Mather Duke was born the moon was full that same day in yr of 1758."

VIII. "May 13th day Margerat Duke was born the moon was in the wan one day to come 1760."

IX. "Novembr. the 12th day Mary Duke was born 1762."

X. "June 17th at 4 in the morning the moon was in the wain one day to come 1765 James Duke was born in 1765."

XI. "March the 20th day at 10 at night Jane Duke was born the 22d day of new moon 1769."

The record then continues with the names of William Duke's children and grandchildren:

"The eage of William Duke's children born in Virginia bartley County" [Berkeley County].

"Margerat Duke was born Ogest 18/1·7·7·8.

"Francis Duke was born November 29 1783.

"John Duke was born May 7, 1786.

"Robert Duke was born August 9 1788.

"Mathus Duke was born Jeneway the 5 1791.

"Nancy Duke was born Aprile the 13 1793.

"Margerat Hendricks died October 5, 1839, aged 61 years and one month and 17 days.

"William Duke, Decd September 13, 1794 [1795] in the 45th year of his age."

The children of Daniel and Margaret Hendricks follow in order named:

"William Hendricks son to Daniel and Margerat Hendricks was born December 22d, 1795.

"Daniel Hendricks was born August 25th 1797.

"John Hendricks was born Oct. 30th, 1799.

"Tobias Hendricks was born year of our Lord 181 [1801] Nov. the 7th.

"Polly Hendricks was born December 13th 1805.

"James Hendricks was born in the year of Our Lord 2 day of July, 1812.

"Eliza Hendricks was born in September 27th 1814.

Sometimes the Hendricks name is spelled "Hendrix" and on one of the pages is written the signature of "Eliza hendrickus."

The little volume contains other domestic chronicles, such as an item referring to the teaching of John Duke's children by the Rev. John Black, who was then itinerating through Virginia and afterward became pastor of Upper Marsh Creek Presbyterian Church, in York Co., Pa.

Another item refers to William Duke: "November the 19, 1767, William Duke went to Youder Spair to larn his trade." This event was probably postponed, as is evident by a subsequent entry: "Jan'ry 14 day, William Duke went to Hans Spair to larn a trade of the blacksmith 1768 and the said Spair is to pay him ten pounds at end of two years help."

THE DUKE GENEALOGY

Gibril (Gilbert) Christian's name appears among other notes as the purchaser of a crop of wheat, in 1770. One of the curious entries is a trading account between John Duke and an employee: Daniel Campbell, against whose wages offset charges are made in the years 1768–69, which include washing, mending, "linnen," "liker," "knife," "wheat," "tabac" and other sundries, as well as for occasional advances of cash, all of which are reckoned in pounds, shillings and pence "Virginia money."

Among the contents one reads receipts for produce sold; of rents paid to Felix O'Neil; levies paid to Sheriff Crane, of Berkeley Co., Va.; quit-rents to Robert Stephens, agent for Lord Fairfax on the purchase of 1764. This obligation, which Thomas, Lord Fairfax, entailed upon all sales of land in the Northern Neck, was abolished in the success of the Revolution, along with other feudal customs of the baronial proprietor. The items of taxes paid to James Crane, the sheriff and justice, extended through the years 1764 to 1778, at which time Duke ceased to pay the quit-rents as well.

As John Duke came from a country that was then the stronghold of Calvinism of the most uncompromising sort, so here he, like the majority of his compatriots in the valley, was a Presbyterian. His neighbors in Frederick County were mostly Scotch-Irish, with a sprinkling of German. The former were largely of the Presbyterian faith and the latter were Lutherans. Their meetings were held at first among individual families until congregations were organized and preaching held at fixed places in the different localities and these were so remote and so widely separated that they could only be reached after travelling long distances; but neither long, tedious journeys and their discomforts diminished the ardor of the steadfast God-serving pioneers, or deterred them from attending on the worship of their hereditary faith.

As soon as the Scotch-Irish got a foothold in the Valley of Virginia places for Presbyterian worship began to be established among the people living in the then wilderness; and as far as western Virginia was thought to extend Donegal Presbytery held jurisdiction over it long before the year 1755, when Hanover Presbytery was created. Among the ministers called upon to supply the various congregations of Hanover Presbytery were John Wright and John Black, whose names appear, with some frequency, upon John Duke's note-book.

Somewhere in the district lying west of the Blue Ridge, between the headwaters of the Bullskin and the Elk Branch, a small church of the Presbyterian denomination had been organized as early as 1745, but its site, however, as well as its history, has long since been forgotten. This same territory, embracing the country from Shepherdstown on the Potomac to Charlestown, and including the locality in which the Duke and Lemon families

296

resided, was served by missionaries and occasionally by stated supplies, and it was not until the latter part of the eighteenth century that the four congregations of that period: Shepherdstown, Tuscarora, Opequon and Front Royal had separate pastors.

Dr. John McKnight, whose name appears in the Lemon family papers, was preaching to the Bullskin meeting in 1775, and on his departure a little time later a division occurred in the congregation, and a part of the worshippers established the Mt. Carmel Church at Mecklenburg (Shepherdstown). The Rev. Moses Hoge was called to officiate here and he took charge in 1787, while the remainder of the Bullskin congregation, sometimes called Hopewell, installed the Rev. Wm. Hill as their pastor, but this was not until 1792, the pulpit in the meantime having been supplied by missionaries. Over the Elk Branch Church the Revs. Hoge and Hill divided their ministrations for a number of years.

The Rev. Moses Hoge, who in after years became one of the foremost clergymen in Virginia, came to Shepherdstown in 1787, from the South Branch of the Potomac, and served this congregation till 1807, when he was chosen president of the Hampden-Sidney College, succeeding the Rev. Archibald Campbell, who had been called to the head of Princeton College, N. J. While at Shepherdstown Rev. Moses Hoge conducted a private school where many men destined to become famous in history obtained their first rudiments in a classical education.

At Shepherdstown the Rev. John Matthews succeeded Dr. Hoge in 1809. It was under the influence of these two beloved Presbyterian ministers that John Duke and his family worshipped. and where many of his children and grandchildren received their spiritual nourishment that in after years was reflected in the purity of character and uprightness of life of many of the family. William Duke worshipped at Shepherdstown and here his youngest daughter, Nancy, became a member at eleven years of age under Dr. Hoge's pastorate. H⸳⸳ son, Rev. John Matthew Clymer, the Presbyterian minister of the church at Ashburn, Loudon Co., Va., was named for Dr. Hoge's successor at Shepherdstown, Rev. John Matthews.

NOTES

1778, June 24. John Duke. Deed of surrender; Wm. Stephens to Andrew Devorer; was proved by the oaths of Samuel Thompson and John Duke, and ordered recorded (Minutes of Yohoghania Co., Va., Court).

SETTLEMENT IN VALLEY OF VIRGINIA

John Duke came to Frederick Co., Va., at a time when it was being rapidly parcelled out to grantees under Lord Fairfax, who held the proprietorship of the Northern Neck by inheritance from his Culpepper ancestors. The "Neck" was a vast domain, millions of acres in area, lying west of the mountains and from which, from time to time, have been carved numerous counties of the two Virginias. Over these extensive possessions Lord Fairfax held feudal court and custom after the baronial fashion in old England. A land office was set up after 1748 and patents were issued for grants of land at a few shillings per acre. Many of these purchases were surveyed by the youthful Washington, who later was destined to become the first ruler of a free and sovereign people. Under Fairfax a system of quit-rents were entailed upon property bought in his domain and by which a perpetual overlordship was intended to be secured to his family in much the same manner as that inaugurated by William Penn in the Province of Pennsylvania.

Great tracts of land along the beautiful streams and in the wilds of western Virginia, thousands of acres in area, were thus disposed of to the first settlers who swarmed into the rich and fertile valleys from the overflowing fountains of emigration in the eastern colonies. Scotch-Irish, Germans and Quakers were among the first to absorb the choicest portions lying at the foot and west of the Blue Ridge. There were many who came merely as speculating adventurers, but the majority of newcomers were well meaning settlers, founding permanent homes.

Winchester, in the heart of this great manor, at first called Fredericktown, was established toward the middle of the eighteenth century. It was at first merely an Indian village, or trading post, and was known along the trails as "Shawnee Cabins," but with an emigrant population constantly pouring into the vicinity, and with increasing conditions of prosperity and favorable location, the post soon became the center of activity for the whole valley lying between the Shenandoah and the South Branch of the Potomac.

In 1738 Winchester was made the county seat and a frontier military post for the Virginia forces, and it was to dominate a territory whose limits extended almost indefinitely toward the west, a country practically unknown to the most adventurous pioneer.

It was at Winchester that George Washington had his headquarters while surveying for Baron Fairfax, and it was here that he, scarcely out of his teens, received his first commission as an officer of the provincial militia of Virginia, and as such he was entrusted with the strengthening of Fort Loudon. It was here, too, he suffered his first political failure, as it was also the scene of his first political success, when the citizens of Frederick County elected him to the House of Burgesses. In the list of freemen who voted for him is found the name of John Duke, several of the Lemons, the Shepherds, Van Metres and others whose names

THE DEED

are more or less connected with this subject. All of these persons
were probably personally known to Washington in a social, business, or in the military way.

John Duke, after trading among the valley people for a few
years, selected and bought a small plantation of 164 acres from
his neighbor, Robert Lemon, at Rocky Marsh. It was situated
a few miles above Harper's Ferry and near where Kearneysville
was established, and but a short distance from the village of
Shepherdstown, on the Potomac River. At this date, 1765, the
farm then was located in Frederick County, but by subsequent
divisions of this county it fell into Berkeley and afterward into
Jefferson Co., W. Va. The property was a portion of a much
larger tract which Lord Fairfax had granted to Robert Lemon
in 1762. Lemon's plantation was called "Southwood Springs."
The Duke homestead adjoined it and lay in part along the main
road leading from Shepherdstown to Winchester, and Duke's
neighbors were the Lemons, William Heath and Burkit Treager.

Over this whole region during the Civil War the armies of
Grant and Lee marched and countermarched as they pursued each
other, until this farm, like many another, was devastated and
almost abandoned. At this period it was occupied by John Spangler, but quite recently by a party named McSherry.

THE DEED

Deed of Lease: This Indenture made this first day of April in the year
of our Lord 1765, Between Robert Leman of the County of Frederick,
Colony of Virginia, of the one part and John Duke of said County of
Frederick of the other part Witnesseth: that for and in consideration of
the sum of 5 shillings current money of Virginia to the said Robert
Leman in hand paid by the said John Duke at or before the sealing and
delivery of these presents the receipt hereof he doth hereby acknowledge
he the said Robert Leman hath granted devised and do farm-let and by
these presents doth grant devise and to farm-let unto the said John Duke
a Certain tract or parcel of land lying and being in the said County of
Frederick and bounded as followeth: Beginning at a locust stump near
and on the west side of the said waggon road that leads from Martinsburg to Winchester and extending thence S. 57° E 94 poles near a locust
sapling in a small valley in the line of Robert Leman's Patent Land thence
N. 20° E. 123 poles to a white oak and locust on a hill corner to William
Heath thence along his line N. 77° 30' W 228 poles near a locust and
black oak on a ridge thence N. 13° 30' E. 60 poles to a locust stake at
Burkit Treager's line thence with the same N. 77° 30' W. 38 poles to two
hickories corner to Leman's Patent thence S. 50° 30' W 110 poles to a
stake in the line thence S. 69° 30' 290 poles to the Beginning Containing
164 acres which tract or parcel of land was granted to the said Leman by
Deed bearing date, &c. from under the hand of the Right Honorable
Thomas Lord Fairfax, Lord Proprietor, &c. as may appear, &c, and all
houses building, orchards, ways waters water courses profits commodities
hereditaments and appurtenances whatsoever to the said premises hereby
granted or any part thereof belonging or in any wise appertaining of in
and to the said premises & all Deeds Evidences & Writings touching or in

anywise concerning—To Have and To Hold the said tract or parcel of land and all and singular the premises hereby granted and devised and every part thereof with their and every of their appurtenances unto the said John Duke his executors administrators for and during unto the full end and term of one whole year from hence next ensuing fully to be completed and ended Yielding & Paying therefor the rent of one ear of Indian corn to the said Robert Leman on the last day of the said term if the same shall be lawfully demanded to the intent and purpose that by virtue of these presents and of the Statute for transferring use unto possession he the said John Duke may be in the more and full and actual Possession of the premises & thereby he be the enabled to accept and take a grant and Release of the Reversions and Inheritance thereof to him and his heirs. In Witness Whereof the said Robert Leman hath hereunto set his hand and seal the day and year above written.

(sig) ROBERT LEMEN. [s. s.]

Sealed and delivered in the presence of:
Wᵐ Heath
Jonathan Mercer
This Deed was acknowledged by Robert Leman in Open Court on the 2ᵈ day of April 1765 and ordered to be recorded. And on the same day a Deed of Release is given by Robert Leman to which his wife Isabella Leman joins—for the same land.

John Duke was a witness to a deed for 116 acres from Robert and Isabella Lemon to William Heath, dated 2 Sept., 1762.

MEMORANDA OF DEED TO JOHN DUKE

Deed dated November 1782 Between Thomas Weckerley of Frederick County, Virginia, Gentleman, and Elizabeth his wife, of the one part and John Duke of the County aforesaid, of the other part for the consideration of 5 shillings current money of Virginia conveys a tract of land situate in the County of Frederick, Va. on the northwest side of the Blue-Ridge part of a larger tract taken up by William Rew, containing 44 acres, with a quit-rent of one pepper-corn payable on Lady Day next if the same be lawfully demanded &c. This instrument as recorded 5 Nov. 1782 bears no signature of grantor or witnesses.

THE WILL OF JOHN DUKE

In the name of God Amen, the ninth day of February in the year of our Lord 1789 I John Duke, Senior, of Berkeley County, in the Commonwealth of Virginia being afflicted and weak in body but of perfect mind and Memory thanks be given unto God therefor calling to mind the Mortality of my body and knowing that it is appointed for all once to die do make and ordain this my last Will and Testament that is to say principally and first of all I give and reccomend my soul into the hands of God that gave it and my body I recomend it to the earth to be buried in Christian-like & decent manner at the discretion of my executors nothing doubting but at the general ressurection I shall receive the same again by the mighty power of God. And as touching such worldly estate wherewith it hath pleased God to bless me with in this life I give dispose and devise of the same in the following manner and form first of all I do allow all my just debts and funeral charges to be paid. Imprimis I

THE WILL OF MARGARET DUKE

give leave and bequeath unto my dearly beloved wife Margerat all my land houses stock farming utensils and household furniture freely to be enjoyed and possessed by her during her natural life and at the decease of my wife Margerat the pewter are to be equally divided among my two daughters Margerat and Jane also each of the aforesaid two are to have a bed and furniture belonging to a bed to each of my daughters Margerat and Jane as also the rest of the household furnishing to be equally divided between my two daughters Margerat and Jane at my wife's decease. And at my wife's decease the land the landstock and farming utensils are to be sold and equally divided amongst all my sons and my daughters and after my just debts are all paid any bond or cash that is due to me is likewise to be equally divided between my sons and daughters and if any of my sons and daughters receive anything of my estate before it is sold and divided that it is to be stopped out of their share except the above mentioned articles that I have left to my daughters Margerat and Jane and I likewise do constitute and ordain David Osbourne, Senr. my well beloved friend and my well beloved wife and my son Robert to be my only and sole executors of this my last Will and Testament and do hereby utterly disannul, revoke disavow all and every other former Testament Will Legacy and Execution by me in any way before this time named willed and bequeathed ratifying and confessing this and no other to be my last Will and Testament. In Witness Whereof I have hereunto set my hand and seal the day and year above written.

(Sig) JOHN DUKE [s. s.].

Witnesses: signed sealed, pronounced
and declared by the said John Duke
as his last Will and Testament
in the presence of us the subscribers
Gasper Walper
James Glenn
Thomas Currey
George Young.
Proved by the oaths of James Glenn and George Young in Berkeley Co. Court 16th June, 1790.

THE WILL OF MARGARET DUKE

In the name of God Amen I Margerat Duke relict of John Duke deceased (living in Berkeley County and State of Virginia) being sick and weak of body but of sound memory and considering this transitory life that it is appointed for all mortals once to die. I bequeath my soul to God who gave it hoping for mercie through the merits of Jesus Christ and my body to the earth from whence it came to be decently interred by my dear husband. As for my temporal affairs which yet remains in my hands I will Settle and Dispose of them as follows: Imp^r. I will that my two daughters to wit: Margerat and Jenny may have the part of the crop that was to be mine to be raised by Mathew Duke and Isaac Bean and my part of the wheat now in the ground to be wholly given to my said daughter—except ten bushels of wheat which I owe to my son John which I allow to be paid out of said Crop I also allow my said daughters the sum of four pounds nine shillings and two pence due to me by my son Matthew Duke which I allow him to pay as soon as possible I appoint the same executors mentioned and appointed by my husband in his will to see all things performed according to the purport of these presents. I likewise revoke any former Wills made by me or in my name verbally

or in writing by any person or persons but this to be my last Will and Testament. Given under my hand and seal this 7th day of May 1790
Witnesses: David Osborn
          Isaac Bean
          Jno MacClay

her
Margerat   X   DUKE [s. s.]
mark

Memo before signing: "Allow my son John to receive $10.00 in lieu of above mentioned wheat"

Acknowledged in open Court by David Osborne and John McClay 20 Sept. 1791.

THE HARPER'S FERRY DUKES

The three eldest sons of William Duke, Francis, John and Robert Duke, aged respectively, at the time of their father's death in 1795, eleven, eight and six years, when they were old enough to do so, learned the blacksmith's trade, which had been successfully carried on by their father, and these boys later developed into skilled machinists and gunsmiths.

The United States Arsenal was established at Harper's Ferry in 1799 and here these brothers spent the later years of their life, first as armorers, then as inspectors of arms in Hall's Rifle Works, a branch of the Arsenal, which the government had taken over for the manufacture of Hall's patent rifle. It was situated on Virginius Island, in the Shenandoah.

During this era, however, Francis and John Duke found time to trudge afoot across the Alleghanies to visit their kindred at West Liberty, on the Ohio. While absent they were employed, for a time, in building flatboats for the Ohio River navigation. The boys in their journey over the mountains had, as part of their provision supply, dried wild turkey breasts, and bread; and from time to time gathered along the forest trails such game as the use of their rifles would bring to their larder. Their parents, William and Mary Duke, had taken the same trip in 1791, but they rode horseback over the mountains, along narrow paths and difficult passes, with a third horse laden with flour and provisions.

Francis and John Duke returned to the Ferry in 1811 and found the clouds gathering for the second war with Great Britain.

John Duke enrolled as a private in the Fifth Virginia Militia under Col. Thomas Davenport, and, on the 18 of May, 1813, was transferred to Captain Langdon Osbourne's Company of the same regiment. He was discharged at Craney's Island, Norfolk, 13 Oct., 1813, and re-enlisting 13 April, 1814, as a private in Captain Matt. McCowan's Company, Fourth Virginia Regiment; served in the defense of Baltimore; was promoted to a sergeancy and transferred to Capt. Thomas Cockrill's Company. Discharged at Lambert's Point, Norfolk Harbor, he re-enlisted the

RUINS OF THE UNITED STATES ARSENAL, HARPERS FERRY, W. VA.

third time 26 Aug., 1814, in Col. Bushrod Taylor's Regiment, and was finally discharged at Washington, 7 Dec., 1814.

Francis Duke enlisted as a private in Capt. John H. Elson's Company, First Virginia Regiment, 16 Sept., 1812; discharged 15 April, 1813; re-enlisted as a private in Capt. Wm. Fowler's Company, Fourth Virginia Regiment, 13 Feb., 1815, and was mustered out at Charlestown, Brooke Co., Va., 11 March, 1815.

John Duke married Lucy Keys Talbot, of Maryland, and at the close of the war settled at Smithfield, Jefferson Co., Va., where he conducted a blacksmithing, wheelwrighting and coopering establishment. When Hall's Rifle Works renewed operations at the Ferry and were requiring skilled mechanics, John Duke and his family returned there and he became an employee of the Arsenal. His home was on Bolivar Heights; to this he added a general store, the first in the neighborhood, and became successful. Another enterprise in which he was interested was in the furnishing of arms and equipment for the Texan Revolutionists, for which his knowledge and experience qualified him. These were sent over the mountains, by pack-horse, to the Ohio, and thence flatboated, by way of the Mississippi, to New Orleans, which was the market where the Texans thronged—the soldier and the settler—in those days of excitement. John Duke was a member of Logan Lodge, F. & A. M., at Harper's Ferry, in his later years.

Francis Duke was associated with his brother John in the business at Smithfield, and when John Duke removed to Harper's Ferry, Francis left for Pennsylvania where he found employment with a gunsmith at Lancaster. While here he met Elizabeth Kendrick to whom he was afterward married at Shepherdstown, Va. From Lancaster, Francis Duke went to Philadelphia and entered the government service as a gunsmith, and was later transferred to Harper's Ferry to fill a similar position in the arsenal at that place, and where, later, he became a rifle inspector. After his marriage, in 1819, he made his residence in one of the government cottages on Virginius Island. The site of his home is now obliterated by Lake Quigley, a body of impounded water now used as the log boom of a paper mill which stands at the head of the island.

Francis Duke met a sad and untimely fate by drowning. It occurred in 1836 and happened while he was residing on the island. He had been calling on some friends in the village, and was returning home about nine o'clock in the evening. Passing along the path which ran beside the Shenandoah from Union Street to the entrance of the island, he started to cross the small bridge which spanned the narrow, but deep and rapid, watercourse flowing between the main street and the island. Afflicted by which is called "night blindness" he made a mis-step and plunged into the swift race-way, which, at this point, rushes be-

tween high-walled banks in its passage to the Shenandoah. As
he fell he gave a cry, the only one he uttered, as it is supposed
that his head struck against the stone wall or the rocks which
filled the bed of the stream. Unconscious and helpless he was
carried fast toward the river. His cry was heard by someone
near and the alarm was given, and an attempt was made to
rescue him, but the current bore him so swiftly along on its ever-
increasing width of water, with the darkness opposing—help
failed, and he was drowned within reach of his friends. At the
lower end of the island to which the alarm had spread and where
the waters emptied into the river, a boat was launched and by the
time the body reached that point the boatmen met it in midstream,
else, in a few minutes more, it would have disappeared in the
rapids of the Shenandoah. A few days later Francis Duke was
interred in the old Harper Cemetery. Business was suspended
in the town while the people paid their last respects to the memory
of a popular and respected citizen, an exemplary father and
husband.

After this event, the widow and her children went to reside
at "Willow Springs" with the widow of Robert Duke, Francis
Duke's younger brother, but later on they returned to her father's
home in Lancaster.

Robert Duke, the youngest of the brothers, was also an em-
ploy of the government at the arsenal, at Harper's Ferry, and
rose to be Chief Rifle Inspector, a position he held at the time
of his death, in 1834. Robert was particularly thrifty in his
habits and by his industry managed to buy a fine farm on the
banks of the Potomac River, about three miles above Harper's
Ferry. "Willow Springs" contained 311 acres, and formerly
belonged to Joseph McMurran from whom it came, by inheritance, to his two sons, William and Samuel and from whom it
was purchased by Robert Duke, in 1830. The plantation contained great quantities of limestone, iron ore and stone which, at
this time, is being extensively quarried; these operations have
been the undoing of the once beautiful farm; it is no longer culti-
vated, as of old, but has been given over to the quarrymen and
railroads, and the latter have literally gridironed it. Here Robert
Duke lived, also his children and grandchildren, until quite recently when "Willow Springs" passed into the ownership of
strangers.

THE DESCENDANTS OF JOHN DUKE

I. ELIZABETH, or "BETTY" DUKE as she is named in the record
written by her father, was born 14 July, 1747, and "dide 1773,"
as stated in the quaint marginal note opposite her name. It is

said that "she married a Blue." No further light is shed upon her history. The Blues, however, were a prominent family and mostly numerous in Hampshire County, around Romney and Springfield, in the vicinity of which their German ancestor settled about 1730.

II. WILLIAM DUKE was born 17 March, 1749, and died in Berkeley County, Virginia, 13 Sept., 1794, in his forty-fifth year. He was the eldest son, and was probably born in Ireland. About 1777 he married Mary Ann, dau. of Nicholas and Christina Lemon, of Harper's Ferry. Her mother was a descendant of Robert Lemon, a soldier and personal friend of Oliver Cromwell, Lord Protector of England, and was born 7 Jan., 1756. She died *circa* 1796, and was buried at "Southwood Springs," near Kearneysville, in Berkeley County. Her mother married, 2d, Rev. Henry Eaty, a Presbyterian minister, by whom she had two daughters and a son: Sebastian Eaty, a well-known justice of the peace in Clark Co., Va., between 1819 and 1840.

In the old grveyard at "Southwood Springs" several of the Lemon family are buried, and here two were interred, John Duke, Jr., his wife Margaret, and some of their children. It is a regretable circumstance that the burial place of these ancestors was swept over by the fiery flame of the Rebellion and its desolating torch, with other changes since that time, has caused the obliteration of their graves. The Duke tombstones were long ago past finding, and in this generation there is only the recollection of a few fragments of a lettered sandstone from one of the graves found in a neighbor's farm-yard wall, and these, too, have now disappeared. Thus memory alone recalls the spot where repose the ashes of our Virginia forefathers and reminds us of the passing of all material things.

In the settlement of the estate of John Duke the homestead was conveyed to Captain James Kearney, April 1, 1792, by Robert Duke, the executor, and in October of the same year, Captain Kearney transferred the title to William Duke. William Duke and Mary, his wife, by deed dated 15 Oct., 1793, for the consideration of £209, Virginia currency, reconveyed to Captain Kearney a portion of the homestead containing 47 acres. This instrument was witnessed by Elisha Boyd, John Riddle and James Kennedy, and recorded at Martinsburg, in Deed Book, No. 11, p. 365.

William Duke died intestate 13 Sept., 1794, and the inventory and appraisal of his personal estate was filed 21 Sept., 1795. The value of the personal property amounted to £156. 11. 1½.; the appraisers were David Moore, David Osbourne and Thomas Lafferty.

INVENTORY AND APPRAISAL

1 old Bay mare	3. 0.0.	1 Flax breake	0. 2.0.
1 Bay Mare	9. 0.0.	1 New wagon	6. 0.0.
1 old Brown Cow	2.10.0.	Dresser Utensils	0.12.0.
1 Brindle yr^{ls}. Calf	1.10.0.	2 Tea Kettles, 1 coffee	
8 Hogs	5. 0.0.	can and pepper-mill	1.13.0.
2 Milch Cows.	8. 0.0.	2 Candle-sticks & snuffers	0. 5.0.
1 set Smith's tools	13.11.3.	2 Flat Irons, salt box &	
364 lbs. Iron partly worked	6.14.4.	knife box	0. 5.6.
3 gridles made and		1 Chair, Table, Butter Crock	0. 6.0.
1 set Plow irons	2.10.9.	2 Frypans, Dutch oven ⎫	
32 lbs steel 9c. per lb.	1. 4.0.	8 griddle pans and skillet ⎬	1. 4.0.
395 lbs Iron @ 3½ c. pr. lb.	5. 0.7½	2 Lamps and stands ⎫	
1 Handsaw, plain & 3 gim-		8 Blue Chairs ⎬	1. 7.0.
lets	0. 6.4.	2 Arm chairs, 12 Spoons ⎫	
pr. steelyards	0. 9.0.	and one tumbler & 1 — ⎬	0.12.0.
1 young Bay mare	12. 0.0.	1 Pewter Teapot & Tea	
1 Grey horse colt	9. 0.0.	ware	0. 9.0.
3 Augurs, 4 chisels, 3 draw-		1 Bundle Table & 12 chests	2.17.0.
Knives, a Broad Axe & 1		2 Axes, Shovel and Spade	1. 0.0.
post axe	1. 5.0.	1 Desk and 1 set Drawers	8. 0.0.
4 hoes, new pr. bellows	6.12.0.	1 smooth bore gun	1.10.0.
Some old Iron	0.10.0.	1 Man's saddle	0.15.0.
1 Dutch oven, 1 cutting		Bed & bedding	3.10.0.
box.	0.18.0.	1 Man's saddle bed and ⎫	
Barrel, Bucket &c.	0. 2.6.	bedding, 2 bolsters ⎬	7.10.0.
6 cags, 1 shoeing horse	0. 6.6.	1 case and some bottles ⎫	
1 Large Iron Kettle	0.15.0.	1 big wheel ⎬	0. 9.0.
some coal & coal rakes	1.16.0.	2 Spinning Wheels @ 6 S.	0.12.0.
1 Coffee Mill, 1 gudgeon	0. 7.0.	Hand Irons	1.10.0.
Shovels, Tongs & pot		1 Dough Trough & Tray ⎫	
Trammels	1. 3.0.	1 old check reel ⎬	0. 7.0.
2 pots	0.12.0.	3 Table Cloths @ 15 ⎫	
1 half bushel, pickling tub	0. 5.0.	2 bed quilts 18 ⎬	1.15.0.
Bed & bedding, old Lumber	2. 8.9.	6 sheets, 2 coverlids	3.16.0.
B. L. Bags, 7 books, powder		1 Little wagon for children	1. 0.0.
Horn, and cotton cards	1.11.0.	some flax	1. 0.0.
1 blanket, 4 bread baskets	0.11.4.	Total	156.11.1½
1 Washing tub	0. 2.6.		

III. FRANCIS DUKE, second son of John and Margaret Duke, born in Ireland(?) 11 Feb., 1751, was killed by the Indians at the seige of Fort Henry (Wheeling), Ohio Co., Va., in an heroic attempt to relieve the besieged post, 1 Sept., 1777. He married, *circa* 1773, Sarah, the third daughter of Colonel David Shepherd and his wife Rachael Teague. Sarah's father, who was a son of Thomas Shepherd, the founder of Shepherdstown, Virginia, was lieutenant of Ohio County, Western Virginia, and commandant of Fort Henry. After the death of Francis Duke, his widow married, 2d, Levi Springer, of Uniontown, Fayette Co., Pa., where she died about 1835 or 1840, after having issue: two sons by her first husband, and several children to her second husband.

"September the first day, 1777, ffrancis Duke was k—led [killed] by the Sagues [savages]."

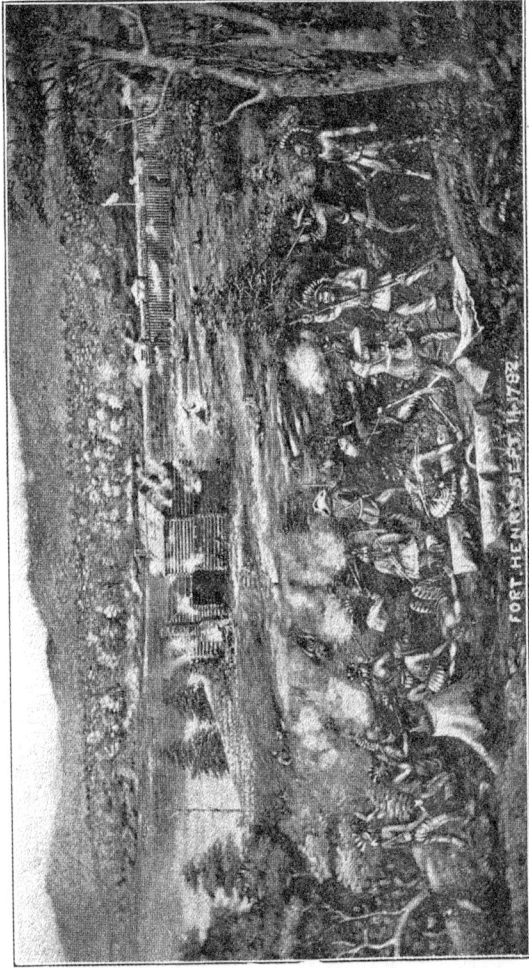

SIEGE OF FORT HENRY (WHEELING, WEST VIRGINIA)

THE DESCENDANTS OF JOHN DUKE

Back of this brief and simple record which John Duke noted in his little book chronicling the death of his son, is a long story of Indian persecution, perfidy and barbarity, that for years harrassed the border settlers, and had its climax in the first siege Wheeling. The incidents leading up to that historic, but tragic event, forms a narrative peculiarly interesting to the descendants and kinsmen of that brave and fearless youth. His martyrdom has been the theme of many writers of border history and may be briefly related in these pages.

On the eve of the War of the Revolution, the various Indian tribes along the western border, were giving endless trouble to the whites, and committing savage atrocities, with appalling frequency, among the settlers in the Ohio Valley. So determined were they to exterminate the people who were encroaching upon their territory to which they had been forced by the advancing settlement and development in the valley of Virginia, that Lord Dunmore, then governor of the province, declared upon them a war of subjugation, and in 1774 took the field and led one of the divisions of volunteer militia against them. With General Andrew Lewis in command of a similar body of troops, both divisions marched upon the Indians. The fierce and disastrous battle of Point Pleasant, fought and won by the provincials, 10 Oct., 1774, at the junction of the Ohio and Kanawha Rivers, was a decided blow, and resulted in the overthrow of the Indians and the flight of the allied tribes, known as the Northern Confederacy, which was under the leadership of "Cornstalk" the great sachem of the Shawnese. These were the "red terrors" of the border.

In the early summer, just before the expeditions set out, Dunmore ordered the erection of Fort Fincastle, being then in Fincastle Co., Va., as an additional post for the protection of the white settlers west of Fort Dunmore (afterward Fort Pitt, now Pittsburg, Pa.). It was built under the direction of Major William Crawford and Angus MacDonald, and was situated on a high bluff, overlooking the Ohio River, at the mouth of Wheeling Creek. The fort was substantially constructed of heavy squared timbers, eight feet high and pointed at the top, and furnished with sentry boxes at the angles; it was parallelogram in form, and covered an area of about three fourths of an acre. The interior of the post contained officers' quarters, barracks, storehouse, well and cabins for families seeking its protection. In strength and importance it ranked next to Fort Pitt. A steep hill rises inland and between it and the river lay a plain from which the forest had been cleared away, so that the fort stood in the open, with a few cabins occupied by the settlers near it.

The Revolution came swiftly on and broke over the colonies in the following year, and with it came an alliance between the English and the Indians, who were previously allies of the French in seeking control of the western waterways. The Indians, aided by the fratricidal English, now lost no time in renewing the reign of terror on the border and in laying waste the flourishing settlements, and to an extent far more cruel and sanguinary than ever before. The compact against the colonists involved not only the worst element of the English, but also the Tory, who proved no less subtle, and equally as dangerous and treacherous as his copper-skinned ally. This then, was the character of the combination arrayed against the patriots in the west.

The fever of freedom, coupled with the need of self-preservation, penetrated to the dwellers in the wilderness with amazing rapidity. Organizations, under experimental, or military government, were quickly formed among the harried settlers along the border. David Shepherd who had been a colonial officer under Lord Dunmore's rule, and had commanded one of the expeditions against the Indians, and had also been second in command at Fort Pitt, at this time, was among the first to throw off the English thralldom, directing all his energies and the benefit of his civil and military experience toward the accomplishment of the cause of liberty. His friend and associate, Dorsey Pentecost, of the Council of West Augusta, recorded the appointment of Col. David Shepherd, on the 4 Sept., 1776, as Commissary of the Virginia troops on the Ohio, then a part of Virginia's territory, but now included in the bounds of Pennsylvania. The frontiers, extending along the Ohio for a hundred miles, was under Shepherd's official supervision.

Colonel David Shepherd was the eldest son of Thomas Shepherd and his wife Elizabeth Van Meter. He married Rachael Teague about 1756, and with the Zanes, Wetzels and other pioneers from the Potomac Valley, emigrated to the western country in 1773, or earlier. On being appointed Commissary of Ohio County, he selected as his deputy, his son-in-law, Francis Duke, the husband of the Colonel's daughter Sarah. Francis Duke was then living on the Ohio; he was about twenty-nine years of age, a strong, brave and fearless frontiersman, and of such who were foremost in the winning of the west.

About 1774, Col. David Shepherd had bought out a tomahawk right from Silas Zane, who had pre-empted a claim at the forks of Wheeling Creek, six miles above its confluence with the Ohio. Here, in the same year, he erected a stockade to which he gave the name of Shepherd's Fort, and brought there his family and several mechanics from among his old neighbors at Shepherdstown. At Beech Bottom, near the mouth of Short Creek, twelve miles above Fort Henry, and about three miles below Wellsburg, was another blockhouse where Commissary Francis Duke was stationed in 1777. The region around it was settled by Scotch-Irish gathered there from York, Pa., and from the Valley of Virginia.

For months before the attack on Wheeling, the ravages on the border continued unabated; whole families were destroyed, and others suffered the loss of one or more of their members. The inhabitants of the entire country bordering on the Ohio River were alarmed, and measures were taken for their safety.

On the 13 of March, 1777, Governor Patrick Henry, of Virginia, appointed Col. David Shepherd, County Lieutenant, and named Fort Henry (that had formerly been called Fort Fincastle, and renamed in honor of Governor Henry) as his headquarters. General Edward Hand, of Pennsylvania, held a like command at Fort Pitt, in the District of West Augusta. In the summer of 1777 the hostiles quietly prepared for an invasion of the valley settlements, and among other depredations planned was an attack to be made on Fort Henry, then a prosperous village, of perhaps thirty cabins, nestling around the fort. Companies of militia were hurried into the region from Virginia, Maryland and Pennsylvania, and were posted at the various blockhouses; scouting parties ranged the trails and along every stream and forest path, and watched and waited to intercept any runner or other means of communication. General Hand, who had received a hint of the danger, from some friendly native, of the proposed attack on Fort Henry, quietly warned Colonel Shepherd to be on his guard. He was ordered to leave his own fort, with his family, and rendezvous all the forces between the Ohio and the Monongahela, at Fort Henry, and strengthen its condition. The men from the settlements were organized and drilled for its defence; the women and children were gathered into the fort and all suitable and proper preparations were made to resist an attack. By Aug. 22, 1777, the date of a letter written by Col. David Shepherd to General Hand, the latter is advised that "the fort is Indian proof." As the foe did not come, however, the idea got abroad, and gained confidence, that it was a false alarm, so that by the end of August the fears of the people were lulled and they had started off to their various homes to finish up their harvesting, and do such other labor as they had been interrupted in by the scare. Several of the militia companies had been dismissed, and were now well on their way back to their various mustering places, and everywhere vigilance was relaxed; all that were left to keep watch and ward at the point of disturbance were two Virginia companies under command of Captains Mason and Ogle, who perfunctorily kept their vigils in the vicinity, one company scouting between Fort Henry and Beech Bottom, and the other watching the country toward Grave Creek. By this time, Captain Boggs and Reazin, with their companies, had reached the neighborhood of Catfish Camp (now Washington, Pa.).

Early on the morning of the first of September, 1777, the garrison at Fort Henry was surprised by a body of between three and four hundred Indians, who had encompassed it on all sides, and opened the attack with savage yells and shot. Before this occurred, however, the Indians had come upon the scouting parties of Mason and Ogle, before their presence in the locality had been suspected, and put them to flight, after the wounding of several of the party, including Captain Ogle. In the fort were only a few men—perhaps a dozen—and a number of women and children, who had remained for a few days longer after the most of the men had gone. The attack began about seven o'clock in the morning, continued all day and into the night, when the Indians, unsuccessful in capturing Fort Henry, withdrew under cover of the darkness.

Many historians of border warfare have written of this siege, and while their accounts differ in detail, they all agree that it was one of the most desperate in the annals of the frontier. Many incidents of bravery and many stories of wonderful escapes have illumined their narratives, but among them all there is none more pathetic, or heroic, than the manner of Francis Duke's death, who, according to all authorities on the subject, endeavored alone to aid in the defense of Fort Henry.

"When intelligence of the investiture of Wheeling, by the savages, reached Shepherd's Fort, a party was immediately detached from it, to try and gain admission into the beseiged fortress and aid in its defense. Upon coming into view, it was found that the attempt would be useless and unavailing, and the detachment consequently prepared to return. Francis Duke (son in law to Col. Shepherd), was unwilling to turn his back on a people straitened as he knew the beseiged must be, and declared his intention of endeavoring to reach the fort, that he might contribute to its defense. It was useless to dissuade him from the attempt,—he knew its dangers, but he also knew their weakness, and putting spurs to his horse, rode briskly forward, calling aloud, ' open the gate! open the gate'!! He was seen from the fort, and the gate was loosened for his admission—but he did not live to reach it,—pierced by bullets of the savages, he fell, to the regret of all. Such noble daring deserved a better fate. . . . Of the garrison none were killed and only two wounded—the heroic Francis Duke was the only white man who fell during the seige " (Wither's Chronicles of the Border, p. 359).

" Just before the withdrawal of the enemy, Francis Duke, son in law of Colonel Shepherd, rode up to the fort and had almost gained the gate, when an Indian shot him. His death was greatly regretted, as he was a brave and generous man, and of much service on the frontier. He had been stationed at Beech-Bottom blockhouse, as assistant commissary and getting information of the attack, mounted his horse and rode with all speed to the scene of the operation, Here alas! to meet untimely death. His remains with those of his brother-in-law William Shepherd, were interred near where the Northwestern Bank stands [at Wheeling, W. Va.]. In consequence of the great loss at Wheeling in September 1777, and the death of Colonel Shepherd's son and son-in-law Francis Duke, it was determined in the Fall of that year to abandon the place and send the families to Redstone [Brownsville, Pa.]. The fort was accordingly evacuated September, 21, 1777, and soon after the Indians burned it to the ground " (De Haas' History of Western Virginia).

THE DESCENDANTS OF JOHN DUKE

Mrs. Lydia Crugar, widow of Moses Shepherd, the youngest, and surviving son of Colonel Shepherd, and daughter of Captain Boggs, gives the following account of the incidents preceding the siege and of the death of Francis Duke, as she related them to Lyman C. Draper the eminent historian.

"It was near the first of September, 1777, in the morning early. D^r. Daniel MacMahon desired to move away and sent out one Boyd with two negroes up the hill to find the horses to remove on; Boyd was shot and scalped by Indians in ambush and the negroes escaped to the fort. This was the first intelligence of the approach of the Indians. Then Captains Ogle and Mason, each having a company of militia there (Mason was from the waters of Ten-Mile near Washington, Pa.), with a party, about ¾ of a mile away [found] the Indians in ambush, in [the] bushes on the creek bottom and while the men were hunting for the trail, the Indians arose from the covert around them and fired upon the whites—shot them down. Mason received a flesh wound in the hip and hid himself in a fallen tree top full of green leaves. Indians hunted all around him; he seeing them, in the night escaped to some neighboring fort. Capt. Ogle escaped to a cornfield with a wounded man and concealed themselves in the high horse-weeds, and while there a wounded Indian, blood running down and crying, and another Indian with him both sitting on the fence within a [few feet] of Ogle, and Ogle expecting every moment to be discovered. He lay with his gun cocked, intending, if discovered, to sell his life as dearly as possible. These Indians remained on the fence and finally went away. In the night Ogle took the wounded man with him into the fort. Three of the men: William Shepherd, eldest son of Col. David Shepherd; Hugh McCullogh [whose sister Rebecca married W^m. Shepherd] and Thomas Glenn, started from the defeated spot for the fort, and young Shepherd as he neared the fort, his foot caught in a grape vine and threw him, and before he could recover the Indians tomahawked and scalped him. Glenn was chased above the fort a little distance up the river, was overtaken and killed, McCullogh reached the fort. John Caldwell escaped to Shepherd's fort, 6 miles above Wheeling, where at the forks of Wheeling the neighborhood forted though Colonel Shepherd was himself at Wheeling; others escaped.

"Town lots had been sold and several had built cabins and lived in them—outside of Fort Henry, and at this alarm, unexpected, the people flew to the fort leaving all their property in their cabins, all of which was plundered and some of the cabins were burned, and others were seized and occupied by the Indians from which to fight.

"Francis Duke, Deputy Commissary, came from Beech Bottom station above, about noon, . . . and made a dash for the fort, so near that the Indians did not go for his scalp until after nightfall when they dragged his body into one of the cabins and scalped and stripped him. The Indian shot down large number of cattle, hogs, sheep, and geese, and took away a good many horses, soon after dark they decamped. Thought to have been about 300 Indians."

By the time the companies of Captains Boggs and Reazin Virgin had arrived from Catfish Camp, which was during the following morning, the Indians had all disappeared. These reinforcements could only help bury the dead and haul the swollen cattle into the river.

After the siege Colonel Shepherd sent his family to Catfish Camp, while he returned to his own settlement to restore, as speedily as possible, something like order out of the terrible ruin spread on every hand. In writing to General Hand at what was then Fort Pitt, in a letter dated 3 September, Colonel Shepherd stoically ignores his own bereavement and personal losses, but gives an account of the affair; but in writing again to General Hand on 15 September he gives the first definite statement of the casualties at Fort Henry, he says that "one Lieutenant and fourteen men killed, one Captain and four men wounded." Francis Duke was likely the lieutenant referred to as his son William was a militiaman in Capt. Mason's Company.

The last entry Francis Duke made in his commissary book is dated at Beech Bottom, August 30, 1777. He left surviving him a widow Sarah, son John, about three years of age, and a son Francis who was a posthumous child born some months after the siege of Fort Henry. His widow afterward married Levi Springer, of Uniontown, Pa.

William Shepherd left surviving him his widow Rebecca; his only child, Elizabeth, was born shortly after its father's death.

Administration on the estate of Francis Duke, deceased, was granted to Col. David Shepherd, 3 Nov., 1778, he having complied with the law, and Jacob Newland, Charles Hedges and John Mitchell were appointed by the court, on that date, to appraise the estate. At a later date (not recorded) they made the following return to the court:

A List of Goods belonging to Francis Duke, dec⁴.

2 Black cows	£40. 0.0	1 Mattock	£1.10.0.
1 Black heifer	7. 0.0.	1 Broad Axe	1.16.0.
1 Bull	7. 0.0.	Old Iron	0.10.0.
1 yearling heifer	7.10.0.	Old Bell	0. 6.0.
1 ditto	4.10.0.	1 Drawing Knife	0.12.0.
1 Pot. wt. 17 lbs.	4.10.0.	2 pr Hames	0.10.0.
2 pr. Irons	6. 0.0.	2 Clevises	1.10.0.
1 old axe	0.10.0.	1 pr. plow irons	6. 0.0.
1 Ten gal. Kittle	10.0.0.	1 adze	1.10.0.
		Total	£102.0.0.

IV. JOHN DUKE, JR., third son of John and Margaret Duke who came from Ireland with his parents, and is supposed to have been born there, was, according to the record in his father's memorandum book, born 20 Aug., 1753, and in the same little book there is found this quaint reference to his death: "Oct. [November] 4th, 1791, John Duke was kled [killed] by the Ingins [Indians] about Sun-Rising in the battle of Ganeral Sinkelear [General St. Clair]." His will, recorded at Martinsburg, seems to be the only other documentary evidence available concerning this son; as no wife is mentioned in the will it is supposed she predeceased her husband.

THE DESCENDANTS OF JOHN DUKE

WILL OF JOHN DUKE, JR.

Second May, 1791, I. John Duke of Berkeley Co., State of Virginia.
. . . I give and bequeath to my well beloved sons: James, William and
John,—my part lately left me by my father of his estate together with all
other debts dues and demands due to me by others to be equally divided
among them share and share alike when they arrive at the age of twenty
one years each. But if any one of them should die before he arrive to
age then his share shall be divided equally amongst the surviving two,
but if any two of them shall die before they arrive at age then the surviving one shall inherit the whole, but provided any one of them shall
"mary" before he arrives at age then he or they shall receive their
full "shear" at or upon their marriage day. Appointing brother William
Duke sole executor.

Witnesses: Thomas Curry, William Duke and George Lafferty.

This will was probated at Martinsburg, Va., 17 January, 1792.
The following account of the estate of John Duke was presented to court by William Duke, his executor:

To Balance due by William Richardson		£11.12. 9.
" James Dukes account		2.11. 3.
" Smith Work		1.19. 6.
" Barbery Clu's account		2. 5. 1.
" John Kearsley's Note		0.15. 0.
" Robert McKnight's account		0. 5. 2.
" John McClay for Schooling		1.18. 8.
" John Norris' note with interest		2. 5. 6.
" Conelius Wyncoop's note & interest 3.3.10. va. currency		3.19. 9.
" Samuel Swearingen's Note		1.19. 0.
" John Daniel's account		0. 9. 2.
" Casper Walpole's account		3.15. 0.
" Fees paid Reed and White, lawyers (£20.13.8)		2. 1. 3.
By Cash for a Judgement against Watson	31.11. 0.	
" Cash H. Bedinger (12 dollars 49 cents)	4.13. 8.	
" Cash T. Lafferty	0. 9. 9.	
" Cash Dennis Stephens	0. 1. 6.	
To Balance due Estate John Duke		0.18.10.
	£36.15.11.	£36.15.11.
To T. Brown account and Receipt	1.12.4.	
" my expenses attending Court	1.10.0.= 3. 2. 4.	
By Estate Balance	0.18.10.	
Due Wm. Duke (Pa. currency)	2. 3. 6.	
" " " (Va. currency)	1.14. 9¾.	

Audited, 15 July 1793 { Cato Moore
{ Joseph Swearingen

Returned to Court and ordered recorded.

15 Oct. 1793.   (sig) JNOS HUNTER C. B. C.

In all the annals of savage warfare, there is no event more
appalling than the story of General St. Clair's defeat; its bar-
barous butchery and the effect of it on the American people in
the infancy of the Republic, and the consequent loss of prestige
of one of its great generals, will ever be remembered to the
Nation's regret.

313

The army of the Northwest was led by one of the most successful Generals of the Revolution, with some of the best and most tried veterans of that campaign under his command, which consisted of 2,700 men and included among its officers: General Richard Butler and Col. Wm Darke: The scene of battle was on the Pickway fork of the Maumee, a branch of the Wabash River, in what is now Mercer Co., Ohio. The attack occurred 30 miles from Fort Jefferson, and was made by a body of 2,000 Indians from ambush, and lasted three hours.

Col. William Darke had command of a body of militiamen from Berkeley and Hampshire Counties, Virginia, and these formed the second line of defense. In that slaughter these battalions made the two terrific charges against the Indians which made Darke's name memorable. The confusion of the army was so great, that St. Clair was unable to hold the ground won by Darke's heroic advance at the head of the Virginians.

The main body of the army had camped where Fort Recovery was afterward erected by General Wayne. The Miami villiages were supposed to be about twelve miles distant. At this place,—the headwaters of the Wabash River,—the army encamped. The front was covered by a creek on the other side of the river, while a creek protected the flank of the second line. There was no suspicion of danger as the army lay down to get some rest. Some few hours before daybreak; and under the expectation of attack, or, at least, to have the men in a state of readiness, —the general had the reveille beaten, and the troopes paraded under arms, thus they stood watchful till daybreak, when they were dismissed to their tents to get some further rest; but the men had scarcely lain down when a rifle, fired by some of the men in front, was followed by an irregular volley in the same direction. The drums beat; the officers formed the men; the militia came pouring in from the front; and in a few minutes, all was stir and confusion. The militia coming in pursued by swarms of Indians, broke over the ranks of the regulars, and bore down all before them. The Indians themselves, penetrated beyond the front ranks and tomahawked some of the wounded officers who had been carried back to have their wounds dressed. In no long time the whole body of the army was encompassed by a livid stream of fire on all sides 'round. St. Clair was suffering from a fever and was unable to mount a horse, but part of the time was carried from place to place on a litter. . . . ; he directed the men to carry him to a place where the firing was the heaviest and where the men were falling on all sides. Here the brave Col. Darke, an officer of Revolutionary distinction, was trying his utmost to allay the consternation of the men, and hold the lines steady.

When St. Clair came up he directed the Colonel and his men to make a sudden and rapid charge with the bayonet; the charge was made with some effect, for swarms of the red backed creatures rose up before the lines of infantry, out of the high grass, and fled before them, but the soldiers could not overtake them, they recovered their courage and soon after, from behind every kind of shelter,—poured such a fire upon the soldiers that they in turn were driven back. A second time was the charge with the bayonet made and followed with same result. When the artillery was brought up the horses and men were destroyed before they could do any service. . . . the men at last gave way and retreated in a panic. The chief of the hostiles in this battle, was " Mishikenakwa," or, " Little Turtle," a son of a Miami chief by a Mohickan woman. He was the chief leader of all the warriors in that part of the country. He died in 1812, and his grave is at Fort Wayne (see History of Westmoreland Co., Pa., p. 219).

Another writer states that

"Every commissioned officer of the Second Regiment, except three,—was killed or wounded. Every artillery officer had been killed—except Captain Ford. 630 men were lost, 80 of whom were from Berkeley Co., Va., and included Col. Darkes's own son Joseph,—a lieutenant, and John Duke. 240 men were wounded, including Colonel Darke" (see Lewis' Hist. of West Virginia; and St. Clair Papers).

Major Denny, aid to General St. Clair, states in his journal, that

"The troops paraded this morning at the usual time and had been dismissed from the lines but a few minutes, *the sun not yet up,* when the woods in front rang with the yells and fire of the savages."

For report of his defeat, including list of officers killed and wounded see St. Clair's Report to Congress, Nov. 9, 1791, in American State Papers, Art. Indian Affairs, Vol. I., pp. 137–138.

Colonel William Darke, to whom repeated reference has been made in these pages, was born in 1736, in Pennsylvania, probably in Falls Township, Pa., near the Delaware River, below Trenton N. J., where the family of that name settled soon after their emigration to America. He came to Virginia with his parents, John and Jane (Rush) Darke, about 1742. They settled in the vicinity of Harper's Ferry. Mary Darke, a sister of Wm. Darke, married Philip Engle, Sr., a pioneer from Lancaster Co., Pa., who had located where Engle station (on the B. & O. R. R.) now stands; through this union their descendants intermarried with the Dukes and other families in the locality. Wm. Darke, as a young man, served in the earlier Indian wars of the border, and the experience gained for him the meritorious distinction he received in service in the War of the Revolution, for he was frequently promoted. After the Indian war in the northwest, in St. Clair's Campaign, he was made a brigadier general for his daring and bravery. His home was midway between Shenandoah Junction and Duffields—two stations on the B. & O. R. R., at a place now called Darkesville—Jefferson Co., W. Va., where he died in 1801. Duffields was formerly known as Elk Branch. A Presbyterian Church was very early established at this place, and in its beginning was used by itinerating clergymen, and it was here that the Darkes, the Dukes, the Clymers and others of that faith, in the neighborhood, worshipped.

V. Robert Duke, born 4 May, 1755, seems to have disappeared entirely from view after April, 1792, at which time, as surviving executor of the wills of his father and mother, he transferred the homestead to James Kearney. Nothing has been found by which his line of posterity—if he left any—can be traced; although, in the course of the inquiry incident to this work, it has developed a family of Dukes who claim a Robert Duke as their ancestor, who lived, about the time of our Robert's period, in Cumberland Co., Pa. *This* Robert Duke, it is said, married a German woman and their descendants are now living in the vicinity of Carlisle, Shippensburg and Chambersburg. A peculiar resemblance in physiognomy, stature and temperament of the descendants of this man seems to argue strongly for the presumption of close relationship; and these hereditary characteristics are so marked that the writer feels justified in adopting this family in kinship relation and will include their line, in its place, upon these pages.

VI. MARY DUKE, born in America, 30 June, 1757, died in childhood.

VII. MATTHEW DUKE, born 5 July, 1758. Very little information regarding him is to be had. At the date of his mother's will, Matthew was farming near the Duke homestead, in Berkeley Co. The family tradition is that he never married, and that he served in the War of the Revolution as a substitute for Daniel Hendricks, the husband of his niece Margaret. He was buried in the family plot on Hendrick's farm, near Uvilla, about 1820.

VIII. MARGARET DUKE, born 13 May, 1760, is another of whom nothing, at present, is known. She was living in 1792 and was mentioned in her mother's will.

IX. MARY DUKE, born 12 Nov., 1762, said to have married some time before the death of her parents, a person by the name of Foutz and to have emigrated to the neighborhood of West Liberty, in Ohio Co., Va. West Liberty was known as Black's Cabin as early as 1777. It was situated at the head of Short Creek, about six miles back from the Ohio River, and was formerly the seat of government of Ohio County. When some of her nephews visited her, about 1830, they found Aunt Polly Fouts a widow, with a son George, living with her at the time.

X. JAMES DUKE, youngest son of John and Margaret Duke, born 17 June, 1765. Thus far nothing has been learned concerning this member of the family.

XI. JANE DUKE, youngest daughter of John and Margaret Duke, born 20 March, 1767. She married Captain James Glenn, of Berkeley Co., Va. A correspondent writes me that " Captain Glenn, as a young soldier, met Jane Duke on her return from Ireland. She was a tall, beautiful blonde, and intelligent. Her three children died young, and she educated her servants." Captain Glenn, after the death of Jane, married again, but at his death he was buried beside his first wife in the Presbyterian churchyard at Shepherdstown, W. Va.

Captain Glenn was one of the first officers to receive a commission in the regular army of the United States.

"Born about 1764, in Berkeley Co., Va., on the sunny slopes of the Blue Ridge, and dowered with a fine physique, and military aspirations inherited from a sturdy ancestry which shares the blood of Robert Bruce and the great scotch clans of Campbell—young Glenn seemed foreordained for a soldier's career. At the age of 14 he ran away from home

DESCENDANTS OF WILLIAM DUKE

to join the army under General Nathaniel Greene. At this time (1779–80), Greene's army, barefooted, half clad, and famished—made a forced march across North Carolina and reached the Dan with only a remnant of his shattered army in which James Glenn served as a sharp-shooter. A year later the conquering armies of Greene and Washington met at York-town, and Glenn shared the glories of Oct. 19, 1781, in the surrender of Cornwallis.

"Upon the reorganization of the Army of the United States, Glenn received his commission as Lieutenant. In 1793, Henry Knox, Secretary of War, assigned him to special service at Pittsburg, in recognition of distinguished merit. The commission hangs upon the walls of his grand-daughter's (Mrs. Lillian Glenn Barnes) home at Snow-Hill, Maryland."

James Glenn was the youngest officer sent by General Arthur St. Clair, as bearer of despatches, to General Washington at Philadelphia, where Congress was then in session. When St. Clair's army retreated from Fort Washington, Captain Darke was killed at the first fire—Glenn took command in his place. All of his own men were killed but eight; of these, only three—O'Neal, Morgan and Glenn—lived to reach Shepherdstown. Glenn's gallantry in saving the life of his friend Raleigh Morgan at this time was an act of extraordinary heroism. He bore Morgan's body from the field; making his bugler dismount he placed the wounded man on his horse and conducted him to a place of safety under fire of three Indians, who followed them and continued to fire and hide behind trees until weary of the pursuit. For his valor and devoted service, General Washington made him adjutant of his regiment. Subsequently, he served as recruiting officer and was finally placed on the retired list of the United States Army on account of continued ill health, the result of hard service and exposure.

He died when he had passed three score years and ten. His age was 63 years. His second wife was Ruth Burns, a native of his own county, and by whom he had three children: Elizabeth, Mary and Capt. James W. Glenn, who lives at the old home-stead "Glenburnie," near Shepherdstown, W. Va.

DESCENDANTS OF WILLIAM DUKE

II. WILLIAM DUKE, eldest son of John and Margaret Duke, born 17 March, 1749, died in Berkeley Co., Va., 13 Sept., 1794; *m. circa* 1777, Mary Ann, dau. of Nicholas and Christina Lemon, of Frederick Co., Va. She was born in the vicinity of Harper's Ferry, 7 Jan., 1756; *d. circa* 1796, and was buried at "Southwood Springs," near Kearneysville, Berkeley Co., Va.   Issue:

1, Margaret, b. 18 Aug., 1778; d. 5 Oct., 1839.
2, Francis, b. 29 Nov., 1783; d. 8 Nov., 1836.
3, John, b. 7 May, 1786; d. 31 March, 1871.
4, Robert, b. 9 Aug., 1788; d. 16 Aug., 1834.

317

5, Matthew, b. 5 Jan., 1791; d. *circa* 1820.

6, Nancy, b. 13 April, 1793; d. July, 1876.

1. MARGARET DUKE (John[1], William[2]), eldest child of William and Mary A. Duke, b. Rocky Marsh, Berkeley Co., Va., 18 Aug., 1778; d. 5 Oct., 1839; *m. circa* 1794, Daniel Hendricks, a farmer, of Berkeley Co., Va., and son of Daniel (?) Hendricks and his wife Rebecca (?) Buckles, dau. of one of the early settlers, who located at "Rattling Springs" on the Potomac River, two miles above Harper's Ferry, Va.

The Hendricks family, of the Valley, into which Margaret Duke married were one of the earliest and thriftiest among the settlers from Pennsylvania. Their ancestors came from the Dutch settlement near Philadelphia which antedated the arrival of Penn and his colonists by several years, and at that time he was prominent in colonial history. Thomas A. Hendricks, former Vice-president of the United States, who died in 1885 after having served only a few months, was, with Grover Cleveland the President, the first to be elected to those offices by the Democratic party since 1857; he too, was of this line, the grandfathers of Thomas A. Hendricks and Daniel W. Hendricks being brothers. The earlier forefather was "Albertus Hendricon, of Locomo"—so runs his will, who was given a patent to lands at what is now Lamokin, about a mile west of Chester Creek, on the Delaware, in Delaware Co., Pa., in the year 1673. He was a constable of the Upland Court in 1676, and a juror of the first court under the Penn government. His death occurred in 1715 and his will recites sons: Tobias, James, Johannes; daughters: Elizabeth Wright, Isabel Venamon and Katharine Haverd; and grandchildren: Albertus Steer and Helchy, the daughter of Tobias; the executors were the son Tobias and John Salkeld, the celebrated Quaker preacher (see Smith's History of Delaware County, p. 468; The American Genealogist, Vol. I., pt. 4, p. 136, 1899).

The Hendricks and Wrights migrated in 1726 to the west side of the Susquehanna, where they became involved in a raging border controversy between the Provinces of Maryland and Pennsylvania, respecting their boundary rights (see Pennsylvania Archives, 1st Series).

Tobias Hendricks settled at what is now known as Oyster Point, at the head of the Cumberland Valley, and about two miles west of Harrisburg. He was one of the Justices of Chester Co., in 1726; died at Oyster Point, in 1739, leaving wife Catherine, and children: Henry, Rebecca, Tobias, David, Peter, Abraham and Isaac.

James Hendricks, the brother of Tobias, both sons of Albertus, was a noted Quaker, and a carpenter; he also settled on the Susquehanna in Lancaster Co., near his brother Tobias, but finally passed down the Cumberland Valley to the new settlements on the Potomac in the vicinity of Martinsburg. He was probably the Major James Hendricks, of the 7th Virginia Line commanded by Col. Mordecai Buckner, in the War of the Revolution (see Records of Spottsylvania Co., Va., pp. 526–533). James Hendricks *m.* Priscilla ——, and died at a venerable age, in Berkeley Co., Va., in 1795. This couple left several children who intermarried with the Lucases, Buckleses, Blues and Van Metres. He was the father of Daniel Hendricks who is said to have married Miss Buckles, of Rattling Springs, and were the parents of Tobias and Daniel; the latter *m.* Margaret Duke.

7, William Hendricks, b. 22 Dec., 1795; d. young and without issue.

8, Daniel Hendricks, b. 25 Aug., 1797; d. 28 Nov., 1852.

9, John Hendricks, b. 30 Oct., 1799; d. s.p.

10, Tobias Hendricks, b. 7 Nov., 1801; d. s.p.

11, Polly Hendricks, b. 13 Dec., 1803; d. ——.

12, James Hendricks, b. 2 July, 1812; d. 10 Aug., 1848.

13, Eliza Hendricks, b. 27 Sept., 1814; d. 28 Aug., 1877.

2. FRANCIS DUKE (John[1], William[2]), eldest son of William and Mary A. Duke, b. Rocky Marsh, 29 Nov., 1783; drowned at Harper's Ferry, Va., 8 Nov., 1836; *m.* 20 Nov., 1819, at Shepherdstown, Va., Elizabeth, dau. of Jacob and Rebecca (McNutt) Kendrick, of Lampeter Square, Lancaster Co., Pa., a lineal descendant of Martin Kendig, a Swiss Mennonite who came to America from the Palatinate in 1709, and settled in the Pequea Valley, Lancaster Co., Pa. He was an agent of the Dutch and Swiss emigrants who settled in that part of Pennsylvania, and himself was a prominent landowner, preacher and citizen. Elizabeth Kendrick was b. 22 Aug., 1802; d. at Philadelphia, Pa., 6 Oct., 1869. Issue:

14, Ann Catharine, b. 31 Jan., 1821; d. 21 Jan., 1863.

15, Mary Margaret, b. 15 Oct., 1823; d. 28 March, 1825.

16, Elizabeth Frances, b. 28 Dec., 1825; d. 18 Feb., 1901.

17, Sarah Jane, b. 27 May, 1828; d. 21 June, 1833.

18, Francis Kendrick, b. 7 Dec., 1830; d. 9 Sept., 1908.

19, John Francis, b. 5 March, 1834; d. 28 Oct., 1898.

20, Rebecca Ellen, b. 14 Jan., 1837; d. 30 Nov., 1899.

3. JOHN DUKE (John[1], William[2]), son of William and Mary A. Duke, b. Rocky Marsh, Va., 7 May, 1786; d. at Harper's Ferry, Va., 31 March, 1871; *m.* 23 Sept., 1813, Lucy Keys Talbot, dau. of Walter and Elizabeth (French) Talbot Shirley, a pioneer settler of Chestertown, Md. Her first husband was George Talbot, of Delaware City, Del., b. 1778; d. at Harper's Ferry, Va., 19 July, 1862. Issue:

21, John William, b. 24 July, 1814; d. 23 Sept., 1822.

22, James Francis, b. 26 Dec., 1816; d. 6 March, 1897, at Charlestown, W. Va.

23, Talbot Shirley, b. 26 June, 1819; d. at Richmond, Va., 29 July, 1862.

24, Elizabeth Goff, b. 20 Dec., 1821; d. 3 Oct., 1844.

25, Virginia, b. 8 April, 1825; d. 8 April, 1825.

26, Mary Ann, b. 21 Oct., 1826.

27, William Vance, b. 7 July, 1829; d. 14 Feb., 1832.

4. ROBERT DUKE (John[1], William[2]), son of William and Mary A. Duke, b. at Rocky Marsh, Va., 9 Aug., 1788; d. at "Willow Springs," near Harper's Ferry, Va., 16 Aug., 1834; m. circa, 1815, Anna Newton Moore, dau. of Rev. Francis Moore, pastor of the Zoar Baptist Congregation (Ketochtin District), and his wife Sally Allnut, only dau. of Jesse, son of James Allnut, one of the original settlers of Dawsonville, Prince George's Co., Md., and his wife, Eleanor Chiswell. The Allnuts were descended—in the Newton line—from the progenitor of Sir Isaac Newton, the great English scientist and mathematician. Anna N. Moore was descended from William Moore who lived in Westmoreland, or Prince William Co., Va., and is said to have been the youngest son of Lord John Moore who came to South Carolina from England. William's son, Jeremiah, m. a Miss Renno, of a prominent Maryland family, and removed to Fairfax Co., Va. The Moores belong to the Church of England, but one day Jeremiah went to hear the Rev. David Thomas preach; he was a well-known Baptist minister of that day, and Jeremiah was much impressed with his doctrines; after this he became a Baptist and entered its ministry as did also his son Francis, who was b. in Fairfax Co., Va., 18 Sept., 1766; m. 8 Nov., 1792, Sarah C. Allnut, and died at Pleasant Valley, 15 Feb., 1831 (Semple's Lives of the Baptists; and Virginia Baptist Ministers, p. 386). Issue:

28, Francis William, b. 9 Sept., 1816; d. in 1821.

29, Robert Newton, b. 18 July, 1818; d. in 1821.

30, Ann Margaret, b. 24 Aug., 1820; d. in 1821.

31, Francis William, b. 29 June, 1822; d. 1 Aug., 1905, Bloomington, Ill.

32, Robert Newton, b. 12 Sept., 1824; d. 21 Nov., 1879.

33, Matthew Allnut, b. 29 Sept., 1826; d. 26 Oct., 1879.

34, Ann Margaret, b. 29 Sept., 1826; d. 28 Aug., 1874.

35, Mary Ellen, b. 24 June, 1832; d. 18 Aug., 1870.

5. MATTHEW DUKE (John[1], William[2]), son of William and Mary A. Duke, b. 5 Jan., 1791; he never married, but lived with his sister, Mrs. Daniel Hendricks. He served as a substitute in the War of 1812. The date of his death is unknown, but he was living in 1822. He was buried in the burial plot on the Hendricks

farm, where his grave is marked by a sandstone with the letters
" M. D." carved upon it.

6. NANCY DUKE (John[1], William[2]), second dau. and youngest
child of William and Mary A. Duke, b. at Rocky Marsh, Va.,
13 March, 1793; d. — July, 1876, and was buried at Rocky Marsh.
She *m. circa* 1818, Isaac Clymer, Jr., son of Isaac Clymer, Sr., of
Reading, Pa., and a cousin of George Clymer, Esq., a merchant
of Philadelphia, and one of the signers of the Declaration of
Independence. Her husband was a soldier in the War of 1812;
one of the Defenders of Baltimore and an eye-witness to the
death of Lord Ross. Isaac Clymer, Jr., was b. *circa* 1779, and
d. 10 Oct., 1870.

"Being recently at Harper's Ferry, West Virginia, a friend and brother
minister who was laboring transiently with me there, proposed to go and
see his aged mother. With my habit of mind in respect to old people, I
was seized with a great desire to see and talk with this venerable christian person, whose mind, I knew, to be richly freighted with memories
of by gone days. . . . we made our way, the five miles that intervened,
over long rough roads, to the rural abode which was the place of our
destination. But if the greater part of the way was hilly and rocky, we
were compensated for this by the enjoyment of the scenery. Part of our
route was along the Potomac, sometimes within a few yards of the
stream; the B. & O R. R. running on the other side of our road; grand
cliffs, that sometimes shape themselves into the forms of midair towers,
and castles overhanging us, and looking down upon the glistening track,
the river surface and the line of the canal beyond, for here the Chesapeake
and Ohio canal runs parallel to the Potomac, which feeds it. And here,
let me say, that M[r]. Jefferson had good cause to write as he did some
ninty-odd years ago, about the passage of the blended waters of the
Shenandoah and the Potomac through the mountains . . . as worth a voy-
age across the Atlantic to see it? I believe there can be few places in our
country or in the world, that afford such a variety of grand and beautiful
scenery as does Harper's Ferry locality.

"Age had made its marks strongly on the once smooth face and active
frame of the friend we went to see, now nearly eighty-five years of age.
It was not hard to turn her mind in the direction that I wished; for old
people, mentally, live much in the past. She talked of the ministers of
other days; had heard the first Moses Hoge preach, and expressed a
strong wish that she just could hear that grandson of his down at
Richmond. The eminent D[r]. John Matthews had been, from her earliest
life and for many subsequent years—her pastor. The Sheperdstown
church was then a large and powerful one, taking in what in now embraced
in that and one or two other congregations. And anyone now visiting
Shepherdstown, and taking a view of the beautiful scenery of the river
from the Potomac bluffs, will notice a pleasant rural residence, on an
eminence, on the Virginia side, commanding a view of the water, where
D[r]. M. once had his pastor's home. . . . She soon got upon the track of
her own religious history; . . . at as early an age as three years, she was
left an orphan. But now after eighty years she remembers, in her
mother's last days, being taken up from where she was lying by her side,
on the bed, for the mother to make a last prayer over and for her. I
could not but think how has that dying mother's prayer brought forth its
fruit! At five years of age her mind was deeply impressed by an exciting dream, in which Death in visible form, appeared to her, to call her
away. She implored him to spare her yet awhile, and he agreed so to do,

bidding her, as his awful form disappeared, to make her preparations, by
the time he should come again. And greatly was I struck, as here the old
lady, interrupting her recital, turned her bright eyes, suffused with tears,
into my face and said, in a very impressive tone 'that is what I have been
trying to do ever since.' Yes, I thought, for these four score years, and
has it been too long a time for such a work? Her mind from that time
for years, continued in a state of distress, her sister with whom she lived,
observed the sadness that seemed to overshadow the child's face, and at
length, one day, while the young sister was rocking the cradle urged her
to tell the reason and she did. Her sister, though a pious woman was
astonished, and exclaimed 'Why, Nancy, you are as innocent as that
baby.' This gave her some comfort for a while; but her distress returned,
for people do not often know of the religious feelings of children or
make much of them if they do, and this little one was a 'stricken deer'
for months and years, till at length, at eleven years of age being at a
sacramental meeting in Shepherdstown, she heard from the late Rev. N.
Scott, so well known in many years after in all this region,—a communion sermon from the text 'Is there no balm, &c.' That text and
sermon drew the barbed arrow and poured in the balm as a dying Christ
was held up before the believing and penitent child. She was soon ready
to profess her faith, and when a proper occasion came for it, appeared
before the session with some older persons, I think, seven in number.
Dr. Matthews uttered his surprise and interest, in an exclamation about
'so young a one coming' in that capacity. Said the child: 'I have lost
my earthly parents, I feel the need of a heavenly one.' Dr. Matthews was
so overcome that he dropped upon his knees before her, almost putting
his head upon her lap, as she sat before him; and poured his emotions in
prayer for this lamb of the fold. No doubt that prayer, too, was one
that blessed her life ever afterward.

"Marrying, becoming a mother, and happy in having a husband whom
everybody in the region knows to have shown him a truly christian
partner. She was in the habit of attending church at Shepherdstown,
sometimes taking 'the baby' before, and another child—behind her, on
the horse; for in those days, good roads and carriages were not much
known. She spoke particularly of 'a great revival' that they had there
in town, and how during that time, she had once risen not very long
after midnight and with the assistance of a faithful servant, ridden the
five miles to town, to a sunrise prayer meeting. In those days we certainly had 'some strong minded women,' in the best sense of the term.
With her growing maternity, she determined at one time, that if the
Lord should give her another son, she would hope and pray for his being
a minister. Another son was born, as he grew up he went to College;
and she spoke of her concern and her prayers for him. He was named
after her pastor Dr. M., though he had removed; and was baptised by him
on a visit to Virginia. That son is now well-known as a faithful, useful minister of Christ. . . . all her children—but one, became hopeful
subjects of grace, most of them in early life, one at eleven years of age.
Several have died, and she spoke of the somewhat remarkable piety and
character of one, a daughter, who died in the bloom of early womanhood. Oh! said a dying aunt of this young christian, 'let Maggie stay
near me,' and added, 'if she could but go with me into the dark river,
and I could hold to her, she would float and I with her.' . . . And when
this young one herself was consciously about leaving this world, calling
a beloved but unconverted brother-in-law to her bedside and having her
head placed upon a pillow, upon his knees, she gazed into his face and
said? Now, Brother—I am going; I have one legacy to leave you; it is
my place at the communion table; will you take it? And that sermon
from dying lips, I believe, was not unheeded for the brother-in-law from

about that time, had been filling the place at the Lord's table, and has now, I believe, joined her in the communion above. . . .
"June was in all its glory, all nature dressed in its fullest garb of summer beauty, in those days, on one of which we drove back, and the evening cast its soft tints over the landscape, and the western sky was lit up with the ethereal beauty of such a day's sunset. I could not but think, the last days of an aged saint are like this . . . (L. N. in " The Christain Observer " of Louisville, Ky., 15 July, 1874).

Issue:

36, Joseph, b. and d. in infancy.
37, Elizabeth, b. 1 Feb., 1820; d. 16 July, 1894.
38, Margaret Ann, b. 7 March, 1822; d. 2 Sept., 1840; *unm.*
39, Isaac, Jr., b. 5 June, 1824; d. 12 Dec., 1890 or 1891.
40, Robert, b. 18 Dec., 1826; d. in infancy.
41, Mary Ann, b. 18 Dec., 1826; d. 16 May, 1842; *unm.*
42, Daniel Hendricks, b. 21 June, 1829; d. 30 Jan., 1864, in Confederate service.
43, John Matthews, b. 29 March, 1831.
44, Eliza Jane, b. — June, 1833; d. ——.
45, Francis Duke, b. 16 Jan., 1835.

8. DANIEL HENDRICKS (John[1], William[2], Margaret[3]), son of Daniel and Margaret (Duke) Hendricks, b. 25 Aug., 1797; d. 28 Nov., 1852; m. Polly Osbourne.   Issue:
46, Blanche, b. 1 Nov., 1830; d. ——.
47, William, b. 31 Dec., 1831; killed in battle of Manassas, Va., 21 July, 1861.
48, Tobias, b. ——; 49, Sarah Taylor, b. 15 Aug., 1824, d. 21 Feb., 1894; 50, Margaret, b. ——.

11. POLLY HENDRICKS (John[1], William[2], Margaret[3]), eldest dau. of Daniel and Margaret (Duke) Hendricks, b. 13 Dec., 1803; m. William Marshall. They removed to Dayton, O. Issue:
51, J. William, b. *circa* 1832; James, b. *circa* 1836.

12. JAMES HENDRICKS (John[1], William[2], Margaret[3]), son of Daniel and Margaret (Duke) Hendricks, b. 2 July, 1812; d. 10 Aug., 1848; m. Sophia Snyder, b. 24 Dec., 1808.   Issue:
53, Mary Ellen, b. 25 March, 1832; d. 3 July, 1876.
54, John William, b. 23 March, 1833; d. ——.
55, Elizabeth Jane, b. 24 Nov., 1834.
56, Susanna, b. 8 Oct., 1836; d. ——.
57, Daniel Webster, b. 26 July, 1838; living at Uvilla, Jefferson Co., W. Va., 1908.
58, Margaret Ann, b. 13 Sept., 1840; d. ——.
59, Virginia Catharine, b. 15 Jan., 1843; d. 1879.
60, James Madison, b. 6 Feb., 1844; d. ——.
61, Alice, b. 15 Feb., 1849; d. ——.

13. ELIZA HENDRICKS (John[1], William[2], Margaret[3]), youngest dau. of Daniel and Margaret (Duke) Hendricks, b. 27 Sept.,

323

1814; d. 28 Aug., 1877; *m.* Edward Lucas (4th), who was b. 1
April, 1811. He was the son of Capt. Edward Lucas (3d), b.
7 Nov., 1783; d. — Sept., 1849; who was the son of Edward
Lucas (2d), b. 3 Dec., 1738; d. 19 March, 1809, who was the
son of Capt. Edward Lucas (1st), b. 24 Dec., 1710; d. 3 Oct.,
1777. Edward Lucas, 1st, who came to Frederick Co., Va.,
in 1725, took up land which is now known as "Cold Spring,"
near Shepherdstown, W. Va. "He was an Indian fighter and
a Revolutionary officer and served in the Virginia volunteers
under Captain William Morgan as first lieutenant, as is attested
by his furlough papers granted by General George Washington
and dated at 'Hd'qrts, N. Y., 1777,' all in Washington's handwriting" (Hon. D. B. Lucas to Miss S. L. Powell). The first
Edward Lucas came from Bucks Co., Pa., and whose ancestor
came thence from Wiltshire, England, and settled, under grant
from William Penn, in Falls Township. (Note: There is a
place called "Cold Spring" in Falls Township, Bucks Co., Pa.
It is located on the ancient Penn's Manor, about midway between
Bristol, Pa., and Trenton, N. J. The Morgans above referred to
may have been of the same family of Morgans who were early
settled at Durham, Bucks Co., Pa., some of whom are known to
have emigrated to the Valley of Virginia, as did the Darkes and
the Lucases at an early date.) Edward Lucas, who was a
brother of Dr. Robert Armisted Lucas and Lewis Shepherd
Lucas, d. 5 Sept., 1873.   Issue:

  62, Benjamin F., b. 2 Oct., 1837; lieutenant, killed at Gettys-
      burg, Pa., 16 Sept.(?), 1864.
  63, Virginia Mary, b. 12 June, 1839; d. 17 June, 1849.
  64, Edward (5), b. 3 Feb., 1843; d. *unm.*
  65, Emily Catharine Shepherd, b. 29 Dec., 1846; d. *unm.* 16
      Jan., 1889.
  66, Margaret Elizabeth, b. 4 May, 1848; d. ——.
  67, William B., b. 4 Jan., 1850; d. 9 Jan., 1851.
  68, John Allen, b. 13 Jan., 1852; d. 1896.
  69, Lula May, b. 15 April, 1855; d. ——.

14. ANN CATHARINE DUKE (John[1], William[2], Francis[3]), eldest
dau. of Francis and Elizabeth (Kendrick) Duke, b. 31 Jan., 1821;
d. 21 Jan., 1863; *m.* 9 Aug., 1843, Thomas H. Mensing, Sr., of
Philadelphia, Pa., son of Frederick Mensing. Thomas H. Mensing was a Union soldier and served in the Civil War. Mustered
into Company H, 118th (Corn Exchange) Regiment, Pa. Vols.,
5 Aug., 1862, as a private; was afterward promoted to be corporal; was wounded at Fredericksburg, Va., 13 Dec., 1862;
transferred to 53d Co., 2d Battalion, Veteran Reserve Corps, 13
Nov., 1863. Member of Ulric Dahlgren Post, No. 14, G. A. R.,
of Philadelphia, Pa.   Issue:

  70, Thomas H. Mensing, Jr., b. 3 June, 1844; 71, John F.

FRANCIS K. DUKE, ESQ.

Mensing, b. 9 May, 1846; 72, Pauline Clara Mensing, b. 1 Feb., 1849; 73, Anna F. Mensing, b. 19 May, 1851; 74, Ida Virginia Mensing, b. 4 March, 1858; 75, Elizabeth M. Mensing, b. 8 May, 1862.

16. ELIZABETH FRANCES DUKE (John[1], William[2], Francis[3]), third dau. of Francis and Elizabeth (Kendrick) Duke, b. Harper's Ferry, Va., 28 Dec., 1825; d. 18 Feb., 1901; *m.* 27 June, 1860, Charles W. Kinsey, of Bristol, Pa., a descendant of one of the early settlers of Bucks Co., Pa., and grandson of William Kinsey, a soldier of the Revolution. He was born in 1829; d. at Philadelphia, 22 Aug., 1883.   Issue:
    76, Elizabeth Frances, b. Philadelphia, 10 May, 1865; d. — Feb., 1900.

18. FRANCIS KENDRICK DUKE (John[1], William[2], Francis[3]), eldest son of Francis and Elizabeth Kendrick Duke, b. Harper's Ferry, Va., 7 Dec., 1830; d. at Cape May, N. J., Sept. 9, 1908; *m.* 13 Oct., 1853, at Chester, Pa., Sophia Louise Eldridge, of Cape May, N. J., dau. of Thomas and Deborah (Ware) Eldridge, and a descendant, in the maternal line, through the Whilldin and Gorham ancestry, of John Howland and his wife, Elizabeth Tilley, who was long supposed to have been the adopted daughter of Governor Carver, of Plymouth (Mass.) colony, passengers on the famous "Mayflower," which landed at Plymouth Rock, 20 Dec., 1620; and also on her maternal side from Joseph Ware and his wife, Martha Becket, of John Fenwick's company, who came in the ship "Griffith" from London, England, landed and settled at Salem, in the Province of West Jersey, 5 Oct., 1675; and also of Peter Corson, whose ancestor settled at Brooklyn, N. Y., *circa* 1660, from whence Peter Corson came and settled at Cape May, *circa* 1690; and also of the Crowell family, early settlers at Cape May from New England, who are said to have been descendants of Oliver Cromwell, Lord Protector of England (see Howland Genealogy, Ware Genealogy, Corson, Crowell, Whilldin and Eldridge family records). Francis Kendrick Duke, one of the honored surviving veterans of the Civil War, received his education in part in the public schools of Lancaster, Pa., which he was obliged to give up at an early age on becoming an apprentice to Parker McLaughlin, a millwright of Quarryville, Pa. He devoted three years to mastering this trade and two years additional at house carpentering, thus combining two useful, but allied industries; and his skill in these lines were his only capital at the outset of his career as journeyman mechanic.

About 1850 Francis Duke drifted to Cape May, N. J., with other mechanics, and secured employment during the erection of the famed hostelry, Mount Vernon. This and other building operations occupied his time for another two years; he then returned to Philadelphia and began business on his own account as a contractor and builder, and was successful in securing several important municipal contracts for bridges and other public improvements. He married Miss Eldridge in 1853, at Chester, Pa., at the home of her sister, Mrs. Henry W. Sawyer, and thereafter, for some years, was associated in business with his brother-in-law. He removed to Bridgeport, N. J., where he resided for a while, finally removing to Philadelphia again, where he was living at the outbreak of the Rebellion. When the call came for volunteers to serve for three years Mr. Duke responded by recruiting and organizing a company in the Kensington District of Philadelphia, and had them prepared for service by June, 1861. Finding the quota of State troops already made up and missing an opportunity of joining his company to Colonel Heintzlemen's regiment, he was obliged to take his men to Wilmington, Del., where he and his men were accepted and mustered into the Second Delaware Regiment of State troops, 10 July, 1861. His company was Company F, and Duke was commissioned second lieutenant of it, and thereafter his personal history forms a part of the annals of that famous regiment.

The Second Regiment of Delaware was the first body of troops to organize in that State, under the call for "three-year men," organizing 21 May, 1861. It did not have its ranks filled up until a few months later, owing to the lack of a State system to aid in the work. This occasioned delay and led to the taking in of companies from outside the State in order that its organization might be more speedily effected. Col. Henry H. Wharton, late a captain in the Sixth U. S. Infantry, was given the command of the regiment, but he resigned it in August, 1861, and Lieut. Col. W. P. Baily was promoted to the command.

The regiment rendezvoused at Camp Brandywine and on Sept. 17, 1861, proceeded to Camp Wharton at Cambridge, Md., where General H. H. Lockwood, late an instructor of mathematics in the Naval Academy at Annapolis, and who had been appointed colonel of the First Delaware Regiment, commissioned Brig. Gen. in August, 1861, instructed them in field tactics.

The Second Regiment moved with the brigade of General Lockwood, Dec. 1, 1861, to Accomac Co., Va., and remained in that locality till March 1, 1862, when it was transferred to Baltimore to do garrison duty. In May of that year it joined the Army of the Potomac and was assigned to Summer's Corps, Richardson's Division, and at the battle of Fair Oaks was placed in the brigade of Gen. W. H. French. Here the first serious duty of the regiment began and continued almost incessantly during the siege of Richmond, participating in the several engagements of Gains's Mill, Savage Station, Peach Orchard, White Oak Swamp and Malvern Hill, from June 27 to July 1, 1862. In the battle of Antietam the regiment held an advanced position and was warmly commended for its bravery. Here they captured the colors of the Sixteenth Mississippi Regiment. Out of 350 men taken into action 70 were killed and wounded. The regiment also took a conspicuous part in the battle of Fredericksburg; here also it was in the front and covered the retreat from that hotly contested field so ably that it attracted the attention of the army (Scharf's History of Delaware, Vol. I., pp. 367 *et seq.;* also New York Times, January 13, 1863).

The personal experience and incidents in the service of Lieutenant Duke are sufficiently interesting to be more particularly related. He visibly bears the scars of battle and the supporting cane he wears are the present-day external evidences of that memorable conflict.

While with his regiment in Accomac Co., Va., Lieutenant Duke was attached to the staff of General Lockwood, having been appointed district marshall for that county. In November, 1861, the Confederates having burned the bridge crossing the Nassowango River, a branch of the Pocomoke, some distance below Snow Hill, Md., Lieutenant Duke was sent by General Lockwood with a detail to rebuild it. While on his way to execute the order the lieutenant's horse took fright and plunged into a fence, breaking the lieutenant's right leg in two places, and he was carried to the hospital. The wound was so severe and the conditions so complicated that it was feared he might not recover; to save him, however, preparations were made by the regimental surgeon and his staff to amputate the injured limb. Lieutenant Duke considered that the loss of the limb was unnecessary and desired to retain it even at the risk of his life. His remonstrances were of no avail; the leg must come off decided the doctors. In the meantime the wife of Lieutenant Duke, who was living in New Jersey, but had been notified of her husband's injury and its possibly dangerous consequences, hurried to Drummondtown, Va., where the regiment was stationed, and had arrived just about the time the doctors had determined upon for the amputation. While Lieutenant Duke was helpless himself to prevent it, he told his wife that if the doctors persisted in proceeding with the operation, that she should take his revolver, which lay beneath his pillow, and shoot the first person who should lay hands upon him for the purpose. When the doctors came into the room and saw the situation they endeavored to persuade the wife also that the only hope of saving her husband's life was to sacrifice his leg, but she as resolutely refused to sanction it, or to leave the room upon their request. The doctors, finding her inflexible in her determination, finally yielded to the lieutenant and his wife, even if the officer had to die to have his own way. After a long and tedious treatment the limb healed and the lieutenant recovered, but he was more or less of a cripple for life; hence his use of the cane; and he has to thank his courageous wife and his own confidence that he has two legs to stand on instead of one, or none.

Lieutenant Duke rejoined his regiment in the following spring and it was to take part in its operation on the Peninsula. At Fair Oaks he went into the fight with his cane and received a bullet in his lame leg, and at Savage Station, 29 June, 1862, he was shot in the neck while leading his men in a charge. The first lieutenant of the company had fallen earlier in the battle, so Second Lieutenant Duke took his place, cane in one hand, sword in the other, led the men, with fixed bayonets, across the field to dislodge the enemy concealed under the cover of the woods, who were rapidly picking off the Union men with unerring deadliness. When hit the lieutenant fell, but almost instantly regained his feet, and rushed his men " double quick " against the sharpshooters. At the critical moment, however, the enemy was reinforced and counter-charging out of their cover forced the Federals to retreat. Seven of the company were captured, but the lieutenant, with the other officers and men, escaped. General French, who had witnessed the charge, came up to Lieutenant Duke while his wound was being dressed, grasped his hand and warmly thanked him for his fearless charge.

Three days after the affair at Savage Station Duke was appointed acting quartermaster. While thus engaged he occupied a position of great danger during the hottest of the fight at Malvern Hill; he, however, successfully performed his duties, though at this time in no condition physically for it. A few days later he was relieved and given command of the Fourth Division of the Convalescent Camp at Alexandria, Va. Gathering together his invalided comrades in the smoke house of the famous Westover mansion, near Harrison's Landing, on the James River, the party was soon transferred by transport to the Invalid Camp at Alexandria.

Remaining at the camp till the 18th of March, 1863, Lieutenant Duke, for longstanding disability and at his own request, was honorably discharged from the service and returned to Philadelphia. His bravery, efficiency and service have been publicly attested by Governor Geary and others prominent in war times and since; years afterward, his old commander, General Lockwood, visited him at Cape May and they rejoiced together over the leg that was saved at Drummondtown and the sword that was wielded at Savage Station.

After the close of the war Francis K. Duke was active in the organization of " The Boys in Blue," the social forerunner in Philadelphia of the Grand Army of the Republic. He also was one of the organizers of John Mecray Post, No. 40, G. A. R., of Cape May, N. J., was one of its earliest commanders and always has been zealous for its growth and success.

Politically Francis K. Duke has always been an active Repub-

DESCENDANTS OF WILLIAM DUKE

lican. His fealty to his party has ever been of the most stalwart
character and uncompromising quality, and it has brought him
his rewards in local political preferment. From 1874 to 1884
he served as justice of the peace in Lower Township, Cape May,
N. J. From 1886 to 1891 he was a member of council of Cape
May City and for two years was presiding officer of that body.
In 1892 he was temporarily in the State of Pennsylvania, remod-
elling the Red Rose Inn on the estate of Frederick Phillips, Esq.,
near Villa Nova. On his return to Cape May in the spring of
1893 Francis K. Duke was elected coroner of Cape May County,
and at the conclusion of his term was elected alderman of Cape
May City for the term ending in 1899. He was re-elected to the
same office in 1902 and has continued to fill the position since
that time.

Mr. Duke for many years has carried on his business as a contracting builder and has erected many of the finest cottages and
hotels on the New Jersey coast. He takes a deep interest in
fraternal organizations and in the commercial advancement, and,
in fact, in anything that tends to maintain the prestige of Cape
May as the " Queen of coast resorts." He is a member of Cape
Island Lodge, No. 30, F. and A. M., the Fire Department and the
Board of Trade of Cape May City, N. J.   Issue:

77, Harriet Louisa, b. Philadelphia, 31 July, 1854; *unm.*
78. Mary Elizabeth, b. Bridgeport, N. J., 13 Jan., 1857.
79, John Francis, b. Mantua, West Philadelphia, 22 Aug., 1861.

19. JOHN FRANCIS DUKE (John[1], William[2], Francis[3]), second
son of Francis and Elizabeth (Kendrick) Duke, b. at Harper's
Ferry, Va., 5 March, 1834; d. Philadelphia, 28 Oct., 1898; *m.*
1st, 1860, at Beverly, N. J., Mrs. Elizabeth Stewart Boat, dau.
of George and Sarah (Bessonett) Stewart; the latter was the
daughter of Charles Bessonett, deputy postmaster-general during
the Revolutionary War, and the first person to establish a coach
line between Philadelphia and New York. His ancestor came
to Bristol, Pa., about 1720, and was descended of that branch of
the Bessonett family seated in Dauphiny, France, who at the
Revocation of the Edict of Nantes fled, first to Ireland, thence to
America and settled at Burlington, N. J., in 1692. Elizabeth
Stewart was the wife of George Boat, a merchant-manufacturer
of Philadelphia, and upon his death, she *m.* 2d John Francis
Duke. She died at Beverly, 12 Aug., 1863. John Francis Duke
m. 2d, 2 Sept., 1873, Louisa Kinsey, of Bristol, Pa., sister of
Chas. W. Kinsey, the husband of J. F. Duke's sister, Elizabeth
Frances. She was also a half-sister of Hon. William Kinsey,
of Bristol, member of the Senate from the seventh senatorial
district of Pennsylvania, and he was also a first cousin of her
husband's first wife, Elizabeth S. Boat, and of the late Hon. B.
Frank Gilkeyson, former banking commissioner of Pennsylvania.

329

Louisa Kinsey Duke d. at Cape May, 27 Aug., 1904.   Issue:
80, Francis K., b. Beverley, N. J., 9 Aug., 1861, by 1st uxor;
m. 22 Aug., 1882, Sarah Emma Williams, of Holmes-
burg; no issue.
81, Herman, b. 5 June, 1874; d. Sept., 1875, by 2d uxor.
82, Beatrice, b. 18 June, 1875; d. May, 1877, by 2d uxor.

20. REBECCA ELLEN DUKE (John[1], William[2], Francis[3]) youngest child of Francis and Elizabeth (Kendrick) Duke, b. at Harper's Ferry, Va., 14 Jan., 1847; d. at Philadelphia, 30 Nov., 1899;
m. 1864, James Wier, late lieutenant in the Delaware troops in
the War of the Rebellion. He predeceased his wife.   Issue:
83, Ellen M., b. 30 April, 1865; d. 16 April, 1866.
84, Elizabeth M., b. 9 Dec., 1866; d. 10 Dec., 1866.

22. JAMES FRANCIS DUKE (John[1], William[2], John[3]), second
son of John and Lucinda K. (Talbot) Duke; b. at Harper's Ferry
(Rocky Marsh), 26 Dec., 1816; d. at Charlestown, W. Va., 6
March, 1897; m. 13 May, 1836, Sophia M. Martin, of Martinsburg, W. Va., b. London, England, 15 July, 1818; d. Champaign,
Ill., 18 July, 1897.   Issue:
85, John Francis, b. 6 July, 1837; d. 2 April, 1849.
86, Lelia, b. 18 Nov., 1838; d. 3 Oct., 1844.
87, Ann Elizabeth, b. 13 May, 1841; d. 29 July, 1841.
88, William Lorrain, b. 27 April, 1845; living at Wilmington,
N. C., 1908.

23. TALBOT SHIRLEY DUKE (John[1], William[2], John[3]), third son
of John and Lucinda K. (Talbot) Duke, b. 26 June, 1819; d.
Richmond, Va., 29 July, 1862; m. 6 June, 1845, Mary T. Brittain,
dau. of Joseph, Sr., and Mary Brittain, of Washington Co., Md.
She d. 22 Jan., 1899, and is buried in Camp Hill Cemetery, Harper's Ferry, W. Va. Talbot S. Duke was superintendent's clerk
at the U. S. arsenal at Harper's Ferry. He was captain of the
Floyd Rifles of Harper's Ferry, was present and took part in
the defense of that town during the invasion of John Brown and
his followers. He later removed to Richmond, became a member
of the Virginia Assembly and was a noted orator. He was
buried in Hollywood Cemetery, Richmond, adjoining the grave
of General Pegram:

". . . From his youth the deceased was of studious habits, and being
fond of reading had acquired a considerable amount of information which
he made practically available. After he was married he read law under
the direction of Hon. Chas. J. Faulkner, of Va., and was admitted to the
Bar. Though a ready speaker, chaste and eloquent, yet he never entered
to any extent upon the practice of his profession. For two sessions he
represented his native country (Jefferson) in the House of Delegates
with credit to himself and acceptability to his constituency. At the commencement of our present national troubles he removed to Fayetteville,
N. C. and subsequently to Richmond, Va. Shortly after his removal to
the latter place he was taken with a severe attack of typhoid fever which

terminated in his death. From the information received concerning his sickness and death we have reason to believe that his end was peace. . . . It was his desire to visit once more the home of his youth and gaze upon its natural beauties which he so much loved, and to see his aged father whose heart had been saddened by death and painful separations, but this looked for privilege was denied him. . . he died away from home toward which his footsteps were tending and for which his heart was longing. A loving wife smoothed his dying pillow and in Hollywood Cemetery stranger friends gently laid his remains whence they will come forth at the bidding of the last day" (from the Methodist Protestant, 1862).

89, Lelia Elizabeth, b. 22 Dec., 1849; *m.* 30 April, 1872, Thomas Ewing King, of Lancaster, O. (T. E. King is the grandson of Christian King, one of the first settlers of Lancaster, Fairfield Co., O., a prominent merchant and one of the founders of the Lutheran Church in that place. In 1832 Christian *m.* a Miss Butler, a native of New York, and a connection of the well-known Butler family of the Mohawk Valley. Their son William was the father of Mr. T. E. King.) They reside in Washington, D. C.; no issue.

90, Walter Robert, b. 18 March, 1846; *unm.*; living in Washington, D. C.

26. MARY ANN DUKE (John[1], William[2], John[3]), third dau. of John and Lucinda K. (Talbot) Duke, b. Rocky Marsh, Harper's Ferry, W. Va., 21 Oct., 1826; living (1909) at Harper's Ferry, W. Va.; *m.* 18 April, 1850, Rev. Joseph Alexander McFaden, whose grandparents came to this country from Londonderry, Ireland. He was b. at Augusta, Ga., 11 Jan., 1825; d. at Harper's Ferry, W. Va., 5 July, 1885. He was an earnest and devoted clergyman and a member of the Maryland Annual Conference of the Methodist Protestant Church.   Issue:

91, John Duke, b. 19 Oct., 1851; 92, Mary Hill, b. 22 June, 1854; 93, George Henry, b. 14 Jan., 1857; 94, Lucinda Shirley, b. 14 May, 1859, d. 13 Aug., 1902, at Harper's Ferry; 95, Lillie Lee, b. 3 Oct., 1861, d. 24 Sept., 1865; 96, Frank Talbot, b. 5 Feb., 1864; 97, Irene Dashiel, b. 2 Nov., 1872.

31. FRANCIS WILLIAM DUKE (John[1], William[2], Robert[3]), third son of Robert and Anna N. (Moore) Duke, b. 29 May, 1822; d. at Bloomington, Ill., 1 Aug., 1905; *m.* 23 Oct., 1855, at Springfield, O., Lydia Thompson; she d. *circa* 1901. In his youth he went west and was lured to California in the gold excitement of 1849, and was one of the first to make the overland trip across the plains. He spent four years among the diggings. During the Civil War he resided in Missouri, but finally removed to Bloomington, Ill., in 1868, where he was engaged in farming for many years. He returned, however, some years ago and has lived in the city of Bloomington since. He was a man of high

THE DUKE GENEALOGY

ideals and his way was very much esteemed in his circle of
acquaintances. Issue:
98, Anna, b. ——, d. 1880; 99, Kate (Catharine), b. 17 Sept.,
1857, d. *circa* 1906.

32. ROBERT NEWTON DUKE (John[1], William[2], Robert[3]), fourth
son of Robert and Ann N. (Moore) Duke of "Willow Springs,"
Jefferson Co., W. Va., b. 12 Sept., 1824; d. 21 Nov., 1879; *m.* his
first cousin, Annie Newton Mohler, 10 Oct., 1846, dau. of George
A. and Sarah Chiswell Moore, who was the dau. of Rev. Jeremiah Moore and sister of Ammishadie Moore, Esq., of Clarke
Co., W. Va. Robert N. Duke was a prominent farmer and a
justice of the peace for the seventh judicial district, Jefferson
Co., W. Va., in 1861–62. Issue:
100, A son, b. 16 Aug., 1847; d. young.
101, George Mohler, b. 15 July, 1848; d. Nov., 1904.
102, Robert Moore, b. 10 Feb., 1850.
103, Anna Frances, b. 24 Dec., 1851; d. Aug., 1887.
104, Sarah Griffith, b. 27 April, 1853; d. 13 Mar., 1880.
105, Emily Newton, b. 9 April, 1855.
106, Anna Newton, b. 2 Sept., 1859.

34. ANN MARGARET DUKE (John[1], William[2], Robert[3]), second
dau. of Robert and Ann N. (Moore) Duke, b. 27 Sept., 1826; d.
28 Aug., 1874; *m.* 29 May, 1851, James William Engle, of "Elm
Springs," near Harper's Ferry, W. Va., b. 5 Aug., 1827; d. 26
Jan., 1904; son of John and Catharine (Melvin) Engle.
The Engles of Jefferson Co., W. Va., are descended from
Melchoir Engle, a German pioneer who emigrated from Lan-
caster Co., Pa., about 1742 and settled at the head-spring of Elk
Branch Creek, near a place now called Duffields, a station of the
B. & O. R. R., a few miles west of Harper's Ferry. His son,
Philip Engle, served in the Carolina Campaign under General
Gates, in the War of the Revolution, and at its conclusion re-
turned to Virginia, where he married 1st Mary Darke, the sister
of General Darke who was a friend and neighbor of the Engles.
He married 2d Isabella Pollock of the family to which President Polk was related. By these two marriages Philip Engle had
eighteen children; on his death, in 1830—according to his physician and biographer—there survived him: eighteen children,
seventy-five grandchildren and forty-six great-grandchildren—a
mighty progeny! Philip Engle, Jr., son of Philip and Mary
(Darke) Engle, b. 1767; d. 1822; was buried in the graveyard on
the Darke homestead; he *m.* Lydia Daniels, b. 1771; d. 1836.
Among his issue of five children was John Engle, b. 1795; d.
1865; one of the most prominent and wealthy of the family; he
owned an estate on the Potomac containing 400 acres, called
"Rattling Springs," three miles above Harper's Ferry, and a
large number of slaves. He was an extensive dealer in grain;

had large grain warehouses and was one of the leading shippers in that part of the country. He married 1st Catharine Melvin; 2d Catharine Daniels; 3d Sarah Ann Engle and had issue by each. James W. Engle was the second son of John and Catharine Melvin Engle. His first wife was Ann Margaret Duke, dau. of Robert Duke, and his second wife was Rebecca Dust, dau. of Isaac Dust, Esq., one of the John Brown jurors. James W. Engle lived at "Elm Springs," a lovely home on the banks of the Potomac adjoining the "Rattling Springs" estate. He was, for forty years, an Elder of the Presbyterian Church, at Duffields; was on the County Board of Education when the free school system was first organized in Virginia, in 1860, and was identified actively with its progress at the time of his death; he was a highly respected citizen of Jefferson County. By his wife Anna M. Duke he had   Issue:

107, Robert Newton, b. 13 March, 1852; 108, James Melvin, b. 29 Nov., 1853; 109, Jessie Allnut, b. 31 Oct., 1855; 110, Williard F., b. 22 Sept., 1857.

111, John Frances, b. 1 Nov., 1859; d. 15 March, 1860.

112, John Francis, b. 13 Jan., 1861; d. 8 Jan., 1888, at Eucitius, California.

113, Ammishadie M., b. 1 June, 1865; 114, Carlton Duke, b. 8 June, 1868; 115, Mary Ella, b. 8 July, 1870, d. 12 Nov., 1870.

35. Mary Ellen Duke (John[1], William[2], Robert[3]), dau. of Robert and Anna N. (Moore) Duke, b. 25 May, 1832 (or 24 June); d. 18 Aug., 1870, at Leipsic, Del.; m. 29 March, 1852, Rev. Levi Towne, son of Samuel Towne of early New England ancestry and a descendant of Richard Town, of Braceby, England, and of William Town who came to Salem, Mass., about 1630 (see Town Genealogy). Levi Town was b. at Arkwright, N. Y., 25 May, 1821; he m. 2d Christina H. Clayton, 21 Nov., 1871.   Issue 1st uxor:

116, William Newton, b. Harper's Ferry, 31 Dec., 1852; d. 10 Oct., 1853.

117, Annie Moore, b. Conneaut, O., 4 March, 1855; lives at Berwyn, Pa.

118, Mary Margaret, b. Conneaut, O., 8 Nov., 1857; m. Winfield Hartman, of Philadelphia.

119, Samuel Francis, b. Centre Road, Pa., 10 Nov., 1861.

120, Robert Duke, b. Warren, O., 4 Jan., 1866.

121, George Levi, b. Warren, O., 4 Dec., 1867; d. 25 Feb., 1873.

122, Carrie, b. Leipsic, Del., 17 July, 1870; d. 16 Aug., 1870.

123, Lavinia, b. Philadelphia, Pa., 29 Dec., 1873; d. ——; by 2d uxor.

THE DUKE GENEALOGY

37. ELIZABETH CLYMER (John[1], William[2], Nancy[3]), eldest dau. of Isaac and Nancy (Duke) Clymer, b. 1 Feb., 1820; d. 16 July, 1894; m. 29 Jan., 1840, Joseph Banes, son of Francis and Susannah Jones (he was Joseph B. Jones), b. 26 Feb., 1812; d. 15 Feb., 1864. The following notes from Pennsylvania marriages may serve to trace the ancestry of Francis Jones. Falls Township meeting (Bucks Co., Pa.), Isaac Ashton m. Deborah Banes, 5 mo. 31, 1701; Susannah Ashton m. Jonathan Jones, 7 mo. 5, 1772; Francis Jones, b. Feb. 1777; d. 1841; his wife Susannah was b. 5 Aug., 1777; d. 1847. Issue of Joseph B. and Elizabeth (Clymer) Jones:

124, Francis Jones, b. 24 Nov., 1840; d. 25 July, 1841.
125, Francis Jones, b. 12 March, 1842; living at Uvilla, Jefferson Co., W. Va., 1908.
126, Isaac, b. 25 Oct., 1843; d. 27 Nov., 1875.
127, George W., b. 25 June, 1846.
128, Margaret, b. 21 Nov., 1848; d. 6 Aug., 1864.
129, Thomas Hammond, b. 26 Oct., 1851; living at Harper's Ferry, W. Va., 1908.
130, Susannah Rebecca, b. 26 Oct., 1852.
131, Mary, b. 3 April, 1856; d. 25 July, 1856.
132, Mary Elizabeth, b. 3 April, 1856; d. 8 Sept., 1856. Nos. 131 and 132 were twins.
133, Nancy Climer, b. 15 April, 1857.
134, Robert Magruder, b. 15 April, 1857. Nos. 133 and 134 were twins.
135, John M., b. 17 Feb., 1860; d. 24 June, 1863.
136, Martha E., b. July, 1863.

39. ISAAC CLYMER, JR. (John[1], William[2], Nancy[3]), second son of Isaac and Nancy (Duke) Clymer, b. 5 June, 1824; d. 12 Dec., 1890; m. 20 Nov., 1860, Lottie Given, dau. of Col. H. Given, of Lewiston, Me., who held a commission in the United States Army prior to the Rebellion, but resigned on the breaking out of the War because his brothers and sisters had married into families divided by its issues. Issue:

137, John William, b. 1861; 138, Charles Woodman, b. 1863; 139, Isaac Henry, b. 1865, d. 19 March, 1866; 140, Humphrey Given, b. 1866, d. 15 April, 1891; 141, Ella Lee, b. 1869; 142, Isaac Newton, b. 1872, d. 10 July, 1885.

43. JOHN MATTHEWS CLYMER (John[1], William[2], Nancy[3]), fifth son of Isaac and Nancy (Duke) Clymer, b. 29 March, 1831; living at Ashburne, Loudon Co., Va.; m. 20 Dec., 1858, at Lewiston, Me., Ella H., dau. of Col. H. Given, and sister of her husband's brother Isaac's wife. She was b. 1839; d. 13 July, 1896, and is buried in Elmwood Cemetery, Shepherdstown, W. Va. Rev. John M. Clymer is a graduate of Delaware College, of

Newark, Del., 1854, and of Union Theological Seminary, of New York, 1858. Licensed, as probationer, to preach in Winchester Presbytery, at Bunker Hill, Berkeley Co., W. Va., 22 May, 1858. Ordained as an evangelist, at Marion, Va., 28 Nov., 1858. Stated supply there, 1858–1859; pastor at Woodstock, Va., Nov., 1859–1871; at Keyser, Va., 1871–1881; and is now preaching the Gospel at Ashburne, Loudon Co., Va. Issue:

> 143, Mary Weston; 144, Frank Lee; 145, Jennie Graham, b. April, 1865; d. 6 May, 1868, at Woodstock, Va.

44. ELIZA JANE CLYMER (John[1], William[2], Nancy[3]), fourth dau. of Isaac and Nancy (Duke) Clymer, b. June, 1833; d. about one year after her marriage to Samuel Knott.

45. FRANCIS DUKE CLYMER (John[1], William[2], Nancy[3]), youngest son of Isaac and Nancy (Duke) Clymer, b. 16 Jan., 1835; living at Baltimore, Md.; m. 1867, O. E. Buckingham, dau. of William and Rebecca (York) Buckingham, of Harford Co., Md. William was the son of Basil and Hannah Buckingham who were of English ancestry, and a soldier of the Revolution. Francis D. Clymer is a Confederate veteran. No issue:

46. BLANCHE HENDRICKS (John[1], William[2], Margaret[3], Daniel[4]), eldest dau. of Daniel and Polly (Osborne) Hendricks, b. 1 Nov., 1830; m. George W. Brantner, 10 April, 1851. Geo. W. Brantner was a Confederate soldier; a son of Samuel Brantner and Betsey Engle. Issue:

> 146, Thomas; 147, William, b. ——, m. Mary Maddox, lives at Shenandoah Junction, Va., and has four children; 148, Hendricks; 149, Tobias; 150, George; 151, Edgar; 152, Lillie; 153, Minnie; 154, Bessie; 155, Harrie; 156, Carrie; 157, Ruth.

47. WILLIAM HENDRICKS (John[1], William[2], Margaret[3], Daniel[4]), eldest son of Daniel and Polly (Osborne) Hendricks, b. 31 Dec., 1831; killed at the battle of Manassas, Va., 21 July, 1861; m. 2 April, 1846, Rhuhama Jane Link, dau. of Adam Link, b. 22 Jan., 1827. Issue:

> 158, Adam Link; 159, Sarah; 160, Mary; 161, Tobias; 162, Ambrose; 163, Minnie; 164, Catharine.

48. TOBIAS HENDRICKS (John[1], William[2], Margaret[3], Daniel[4]), second son of Daniel and Polly (Osborne) Hendricks, b. ——; d. ——; m. Margaret Coffenburger.

49. SARAH TAYLOR HENDRICKS (John[1], William[2], Margaret[3], Daniel[4]), eldest dau. of Daniel and Polly (Osborne) Hendricks, b. 15 Aug., 1824; d. 21 Feb., 1894; m. 21 Nov., 1843, Adam, son of Alexander and Nancy Link, b. 16 Oct., 1817; d. 26 April, 1885. Issue:

> 165, Thomas J., b. 13 Sept., 1844; 166, Henry Taylor, b. 23

THE DUKE GENEALOGY

Feb., 1847; 167, Mary Alexander, b. 31 Jan., 1849, *m.*
—— Jones; 168, Catharine Melissa, b. 22 Jan., 1851, d.
9 June, 1852; 169, Adam Smeltzer, b. 24 Dec., 1852;
170, William Harman, b. 6 Jan., 1855; 171, John Luther,
b. 1 Jan., 1857; 172, Margaret Esther, b. 14 April, 1864.

50. MARGARET HENDRICKS (John[1], William[2], Margaret[3],
Daniel[4]), youngest dau. of Daniel and Polly (Osborne) Hendricks, b. ——; d. ——; *m.* Daniel Nichols.

53. MARY ELLEN HENDRICKS (John[1], William[2], Margaret[3],
James[4]), eldest dau. of James and Sophia (Snyder) Hendricks,
b. 25 March, 1832; d. 3 July, 1876; *m.* George W. Johnston.
Issue:
173, Annie; 174, John W.; 175, Virginia; 176, Hester; 177,
George T.; 178, David N.; 179, James H.; 180, Walter
M.; 181, Kate; 182, Daniel W.; 183, Abraham.

54. JOHN WILLIAM HENDRICKS (John[1], William[2], Margaret[3],
James[4]), eldest son of James and Sophia (Snyder) Hendricks,
b. 13 March, 1833; *m.* Catharine Snyder.   Issue:
184, Milton B., b. 6 Sept., 1857; 185, Elizabeth, b. 1 Aug., 1859.

55. ELIZABETH JANE HENDRICKS (John[1], William[2], Margaret[3],
James[4]), dau. of James and Sophia (Snyder) Hendricks, b. 24
Nov., 1834; d. ——; *m.* Robert B. Evans.   Issue:
186, Kate; 187, William; 188, Elizabeth; 189, Rebecca; 190,
Virginia.

57. DANIEL WEBSTER HENDRICKS (John[1], William[2], Margaret[3],
James[4]), son of James and Sophia (Snyder) Hendricks, b. 26
July, 1838; living at Uvilla, Jefferson Co., W. Va.; *m.* 9 Nov.,
1858, Sarah M. Link.   Issue:
191, Newton Madison, b. 17 May, 1862; 192, Annie L., b. 12
June, 1866; 193, Harvey, b. 2 March, 1869; 194, James
Allen, b. 25 Dec., 1871; 195, Esther, b. 6 April, 1874;
196, Leroy, b. 17 July, 1876; 197, Daniel Webster, Jr.,
b. 24 Dec., 1877.

58. MARGARET ANN HENDRICKS (John[1], William[2], Margaret[3],
James[4]), dau. of James and Sophia (Snyder) Hendricks, b. 13
Sept., 1840; *m.* Cephas Sancey (Sensing).   Issue:
198, Emma.

59. VIRGINIA CATHARINE HENDRICKS (John[1], William[2], Margaret[3], James[4]), dau. of James and Sophia (Snyder) Hendricks,
b. 15 Jan., 1843; d. 1879; *m.* James M. Snyder.   Issue:
199, Virginia; 200, Etta.

60. JAMES MADISON HENDRICKS (John[1], William[2], Margaret[3],
James[4]), son of James and Sophia (Snyder) Hendricks, b. 6
Feb., 1844; *m.* Ella (or Sarah) Knott.   Issue:
201, Maggie; 202, James; 203, Samuel; 204, Nellie; 205,
Hattie.

 DESCENDANTS OF WILLIAM DUKE

61. ALICE HENDRICKS (John[1], William[2], Margaret[3], James[4]), dau. of James and Sophia Snyder Hendricks, b. 15 Feb., 1849; *m.* Robert Gordon. Issue: 206, Evans; 207, Sophia; 208, Hendricks.

66. MARGARET ELIZABETH LUCAS (John[1], William[2], Margaret[3], Eliza[4]), third dau. of Edward and Eliza (Hendricks) Lucas, b. 4 May, 1848; *m.* 1st Isaac Jones, son of Joseph Banes and Elizabeth Clymer Jones (No. 126); no issue; *m.* 2d Milton Wisler *circa* 1884, of Philadelphia, Pa.; no issue.

68. JOHN ALLEN LUCAS (John[1], William[2], Margaret[3], Eliza[4]), son of Edward and Eliza (Hendricks) Lucas, b. 13 Jan., 1852; d. 1896; *m.* 2 Jan., 1876, Martha Porter. They live at Brunswick, Md. Issue:
209, Edna May, b. *circa* 1877; 210, Gertie Etta, b. *circa* 1878; 211, Julia, b. *circa* 1881; 212, Henry Allen, b. *circa* 1884; d. *circa* 1897; 213, Levi, b. *circa* 1887.

69. LULU MAY LUCAS (John[1], William[2], Margaret[3], Eliza[4]), youngest dau. of Edward and Eliza (Hendricks) Lucas, b. 15 April, 1855; d. *circa* July, 1906; *m.* 4 Jan., 1876, William R. Miller, of Shepherdstown, W. Va. Issue:
214, Edward Holland, b. 8 Oct., 1877; 215, Imogen, b. 26 Oct., 1878; 216, Florence H., b. 10 May, 1880; 217, Milton, b. 16 July, 1881; 218, Maggie Steel, b. 28 May, 1883; 219, Elizabeth, b. 28 Jan., 1886; 220, Raymond W., b. March, 1888.

70. THOMAS H. MENSING, JR. (John[1], William[2], Francis[3], Ann C.[4]), eldest son of Thomas and Ann C. (Duke) Mensing, b. 3 June, 1844; living at 3142 Howell St., Wissinoming, Philadelphia, Pa.; *m.* 4 May, 1869, at Free Church of St. John, Philadelphia, Elizabeth Coleman, dau. of William and Elizabeth (Lee) Coleman. The latter's father is said to have been a kinsman of Gen. Robert E. Lee, late Commander of Confederate States' Army, and a descendant of a former Lord Mayor of London, England. Thos. H. Mensing, Jr., was mustered into Company H, 118th (Corn Exchange) Regiment, Pennsylvania Volunteers, 5 Aug., 1862, as a private for three years; later he became a corporal; was mustered out of the service at Washington, D. C., June, 1865. He served on detached service in Battery E, 5th Artillery, Mass., under Capt. Asa Phillips. Wounded in action at Laurel Hill, Spottsylvania Court House, Va., 12 May, 1864; shell wound in right shoulder. Was in thirty engagements from South Mountain to Appomattox. Was detailed to receive all the battle flags at the surrender of General Lee's Army, 10 April, 1865. Member and Past Commander of Colonel Ulrich Dahlgren's Post, No. 14, G. A. R. Vice-president of Survivors Association, 30 June, 1882 (see History Corn Exchange, or 118th

23 337

Regiment, Pennsylvania Volunteers). At present in the United
States Navy Department, at League Island, Philadelphia.

Issue:

221, Thomas William, b. 10 Oct., 1870; 222, Elizabeth Clara,
b. 15 July, 1872; 223, Anna May, b. 19 Feb., 1874, d. 9
April, 1876; 224, Gertrude Viola, b. 21 June, 1877;
225, William John, b. 8 Aug., 1879, d. 13 Sept., 1879;
226, Laura May, b. 8 March, 1882.

71. JOHN FREDERICK MENSING (John[1], William[2], Francis[3],
Ann C.[4]), son of Thomas H. and Ann C. (Duke) Mensing, b. 9
May, 1846; d. ——; m. 1st Matilda Grey; m. 2d Anne Trephagen.

Issue:

227, Edward, b. — 1872; 228, Eleanor, twin to 229, Albert;
230, Matilda.

72. PAULINE CLARA MENSING (John[1], William[2], Frances[3],
Ann C.[4]), dau. of Thomas H. and Ann C. (Duke) Mensing, b.
1 Feb., 1849; living at Tacony, Philadelphia, Pa.; m. 22 March,
1874, John Armstrong, b. 1 April, 1841; d. 7 Feb., 1885. Issue:

231, Francis Charles, b. 27 April, 1875; 232, James Given, b.
3 Feb., 1877; 233, William John, b. 9 Aug., 1878; 234,
Ann Eliza, b. 24 April, 1880; 235, George Elmer, b.
16 Oct., 1882, d. 2 Oct., 1884.

73. ANNA FLORELLA MENSING (John[1], William[2], Francis[3],
Ann C.[4]), dau. of Thomas H. and Ann C. (Duke) Mensing, b.
19 May, 1851; living at Tacony, Philadelphia, Pa.; m. 13 July,
1868, Benjamin Taylor, b. Leeds, Eng., 25 Oct., 1844. He enlisted in the United States naval service at Philadelphia, Pa., 22
Sept., 1864; discharged 18 July, 1867; served on United States
steamer "Tacony." Was at Vera Cruz, Mexico, when General
Santa-Anna was taken; the "Tacony" convoying the steam-
ship "Virginia" which brought Santa-Anna to the north. Member Walter H. Newhall Post, No. 7, G. A. R. of Pennsylvania.

Issue:

236, James Henry, b. 27 March, 1869; d. 1 July, 1869.
237, Anna Drusilla, b. 27 May, 1870; d. 3 Dec., 1871.
238, Benjamin William, b. 30 Aug., 1872; m. 23 Oct., 1901,
Anna May Chester.
239, Harry Wilkinson, b. 19 July, 1874.
240, Ida Virginia, b. 16 Jan., 1877.
241, Chas. Augustus, b. 5 Nov., 1878; d. 27 Aug., 1879.
242, Florella May, b. 29 Dec., 1880.
241, Harvey Elmer, b. 15 July, 1891.

74. IDA VIRGINIA MENSING (John[1], William[2], Frances[3], Ann
C.[4]), dau. of Thomas H. and Ann C. (Duke) Mensing, b. 4
March, 1858; living at Philadelphia, Pa.; m. John Raynor, 19
March, 1879; b. 3 Nov., 1851; d. 25 Feb., 1901. He served as a
bugler in the United States cavalry, 1874. Issue:

SAMUEL GORDON SMYTH

MRS. MARY E. DUKE-SMYTH

242, John Shepherd, b. 29 Nov., 1879; 243, William Derrick, b. 13 Dec., 1882; 244, Wesley, b. 4 Nov., 1885, d. 4 June, 1887; 245, Ida Virginia, b. 21 Jan., 1889; 246, Naomi May, b. 12 March, 1891; 247, Eliza Viola, b. 14 April, 1893; 248, Thomas Henry, b. 3 July, 1895.

75. ELIZABETH MARIA MENSING (John[1], William[2], Frances[3], Ann C.[4]), dau. of Thomas H. and Ann C. (Duke) Mensing, b. 8 May, 1862; m. 1885, Samuel Laverty, b. 7 Feb., 1858.   Issue: 249, Ida Elizabeth, b. 27 Dec., 1885; 250, Ella Mary, b. 18 Feb., 1888; 251, John H., b. 25 June, 1890; 252, Samuel H., Jr., b. 18 June, 1892; 253, Benjamin W. Taylor, b. 14 Sept., 1895.

76. ELIZABETH FRANCES KINSEY (John[1], William[2], Francis[3], Elizabeth F.[4]), only child of Chas. W. and Elizabeth Francis (Duke) Kinsey, b. 10 May, 1865; d. Feb., 1900; m. 13 Sept., 1883, Charles Crumlie, of Philadelphia.   Issue: 254, Amanda Frances, b. 12 July, 1884; 255, a child, d. 1886; 256, Charles Wesley, b. Jan., 1887; 257, Eva Mary, b. 30 May, 1889; 258, Rebecca Ellen, b. 1890, d. 1894; 259, Albert Edward, b. 15 March, 1894.

78. MARY ELIZABETH DUKE (John[1], William[2], Francis[3], Francis K.[4]), second dau. of Francis K. and S. Louisa (Eldridge) Duke, b. 13 Jan., 1857, at Bridgeport, N. J.; living at West Conshohocken, Pa.; m. 24 July, 1879, at the parsonage of the Cold Spring Presbyterian Church, Cape May Co., N. J., by Rev. Thos. S. Dewing, to Samuel Gordon Smyth, eldest surviving son of Jonathan and Elizabeth (Ritchie) Smyth, formerly of Newtown, Bucks Co., Pa.; b. Pennsbury Manor, Falls Township, Bucks Co., Pa., 24 July, 1859. His ancestors, in the paternal line, were Scotch and English covenanters who, when the family were divided by religions differences, were forced to flee from their home on the Cumberlandshire border in England, to the lowlands of Scotland and from thence, later, to the north of Ireland, settling in Armoy, County Antrim, Province of Ulster, about 1650. From this place descendants of the Smyths scattered into other townlands of Ulster, still retaining their Puritan faith. Many emigrated to America at different periods where some of them served in the War of the Revolution. Jonathan Smyth came to America about 1840 and settled in Philadelphia where he m. Elizabeth Ritchie, daughter of John and Margaret (MacAlees) Ritchie, of Bridgeport, Montgomery Co., Pa. Jonathan Smyth was the eldest son of James and Martha (Grey) Smyth, of "The Mullans," Finvoy, County Antrim, Ireland, where he was b. 4 Sept., 1814. Elizabeth Ritchie's descent is derived from a Hanoverian soldier in William of Orange's army, who came into Ireland about 1688. The family name was originally Riché. Elizabeth was born in

Kilrea, Ireland, 11 July, 1831. Samuel G. Smyth was their
fourth child and was born on Penn's Manor, formerly the residence of William Penn, on the Delaware River, in Bucks Co., Pa.
Samuel received a common school education at Newtown, Pa.,
to which place his parents removed in 1866; on the death of his
father, in 1873, the boy left home to earn his own living. He
entered the marine service of the Philadelphia and Reading Coal
and Iron Co., first as cabin boy, and afterward became steward.
Leaving this service in 1877, owing to ill-health, he went to Cape
May, N. J., where he became apprenticed to J. H. Benezet Bro.,
heater and hardware merchants, and remained with them till
his marriage in 1879, when he removed to Philadelphia, and
after varied employment there, and in Washington, D. C., he
finally entered the commercial house of Moro Phillips, Esq., the
prominent chemical manufacturer, in 1881. From the position
of shipping clerk at that time he has risen to his present position
of secretary and treasurer of The Villa Nova Co., Limited—an
outgrowth of the Phillips interests—Real Estate Operators.
Politically, Mr. Smyth is an ardent Republican; has served in the
local Board of Health and in the Councils of the Borough of
West Conshohocken, Pa., for several terms and as president of
these bodies a part of the time. He is a ruling elder in the Presbyterian Church of Conshohocken, Pa., since 1894, and a member
of its Board of Trustees; chosen a commissioner to the Synod
of Pennsylvania, meeting at Bellefonte, Pa., 1896; a member of
the Historical Society of Pennsylvania, and also those of Bucks
and Montgomery Counties, Pa.; a past-master and trustee of
Fritz Lodge, No. 420, F. & A. M. of Conshohocken; a past-grand
of Philadelphia-National Lodge, No. 223, I. O. O. F. of Philadelphia; a member and one of the organizers of George Clay
Fire Co. of West Conshohocken, Pa., and a Delegate to the
Republican State Convention which met in Harrisburg, Pa., 1904.
He is a prolific writer and has contributed many historical papers
—from original research—to magazines and other publications.
Resides at "Rylmont," West Conshohocken, Pa. (see Cyclopædia
and Biography of Montgomery Co., Pa.).   Issue:
   260, Francis Alison, b. Philadelphia, Pa., 7 June, 1880; 261,
      Marion May, b. Philadelphia, Pa., 16 May, 1885; 262,
      Samuel Gordon, Jr., b. Philadelphia, Pa., 21 Nov., 1891.

   79. JOHN FRANCIS DUKE (John[1], William[2], Francis[3], Francis
K.[4]), only son of Francis K. and S. Louisa Eldredge) Duke, b.
at Philadelphia, 22 Aug., 1861, living in Atlantic City, N. J., com-
positor; m. 24 July, 1881, at Cape May, N. J., Kate Godwin, of
Philadelphia; b. in Kentucky, 1861; d. in Atlantic City, N. J., 24
Nov., 1905.   Issue:
   263, Earle Francis, b. 12 Dec., 1882; d. 8 Feb., 1888; 264,
      Louis, b. 2 July, 1886; living in Atlantic City, N. J.

88. WILLIAM LORRAIN DUKE (John[1], William[2], John[3], James F.[4]), youngest son of James Francis and Sophia (Martin) Duke, b. Harper's Ferry, Va., 27 April, 1845; living in Wilmington, N. C.; *m.* 9 Oct., 1871, Emma J. Vann. He entered the Confederate service early in the spring of 1862, having run away from home to enlist; private in Company B, 13th Battalion Light Artillery, C. S. A., until 15 July, 1865, when his command surrendered with Johnson's army to General Sherman, near High Point, N. C. He returned to Tallahassie, Ala., where his family then lived and afterward removed to Richmond, Va., in 1868 again removing to Wilmington, N. C. Mr. Duke has a responsible position with the Atlantic Coast Line Railway Co., in which service he has continued since 1868.   Issue:
    265, Alice E., b. 1 July, 1873, d. 7 Dec., 1878; 266, Minnie L., b. 12 Jan., 1875, d. 1 June, 1877; 267, George F., b. 22 Feb., 1878; 268, Willie T., b. 15 Jan., 1881, d. 25 Oct., 1883; 269, Lillie L., b. 25 Dec., 1885; 270, Mary Stewart, b. 24 July, 1895.

91. JOHN DUKE MCFADEN (John[1], William[2], John[3], Mary Ann[4]), son of Rev. Joseph A. McFaden and Mary Ann (Duke) McFaden, b. 19 Oct., 1851, at Concord, Franklin Co., Pa.; *m.* 31 Dec., 1879, at Willow Grove, Kent Co., Md., Lucinda Dill. Rev. John D. McFaden was born and reared at Harper's Ferry, and at the age of nineteen years was converted and joined the Methodist Protestant Church and thenceforth determined to devote his life to the ministry. He was prepared for his future work in the private school of Joseph Barry at "the Ferry" and after successfully completing his studies was ordained and has since filled acceptably some prominent pulpits, with great credit, and has drawn many hundred of persons to the service of Christ. He has also organized churches at several places. His charges have been Hagerstown, Md., Berlin and Philadelphia, Pa., and in the city of Chicago. For the last ten years he has labored at Carlton, Neb. He also studied medicine and practices that profession in connection with his pastoral work. In addition to practice in these professions he is an expert phrenologist, and was a demonstrator and lecturer of this science while living in Philadelphia, being a graduate of the American Institute of Phrenology and a member of the New York Academy of Anthropology. Dr. McFaden has considerable ability as a lecturer and his filled many engagements in the chief cities of the country. In 1893 he was elected by the National Conference to represent them in the Parliament of Religion held at Chicago. He addressed that body and when Rand, McNally and Company compiled a collection of select addresses made before the Parliament, Dr. McFaden's was one of those chosen. His own publication, "Our Bible, Our Church and Our Country," his exceeded a cir-

culation of 500,000 copies. "The Story of Jesus" also has had extensive circulation. Dr. McFaden has established a sanitarium at Concordia, Kan., and it is said that he has the largest percentage of cures on record in the west. These various activities reflect the wonderful energy and resourcefulness that Dr. McFaden it putting forth in behalf of mankind. He resides at Carlton, Neb. Issue:

271, Alexander Duke, b. 4 Oct., 1880, at Baltimore, Md.; 272, Mary Emma, b. 16 Sept., 1883, at Willow Grove, Kent Co., Md.; 273, Shirley, b. 23 Sept., 1892, at Berlin, Pa.

93. GEORGE HENRY MCFADEN (John[1], William[2], John[3], Mary Ann[4]), second son of Rev. Joseph A. and Mary A. (Duke) McFaden, b. 14 Jan., 1857, in Dorchester Co., Md.; m. at Bay View, Norfolk Co., Va., 19 Sept., 1888, Lillian McWhorter, of Norfolk, Va. Like his brother, George H. McFaden chose the ministry for his profession. He became a member of the Virginia Conference of the Methodist Episcopal Church South, in 1886. His first charge was at Oaklette and Bethel in Norfolk Co., Va., and then labored in Prince Edward Co., Va. After two years' service in this field he was assigned to the Cartersville circuit and did effective work in the ministry there. From Cartersville he went to Matthews Co., Va.; twice, to the great satisfaction of the people of his charge, he was returned to them. His next assignment was at Gloucester Point; from thence he was transferred to Hanover, then to Manchester, Crewe, and, later, to the Wright Memorial Church at Portsmouth, Va. At the latter place his labor met with marked success. The Sabbath School connected with this church is one of the largest in the South, numbering about 500 scholars and the Pastor's Bible class having a membership of 65. The church and school have both rapidly developed in membership and usefulness under Rev. McFaden's pastorate. A cotemporary journal thus characterizes him: "As a preacher, he is sound, impressive and at times truly eloquent. His manner of speaking is rapid and marked by earnestness which inspires a strong belief in his sincerity and deep conviction." Since 1906 Rev. George H. McFaden has been called to Richmond and is doing a good work in building up a congregation in the newer residential district in the vicinity of the Washington monument in the western part of the city. Issue:

274, William Alexander, b. Bay View, Norfolk Co., Va., 11 May, 1891.

275, George Henry, b. Norfolk Co., Va., 18 Sept., 1900; d. 25 Sept., 1900.

94. LUCINDA SHIRLEY MCFADEN (John[1], William[2], John[3], Mary A.[4]), dau. of Rev. Joseph A. and Mary A. (Duke) McFaden, b. 14 May, 1859; d. at Harper's Ferry, Va., 13 Aug., 1902; m. 6 Jan., 1892, at Harper's Ferry, W. Va., Daniel H.

REV. FRANK T. McFADEN, D.D.

Nichols, son of Lewis and Elizabeth Nichols, of Charlestown, Jefferson Co., W. Va. He is a contractor and builder and resides at Harper's Ferry, and was deputy sheriff of Jefferson County 1901–1904.   Issue:
   276, Lewis, b. 2 Jan., 1893; 277, Daniel Shirley, b. 25 Dec., 1895; 278, Frances Minge, b. 21 April, 1897; 279, Joseph McFaden, b. 19 June, 1899.

   96. FRANK TALBOT McFADEN (John[1], William[2], John[3], Mary A.[4]), youngest son of Rev. Joseph A. and Mary Ann (Duke) McFaden, b. 5 Feb., 1864; m. 10 April, 1890, Mary Minge Friend, dau. of Charles Friend, Esq., of Petersburg, Va., and Mary (Atkinson) Minge, and is a descendant of John Minge, of "Weyanoke," Charles City Co., Va., who m. Sarah, dau. of Benjamin Harrison of "Berkeley." She is also related to the Pages, Nelsons, Lightfoots, Carys and other old Virginia families; a sister of Rev. Charles Friend, of Buchanan, Va.; Jennie, wife of Rev. P. D. Stephenson, of Woodstock, Va.; Nathalie, wife of Rev. James Smith, of Fredericksburg, Va., and of Bessie, wife of Professor Willis Bocock, of Athens, Ga.; and is also a kinswoman of Robert A. Mayo, of "Powhattan's Seat," Richmond, Right Rev. Thomas Atkinson, of North Carolina, and Rev. Dr. J. P. M. Atkinson, who for twenty-five years was president of Hampden-Sidney College in Virginia.
   Rev. Frank T. McFaden was born at Salisbury, Md., graduate A.B. and B.Litt., Hampden-Sidney College, class 1886; Union Theological Seminary, B.D., 1889; trustee Hampden-Sidney College, 1894; pastor of the Presbyterian Church at Marion, Va., 1889–1896, and from the latter date to 1903 of the First Presbyterian Church of Lynchburg, Va., and since 1903 he has been the efficient minister of the old First Presbyterian Church of Richmond, Va. He was commissioner to General Assembly at Nashville, Tenn., 1894, and at Atlanta, Ga., 1901; is the Grand Regent of the Grand Camp, Royal Arcanum of Virginia, and Grand Commander of the Grand Camp, Knights Templar. The degree of D.D. was conferred upon him by Washington and Lee University in June, 1902.   Issue:
   280, Mary, b. 15 May, 1891; 281, Natalie Friend, b. 1 Jan., 1895; 282, Frances Talbot, b. 29 April, 1899; 283, Frank Talbot, Jr., b. 17 Sept., 1901.

   97. IRENE DASHIEL McFADEN (John[1], William[2], John[3], Mary A.[4]), youngest dau. of Rev. Joseph A. and Mary A. (Duke) McFaden, b. 2 Nov., 1872; living at Cumberland, Md.; m. 27 June, 1900, J. E. Wilmer Benjamin, of Harper's Ferry.   Issue:
   284, Joseph Wilmer, b. 11 Oct., 1902.

   99. KATE (CATHARINE) DUKE (John[1], William[2], Robert[3], Francis W.[4]), second dau. of Francis W. and Lydia (Thompson)

Duke, b. Bloomington, Ill., 17 Sept., 1857; d. Bloomington, Ill., 1906; m. 11 Sept., 1878, Robert Murray, of Leroy, Ill.; d. 1898.
Issue;
285, Edna, d. young; 286, Charles B., living at St. Paul, Minn.; 287, Frank R., living at Spokane, Wash.; 288, Madge, living at Bloomington, Ill.; 289, a dau., m. Walter Brand.

101. GEORGE MOHLER DUKE (John[1], William[2], Robert[3], Robert N.[4]), son of Robert N. and Ann N. (Mohler) Duke, b. 15 July, 1864; d. Nov., 1904; m. 3 Oct., 1880, Frances E. Chiswell, of Maryland; d. Washington, D. C., 1906.
Issue:
290, Joseph Chiswell, b. 31 July, 1885; 291, George Francis, b. 11 Jan., 1889, d. 21 Aug., 1889; 292, Raymond White, b. 12 Aug., 1890.

102. ROBERT MOORE DUKE (John[1], William[2], Robert[3], Robert N.[4]), son of Robert N. and Ann N. (Mohler) Duke, b. 10 Feb., 1850; m. 9 Feb., 1875, Mary Hester McGary, of Baltimore, Md.
Issue:
293, Walter McGary, b. 28 Oct., 1875, m. Aug., 1907, Florence E. Jacques; 294, Ann Newton, b. 12 Sept., 1877; d. 21 July, 1879; 295, John William, b. 26 May, 1879; 296, Robert M., Jr., b. 2 Nov., 1881; 297, Ann Alena, b. 26 March, 1886, d. 21 March, 1887; 298, Leslie Daniel, b. 29 March, 1889.

103. ANN FRANCES DUKE (John[1], William[2], Robert[3], Robert N.[4]), dau. of Robert N. and Ann N. (Mohler) Duke, b. 24 Dec., 1851; d. Aug. 1887; m. 27 Oct., 1887, Joseph T. White. Issue:
299, Aldah, b. 1888; 300, Sallie, b. 1892.

104. SARAH GRIFFITH DUKE (John[1], William[2], Robert[3], Robert N.[4]), dau. of Robert N. and Ann N. (Mohler) Duke, b. 27 April, 1853; d. 13 March, 1880; m. 17 Feb., 1880, John H. Engle, son of John Engle, Sr., of "Rattling Springs," and half-brother of James W. and Captain Jacob Engle, of Engle's Station, on the B. & O. R. R., Jefferson Co., Va. John H. Engle served in the Confederate army for a short time, 12th Virginia Cavalry, but being in ill health returned home and resumed farming. No issue.

108. JAMES MELVIN ENGLE (John[1], William[2], Robert[3], Ann M.[4]), son of James W. and Ann Margaret (Duke) Engle, b. at Harper's Ferry, Va., 29 Nov., 1853; living in Washington, D. C.; m. 20 Dec., 1886, Lavinia Hawke, dau. of John S. Hawke, atty.-at-law, Washington, D. C., formerly of Springfield, O. Mr. Engle is a registrar in the Sixth Auditor's Office, Treasury Department, and was appointed immediately after the adoption of the Civil Service Rule law, 23 July, 1883. Issue:
301, Claude, b. 1887; 302, Lavinia, b. 1889; 303, Rilla, b. 1891;

DESCENDANTS OF WILLIAM DUKE

304, Melvin, b. 1893; 305, Elizabeth, b. 1894; 306, Parke, b. 1896.

109. JESSIE ALLNUT ENGLE (John[1], William[2], Robert[3], Ann M.[4]), son of James M. and Ann M. (Duke) Engle, b. 31 Oct., 1855; *m.* 1875, Mary L. Mohler. He was county superintendent of public schools, 1896, re-elected 1904. Issue:
307, Carroll Anderson; 308, Carrie; 309, Forrest.

110. WILLIARD FLETCHER ENGLE (John[1], William[2], Robert[3], Ann M.[4]), son of James M. and Ann M. (Duke) Engle, b. 22 Sept., 1857; *m.* Jennie Royston, of Ohio, 1874. Issue:
310, Ethel; 311, William; 312, Omer.

113. AMMISHADIE MOORE ENGLE (John[1], William[2], Robert[3], Ann M.[4]), son of James M. and Ann M. (Duke) Engle, b. 1 June, 1865; living at Berkeley Springs, W. Va.; *m.* 1890, Maggie Mohler, dau. of William Mohler. Rev. A. M. Engle is pastor of the Presbyterian Church at Berkeley Springs, W. Va. Issue:
313, Margaret; 314, James Watt; 315, Elizabeth.

114. CARLTON DUKE ENGLE (John[1], William[2], Robert[3], Ann M.[4]), son of James M. and Ann M. (Duke) Engle, b. 8 June, 1868; living in Baltimore, Md.; *m.* 1893, Bertie Shader. Issue:
316, a child.

117. ANNA MOORE TOWN (John[1], William[2], Robert[3], Mary E.[4]), eldest dau. of Rev. Levi and Mary Ellen (Duke) Town, b. at Conneaut, O., 4 March, 1855; living at Berwyn, Pa.; *m.* 20 June, 1876, Theodore F. Van Meter, b. Woodstown, N. J., 27 Sept., 1844, son of John Van Meter, of Salem, N. J. Mrs. Van Meter is actively interested in the work of the Baptist Church and is president of the Ladies' Aid Society of the Church at Newtown Square, Delaware Co., Pa. Issue:
317, Anna A., b. at Pittsgrove, N. J., 6 April, 1877, d. 23 July, 1877; 318, Theodore L., b. at Pittsgrove, N. J., 21 June, 1878; 319, Florence, b. at Pittsgrove, N. J., 24 July, 1880; 320, Howard, b. at Camden, N. J., 25 May, 1884; 321, Mary E., b. at Camden, N. J., 18 Dec., 1885; 322, Warren R., b. at Newtown Square, Pa., 29 Oct., 1893.

119. SAMUEL FRANCIS D. TOWN (John[1], William[2], Robert[3], Mary E.[4]), son of Rev. Levi and Mary Ellen (Duke) Town, b. Centre Road, Pa., 10 Nov., 1861; living at Germantown, Philadelphia; *m.* 27 June, 1889, Clara Louisa, dau. of Dr. Camm, of Philadelphia. Issue:
323, Norman Wesley, b. 23 Sept., 1890; 324, Robert Frank, b. 30 May, 1893; 325, Ethel Camm, b. 5 Dec., 1894; 326, Mary Louise, b. 14 June, 1899.

120. REV. ROBERT DUKE TOWN (John[1], William[2], Robert[3], Mary E.[4]), son of Rev. Levi and Mary Ellen (Duke) Town, b.

Warren, O., 4 Jan., 1866; *m.* 28 June, 1888, Maude A. Barack-man. The personal history of Robert D. Town, writer, author, lecturer and humorist, is best told in his own words as appear in the Town Genealogy:

"I moved around pretty lively with my parents the first few years of my life, either going wherever they went or they going wherever I went, in this way I lived in quite a number of states before I was really able to decide which was best suited to my purposes, but finally located in West Virginia, on a plantation of 500 acres when I was four or five years old. With the assistance of an uncle and quite a number of hands who did the heavy work I carried on this farm for a few years, then went to Baltimore and served as a clerk in a grocery store, then in a laundry establishment, then painted bedsteads in a furniture factory, made trunks; afterwards ran a flouring mill, entered the University of Pennsylvania and assisted the Medical faculty in their department. Graduated from a Divinity School and got married. I then became an editor, and have been a plain newspaper man ever since. As I look back over my life, I can see how my diverse employments have all been beneficial. The farm brought me industry. In the furniture factory I learned to appre-ciate beauty in painting, in the laundry I learned the value of cleanliness and neatness of dress, in fact, I can now see that everything I know has been learned as I went along. Doubtless if I had more time I might have acquired more knowledge. All in all, I have a very interesting life. It is even more interesting to look back upon than it was at the time."

Editor "Judge," New York, 1906, elected vice-president of the "Humorist's Association," June 7, 1906.　　　　Issue:
　　327, Wendell Phillips Duke, b. 24 March, 1889; 328, Marion
　　　　Etta, b. 2 Oct., 1890; 329, Bertha Violet, b. 7 May, 1896.

125. FRANCIS JONES (John[1], William[2], Nancy[3], Elizabeth[4]), son of Joseph B. and Elizabeth (Clymer) Jones, b. 12 March, 1842; living at Uvilla, Jefferson Co., W. Va.; *m.* 10 March, 1868, Mary Alexander Link, dau. of Adam and Sarah (Hendricks) Link, of Bakerton, W. Va. Francis Jones enlisted in the Con-federate army, became captain in the First Virginia Cavalry, serving under Colonel William Morgan in General J. E. B. Stuart's Division; was assigned to special duty on the staff of General Stuart. Mrs. Jones d. April, 1909.　　　　Issue:
　　330, Sarah Elizabeth, b. 12 Nov., 1869; 331, Elmer Taylor, b.
　　　　20 June, 1873, d. 15 April, 1875; 332, Adam Francis, b.
　　　　20 Aug., 1875; 333, Robert Luther, b. 24 Oct., 1877; *m.*
　　　　Helen Blackford; 334, Ernest Drawbaugh, b. 23 April,
　　　　1880; 335, Joseph Carlton, b. 2 May, 1882; 336, Jessie
　　　　Allen, b. 19 Jan., 1884, d. 2 Oct., 1901; 337, William
　　　　Morgan, b. 16 Dec., 1891.

127. GEORGE W. JONES (John[1], William[2], Nancy[3], Elizabeth[4]), son of Joseph B. and Elizabeth (Clymer) Jones, b. 25 June, 1846; *m.* 1874, Ann Nichols.　　　　Issue:
　　338, Joseph; 339, Eliner; 340, Maggie Link, b. June, 1875;
　　　　341, Lillian Bell, b. 1869, d. 30 June, 1870.

129. THOMAS HAMMOND JONES (John[1], William[2], Nancy[3], Elizabeth[4]), son of Joseph B. and Elizabeth (Clymer) Jones, b. 26 Oct., 1851, liveryman at Harper's Ferry, W. Va.; m. 26 March 1873, Sarah Fanny, dau. of Thomas S. and Mary E. (Daily) Rockenbaugh.   Issue:
  342, Joseph M., b. 31 Dec., 1874; m. Jessie, dau. of Albert
      Benton, of Bolivar Heights, Harper's Ferry, W. Va.
      She d. Feb., 1909.
  343, Charles N., b. 10 Aug., 1876; 344, Colby E., b. 19 June,
      1880; 345, Robert Ashton, b. 15 Sept., 1881; 346, Pres-
      ton, b. 18 Sept., 1888, d. 7 Aug., 1889; 347, Layne, b. 22
      May, 1892.

130. SUSANNAH REBECCA JONES (John[1], William[2], Nancy[3], Elizabeth[4]), dau. of Joseph B. and Elizabeth Clymer Jones, b. 26 Oct., 1852; m. Daniel Taylor Morrison; living at Charlestown, W. Va.   Issue:
  348, Lily, b. circa 1874; 349, Edna Browne, b. circa 1876; 350,
      William Earl, b. circa 1879; 351, Elizabeth, b. circa 1883;
      d. young.

133. NANCY CLYMER JONES (John[1], William[2], Nancy[3], Elizabeth[4]), dau. of Joseph B. and Elizabeth (Clymer) Jones, b. 15 April, 1857; living at Bakerton, W. Va.; m. her cousin, Daniel Hendricks Nichols, 9 June, 1880; he d. 31 March, 1895, aged 42 years.   Issue:
  352, Anne Pearl, b. 26 Aug., 1881; m. 14 Dec., 1905, Henry
      Acher, of Baltimore.
  353, Mattie Florence, b. 24 Oct., 1884; 354, Robert Magruder,
      b. 16 Oct., 1886.

137. JOHN WILLIAM CLYMER (John[1], William[2], Nancy[3], Isaac[4]), son of Isaac, Jr., and Lottie (Given) Clymer, b. 1861; m. —— ——.   Issue:
  355, Hazel Bergen, b. 19 May, 1893; 356, Nellie Virginia; 357,
      William Roland.

141. ELLA LEE CLYMER (John[1], William[2], Nancy[3], Isaac, Jr.[4]), dau. of Isaac, Jr., and Lottie (Given) Clymer, b. 1869; m. Frank Ronemous.   Issue:
  358, Elmer Clymer; 359, Frank Davis; 360, Edna.

143. MARY WESTON CLYMER (John[1], William[2], Nancy[3], John M.[4]), dau. of John M. and Ella H. (Given) Clymer; m. 28 Oct., 1884, at Keyser, Va., Rev. F. W. T. Pitman, pastor of Pooles-ville Presbyterian Church in Washington Co., Md., 1896.   Issue:
  361, Ella Minetta, b. 22 Jan., 1888; 362, Mary Latimer, b. 2
      Sept., 1890; 363, John Matthews, b. 21 July, 1893; 364,
      Lawrence, b. 28 Nov., 1895.

144. FRANK LEE CLYMER (John[1], William[2], Nancy[3], John M.[4]), son of John M. and Ella H. (Given) Clymer; m. at

Keyser, Va., 18 Aug., 1897, Elizabeth Buckalough. Mr. Clymer is a physician living at Midlothian, Alleghany Co., Md.   Issue: 365, Frank Lee Clymer, Jr., b. 15 May, 1902.

147. WILLIAM BRANTNER (John[1], William[2], Margaret[3], Daniel[4], Blanche[5]), son of George W. and Blanche (Hendricks) Brantner; m. Mary Maddox; living at Shenandoah Junction, W. Va. Issue: 366, 367, 368, 369.

165. THOMAS J. LINK (John[1], William[2], Margaret[3], Daniel[4], Sarah[5]), son of Adam and Sarah T. (Hendricks) Link, b. 13 Sept., 1844; m. 6 Nov., 1878, Jennie H. Maddox; living at Shepherdstown, W. Va.   Issue:
370, Talzie J., b. 17 June, 1879, d. 17 May, 1880(?); 371, William Boyd, b. 6 Sept., 1880; 372, Mamie Esther, b. 19 Aug., 1885.

191. NEWTON MADISON HENDRICKS (John[1], William[2], Margaret[3], Daniel[4], Daniel W.[5]), son of Daniel W. and Sarah M. (Link) Hendricks, b. 17 May, 1862; m. 1st Miss Mohler; 2d Miss Warfield.   He is a physician.   Issue:
373, Mabel; 374, Arnold; 375, Lister; 376, Margaret.

192. ANNIE L. HENDRICKS (John[1], William[2], Margaret[3], James[4], Daniel W.[5]), dau. of Daniel W. and Sarah M. (Link) Hendricks, b. 12 June, 1866; m. W. M. Dick.

193. HARVEY HENDRICKS (John[1], William[2], Margaret[3], James[4], Daniel W.[5]), son of Daniel W. and Sarah M. (Link) Hendricks, b. 2 March, 1869; m. Minnie Brantner.   Issue:
377, Garland; 378, Marge; 379, Elizabeth.

194. JAMES ALLEN HENDRICKS (John[1], William[2], Margaret[3], James[4], Daniel W.[5]), son of Daniel W. and Sarah M. (Link) Hendricks, b. 25 Dec., 1871; m. Lou Lemon.   Issue: 380, Allen.

195. ESTHER HENDRICKS (John[1], William[2], Margaret[3], James[4], Daniel W.[5]), dau. of Daniel W. and Sarah M. (Link) Hendricks, b. 6 April, 1874; m. Jesse Engle.

196. LEROY HENDRICKS (John[1], William[2], Margaret[3], James[4], Daniel W.[5]), son of Daniel W. and Sarah M. (Link) Hendricks, b. 17 July, 1876; m. Miss Moore.   Issue: 381, Cora.

197. DANIEL W. HENDRICKS, JR. (John[1], William[2], Margaret[3], James[4], Daniel W.[5]), son of Daniel W. and Sarah M. (Link) Hendricks, b. 24 Dec., 1877; m. Sallie Link.   Issue: 382, Gilbert; 383, Mary.

221. THOMAS WILLIAM MENSING (John[1], William[2], Francis[3], Ann C.[4], Thos. H., Jr.[5]), son of Thomas H. Mensing, Jr., and

Elizabeth (Coleman) Mensing, b. 10 Oct., 1870; *m.* 14 Aug., 1895, Ellen E. Rollinson, dau. of Joseph and Maria Rollinson, of Philadelphia, Pa.   Issue:
384, Walter Williard, b. 17 May, 1896; 385, Clarissa, b. 8 Aug., 1899, d. 21 Aug., 1899; 386, a child, b. and d. 28 Sept., 1900; 387, Mabel, b. 27 April, 1902, d. 4 May, 1902.

222. ELIZABETH CLARA MENSING (John[1], William[2], Francis[3], Ann C.[4], Thos. H., Jr.[5]), dau. of Thomas H. and Elizabeth (Coleman) Mensing, b. 15 July, 1872; *m.* 27 Nov., 1895, Benjamin Franklin Cook, son of Moses F. and Kate Cook, of Wissonoming, Philadelphia, Pa.   Issue:
388, Abraham, b. 11 Nov., 1896; 389, Clarissa Markley, b. 22 Sept., 1899; 390, Laura, b. 12 March, 1902; 390*a,* Charlotte Florence, b. 1 June, 1908; 390*b,* Elizabeth M., b. 1 June, 1908. Nos. 390*a* and 390*b* are twins.

224. GERTRUDE VIOLA MENSING (John[1], William[2], Francis[3], Ann C.[4], Thos. H., Jr.[5]), dau. of Thomas H., Jr., and Elizabeth (Coleman) Mensing, b. 21 June, 1877; *m.* 20 April, 1897, Walter Duffield Williard, son of David D. and Ellen Smith Williard, the latter the dau. of Martin Smith, of Doylestown, Bucks, Co., Pa.
Issue:
391, Gertrude Viola, b. 12 June, 1898.

226. LAURA MAY MENSING (John[1], William[2], Francis[3], Ann C.[4], Thos. H., Jr.[5]), dau. of Thomas H., Jr., and Elizabeth (Coleman) Mensing, b. 8 March, 1882; *m.* 2 May, 1892, Louis Ferdinand Schaefer, b. Germany, 18 Feb., 1882; son of Ferdinand and Elizabeth Hackerth Schaefer.   Issue:
392, Ferdinand and Thomas, b. 7 Jan., 1903.

231. FRANCIS CHARLES ARMSTRONG (John[1], William[2], Francis[3], Ann C.[4], Pauline[5]), son of William J. and Pauline (Mensing) Armstrong, b. 27 April, 1875; *m.* May Viola Wolf.   Issue:
393, Frank, b. 16 May, 1906.

232. JAMES GIVEN ARMSTRONG (John[1], William[2], Francis[3], Ann C.[4], Pauline[5]), son of William J. and Pauline (Mensing) Armstrong, b. 3 Feb., 1877; *m.* 3 Feb., 1893, Mary Edmunds.
Issue:
394, Frank Leroy E.; 395, Walter Williard; 396, Anna C., b. 10 Oct., 1905.

240. IDA VIRGINIA TAYLOR (John[1], William[2], Francis[3], Ann C.[4], Anna F.[5]), dau. of Benj. and Anna F. (Mensing) Taylor, b. 16 Jan., 1877; *m.* 29 Nov., 1895, Samuel Carless, b. 1 May, 1874, in Staffordshire, England.   Issue:
397, Drusilla May, b. 22 Jan., 1902.

249. IDA ELIZABETH LAVERTY (John[1], William[2], Francis[3], Ann C.[4], Elizabeth M.[5]), dau. of Samuel and Elizabeth M. (Mensing)

Laverty, b. 27 Dec., 1885; *m.* August Pfeiffer.   Issue:
398, Gertrude V., b. 8 Sept., 1904; 399, Wm. Edward, b. 20
Feb., 1905.

260. FRANCIS ALISON SMYTH (John[1], William[2], Francis[3],
Francis K.[4], Mary E.[5]), son of Samuel Gordon and Mary E.
(Duke) Smyth, b. Haddington, Philadelphia, 7 June, 1880; *m.*
3 July, 1899, at Cape May, N. J., Florence May, dau. of Abraham and Emma S. Cavanaugh, of Conshohocken, Pa., No issue.
F. A. Smyth is a graduate of the Conshohocken High School, and
entered State College at Bellefonte, Pa., but during the progress
of the Spanish-American War he left college and enlisted, 12
Aug., 1898, as a private in the United States Army; was sent
to Fort St. Phillip, La., and assigned to duty in Company D,
1st Regiment, United States Heavy Artillery; some months later
was transferred to the infantry arm of the service at Newnam,
Ga., and from there proceeded with his regiment to join the
army of occupation in Cuba, during the armistice. While stationed in the Province of Puerto-Principe was attacked with
fever and invalided home. Through the personal interest of
General Merritt, he was permitted to return home, under furlough, to convalesce. As his disability continued, he was honorably discharged from the service. Upon recovering his health
he re-enlisted in the army, doing duty in the Philippines, in
Hawaii, and was in San Francisco when the earthquake destroyed
that city; here he performed special service in connection with
the restoration of order and provisioning the destitute. Was
promoted to be corporal in the Marine Service; his malady, re-
appearing, however, after a few months' service, and not yielding to treatment he was finally honorably discharged the service
for continued disability. Now resides in Manitoba, Canada.

264. LOUIS DUKE (John[1], William[2], Francis[3], Francis K.[4],
John F.[5]), son of John F. and Kate (Godwin) Duke, b. Cape
May, N. J., 2 July, 1886; *m.* 1906, at Atlantic City, N. J., Mamie
Llewellyn of that city.   Issue:
399½, Violet Catharine, b. Atlantic City, 10 July, 1909.

267. GEORGE F. DUKE (John[1], William[2], John[3], James[4], William L.[5]), son of William L. and Emma J. (Vann) Duke, b.
Wilmington, N. C., 22 Feb., 1878; *m.* 30 Nov., 1898, Lee Yapp.
He enlisted for service in the Spanish-American War, 27 April,
1898; served in Company K, 2d North Carolina Regiment, at
Brunswick, Ga., where the regiment lay camped on waiting orders
until mustered out, 18 Nov., 1898.   Issue:
400, Thelma F.; 401, Evelyn E.; 402, a son, b. 1 Feb., 1904.

269. LILLIE L. DUKE (John[1], William[2], John[3], James[4], William L.[5]), dau. of Wm. L. and Emma J. (Vann) Duke, b. 25

Dec., 1885; *m.* 26 July, 1904, William W. Christian; living at Wilmington, N. C.   Issue:
403, Emily, b. 1905; d. 1907.

318. THEODORE L. VAN METER (John[1], William[2], Robert[3], Mary E.[4], Anna M.[5]), son of Theodore F. and Anna M. (Town) Van Meter, b. 21 June, 1878; living at Berwyn, Pa.; *m.* 26 Nov., 1901, Anna C. Bradford, of Newtown Square, Pa.   Issue:
404, a child, b. and d. 1902; 405, Anna E., b. Feb., 1904; 405a, Florence, b. 23 March, 1906.

319. FLORENCE VAN METER (John[1], William[2], Robert[3], Mary E.[4], Anna M.[5]), dau. of Theodore F. and Anna M. (Town) Van Meter, b. 24 July, 1880; *m.* 25 Oct., 1905, E. P. S. Spooner. Their dau. Florence was b. 21 Sept., 1907.

322. ADAM FRANCIS JONES (John[1], William[2], Nancy[3], Elizabeth[4], Francis[5]), son of Francis and Mary A. (Link) Jones, b. 20 Aug., 1875; *m.* 1903, Alice Lemon, of Shepherdstown, W. Va., his cousin.   Issue:
406, a child, b. 1904.

345. ROBERT ASHTON JONES (John[1], William[2], Nancy[3], Elizabeth[4], Thos. H.[5]), son of Thomas H. and Sally Fanny (Rodenbaugh) Jones, b. 15 Sept., 1881; *m.* 20 April, 1905, Victor Peach Cassell, b. 29 May, 1890.

ADDENDA

250. ELLA MAY LAFERTY (John[1], William[2], Francis[3], Ann C.[4], Elizabeth M.[5]), dau. of Samuel and Elizabeth Marie (Mensing) Laferty, b. 18 Feb., 1888; *m.* James Deering, who was b. 24 March, 1876.   Issue:
a, James M., b. 6 April, 1906; b, Drusilla M., b. 10 March, 1909.

251. JOHN LAFERTY, enlisted in the United States Naval Service; was assigned to duty on U. S. S. "Tennessee," which acted as one of the scout ships to the world-encircling fleet, and returned to Hampton Roads, 22 Feb., 1909.

252. SAMUEL H. LAFERTY also enlisted in the United States Navy in Aug., 1907; was assigned to duty on U. S. S. "Missouri," and made the tour with the fleet, which returned on 22 Feb., 1909, and was reviewed by President Roosevelt, at Hampton Roads, Virginia.

242. JOHN SHEPHERD RAYNOR (John[1], William[2], Francis[3], Ann C.[4], Ida V.[5]), son of John and Ida V. (Mensing) Raynor, b. 29 Nov., 1879; *m.* in New York, 19 May, 1906, Irene Hartman, b. 25 April, 1887.
a, a child, b. and d. 6 Sept., 1907; b, John Shepherd, Jr., b. 28 Jan., 1909.

321. MARY E. VAN METRE (John[1], William[2], Robert[3], Mary E.[4], Anna M.[5]), dau. of Theodore F. and Anna M. (Town) Van Metre, b. 18 Dec., 1885; *m.* James Brooke.   Issue: *a,* Elizabeth, b. 24 Sept., 1906.

343. CHARLES NEAL JONES (John[1], William[2], Nancy[3], Elizabeth[4], Thomas H.[5]), son of Thomas H. and S. Fanny (Rodenbaugh) Jones, b. Harper's Ferry, W. Va., 10 Aug., 1876; *m.* 1901, Bertha, dau. of David Beck, of Harper's Ferry.   Issue: *a,* Leslie, b. 1901; *b,* Paul, b. Jan., 1904.

349. EDNA BROWNE MORRISON (John[1], William[2], Nancy[3], Elizabeth[4], Susannah R.[5]), dau. of Daniel T. and Susannah R. (Jones) Morrison, b. *circa* 1876; *m.* a Victor Harder, of Charlestown, W. Va.   Issue: *a,* Ralph Keith, b. *circa* 1896; *b,* a son, b. *circa* 1903.

DESCENDANTS OF FRANCIS DUKE

III. FRANCIS DUKE, second son of John and Margaret Duke, born (sup.) in Ireland, 11 Feb., 1751; was killed by the Indians, 1 Sept., 1777, in an heroic attempt to relieve the beseiged garrison at Fort Henry (Wheeling), Ohio Co., Va.; *m. circa* 1773, Sarah, third dau. of Col. David Shepherd and his wife Rachael Teague. After the death of Francis Duke his widow *m.* 2d Levi H. Springer, by whom she had issue: Sarah, Hannah, Elizabeth, Lydia, Rachael, David, Dennis and Job Springer. Sarah Shepherd was born at Shepherdstown, Va., *circa* 1758/60; *m.* Levi Springer, 1780, at Uniontown; died there 25 Oct., 1832. Levi H. Springer was a resident of Uniontown, Fayette Co., Pa. Sept. 3, 1796, he purchased of Jacob Beeson a tract of ground adjoining Uniontown, being part of "Coal Run Tract," afterward known as Mt. Vernon. This property now belongs to his descendants. His father came from New Jersey and settled on the "Apple Pye Ridge," on land surveyed by George Washington for Lord Fairfax. Here Levi H. Springer first married and after two of his children were born, Levi moved to Fayette Co., about 1773 (see History of Fayette Co., Pa.). His first wife was Ann Gaddis whom he *m.* 1768; she d. 1778. He was b. 4 May, 1744; d. 26 March, 1823. Issue by his first wife, Ann, were: Drusilla, Abner, Ruth, Annie, William, Zadoc and Levi H., Jr. The latter *m.* the widow Catharine Todd in 1828. Issue of Francis and Sarah Shepherd Duke:

    1, John Duke, b. Ohio Co., Va., 24 June, 1774; d. 14 Jan.,
        1849 (from dates inscribed upon his tombstone).
    2, Francis Duke, Jr., b. Ohio Co., Va., 1777; d. near Johnstown, Ohio.

    1. JOHN DUKE (John[1], Francis[2]), eldest son of Francis and

Sarah Shepherd Duke, b. Ohio Co., Va., 24 June, 1777; d. in
Jones Co., Iowa, 14 Jan., 1849; *m.* 1st Catharine Hoover, presumed to have been the dau. of Jacob Hoover, formerly of
Dunkard's Creek, Pa., and later of Capon Springs, Hampshire
Co., Va. She was living in Johnstown, Ohio, at time of her
marriage; d. in Licking Co., O., 10 Oct., 1813, and was buried
in the Canton graveyard in Jackson Co., Ia. She had nine children. John Duke *m.* 2d Mrs. Elizabeth Wheeler, *circa* 1821, by
whom he had six children. After the death of John Duke his
widow is said to have married again, to Thomas Burrowes, in
1852, who d. in 1858, without issue, leaving her a widow for the
fourth time. Papers signed by her, in 1868, bear the name of
"Elizabeth Duke." John Duke removed from Brooke Co., Va.,
to Ohio, in 1803, with his wife and five small children. He removed from Ohio to Jones Co., Iowa, with his second family
when he was at an advanced age. John Duke was the first Justice
of the Peace of Granville Twp., Licking Co., O. When he first
came to Licking Co., in 1803, there were only about fifteen residents in the County. As heir-at-law of his father, Francis Duke,
the following record of the survey of the lands which he inherited
is taken from Survey Book, No. 1, p. 227, dated Wheeling, Va.,
Oct. 15, 1785.

"Surveyed for John Duke, heir-at-law of Francis Duke, deceased, 400
acres of land in Ohio Co. Va., including his settlement made in 1773,
by virtue of a certificate from the Commissioners bearing date the 18
January, 1780, situate on the waters of Short Creek and bounded as
followeth, to wit: Beginning at a sugar-tree corner to Joseph Kyle and
with his lines N. 67° E. 28 per. to a black oak and sugar tree thence S.
65 E 200 per. to two sugar trees corner to James Garrison with his line
East 160 per. to an Elm corner to Charles Hedges, and with his lines N.
17 W. 110 per. to a beech tree thence N. 37 W. 40 per to a sugar tree
thence N. 12 E. 62 per. to a sugar tree in W^m. Bonar's line and with
his line N. 69 W. 49 per. to a sugar tree, N. 77 W. 100 per. to a wash in
Jemima White's line and with her line S. 14 W. 28 per. to a hickory thence
N. 73 W. 140 per. to a walnut corner to W^m. Dunlap and with his line
S. 30 W. 26 per. to a poplar thence S. 21, W. 66 per. to a beech tree S.
12. E. 111 per to the beginning. Variation 21' East."

ROBERT WOODS, *Surveyor.*

This tract of land, lying on Short Creek, was afterward disposed of by John and Catharine Duke, his wife, in five different
transactions, to wit:

To Joseph Hedges, son of Charles Hedges, 7 Mar. 1796, 30 a. 126 poles,
$330.00
To Joseph Connell of Brooke Co., Va., 24 Oct., 1797, 136 a., $900.00.
To Samuel Hedges of Brooke Co., Va., 30 Jan. 1804, 141 a., $1269.00.
To Joseph Hedges of Brooke Co., Va., 30 Jan., 1804, 12 a. 120 poles,
$664.75.
To Francis Duke, his brother, 30 Jan. 1804, 100 a., $600.00.

24   353

Issue of John and Catharine (Hoover) Duke:
3, Levi Hoover, b. Brooke Co., Va., 12 May, 1795.
4, David, b. Brooke Co., Va., 27 May, 1797.
5, William, b. Brooke Co., Va., 13 June, 1799.
6, Sarah, b. Brooke Co., Va., 26 April, 1802; d. 20 June, 1866.
7, Henry, b. Licking Co., O., 9 Oct., 1806; d. 20 April, 1860.
8, John Shepherd, b. Licking Co., O., 9 Aug., 1808; d. *unm.*
    circa 1830.
9, George, b. Licking Co., O., 13 Sept., 1811.
Issue of John and Elizabeth Wheeler Duke:
10, Ruhahma, b. Licking Co., O., 2 April, 1822.
11, Clarissa, b. Licking Co., O., —— 1825; d. 22 June, 1843.
12, Calvin, b. Licking Co., O., 9 Dec., 1826.
13, Lydia, b. Licking Co., O., 25 March, 1829.
14, Calista, b. Licking Co., O., 26 May, 1831.
15, Hannah, b. Licking Co., O., 10 Feb., 1834.

2. FRANCIS DUKE (John[1], Francis[2]), second son of Francis
and Sarah (Shepherd) Duke, b. Ohio Co., Va., 1777, a few
months after his father's tragic death. He died at an advanced
age, at the home of his daughter Elizabeth Prefect, near Johnstown, O. Major S. A. Duke writes (1903): "I can remember
him well; he was a great rifle shot and could kill more squirrels
than I could carry." He acquired by purchase the following
tracts of land in Ohio and Brooke Counties, Va.:
    a. 29 January, 1795. David Shepherd (his grandfather) con-
veys a tract of 42 acres which was granted to the said David
Shepherd by Patent Deed, dated 25 July, 1788, on waters of Short
Creek; consideration £20 Virginia currency (Deed Book 3, p. 114,
Wheeling, W. Va.). This land adjoined lands of John Duke,
Morgan Van Metre, John Van Metre and Wm. Dunlap. Wit-
nesses: David McIntire, William Shepherd (uncle) and Hezekiah
Thornburg.
    b. 30 January, 1804. John (brother) and Catharine Duke, of
Brooke Co., Va., convey 100-acre tract on waters of Short Creek
for consideration of $600 (Deed Book 3, p. 183, Wellsburg,
Brooke Co., W. Va.). This tract adjoined lands of Daniel Rob-
erts, Wm. Dunlap and Joseph Kyle.
    c. 25 June, 1810. John Morgan and Sarah, his wife, of Ohio
Co., Va., convey a tract of land in Brooke Co., Va., containing
3 roods and 20 perches, for a consideration of $1.00 (Deed Book
4, p. 306, Wellsburg, Brooke Co., Va.).
    The above lands were disposed of by Francis and Margaret
Duke as follows:
    To Daniel Tilton, of Washington Co., Pa., 48 acres; considera-
tion $96.00.
    To John Morgan, of Ohio Co., Va., 6 acres, 1 rood, 30 perches;

DAVID DUKE

consideration $10.00. Both of these transfers were dated 10 May, 1804.

To Edward Morgan, of Ohio Co., 96 acres on Short Creek, Va., for a consideration of $750, dated 30 Jan., 1826 (Wellsburg, Va., Records, Deed Books, Nos. 3, 4 and 7).

Edward Morgan *m.* Elizabeth Hedges, 13 Jan., 1829.

Francis Duke *m. circa* 1799, Margaret Jackway (or Jacques). Issue:

16, Mary, b. 1800, d. ——, *m.* William H. B. Wilson; 17, Rachael, b. 1802, d. *unm.* 1819; 18, Shepherd, b. 1 Sept., 1805, d. 19 Aug., 1872; 19, Elizabeth, b. 1807; 20, Robert, b. 1809; 21, Sarah, b. 1813; 22, Nancy, b. 1819.

3. LEVI HOOVER DUKE (John[1], Francis[2], John[3]), eldest son of John and Catharine (Hoover) Duke, b. Brooke Co., Va., 12 May, 1795; *m.* Persis ——; both living in Licking Co., O., in 1853 (Deed Book 53, p. 333, Wheeling, W. Va.). Issue:

23, Milton (probably), *m.* Mary Fulton, of Ohio Co., W. Va.

4. DAVID DUKE (John[1], Francis[2], John[3]), son of John and Catharine (Hoover) Duke, b. Brooke Co., Va., 27 May, 1797; d. Licking Co., O., 23 Sept., 1888; *m.* 1st Martha Larue, 1 Jan., 1821, by whom he had one child: Harvey; *m.* 2d 1 March, 1827, Sarah, dau. of Nathan (d. 10 Sept., 1854) and Hannah Butcher Conrad, emigrants from Loudon Co., Va., where Nathan was b. 5 June, 1779. Hannah was his second wife, she was born in Hampshire Co., Va., 7 Jan., 1779, and d. Licking Co., O., 28 Jan., 1871. Nathan and Hannah Conrad settled in the upper valley of the North Fork, Licking Co., O., in 1807. David Duke had nine children by his second wife. He was a carpenter by trade and came to Licking Co., O., with his parents, from Brooke Co., Va., now one of the "Pan Handle Counties." The Indians were still in the Ohio forests and David learned from the Indian boys the art of archery and was very skillful at it. The Indian boys were his playmates for several years. It is written of David Duke that "he was an honest man—the noblest work of God." His second wife, Sarah Conrad, to whom he was *m.* 1 March, 1827, was b. 24 March, 1805, and d. in Licking Co., O., 20 Sept., 1877. Issue:

24, Harvey Larue, b. 27 May, 1823; 25, Salathiel Allen, b. 14 Jan., 1828; 26, John Crawford, b. 3 March, 1830, d. 15 Jan., 1904; 27, Nathan W., b. 1 Dec., 1832; 28, Jonah Bowman, b. 15 March, 1835, d. 1908 at Mountain Home for Invalid Veterans, Union Army, Tenn.; 29, David Milton, b. 25 May, 1838; 30, Sarah Elizabeth, b. 2 Dec., 1840; 31, William Benton, b. 21 Feb., 1843; 32, Joseph Wesley, b. 4 Oct., 1845, d. Licking Co., O., 9 Oct., 1855; 33, Lewis Cass, b. 18 April, 1848, *unm.,* lives in Montana.

5. WILLIAM DUKE (John[1], Francis[2], John[3]), son of John and Catharine (Hoover) Duke, b. Brooke Co., Va., 13 June, 1799; m. Hannah, dau. (probably) of Henry Bigelow, who laid out Johnstown, Licking Co., O., in 1813. Issue:
    34, Lydia A. B.; 35, Henrietta; 36, William H.; 37, George B.; 38, Hamilton, b. Johnstown, O., 25 May., 1829, d. 14 March, 1886.

6. SARAH DUKE (John[1], Francis[2], John[3]), dau. of John and Catharine (Hoover) Duke, b. 26 April, 1802; d. 20 June, 1866; m. 20 Nov., 1820, Nesbit Aldin, who d. at Emmaline, Ia., 27 Jan., 1859. Issue:
    39, John Ransom, b. 11 Aug., 1821, d. 19 March, 1856; 40, Phoebe, b. 31 Aug., 1824, d. y.; 41, Margaret, b. ——, 1826; 42, Mary, b. 28 Nov., 1828, m. 28 Oct., 1849, Samuel Clark, no issue; 43, Levi, b. 25 April, 1830; 44, Lloyd, b. 24 Oct., 1834; 45, Esther, b. 26 March, 1837; d. ——, 1839; 46, Horton E., b. 13 June, 1840, d. 14 March, 1873; 47, Albert W., b. 1 June, 1844, d. 15 Nov., 1861.

7. HENRY DUKE (John[1], Francis[2], John[3]), son of John and Catharine (Hoover) Duke, b. at Homer, Licking Co., O., 9 Oct., 1806; d. Johnson Co., Ia., 20 April, 1860; m. Catharine Willis, b. 1811; d. May, 1882, aged 71 years. Issue:
    48, Sarah Emily, m. Mr. Higgins, living at Shenandoah, Ia.; 49, Ruth; 50, Louise, m. Mr. Shepherd, living at Pierre, Ia.; 51, John Grafton, m. —— ——, lives Chalk Level, Mo.; 52, James Crawford, b. 27 Sept., 1842, living at Shenandoah, Ia.; 53, Henry Wesley.

9. GEORGE DUKE (John[1], Francis[2], John[3]), son of John and Catharine (Hoover) Duke, b. in Licking Co., O., 13 Sept., 1811. Issue:
    54, Calvin, b. 13 Nov., 1833, m. Martha Birge; 55, Mary, b. 6 Sept., 1835, d. 20 Sept., 1899; 56, Nesbit Allen, b. 25 Dec., 1837, d. 13 Feb., 1888; 57, Zenus, b. 8 Dec., 1839; 58, Sarah, b. 25 Oct., 1841; 59, Matilda, b. 13 Aug., 1843; 60, John, b. 13 March, 1845; 61, Eliza, b. 11 June, 1847, m. William Davis; 62, Zena, b. 11 Oct., 1849, d. y.; 63, Christina, b. 22 Feb., 1852; 64, Salathiel Allen, b. 3 May, 1854.

10. RUHAMAH DUKE (John[1], Francis[2], John[3]), eldest dau. of John and Elizabeth (Wheeler) Duke, b. in Licking Co., O., 2 April, 1822; d. ——; m. 1 Jan., 1843, William Parr (same, perhaps, who was sheriff of Licking Co., O., 1848–1852; member of Ohio Legislature 1858–1862, 1868–1872. Issue:
    65, Elizabeth; 66, Elliott; 67, John; 68, Richard; 69, Sabrey; 70, Malissa; 71, Charles Francis; 72, Hiram; 73, Albert.

DESCENDANTS OF FRANCIS DUKE

12. CALVIN DUKE (John[1], Francis[2], John[3]), son of John and Elizabeth (Wheeler) Duke, b. in Licking Co., O., 9 Dec., 1826; *m.* 17 Aug., 1848, Eliza Ann Mackerd; living at Canton, Jones Co., Ia.   Issue:
74, Joel Francis, b. 12 Sept., 1849; 75, Henry Allen, b. 16 Nov., 1851; 76, George Ransom, b. 24 Jan., 1859, d. 24 Sept., 1889.

13. LYDIA DUKE (John[1], Francis[2], John[3]), dau. of John and Elizabeth (Wheeler) Duke, b. in Licking Co., O., 25 March, 1829; d. ——; *m.* 17 Dec., 1846, Aaron French.   Issue:
77, John; 78, Joseph; 79, Calvin; 80, Ira; 81, William; 82, Simon; 83, Elizabeth; 84, Eliza; 85, Isaac; 86, Abigail; 87, Rose; 88, Sarah.

14. CALISTA DUKE (John[1], Francis[2], John[3]), dau. of John and Elizabeth (Wheeler) Duke, b. in Licking Co., O., 26 May, 1831; *m.* 19 May, 1849, Simon Parr; living at Monticello, Jackson Co., Iowa.   Issue:
89, Endorra; 90, Byron Clinton; 91, Eddie Dorr; 92, Sarah; 93, Sylvia.

15. HANNAH DUKE (John[1], Francis[2], John[3]), youngest dau. of John and Elizabeth (Wheeler) Duke, b. Licking Co., O., 10 Feb., 1834; d. at Philadelphia, Pa.; *m.* Alexander R. Rehm, a German. No issue. Hannah was a woman of enormous size, her weight being about 600 lbs.

18. SHEPHERD DUKE (John[1], Francis[2], Francis[3]), eldest son of Francis and Margaret (Jacques) Duke, b. near Bethany, W. Va., 1 Sept., 1805; d. at Plattesmouth, Neb., 19 Aug., 1872; *m.* 14 March, 1826, Lavinia Snedaker.   Issue:
94, Garrett Francis, b. 12 Dec., 1826, d. *unm.*, 1850; 95, Rachael, b. 14 Dec., 1828, d. 24 April, 1830; 96, John Shepherd, b. 2 Feb., 1831; 97, Edwin M., b. 7 Aug., 1833, d. 13 July, 1834; 98, Margaret Louise, b. 13 June, 1835, *m.* 1859, Lloyd D. Bennett, Plattesmouth, Neb.; 99, Belinda, b. 7 Nov., 1836; 100, Edward Truman, b. 14 Aug., 1838; 101, Lenora, b. 15 Jan., 1841, d. 1 June, 1842; 102, Roxalena Ellen, b. 6 Sept., 1843.

19. ELIZABETH DUKE (John[1], Francis[2], Francis[3]), dau. of Francis and Margaret (Jacques) Duke, b. 1807; d. ——; *m.* Truman Perfect, of Delaware Co., O., uncle of Judge Lee Estelle, of Omaha, Neb.   Issue:
103, Douglass; 104, a son.

21. SARAH DUKE (John[1], Francis[2], Francis[3]), dau. of Francis and Margaret (Jacques) Duke, b. ——, 1813; d. ——; *m.* David Corbin.   Issue:
105, Francis; 106, Truman; 107, Shepherd; 108, Sarah.

22. NANCY DUKE (John[1], Francis[2], Francis[3]), youngest dau. of Francis and Margaret (Jacques) Duke, b. ——, 1819; d. ——; m. Levi Corbin.

24. HARVEY LARUE DUKE (John[1], Francis[2], John[3], David[4]), eldest son and only child of David and Martha (Larue) Duke, b. 27 May, 1823; m. Rhoda Conard, dau. of Edward, the son of Anthony Conard, who was cousin to Nathan Conard. Harvey L. and Rhoda C. Duke resided at Fithian, Ia.

109, Alice; 110, David Raymond, b. 17 Aug., 1852.

25. SALATHIEL ALLEN DUKE (John[1], Francis[2], John[3], David[4]), eldest son of David Duke and his second wife, Sarah Conrad, b. near Johnstown, Licking Co., O., 14 Jan., 1828; living (1909) at Baxter, Drew Co., Ark.; m. 24 Dec., 1849, Ruth Elizabeth Barnes, whose parents emigrated west from Virginia and were of German origin. She was b. 27 March, 1828; d. at Baxter, Ark., 19 Oct., 1900. Mr. Duke is a wonderfully energetic and remarkably successful member of the Duke family; he is now (1909) in his eighty-first year and as virile as a youth, a typical son of the pioneer in his ability to take care of himself. To use his own words, he "was born in the woods," and ran away from home when he was but fourteen years of age, not only because he had been chastised by his father as a result of a quarrel between the boy and his elder half-brother over the ownership of a rifle, but as much for the reason that it afforded him the excuse and the opportunity of obtaining that which his parents could not afford —an education— and the chance to learn a trade and be independent. He made his way to Newark, O., and there found employment at odd jobs, and when he reached Circleville, sixty miles from home, he wrote his parents that he would return if they would agree to put him at a trade. A treaty of peace was negotiated on this basis and he came back and was apprenticed to one George Brown, a Dutch shoemaker, to serve two and a half years. After a year or more, during which time young Duke was maltreated and half-starved, public indignation caused the agreement to be cancelled, but the boy continued to find employment at it until he became a proficient journeyman, after which he was employed at St. Louis, Burlington and Keokuk. At the latter place he decided to go into the mercantile branch of his business and formed a partnership with James R. Phillips. Between them $100 was put in at the start; a year or two later Phillips sold his interest to Duke, who made rapid progress toward success. At the end of five years Duke sold out his business and cleared about $35,000 at a time when Keokuk was "booming," and after Duke had put all his surplus means into real estate. At the close of another five years this fortune, through the misconduct of a business confidant, had been dissipated, and Duke "found himself broken up and ready to go to

HON. S. A. DUKE

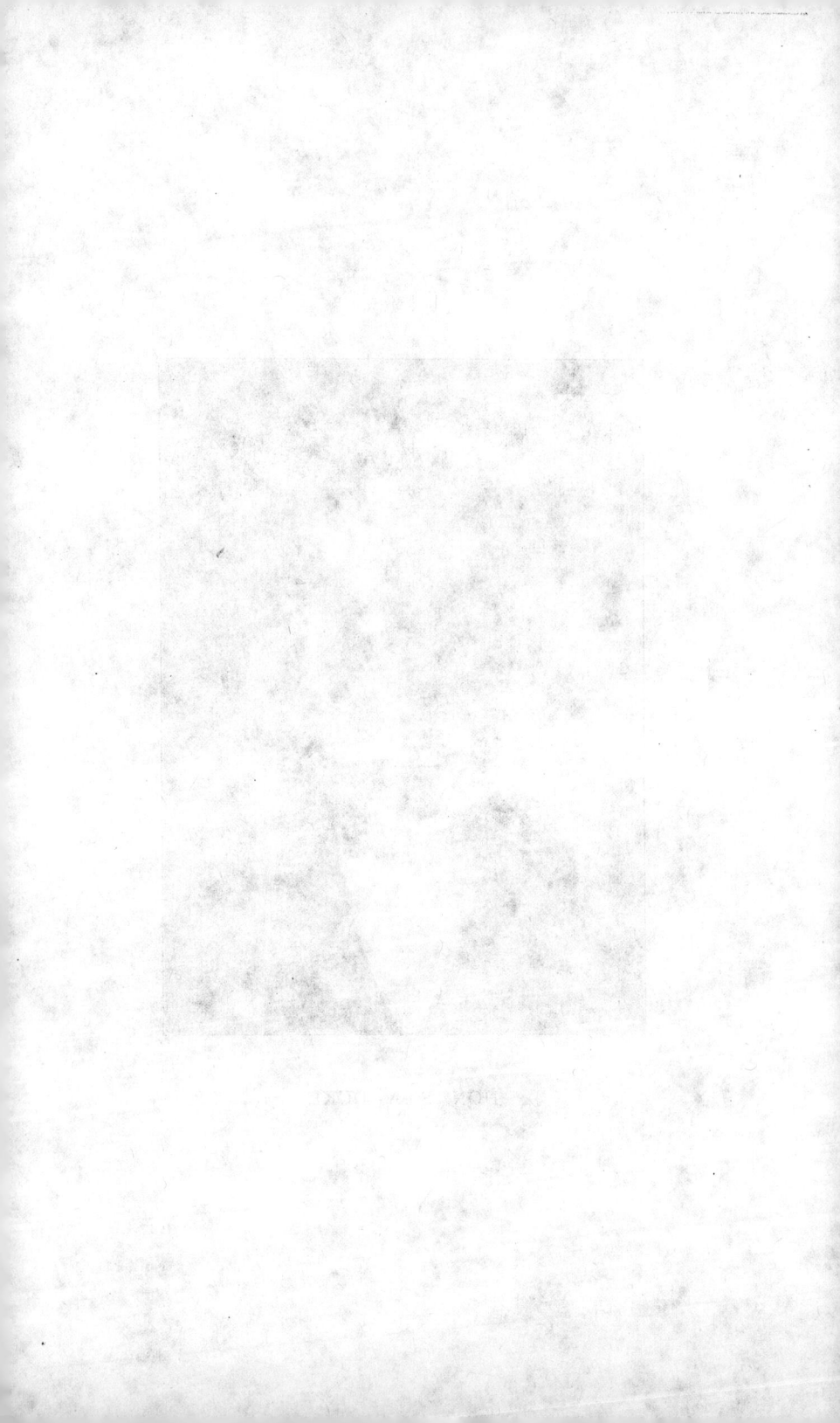

DESCENDANTS OF FRANCIS DUKE

Denver, or the War." Before this time, however, Mr. Duke, like his father and other male members of his family, had been a Democrat and was active in the affairs of that party, but in 1852 he quit the party on issues arising out of the Kansas-Nebraska Bill, and finally became a strong "Wilmot Proviso" adherent. When the Republican party was organized in 1856 he allied himself with it and has ever since remained one of its faithful and steadfast supporters, and has taken prominent part in its councils from local politics to those of national importance, and is still one of its ruling factors in his adopted State. I first met him shortly after he had come to Philadelphia as a National delegate to the Republican Convention which met in that city in June, 1900. In a letter to me, referring to the approaching Golden Jubilee of the Republican party, which was to be celebrated in Philadelphia in June, 1906, he writes:

"I will try to attend the Convention (of Young Republican Clubs), if not as a Delegate—then as a private citizen who has voted for every Republican candidate for President; and who attended the Convention in the Chicago Wigwam that put Lincoln in nomination the first time."

Mr. Duke attended the Philadelphia Jubilee of 1906 and took his place among the Fremont veterans on that occasion. Mr. Duke was a resident of Keokuk, Ia., during the war; here all his children were born and here all died in infancy save one—the youngest son—Charles T. Duke, who now resides at Monticello, Ark. On the breaking out of the Rebellion, and although he had taken little part in the public agitation up to this time, yet when Lincoln's Proclamation of Emancipation was published to the world Mr. Duke declared his pro-Union sentiments and his determination to aid in maintaining the integrity of the Union.

"When the Emancipation proclamation was issued, I immediately wrote Gen. S. R. Curtis, then located at St. Louis and in command of the Department of the Missouri,—that as the negroes were now emancipated, I was ready to take a hand in putting them into service, that by the shedding of their blood they might seal their freedom. Gen. Curtis at once gave me authority to raise a regiment of negroes at Helena, Miss. (Vicksburg then being in the hands of the Confederates), where there were thousands of them hanging lazily on the heels of the Union Army; many of them had escaped from their southern owners and gathering in numbers with the progress of the Federal troopes these contrabands became a positive nuisance about Helena. But Helena having been taken out of Gen. Curtis' charge immediately after he had written me, and placed in Gen. Grant's department to facilitate his operations against Vicksburg, my plan was halted until Gen. Lorenzo Thomas came out to organize negro troopes along the Mississippi River and to demonstrate, if possible (for the Rebels and the Copperheads had said that soldiers could not be made of them), that the negro could be made a military factor, or work as free laborers. They were concentrated at Lake Providence; organized, drilled, equipped and prepared for the field. As I had foreseen, the white officers, and men in superabundance, sought promotion in negro regiments, and when I had revisited a part of the regiment which I had undertaken to organize, I found that a Lieut. Col. of an Indiana regi-

359

ment of Cavalry wanted, and was made Colonel of my regiment: The First Arkansas; a Major who wanted to be Lieut. Col. was advanced, and a Captain who wanted to be its Major accepted the promotion, so I found that my chances for duty in that line of service was at an end, and promptly realized that I had received no military training it was of importance that the negroes should be quickly trained for they were much needed in 1863!

"Gen. Thomas told me to continue with him and to help put the plantation business in shape, I did this and it was in this way that I became a cotton-planter and a demonstrator of the fact that a bull-whip was unnecessary to make a negro work. Many of the cotton plantations along the Mississippi had been abandoned by their Confederate owners and turning my attention to them I organized the free labor plantations, useing the negroes, who were unfitted for military duty, and leasing them many of the confiscated plantations and upon which the freedman worked and raised cotton successfuly. In connection with this period I was appointed by President Lincoln a special Agent of the Treasury, for the collection of cotton crops on the abandoned plantations, the crops were sold in the New Orleans market for the benefit of the War Treasury.

"My first plantation I acquired in 1863; it was called "The Outpost" and lay 2½ miles back from Goodrich's Landing and it was by 'holding the fort' in rather an unusual manner that I got possession of the Goodrich plantations and storehouse which used as a trade store. This was granted me without solicitation for what the authorities were pleased to call my 'heroism' in holding it, although, as I look back I can see that it was only a foolhardy reluctance to retreat."

This active service was of a unique character and fittingly exhibited Mr. Duke's resourcefulness, energy and intrepidity—traits quite typical of the pioneer fathers. The circumstances connected with the holding of "The Outpost" were, no doubt, owing to the modesty of the principal actor in it, never noticed by writers of war history; the facts were, however, gathered and published later in an Iowa newspaper among its war reminiscences and recently confirmed by Mr. Duke in a conversation with the compiler.

"In the winter of 1863-4 I held Fort Goodrich for ten weeks while the troops were withdrawn from this post, and my only defensive armament was smallpox! I found, among some four or five thousand negroes who congregated at the Fort from surrounding plantations, about a hundred cases of smallpox. I had never been vaccinated, but had attempted doing it myself with a darning needle, when a boy of 12 years. I decided to take my chances with such a defense rather than fly as all other free labor planters did—to Vicksburg, and other places of safety. The country back of Goodrich's Landing was infested with the bloodiest guerrilas of the war times, among whom were many of Quantrell's band, including the James and the Younger boys. I at once got it into my head that all desperadoes were moral cowards, and while they seemed to take desperate chances, they always did so after getting the 'drop,' so I, to forestall them, took the 'drop' on them, and while I was often reported as dead; having had my throat cut; and all such ghastly descriptions of my mode of death, I came out without a scratch notwithstanding the guerillas came within a mile of the Fort on an intended raid, but learning that I had a smallpox hospital across the gate of the Fort, they turned away and massacred all the negroes and Union men they could find at Milliken's Bend, 10 miles below Goodrich's Landing."

DESCENDANTS OF FRANCIS DUKE

After the close of the war Major Duke, who had been complimented by this title as a courtesy for his services in organizing the colored troops, disposed of his interests at Keokuk, Ia., and removed to southern Arkansas, where he bought extensively of rich bottom timber and cotton lands and went there to stay. His estate, which comprises many thousands of acres, is located in Drew County and bisecting it is the Little Rock, Mississippi and Texas Railroad. Upon his large possessions Major Duke has founded two prosperous towns, Baxter and Dermott; both are populous and enterprising. The former town was named for his former friend and political associate, ex-Governor Baxter, and for many years Major Duke was its postmaster. In this town is located the extensive warehouses and general stores of the plantation. Mr. Duke, who has always been the active and practical friend of the negro and a firm believer in the higher destiny and usefulness of the freedmen, employs many hundreds of them, and there are many others to whom he leases portions of his estate under conditions and environment so favorable they have progressed and developed rapidly, fully justifying the Major's point of view with regard to their capabilities. His influence among them has been a leading one, and he has also supported and encouraged them in all their civil rights and privileges. With respect to this subject of the negro, Mr. Duke wrote me not long ago his sentiments concerning the problem that is disturbing the public's peace of mind:

"The negro 'bug-a-boo' that is dwarfing our statesmanship, is truly alarming. Our people seem to be losing sight of great national questions while they root up from the ground, the lowest sentiments based on a hysterical fact, that some time, the negro will acquire the status of equality; and while they are doing this, the Negro is gradually evolving. The white man makes laws and constitutions to compel educational qualifications in the negro for suffrage, that, at the same time, they expressly exempt the white man from. And they are so blinded by their foolish fear that they seem not to look beyond present safety. They are hiding their heads in the sand. God and the future generations must work out the problem, not we of this generation."

In the state political campaign of 1868 Mr. Duke was elected by a portion of the people—the Reconstructionists—to the House of Assembly of Arkansas without his consent, and being unable to resign a position which came from the people, declined to attend the sessions of the Assembly. This period, which followed the war, was filled with general unrest and apprehension. It was a trying epoch in the South, fraught with dangerous perils and events frequently occurred which tried many a courageous man; the outrages of the time cost many men their lives. During the period antedating the election of Mr. Duke many of the most respected and influential white citizens were disfranchised because of their participation in the cause of the Confederacy, while the negroes, by Constitutional Amendment, had been given the right of franchise almost coincident with their emancipation; hence Major Duke would not serve in a legislature growing out of such conditions. Matters grew worse and the Republicans became more and further disregardful of the common rights of the people, and all this time the "Ku-Klux" were growing more active throughout the South; men identified with the Federal administration living in that section, and sympathizers of the rehabilitation of the devastated country, were harassed, tormented and made to flee for their lives. Major Duke was one of those who was sought but not driven, until his experiences became like those of Servoss in Judge Tourgee's novel, "A Fool's Errand," and in one particular it was quite similar, except that in Servoss' case *his* daughter married a son of the Confederacy, while Major Duke's son married a daughter of the Confederacy! At one time during the election of 1868 the Major thought "discretion the better part of valor," and in order that he might prolong his stay in this world with comfort, he wisely sought seclusion in New Orleans until the excitement caused by a report that he was secreting arms and encouraging a negro uprising had quieted down. An incident occurred about this time which clearly enough showed the temper of his southern neighbors. A negro resident, replying publicly to a taunt that "the South was going to put the negroes back into slavery," said that, "if the South could not do it in 1865, when she had only the Yankees to whip, how could she expect to do it now, she would have to whip the Yankees and negroes both!" For this audacious utterance the negro was "brought out" by the Klan, shot and left hanging as a warning to others to guard their tongues. The consequences of this act became almost tragical for the Major. During his campaign for State Senator in 1872, in addressing an audience in his locality, he publicly arraigned some of them with complicity in the negro's murder; but, while the challenge remained unanswered for the moment, the Major stood upon the verge of a volcano caused by his expressions; the excitement ran high. He learned of it a long time afterward, when one of his staunchest friends of later days told him that he was present at that meeting and at its conclusion had tried to organize a squad "to take the Major out" and hang him, but he had not succeeded. The Major told him that had such a thing been attempted there would have been the worst kind of trouble, for in that meeting were many men who were members of the militia regiment of which Mr. Duke was lieutenant colonel, and in citizen's clothes, and had any demonstration against the speaker taken place, the militiamen would have taken a hand in the affair. In 1872 Major Duke was elected to the Senate of Arkansas from the district composed of the four counties of Chicott, Ashley, Drew and Deshan. Just before the open-

ing of the session Mr. Duke had the misfortune to get his left
hand caught in a cotton-gin and the accident nearly cost him his
life; it also kept him home during the first half of the session of
the legislature. When he was able to attend, he found that a great
outrage was about to be perpetrated on the State by the leaders
of his party, in sheer violation of what they had been promul-
gating on the stump during the campaign. The situation, in a
nutshell, was like this: thinking that the State would fill up and
progress like the territories had done when opened to settlement
with enterprising, hustling people of the north, the first legisla-
tors had made liberal laws encouraging the building of railways
throughout the State and providing for guaranteeing the payment of railroad bonds and their interest, taking first mortgage
on the roads as security; this plan would have been good enough
had the scheme worked, but it depended upon a boom which never
came. In the midst of other troubles the "Ku Klux" organized
and all sensible northern men who could left the State and took
their enterprises and enterprising "spurt" along with them; but
there had been fifteen or twenty millions of railroad bonds issued
for which the State stood sponsor. The Democracy charged this
as a State debt, but the Republicans urged that it was only a
guarantee to be paid by the State in finished roads. However,
a bill was introduced in the Senate by which the State was made
directly responsible for all the bonds, thus relieving the railroads
of their obligations. Mr. Duke, who had now taken his seat,
took a strong stand against the bill and did all in his power to
defeat it. Baxter, the governor, was also opposed to it on the
same ground, that it was inconsistent with his representations
before the people. After a long and arduous fight the bill was
defeated. The controversy between Brooks and Baxter, rival
candidates for governor, grew out of this question. Baxter
having been elected and Brooks defeated, the latter carried the
contest up to the Supreme Court of the State; that body decided
in his favor and Baxter was notified to vacate his seat as governor. Brooks was sworn in and placed in possession of the
capitol. Baxter retired to St. John's College and appealed to
President Grant, who recognized and sustained him as the right-
ful governor, and Brooks was forced to capitulate. While these
legal questions were being adjusted a bitter and bloody feud was
waged in the city of Little Rock between the rival factions. This
affair has come down in history as "The Brooks and Baxter War
of 1874." In this struggle Major Duke was a firm supporter of
Governor Baxter.

Thus we have again the view of the strong, courageous and
rugged personality of S. A. Duke, a typical southwesterner in
dominance and forcefulness, and a man who lives up to and practices the principles of right and honor.   Issue:

111, Horace Barnes, b. 7 Oct., 1850, d. 10 Feb., 1853; 112, a daughter, b. 14 Feb., 1853, d. 18 Feb., 1853; 113, Alice Minerva, b. 18 May, 1854, d. 18 Nov., 1855; 114, Jessie Attica, b. 10 Dec., 1856, d. 22 Nov., 1858; 115, Charles Talbot, b. 21 April, 1860.

All these children were born at Keokuk, Ia.

26. JOHN CRAWFORD DUKE (John[1], Francis[2], John[3], David[4]), son of David and Sarah (Conard) Duke, b. 3 May, 1830; d. Boulder, Colo., 15 Jan., 1904; m. 1850, Jane Ulm. Issue:
116, Rhoda Minerva, b. 1851; 117, Horace Allen, b. 1853; 118, Wesley Lewis, b. 1855, m. —— ——, lives in Mexico; 119, Charles Douglass, b. 1858.

27. NATHAN WARREN DUKE (John[1], Francis[2], John[3], David[4]), son of David and Sarah (Conard) Duke, b. 1 Dec., 1832; d. —— ——; m. 20 March, 1856, Phoebe Baker. Issue:
120, Albert Leroy, b. 7 Jan., 1857, d. 14 Jan., 1857; 121, Elmer Clark, b. 9 Jan., 1859; 122, Charles Elbert, b. 28 —, 1862; 123, Leona Dill, b. 13 June, 1864, d. 28 Nov., 1885; 124, Ora Bell, b. 20 March, 1866; 125, Mary Alvada, b. 7 July, 1868; 126, Angie Maud, b. 4 Feb., 1872, d. 25 Sept., 1873; 127, Vina Estella, b. 28 Nov., 1876.

29. DAVID MILTON DUKE (John[1], Francis[2], John[3], David[4]), son of David and Sarah (Conard) Duke, b. 25 May, 1858; m. 29 Nov., 1862, Sarah Smith, b. Licking Co., O., 26 March, 1843. Issue:
128, Amy Estelle, b. Licking Co., O., 15 Sept., 1863.
129, Ida Ethel, b. Licking Co., O., 12 Dec., 1864.
130, Williard Leslie, b. Licking Co., O., 31 May, 1869.

30. SARAH ELIZABETH DUKE (John[1], Francis[2], John[3], David[4]), eldest and only dau. of David and Sarah (Conard) Duke, b. 2 Dec., 1840; d. ——; m. Miles Sinkey; living at Richwood, Ohio. Issue:
131, Blanche, b. 14 Nov., 1866; 132, Benton, b. 17 Feb., 1868; 133, Quinney, b. 8 April, 1874, d. 12 Aug., 1880; 134, Olive, b. 8 May, 1878.

31. WILLIAM BENTON DUKE (John[1], Francis[2], John[3], David[4]), son of David and Sarah (Conard) Duke, b. 21 Feb., 1843; m. 16 Sept., 1869, Laverna V. Trevitt, b. at Alexandria, Licking Co., O., 25 April, 1847; d. Richwood, Ohio, 16 June, 1907. She was a woman of high Christian character and virtues. Issue:
135, Maud; 136, Hermon Clyde, b. 16 Sept., 1875.

34. LYDIA A. B. DUKE (John[1], Francis[2], John[3], William[4]), eldest dau. of William and Hannah (Bigelow) Duke, b. ——; m. Rev. Marks.

DESCENDANTS OF FRANCIS DUKE

38. HAMILTON DUKE (John[1], Francis[2], John[3], William[4]), son
of William and Hannah (Bigelow) Duke, b. Johnstown, O., 25
May, 1829; d. 14 March, 1886; *m.* 1st 11 July, 1850, Hannah
Hebson, b. England, 20 Dec., 1828; d. Johnstown, O., 27 Dec.,
1857; leaving two children; *m.* 2d Anna L. Wood, 12 April, 1858;
d. 23 May, 1895; leaving four children. Hamilton Duke served
in the Union Army under General Curtis. Issue:
   137, William Fenton, b. Johnstown, O., 17 July, 1851; 138,
      Ella Ventura, b. Johnstown, O., 4 Sept., 1853, *m.* ——
      ——; 139, George Curtis, b. 8 Feb., 1861; 140, Jimmie
      Grant, b. 16 Sept., 1862; 141, Friend Walter, b. 16 July,
      1867; 142, Essie May, b. 13 May, 1871.

39. JOHN RANSOM ALDIN (John[1], Francis[2], John[3], Sarah[4]),
eldest son of Nesbit and Sarah (Duke) Aldin, b. 11 Aug., 1821;
d. 19 March, 1856; *m.* Sarah J. Wilson. Issue:
   143, Mary, *m.* —— Woodruff, lives at Burns, Mo.; 144, George
      Ransom, lives at Cedar Rapids, Mich.; 145, Harvey
      Darwin, b. 17 Nov., 1853.

44. LLOYD ALDIN (John[1], Francis[2], John[3], Sarah[4]), son of
Nesbit and Sarah (Duke) Alden, b. 24 Oct., 1834; d. —— ——;
m. Julia Shoemaker. Issue:
   146, Augusta; 147, Mary; 148, Morris; 149, Mary Ann; 150,
      Nora.

46. HORTON E. ALDIN (John[1], Francis[2], John[3], Sarah[4]), son of
Nesbit and Sarah (Duke) Aldin, b. Ohio, 13 June, 1840; d. 14
March, 1873, in Wisconsin; *m.* 1st 22 March, 1863, Mate Sutton;
m. 2d 10 July, 1870, Melissa J. Fox. Issue:
   151, Fred. M., b. 2 Jan., 1864, living at Maquoketa, Ia.; 152,
      Leona, b. 7 Sept., 1867, living at Monmouth, Ia.; 153,
      Lloyd, living at Anita, Ia.; 154, Charles C., b. 3 Sept.,
      1871, living at Great Falls, Mont.; 155, Claude Leroy,
      b. 3 Sept., 1873, d. 31 Jan., 1874.

49. RUTH DUKE (John[1], Francis[2], John[3], Henry[4]), dau. of
Henry and Catharine (Willis) Duke, b. ——; d. ——; *m.* John
Cossan Ferneau. Issue:
   156, James M., b. 14 Oct., 1867; 157, John O., b. 14 Dec.,
      1871; 158, Nora Mae, b. 27 June, 1876.

52. JAMES CRAWFORD DUKE (John[1], Francis[2], John[3], Henry[4]),
son of Henry and Catharine (Willis) Duke, b. Homer, Licking
Co., O., 27 Sept., 1842; *m.* 26 Sept., 1869, Belle Oppenheimer.
James C. Duke served in Company F, 22d Regiment, Iowa Volunteers, in the Union Army. They live at Shenandoah, Iowa.
Issue:
   159, Ella May; 160, Clifford W.; 161, Iva Bell.

54. MARY DUKE (John[1], Francis[2], John[3], George[4]), eldest dau. of George and —— Duke, b. 6 Sept., 1835; d. 20 Sept., 1899; *m.* 1859, Edward Wilson.   Issue:

162, Alpha, b. 8 May, 1860; *m.* 1st Henry Mayo; *m.* 2d Daniel Mayo; *m.* 3d Jack McKenzie.

163, Horton A., b. 18 Jan., 1862; *m.* Jane Winslow. They live at Hockspur, Washington.

164, Laura, b. 4 Oct., 1864; *m.* M. W. Garrabrant; lives at Waterloo, Iowa.

165, Melsena, b. 20 July, 1866; *m.* George Rohrer; live at Waterloo, Iowa.

166, Edward, b. 11 June, 1868; *m.* Lily Oliver; live at Wycena, Wisconsin.

167, Alfred, b. 8 May, 1870.

168, Albert, b. 19 Nov., 1872; *m.* Mate Vaughan; live at Bethhurst, Miss.

169, Charles, b. 9 Jan., 1874; *m.* Wealthy Patterson; live at Butte, Mont.

56. NESBIT ALLEN DUKE (John[1], Francis[2], John[3], George[4]), son of George and —— Duke, b. 25 Dec., 1837; d. 13 Feb., 1888; *m.* Ella Hilborn.   Issue:

170, Clara Louella, b. 24 Oct., 1858; *m.* Isaac Leekington.

171, Rufina Helen, b. 20 Oct., 1859.

172, Burris B., b. 24 April, 1861.

173, Alton A., b. 22 Nov., 1862; *m.* Augusta Fischer.

174, John W., b. 2 July, 1864.

175, George A., b. 16 Oct., 1866; *m.* Jane Fisher.

176, James A., b. 12 Nov., 1868; *m.* Eliza Cossy.

177, Cora A., b. 28 Sept., 1870; *m.* George Colvin.

178, Jessie M., b. 9 Feb., 1873; *m.* Henry Smith.

179, Harry A., b. 8 June, 1876; *m.* Eva Haller.

180, Cordia E., b. 4 Dec., 1878; *m.* Will Fish.

57. ZENUS DUKE (John[1], Francis[2], John[3], George[4]), son of George and —— Duke, b. 8 Dec., 1839; d. ——; *m.* 1st Eliza Berry; *m.* 2d Hettie Bull Mullarky. Zenus Duke served as a private in the Union Army.   Issue:

181, Israel, b. 10 April, 1866; 182, Lafayette, b. 13 April, 1868, *m.* Aggie Tisdall, reside at Arsdale, Butler Co., Ia.

183, Ralph, b. 6 July, 1871; 184, Minnie E., b. 16 July, 1875, *m.* Charles Guy, reside at Waterloo, Ia.

58. SARAH DUKE (John[1], Francis[2], John[3], George[4]), dau. of George and —— Duke, b. 25 Oct., 1841; d. ——; *m.* Alexander L. Wilson; living at Denver, Colo.   Issue:

185, George B.; 186, Emma E., 187, Beatrice, *m.* C. A. Wilson, of Denver, Colo.; 188, Orlando H.; 189, Martha Attia.

59. MATILDA DUKE (John[1], Francis[2], John[3], George[4]), dau. of George and —— Duke, b. 13 Aug., 1843; d. ——; *m.* William Stead; living at Denver, Colo.

60. JOHN DUKE (John[1], Francis[2], John[3], George[4]), son of George and —— Duke, b. 13 March, 1845; *m.* Charlotta Gray. Issue:
190, Fred. A., b. 28 March, 1870; *m.* Nettie Shaeffer; live at Oelwine, Ia.
191, Francis, b. 16 May, 1872; *m.* Annie Bowder; live at Oelwine, Ia.
192, Emma C., b. 3 July, 1875.

63. CHRISTINA DUKE (John[1], Francis[2], John[3], George[4]), dau. of George and —— Duke, b. 22 Feb., 1852; *m.* 1st William Johnson; *m.* 2d Wm. H. Brott; living at Waterloo, Ia. Issue:
193, Pearl, b. *circa* 1878; 194, Ralph, b. *circa* 1882.

64. SALATHIEL ALLEN DUKE (John[1], Francis[2], John[3], George[4]), son of George and —— Duke, b. 3 May, 1854; d. ——; *m.* 26 June, 1877, Sarah Dillenbuck. They live at Reinbeck, Ia. Issue:
195, Lizzie Edith, b. 2 April, 1879, *m.* C. H. Miller, living in Minneapolis, Minn.; 196, Eugene Moses, b. 26 Jan., 1882; 197, Leo Fern, b. 12 June, 1884; 198, Ethel Blanche, b. 12 Dec., 1887.

75. HENRY ALLEN DUKE (John[1], Francis[2], John[3], Calvin[4]), son of Calvin and Eliza A. (Mackerd) Duke, b. 16 Nov., 1851; *m.* 29 Oct., 1875, Rosella-Mackril. They live at Canton, Ia. Issue:
199, Horton Oscar, b. 12 Aug., 1876; 200, Allen Leroy, b. 17 Sept., 1880; 201, Idell Floy, b. 19 Jan., 1885, living at Onslow, Ia.; 202, Louis Benton, b. 15 July, 1890, living at Canton, Ia.; 203, Lotus E., b. 7 July, 1894.

96. JOHN SHEPHERD DUKE (John[1], Francis[2], Francis[3], Shepherd[4]), son of Shepherd and Lavinia (Snedaker) Duke, b. 2 Feb., 1831; *m.* 1853, Rachel L. Hambleton. Issue:
204, Edgar Hambleton, b. *circa* 1854; 205, Charles Elbert, b. *circa* 1857.

100. ELBERT TRUMAN DUKE (John[1], Francis[2], Francis[3], Shepherd[4]), son of Shepherd and Lavinia (Snedaker) Duke, b. 14 Aug., 1838, at Charlestown, W. Va.; *m.* 9 April, 1863, Carolina Aurelia Sage; living at Omaha, Neb.. Issue:
206, Charles Sage, b. 5 July, 1864, living at Omaha, Neb.; 207, John Shepherd, b. 27 Feb., 1865, living at St. Paul, Minn.; 208, Frankie Eloise, b. 1872, *m.* Fred. S. Knapp, 1892, at Omaha, Neb.

102. ROXALENA ELLEN DUKE (John[1], Francis[2], Francis[3], Shepherd[4]), dau. of Shepherd and Lavinia (Snedaker) Duke,

b. 6 Sept., 1843; d. 2 April, 1863; *m.* Steans Fisher Cooper, b. Logansport, Ind., 24 March, 1838; d. Chicago, Ill., 3 March, 1876. He was captain of Company M, 2d Nebraska Cavalry, in the Union Army; was transferred to the Veteran Reserve Corps; in command of 98th Company, and also commanded the fort at Quincey, Ill. After the Company was mustered out he was transferred to Washington, D. C., and was in charge there of the guard at Sewards' mansion after the attempted assassination of the Secretary. He was mustered out of the service, spring of 1866.

Issue:

207, Mattie F., b. 23 Feb., 1864; 208, Leonora, b. 4 April, 1870, d. 1870.

109. ALICE DUKE (John[1], Francis[2], John[3], David[4], Harvey[5]), dau. of Harvey L. and Rhoda (Conard) Duke; *m.* M. H. Love; living at Hot Springs, South Dakota.

110. DAVID RAYMOND DUKE (John[1], Francis[2], John[3], David[4], Harvey L.[5]), son of Harvey L. and Sarah (Conard) Duke, b. 17 Aug., 1852; *m.* 9 Aug., 1874, Martha Stevenson.   Issue:
207, Lew H., b. 5 Sept., 1875; living at Fithian, Ill.
208, Arlington Ira, b. 6 Aug., 1877; living at Alexis, Ill.
209, Gertrude Alice, b. 9 March, 1879; living at Fithian, Ill.
210, Holly Clay, b. 26 Feb., 1881; living at Omaha, Neb.

115. CHARLES TALBOT DUKE (John[1], Francis[2], John[3], David[4], Salathiel A.[5]), youngest and only surviving child of Salathiel A. and Ruth E. (Barnes) Duke, b. Keokuk, Ia., 20 April, 1860; now residing at Monticello, Ark.; *m.* 25 March, 1885, Willie, dau. of Col. W. F. Slemmons, former Representative from the VI. District of Arkansas to the Congress; late Colonel in the Confederate States Army, and now County and Probate Judge of Drew County, Ark. Chas. T. Duke received a classical education at the Vanderbilt University, Nashville, Tenn., and later completed his course in business and commercial law at the Poughkeepsie Business College, Poughkeepsie, N. Y. He was associated with his father in the firm of Duke & Co., in the management of their large interests in Drew Co., Ark. He was formerly Register in the United States Land Office, at Camden, Ark., but resigned the position to devote his time more fully to the development of the firm's business interests. He was Lieutenant-Colonel of the 2d Regiment, N. G. of Arkansas; is an executive officer and director in several prominent trust and investment companies in the southwest; is an ardent Republican and had done active and efficient service for the party, and has been brought forward a number of times for nomination to prominent offices, but more recently was urged to accept the nomination for Governor, but as the state is almost overwhelmingly Democratic he failed to see the utility of standing against such large majorities, particularly

COL. CHAS. TALBOT DUKE.

DESCENDANTS OF FRANCIS DUKE

after being defeated for Secretary of State at a former election.
He was one of the "Big Four" Delegates to the National Convention held in Chicago in June, 1904. He is also a Mason of
high degree; is personally very popular, a man of pleasant presence, easy conversation and prominent in society.   Issue:
    211, Elizabeth, b. Baxter, Ark., 21 April, 1886.
    212, Charles Edward, b. Baxter, Ark., 10 Dec., 1887; d. 22
        July, 1896.
    213, Marguerite, b. Baxter, Ark., 5 Dec., 1889.
    214, Martha, b. Monticello, Ark., 18 July, 1892; d. Monticello,
        16 Sept., 1892.
    215, David Francis, b. Monticello, Ark., 1 Sept., 1893; d. 31
March, 1895.
    216, Catharine, b. Monticello, Ark., 4 Aug., 1894.

116. RHODA MINERVA DUKE (John[1], Francis[2], John[3], David[4],
John C.[5]), dau. of John C. and Jane (Ulm) Duke, b. 1851; m.
1874, James Edward Hubbard; living at Denver, Colo.   Issue:
    217, James Hobart, b. 5 Jan., 1875; 218, John Charles, b. 6
        April, 1879; 219, Edward, b. 8 Aug., 1883; 220, Mary,
        b. 9 Feb., 1887; 221, Helen, b. 24 Nov., 1890; 222, Stella
        Marguerite, b. 22 Dec., 1894.

122. CHARLES ELBERT DUKE (John[1], Francis[2], John[3], David[4],
Nathan W.[5]), son of Nathan W. and Phoebe (Baker) Duke, b.
1862; m. 26 Aug., 1886, Emma Smith, b. 11 Nov., 1866. Issue:
    223, Clyde E., b. 14 May, 1887; 224, Warnley C., b. 24 Jan.,
        1889; 225, Helen M., b. 9 May, 1896.

123. LEONA DILL DUKE (John[1], Francis[2], John[3], David[4], Nathan W.[5]), dau. of Nathan W. and Phoebe (Baker) Duke, b. 13
June, 1864; d. 28 Nov., 1885; m. 1 May, 1884, D. C. Capell.
                                                         Issue:
    226, Guy, b. 5 Nov., 1885.

124. ORA BELL DUKE (John[1], Francis[2], John[3], David[4], Nathan
W.[5]), dau. of Nathan W. and Phoebe (Baker) Duke, b. 20 March,
1866; m. 25 Nov., 1886, M. V. Corbin.   Issue:
    227, Ethel L. Duke.

125. MARY ALVADA DUKE (John[1], Francis[2], John[3], David[4],
Nathan W.[5]), dau. of Nathan W. and Phoebe (Baker) Duke, b.
7 July, 1868; m. 6 Oct., 1887, D. C. Capell, widower of No. 123.
                                                         Issue:
    228, Inez, b. 6 Oct., 1892; 229, Bessie, b. 26 April, 1895; 230,
        Nelson, b. 22 April, 1901; 231, Dorothy, b. 29 March,
        1904.

128. AMY ESTELLE DUKE (John[1], Francis[2], John[3], David[4],
David M.[5]), dau. of David M. and Sarah (Smith) Duke, b. Lick-

ing Co., O., 15 Sept., 1863; *m.* 20 June, 1890, Oliver Leonard Babcock, b. in New York City, 3 Sept., 1862.   Issue:
232, Beatrice Olive, b. at Fort Wayne, Ind., 23 July, 1898.

129. IDA ETHEL DUKE (John[1], Francis[2], John[3], David[4], David M.[5]), dau. of David M. and Sarah (Smith) Duke, b. Licking Co., O., 12 Dec., 1864; *m.* 4 Jan., 1883, Samuel Miller, b. at Van Wert, O., 15 April, 1861.   Issue:
233, Blanche Marguerite, b. at Fort Wayne, Ind., 16 July, 1891.

130. WILLIARD LESLIE DUKE (John[1], Francis[2], John[3], David[4], David M.[5]), son of David M. and Sarah (Smith) Duke, b. in Licking Co., O., 31 May, 1869; *m.* 20 June, 1900, Caroline Miller, b. 11 March, 1880.   Issue:
234, Lawrence Clifford, b. at Fort Wayne, Ind., 10 May, 1902.

131. BLANCHE SINKEY (John[1], Francis[2], John[3], David[4], Sarah E.[5]), dau. of Miles and Sarah E. (Duke) Sinkey, b. 14 Nov., 1866.   Issue:
235, Rudy, b. 11 March, 1888; 236, A. Carl, b. 2 March, 1890; 237, Frank, b. 8 Nov., 1892; 238, Clifford, b. 24 April, 1895; 239, Clarence, b. 4 Aug., 1899.

136. HERMAN CLYDE DUKE (John[1], Francis[2], John[3], David[4], William B.[5]), son of Dr. William B. and Lavinia V. (Trevitt) Duke, b. Richwood, O., 16 Sept., 1875; *m.* 16 Sept., 1899, Laura J. Cahill, dau. of Benton and Lavinia (Howland) Cahill. Graduate of Richwood High School, 1895; Eclectic Medical Institute, Cincinnati, O., May, 1898; practicing physician at Richwood, O.
Has issue.

137. WILLIAM FENTON DUKE (John[1], Francis[2], John[3], William[4], Hamilton[5]), son of Hamilton and Hannah (Hebson) Duke, b. Johnstown, O., 17 July, 1851; *m.* 16 Jan., 1879, at Drakesville, Ia., Matilda Shepherd, of same.   Issue:
240, Mozelle S., b. 13 Nov., 1879; 241, Louella, b. 11 Jan., 1881; 242, Hamilton H., b. 15 July, 1883, d. July, 1885; 243, Iona Hannah, b. 15 June, 1885; 244, John J., b. 10 April, 1887; 245, Essie E., b. 3 Dec., 1891.

142. ESSIE MAY DUKE (John[1], Francis[2], John[3], William[4], Hamilton[5]), dau. of Hamilton and Ann L. (Wood) Duke, b. 13 May, 1871; living at Oscaloosa, Ia.; *m.* 31 Dec., 1891, Lora E. Sayles, of Drakesville, Ia.   Issue:
246, Donald Duke, b. 16 April, 1894; 247, Bonnie Beatrice, b. 2 Jan., 1897.

144. GEORGE RANSOM ALDIN (John[1], Francis[2], John[3], Sarah[4], John R.[5]), son of John R. and Sarah (Duke) Aldin; *m.* 1st 1874, Pheobe F. Ashley; *m.* 2d 1891, Mary S. Mann.   Issue:
248, Nina, b. 3 Feb., 1875, *m.* —— DeLong, living at Fond du Lac, Wis.; 249, John R., b. 1 June, 1877; 250, Alice, b.

15 Nov., 1879, *m.* Roy Wilson, living at Marion, Ia.; 251, Lewis A., b. 22 Oct., 1880; 252, Gertrude, b. 10 Sept., 1882, *m.* Fred. Hurst, living at Huntsville, Ia.; 253, Clifford, b. 13 Oct., 1884; 254, Beulah, b. 25 Jan., 1892; 255, Leslie, b. 17 Oct., 1894.

145. HARVEY DARWIN ALDIN (John[1], Francis[2], John[3], Sarah[4], John R.[5]), son of John R. and Sarah Duke Aldin, b. 17 Nov., 1853; *m.* 2 July, 1878, Charlotte Clark, b. 27 Aug., 1858. Issue: 256, Gertrude Sarah, b. 19 Sept., 1879, *m.* 25 Jan., 1900, S. M. Propet; 257, Arthur Darwin, b. 5 Dec., 1882, d. 26 March, 1883; 258, Wylie Evered, b. 11 April, 1885; 259, Nellie Warda, b. 15 May, 1888; 260, Dale Clifton, b. 17 Nov., 1893; 261, Orman Kyle, b. 23 Nov., 1897.

151. FREDERIC M. ALDIN (John[1], Francis[2], John[3], Sarah[4], Horton E.[5]), son of Horton E. and Mate (Sutton) Aldin, b. 2 Jan., 1864, at Ozark, Ia.; *m.* 14 June, 1884, Mary L. Houston; living at Maquoketah, Ia.
262, Clyde C., b. 28 Oct., 1885; 263, Norman H., b. 4 July, 1888; 264, Harold B., b. 6 July, 1891, twin; 265, Edith A., b. 6 July, 1891, twin, d. 18 Aug., 1895.

152. LEONA ALDIN (John[1], Francis[2], John[3], Sarah[4], Horton E.[5]), dau. of Horton E. and Mate (Sutton) Aldin, b. 7 Sept., 1867; *m.* Thomas W. Hamilton; living at Monmouth, Ia. Issue: 266, Ernest, b. 23 June, 1884; 267, Albert Paul, b. 22 May, 1886; 268, Arthur Lee, b. 28 Oct., 1888; 269, Effie Rose, b. 1 Aug., 1891; 270, Mabel Bernice, b. 5 March, 1893.

156. JAMES M. FERNEAU (John[1], Francis[2], John[3], Henry[4], Ruth[5]), son of John C. and Ruth (Duke) Ferneau, b. 14 Oct., 1867; *m.* 29 Aug., 1892, Clara Williams, b. 19 Aug., 1872. Issue: 271, Ross, b. 26 Oct., 1893; 272, Donald Claude, b. 11 Sept., 1903.

157. JOHN O. FERNEAU (John[1], Francis[2], John[3], Henry[4], Ruth[5]), son of John C. and Ruth (Duke) Ferneau, b. 14 Dec., 1871; *m.* 2 Dec., 1899, Dora Collins. Issue: 273, Junietta Bethayne, b. 2 Jan., 1900; 274, Dorothy, b. 12 July, 1901; 275, Laverne, b. 29 July, 1903.

158. NORA MAE FERNEAU (John[1], Francis[2], John[3], Henry[4], Ruth[5]), dau. of John C. and Ruth (Duke) Ferneau, b. 27 June, 1876; *m.* 9 Jan., 1901, George R. Estabrooke, b. 24 July, 1859; secretary and general manager, The Fisher Governor Co., of Marshalltown, Ia. Issue: 276, Kenneth Ferneau, b. 5 Jan., 1902.

160. CLIFFORD W. DUKE (John[1], Francis[2], John[3], Henry[4], James C.[5]), son of James C. and Belle (Oppenheimer) Duke, *m.* Crissa D. ———. Issue: 277, Vernon J., b. *circa* 1902; 278, Mildred E., b. *circa* 1904.

172. BURRIS B. DUKE (John[1], Francis[2], John[3], George[4], Nesbit A.[5]), son of Nesbit A. and Ella (Hilborn) Duke, b. 24 April, 1861; *m.* Ida Huckins. Issue:
   279, Fay Eleanor, b. 12 Jan., 1887; 280, Nina May, b. 7 April, 1896.

186. EMMA E. WILSON (John[1], Francis[2], John[3], George[4], Sarah[5]), dau. of Alexander L. and Sarah (Duke) Wilson, b. Waterloo, Ia., Jan. 31, 1868; *m.* in South Dakota, 5 Nov., 1890, G. Frank Emmert; she d. in Denver, Colo., 27 June, 1907. Issue:
   281, Raymond, b. *circa* 1892.

188. ORLANDO H. WILSON (John[1], Francis[2], John[3], George[4], Sarah[5]), son of Alexander L. and Sarah (Duke) Wilson; *m.* Bessie ——. Issue:
   282, Leonard H., b. *circa* 1905.

189. MARTHA ATTIA WILSON (John[1], Francis[2], John[3], George[4], Sarah[5]), dau. of Alexander L. and Sarah (Duke) Wilson; *m.* Chas. A. Wilson. Issue:
   283, Lee Otto, b. *circa* 1892; 284, Claudius Clinton, b. *circa* 1898; 285, Bessie Nora, b. *circa* 1902; 286, a daughter, b. *circa* 1906.

192. EMMA C. DUKE (John[1], Francis[2], John[3], George[4], John[5]), dau. of John and Charlotte (Guy) Duke, b. 3 July, 1875; *m.* Lamor Sinard; living at Waterloo, Ia. Issue:
   287, Marie; 288, Duke.

205. CHARLES ELBERT DUKE (John[1], Francis[2], Francis[3], Shepherd[4], John S.[5]), son of John S. and Lavinia (Snedaker) Duke, b. 1857; *m.* 1884, Lena Levins. Issue:
   289, Halsey Hambleton, b. 1885; 290, Gladys.

206. CHARLES SAGE DUKE (John[1], Francis[2], Francis[3], Shepherd[4], Elbert T.[5]), son of Elbert T. and Carolina A. (Sage) Duke, b. 5 July, 1864; *m.* 1st —— ——; m. 2d Ella S. Stratton. Issue:
   291, Carrie E., b. 1882; 292, Sidney Elias, b. 1894.

207. JOHN SHEPHERD DUKE (John[1], Francis[2], Francis[3], Shepherd[4], Elbert T.[5]), son of Elbert T. and Carolina A. (Sage) Duke, b. 27 Feb., 1865; *m.* 1887, Mary J. Kinser; living at St. Paul, Minn. Issue:
   293, Bernerice, b. 1888.

209. GERTRUDE ALICE DUKE (John[1], Francis[2], John[3], David[4], Hervey L.[5], David R.[6]), dau. of David R. and Martha (Stevenson) Duke, b. 9 March, 1879; *m.* George Cannon; living at Fithian, Ill. Issue:
   294, Bessie, b. 12 April, 1901.

DESCENDANTS OF JOHN DUKE, JR.

IV. JOHN DUKE, JR., third son of John and Margaret Duke, b. probably in Ireland, 20 Aug., 1753; was killed in the defeat of General St. Clair's forces on the Wabash River, 4 Nov., 1791. His wife's name is not known. At the date of John Duke's will, 2 May, 1791, she is not mentioned in it and the assumption is that she predeceased her husband. The will was probated at Martinsburg, Va., 17 January, 1792, and the children therein named were all stated to be under age when their father made the instrument. Issue:

1, James, b. *circa* 1774; 2, William, b. *circa* 1776; 3, John, b. *circa* 1778.

2. WILLIAM DUKE (John[1], John[2]), was living in the vicinity of Shepherdstown, Va., in 1826.

3. JOHN DUKE (John[1], John[2]), is said to have married in Berkeley Co., Va., and settled near Shepherdstown; after some time he emigrated to Ohio and had several children, some of whom remained near the old home in Virginia and died there. This John Duke, it is asserted, served in the War of 1812. Those who were in possession of the family records lost them during the Civil War when the Valley of Virginia was overrun and fought over by the rival armies. The following is from the traditions of one of his descendants now living in Cumberland, Md.

4. WILLIAM, bridgekeeper of the old Blue Bridge at Harper's Ferry, W. Va.; d. at Chase Station, Baltimore Co., Md.

5, JOHN, lived near Kearneysville, Jefferson Co., Va.; 6, EVALINE; 7, GEORGE, lived near Kearneysville, Va.; 8, SARAH; 9, LEWIS; Sarah and Lewis removed to Ohio and there died.

9. LEWIS DUKE (John[1], John[2], John[3]), son of John Duke, 3d, born and died near Shepherdstown, Va.; twice married; 2d wife was Catharine Koonce, who survived her husband and again married. She had a daughter (10) by her first husband; the child died at three weeks of age.

11. JOHN H., b. 12 March, 1841, at Shepherdstown, Va.; now living at Cumberland, Md., a bachelor; calls himself John Duke, Jr., and says that his father frequently referred to the Dukes of Harper's Ferry and of " Willow Springs " as cousins of his own.

12. GEORGE W., born near Bunker Hill, Berkeley Co., Va., *circa* 1833; *m. circa* 1854, Emily Jones, of Frederick, Md. Issue:

13, Ellen, now deceased; 14, Thomas, now deceased.

DESCENDANTS OF ROBERT DUKE.

V. ROBERT DUKE, fourth son of John and Margaret Duke, supposed to have been born in Ireland, 4 May, 1755. Subsequent history of this son after 1792 is unknown. At that date he gave title to the Duke homestead near Kearneysville to Captain James Kearney, as executor of his parents' wills.

A Robert Duke of this period was living after 1792 on the Conondequinett Creek, in Cumberland Valley, Pa., whom we have reason to believe may have been the son of John and Margaret Duke, of Berkeley Co., Va. He married a German woman and had a numerous offspring; the names of only two of them, however, are recalled by their descendants and the line of the one son is here given for the benefit of his posterity in case future developments may prove the above Robert to have been the son of John Duke, the emigrant ancestor. Issue:

1, John (Robert²), d. 8 Dec., 1845.

2, A daughter of Robert, who d. three weeks after her marriage to Jacob Gottschau, or Gottschall.

1. JOHN DUKE, son of Robert Duke, of Cumberland County, d. 8 Dec., 1845; m. at Lancaster, Pa., Abigail Kline, who was b. in Lancaster Co., Pa., and d. 17 Dec., 1849. This family lived near Shippensburg, Pa., and had issue:

3, John; 4, Samuel, d. 1 March, 1846; 5, David; 6, George, d. 2 April, 1874; 7, Daniel, d. 9 Aug., 1852; 8, Benjamin; 9, Adam; 10, Jacob, d. 16 March, 1879; 11, Mary; 12, Sarah, d. 10 Feb., 1892; 13, Elizabeth, b. 17 March, 1801, d. 19 Jan., 1892; and 14, Margaret, d. 15 Jan., 1893.

3. JOHN DUKE (Robert², John³), son of John and Abigail (Kline) Duke; m. Jane Parks, of Cumberland Co., Pa. They had issue:

15, William; 16, Rebecca; 17, Sarah; 18, Adeline.

4. SAMUEL DUKE (Robert², John³), son of John and Abigail (Kline) Duke, d. 1 March, 1846; m. Elizabeth Ware, of Piketon, O.; she d. May, 1883. Issue:

19, John K., b. Piketon, O., 20 Aug., 1844; 20, Sarah, b. *circa* 1846.

5. DAVID DUKE (Robert², John³), son of John and Abigail (Kline) Duke; m. Miss Jones. Issue:

21, Alexander; 22, Hattie; 23, Sadie; 24, David, Jr.; 25, George. This family resides at Kokoma, Ind.

6. GEORGE DUKE (Robert², John³), son of John and Abigail (Kline) Duke, d. 2 April, 1874; m. 1 Nov., 1856, Annie Siebert, of Springfield, O.; she d. 3 Feb., 1891, leaving issue:

26, Margaret; 27, Eva C.; 28, Ida; 29, Nora; 30, Sarah; 31, Anna. The three latter reside at Springfield, O.

7. DANIEL DUKE (Robert[2], John[3]), son of John and Abigail (Kline) Duke, d. 9 Aug., 1852; *m.* Sophia Thrush.   Issue: 32, John Edgar, b. 5 Dec., 1836; 33, Henry, b. 1 Dec., 1839; 34, Robert H., b. 1841; 35, George; 36, Abbie; 37, Sarah.

8. BENJAMIN DUKE (Robert[2], John[3]), son of John and Abigail (Kline) Duke, *m.* Miss Wallis and had issue: 38, Mary; 39, Lizzie; 40, John.

9. ADAM DUKE (Robert[2], John[3]), son of John and Abigail (Kline) Duke, *m.* Anne Meredith.   They had issue: 41, Kate; 42, Israel; 43, Charles; 44, Abbie; 45, Burd; 46, Ida; 47, George, who was drowned in Texas.

10. JACOB DUKE (Robert[2], John[3]), son of John and Abigail (Kline) Duke, b. 13 April, 1801; d. 19 March, 1879, at Chambersburg, Pa.   He was a miller and with his family resided at Chambersburg, Pa.; *m.* Mary Kunkle.   They had issue: 48, Benjamin, b. 12 Aug., 1835, in Green Township, Franklin Co., Pa., a blacksmith; 49, —— ——.

11. MARY DUKE (Robert[2], John[3]), dau. of John and Abigail (Kline) Duke, *m.* William Griffin.   Issue: 50, Laura; 51, Anna; 52, James; 53, Alice.

12. SARAH DUKE (Robert[2], John[3]), dau. of John and Abigail (Kline) Duke, d. 10 Feb., 1892; *m.* Ephraim Muse. No issue.

13. ELIZABETH DUKE (Robert[2], John[3]), dau. of John and Abigail (Kline) Duke, b. 17 March, 1801; d. 19 Jan., 1892; *m.* 1843, Jacob Powder; reside at Abilene, Kan.   They had issue: 54, Margaret; 55, Ella.

14. MARGARET DUKE (Robert[2], John[3]), dau. of John and Abigail (Kline) Duke, b. 1820; d. 15 Jan., 1893, at Springfield, O.; *m.* —— Fletcher. No issue.

19. JOHN K. (Robert[2], John[3]), son of Samuel and Elizabeth (Ware) Duke, b. Piketon, Pike Co., O., 20 Aug., 1844; *m.* 27 Oct., 1870, Lola C. Lloyd, dau. of Thomas J. Lloyd, of Portsmouth, O.   They had issue: 56, John K., Jr.   John K. Duke was two years of age when his father died.   He attended the common schools, enlisted in Company F, 53d Regiment, Ohio Volunteer Infantry, in 1864; joined his regiment in Alabama.   After the war taught school, held position in First National Bank till 1874; financial manager and accountant of the Illinois Sewing Machine Co., of Chicago.   Failing in health, he returned to Portsmouth, O., and engaged in the real estate and insurance business.   A life-long member of the Methodist Church; was treasurer of the Board of Education for several years; is at present engaged with

THE DUKE GENEALOGY

his father-in-law in business (see History of 53d Regt., Ohio Vol. Inf.).

26. MARGARET DUKE (Robert², John³, George⁴), dau. of George and Annie (Siebert) Duke, *m.* July, 1874, William Lewis; residing at Springfield, O.   Issue:
57, Frank; 58, Jessie; 59, Albert; 60, Carl; 61, Edith; 62, Elsie; 63, Anna.

27. EVA CATHARINE DUKE (Robert², John³, George⁴), dau. of George and Annie (Siebert) Duke, *m.* William Pickard. Issue: 64, George; 65, Dollie.

28. IDA DUKE (Robert², John³, George⁴), dau. of George and Annie (Siebert) Duke, *m.* Otto Eglinger; residing at Springfield, O.

32. JOHN EDGAR DUKE (Robert², John³, Daniel⁴), son of Daniel and Sophia (Thrush) Duke, b. 5 Dec., 1836; residing at Cumberland, Md.; *m.* 1860, Elizabeth J. Kerney, dau. of Uriah Kerney, of Jefferson Co., W. Va. She is of Scotch-Irish descent. J. Edgar Duke left his home in the Cumberland Valley in 1853 and went to Jefferson Co., W. Va., where he was married in 1860. He enlisted and served four years in the Southern army and he gives us a unique record of his service in the Confederacy. In the history of the Civil War he is referred to as " the man who stole the locomotives from the Baltimore and Ohio Railroad." It was under his directions that the engines were removed from the tracks of the B. & O. R. R. at Martinsburg, Va., and hauled over the rough pike road to Winchester in July, 1861. The "steal" consisted of taking physically nineteen engines, with their tenders, over the highway for forty miles, that they might be put to use in the Confederate service. Mr. Duke at the time of his army enlistment was confidential clerk for Thomas R. Sharp, a civil engineer in the corps of the B. & O. R. R. Co. Later Mr. Sharp became a colonel and acting quartermaster in the Southern army. Mr. Duke was detailed for duty in Colonel Sharp's department and was personally responsible for the despoilation of the railroad property. A good account of this incident in the Rebellion may be found in "The Royal Blue Book," a monthly publication of the passenger department of the B. & O. R. R. Co., for January, 1898. Mr. Duke, notwithstanding the part he played in this particular phase of the events of 1861 against the property of his employers, is still in the service and now occupies a very responsible position with the Baltimore and Ohio Railroad Co. While Mr. J. E. Duke was serving in the Confederate army two of his brothers were serving in the Union army; thus was "a house divided against itself" by the issues of the war for the preservation of the Union.   Issue:
66, Mary Woods, b. 7 June, 1862, at Staunton, Va.; 67, Fred-

HENRY J. DUKE

erick; 68, Edgar Thrush, b. 20 Nov., 1865; 69, Harry K.; 69½, Mary, *m.* —— Campbell.

33. HENRY J. DUKE (Robert[2], John[3], Daniel[4]), son of Daniel and Sophia (Thrush) Duke, b. near Shippensburg, Pa., 1 Dec., 1839, and there residing; *m.* 1864, Mary E. Obelman. Issue: 70, Carlton, b. 1867; 71, William, b. 1873, *m.* Annie Kauffman, of Harrisburg, Pa.; 72, Mary E. Eveline, b. May, 1881.

34. ROBERT H. DUKE (Robert[2], John[3], Daniel[4]), son of Daniel and Sophia (Thrush) Duke, b. 1841; living at Shippensburg, Pa.; *m.* Mary Dietrich, of same place. He is an architect and builder; served in 130th Regt. Pa. Vols. Issue: 73, Robert, b. 1888.

35. GEORGE K. DUKE (Robert[2], John[3], Daniel[4]), son of Daniel and Sophia (Thrush) Duke, b. 1845; *m.* Jane Mill. George enlisted as a private in a Union cavalry regiment when fifteen years of age and served a part of his time as dispatch bearer for General P. H. Sheridan. Issue: 74, A son; 75, Nellie, who *m.* Joseph Conner; 76, Annie, who *m.* Frank Hinkle; 77, Robert.

40. JOHN DUKE (Robert[2], John[3], Benjamin[4]), son of Benjamin and —— (Wallis) Duke, b. ——; *m.* Josephine Dietrich and had issue: 78, Josephine Gotwals; 79, Rhetta, *m.* and has issue; 80, William; 81, Mary.

42. ISRAEL M. DUKE (Robert[2], John[3], Adam[4]), son of Adam and Anne (Meredith) Duke; *m.* 3 Sept., 1879, Mary Etter. Issue: 82, Sarah, *m.* Mr. Barrach and has issue; 83, Mary; 84, Nina; 85, Laura; 86, John; 87, Nellie; 88, Amanda.

43. CHARLES DUKE (Robert[2], John[3], Adam[4]), son of Adam and Anne (Meredith) Duke; *m.* Miss Grove and had issue.

44. ABBIE DUKE (Robert[2], John[3], Adam[4]), dau. of Adam and Anne (Meredith) Duke; *m.* Alfred Shugars and had issue.

45. BURD DUKE (Robert[2], John[3], Adam[4]), son of Adam and Anne (Meredith) Duke; *m.* Miss Wilt and had issue.

46. IDA DUKE (Robert[2], John[3], Adam[4]), dau. of Adam and Anne (Meredith) Duke; *m.* Mr. Sidars and had issue.

48. BENJAMIN DUKE (Robert[2], John[3], Jacob[4]), son of Jacob and Mary (Kunkle) Duke, b. 12 Aug., 1835, in Green Township, Franklin Co., Pa.; *m.* 5 Jan., 1856, Margaret Boles, dau. of Adam and Jemima Boles. Issue: 89, William; 90, Ellen; 91, Samuel; 92, Frank; 93, Edward; 94, Charles; 95, Alice; 96, Harry; 97, Lillie; 98, Benjamin; 99, Albert; 100, Elmer, *m.* Edith Waltrich, resides Chambersburg, Pa.; 101, Bessie.

55. ELLA V. POWDER (Robert[2], John[3], Elizabeth[4]), dau. of Jacob and Elizabeth (Duke) Powder, b. 1849; *m.* 1874, Jacob Burkholder; resides at Abilene, Kan. Issue:
102, Alice; 103, Price; 104, Mary; 105, Raymond; 106, Bertha.

66. MARY WOOD DUKE (Robert[2], John[3], Daniel[4], John E.[5]), dau. of J. Edgar and Elizabeth (Kerney) Duke, b. Staunton, Va., 7 June, 1862; *m.* 13 June, 1883, William Pendleton Campbell, b. at Charlestown, W. Va., 6 Sept., 1857. Issue:
107, Ellenor Duke, b. 2 April, 1884, at Cumberland, Md.

68. EDGAR THRUSH DUKE (Robert[2], John[3], Daniel[4], John E.[5]), son of Major John E. and Elizabeth (Kerney) Duke, b. Charlestown, W. Va., 20 Nov., 1865; d. Cumberland, Md., April, 1909; *m.* 29 Dec., 1898, Mary A., dau. of James and Charlotta (Marburg) Gardner. He was a practicing physician at Cumberland, Md.; graduate University of Maryland; member of Allegany Co. (Md.) Medical Society; Cumberland Academy of Medicine; American Medical Association; Society for the Prevention and Cure of Tuberculosis, and an elder in the First Presbyterian Church of Cumberland. He is buried in Rose Hill Cemetery, Cumberland, Md. Issue:
108, John.

70. CARLTON DUKE (Robert[2], John[3], Daniel[4], Henry J.[5]), son of Henry J. and Mary (Obelmann) Duke, b. Shippensburg, Pa., 1867; *m.* Laura Boyer, of Harrisburg, Pa.; real estate broker, residing at Philadelphia, Pa. Issue:
109, Helen, b. 1892; 110, Carlton, b. 1897.

91. SAMUEL DUKE (Robert[2], John[3], Jacob[4], Benjamin[5]), son of Benjamin and Margaret (Boles) Duke, *m.* Belle Reisher. Issue:
111, Nellie; 112, Benjamin; 113, Daniel; 114, Bertha.

92. FRANKLIN DUKE (Robert[2], John[3], Jacob[4], Benjamin[5]), son of Benjamin and Margaret (Boles) Duke, *m.* Emma Shoe; blacksmith, Chambersburg, Pa.
115, Russell; 116, Edwin.

93. EDWARD DUKE (Robert[2], John[3], Jacob[4], Benjamin[5]), son of Benjamin and Margaret (Boles) Duke, blacksmith; resides at Chambersburg, Pa.; *m.* Virginia Reisher. Issue:
117, Susie; 118, Daniel; 119, Benjamin; 120, Mary.

94. CHARLES DUKE (Robert[2], John[3], Jacob[4], Benjamin[5]), son of Benjamin and Margaret (Boles) Duke, *m.* Sophia Marx; machinist, Chambersburg, Pa. Issue:
121, Charles; 122, George; 123, Trevor.

97. LILLIE DUKE (Robert[2], John[3], Jacob[4], Benjamin[5]), dau. of Benjamin and Margaret (Boles) Duke, *m.* George Gillespie. Issue:
124, Garnet.

JAMES DUKE, OF CHARLESTOWN, W. VA.

99. ALBERT DUKE (Robert[2], John[3], Jacob[4], Benjamin[5]), son of
Benjamin and Margaret (Boles) Duke, *m.* Nellie Stratton; machinist, resides at Altoona, Pa.   Issue:
125, Franklin.

JAMES DUKE, OF CHARLESTOWN, W. VA.

I. JAMES DUKE, descendant of Col. William Duke, an officer
of cavalry in the army of William of Orange, who came into
Ireland, in 1691, was a cousin of John Duke, Sr., of Berkeley Co.,
Va. James Duke evidently belonged to a family of Dukes that
were living in Newry Parish, Newry Barony, County Down, Ireland, where one Mark Duke is listed among " Protestant Householders," in 1740; and in 1781, one Mark Duke is found among
the list of "Taxable Freemen" in Cumberland Co., Pa., in
Middletown Township, where he owned much property. This
circumstance is mentioned because it was this same township
that the above James Duke came and settled after the War of
the Revolution, in 1785. It is possible that Mark and James were
brothers, perhaps, father and son.
James Duke sailed from Warren's Point, at mouth of Newry
River, County Down, Ireland, 13 June, 1774, and landed at
Philadelphia nine weeks and three days later. He was b. 2 Feb.,
1755; *m.* 11 Nov., 1779, at Philadelphia, to Judith Crane, and
d. at Charlestown, Va., Oct., 1825. He was a soldier in the
Revolution, enlisting as a substitute, at Philadelphia, 25 June,
1777, in Capt. Peter Mehrling's Company, 2d Battalion of Foot,
in Philadelphia Brigade, commanded by Sharp Delaney, Colonel,
and was mustered out at Billingsport, N. J., 12 July, 1777 (Pennsylvania Archives, Second Series, Vol. XIII., pp. 633, 634); 29
June, 1780, recorded as a private in Capt. Nathaniel Twining's
Company, 5th Battalion of Volunteers, Philadelphia City and
Districts, 3d Company (Pennsylvania Archives, 2d Series, Vol.
I., p. 751); and discharged from Capt. Jacob Bower's (Colonel's
Company) seven months men, 6th Pennsylvania Continental Line,
under Col. Robert Magaw, 26 Aug., 1780 (Pennsylvania Archives,
2d Series, Vol. I., p. 592). His wife, Judith, d. *ante* 1825. Both
were living 8 June, 1799, at which time they conveyed a lot in
the town of Charlestown, Va., to Margaret Worthington, which
was formerly the property of " Capt. Samuel and Dorothea Washington, he being the son of Major Charles Washington and
Mildred Thornton, his wife, etc." Margaret Worthington was
the dau. of Ephraim and Essie Worthington. Issue of James
and Judith Duke:
1, William, b. 4 Aug., 1780.
2, Sarah, b. 12 April, 1782.
3, Susannah, b. 28 July, 1784; d. ——; *m.* Richard McMakin.

4, James, b. 16 Feb., 1786; d. "Easter Sunday, 1825."
5, Mark, b. 24 Feb., 1789.
6, Catharine, b. 20 Feb., 1791; *m.* 16 Dec., 1841, Henry Eby, her brother-in-law.
7, Thomas, b. 15 May, 1793.
8, Ailcey, b. *circa* 1795; *m.* Henry Eby and had issue.

1. WILLIAM DUKE, son of James and Judith Duke; *m.* 1st 19 March, 1805, Ellen Lewis, no issue; *m.* 2d 12 May, 1807, Sarah Fletcher, she d. 18 Sept., 1807; *m.* 3d the widow Figgins, in 1810; William Duke afterward emigrated to Georgia.   Issue:
9, Juliet, b. 18 May, 1812.

2. SARAH DUKE, dau. of James and Judith (Crane) Duke, *m.* 1 Aug., 1799, John Anderson, by Rev. John Huyett. John Anderson owned a tract of land on Long Marsh, adjoining John Vance's land, the tract was surveyed by George Washington, 19 Oct., 1750; he was associated with George Hite as an official of the Charlestown Jockey Club, in 1808, and was licensed in 1811 to keep an ordinary in Jefferson Co., Va.   Issue:
10, John Anderson, b. 18 Sept., 1800.
11, Elizabeth, b. 19 Aug., 1802; d. 29 Aug., 1803.
12, James, b. 29 May, 1804; d. 3 Oct., 1805.
13, Hannah, b. 9 Aug., 1806; *m.* Robert Muse, of Berryville, Va., but had no issue.
14, Emelia, b. 6 Feb., 1809.
15, George W., b. 25 Jan., 1812.
16, Thomas Duke, b. 6 Aug., 1814.
17, Joseph, b. 19 March, 1824; d. 13 April, 1824.

5. MARK DUKE, son of James and Judith (Crane) Duke, *m.* 25 Feb., 1818, Margaret McCarty, of Charlestown, Va.   Issue:
18, Samuel, b. 27 Nov., 1818.
19, James William, b. 15 Feb., 1820; d. 1855; *m.* Miss Tracey, of Maryland.
20, Mark Andrew, b. *circa* 1821; d. *circa* 1857; *m.* 1st Miss Dunham, of Baltimore; *m.* 2d Miss Meredith, of Baltimore.
21, Peter Thomas, b. *circa* 1823; d. *circa* 1863; *m.* Miss Hamilton.
22, George Samuel, b. *circa* 1825; d. *circa* 1830.
23, Margaret Ann, b. *circa* 1831; living 1906 at Charlestown, W. Va.
24, Julia Rebecca, b. *circa* 1835; d. *circa* 1863; *m.* George Everett, of Philadelphia.

7. THOMAS DUKE, son of James and Judith (Crane) Duke, *m.* 17 Aug., 1817, at Charlestown, Va., Sidney Johnston. She d. in Iowa, 1874; he d. in Logan Co., O., 8 Jan., 1857. Thomas Duke removed from Virginia to Logan Co., O., in 1853. After

his death there, in 1857, his family removed to Jefferson Co., Ia. He was a soldier in the War of 1812; was present at the bombardment of Fort McHenry, in Baltimore harbor, and "was anxious, when day dawned to see if the flag was still there." Issue: 25, James, b. 4 June, 1819; 26, Susannah, b. 2 May, 1821, d. 28 March, 1822; 27, Thomas Hammond, b. 24 June, 1823; 28, David, b. 3 Feb., 1825; 29, Mary Jane, b. 18 May, 1827; 30, Sarah Frances, b. 18 Sept., 1829; 31, John R., b. 19 Aug., 1832; d. 2 Aug., 1834; 32, Hugh R., b. 28 Nov., 1836, living, 1904, at Woodburne, Ia.; 33, Catharine Ann, b. 11 Sept., 1839; 34, Julia, b. 11 Sept., 1839, Nos. 33 and 34 were twins; 35, William Luther, b. 30 June, 1845.

8. AILCEY DUKE, dau. of James and Judith (Crane) Duke, *m.* Henry Eby, who, after her death *m.* 2d her sister Catharine. Issue:

36, Warren; 37, Laura.

14. EMELIA ANDERSON, dau. of John and Sarah (Duke) Anderson, *m.* Frank Mellhorn. Issue:

38, Jennie; 39, Cornelia; 40, Ella; 41, Harry.

23. MARGARET ANN DUKE, dau. of Mark and Margaret (McCarty) Duke, *m.* F. A. Smith, a photographer, of Columbus, O. Mrs. Smith informed me in 1906 that her descendants are now known by the name of "Dukesmith," which has grown out of the act of her son, in having his name changed from *Smith* to *Dukesmith*, by Legislative Act of the State of California. Issue: 42, Julian, *m.* Alice Taylor, she *m.* 2d Dr. Williams; 43, Rebecca; 44, Frank Hutchinson; 45, Daniel Lucas; 46, Margaret Gertrude.

28. DAVID DUKE, son of Thomas and Sidney (Johnston) Duke, b. 3 Feb., 1825. Issue:
47, William, d. ——; widow lives at Ottumwa, Ia.

32. HUGH R. DUKE, son of Thomas and Sidney (Johnston) Duke, was born in Clarke Co., W. Va., 19 Aug., 1836; is now living at Woodburn, Ia.; enlisted 18 July, 1861, in Company K, 7th Regiment, Iowa Volunteers, for service in the Union Army; was mustered out 22 July, 1865; *m.* 13 June, 1867, Mary C. Frush.

35. WILLIAM LUTHER DUKE, son of Thomas and Sidney (Johnston) Duke, *m.* 13 June, 1867, Mary J. McCreary; now living Trenton, Grundy Co., Mo. Issue:
48, Anna Belle, b. 20 July, 1868; 49, George T., b. 21 Sept., 1870; 50, Sidney Mae, b. 3 Aug., 1873, d. ——, *m.* 3 Aug., 1893, George Carpenter; 51, Luther Franklin, b. 13 Jan., 1876; 52, Orville, b. 17 Jan., 1879, d. 22 Feb.,

1879; 53, William W., b. 17 Dec., 1880; 54, Jessie R., b. 27 March, 1883; 55, Mary Mabel, b. 30 May, 1886; 56, Lena Viola, b. 20 Jan., 1889.

36. WARREN EBY, son of Henry and Ailcey (Duke) Eby, *m.* Virginia Locke.   Issue:
57, Willemina French, b. 1850; 58, Henry Jason, b. 1852; 59, Rachael Alice, b. 1854, d. 1890, *m.* Robert B. Mitchell; 60, Lucy, b. 1855, died during Civil War; 61, Warren, b. Dec., 1857, died in 1903; 62, Clarence, b. Jan., 1858; 63, Catharine, b. 1866; 64, Sue Carroll, b. 1870.

37. LAURA EBY, dau. of Henry and Ailcey (Duke) Eby, *m.* J. H. Marsh, of Woodstock, Va.   Issue:
65, Mamie, *m.* Hon. Matt. Walton; 66, Blanch; 67, Minnie; 68, Ellen; 69, Kate, *m.* Dr. Bell.

42. JULIAN DUKESMITH, son of F. A. and Margaret Ann Dukesmith, *m.* Alice Taylor; she *m.* 2d Dr. Williams.   Issue:
70, Blanche Florine, living at Philadelphia, Pa.

43. REBECCA DUKESMITH, dau. of F. A. and Margaret A. Dukesmith, *m.* John Q. Fleming.   Issue:
71, Glenn Colston; 72, Elizabeth Gertrude.

44. FRANK HUTCHINSON DUKESMITH, son of F. A. and Margaret A. Dukesmith, *m.* 1st Mary Burke; *m.* 2d Margaret Patton. Issue by 2d *m.* (Margaret):
73, Margaret Wilson; 74, Anna Newcome; 75, Ruth Gamble.

46. MARGARET GERTRUDE DUKESMITH, dau. of F. A. and Margaret A. Dukesmith, *m.* David Herz.   Issue:
76, Frank H.

47. WILLIAM DUKE, son of David Duke, of Ottumwa, Ia.
                                                                                                                    Issue:
95, Lloyd L., living at Des Moines, Ia.

48. ANNA BELLE DUKE, dau. of William Luther and Mary J. McCreary Duke, *m.* 21 March, 1889, Edw. Woolums.   Issue:
77, Irl, b. 20 Feb., 1890; 78, Don. L., b. 15 May, 1895.

49. GEORGE T. DUKE, son of William Luther and Mary J. McCreary Duke, *m.* 23 Sept., 1889, Hattie McVey.   Issue:
79, Miner Mac., b. 4 May, 1891; 80, Leo Lex, b. 7 Sept., 1894; 81, Eva Belle, b. 4 Sept., 1899.

51. LUTHER FRANKLIN DUKE, son of William Luther and Mary J. McC. Duke, *m.* 4 July, 1897, Jennie Betz.   Issue:
82, Franklin W., b. 1 Jan., 1898; 83, Leland I., b. 13 Feb., 1900; 84, Buford B., b. 4 May, 1902.

54. JESSE R. DUKE, son of William Luther and Mary J. McCreary Duke, *m.* 25 Dec., 1901, Katie Gates.   Issue:
85, Morton C. Duke, b. 18 Oct., 1902.

58. HENRY JASON EBY, son of Warren and Virginia (Locke) Eby, m. Ella Locke, of Charlestown, W. Va.   Issue:
  86, Eugene, b. 1880; 87, Henry, b. 1882; 88, William, b. 1884;
        89, John, b. 1888; 90, Shirley, b. 1892; 91, Judith Ann.

62. CLARENCE EBY, son of Warren and Virginia Locke Eby, m. Rose Thomas Hardesty, of Berryville, Clarke Co., Va. Issue:
  92, Marion Paul, b. 1884; 93, Winnie Baron, b. 1888; 94, Cecil de Grate, b. 1890.

DUKE, OF NORFOLK CO., VA.

The families of Duke now found so extensively in Norfolk and Nansemond Counties of Virginia, are doubtless descendants of earlier ones of the name who located on lands in the Upper Parish of Nansemond toward the close of the seventeenth and the forepart of the eighteenth centuries. According to the Land Office Records at Richmond, are found several entries of grants made to the newcomers, who were probably representatives of the Duke families of Wiltshire and Devonshire. The following are abstracts from the foregoing records:

9 April, 1681, to Thomas Duke, 430 acres, by Governor Chickely, for bringing into the colony five persons, among whom was the grantee, his son, Thomas Duke, Jr., and Francis Mace. Mace probably originated in Devonshire where the Maces, like the Dukes, were quite numerous.

24 April, 1682, to Thomas Duke, 350 acres adjoining Barbicue Swamp, by Governor Chickely, for bringing into the colony seven persons, among whom was Thomas Pryor.

28 Oct., 1702, to Thomas Duke, Jr., by Governor Francis Nicholson, 350 acres "at a place called 'Sarum,' for transporting into ye colony seven persons." "Sarum," in old England, was in Wiltshire, and in the neighborhood of Salisbury Plain where the Dukes of Balford were seated.

24 April, 1703, to John Duke, by Governor Nicholson, 113 acres on southwest side of Cypress Swamp, for bringing three persons into the colony.

28 April, 1711, to Thomas Duke, Jr., and his brother, John Duke, 49 acres of land, in same parish, on west side of the southern branch of the Nansemond River, and "near their father, Thomas Duke's line"; also, adjoining Francis Mace's land; and also, Governor Spottswood granted:

14 July, 1718, to Francis Duke, 231 acres of land on west side of Barbicue Swamp, in Upper Parish of Nansemond, and adjoining lands of Thomas Duke and others.

14 Feb., 1761, to Francis Duke, 480 acres of land, adjoining his own and Thomas Duke's land, by Governor Francis Fauquier.

THE DUKE GENEALOGY

There were also recorded in the Land Grant Books at different periods, beginning about 1728, grants of land to William, John and John Taylor Duke, in Brunswick and Lunenburg Counties, Virginia. These grantees may or may not have been descendants of the earlier Dukes of Nansemond Co., for we find them moving down into North Carolina, South Carolina and Georgia where there were several of them bearing the hereditary baptismal names and who served in the Continental Army during the War of the Revolution. James Duke, son of John Duke, of Great Bridge, Norfolk Co., Va., was the father of Thomas, Gideon and James, Jr.; Thomas died young; Gideon was a mariner and died in Liverpool, England.

JAMES DUKE, JR., of North Carolina, b. 1 Nov., 1813; d. at Shiloh, N. C., March, 1890; m. 1st Pollie Grey; m. 2d Caroline ——; m. 3d Cordelia Humphreys; d. 1881.   Issue:
   1, Martha, b. 28 Oct., 1838, d. 21 Aug., 1882; 2, Thomas, b. 13 Nov., 1841, d. 1893; 3, William, b. 9 Aug., 1845, d. 1878; 4, James Edward, b. 12 Sept., 1867, living at Norfolk, Va.; 5, Pollie; 6, Elizabeth.

   1. MARTHA DUKE, b. Great Bridge, Va., 28 Oct., 1838; d. Shiloh, Camden Co., N. C., 21 Aug., 1882; m. 28 Dec., 1865, Wm. H. Elliott, of English ancestry, b. 13 Feb., 1838. He served in General Johnson's Division in the Confederate service during the Civil War.   Issue:
   a, Enola, b. 15 Dec., 1866; b, Mary M., b. 16 June, 1872; c, John P., b. 3 April, 1875; d, William, b. 28 Aug., 1877.

   4. JAMES EDWARD DUKE, son of James and Cordelia H. Duke, b. Manchester, Va., 12 Sept., 1867; m. 20 Nov., 1895, Mary Rose Loughran, dau. of Daniel and Mary (Fitzhugh) Loughran, of Washington, D. C. Jas. E. Duke is a member of the firm of Duke & Smith, of the Southampton Lumber Co., of Norfolk, Va. Graduate of King's Mountain College, and Bingham Military Institute.

   6. ELIZABETH DUKE, dau. of James and Cordelia H. Duke, m. W. J. Cowell.
   a, Enola Elliott, dau. of William H. and Martha (Duke) Elliott, of Camden Co., N. C., b. 15 Dec., 1866; living at Elizabeth City, N. C.; m. 29 Dec., 1886, John Newbold.   Issue:
   i, Ruth, b. 28 Feb., 1888; ii, Edna, b. 10 Jan., 1890; iii, Margaret, b. 28 Oct., 1891; iv, Henry, b. 9 Oct., 1893; v, Mary, b. 26 Nov., 1901.

JACOB DUKE, of Nansemond Co., Va., m. Penniniah Booth; both living 7 Sept., 1825.   Issue:
I, Abraham Duke, b. in Nansemond Co., Va., 22 Nov., 1818; d.

23 July, 1886; *m.* 1st Sarah C. Daughty, 6 March, 1845; *m.* 2d Sarah L. Daughty, 9 Nov., 1860; she d. after 1886.

Issue:

1, Sarah Jane, b. 30 Dec., 1845; d. Aug., 1875; *m.* 29 Feb., 1872, B. Stephenson, and had issue: Harry J. Stephenson.

2, Mary Elizabeth, b. 26 Jan., 1850; *m.* 22 Dec., 1878, Jethro Raiford, now of Carrsville, Va.; they had issue:

   a, Annie S., b. 19 Nov., 1879; *b,* Sallie M., b. 17 Dec., 1883; *c,* B. Wesley, b. 18 Aug., 1886; *d,* Fannie B., b. 18 Sept., 1888.

3, Martha Ann, b. 22 July, 1852; *m.* Christian Duck, 22 Dec., 1878.

4, Charles, b. Nov., 1863; d. 1865.

5, Walter C., b. 17 July, 1866; *m.* 18 June, 1899, Estelle Butt; reside at Lake City, N. C.

6, Shelton H., b. 28 Jan., 1871.

II, Christian Duke, *m.* M. Harrell; III, Maggie Duke; IV, Daniel Duke, *m.* M. Williams; V, Edwin Duke, *m.* E. Copeland.

VI, Robert Duke, *m.* Margaret A. ——. Issue:

   1, Mary Jane, *m.* —— Holland; Emma Lee; Henry Littleton.

VII, Ely Duke.

VIII. James Duke, *m.* E. Lawrence.

HENRY DUKE, b. in North Carolina, 1796; d. in Virginia, 1891; *m.* Betsey ——. Issue:

I, Andrew; II, John; III, David; IV, Frank; V, Hardy, b. Nansemond Co., Va., 1831, d. Delaware Co., Pa., 1890, *m.* 1856, Sarah Morgan, who d. in Delaware Co., Pa., 1875. Issue:

   1, Henry Morgan Duke, b. in Virginia, 27 Sept., 1865; living at Norwood, Delaware Co., Pa.; *m.* 28 June, 1891, Mary Baier, of Norwood. Issue:

      a, Harry; *b,* Frank; *c,* Horace; *d,* Charles; *e,* Ruth.

HENRY DUKE, of Norfolk Co., Va., *m.* Harriet ——. Issue:

1, John M. Duke, d. at Richmond, Va., 1883; *m.* Mary Miller and had issue:

   a, George Henry Duke, b. Norfolk Co., 1869; *m.* 9 March, 1892, Jessie Sanderlien. Issue:

      i, Clarion; ii, Irene; iii, Lloyd.

WHITEMAN DUKE, of Nansemond Co., Va., b. 1774; d. 1866; *m.* Susan ——; she d. 1861. They had eleven children. Issue:

I, Hardy Duke, who came to Norfolk Co., Va., 1855; was b. 28 March, 1832; *m.* 31 March, 1860, Margaret Raby, dau. of Abraham and Catharine Raby. Issue:

1, Charles L., b. 1868, d. 1872; 2, Maggie R., b. 1872; 3, Harry R., b. 1877, d. 1878.

II, Henry Duke, b. Nansemond Co., Va.; b. 1844; d., *m.* 1869, Elizabeth A. Meers, b. 18—; d. Jan. 16, 1902.

—— DUKE, of Nansemond Co., was the father of two sons:
I, Elisha Duke, d. *circa* 1868. Issue:
  a, Elisha Duke, Jr., who *m.* Barberry Ann ——. Issue:
    I, John T.; II, Charles A.; III, Molly Lee Jones; IV, Francis; V, Mirabou; VI, Elizabeth; VII, Matilda, *m.* —— Ballard.
II, Parker Duke, of Holly Neck District, Norfolk Co., Va., d. *circa* 1882; *m.* —— ——. Issue:
  a, Burwell Duke, *m.* —— —— and had:
    i, Jesse P. Duke; ii, a daughter, *m.* —— Babb and had issue: Geo. A. Babb.
I, Benjamin Duke, of Cypress District. Issue:
  a, Nelson Duke, *m.* Mary Elizabeth ——; *b,* David Duke, *m.* —— Cissy. Issue:
    I, James W. Duke; 2, Laura Ann, *m.* —— Byrd, issue May Ida Byrd; 3, Alice, *m.* Jos. Alfred Saunders.

DAVID O. DUKE, d. 1865; *m.* Catharine I. ——. Issue: Owen J. Duke, of Beaufort, S. C.

CAROLINE DUKE, *m.* —— Duke. Issue:
I, David, II, James A., *m.* Louisa E. ——, and had issue:
  1, John F.; 2, James A.; 3, Minnie Lou.
III, Warner D.; IV, Elizabeth, *m.* —— Wells; V, Mary S., *m.* —— Outland.

ADONIRAM I. DUKE, *m.* Mary C. Nash. Issue:
I, Marjorie M. E., *m.* Thomas W. Babb; II, Isaac T. Duke, of Yates Co., N. C.; III, Henry F. Duke, of Yates Co., N. C.; IV, James A. Duke, of New Hanover Co., N. C.

DUKES OF BROOKE CO., W. VA.

A family of Dukes settled early near Harper's Ferry, Va., and by tradition were said to be of English origin, the head of whom served as a major in the British army then in America. This man left two sons, one of whom, whose name has not been preserved, remained in Virginia and the other was Alexander Duke, born near Harper's Ferry about 1772 and left an orphan at about five years of age. While yet a boy he left Virginia and settled first in the vicinity of Cincinnati, where he *m.* 1st Jane Eckles; *m.* 2d 1796, Mary Eckles; *m.* 3d 7 Jan., 1826, Elizabeth Wells, of Wellsburg, in what is now Brooke Co., W. Va. By the latter marriage there was no issue. Both Alexander Duke and Elizabeth, his wife, died in 1858, Elizabeth in March and Alexander in September of that year. Alexander Duke had by his first wife: Thomas, Elizabeth and Benjamin Franklin Duke; and children by his second wife were: Mary, Catharine Parmelia, Hezekiah and Rachael.

The following record regarding Alexander Duke is found in Deed Book No. 2, p. 213, at Wellsburg, Brooke Co., W. Va., and is of interest in this connection:

"We the undernamed Subscribers do Certify that Whereas Alexander Duke says that he was caught by a number of persons unknown to him in the night of 2ᵈ day of December 1799 and sorely beat & abused, and a part of his ear cut off, which was supposed to be done to him on account of his having returned some stillers for not having a legall entry of their stills. These is to certify that is supposed to be very Vilanously done, and that he has no fellonous trial to cause it to be done as given under our hands this 5ᵗʰ day of December, A. D., 1799

Signed   Andrew Campbell
John Swearingen,   Richard Campbell
Daniel Kelley,   James Campbell "

I. Thomas Duke, born about fifty miles north of Cincinnati, 9 Feb., 1798; d. Washington, Ia., 9 Jan., 1885. His mother died when he was a small boy and afterward he was taken and raised by an uncle, Chas. Eckles, of Bellaire, O. He m. 21 Jan., 1824, Nancy Garrett, who was b. 25 March, 1798, and d. at Washington, Ia., 21 July, 1880. After his marriage Thomas removed first to Marion Co., O., and later (in 1851) to Washington, Ia.; corporal, Brooke-Oakes Guards, 1851.   Issue:

  1, John Anderson Duke, born Iberia, O., 21 Dec., 1824; d. in Confederate prison at Macon, Ga., 6 Oct., 1862. He was a corporal in the 8th Regt. Iowa Vols., was taken prisoner at Shiloh and died on the morning of the day he was to have been paroled. He m. 3 April, 1852, Julia Ann Eckles.   Issue:

   a, Mary Catharine, b, Washington, Ia., 23 Jan., 1853; residing at Laporte, Ind.; m. William Harvey Tedford, who was b. near Marysville, Tenn., 13 Sept., 1844.   Issue:

    i, Samuel L.; ii, Leroy; iii, Beulah Luetta; iv, Coralie Geneva; v, Iva Bell; vi, Media Alice; vii, Joseph Guy; viii, William Homer; ix, John Arthur; x, Thomas Duke; xi, Julianna Paul.

  2, Margaret Jane Duke, b. 20 Oct., 1826; d. at Washington, Ia., 5 July, 1898.

  3, Andrew Garrett Duke, b. Marion, O., 30 Dec., 1830; living 1903 in Chicago, Ill.; m. 23 Sept., 1856, Elizabeth, dau. of James Currie, an emigrant from Virginia.   Issue:

   a, James Thomas; b, Agnes M.; c, Sadie S.; d, Laura, m.

—— Babcock; *e,* Cora, b. Washington, Ia., 1875, *m.* 10 Oct., 1899, John M. Winchester, a descendant of the Bradfords, Mayflower Pilgrims, and a cousin of Hon. Levi P. Morton, late Vice-President of the United States.

    i, Morton Duke Winchester.

4, Mary Elizabeth Duke, b. 11 Nov., 1833; d. at Chicago, Ill., May, 1894; *m.* Capt. J. A. Beyer.

III. BENJAMIN FRANKLIN DUKE.   Issue:

    1, Elizabeth, *m.* —— Hood, living at Olivet, Ia.; 2, Thomas, living at St. Louis, Mo.

V. CATHARINE DUKE, *m.* at Wellsburg, Va., 29 Jan., 1829, Andrew Groves.

DUKES OF DURHAM, N. C.

Henry Duke (captain, afterward major, in the Georgia line of the Revolutionary army), emigrated from lower Virginia to Orange Co., N. C., some time prior to the Revolution. He was probably a descendant of a John Duke, who was granted lands in Brunswick Co. and Lunenburg Co., Va., by successive governors of that colony at various times from 1728 to 1750, and of his (supposed) son, John Taylor Duke, to whom also lands in Brunswick and Lunenburg Counties in Virginia were granted at different periods between 1738 and 1760.

In correspondence with Washington Duke, Esq., of Durham, N. C., some years ago he informed me that his grandfather, Major Duke, with two brothers, William and Hardiman Duke, came to Orange Co., N. C., from Virginia before the Revolution, but that he was without definite information as to the facts.

In a list of soldiers of the Georgia line the name of Captain and Major Henry Duke is found (Third An. Report Nat. Soc. D. A. R., p. 375, 1900), and in another reference to soldiers serving in the Georgia line are found the names of Lieutenants William and Andrew Duke; privates James, Buckner, John Taylor, John Taylor, Jr., and Taylor Duke. These are confirmed in part and supplemented by the list of Revolutionary soldiers in North Carolina archives (Vol. X., p. 517).

Taylor Duke, son of Major Henry Duke, b. 1770; d. 1847, was a captain of militia and a deputy sheriff of Orange Co., N. C. He *m.* Dicie Jones and they had a large family of children, among whom were: Robert, Brodie, Kirkland, John Taylor, William J., Washington, Malinda, who d. *unm.*; Amelia (Riggs), Rena (Clinton).

I. JOHN TAYLOR DUKE, son of Taylor and Dicie (Jones) Duke, was b. 18 March, 1818; d. 20 April, 1893; *m.* 1st Miss Whittemore, by whom he had three children; *m.* 2d Mrs. Taliaferro (*neé* Yancey), by whom he had five children, one of whom, Lockie Duke, now lives at Milan, Tenn.

II. WASHINGTON DUKE, b. near Bahama, Orange Co., N. C., 20 Dec., 1820; d. at Durham, N. C., 8 May, 1905; was the founder of the famous tobacco manufacturing firm of W. Duke's Sons, of Durham, N. C.; a broad and public-spirited citizen and philanthropist, and the benefactor of Trinity College, of Durham, N. C. Mr. Duke, from a poor planter at the close of the Civil War, in which he was a participant as a Confederate private, became one of the most successful growers, curers and manufacturers of tobacco products of this country, and at his death left an immense plant and business enterprise. In connection with this subject the writer was present and witnessed a remarkable occurrence in the summer of 1906 while in Richmond, Va.

One pleasant morning in July, 1906, the Hon. S. A. Duke, of Arkansas, with the writer, under the personal escort of a mutual kinsman, Rev. Dr. F. T. McFaden, of Richmond, Va., were invited to visit the studio of Mr. J. G. Valentine, the eminent sculptor of that city, to view the statue of ex-President Jefferson Davis, then being completed by the artist. The party were met in the studio gardens by Mr. Valentine and, after introductions, were ushered into the studio. Just within the door, a few feet away, rested a nearly finished bust upon a rough pedestal. Mr. Valentine, as he approached it, turned to the group and said: "Do you know whom this bust represents?" And glancing quickly again toward the bust and back again to Mr. Duke of our party, with an expression of surprise upon his face, exclaimed: "Why, how remarkable! This is Washington Duke, of Durham; was he a relative of yours?" On being informed that no relationship was known to exist, the artist said: "Well, there must have been somehow; why," said he, "you have the very physiognomy of the Carolinian, except for the beard; there are certain details of the features common to you both. Look at the ears; you have the very ears of the family, and now, I remember, there is a particular detail I want to complete, will you let me pose you, please, for a few moments, while I put the finishing touches to the marble?" Placing my friend in a suitable position, the artist rapidly wrought with his chisel the desired effect and then thanking the major for his courtesy, and with some further remarks about family types and characteristics, led the way toward the statue of the great chief of the Confederacy. Washington Duke was twice married; 1st to Mary Caroline Clinton, dau. of Jesse Clinton, of Durham, 1844, who died in 1847, and 2d 9 Dec., 1852, to Artelia Roney, of Alamanse Co., N. C. By his first wife he had two children:

1, Samuel T., b. 1845, d. 1859; 2, Brodie Lawrence, b. 17 Sept., 1846.

By his second wife he had:
3, Mary Elizabeth, d. 1893; 4, Benjamin Newton, b. 27 April, 1855; 5, James Buchanan, b. 23 Dec., 1856.

2. BRODIE L. DUKE, *m.* 1st —— ——, by whom he had six children; *m.* 2d 19 Dec., 1904, Alice Webb, by whom no issue.
6, Lawrence; 7, Mabel, *m.* 22 Sept., 1901, Harry L. Goodall, of Richmond, Va. (children of 1st wife).

3. MARY ELIZABETH DUKE, *m.* Robert E. Lyon, and had issue:
8, Mary W., who *m.* G. E. Stagg; 9, George L.; 10, Buchanan.

4. BENJAMIN NEWTON DUKE, *m.* 21 Feb., 1877, Sarah Pierson, dau. of M. A. Angier.   Issue:
11, Washington; 12, Angier B., b. *circa* 1885; 13, Mary Lillian.

5. JAMES BUCHANAN DUKE, *m.* 1st 29 Nov., 1904, Mrs. Lillian McCredy; 2d 23 July, 1907, Mrs. Adeline Inman.

THE DUKES OF INDIANA

John Duke, a soldier of the Revolution, born in Great Britain, 25 June, 1756, came to America in early youth and after the War of Independence settled in Botetourt Co. (afterward set off as Alleghany Co.), Va. On May 5, 1776, he enlisted as a private in Capt. Charles Craig's company, First Pennsylvania line, and was in the battles of Brandywine, Trenton, Princeton, Fort Washington and White Plains, New York. In October and November, 1777, his name is recorded among the privates in Pennsylvania Invalid Regiment at Philadelphia. On September 12, 1778, he re-enlisted to serve during the war under Capt. John Pearson at Philadelphia, and served in Col. Walter Stewart's 2d Pennsylvania Regiment and in Col. Richard Butler's 9th Pennsylvania Regiment. His name appears among the Revolutionary pensioners of Pennsylvania, dated Feb. 5, 1830, then residing in Johnson Co., Ind. A part of his military service was rendered as a volunteer in the Pennsylvania navy; he had the experience of having been captured and held a prisoner on a British man-of-war in New York harbor (see Pennsylvania Archives, 2d Series, X.–XI.; 3d Series, Vol. XXIII., and Pennsylvania Magazine of History and Biography, Oct., 1901, p. 423).

John Duke, after the war, went to the settlements in western Virginia, where he *m.* 12 Feb., 1789, Sally McNeal, of Covington, Botetourt (or Fincastle) County, and then removed to the region of Jackson's River and engaged in farming. At the time of his application for a pension he was resident in Alleghany Co., Va., but when his claim was allowed he was living in Johnson Co., Ind.

While residing in Virginia one of his daughters *m.* a John Jordan, of Alleghany County, and another *m.* Robert Branch, of Kentucky, who afterward removed to Nebraska.

In the new west John Duke is said to have ridden eighty miles on horseback from his home through the wolf-infested and Indian-haunted forests to Madison, Ind., where he received his pension money. He d. 9 April, 1841, and his widow is said to have remarried twice and to have had several children from these later unions.
Issue:

1, Hugh, d. Morgan Co., Ind.; 2, George, b. 8 Oct., 1796, d. 5 May, 1872; 3, John, b. 16 July, 1800, d. 10 Nov., 1875; 4, William, b. 8 Jan., 1802, d. 22 July, 1884; 5, James; 6, Robert, d. *unm.*; 7, Mary; 8, Elizabeth, *m.* Daniel Etter, of Indiana, no issue; 9, Washington, b. 5 March, 1814, d. 31 Jan., 1854; 10, a daughter, *m.* J. Jordan; 11, a daughter, *m.* Robert Branch, of Kentucky.

1. HUGH DUKE, son of John and Sally (McNeal) Duke, *m.* Pauline White and had issue:
12, Thomas, who d. *unm.;* 13, Robert, who d. *unm.;* 14, Allen G.; 15, Winfield; 16, Columbus; 17, John; 18, James H.; 19, Mary; 20, Ella; 21, Emmaline; 22, Adaline; 23, Paulina; 24, Martha.

2. GEORGE DUKE, son of John and Sally (McNeal) Duke, b. 8 Oct., 1796; d. 5 May, 1872; *m.,* in Virginia, Mary Brummond and had issue:
25, Martha; 26, John; 27, Jacob C.; 28, James; 29, Mary.

3. JOHN DUKE, son of John and Sally (McNeal) Duke, b. 16 July, 1800; d. 10 Nov., 1875; *m.* Judith Humphries, a descendant of the Howard family of Virginia, and had issue:
30, Morgan H., b. 1832, d. 6 July, 1906, at Franklinville, Johnson Co., Ind.; 31, Sarah; 32, Elizabeth, *m.* in Virginia, James Humphries. She d. in Morgan Co., Ind.

4. WILLIAM DUKE, son of John and Sally (McNeal) Duke, b. in Virginia, 8 Jan., 1802; d. in Morgan Co., Ind., 22 July, 1884; *m.* in Alleghany Co., Va., 16 March, 1829, Nancy Glassburn, of Covington, Va., whose father, a soldier of the Revolution, was seriously wounded, yet lived to be 100 years of age. William Duke removed to Indiana in 1832.
Issue:
33, Sarah E.; 34, Robert; 35, Mary; 36, Paulina; 37, Eliza E.; 38, John W. (late of Banta, Johnson Co., Ind.).

5. JAMES DUKE, son of John and Sally (McNeal) Duke, *m.* in Indiana, afterward removed to Illinois.
Issue:
39, John; 40, Mahala; 41, Delilia; 42, Emma; 43, Minerva; 44, James W.; 45, Franklin P.; 46, Jerome.

7. MARY DUKE, dau. of John and Sally (McNeal) Duke, *m.* George Brummond, and had issue:

47, Anthony; 48, William; 49, Sarah; 50, Catharine; 51, Charlotta.

9, WASHINGTON DUKE, son of John and Sally (McNeal) Duke, b. 5 March, 1814, d. in Morgan Co., Ind., 31 Jan., 1854; *m.* Roxanna Etter. Issue:
 52, Robert J.; 53, Catharine; 54, Elizabeth; 55, Adaline; 56, Daniel.

38. JOHN W. DUKE, son of William and Nancy (Glassburn) Duke, b. Morgan Co., Ind., 23 Dec., 1840; d. at Banta, Johnson Co., Ind., 16 Oct., 1907; *m.* 4 Jan., 1874, Elvira E. Tressler of Indiana, but of Virginia ancestry.

"John W. Duke had long been a prominent citizen of White River township and was one of its successful farmers. He was a leading member of the Masonic fraternity at Waverley and had taken the Scottish Rite degree. In his life he exemplified the principles of the Order in his every walk in life. Personally he was a man of quiet ways but warm and true in his friendship. His disposition was to uphold what is right and to deal honorably and charitably with all men. He was a member of the Bluff Creek Christian Church. M^r. Duke had long been a correspondent of the Agricultural Department at Washington, making reports to the Department from his locality. He had also been the "Democrat's" correspondent for many years at Banta and was always faithful and efficient as a reporter of the interesting events in the neighborhood. . . . he leaves behind him the record of an honest and upright life, a legacy that can never be prized too highly." Providence Democrat.
Issue:
 57, Robert M., b. 12 Nov., 1874; *m.* 9 Nov., 1893, Nora Abraham.
 58, Ella J., b. 5 Nov., 1875; *m.* 10 Jan., 1900, Herbert V. Briggs.
 59, William E., b. 12 Oct., 1877; *m.* 17 Aug., 1899, Myrtle C. Beck.
 60, John W., b. 4 April, 1882; *m.* 7 Dec., 1904, Mattie Deer.
 61, Anna M., b. 16 Aug., 1885; *m.* 16 Aug., 1905, Russell G. Etter, of Providence, Ind.

58. ELLA J. DUKE, dau. of John W. and E. V. (Tresslar) Duke, of Banta, Ind., b. 5 Nov., 1875; living at Indianapolis, Ind.; *m.* 10 Jan., 1900, Herbert V. Briggs. Issue:
 62, Basil.

OTHER DUKE FAMILIES

THOMAS DUKE (son of David Duke, of Ireland), b. 1780, at Williamsburg, S. C.; d. 1858, at Kingston, S. C.; *m.* 1805, Sarah McClary. Issue:
 I, David M. Duke, b. 1812; d. Kingston, S. C., 1874; *m.* 1835, Adelaide Gamble. Issue:
  1, Robert E. Duke, b. Kingston, S. C., 31 Aug., 1844;

JOHN W. DUKE

residing at Lake City, S. C.; *m.* 28 Nov., 1872, Mary L. E. Hanna. Issue: *a,* John; *b,* Elizabeth M.; *c,* Julius C.; *d,* W. C.; *e,* Rubio V.; *f,* Harley P.; *g,* Lenia V. Fluvia A. Duke, of Workman, S. C., is a relative.

JAMES DUKE (b. sup. England), *m.* —— ——. Issue: I, James Duke, b. ——; d. Wolf City, Texas, *post.* 1890; *m.* Ann Amelia Miller, residing at Pendleton, S. C. Issue:
 1, Martha Duke, who *m.* —— Paris, residing at Benton, Polk Co., Tenn.
 2, John Calhoun Duke, b. Pendleton, Anderson Co., S. C., 4 Feb., 1844; d. 23 Oct., 1880; *m.* 21 March, 1870, Henrietta Frances Breakey. Issue:
  a, Henry Everdell Duke, resides at 396 St. Nicholas Ave., New York City; *b,* John Francis Duke.

JOHN MASTON DUKE (son of John Duke), *m.* 1886, Sarah Ann Garber. Issue:
 I, John; II, Lillian; III, Maude, residing at 510 Nicholson St., Richmond, Va.

GREEN R. DUKE, d. Jefferson, Jackson Co., Ga., 1867; *m.* Miss Pollard. Issue:
 I, R. S. Duke; II, W. M. Duke; III, M. N. Duke, *m.* 1st Julia, dau. of Dr. John Venables. Issue:
  1, Lillian May Duke, graduate of Grady Training School for Nurses, Atlanta, Ga.; *m.* 2d Mollie Long, of Athens, Ga. Issue:
   a, John R. Duke; *b,* Marshall N. Duke; *c,* Clarence D. Duke; *d,* David Duke; *e,* a dau.
 IV, Eliza Duke; V, Emma Duke; VI, Ella Duke.

JOHN DUKE, a soldier of the Revolution. Issue:
 I, Maston S. Duke, b. Hanover Co., Va.; d. Richmond, Va., 1863; *m.* 10 April, Margaret Kilgour. Issue:
  1, Maston S. Duke, Jr., *m.* Nov., 12, 1884, Rebecca ——; she was b. Henrico Co., Va., 22 Feb., 1860. Issue:
   a, James Henry Duke; *b,* Allie Maston Duke.

JOHN DUKE, b. ——; d. Sparta, Ga,; *m.* widow McClary. Issue:
 I, John Duke; II, Adam Duke; III, Henry Duke.
 IV, Joel Emerson Duke, b. Sparta, Ga., 1800; d. Buena-Vista, Ga., 1881; *m.* 1827, Martha Pugh, dau. of William and Clarimond Pugh, of Ga., formerly of Conecah Co., Ala., 1812. Issue:
  1, William J.; 2, Walter N.; 3, Lafayette; 4, James H.; 5, Clarimond, b. Turnbull, Monroe Co., Ala.; *m.* 1852, Dr. John D. Lindsay, son of Larkin W. Lindsay, of Monroe Co., Ala. Issue:

393

THE DUKE GENEALOGY

a, John D., Jr.; *b,* William W.; *c,* Joseph S.; *d,* Clara
Anna Lindsay, *m.* R. S. Wilson, of Jackson,
Clark Co., Ala.; *e,* Lulu, *m.* W. H. Tomlinson,
of Shelby Co., Ala.; *f,* Mattie, *m.* M. Dawson,
of Gulfport, Miss.; *g,* Ida J., *m.* Geo. M. Phase,
of Canton Bend, Wilcox Co., Ala.
V, Ellen Duke, *m.* William Owen.
VI, Ann Duke, *m.* Capt. M. Patterson.

LAFAYETTE W. DUKE (Rev.), son of the foregoing John Duke,
of Sparta, Ga., b. Turnbull, Monroe Co., Ala., April, 1843; resides at Lexington, Texas; *m.* 1st Oct., 1867, Mrs. S. E. Owen
(*neé* Garlington). Issue:
    1, W. B. Duke; 2, E. L. Duke; 3, Martha J. Duke; 4, Susie E.
    Duke; 5, Clara Duke.
Lafayette W. Duke *m.* 2d May 1, 1889, Sue, dau. of Judge
Granberry, of Texas, formerly of Mississippi. Issue:
    7, B. P. Duke; 8, L. T. Duke; 9, E. Duke.
Note.—Sisters of John Duke, of Sparta: Mrs. Hopkins, Allen-
town, Ala.; Mrs. Lewis, of Greenville, Ala.; Mrs. Taylor, of
Belmont, Ala.

BERNARD DUKE, b. Longfort, Ireland; d. at Philadelphia *circa*
1848; *m.* 1835, Emily Francis. dau. of Abraham Ogden, a manufacturer of Manchester, England, and Mary McMahon, his wife,
of County Monaghan, Ireland. Issue:
I, Bernard McMahon Duke, b. at Philadelphia, 30 April, 1840;
    d. at Washington, D. C., 18 Dec., 1899; *m.* 17 Feb.,
    1870, Otilia M. Newbaur, dau. of a French architect.
    Bernard M. Duke was educated in part at St. Thomas
    College at Villa Nova, Pa.; later studied medicine at
    Jefferson College and dentistry at Philadelphia College
    of Dentistry; practiced in New York till 1875 and then
    removed to Washington, D. C. Issue:
    1, Bernard Angelo Duke, b. at New York, 1870; *m.* June,
        1890; no issue.
    2, Mary Ada Duke, b. at New York, 1873; *m.* 2 Aug.,
        1892, Edward J. McQuade. Issue:
        a, Edith Nevins McQuade, b. 13 May, 1893.
    3, Emma Duke, b. at Washington, D. C., 1876.
    4, Harry W. Duke, b. at Washington, D. C., 1879.

DUKES IN THE FIRST UNITED STATES CENSUS

Names.	Location.	Condition.			Year.
		Free white males and females over 16 years.	Free white males and females under 16 years.	Free white males and females no age limit.	
Thomas,	Conestoga Twp., Lancaster Co., Pa.	I	—	—	1790
Daniel,	Martic " " " "	I	I	2	"
Mark,	———— Washington Co., Pa.	I	3	2	"
Philip,	Germantown, Philadelphia Co., Pa.	I	2	2	"
Thomas,	" " " "	I	—	3	"
Burnley,	———— Hanover Co., Va.	6	white persons		1782
Thomas,	Precinct No. 5 " " "	6	" "		"
John,	———— " " "	13	" "		"
Ashel,	John Coles' List., Nansemond Co., Va.	6	" "		1784
James,	" " " " " "	12	" "		"
Thomas,	" " " " " "	7	" "		"
Elisha,	" " " " " "	7	" "		'
Hardy,	" " " " " "	5	" "		
Jacob,	" " " " " "	9	" "		

PART IV
APPENDIX

THE VAN METERS OF FAIRFIELD COUNTY, OHIO

Reference has been made in these pages to Daniel, John and Jacob Van Meter, who were early settlers in the vicinity of the Hockhocking River, near Lancaster, O., in the years 1799 and 1801 respectively. Mr. C. M. L. Wiseman, in his Pioneers of Fairfield County, Ohio, gives further account of them; he says: "Jacob Van Metre, who settled east of Lancaster, was the grandson of John, one of the grantees under Governor Gooch. Daniel Van Metre, who settled west of Lancaster, was descended from Isaac, the brother of John and one of the co-grantees. . . . Among the first lot purchasers at the sale of lots in the new town of Lancaster, in November, 1801/2, was John Van Meter (Centennial Lancaster). . . . Jacob and Daniel Van Meter were natives of Virginia, but came to Fairfield Co., Ohio, from Westmoreland Co., Pa. They were cousins and friends, but entered land ten miles apart in this county. They came with families in 1799. Daniel settled on the edge of Muddy Run prairie, eight miles west of Lancaster, and became the owner of a large and productive farm. In 1803 he was appointed assistant judge of the Court of Quarter Sessions. He met with reverses later in life and involved his cousin Jacob. He had one son, who went to Cincinnati, studied and practiced law there. His sister Mary lived with him. Both are long since dead and their names are unknown to the present generation."

Jacob Van Meter entered 1,208 acres of land, a part of which has been known as Van Meter's prairie. This was a body of land between the glass works and the steam quarry and was often from one to three feet under water. Van Meter's land was one mile long and two miles wide. His cabin stood where Applegate's house now stands and there he lived and died. In 1803 he was appointed by the Court one of the county commissioners. He was an old-fashioned Virginia gentleman, who took life easy and enjoyed the amusements of the neighborhood; he was fond of live stock; was a fox hunter, and many of his descendants possess the same traits. He bailed his cousin at one time and was compelled to sell 500 acres of his lands to pay the debt. The name of his wife was Catharine DeMoss. She was born in 1752 and died in 1816, aged 64 years; was a Dutch-French woman of good qualities. Jacob Van Meter was born in 1745 and lived to be 93 years of age; died in 1838. His daughter Josina *m.* Rev. Hickman of the Baptist Church while they lived in Virginia;

this family removed to Indiana. Rebecca *m.* James Pearse in Virginia; they came to Fairfield County in 1800. Elsie Van Meter *m.* Walter Applegate; they lived upon the old home place on Pleasant Run. Sarah Van Meter *m.* Samuel Crawford; they farmed in Walnut Township, and there raised a large family. Catharine Van Meter, the youngest daughter, *m.* 1st Thomas Armstrong; he built a carding mill on Pleasant Run near the old Hull cabin. She *m.* 2d Robert S. Hull, of New York State. Col. John Van Meter lived and died on the prairie; b. 1771; d. 1845, aged 64. His house stood just west of Ashbaugh's spring; served in the War of 1812, in Captain Sanderson's company, and was made first sergeant; was paroled at Detroit; re-enlisted in 27th U. S. Infantry; *m.* 1st Ann Neely; *m.* 2d, Margaret Young. He was colonel of Ohio militia, and also filled many minor offices. After his death his family received a land warrant for 160 acres. His son Jacob located the warrant and lives on the land in the State of Iowa. Rebecca Van Meter *m.* Jacob Heberling, a butcher; they had several children. Cynthia Ann Van Meter *m.* John Shreives, a native of Rhode Island, also a butcher, and they had several sons (Pioneers of Fairfield Co., O., pp. 335–345).

THE KENTUCKY VAN METERS

Beginning with the year 1889 there appeared in the columns of the Elizabethtown News (Elizabethtown, Ky.) a series of fifty-eight letters of a general nature and treating of a variety of subjects. The writer was Hon. Samuel Haycroft, son of Samuel Haycroft, and his wife, Margaret Van Meter. Through the courtesy of the editor, Mr. Harry Sommers and the zeal and generous labor of Mrs. W. W. Van Meter, of New Orleans, the compiler is enabled to give additional data in the form of abstracts culled from these articles. The records of Hardin County do not go farther back than 1792, those of prior date being at Bardstown, the county seat of Nelson Co., Ky.

At the court house at Elizabethtown was found the following:
" Nov. 7th, 1807, License granted to Abraham Van Meter and Sallie Van Meter."
" Nov. 8th, 1807, Abraham Van Meter and Sallie Van Meter, *m.* by B. Ogden."

ABSTRACTS FROM ELIZABETHTOWN NEWS

I received my information from Jacob Van Meter, who was the younger Jacob Van Meter in the original constitution of the church.
The Van Meters, Bells and others were Valley settlers.
Henry Rhodes mentioned as one of the three commissioners appointed by the Legislature to manage and settle the estate of Jos. Barnett.

Jack Thomas died in 1865. (He was a friend of the writer.)
Among early settlers of this town was Hardin Thomas.
About the fall of 1779, winter of 1780, the early settlers were Capt. Thos. Helm, Col. Andrew Hynes and Samuel Haycroft, each of whom built forts with blockhouses.

The colony which came to Kentucky with my father, Samuel Haycroft, consisted of his wife, my mother; Jacob Van Meter and wife, Jacob Van Meter, Jr., Isaac and John Van Meter, Rebecca Van Meter, Susan Gerrard and John, her husband; Rachael Van Meter, Ailsey Van Meter, Elizabeth Van Meter and Mary Hinton. All of them, with my mother, were sons, sons-in-law and daughters of Jacob Van Meter, Senior. Hinton was drowned on the way in the Ohio River. There was also a family of slaves belonging to the elder Van Meter; these all settled for a time in the Valley.

My memory extends far back, for I distinctly remember the burial of my grandfather, Jacob Van Meter, on the seventeenth or eighteenth day of November, 1798.

Jacob Van Meter was my grandfather. He, with his family emigrated from Monongahela in 1779 and in the year 1780 came to Severen Valley and settled on a farm now owned by Geo. W. Strickler, two miles from Elizabethtown, on Valley Creek, at the mouth of Billy's Creek, on which last named creek he built a grist mill for corn and wheat, and, although there remains at this day not a vestige of this mill, yet I ought to know where it stood, as my father carried on a one-horse distillery, and when I was about eight years old it was my daily business (Sunday excepted) to go with a bag of corn three times a day. My grandfather continued to reside there until his death, which occurred on the sixteenth day of November, 1798. He was in the original constitution of the Severen's Valley Baptist Church on the seventeenth day of June, 1781. His wife (my grandmother), his son Jacob and his negro man, Bambo, were also members. At his death he left a large family, all grown. It is now nearly seventy-two years since his death, and, like the patriarch Jacob, his descendants have multiplied like a fruitful vine that ran over the wall, for they are scattered east, west, north, south, and may be found in every State and Territory of the Union, and from the least calculation that can be made they now number at least 3,000 souls. And that will not appear so surprising when you find that one out of his numerous grandsons had his *thirtieth* child born the night of his death. But that was over the average of the family, as the number of his descendants to each family ran on an average from nine to eleven children, but frequently exceeded these numbers. My mother had eleven.

My grandfather was buried on his own farm. I was present at his interment, being then three years and three days old and have a distinct recollection of the occasion. His son Jacob procured a sand rock and cut a tombstone which is yet in a good state of preservation and every letter distinct at this day. On the fifth day of February, 1849, I visited the grave, having a little grandson with me, and pointed out to him the spot which contained the remains of his great-great-grandfather. And as the inscription itself on the stone is a piece of antiquity, particularly as to its orthography, I will here give something like a fac-simile of it:

> Here Lizes
> The Body of
> Jacob Van Mater
> Died in the 76
> Yare of his Age
> November the 16
> 1798

APPENDIX

The spelling is rather of the normal style and is an honest attempt to carry out the sound. . . . Therefore, let no man pretend to criticise it or alter it. It is a jewel to me, so all mankind let it alone. It is the honest, homespun epitaph of a good man and a Christian, who braved all the perils and dangers of his day; honorable, kind, hospitable and generous, and truly a patriarch.

Jacob Van Meter, the second, was born in Pennsylvania(?) about the year 1761; became a member of the Baptist Church at eleven years of age. At nineteen years of age, say 1779–80, he came with his father to Kentucky and settled in the Valley. . . . At the death of his father he inherited the old homestead. On the advent of the Geoghegan family he sold them his farm and settled at the forks of Otter Creek, where he built a large stone house and resided in it until late in life. When all his children had married and left him he sold out and with his wife resided with his son John until he died. . . . He departed this life on the twenty-first day of October, 1850, in his eighty-ninth year, having been a member seventy-eight years and forty-five of this time a deacon of the Baptist Church, leaving thirteen children, the youngest upward of forty years of age. Out of his ten sons seven were deacons in the Baptist Church. . . . Thus lived and died the last survivor of the pioneers of Elizabethtown.

Abraham Van Meter, son of the last named Jacob, was born in Hardin County, two miles from Elizabethtown, in the year 1788. He resided in Hardin County up to the year 1831, when he removed to Tazewell County, Illinois, where, in 1866, he lost his faithful wife, who for sixty years had been a Christian helpmate in the true sense of the word. Shortly after the death of his wife he sold out and took up his residence with his son, Edward A. Van Meter, a merchant in Burlington, Iowa, and there resided until his death on November 11, 1868, in his eightieth year. He was the father-in-law of Rev. Dr. Weston, an eminent preacher of the city of New York, and was the father of Rev. William C. Van Meter, now of the same city, who is known nearly world-wide for his labors in the Five Points of that city . . . a full account of whose labors and the stirring scenes through which he has passed would make a volume of thrilling interest.

MORGAN VAN METRE

Mr. Morgan Van Metre, one of the best known residents of Berkeley Co., W. Va., died at his home along the Opequon Creek, on the Shepherdstown road, about two miles east of Martinsburg. Mr. Van Metre's was one of the very oldest families in this section, his ancestors having come here almost two hundred years ago. The farm on which he was born and where his long life was spent, was taken up by the first Van Metre in 1730, and has ever since remained in the family. The original dwelling was abandoned in 1780, when a substantial stone mansion was erected. This was the home of the family from generation to generation until about three years ago when it was destroyed by fire. The third structure, a brick house, was then built and has ever since been occupied as a family home. Mr. Van Metre was a Confederate veteran, having been a member of Company F, First Virginia Cavalry. He was a faithful and courageous soldier and served with gallantry until the surrender at Appomattox, taking part in the very last of the fighting. Mr. Van Metre was 73 years of age. He was a son of Abram Van Metre, his mother before her marriage was a Miss Isabella Tabb, of another prominent Berkeley family. He is survived by his wife and by a sister, Mrs. Georgetta Noland, of South Bend, Ind. (Shepherdstown Register, Aug. 19, 1909).

The above Morgan Van Metre was a descendant of John[1] Van Metre, through the following lines: Henry[2], Nathan[3], Joseph[4] (see Van Metre VII., No. 64), who was the son of Nathan and Mary Ann (Pyle) Van Metre. He was born in Virginia and is said by the late J. B. Kerfott, Esq., to have *m.* a Van Metre. Joseph lived for a time in Kentucky, where he was known among the family as "Virginia Joe." His son, Abraham P., *m.* Isabella Tabb, a daughter of Thomas Tabb and his wife Elizabeth Van Metre, who was the daughter of Jacob and Isabella (Evans) Van Metre.

HEDGES

1. SILAS HEDGES (John[1], Rebecca[2], Silas[3]), son of Silas and Margaret (Hoagland) Hedges, *m.* in Brooke Co., Va., Mary Cox. He died at Mountsville, Morgan Co., O., in 1873. He was a taxable in West Liberty Township, Brooke County, 1806-1817; afterward went to Federal Creek, O., and took possession of his soldier's claim (land) for services in War of 1812.   Issue:
   1, Allen, supposed to have been killed by Indians.
   2, Isaac; 3, Israel; 4, William F.; 5, Elson, b. at Wellsburg, *m.* Katharine Fulton, resided near Wrightsville, Athens Co., O.; 6, Catharine, *m.* William Rodgers; 7, Nancy, *m.* Absalom Fouts; 8, Jane, *m.* Henry Maguire; 9, Elizabeth, *m.* Joseph Moore; 10, Margaret, *m.* Jacob Fouts.

2. ISAAC HEDGES (John[1], Rebecca[2], Silas[3], Silas[4]), son of Silas and Mary (Cox) Hedges, b. at Wellsburg, 1809; d. 16 Feb., 1887; *m.* Lucinda Preston. They lived for a time on a farm near Amesville, Athens Co., O. In 1845 resided on the Muskingum for six months, then moved to Malta, O.   Issue:
   11, Tina, b. 1838; *m.* and had an only child who d. aged 2 years.

3. ISRAEL HEDGES (John[1], Rebecca[2], Silas[3], Silas[4]), son of Silas and Mary (Cox) Hedges, b. Wellsburg, Va., 31 Oct., 1812; *m.* Mary Ann Jenkins in Morgan Co., O.   Issue:.
   12, Rose Mary, *m.* —— Carey, and had a son, *a*, Verne Carey Hedges, living at Independence, Oregon; *b*, Sarah, *m.* —— Thorpe, lives at Independence, Oregon.
   13, David Lyman, living at Independence, Oregon; 14, Eli; 15, William; 16, Purley.

4. WILLIAM F. HEDGES (John[1], Rebecca[2], Silas[3], Silas[4]), son of Silas and Mary (Cox) Hedges, b. at Wellsburg, Va., 1816; d. 1880; *m.* Sarah McElhany. They lived on the paternal homestead

at Federal Creek, six miles from Amesville, O.; his father, Silas, resided with them. At a later date they removed to Mountsville, Morgan Co., O., where William, his wife, his father, Silas, and four children are buried. Those living are: 17, Sadie; 18, Silas E., who is now Mayor of Athens, O.

VAN METRE–MITCHELL–FUNSTON

The following communication appeared a few years ago in the Indianapolis Journal and is here given with additional notes gathered from some recent correspondence with prominent members of the above families:

As a cousin of General Frederick Funston and Lieutenant Burt Mitchell, I take the liberty of correcting some mistakes in the various accounts of them that have appeared in the Journal. Lieutenant Mitchell is not a nephew of General Funston, but a cousin, a son of Asa N. Mitchell, who served as a sergeant in the Sixteenth Ohio Battery. The Funston family were at no time residents of Indiana. E. H. Funston was born in Bethel township, Clark County, Ohio, was raised there, graduated at Linden Hill Academy, New Carlisle, O., served as a lieutenant in the Sixteenth Ohio Battery during the four years of the Rebellion, and then moved to Kansas. A few facts known to the family which might account for the adventurous and fighting qualities of both Funston and Mitchell may, perhaps, be of interest to the public at this time. Their ancestry fought in every American war. While General Funston's father was a brave soldier in the Civil War, it is from his mother's family, the Mitchells, he inherits his military tendencies. Pomroy Mitchell, great-grandfather of both young men, was a soldier of the Revolution, as was also their great-grandfather, Philip Sweigart. Their great uncles, John and Archibald Mitchell, fought in the War of 1812, and their great uncles, Charles and Anderson Mitchell, were in the Mexican War, Anderson losing his life at the battle of the City of Mexico. Their great-grandmother, *Margaret Van Meter,* was a *niece* of *Daniel Boone* and a *cousin* of *General George Rogers Clark;* she also was the *daughter* of a *soldier of the Revolution,* who fought at the battle of King's Mountain. This woman probably had a military record unsurpassed in American history, having thirty grandsons in the Civil War. The aggregate military service of these men amounted to sixty years. One of these grandsons, Anderson Mitchell, captain of the Sixteenth Ohio Battery, was killed at the battle of Champion Hill. This battery served in General McGinnis's brigade during the Vicksburg campaign, and the fathers of both Funston and Mitchell were members of the battery.

A. B. MITCHELL.

INDIANAPOLIS, March 30.

The Margaret Van Metre referred to in the foregoing sketch was born on the Yadkin River, North Carolina, in 1769. Her parents, probably Abraham Van Metre (son of Jacob, 1st), whose wife was possibly a Boone or a Morgan, were pioneers like the Boones, Bryans and others of the same neighborhood that formed there the settlement of emigrants from Pennsylvania and Virginia about 1750 or later. Family traditions uniformly agree that Margaret was a near relative of both Daniel Boone and Captain Meriwether Lewis, men so famous in the annals of colonization and exploration in the early days of the western frontiers that little, if anything, further can be said of them that would add to the prestige of their names or the glory of their achievements.

With the migratory movements of these Carolina settlers to and from Kentucky Margaret Van Metre and her parents formed a part. They were with Boone's party and she a child of eight years when Boonesborough was attacked by the Indians in 1777, and her recollections of those days were vividly recalled as she related their experiences and the adventures of her own early life upon the borders to her children and grandchildren. She *m.* early in life a man by the name of Neel or Neal, who survived but a short time, leaving her a widow with one son, William Neal, who later married and reared a family and saw service in the War of 1812.

Margaret Van Metre's second marriage was to Pomroy Mitchell, a native of Culpeper Co., Va. He, too, was a veteran of the Revolution, as her father and one or two brothers had been. The Mitchells resided near Culpeper Court House, where their children were all born and reared. Their names were: Charles, John, Archibald, Nelson, James, Anderson and Mary. After the death of her second husband Margaret Mitchell and her children removed in 1804 to Clarke Co., O., where she married for the third time a person by the name of McClure and from which union there was no issue. The Mitchell household soon dispersed: Charles married and went to Indiana; a son is Hon. Leander P. Mitchell, assistant comptroller of the Treasury at Washington, D. C. John also married and removed to Indiana, probably by way of the Ohio River Valley, where traces of a John Mitchell as a pioneer of prominence figure in the records of the settlements along this popular waterway. Nelson lived at Springfield, O., where he died in 1856. Anderson drifted to New Orleans when a youth and was never heard of again.

Archibald Mitchell was born in Virginia in 1796. He served in the War of 1812; *m.* 1824, Sarah Sweigert, a daughter of Philip Sweigert and his wife, who was a Miss Garver, a native of Maryland. Philip Sweigert was also a soldier of the Revolution. Archibald d. in Clarke Co., O., in 1873 and left a family of five sons and four daughters, of whom the Hon. Pomroy Mitchell, Mayor of New Carlisle, O., is one and another, the youngest, is A. B. Mitchell, of southwestern Texas. All five of the brothers, together with twenty-seven of their cousins, served in the Union army in the War of the Rebellion. James A., the eldest, was captain of the 16th Ohio Battery and lost his life at the battle of Champion's Hill, Miss. It was in the son Archibald's home that Margaret Mitchell resided in her later years; there she died in 1848 and was buried in the village cemetery at New Carlisle, O.

APPENDIX

James Mitchell, another son of Pomroy, *m.* Elizabeth Sweigert, a sister of Sarah, who married Archibald Mitchell, and a
daughter also of Philip Sweigert. She was born in Ohio 23
Aug., 1810, and died at Iola, Kan., 25 July, 1894. From the lips
of her mother-in-law, Margaret Van Metre Mitchell, Mrs. James
Mitchell learned many accounts of her early life on the frontiers
of North Carolina and Kentucky and repeated them to her grandson, General Funston, in his boyhood. James Mitchell died at
New Carlisle, O., in 1858. His daughter, Anna Eliza, b. 1843,
m. Edward H. Funston, of New Bethel Township, Clarke Co.,
O. He was a lieutenant in Capt. James A. Mitchell's 16th Ohio
Battery and a member of Congress, 1884–1894. Their son,
Frederick Funston, was b. at New Carlisle, O., 9 Nov., 1865, and
m. 23 Oct., 1898, Edna Blanhart. After some service under
Gomez in Cuba, Frederick Funston joined the volunteers in the
war with Spain and rapidly attained preferment. As colonel of
the 20th Kansas Infantry he was sent to the Philippines in 1898,
and there took part in several engagements in which his courage
and abilities were conspicuous.

"For his action in crossing the Rio Grande River at Calumpit
on a small bamboo raft in the face of heavy firing and establishing a rope ferry by which means the troops were enabled to cross
and win the battle, he was promoted to Brigadier General U. S.
Vols., 2d May, 1899, and awarded a medal of honor, 14 Feb.,
1900. He organized and commanded the expedition which resulted in the capture of Aguinaldo, head of the Philippine insur-
rection, and was appointed Brigadier General U. S. A., 30 March,
1901, commanding Department of California" (see Who's Who
in America).

EXTRACTS FROM THE SHEPHERD MANUSCRIPTS IN
THE CUSTODY OF THE WISCONSIN HISTORICAL
SOCIETY, MADISON, WISCONSIN

From October 10, 1776 to the fourth day of December, 1776, Francis
Duke delivered for the use of Capt. Thos. Gaddis' company of Virginia
militia 2,691 lbs. of beef and 1,187 lbs. of Indian meal.

Abraham Shepherd wrote his brother, Col. David Shepherd, 4 Aug.,
1778, that price of salt is £6 per bushel, powder 10 shillings per lb. and
blankets sell at £6. On 2 Nov., 1778 he quotes salt at £9 per bushel, and
suggests a "corner" in salt.

Extracts from Francis Duke's account book as commissary at Fort Henry
(Wheeling):

1777, 3 June, 127 lbs. Flour [issued] to Capt. Ogle's company.
1777, 5 June, to Capt. Benjamin Harrison's company—flour and bacon.
1777, 5 June, Received of John Biggs 101 lbs. bacon for Capt. Ogle's
Company.
1777, 7 June, Received of Silas Hedges 607 lbs. bacon for use of militia.
1777, 7 June, Received of And^w Fouts 425 lbs. bacon for use of militia.
1777, 8 June, To Capt. John Van Metre's Co. Indian meal; Capt. Reason's men some bacon.

1777, 8 June, To Capt. John Van Metre—Sergt. Lemon 503 lbs. bacon.

1777, 12 June, To Lieut. Cox's men—bacon and meal.

1777, 16 June, To Capt. John Van Metre—Sergt. Coons 500 lbs. bacon.

1777, 17 June, Received of Jacob Rice 125 lbs. bacon for use of militia.

1777, 16 June, Capt. John Vanmetre's men 5 lbs. bacon, 5 lbs. flour.

1777, 18 June, Capt. John Lemon's bacon and flour.

1777, 18 June, Sent to the mill 148 lbs. bacon for the use of the men, for the use of part of Capt. Ogle's men stationed there.

1777, 27 June, Issued to Arbuckle's company 145 lbs. bacon; Capt. Ogle's, 191 lbs. meal; Capt. John Van Metre's, 37½ lbs. meal, 17½ lbs. bacon.

1777, 27 June, Received of Andrew Foust and John Beckett 376 lbs. bacon, use of militia.

1777, 1 July, Received of James Miller 256 lbs. bacon for use of militia.

1777, 1 July, Received of Richard Rosebright one beef £2 for use of militia.

1777, 1 July, Issued to Capt. Ogle's men 273 lbs. meal, 150 lbs. beef for use of militia.

1777, 2 July, Issued to Capt. Ogle's men 109 lbs. bacon.

1777, 3 July, Issued to Capt. Ogle's men 14 lbs. bacon, 24 lbs. meal.

1777, 7 July, Issued to Capt. Ogle's men 166 lbs. beef, 32 gills salt for the mill party and 7 qts. & a pt. of salt for militia.

1777, 12 July, Issued to Capt. Ogle's men 579 lbs. meal, 273 lbs. beef.

1777, 20 July, Issued to Capt. Ogle's men 100 lbs. bacon.

1777, 22 July, Issued to Capt. Ogle's men 453 lbs. meal, 100 lbs. bacon, 272 lbs. flour.

1777, 22 July, Account of Indian meal between Jonas Lemon & Francis Duke—1400 cwt.

1777, 23 July, Received from Col. Shepherd a batteaux load of bacon 500 cwt. wh. and Tarr, and 2: 1—16 tare 22. 2: 1: 10 tare 21, &c &c.

1777, 24 July, Issued to Capt. Ogle's men 162 lbs. pork.

1777, 31 July, Issued to the party at the mill 93 lbs. flour, 94 lbs. bacon.

1777, 3 Aug., Issued to Capt. Ogle's men 17 lbs. flour, 12 lbs. bacon.

1777, 4 Aug., Issued to Capt. Ogle's men 84¼ lbs. bacon, 265 lbs. meal, 35 gills salt.

1777, 6 Aug., Issued to Capt. Ogle's men 117 lbs. bacon, 350 lbs. beef, 80 lbs. flour and 32 gills salt.

1777, 7 Aug., Received of Capt. Jos. Ogle 316 lbs. beef for use of militia.

1777, 15 Aug., Received of Lawrence Van Buskirk 217 lbs. beef for use of militia.

1777, 18 Aug., Issued to Capt. Ogle's men, 217 lbs. beef, 123 lbs. pork, 145 lbs. meat, and 39½ gills of salt.

1777, 19 Aug., Issued to Capt. Ogle's men, 384 lbs. meal.

1777, 20 Aug., Received from Jos. Hedges 226 lbs. beef for use of militia.

1777, 27 Aug., Received from Jos. Hedges 267 lbs. beef for use of Capt. Ogle's Co. of militia in actual service.

1777, 27 Aug., Issued to Benjamin Harrison's men, Aug 23, 12 lbs. meal, 10 lbs. fresh beef, and Aug. 27, 5½ lbs. beef, and 9 lbs. meal.

1777, 27 Aug., Issued to Capt. Ogle's men, 267 lbs. beef.

1777, 30 Aug., Received of Isaac Newlands 314 lbs, beef for use of militia.

[Issued to Capt. Ogle's men 308 lbs. beef, 262 lbs. meal. Issued to Capt. Jos. Ogle's Company July 22, 111 lbs. flour, 203 lbs. bacon. Issued to Capt. Ogle's men July 30, 300 lbs. beef, 31 gills salt. Account of Indian meal between Jonas Leman & Francis Duke: Aug. 3, 265 lbs.; Aug. 12, 145 lbs.; Aug. 19, 384 lbs.; Aug. 30, 262 lbs. These items were overlooked in transcribing in chronological order.]

APPENDIX

1777.	No. of men.	bacon.	meal.	gills salt.	beef.	flour.	pork.
Aug. 4.	32	84¼	265				
Aug. 6.		135	1060	67		94	
Aug. 18.	37		145	37	217		21
Aug. —.	44		384	2½	226	202	
Aug. —.	42		262	44	267		
Aug. 31.	38			38	314		

This is the last entry by Francis Duke (who was Col. Shepherd's son-in-law). He was killed by Indians Sept. 1, 1777; Sept. 3d and 4th some entries were made in another and better handwriting and the accounts are added and footed in the figures of this better penmanship. This is another evidence that the siege of Wheeling took place Sept. 1, as Withers says, and not Sept. 27, as McKiernan asserts in the American Pioneer. (Memo by L. C. D.)

REZIN D. SHEPHERD

Rezin D. Shepherd (IX, 2) was born in Shepherdstown on the site now occupied by the State Normal School, formerly " Shepherd's College," which was built originally by Mr. Shepherd for the county court house and public buildings at the time when an effort was being made to make Shepherdstown the county seat of Jefferson County. He built also out of his private funds the building for the county jail. The latter is now being used for the public school and is said to be one of the best conducted schools in the State. Mr. Shepherd was largely instrumental in the erection of Trinity Episcopal Church in Shepherdstown and contributed a very large part of the funds as a memorial to his mother, Mrs. Eleanor Strode Shepherd; gave the ground upon which the rectory was built. She was of a deeply religious nature, a consistent member of the organization and generous in her benefactions to the church.

HENRY SHEPHERD

Henry Shepherd (IX., 29), born in Shepherdstown, went early to New Orleans, where he became a merchant and was successful; he made profitable investments in real estate and greatly increased his fortune. While a resident of New Orleans he married Miss Azemia McLean. Ill health forced him to retire from business and to return to his ancestral home at Shepherdstown, where he devoted his remaining years and a good portion of his means to public benefactions and enterprises. Out of his abundant resources he built and maintained until his death 30 Sept., 1891, the fine highway known as " Shepherd's Grade." At his death it was given to the county. The Shepherd Fire Company was another object of his deep interest. It was equipped and largely supported by Mr. Shepherd. Many other instances of his liberality toward public institutions are related of him. He was a zealous churchman, but of pronounced views and a strict disciplinarian, yet ever responsive in its aid. He was a man of great energy, keen executive ability and fine business qualities. He left four sons: Rezin D. (R. D. McLean), the Shakesperian tragedian; Augustus M. (Augustus McLean), also an actor in Shakesperian rôles; Henry, a fancy stock breeder and farmer, who d. in 1896, and William J., all born and reared in New Orleans.

INDEX

DUKE, SHEPHERD AND VAN METRE SURNAMES

Dook, Duc, Duke.

Abbie, 375, 377; Abraham, 384; Adam Le, 259, 374, 375, 393; Adeline, 374, 391, 392; Ailsey, 380, 381; Adoniram, 386; Agnes M., 387; Albin G., 271; Alice, 273, 358, 368, 377, 386; Alice E., 341; Alice M., 364; Allie M., 393; Albert, 275, 377, 379; Albert F., 364; Alberta N., 275; Alexander, 275, 342, 374, 386; Alfred, 274; Alfred N., 274; Alton A., 366; Allen G., 391; Allen L., 367; Amanda, 270, 377; Amediah, 269, 273; Amelia, 271; Amy, 269; Amy E., 364, 369; Angier B., 390; Angie M., 364; Andrew, 259, 262, 292, 385, 388; Ann, 267, 269, 270, 273, 275, 277, 394; Ann C., 319, 324; Ann E., 330, 344; Ann F., 344; Ann M., 320, 332, 333; Ann M., 344; Anna, 332, 375; Anna B., 381, 382; Anna F., 332; Anna M., 392; Anna N., 332; Anne, 275, 377; Anthony, 392; Archibald, 269, 270; Archibald B., 270; Arlington I., 368; Ashel, 395.

B. P., 394; Barbara A., 276; Bartholomew, 262; Bazil, 264, 392; Beatrice, 330; Benton, 364; Benjamin, 274, 374, 375, 377, 378, 386; Benjamin F., 276, 387, 388; Benjamin N., 390; Belinda, 357; Bernard, 394; Bernard A., 394; Bernard M., 394; Bernerice, 372; Bertha, 378; Bessie, 377; Betty, 294; Blanche, 364; Brodie, 388; Brodie L., 389, 390; Buford B., 382; Buchanan, 370; Buckner, 388; Burd, 375, 377; Burnley, 273, 274, 275, 395; Burris B., 366, 372; Burwell, 386.

Calista, 354, 357; Calvin, 354, 356, 357; Caroline, 270, 386; Caroline F., 274; Carrie E., 372; Carlton, 377, 378; Catharine, 268, 275, 353, 369, 380, 381, 388, 392; Catharine A., 381; Charlotta, 270, 392; Christina, 356, 367, 385; Charles, 270, 375, 377, 378, 385; Charles A., 386; Charles C., 271; Charles D., 364, 367; Charles E., 364, 369, 372; Charles L., 386; Charles R. H., 276; Charles S., 367, 372; Charles T., 359, 364, 368; Clara, 394; Clara L., 366; Clarence D., 395; Clarion, 385; Clarimond, 393; Clarissa, 354; Clementine A., 272; Clifford W., 365; Cliveures, 267, 269, 270, 271, 273; Clyde E., 369; Cora, 388; Cora A., 366; Cora de J., 272; Cordia E., 366; Cordelia, 384; Columbus, 391; Cornelia, 270; Cornelia T., 271; Cosby, 268, 269, 271, 272.

Daniel, 374, 378, 385, 392, 395; David, 354, 355, 374, 381, 385, 386, 393; David F., 369; David M., 355, 392; David O., 386; David R., 358, 368; Deliliah, 391; Dennie, 270.

E., 394; Earle F., 340; Edgar T., 377, 378; Edgar H., 367; Edward, 259, 262, 377, 378; Edward T., 357; Edwin, 378, 385; Edwin M., 357; Edwin P., 271; Elbert T., 367; Elmer, 377; Elmer C., 364; Elizabeth, 259, 266, 267, 269, 270, 272, 273, 275, 276, 304, 355, 357, 369, 374, 375, 384, 386, 387, 388, 391, 392, 393; Elizabeth A., 274; Elizabeth B., 273, 275; Elizabeth F., 319, 325, 329; Elizabeth G., 320; E. L., 394; Elizabeth M., 393; Emma, 274, 275, 276, 391, 394; Emma C., 367, 372; Emma L., 385; Emma V., 393; Emmaline, 391; Emily, 270; Emily N., 332; Elisha, 386, 395; Eliza, 356; Ella, 277, 391, 393; Ella J., 392; Ella M., 365; Ella V., 365; Ellen, 276, 373, 377, 394; Elvira, 277; Ely, 385; Essie E., 370;

411

INDEX

Essie M., 365, 370; Ethel B., 367; Eugene M., 367; Eva B., 382; Eva C., 375, 376; Evaline, 373; Evelyn, 350; Everetta, 275.

Fay E., 372; Florence, 270, 276; Fluvia A., 393; Fontaine, 277; Fontaine P., 277; Frederic, 275, 377; Fred. A., 367; Frederick C., 271; Frances E., 272, 276; Francis, 46, 101, 172, 173, 175, 185, 186, 191, 202, 217, 262, 264, 267, 294, 295, 302, 303, 304, 306, 308, 310, 311, 317, 319, 352, 353, 355, 357, 383, 386, 406, 407; Francis J., 272; Francis K., 319, 325, 326, 330; Francis W., 320, 331, 365; Frank, 276, 377, 385; Frank M., 276; Frank W., 272; Frankie E., 367; Franklin, 378, 379; Franklin P., 391.

Garland, 276; Garnett, 378; Garret F., 357; George, 259, 264, 267, 268, 275, 292, 354, 356, 373, 374, 375, 378, 391; George A., 366; George B., 356; George C., 365; George F., 341, 344, 350; George H., 385; George L., 390; George M., 332, 344; George R., 357, 377; George S., 380; George T., 381, 382; George W., 274, 276, 373; Gertrude A., 368, 372; Gideon, 384; Gladys, 372; Grace, 277; Green, 279, 290, 393.

Halsey, H., 372; Hamilton, 356, 365, 370; Hannah, 354, 357; Hardin, 269, 275; Hardin L., 277; Hardenia, 270; Hardiman, 388; Hardy, 385, 395; Harley P., 393; Harriet L., 329; Hattie, 374; Harry, 377; Harry K., 377; Harry R., 386; Harry W., 394; Harvey A., 366; Harvey D., 365; Harvey L., 355; H. L., 358; Helen, 378, Helen M., 369; Helen R., 271; Henrietta, 356; Henry, 261, 262, 266, 267, 268, 269, 354, 356, 375, 385, 386, 388, 393; Henry A., 357, 367; Henry F., 386; Henry J., 377; Henry L., 385; Henry M., 385; Henry W., 356; Herman, 330; Herman C., 364, 370; Horace, 270; Horace A., 364; Horace B., 364; Holly C., 368; Horton O., 367; Hugh R., 381, 391.

Ida, 276, 375, 376, 377; Ida E., 364, 370; Ida J., 394; Idell F., 367; Indiana L., 279; Iona H., 370; Isabel, 276; Israel, 366, 375; Isaac C., 386; Irene, 385; Irving T., 277; Iva B., 365.

John, 98, 134, 191, 259, 271, 272, 275, 277, 278, 291, 297, 298, 299, 300, 301, 302, 305, 306, 312, 313, 315, 317, 319, 352, 356, 367, 373, 374, 375, 378, 383, 384, 385, 390, 391, 393, 394, 395; John A., 387; John B., 274, 277; John C., 355, 364, 393; John D., 394; John E., 276, 375; John F., 319, 329, 330, 340, 366, 393; John F. S., 271; John G., 356; J. G., 365; John H., 277, 373; John J., 370; John K., 374, 375; John L., 271; John M., 385, 393; John R., 365, 381, 393; John S., 354, 357, 367, 372; John T., 386, 388; John W., 319, 344, 366, 391, 392; James, 261, 264, 266, 269, 291, 295, 313, 316, 373, 379, 380, 381, 384, 385, 388, 391, 393, 395; James A., 366, 386; James B., 269, 276, 390; James C., 356, 365; James E., 384; James F., 275, 320, 330; James H., 391, 393; James L., 277; James N., 272; James T., 387; James W., 380, 386, 391; Jane, 265, 274, 301, 316; Jane E., 277, 295; Jabez, 277; Jacob, 375, 384, 395; Jacob C., 391; J. Taylor, 384; Jemima, 275; Jerome, 391; Jesse A., 364; Jessie M., 366; Jesse P., 386; Jesse R., 382; Joel E., 393; Joel F., 357; Jonah B., 355; Joseph C., 344; Josephine G., 377; Joseph S., 394; Joseph W., 355; Julia, 381; Julia R., 276, 380; Juliet, 380; Julius C., 393.

Kate, 270, 332, 343, 375; Keziah, 269; Kirkland, 388.

Lafayette, 366, 393; Lafayette W., 394; Laurence, 390; Laura, 270, 377, 387; Laura A., 386; Lavina, 277; Lawrence C., 370; Lelia, 330; Lelia E., 331; Lena M., 276; Lena V., 382; Lenora, 357; Leona D., 364, 369; Leo F., 367; Leo L., 382; Leslie D., 344; Levi H., 354, 355; Lenia V., 393; Lewis, 274, 275, 276, 279, 373; Lewis C., 355; Lew. H., 368; Lillie, 377, 378; Lillie L., 341, 350; Lillian M., 393; Lizzie, 375; Lizzie E.,

---

Shepherd.

INDEX

Laura, 246; Leah, 146; Lewis, 218, 219; Louisa E., 223; Louisa V., 246; Lucy, 245; L. Vernon, 234; Lydia, 188, 225; Lyle, 233, 234.

Maggie, 234; Margaret, 144, 219, 222, 230, 233; Margaret B., 232; Martin, 219; Marie, 231; Martha, 148, 152, 219, 230, 231, 235; Marshall, 231; Mary, 58, 142, 148, 152, 218, 219, 222, 224, 229, 230, 231, 234, 245; Mary A., 233; Mary E., 222, 226, 227, 233, 245; Mary F., 246; Mary H., 223; Mary J., 219, 232; McDonald, 219; Melinda, 219; Milton, 233; Moses, 155, 168, 180, 185, 186, 187, 191, 192, 202, 205, 311.

Nancy, 230, 231; Nancy A., 231; Nancy B., 233; Nelson, 231, 233; Nathan, 144, 229.

Ophelia, 219, 222; Orlanda, 219, 222.

Polly, 230, 231.

Rachael, 145, 166, 186; Reazin, 231, 233; Reazin D., 244, 246, 247, 408; Rezin S., 245; Richard, 246; Robert D., 243; Robert F., 245; Ruhamah, 219; Ruth, 191.

Salome C., 225; Sarah, 142, 144, 146, 148, 152, 153, 191, 201, 218, 219, 222, 230, 231, 306; Sarah A., 231, 233; Sarah C., 222, 225; Sarah M., 234; Smiley, 230, 232; Susan, 222, 224; Susan R., 223; Susannah, 148, 151, 152.

Thomas, 25, 28, 30, 34, 35, 36, 57, 133, 142, 143, 144, 145, 146, 147, 148, 149, 150, 152, 153, 155, 156, 157, 158, 162, 165, 167, 190, 202, 218, 228, 306, 308; Thomas A., 226; Thomas B., 223, 226; Thomas C., 147, 222, 223.

Valeria, 245.

William, 98, 142, 143, 144, 148, 150, 151, 152, 153, 154, 156, 167, 172, 173, 178, 190, 191, 217, 218, 219, 222, 230, 231, 233, 310, 311, 312, 354; William B., 223, 226; William C., 225; William J., 246, 409; William M., 245; William W., 233, 234; Wilbur L., 234; Wilson N., 233; Worcester, 231.

Van Meter, Van Metre, Van Metere, Van Meteren, etc.

Abner, 87, 107, 112, 114; Addie, 119; Agnes, 106, 107; Abishua, 42, 100, 104, 105, 109; Abraham, 16, 30, 31, 34, 35, 38, 39, 40, 42, 46, 57, 58, 61, 62, 63, 64, 65, 66, 96, 97, 98, 99, 100, 102, 103, 104, 105, 106, 108, 111, 113, 115, 123, 125, 127, 128, 129, 133, 175, 400, 403, 406; Abraham C., 129, 131; Abraham E., 40, 103, 108; Abraham H., 110, 116; A. Morgan, 71; Abraham P., 104, 111; Abraham W., 128; Absalom, 62, 63, 66, 71, 107; Alice, 57, 63, 67, 112, 119, 190; Ailsey, 106, 112, 124, 401; Alcinda, 125, 127; Allen, 115; Ann, 18; Anna, 88, 104, 109, 111, 115, 117; Anna A., 345; Anna E., 351; Anna R., 131; Ashahel, 42, 100, 103, 104, 105, 109; Amanda J., 119, 121; Aug. A., 114, 120.

Barney, 115; Benjamin, 26, 120; Benjamin F., 99, 134; Betsey, 218.

Carl, 131; Caroline, 73; Caroline E., 69; Cassander P., 131; Cassius E., 114; Catharine, 10, 18, 39, 40, 63, 88, 106, 111, 113, 400; Charles, 112; Charles A., 112; C. E., 42, 62; Chas. H., 130; Charles J., 69, 74; Cornelia, 26; Cornelius, 8; Claude, 131; Clinton C., 69; Cynthia, 106, 113, 126; Cynthia A., 400; Cyrenus, 26; Cyrus, 66, 107, 112, 114, 126.

415

INDEX

Daniel, 65, 71, 88, 99, 102, 127, 399; Darby, 112; Dinah, 42; David, 71, 88, 102, 106, 107, 112, 127; David P., 114; David R., 129, 130; David S., 62, 79, 87; Drusilla, 99, 113.

Earl, 116; Edwin, 64, 107; Edward A., 128, 402; Elijah, 116; Elijah W., 109; Elizabeth, 16, 34, 35, 42, 57, 58, 59, 63, 68, 94, 100, 104, 105, 108, 111, 112, 118, 120, 124, 125, 126, 128, 130, 133, 148, 157, 222, 244, 308, 401, 403; Eliza, 39, 40, 112; Eliza K., 110; Eliza M., 108; Eleanor S., 119; Ellen, 88, 116, 125; Ellen J., 109; Ellen M., 69; Elma, 107; Elsie, 67, 113, 400; Emma, 119, 131; Emmanuel, 3, 8; Endemile, 128; Ernest, 115; Esther, 25; Estina, 130; Ezra, 37; Evans, 103; Eva, 65.

Frances, 126; Francis, 105; Frank, 131; Frederick, 119; Florence, 345, 351.

Gabriel, 41, 105; Geertje, 10, 14; George, 87; George W., 110, 130; Gilbert, 24, 26; Grotias, 129; Guy, 131; Gysbert Janse, 10, 14, 26.

Hattie, 131; Hannah, 58, 59, 61, 62, 63, 64, 68, 99, 100, 102, 106, 113; Hannah M., 119, 121; Harrison, 106, 112; Helen, 131; Hendrix, 15; Henry, 13, 16, 18, 19, 30, 32, 42, 58, 59, 62, 63, 64, 65, 67, 94, 95, 99, 104, 106, 109, 113, 119, 127, 129, 134, 136, 137, 214, 216, 403; Henry C., 108; Henry J., 107, 114; Henrietta, 111, 117; Herschel D., 120; Hester, 59, 65, 94; "Honce," 42; Hoot, 88; Howard, 345; Hubbard, 128.

Ida, 130; Ida V., 70; Isaac, 13, 15, 16, 17, 18, 19, 20, 21, 22, 32, 33, 40, 42, 48, 56, 59, 61, 62, 63, 64, 65, 69, 98, 99, 100, 102, 103, 104, 105, 106, 108, 119, 123, 124, 125, 126, 128, 133, 147, 156, 190, 399; Isaac D., 110; Isaac H., 126; Isaac T., 105; Isabel, 104, 105, 107, 109, 115; Isabella, 100, 403.

Jacob, 8, 16, 30, 32, 33, 36, 37, 38, 42, 58, 59, 60, 63, 64, 65, 69, 95, 100, 103, 105, 106, 112, 119, 122, 123, 124, 125, 126, 127, 128, 133, 136, 145, 169, 217, 242, 399, 401, 403; Jacob C., 130; Jan, 16, 20; Jan Joost, 24, 25; Jan Joosten, 10, 11, 12, 13, 14, 15; James, 104, 110, 113, 119, 137; James H., 109, 116, 129, 131; James L. E., 103; James M., 110; Jap, 42; Jasper, 113; Jennie, 108, 111; Jeremiah, 128; Jesse, 63; Joanna, 36, 100; Johannes, 30, 36, 37, 42, 57; John, 12, 13, 14, 17, 18, 19, 20, 21, 22, 29, 36, 39, 40, 42, 48, 56, 59, 60, 61, 62, 63, 64, 66, 96, 98, 105, 106, 109, 112, 113, 119, 123, 125, 126, 127, 128, 129, 130, 133, 135, 137, 145, 147, 148, 149, 152, 156, 165, 190, 293, 354, 399, 400, 401, 406; John C., 125; John D., 107; John E., 40, 105, 108; John H., 109; John N., 119; John T., 104; John W., 130; Joost Jans, 10, 14, 15, 20; Joseph, 26, 41, 42, 57, 58, 59, 62, 63, 65, 66, 69, 71, 94, 98, 99, 100, 101, 103, 104, 105, 106, 113, 114, 119, 127, 128, 129, 136, 403; Joseph B., 71; Joseph D., 107; Joseph H., 128; Jos. J., 107; Joseph V., 111; Jos. W., 41, 105, 111; Josephine, 119; Joshua, 59, 65, 94; Josiah, 42, 100; Josina, 39, 40, 42, 104, 105, 108, 399; Julia A., 69, 73; Julia C., 120.

Kryn Jans, 25; Kathleyn, 20.

Laura, 118; Laetitia, 64, 106; Laetitia A., 114; Leah S., 119, 121; Letitia, 126; Letty, 130; Lewis, 114; Louisa, 116; Lillian, 114; Luella B., 131, 132; Lula, 119; Luther, 107; Lysbeth, 10, 14, 15.

Mahala, 64; Magdalena, 35, 40, 100, 103, 132; Maria, 16, 66, 71; Marie, 39, 42, 107, 108, 114, 120; Marie E., 107; Margaret, 14, 16, 31, 57, 62, 102, 103, 105, 106, 107, 111, 112, 113, 114, 117, 125, 126, 400, 404, 405;

INDEX OF OTHER SURNAMES

INDEX OF OTHER SURNAMES

BAILEY, Ellis, 193; Col. W. P., 326.
BAINBRIDGE, Peter, 144.
BAIRD, Nancy, 230, 231; Mary, 233.
BALDWIN, Amelia, 209, 212; John, 190; Pauline, 81.
BALLARD, 386; Lucy, 270; Thomas, 270.
BALLINGER, Henry, 43.
BANES, Deborah, 334.
BARRACK, 377.
BARRACKMAN, Maude A., 344.
BARCLAY, Harriet, 68; Margaret, 68; Mary, 68.
BARKER, Hannah, 233.
BARHAM, Hannah, 283.
BARLOW, Elizabeth, 50.
BARNES, Alice, 273; Lillian G., 317; Ruth E., 358.
BARNETT, Joseph, 398.
BARR, Mary E., 194, 197, 238.
BARRY, Joseph, 341.
BARRETT, John, 50.
BASSETT, Hester, 231.
BATES, Elizabeth, 218, 219, 222; James L., 239; Lucy K., 239; Mary, 222.
BATSON, George, 145, 146.
BAUGHMANN, Melissa, 91; Silas F., 209.
BAUM, Adam, 80.
BAYS, Charles, 88.
BAYLESS, Ella, 120; Henry, 115, 120; Jesse, 120; Lottie, 120; Loyd, 120; Margaret, 120.
BEALOR, William, 109.
BEALL, 141.
BEAN, William B., 73; Isaac, 301, 302.
BECKHAM, 235.
BECK, Bertha, 352; B. Lydia, 63; David, 352; Hester, 63, 68; Jacob, 63; Myrtle C., 392.
BECKET, John, 407; Martha, 325.
BECKWITH, Gladys, 276; Sidney, 276.
BEDINGER, H., 313; Jacob, 146.
BEESON, Jacob, 352.
BELL, Alexander, 91; Dr. Bell, 382; Eli, 103; Elizabeth, 232; Melissa, 91; Marian J. W., 130; Mary, 91, 104; Sarah, 106; Sydney, 91; William, 91.
BENEZET, John H., 340.
BENHARDT, Clinton N., 89.
BENJAMIN, J. E. Wilmer, 343; Joseph W., 343.
BENNETT, Adrian, 26; Capt. Van, 223.
BENTON, Jessie, 347.
BENTLEY, Ruth, 98.
BERKELEY, Sir William, 264.
BERRY, Lieutenant, 182.

BERSHARES, Anna, 117.
BESSONETT, Charles, 329; Sarah, 329.
BETTS, Rev. A. D., 283; Marioll, 283.
BETZ, Jennie, 382; Polly, 218, 219.
BEYER, J. A., 388.
BIGELOW, Hannah, 356; Henry, 356.
BIGGARS, Mary, 269, 270.
BIGGS, John, 404.
BIGNALL, Col. Robert, 280; Anne, 289.
BILLS, John H., 270.
BILLMYER, Thomas, 211; Charles, 211; William, 211.
BINKHAME, 196.
BIRGE, Martha, 356.
BIRD, Fannie, 286.
BIRKETT, William, 268.
BIXLER, 207.
BLACK, Adam, 113; John, 295, 296; Mary, 113, 119.
BLACKBURN, Chester, 211; Ethel, 211; Maj., 190; Samuel, 211.
BLACKFORD, Helen, 346; John, 145, 146, 147.
BLACKWELL, William, 272.
BLADES, Elizabeth, 276.
BLAIR, Mary, 287.
BLAKEY, John W., 224.
BLANCHAN, Catharine, 22, 23; Mathese, 22.
BLANHART, Edna, 406.
BLUE, 305; John, 110; Priscilla, 107.
BOAT, Elizabeth S., 329.
BODINE, 12; Isaac, 13, 16, 20; Sarah, 16, 37.
BOCOCK, Bessie, 343; Willis, 343.
BOGERT, Eleanor B., 120; J. Henry, 115, 120; Mary K., 120.
BOGGS, 309; Captain, 179; Lydia, 192.
BOLS, Weaverford, 110.
BOLES, Adam, 377; Jemima, 377; Margaret, 377.
BOLEY, Benjamin, 104; Nancy, 107.
BOLLING, John, 275.
BONAR, William, 353.
BONE, Mary, 89.
BONER, Averilla, 93.
BONNETT, Harriet, 118; Lewis, 187, 192, 217.
BOONE, Daniel, 404; Squire, 98.
BOPES, Charles, 254; Robert F., 254; Victoria H., 254.
BOOTH, Penneniah, 384.
BOTELER, Elizabeth S., 246.
BOYD, 311; Anne B., 286; Anne J., 286; Daniel, 84; Elisha, 305; Henry A., 282, 285; John, 282; John E., 282; Marion M., 286; Mary, 84; Mary S., 285; Parthenia

419

INDEX OF OTHER SURNAMES

A., 282, 285; Pattie R., 286; Rebecca, 84; R. B., 283; Walter B., 282; William J., 286; William M., 286.
BOWLES, David, 147.
BOWN, Capt., John, 25.
BOWEN, Elizabeth, 68; Darwin, 231.
BOWMAN, Joseph, 64.
BOWYER, 114.
BOYER, Laura, 378.
BOYCE, Ida M., 197.
BOYLE, Theresa, 71.
BRADY, Capt. Sam., 49, 184.
BRADDOCK, General, 162.
BRADFORD, Anna C., 351; John, 142; Sarah, 20.
BRADLEY, John, 236.
BRAGONIER, Richard K. C., 228; Joseph S., 228.
BRAGG, General, 228.
BRANCH, Robert, 391.
BRAND, Walter, 344.
BRANDENBURG, Solomon, 62.
BRANDON, Aurelia, 112; Martha, 112.
BRANDT, 113.
BRANDMEULLER, John, 134.
BRANTNER, Bessie, 335; Carrie, 335; Edgar, 335; George, 335; George W., 335; Harrie, 335; Hendricks, 335; Lillie, 335; Minnie, 335, 348; Ruth, 335; Thomas, 335; Tobias, 335; William, 335, 348.
BREAKEY, Henrietta F., 393.
BRENT, Marie E., 247.
BRENTIGO, Peter, 142.
BRICKER, Clara, 91; Dennis, 91; Lorin, 91.
BRIERY, 207.
BRIGGS, Herbert J., 392.
BRICKET, Lester, 130.
BRISTOW, Benjamin H., 131; Emily, 131; Francis M., 131.
BRITTAIN, Joseph, 330; Mary, 330; Mary T., 330.
BRISCOE, Abbie, 130, 131; Eleanor M., 245; Fanny E., 245; John, 245; Nannie, 130; Walter, 127; William, 129, 130.
BROERSEN, Jan, 11.
BROADHEAD, Daniel, 176.
BRODIE, Estelle, 285.
BROOKES, 222; De Lorme, 195; Elizabeth, 352; Fannie, 246; Gorham, 246; James, 142, 352; Peter G., 246; Roxa, 195; Thomas, 195.
BROTT, Pearl, 367; Ralph, 367; William H., 367.
BROWN, 12; A., 199; A. S., 86; Anna L., 86, 120, 121; Benjamin, 268;

274; Balaam M., 224, 227; Barry W., 205; C., 194; Edmund, 274; E. D., 216; Elizabeth, 205; Elizabeth K., 226; Ethel, 56; E. S., 213; Fanny M., 227; George, 358; George W., 205; Hannah M., 205; Huldah, 274; Ida B., 227; Isaac V. M., 119; James, 189; James W., 113, 120; John, 40, 205, 330; Louretta, 216; Morgan, 216; Martha, 82, 205, 113; Mary E., 120; Sarah, 113, 205, 206; Sarah L., 113; Shepherd, 205, 206; T., 313; Thomas, 205; Thomas A., 205; William, 151, 162, 205, 206, 218; William J., 113.
BROWNFIELD, Sally, 195.
BRYAN, 207; Morgan, 135; Samuel, 58.
BRUMMOND, Mary, 391.
BURNS, Abner, 103; Abraham, 103, 110; Alice, 103; Alsie, 103; B. F., 104; Caleb, 103; Catharine, 108; Daniel, 103, 110; Elizabeth, 40, 100, 103; Eliza H., 104, 110; George, 39, 40; Hannah, 39, 40, 41, 103, 110; Isaac, 103; Isabella, 39, 41; Isabel, 103; Jacob, 103; Joanna, 103; John, 39, 103, 108; Jonathan, 103, 108; Joseph, 39, 40; Margaret, 39, 40, 41; Mary, 39, 40, 103, 108, 115; Rachael, 103; Rebecca, 39, 103; Robert, 39, 41; Ruth, 39, 40, 103, 317; Ruth S., 41; William, 38, 100, 103.
BUCHANON, Samuel, 235.
BUCKALOUGH, Elizabeth, 348.
BUCKINGHAM, Basil, 335; Hannah, 335; O. E., 335; William, 335.
BUCKLES, Robert, 216; Rebecca, 318.
BUCKNER, Mordecai, 319.
BUGBY, Miss, 287.
BUCKEY, Jemima, 59, 66; John, 59, 61, 62; Zachariah, 59.
BUMPASS, C. W., 276; Thomas, 276.
BURDEN, Benjamin, 28, 29, 63.
BURK, Charles, 293.
BURCHFIELD, Edward, 238.
BURKE, Mary, 382.
BURKHOLDER, Alice, 378; Bertha, 378; Jacob, 378; Mary, 378; Price, 378; Raymond, 378.
BURNLEY, Elizabeth, 273; James, 274; John, 273; Keziah, 269.
BURKETT, William, 18.
BURR, Aaron, 18.
BURROWES, Thomas, 353.
BURSON, Isaac, 68.
BURTON, Olive, 283; R. C., 280.
BUSH, Hattie, 204; Matilda, 236.

420

INDEX OF OTHER SURNAMES

INDEX OF OTHER SURNAMES

INDEX OF OTHER SURNAMES

Samuel M., 254; Thomas W., 254; William A., 286.

GRANBERRY, Sue, 394.

GRAY, Charlotta, 367; William, 162; John, 182.

GREEN, Mary, 278; Gen. Nathaniel, 317; Thomas E., 278.

GREGORY, Charles, 56; David, 55; Jemima, 54; John, 54; Mary, 55; Ninian, 55, 56; Samuel, 55; Samuel P., 56; Sue, 55; Susan, 68; Warner R., '55; William, 54.

GREENWOOD, Anna M., 215; Benjamin, 208; Benjamin E., 211, 215; Benjamin H., 208; C. Frank, 211; Clara B., 215; Edna L., 215; Elizabeth, 208; Harvey H., 215; H. L., 215; Harry S., 215; H. W., 215; James, 208; James W., 211, 215; Laura, 215; Lillian M., 215; Milford, 215; Matilda, 208; Margaret, 211; Margaret E., 215; Peraquin, 208; Raymond R., 215; Sebastian E., 208; Sally A., 208, 211; Shepherd McD., 208, 211; Thomas C., 211, 215.

GREY, 225; Martha, 339; Matilda, 338; Pollie, 384.

GRIFFIN, Alice, 375; Anna, 375; James, 375; Laura, 375; Mary F., 203; William, 375.

GRIFFITHS, John, 143; Phoebe, 81; West, 81.

GROFF, Hans, 205; Jacob, 205.

GROSE, George R., 240.

GROUND, George, 146; John, 206; Philip, 146.

GROVES, Andrew, 380.

GROVE, Ann, 210; Bertha, 211; Corena B., 210; Calvin, 207; Catharine 205, 207; Carl, 215; Elizabeth, 206, 207, 208, 211; Eleanor, 207; Emma, 207; Ettie C., 210; Frank L., 211; Grace, 215; Hannah M., 206, 207, 208; Harvey, 206, 207; Harvey E., 211; Jacob, 205; John, 162, 205, 207; Kessia, 206; Levi, 206; Mary, 206, 207, 215; Mary B., 162; Mary L., 208, 210; Melvina, 209; Minnie A., 210; Mills, 209; Miss, 377; Naomi, 208, 210; Porter, 215; Parry, 206, 207; Reuben, 208, 210; Rhoda, 208; Shepherd, 205; Sarah, 205, 206, 207; Stephen, 206, 207; Uriah H., 211; William, 207; William B., 206; William E., 210, 215.

GROVER, Hester, 25; James, Sr., 25; James, Jr., 25.

GRUND, George, 208; James, 208; Jefferson, 208; John, 208; Hannah H., 208; Mary, 208.

GUY, James, 113; Charles, 365.

GUNNELL, John, 269.

GWYNNE, Samuel, 210.

GYSBERTSEN, Jan, 25.

HAAS, S. W., 92; Laurence E., 93.

HAGGARD, Lydia, 225.

HAGGERTY, Minnie G., 253.

HAHN, Elizabeth, 81.

HAILE, Thomas J., 78.

HAIR, Jane, 238.

HALLIDAY, Jane O., 275; Elizabeth L., 276.

HALLOCK, Frederick A., 212; Florence E., 212.

HALSEY, Major W. H., 86.

HATTON, Sir Christopher, 261.

HALL, Catharine H., 208, 212; Charles S., 211; E. Groove, 208; Elizabeth, 206; Ellen V., 208; Ella V., 211; Emma F., 208, 211; Eugene G., 211; Frank, 109; Fred. A., 208, 212; George B., 208, 212; Gertrude, 212; Helen, 212; James, 84; James S., 206; John, 206; Lemuel, 205, 206; Leroy K., 206, 208; Martha, 206; Mary, 206; Matilda, 206; Rosamunda, 252; Sarah, 17; Sarah E., 208, 212; Thomas, 17; William, 18, 206; William L., 208.

HALE, Rosamunda, 225.

HAMEL, Jan, 11, 12, 14.

HAMBLETON, Rachael, 367.

HAMILTON, Agnes, 12; Albert P., 371; Alexander, 262; Andrew, 12; Arthur L., 371; Effie R., 371; Ernest, 371; Sarah, 117; Mabel B., 371; Miss, 380; Thomas W., 371.

HAMMOND, Mary, 245; Thomas, 245.

HAMPTON, Noah, 58.

HAMTRANECK, Florence, 245.

HAND, Gen. Edward, 100, 173, 309.

HANGER, Andrew, 73, 83; Azariah, 73, 83; Caroline, 73; Ellen, 73; Elza, 83; Harriet, 84; Jackson, 73, 83; Jacob, 73, 84; Mary, 73, 84; Peter, 73; Rhoda, 73; Sarah, 73, 83, 84.

HANNA, Mary L. E., 393.

HANSCHER, William, 63.

HANSFORD, Lydia, 266.

HARBAUGH, Dennis, 195; Elizabeth, 195; Jacob, 195, 198; Lila, 195; M. Josephine, 198; Porter W., 198; Rachael, 195; Sarah, 195, 199; Springer, 195; Susan, 195; William, 194, 195.

427

INDEX OF OTHER SURNAMES

INDEX OF OTHER SURNAMES

INDEX OF OTHER SURNAMES

432

INDEX OF OTHER SURNAMES

MEEK, Isaac, 50, 51, 53, 179; James, 198; Joshua, 50; Melissa, 54; Ruth, 48; William, 53, 55.
MEERS, Elizabeth A., 386.
MELHORN, Cornelia, 381; Ella, 381; Frank, 381; Harry, 381; Jennie, 381.
MELVIN, Catharine, 332, 333.
MELTON, Francis, 191.
MENSING, Albert, 338; Anna F., 325, 338; Anna M., 338; Clarissa, 349; Edward, 338; Eleanor, 338; Elizabeth C., 338, 349; Elizabeth M., 325, 339; Frederick, 324; Gertrude 338, 349; Ida V., 325, 338; John F., 325, 338; Laura M., 338, 349; Mabel, 349; Matilda, 338; Pauline C., 325, 338; Thomas H., 324, 337; Thomas W., 338, 348; Walter W., 349; William J., 338.
MENT, George, 286; James S., 286; Tempie, 286.
MERCER, John R., 285; Jonathan, 300; Lenoir C., 285; Margaret E., 285, 287; Mary F., 285, 287; Routh S., 285; William, 285; Mary S., 285.
MERCHANT, Capt., 182.
MEREDITH, Anne, 375; Miss, 380.
MERLOT, Abraham, 95.
MESTREZETT, Frederick, 206.
METLER, George, 224.
MERVINE, John, 268; William, 268.
MIDDLETON, 196.
MIFFLIN, Governor, 183.
MILLS, Adaline, 219; Amassa, 231; Andrew J., 220; Ashford, 219; Benjamin, 218, 219, 220; Campbell, 231; Cardine, 194; Catharine, 194; Cornelia, 286; Edward, 212; Elizabeth, 54, 191, 194, 220; Elizabeth D., 218; Emily, 219; Gabriel, 219; James, 219, 231; Jane, 377; Lieut. John, 143; John, 186, 187, 191, 194, 218, 219, 231; Juliet, 191, 194; Levi, 218; Lydia, 191; Mary A., 219; Milton, 220; Minerva, 194; Margaret J., 231; Moses, 191; Rebecca, 218, 219, 220; Ruhamah, 200, 219; Ruth, 188, 194, 196; Sarah, 191, 194, 219, 220; Sarah J., 194; Sarah M., 231; Shepherd, 231; Susannah, 231; Thomas, 143, 219, 220; Warner, 219; Williis, 231; William, 191, 194, 218, 230, 231; William S., 220.
MILLAR or MILLER, 121, 204; Ada, 274; Alpha, 93; Ann M., 393; Anna R., 120; Bertie D., 91; Blanche, 274; Blanche M., 370; Brunella F.,

121; Calvin, 84; Catharine, 107; Caroline, 370; Cinderella, 84, 91; Ch., 367; Charles, 84, 91; Charles E., 121, 122; Charles J., 120; Clyde, 91; Dr., 107; Edwin H., 337; Edward S., 215; Effie, 91; Eleanora, 122; Eliza, 114; Elizabeth, 337; Ella, 84, 222, 223; Emma A., 84, 91; Evangeline, 106; Eugene, 74; Frederick, 120, 191; Florence, 274; Florence H., 337; Florence S., 120; George, 73, 274; Henry, 91; Imogen, 337; Ira V., 34, 92; James, 407; Jesse G., 93; J. N., 228; Joseph, 106; John, 18, 55, 73, 84, 91, 203; John C., 274; John F., 84, 91; King, 91; Lawrence V., 92; Levin, 122; Lillian, 84; Lillian C., 92; Lydia, 93; Mabel L., 120; Maggie S., 237; Margaret, 202; Mary, 73, 91, 385; Mary A., 110; Mary B., 120; Mary E., 84, 91; Milton, 337; Milton S., 115, 120; Myrta, 91; Nannie, 203; Nellie, 91; Nora C., 203; Rachael, 84, 91; Rebecca, 110; Raymond W., 337; Ruth, 73; Sarah 49; Sophia, 106; Sophia C., 203; Samuel, 370; Susannah, 49; T. B., 215; William, 73, 84, 91; William R., 337.
MILLISACK, Jacob, 235.
MINUIT, Peter, 5.
MILLHOLLAND, Geo. H., 254; James H., 254; Mary A., 254; Paul D., 254.
MING, 218.
MINGE, John, 343; Mary A., 343.
MILNOR, Asa, 238; Edward, 238; George, 238; Isaac, 238; Jane, 238; Jesse, 238; John, 238; Joseph, 235, 238; Joseph W., 238; Martha, 238; Rezin, 238; Sarah, 238.
MITCHELL, Alice, 228; Anderson, 404; Asa N., 404; Ann E., 406; Ann H., 226, 228; Archibald, 405; Charles, 404; Charles H., 226; Catharine, 228; Burt, 404; Edward, 228; Edward L., 226; Elizabeth R., 226; Ellen J., 226; James, 405; James A., 405; James L., 226; John, 101, 312, 404; John L., 226, 228; Leander P., 405; Margaret, 405, 406; Mary, 405; Nathaniel, 223, 225; Nelson, 405; Pomroy, 404, 405; Robert A., 382; Ruth L., 225; Virginia, 228; Virginia L., 226, 228; William K., 226, 228; William K., Jr., 228.
MORFERD, Abraham, 194.

29 433

INDEX OF OTHER SURNAMES

PUFFER, Charles, 130.
PUGH, Clarissa, 393, 394; Martha, 393; William, 393.
PUMPHREY, Emily E., 236.
PURSELL, James, 205.
PUTNAM, Charles, 88.
PYLE, Ann, 226; Elizabeth, 58, 65; Hannah, 65, Lawson, 227; Mary A., 65; Mildred, 227.

QUEEN, Christina, 5.
QUICK, Jonas, 102; Tunis, 102.
QUARRIER, Helen S., 249.

RABY, Margaret, 385.
RAINEY, 70.
RAYMER, Michael, 38, 133.
RAIFORD, Annie S., 385; Fanny B., 385; Jethro, 385; Sallie M., 385; Wesley B., 385.
RALEIGH, Sir Walter, 261, 264, 277, 280.
RAMAGE, Cordelia, 214.
RAMSEY, 104; Cornelia, 210.
RANDOLPH, Gov. Beverley, 47, 178; Ona, 130.
RANSOM, 365; James, 269; Matt, 289; Mary, 279, 280; Robert, 289; Seymour, 279.
RAY, Eliza, 109, 111; Julia C., 111; Lou, 225, 227; Margaret, 111; Sallie, 111; Thomas, 111; William, 111.
RAYNOR, Eliza V., 339; Ida V., 339; John, 338; John S., 339, 351; Naomi M., 339; Thomas, 265; Thomas H., 339; William D., 339.
REAZIN, 309.
REDD, Samuel, 269.
REEKS, Josephine S., 285.
RENFORTH, Mary, 220; James, 220.
REHM, Alexander R., 357.
REISHER, Belle, 378; Virginia, 378.
RENCH, Cassandra, 220; Catharine, 220; Eli K., 220; Levi, 220; Mary N., 220; Otto, 220; Sarah, 220; Ullysees, 220.
RENVO, Miss, 320.
REW, William, 300.
REYNOLDS, 276; Kate, 276.
RHODES, Catharine, 63; Elizabeth, 127; Henry, 127; 398; James, 127.
RICE, Emmaline, 199, 201; Jacob, 407.
RICHMAN, John, 19.
RICHARDSON, Betsey, 277; Sarah L., 275; Tom, 276; William, 276, 313.
RIDDLE, John, 305; William, 114.
RIDDLEBURGER, Charles, 115; Jennie, 115; Lou, 115; William, 115.

RIDGELEY, Eugene, 61.
RIDGEWAY, Elizabeth, 109.
RIFFE, Peter B., 78.
RIGGS, Amelia, 388.
RIHON, D., 274.
RILEY, Mary, 110.
RINEHART, 247; William, 199.
RINKER, Margaret, 114.
RITCHIE, Elizabeth, 339; John, 339.
RITTENHOUSE, David, 135.
RIZZER, Albert J., 195, 199; Albert A., 199; Benjamin H., 201; Charles W., 201; Florence M., 199, 201; George S., 199, 201; Louis R., 201; Lucy A., 201; Lydia F., 201; Henry B., 199; Mary F., 199.
ROBERTS, Alfred, 111; Daniel, 354; D. W., 111; Edmund L., 248; Ellen L., 248; Elizabeth, 105, 111; Eliza, 105; Elvira, 111; George, 236; Isaac, 111; John, 105; John C., 130; Josiah, 105; Joseph, 105, 111; Julia, 111; Laura P., 248; Melvina, 111; Naomi, 105; Oregon, 111; Rovilla, 111; Samuel, 41, 96, 100, 105; William S., 248; W. T., 248.
ROBINS, James, 262.
ROBINSON, 232; Aaron, 49, 50, 53; Abraham, 53; Adonijah, 232; Allen, 53; Benoni, 53; Catharine, 53; Elbridge, 53; Elizabeth, 50, 53; Isaac, 50, 53; Israel, 49, 50, 53; Jacob M., 53; James, 50; Jefferson, 53, Jehu, 53; Lewis, 50, 53; Lucinda, 53; Louisa, 53; Mahala, 53; Warne, 53; Mercy, 50, 53; Mergaline, 53; Peggy, 50; Priscilla, 233; Rebecca, 50, 53; R. A., 271; Sarah, 50, 53; Silas, 50, 53; Zill, 53.
ROBERTSON, Elizabeth, 52.
ROCKENBAUGH, S. Fanny, 347; Thomas S., 347.
ROCKWELL, Ellatta T., 203.
RODGERS, Alexander, 54; Bert, 117; Charles C., 54; David, 171, 172; Ella M., 54; Isaac F., 54, 55; Mary, 89; Mary C., 54, 55; William, 403.
ROE, Edwin, 235.
ROHRER, George, 366.
ROLFE, 274.
ROLLINGER, 125.
ROLLINSON, Ellen E., 349.
ROLLINGS, Rebecca, 63.
RODES, Clifton, 79; Mary, 270; Gen. Robert E., 270.
RONEMOUS, Edna, 347; Elmer C., 347; Emma J., 211; Frank, 347; Frank D., 347.
ROMINE, James, 80.

438

INDEX OF OTHER SURNAMES

INDEX OF OTHER SURNAMES

B. Franklin, 82; Belle, 88, 92; Bessie, 89; Byram, 265; Carrie, 89; Caroline, 72, 228; Caroline C., 83; Camilious R., 83; Cecil, 92; Charlotta N., 117; Charles H., 89; Cornelia, 72, 81, 83; Earle, 89; Eliza H., 82, 89; Gen. E. Kirby, 85; ·Elizabeth, 67; Emma, 369; Emma F., 90; Emma V., 82, 89; Fanny, 225; Floyd, 89; Francis A., 227, 381; George M., 82; George W., 227; Grace, 227; Gussie, 117; Guy, 89; Harry, 89; Henry, 67; Henry D., 72, 82; Henry H., 225, 227; Henry L., 90; Isaac, 89; James, 81, 179; Rev. James, 343; James H., 72, 82; Jessie, 92, 227; Capt. John, 8; John, 19, 72, 89; John J., 81, 88; Jefferson D., 82, 89; Joseph H., 225, 227; Julia A., 82; Kossuth, 82; Lafayette, 82; Lafayette N., 89; Leander, 8, 81, (?); Leonidas, 81; Lillian, 227; Louisa M., 82; Lucy, 269; Mabel, 89; Mabel H., 90; Melvina B., 88, 92; Mandie, 93; Martha, 67; Martha A., 82, 89; Martha J., 82; Mary, 72; Mary A., 82, 90; Mary H., 67; Mary P., 225, 227; Mattie, 272; Mina, 88; Nancy, 71; Nathalie, 343; Nina, 92; Overna, 89; Paul, 89; Pearl, 89, 92; Phoebe, 81; Rachael, 67, 72, 83; Rebecca, 67, 82; Rebecca A., 72; Rees, 72, 82, 83; Reuben, 275; Robert, 244; Roy S., 89; S. B., 222, 224; Sarah, 67, 364; Sarah A., 72, 82; S. Carolina, 82, 89; Susan, 89; Thomas C., 225; William, 67, 81, 225, 227, 275; William W., 270; Zoe, 92.

SMITHERS, Benjamin S., 252; David S., 251; Margaret E., 252; Rose C., 252.

SMALL, 225.

SMOOT, Dee C., 252; Helen L., 252.

SMYTH, Francis A., 340, 350; James, 339; Jonathan, 339; Marion M., 340; Mary E., 339, 340; Samuel G., 339; S. Gordon, Jr., 340.

SNEDAKER, Lavinia, 357.

SNEED, 71.

SNIDER, Frank, 209, 213; Frank L., 213; John, 114; Joseph L., 213; Marguerite, 213; Mary I., 213; Thomas W., 213; Will T., 114.

SNIVELEY, John, 63.

SNYDER, Catharine, 336; Etta, 336; James M., 336; J. Walper, 110; Sophia, 323; Virginia, 336.

SOMERVILLE, Catharine, 282; Eliza J., 286; Joseph B., 282; Mary S., 282; Nannie B., 286; Rosa C., 282, 286; Sallie G., 282; Tempie J., 282, 286; Walter E., 282; William J., 282.

SOUTHERLAND, Elijah J., 231; George, 231; Harvey, 231.

SOUTHWOOD, Fanny, 40; Rebecca, 40; Sarah, 103.

SOWERS, 103.

SPRINGER, Abner, 186, 352; Albert, 195; Ann, 193, 196; Anna, 352; Athellia, 199; Caroline, 196; Catharine, 195, 199; Charles A., 199; Daniel, 195, 199; David, 192, 195, 199, 200, 352; David M., 199; Dennis, 192, 193, 195, 352; Drusilla, 352; Ellen J., 196; Elizabeth, 192, 193, 195, 200; Elizabeth B., 195; Eliza, 195, 200; Elva E., 200; Emma G., 199; Ewing B., 195, 200; Hannah, 192, 196; Hannah F., 199; Hervey, 193; Isaac, 199; Isaiah, 195; Jacob, 193, 195, 196, 200; Jacob L., 195; James T., 199; James L., 200; Job, 192, 193, 195, 196, 352; John, 199; John C., 199; John S., 199; John W., 200; Jonathan, 193; Josiah, 199; Julia, 200; Kate, 211; Lafayette, 199; Levi, 162, 163, 191, 193, 195, 306, 312; Levi B., 195; Lydia, 192; Lydia J., 195, 199; Margaret, 199, 201; Mary A., 195; Mary D., 200; Mary R., 199; Marshall, 195, 199; Morgan, 193; Nathan, 195; Oliver, 195; Rachael, 192, 195, 199, 352; Rebecca, 199; Ruth, 200, 352; Ruth A., 195; Sarah, 186, 188, 192, 194, 195, 200, 352; Sarah E., 199; Shepherd, 195, 199; Thomas W., 199; S. William, 193; William, 196, 199, 352; William E., 199; Virginia, 196; Zadoc, 193, 196, 352.

SPAIR, Youder, 295.

SPAHN, Mrs. John, 60; John, 98, 99, 102.

SPANGLER, John, 299.

SPARK, 111; Adaline, 206; John, 205, 206.

SPEAK, Col. Thomas, 58.

SPEED, Joseph, 280; Mary A., 280; Sir Joseph, 280.

SPOONER, E. P. S., 351; Florence, 351.

SPONG, J., 162; Mathias, 146, 147; Sarah, 147.

SPOTTSWOOD, Governor, 383.

440

INDEX OF OTHER SURNAMES

441

INDEX OF OTHER SURNAMES

442

443

www.ingramcontent.com/pod-product-compliance
Lightning Source LLC
Chambersburg PA
CBHW071823270326
41929CB00013B/1888